PHILOSOPHICAL FOUNDATIONS OF CHILDREN'S AND FAMILY LAW

Philosophical Foundations of Children's and Family Law

Edited by
ELIZABETH BRAKE
and
LUCINDA FERGUSON

Great Clarendon Street, Oxford, OX2 6DP,
United Kingdom

Oxford University Press is a department of the University of Oxford.
It furthers the University's objective of excellence in research, scholarship,
and education by publishing worldwide. Oxford is a registered trade mark of
Oxford University Press in the UK and in certain other countries

© The several contributors 2018

The moral rights of the authors have been asserted

First Edition published in 2018

Impression: 1

All rights reserved. No part of this publication may be reproduced, stored in
a retrieval system, or transmitted, in any form or by any means, without the
prior permission in writing of Oxford University Press, or as expressly permitted
by law, by licence or under terms agreed with the appropriate reprographics
rights organization. Enquiries concerning reproduction outside the scope of the
above should be sent to the Rights Department, Oxford University Press, at the
address above

You must not circulate this work in any other form
and you must impose this same condition on any acquirer

Crown copyright material is reproduced under Class Licence
Number C01P0000148 with the permission of OPSI
and the Queen's Printer for Scotland

Published in the United States of America by Oxford University Press
198 Madison Avenue, New York, NY 10016, United States of America

British Library Cataloguing in Publication Data

Data available

Library of Congress Control Number: 2017958201

ISBN 978-0-19-878642-9

Printed and bound by
CPI Group (UK) Ltd, Croydon, CR0 4YY

Links to third party websites are provided by Oxford in good faith and
for information only. Oxford disclaims any responsibility for the materials
contained in any third party website referenced in this work.

Acknowledgements

Many of the chapters contained in this volume were discussed at an interdisciplinary workshop held at Oriel College, Oxford. We would like to thank the University of Oxford Faculty of Law's Research Support Fund and the Society of Legal Scholars' Legal Scholarship Fund for their financial support for the workshop, as well as Oriel College for providing the meeting space and related administrative support. We are particularly obliged to Naomi Webber for all of her hard work as the workshop assistant.

We are indebted to the participants at the workshop—students, visitors to Oxford, and members of the Faculty of Law and Faculty of Philosophy. Their thoughtful contributions much improved the final collection.

We are grateful to the team at Oxford University Press, especially Eve Ryle-Hodges, without whom this interdisciplinary vision would not have come into being.

This collection is missing a chapter—that of our colleague, Helen Reece, who very sadly passed away. She was so generous, both as a person and an academic, and with a talent for seeking out the heart of the matter. Her original voice is greatly missed.

Contents

Table of Cases	ix
Table of Statutes and other Instruments	xiii
List of Contributors	xv
Abstracts	xix

Introduction: The Importance of Theory to Children's and Family Law   1
Lucinda Ferguson and Elizabeth Brake

I. DEFINITIONS

1. Family Law and Legal Theory   41
   John Eekelaar
2. Family and Family Law: Concepts and Norms   59
   David Archard

II. RELATIONSHIPS

3. Paid and Unpaid Care: Marriage, Equality, and Domestic Workers   75
   Elizabeth Brake
4. A Perfectionist Argument for Legal Recognition of Polyamorous Relationships   95
   Ronald C. Den Otter
5. Cohabitants, Choice, and the Public Interest   115
   Robert Leckey
6. Heteronormativity in Dissolution Proceedings: Exploring the Impact of Recourse to Legal Advice in Same-Sex Relationship Breakdown   134
   Charlotte Bendall and Rosie Harding
7. The Rights of Families and Children at the Border   153
   Matthew Lister

III. RIGHTS AND OBLIGATIONS

8. Moral and Legal Obligations to Support 'Family'   173
   Diane Jeske
9. Are Children's Rights Important?   191
   Colin M. Macleod
10. Parental Control Rights   209
    Scott Altman
11. An Argument for Treating Children as a 'Special Case'   227
    Lucinda Ferguson

IV. REGULATION AND INTERVENTION

12. **Private Ordering in Family Law**   257
    Brian H. Bix
13. **Regulating Child Rearing in a Culturally Diverse Society**   273
    James G. Dwyer
14. **Surrogacy: Reconceptualizing Family Relationships in an Age of Reproductive Technologies**   293
    Mary Lyndon Shanley

Bibliography   313
Index   333

Table of Cases

A (Children) (Conjoined Twins: Surgical Separation) [2001] Fam 147 28
A v The United Kingdom (1999) 27 EHRR 611 48
Agar-Ellis (1883) 24 Ch D 317 53
Alcock v Chief Constable of South Yorkshire [1991] UKHL 5 17
Ampthill Peerage Case [1977] AC 547 19
Baby M 525 A2d 1128 (Superior Court, Chancery Division, 1987) 298–9, 300
Baby M 537 A2d 1227 (NJ 1988) 266
Borelli v Brusseau, 12 Cal App4th 47, 16 Cal Rptr 16 (1993) 264
Burden and Burden v United Kingdom (App No 13378/05) [2006] ECHR 1064; [2008]
    STC 1305; [2008] 2 FLR 787 (ECtHR (Grand Chamber)) 3, 79
Caban v Mohammed 441 US 380 (1979) 296
Charman v Charman [2007] EWCA Civ 503 .... 25, 149
Christine Goodwin v The United Kingdom (2002) 35 EHRR 447 49
Davis v Davis 842 SW2d 588 (Tenn 1992) 298–9
Diosdado v Diosdado 118 Cal Rptr 2d 494, 97 Cal App4th 470 (Cal App 2002) 264
EB v France (2008) 47 EHRR 21 49
EG, 515 NE2d 286 (Ill App Ct 1987) 289
Elsholz v Germany (2002) 34 EHRR 58 .... 35, 230
Evans v United Kingdom (2006) 43 EHRR 21 41
Ex parte Williams 617 So2d 1033 (Ala 1992) 270
Fitzpatrick v Sterling Housing Ltd [1999] UKHL 42, 44
Görgülü v Germany [2004] 1 FLR 894 (ECtHR) 35
Gow v Grant [2012] UKSC 29 120
H & Ors (Minors) (Sexual Abuse: Standard of Proof 1996] AC 563 33
Hartshorne v Hartshorne 2004 SCC 22, [2004] 1 SCR 550 121
Hokkanen v Finland (1995) 15 EHRR 139 35
Holler v Holler 612 SE2d 469 (SC App 2005) 270
Hoppe v Germany (2004) 38 EHRR 15 35
Hussemann v Hussemann 847 NW2d 219 (Iowa 2014) 268
Hyman v Hyman [1929] AC 601 121
J (Children) [2013] UKSC 9 5
Jacobson v Massachusetts 197 US 11 (1905) 275
Jason P v Danielle S, 226 CalApp4th 167 (Cal App 2014), review denied, 30 July 2014 .. 267
JB v MB 783 A2d 707 (NJ 2001) 267
Johansen v Norway (1997) 23 EHRR 33 .... 35, 230
Johnson v Calvert 5 Cal4th 84, 851 P2d 776 (1993) 266
Jones v Kernott [2011] UKSC 53, [2012] 1 AC 776 .... 117–20, 127, 130
Kass v Kass 696 NE2d 174 (NY 1998) 267
Kerr v Baranow 2011 SCC 10, [2011] 1 SCR 269 .... 117–20, 127
KMH 169 P3d 1025 (Kan 2007) 267
Lawrence v Gallagher [2012] EWCA Civ 394 .... 27, 136
Lawrence v Texas 539 US 558 (2003) 97, 178
Lehr v Robertson 463 US 248 (1983) 296
Loving v Virginia 388 US 1 (1967) 158
M (Child's Upbringing) [1996] EWCA Civ 1320 229
M (Children) [2016] EWCA Civ 1059 252
MacLeod v MacLeod [2008] UKPC 64 270
Marc Rich & Co AG v Bishop Rock Marine Co Ltd (The Nicholas H) [1994] 1 WLR 1071 17

Marriage of Cooper 769 NW2d 582 (Iowa 2009) 264
Marriage of Witten 672 NW2d 768 (Iowa 2003) 267
Mason v Dwinnell 660 SE2d 58 (NC App 2008) 267
McGuire v McGuire 59 NW2d 336 (Neb 1953) 261
Meyer v Nebraska 262 US 390 (1932) 158
Michael H v Gerald D 491 US 110 (1989) 296
Mikulić v Croatia (App No 53176/99) [2002] 1 FCR 720 41
Miller v Miller 42 NW 641 (Iowa 1889) 264
Miller v Miller; McFarlane v McFarlane [2006] UKHL 24, [2006] 2 AC 618 . . . . 25, 127
Moge v Moge [1992] 3 SCR 813 120
N v N [1999] 2 FLR 745 37
Neulinger v Switzerland (2012) 54 EHRR 31 35
Newham London Borough Council v AG [1993] 1 FLR 281 5
Nova Scotia (Attorney General) v Walsh [2002] 4 SCR 325, 2002 SCC 83 129
Obergefell v Hodges 576 US _ (2015), 135 S Ct 2584 (2015) 10, 55, 97, 158, 271
Ofer v Sirota 116 AD3d 509, 984 NYS2d 312 (2014) 268
Owens v Owens [2017] EWCA Civ 182 6
Paradiso and Campanelli v Italy (App No 25358/12) (24 Jan 2017) (ECtHR
 (Grand Chamber)) 13
Parlour v Parlour [2004] EWCA Civ 872 27
Peter v Beblow [1993] 1 SCR 980 117–20
Pettkus v Becker [1980] 2 SCR 834 117
Piglowska v Piglowski [1999] 3 All ER 632 . . . . 2, 50
Pratten v British Columbia 2012 BCCA 480 305
President and Directors of Georgetown College 331 F2d 1000, 1007 (DC Cir), cert denied,
 377 US 978 (1964) 289
Prest v Petrodel [2013] UKSC 4 16
Quebec (Attorney General) v A 2013 SCC 5, [2013] 1 SCR 61 . . . . 129, 132
Quilloin v Wolcott 434 US 246 (1978) 296
R (on the application of Begum) v Headteacher and Governors of Denbigh High School
 [2006] UKHL 15 28
R (on the application of SG) and Others v Secretary of State for Work and Pensions
 [2015] UKSC 16 253
R v Brown [1994] 1 AC 212 122
R v R [1952] 1 All ER 1194 144
R v R [1991] UKHL 12 49
Radmacher v Granatino [2010] UKSC 42 . . . . 37, 121, 127, 129, 263
Romer v Evans 517 US 620 (1996) 97
Roth Steel Products v Sharon Steel Corp 705 F2d 134 (6th Cir 1983) 270
S (A Child) [2002] EWCA Civ 1795 . . . . 246, 252
S (Transfer of Residence) [2010] EWHC 192 (Fam); [2011] 1 FLR 1789 54
S v HM Advocate 1989 SLT 469, 473 49
S v S [2014] EWHC 7 (Fam) 268
Santosky v Kramer 455 US 745 (1982) 266
Schalk and Kopf v Austria (App No 30141/04) [2011] 2 FCR 650 . . . . 41, 49
Scott v United Kingdom [2000] Fam LR 102 (ECtHR) 35
Skinner v Oklahoma 316 US 535 (1942) 158
ST 467 SW3d 720 (Tex App 2015) 266
Stack v Dowden [2007] UKHL 17, [2007] 2 AC 432 . . . . 117–20, 125, 130
Stanley v Illinois 405 US 645 (1972) 266, 296
Steinfeld and Keidan v Secretary of State for Education [2016] EWHC 128 (Admin);
 [2017] EWCA Civ 81 10
Stokes v Stokes 246 Ga 765m 273 SE2d 169 (1981) 2

Süss v Germany [2006] 1 FLR 522 (ECtHR) 35, 230
T (A Minor) (Wardship: Medical Treatment) [1997] 1 All ER 906 (EWCA) 229
TF v BL 813 NE2d 1244 (Mass 2004) 266
TP and KM v United Kingdom (2002) 34 EHRR 2 35
Troxel v Granville 530 US 67 (2000) 32, 232, 266
Turner v Safley 482 US 78 (1987) 158
US v Windsor 570 US _ (2013) 97
W (Children) [2010] UKSC 12 252
White v White [2000] UKHL 54, [2001] 1 AC 596 .... 127, 136, 150
WW v HW [2015] EWHC 1844 (Fam) 259
X (A Child) (Surrogacy: Time limit) [2014] EWHC 3135 (Fam) 9, 16
Yousef v The Netherlands (2003) 36 EHRR 20 .... 35, 230
Zablocki v Redhail 434 US 374 (1978) 158
Zimmie v Zimmie 464 NE2d 142 (Ohio 1984) 270

Table of Statutes and other Instruments

Canada
Family Law Act 2003 C F-4.5 (AB)
   s 32 6

France
Code Civil ....
   art 371 45
   art 371.3 45

Germany
Civil Code ....
   s 1618a 45
   s 1619 45

Poland
Family and Guardianship Code ....
   art 91(1) 45

United Kingdom
Adoption and Children Act 2002, c 38
   s 1(2) 245
Children Act 1989, c 41
   s 1 229
   s 1(1) 227, 231–2
   s 3(1) 17, 21, 30
   s 8 6
   s 10(2)(b) 244
   s 10(8) 244
   s 41 244
Children and Families Act 2014, c 6
   s 11(2) 50
Civil Partnership Act 2004, c 33
   s 72 27
   s 168 144
Family Law Act 1986, c 55
   s 55A 251
Guardianship of Infants Act 1925
   s 1 231
Guardianship of Minors Act 1971
   s 1 231
Human Fertilisation and Embryology Act 1990, c 37
   s 13(5) 70
   s 30 56
Human Fertilisation and Embryology Act 2008, c 22
   s 42(1) 56
   s 54 56
   s 54(3) 8
Inheritance (Family Provision) Act 1938, c 45 50
Intestates' Estate Act 1952, c 64 50
Marriage (Same Sex Couples) Act 2013, c 30
   sch 4 145
Matrimonial Causes Act 1878, c 19 46
Matrimonial Causes Act 1973, C 18
   s 1 144
   s 1(1) 6
   s 1(2)(b) 6
   s 1(6) 145
   Part II 1
   s 24(1)(a) 16
   s 25(1) 229
   s 25A 229
Poor Law Amendment Act 1834, c 76 45
Poor Relief Act 1601
   s 7 45
Social Security Act 1975, c. 14
   s 44 46
   s 45 46
   s 46 46
   s 47 46
   s 66 46
Statute of Uses 1535 263

United States
Arkansas Code ....
   ss 9-22-801 – 9-11-811 265
Arizona Revised Statutes ....
   ss 25-901 – 25-906 265
Connecticut General Statutes ....
   s 46b-86 268
Illinois Gestational Surrogacy Act 266
Illinois Compiled Statutes 750 ILCS ....
   ss 47/1—47/75 266
   s 47/20(2) 260
Illinois Presumptively Void Transfers Act (Pub Act 98-1093) 75
Louisiana Revised Statutes ....
   ss 9:272 – 9:276 265
Massachusetts Code ....
   chap 210, s 2 268

Minnesota Statutes.........................
  s 518.18(a)........................... 268
  s 518.18(e)........................... 268
North Carolina Family Law Arbitration Act... 268
North Carolina Statutes......................
  ss 50-41 to 50-62 268
Ohio State Constitution......................
  art XV, s 11 270
Uniform Commercial Code ....
  s 2-209............................. 270
U.S. Civil Rights Act 1964
  Title VII............................. 157
U.S. Code...................................
  Title 42, s 3601-19 157
  Title 42, s 3631 157
U.S. Code of Federal Regulations..............
  Title 8, s 204.11....................... 170
U.S. Constitution ....
  Amendment 1......................... 48
U.S. Fair Housing Act 1968, as am in
  1974, 1988......................... 157
U.S. Immigration and National Act............
  s 204(a)(iii)(II) 166
  s 212(a)(4)........................... 165
  s 240A(b)(2) 166
  s 265................................ 167
Washington Statutes.........................
  s 26.33.295........................... 266

European and International
Convention for the Protection
  of Human Rights and
  Fundamental Freedoms
  (European Convention on
  Human Rights, as amended) 1950
  art 8 .... 13, 41, 71, 234
  art 14 253
  First Protocol, art 2 48
Council Directive 90/ 364, 1990 OJ (L 180)... 26
  art 1 165
Council Directive 90/ 365, 1990 OJ (L 180)... 28
  art 1 165
Council Directive 93/ 96, 1993 OJ (L 317) ... 59
  art 1 165
United Nations' Convention
  on the Rights of the
  Child, 20 November 1989, 1577
  UNTS 3 .... 32, 168, 192, 230,
                         232-3, 237, 239
  Preamble 238, 243
  art 3 253
  art 3(1)............................. 230
  art 18(1)............................ 243
  art 24 251
  art 24(1)............................ 251
  art 24(3)............................ 251

List of Contributors

Scott Altman is the Virginia S. and Fred H. Bice Professor of Law at the University of Southern California, where he teaches Family Law and Property. His scholarship focuses on philosophical issues in family law. He has written on fairness in child custody and relocation, justifications for child support, intimacy and parental rights, a child's right to an open future, and coercive negotiations at divorce.

David Archard is Professor of Philosophy at Queen's University Belfast, and has written extensively in applied ethics, political and moral philosophy, especially on the subject of children's rights, the family and the state. His books include *Procreation and Parenthood* (2010), and *The Family: A Liberal Defence* (2010). The 3rd edition of his *Children, Rights and Childhood* was published in 2015. He has been Visiting Fellow at the Universities of Melbourne, South Florida, Bergen, Beijing Normal University, Chinese University of Hong Kong, and the Ethik-Zentrum, University of Zurich. He is Vice-President of the Society for Applied Philosophy.

Charlotte Bendall is a Lecturer in Law at the University of Birmingham. She has recently completed a doctoral research project on the ways in which civil partnership (and, by extension, same-sex marriage) can challenge social and legal constructions of gender in intimate relationships, focusing specifically on the provision of legal advice on civil partnership dissolution. Her interests span family law, feminist legal studies, and law, gender, and sexuality.

Brian H. Bix is the Frederick W. Thomas Professor of Law and Philosophy at the University of Minnesota. He holds a DPhil (doctorate) from Oxford University and a JD from Harvard University. He teaches in the area of Family Law, Jurisprudence, and Contract Law. His publications include *Contract Law: Rules, Theory, and Context* (Cambridge University Press, 2012); *Oxford Introductions to U.S. Law: Family Law* (Oxford University Press, 2013); *Jurisprudence: Theory and Practice*, 7th edn (Sweet & Maxwell, 2015); *A Dictionary of Legal Theory* (Oxford University Press, 2004); and *Law, Language, and Legal Determinacy* (Oxford University Press, 1993). He is a Member of the Bars of the States of Minnesota, Connecticut, and Massachusetts, and a Member of the American Law Institute.

Elizabeth Brake is an Associate Professor of Philosophy at Arizona State University. She holds a BA in Classics and English from Magdalen College, Oxford, and an MLitt. and PhD in Philosophy from the University of St. Andrews. Her research is primarily in ethics and political philosophy. She is the author of *Minimizing Marriage: Marriage, Morality, and the Law* and editor of *After Marriage: Rethinking Marital Relationships* (both with Oxford University Press). She has held a Murphy Institute Fellowship at Tulane, a Canadian SSHRC Grant, and an ASU Provost's Humanities Fellowship. She is currently working on a project on the state's role in disaster response.

Ronald C. Den Otter (Professor, Political Science, California Polytechnic State University) received his JD from the University of Pennsylvania and his PhD in political science from UCLA. His research occupies the space where American constitutional law and normative political theory intersect. In 2009, Cambridge University Press (CUP) published his first book, *Judicial Review in an Age of Moral Pluralism*. In 2015, Cambridge University Press published his second book, *In Defense of Plural Marriage*, which is the first book-length treatment of the constitutional arguments for and against plural marriage (being able to marry more than one person at the same time).

James G. Dwyer is Professor of Law at the College of William & Mary in Virginia, USA, where he teaches courses in youth law, family law, and law & social justice. He has authored several books and dozens of articles on the rights of children in various family law contexts.

John Eekelaar taught family law at Pembroke College, Oxford from 1965 to 2005, and was its Academic Director from 2005 to 2009. He was Lecturer (later Reader) in Law at Oxford University from 1965 to 2005, a founder member of the International Society of Family Law, of which he was President from 1985 to 1988, and founding co-editor of the International Journal of Law, Policy and the Family. He was elected a Fellow of the British Academy in 2001 and Distinguished Visiting Fellow by the New Zealand Law Foundation in 2005. Books include *Family Law and Social Policy* (1978, 1984), *Regulating Divorce* (1991), and *Family Law and Personal Life* (2006) (Second edition, 2017) and a series of empirical studies from *Child Protection: State Intervention and Family Life* (with Robert Dingwall and Topsy Murray) (1983) to *Lawyers and Mediators: The Brave New World of Services for Separating Families* (with Mavis Maclean) (2016). He edited, with Rob George, the *Routledge Handbook of Family Law and Policy* (2014).

Lucinda Ferguson is Associate Professor of Family Law at the University of Oxford; Tutorial Fellow in Law at Oriel College, Oxford; and an Associate Member of 1 King's Bench Walk. Her research and teaching focuses on family law, children's law, and education law and she has published widely in these areas. She has been commissioned to produce research for government law reform bodies, and her work has been cited in leading court decisions. She is a contributing editor of the *Education Law Journal*. She holds an MA in Jurisprudence (English Law with German Law) from Magdalen College, Oxford, as well as a BCL from the University of Oxford. She also holds an LLM from Queen's University, Canada. She is a Senior Fellow of the Higher Education Academy, and was a finalist for OUP's Law Teacher of the Year 2016.

Rosie Harding is Professor and Chair in Law and Society at the University of Birmingham and a 2016/17 British Academy Mid-Career Fellow. Her research focuses on the everyday regulation and legal recognition of intimate and caring relationships. She is author of *Duties to Care: Relationality, Dementia and Law* (Cambridge University Press, 2017), and *Regulating Sexuality* (Routledge Social Justice, 2011; winner of the

2011 SLSA-Hart Book Prize and the 2011 SLSA-Hart Early Career Prize), and editor of *Ageing and Sexualities: Interdisciplinary Perspectives* (Ashgate, 2016), *Law and Sexuality* (Routledge Critical Concepts, 2016), and *Revaluing Care in Theory, Law and Politics: Cycles and Connections* (Routledge Social Justice, 2017).

Diane Jeske received her PhD from the Massachusetts Institute of Technology in 1992. Since then, she has been on the faculty of the University of Iowa, where she is now Professor of Philosophy. Her work has focused on the nature of intimacy and of its attendant obligations. She is the author of *Rationality and Moral Theory: How Intimacy Generates Reasons* (Routledge), and is the co-editor, with Richard Fumerton, of *Introducing Philosophy Through Film* (Blackwell) and *Readings in Political Philosophy: Theory and Applications* (Broadview).

Robert Leckey is Dean of the Faculty of Law and holds the Samuel Gale Chair in Law at McGill University. He is the author of *Bills of Rights in the Common Law* (2015) and *Contextual Subjects: Family, State and Relational Theory* (2008) and the editor of *After Legal Equality: Family, Sex, Kinship* (2015) and *Marital Rights* (2017). He has received the Canada Prize of the International Academy of Comparative Law, the *Prix de la Fondation du Barreau du Québec*, and the McGill Principal's Prize for Excellence in Teaching.

Matthew Lister is a Senior Lecturer (Associate Professor) in the law school at Deakin University in Melbourne, Australia, and a Senior Fellow at the Zicklin Center for Business Ethics Research at the University of Pennsylvania. Additionally, Lister is the current chair of the American Philosophical Association's Committee on Philosophy and Law. He has published papers in peer-reviewed journals and law reviews on most aspects of immigration law, as well as on international law, legal and political philosophy, and criminal law theory. He is currently working on several papers on the intersection of immigration and business ethics, including papers on ethical issues relating to unauthorized immigration.

Colin M. Macleod is Professor of Philosophy and Law at the University of Victoria. He is currently chair of the Philosophy Department. His research focuses on issues in contemporary moral, political, and legal theory with a special focus on distributive justice and equality; children, families and justice; and democratic ethics. He is the author of *Liberalism, Justice, and Markets* (Oxford University Press, 1998), co-editor with David Archard of *The Moral and Political Status of Children* (Oxford University Press, 2002) and co-author with Ben Justice of *Have A Little Faith: Religion, Democracy and the American Public School* (University of Chicago Press, 2016).

Mary Lyndon (Molly) Shanley is Professor of Political Science Emerita on the Margaret Stiles Halleck Chair at Vassar College. Her scholarship examines social justice issues in law and public policy concerning marriage and family formation, and she writes now on college education in prisons and jails. She is author of *Feminism, Marriage and the Law in Victorian England* (Princeton, 1989); *Just Marriage*, ed. D Chasman and J Cohen (Oxford, 2004); and *Making Babies, Making Families* (Beacon, 2001). She edited, with

Carole Pateman, *Feminist Interpretations and Political Theory* (Penn State, 1990); with Uma Narayan, *Reconstructing Political Theory* (Penn State, 1997); and with I. M. Young and D. I. O'Neill, *Illusion of Equality: Engaging with Carole Pateman* (Penn State, 2008). In her local community, she teaches a pre-college course and leads writing groups at the Dutchess county jail, sings in a community chorus, and is an ardent back-packer.

Abstracts

Philosophical Foundations of Children's and Family Law

This volume brings together new essays in law and philosophy on a broad range of topics in children's and family law. It is the first volume to bring together essays by legal scholars and philosophers for an integrated, critical analysis of key issues in this area, marking the 'coming of age' of the comparatively new field of family law. Debates in children's and family law are at once theoretical and empirical in nature. Not only does children's and family law have significant consequences for individuals' intimate lives, the field's impact on lived experience highlights the socially constructed nature of law. Approaching this area of law often involves exploring a legal concept familiar from daily life, such as the very notion of 'marriage' or 'family', and examining it within its social, economic, and historical context. The normative basis for law regulating intimate personal and family life extends beyond any narrow legal philosophy or social context to its broader foundations in theories of morality or justice. The chapters included bring together a representative and broad range of pieces that engage with long-standing and contemporary debates. A wide range of perspectives is represented on topics such as same-sex marriage, polygamy and polyamory, alimony, unmarried cohabitation, gestational surrogacy and assisted reproductive technologies, child support, parental rights and responsibilities, children's rights, family immigration, religious freedom, and the rights of paid caregivers. There is also philosophical discussion of concepts such as care, intimacy, and the nature of family and family law itself.

1 Family Law and Legal Theory, John Eekelaar

This chapter will be about family law and legal theory. Understandably, Brian Bix baulked at the idea that a single theory of family law could be constructed, at least for the US. Given the scope of its subject matter, I also think a quest for one overarching theory for family law will prove elusive. But I will argue that there is a pervasive feature about family law which is central to understanding both how family law operates and how it should operate.

It will be argued that understanding the way legal and social norms interact should be central to theorizing about family law. In fact, there may need to be a number of theories explaining, or justifying, the specific interactions in the various circumstances in which they occur. It will be seen that these invariably revolve around the issue of power: who has it and how it can be controlled.

2 Family and Family Law, David Archard

Much contemporary writing on 'family' and 'family law' cites extensive changes to the family as evidence that the very concept of the 'family' is redundant, or that the family has disappeared.

Conceptual questions (What counts as a family?) should be distinguished from normative ones (Is the family a good thing? Are some families better than others?). The use of the term 'the family' can be normatively innocent such that there are different family forms none of which should be privileged.

Having distinguished 'the family' as an extra-legal concept and as a legal construct, I defend a functional definition of the family. This value-free definition can serve as the basis of evaluative judgments about the family.

There are good reasons why law might recognize the family, consistent with law also recognizing non-familial personal relations. Nevertheless we need not accord familial status to such relations, or abandon the term 'family'.

3 Paid and Unpaid Care, Elizabeth Brake

This chapter argues that relationships between paid caregivers and care recipients should be eligible for equivalent legal protections to other adult caring relationships. Care workers (or intimate workers, or domestic workers) are a vulnerable group; in law, they are not fully protected as workers or as family members, although they often form close, reciprocal caring relationships with the people they care for. While some legal theorists have recently addressed their rights as workers, this chapter considers their eligibility for rights as family members. It extends my earlier arguments for marriage equality, that marriage law (or a marriage-like law with reduced legal entitlements which I call 'minimal marriage') should protect a wider variety of relationship types than law currently does, on grounds of equal treatment. After reviewing these earlier arguments, I make the case for their application to care workers, addressing both theoretical and practical objections.

4 A Perfectionist Argument for Legal Recognition of Polyamorous Relationships, Ronald C. Den Otter

Although several American legal scholars have defended the constitutional right to marry more than one person at the same time on substantive due process or equal protection grounds, few have underscored the possibility that plural marriage could be beneficial. The standard liberal approach eschews comparative judgments between monogamy and polyamory, ultimately depending on the value of the exercise of autonomy for its own sake. The problem is that those who employ it must remain reticent about the benefits that the legal recognition of polyamorous marriage may produce. In this chapter, I formulate an atypical constitutional argument for polyamorous marriage, drawing inspiration from John Stuart Mill's well-known idea of experiments in living, rooted in the benefits of unconventional beliefs and practices. I try to explain why polyamory can be a superior marital arrangement for some people under some circumstances. Such marital experiments also may assist polyamorists in becoming better human beings.

5 Cohabitants, Choice, and the Public Interest, Robert Leckey

Through the narrow entry of property disputes between former cohabitants, this chapter aims to clarify thinking on issues crucial to philosophical examination of family law. It refracts big questions—such as what cohabitants should owe one another and the balance between choice and protection—through a legal lens of attention to institutional matters such as the roles of judges and legislatures. Canadian cases on unjust enrichment and English cases quantifying beneficial interests in a jointly owned home are examples. The chapter highlights limits on judicial law reform in the face of social change, both in substance and in the capacity to acknowledge the state's interest in intimate relationships. The chapter relativizes the focus on choice prominent in academic and policy discussions of cohabitation and highlights the character of family law, entwined with the general private law of property and obligations, as a regulatory system.

6 Heteronormativity in Dissolution Proceedings, Charlotte Bendall and Rosie Harding

This chapter explores how heteronormativity, normative ordering of society to correspond with heterosexuality, shapes experiences of dissolution of formally recognized same-sex relationships. We present qualitative data from in-depth interviews with both clients and solicitors with direct experience of civil partnership dissolution. Drawing on insights from legal consciousness studies, we explore the extent to which legal intervention in relationship breakdown creates an arena of strategy and self-interest. Overall, these data demonstrate the ways in which 'law' is conceived of as a product of its actors, rather than as being an entity of 'the state'. We show that heteronormative understandings of gender roles in relationships have been carried over from (different-sex) marriage into civil partnership proceedings. We argue that lesbians and gay men retain a level of resistance to this legal heteronormativity that has the potential to have transformative effects on contemporary understandings of the place of gender in marriage.

7 The Rights of Families and Children at the Border, Matthew Lister

Families and children pose several problems for states in migration policies. All states provide some family migration benefits, and often special benefits for children, yet many of these states have sought to limit family immigration and the rights of children. This chapter explains why just immigration policies must offer family-based immigration and why this does not imply immigration rights in other relationships, such as friendships. It argues that a right to intimate association grounds a basic right to form family units across borders—a right inhering primarily in current citizens. It also explores how this right may be limited, including by 'public charge' type provisions, and how far these rights should ground protection from deportation for non-citizen family members, arguing that reasons that justify family immigration rights also justify protection from deportation. It finishes with a discussion of special protections owed, as a matter of justice, to children.

8 Moral and Legal Obligations to Support 'Family', Diane Jeske

We have various kinds of moral obligations to take care of those to whom we stand in intimate relationships, and, for many of us, some of those whom we consider family are among our most important intimates. These moral obligations have various grounds; some are unique to intimate relationships while others also occur in non-intimate relationships. Given the centrality of intimate relationships and their attendant moral obligations to our lives, we need to consider what role, if any, political and legal institutions ought to play in protecting, enforcing, and/or regulating intimacy, whether familial or not. I consider various approaches that the state might take to intimate familial relationships and their possible justifications. I then consider state regulation of spousal support after the dissolution of a marriage to see what approach the state seems to take and whether this has implications for how it ought to proceed in other cases.

9 Are Children's Rights Important?, Colin M. Macleod

This chapter explores the nature and justificatory basis of children's rights with a view to determining whether children's rights are important. Although children's rights are frequently invoked in legal and political discourse, they often generate controversy: their practical and theoretical significance is sometimes challenged. Many states acknowledge children's rights and yet fail to secure many of the most basic interests of children putatively protected by their rights. Moreover, the suggestion that children are the bearers of genuine moral rights is sometimes met with philosophical scepticism. This chapter distinguishes different forms of scepticism about children's rights and explores whether doubts about the theoretical and practical importance of children's rights can be vindicated. I argue that reticence about children's rights is not justified. Given a proper construal of children's rights it is appropriate both to treat children as genuine bearers of rights and to view their rights as morally and politically important.

10 Parental Control Rights, Scott Altman

Parents typically direct many aspects of their children's lives and often believe that they deserve protection from interference by governments and third parties. Justifications for such parental control rights sometimes rely on the interests of children or of society. But they can also rely directly on parental interests. This chapter considers whether parental control rights can be justified based on parental interests. It first considers two parental interests sometimes put forward as warranting parental control rights: an interest in intimacy and an interest in acting as a fiduciary. The first fails as a justification for parental rights because intimacy is unlikely to be undermined by most intrusions. The second fails because it misunderstands the nature of fiduciary roles. The chapter then considers an alternative parental interest in nurturing, counselling, and educating. This interest requires both authenticity and discretion to play a meaningful role in a parent's life and facilitating this interest warrants protecting parental control rights.

11 An Argument for Treating Children as a 'Special Case', Lucinda Ferguson

This chapter's argument stems from the premise that legal language should speak for itself. The 'paramountcy' principle suggests the prioritization of children's interests, and 'children's rights' suggests some aspect of distinctiveness to children's interests. But there is academic consensus of both that children's interests cannot and should not be prioritized over those of others. This chapter examines the justification for the contrary perspective, and for treating children as a prioritized 'special case' in all legal decisions affecting them.

Four key counter-arguments frame the discussion. First, the 'social construct' objection: as a social construct, childhood cannot sustain the prioritization of children's interests over those of others. Second, the 'vulnerability' objection: children's vulnerability is either not unique or suggests dependency or interdependency, not prioritization. Third, the 'family autonomy' objection: parents' rights and the family unit justify deference of children's interests. Fourth, the 'equality' objection: equal moral consideration makes prioritization unjustifiable.

12 Private Ordering in Family Law, Brian H. Bix

The chapter begins by clarifying what is meant by 'private ordering' in family law—where the primary focus is usually not on the *fact* of private ordering, but the question of *state recognition* or *enforcement* of private choices. Additionally, the analysis considers the distinction between agreements regarding substantive outcomes (e.g. who should have parental rights), and agreements regarding procedure (e.g. having a dispute settled by arbitration). The chapter offers an overview of the moral and policy arguments that had been raised when private ordering had been strongly discouraged (e.g. various social goods, and the protection of vulnerable parties), and the changing arguments being offered now that private ordering is more frequently encouraged, or at least condoned. Finally, the chapter will consider why some forms of private ordering (e.g. separation agreements at divorce) are encouraged, while others (e.g. co-parenting and surrogacy agreements) continue to be treated with suspicion.

13 Regulating Child Rearing in a Culturally Diverse Society, James G. Dwyer

Common complaints against state agencies that regulate parental conduct are that they are insensitive to cultural diversity, unfairly force adult members of cultural minorities to conform to majoritarian norms, and consequently both disrupt parent–child relationships to children's detriment and threaten the very survival of minority cultures. This chapter will address the difficult question of whether and to what extent state agencies should modify child welfare standards to fit different practices of minority cultural groups. Answering this question entails: clarifying the state's role generally in the lives of non-autonomous persons, considering who is the best alternative decision maker for them, articulating the value commitments of modern liberal societies, assessing the appropriateness of applying those commitments to state regulation of care for non-autonomous persons, and critically examining claims of adult entitlement to dictate the course of particular young persons' lives.

14 Surrogacy, Mary Lyndon Shanley

The development of assisted reproductive technologies sharpened perceptions of the differences among three major criteria for parental status—biological (genetics and gestation), volition/intention, and caregiving/functional. This chapter surveys the development of these justifications. It argues that of these, caregiving—and the underlying philosophic framework of the ethics of care—is the most satisfactory grounding of parental status for three reasons: first, it places relationship at the centre of its theoretical and practical concerns; second, caregiving focuses attention on the child; and third, thinking about relationships of care ensures that we consider the impact of social factors, such as race and class, on reproduction and family formation. But despite the centrality of caregiving to grounding recognition of a parent-child relationship, this chapter concludes that caregiving is not fully satisfactory. It advocates a pluralistic account that regards the relationships established by all three criteria as significant to both social and legal groundings of parental status.

Introduction

The Importance of Theory to Children's and Family Law

Lucinda Ferguson and Elizabeth Brake

I. Introduction

What defines family law? Is it an area of law with clean boundaries and unified distinguishing characteristics, or an untidy grouping of disparate rules and doctrines? What values or principles should guide it—and how could it be improved? Indeed, even the scope of family law is contested. Whilst some law schools and textbooks separate family law from children's law, this is invariably effected without asking what might be gained or lost from treating them together or separately. Should family law and children's law be distinguished or treated together?

One would expect disagreement on these questions in any context. In bringing together theorists from multiple jurisdictions and at least two primary disciplines, we should not be surprised to find deep differences in approach reflecting different methodologies and foundational questions. The tension between them, we hope, can illuminate and enrich discussion on all sides. Further, through combining insights from law and philosophy, we also intend to add another layer to the current trend to focus on the empirical in family law research, and highlight how critical debates in children's and family law are at once theoretical and empirical in nature. Understanding the nature and content of a child's 'best interests' as contained in multiple jurisdictions' legal frameworks regulating private and public law concerning children, for example, requires us to approach the matter both conceptually—in order to adjudicate between frameworks—and in terms of fit with evidence from research. This immediately makes any satisfactory resolution more uncertain, contested, and subject to criticism. It is in this context that we hope that the conversations between law and philosophy, their points of agreement and divergence, can advance stalled debates.

International differences correspond, of course, to differences in law, policy, and procedure. Contrast, for example, England and Wales' 'single-pot' approach to the distribution of property and maintenance upon marriage breakdown[1] to the more common, 'pillarised'[2] treatment of matrimonial property, pensions, and maintenance. The difference in system design necessarily affects the available potential justifications. As a more nuanced aspect of the impact of system design, one might consider the normative

---

[1] Matrimonial Causes Act 1973 C 18, Part II (England and Wales).
[2] Dutta, cited by JM Scherpe, 'Towards a Matrimonial Property Regime for England and Wales' in R Probert and C Barton (eds), *Fifty Years in Family Law: Essays for Stephen Cretney* (Intersentia 2012) 133, 138.

Philosophical Foundations of Children's and Family Law. First Edition. Edited by Elizabeth Brake and Lucinda Ferguson. Introduction © Lucinda Ferguson and Elizabeth Brake 2018. Published 2018 by Oxford University Press.

difficulties created by the variation in default regimes adopted in relation to matrimonial (or marital) property between US states.[3] Facing jurisdictional differences—like considering historical changes within one's own jurisdiction—can yield an awareness of the context-specificity of one's own starting points. And awareness of how things are done differently can lead us to call into question our own ways of doing things. Such awareness might alert us to unintended consequences of legislation or to innovative solutions. And, more fundamentally, it might cause us to interrogate what we take as the core, the normal, or even the natural. This is where philosophical investigation becomes indispensable.

In section II, we outline a number of respects in which the approaches taken by (academic) lawyers and philosophers writing in this field tend to differ, as well as how the structure of this collection seeks to cut across and highlight both these divergences and shared accounts. In section III, we introduce the key themes that underpin the collection, which demonstrate the potential for cross-fertilization between legal contexts as well as between legal and philosophical perspectives. When we refer to 'lawyers' and 'philosophers', we have in mind those working in family law and children's law in particular.

II. Disciplinary Peculiarities

Perhaps even more telling than international differences are disciplinary divides. Whilst many of us would describe our work as inter-disciplinary, differences in training tell in authors' focus and argumentative starting-points and aims, their chosen methodology, and the nature of the conclusions reached.

A. Focus and aim

The questions asked of Family Division judges very often involve value judgments. As Lord Hoffman reasoned in *Piglowska v Piglowski*, a case concerned with discretionary decision making on financial provision upon divorce:

> These guidelines, not expressly stated by Parliament, are derived by the courts from values about family life which it considers would be widely accepted in the community. But there are many cases which involve value judgments on which there are no such generally held views.... *These are value judgments on which reasonable people may differ. Since judges are also people, this means that some degree of diversity in their application of values is inevitable* and, within limits, an acceptable price to pay for the flexibility of the discretion conferred by the Act of 1973. The appellate court must be willing to permit a degree of pluralism in these matters.[4]

Judicial decisions that embody fact-specific and pluralistic value judgments pose an interesting dilemma for philosophical writing about family and children's law, which highlights the importance of recognizing that arguments in law and philosophy may

---

[3] Contrast, eg, California's 'community of property' default regime (Fam C s 751 s770) with the judicial 'equitable distribution' default in Georgia (*Stokes v Stokes*, 246 Ga 765m 273 SE2d 169 (1981)).
[4] *Piglowska v Piglowski* [1999] 3 All ER 632, 644D-G (UKHL) (Lord Hoffmann) (emphasis added).

have critically different drivers. This is because, within philosophy, much ethical theory rejects evaluative pluralism; its mission is to ascertain the correct (whether true, or most reasonable) answer to such moral and evaluative questions. Whilst much contemporary political philosophy addresses the problem of political decision making within a society characterized by a diversity of religious and ethical views, it also often argues for non-pluralistic principles of justice—which may differ significantly from existing bodies of law. (It is worth noting that ethical and political theorists do not always claim these moral and political principles are ahistorical and transcendental; they may be justified as reflecting the deep shared norms of an existing society, for example.)

By contrast to philosophy's focus on discerning true—or at least reasonable—norms, the nature of legal practice encourages (academic) lawyers to be purposive in their focus on normative issues. This can suggest inconsistency to the external observer since normative argumentation is diversely employed—as a means to win cases in court, to underpin criticism of the justifiability of current legal regulation, or as a basis to argue for law reform. Hence, this is why the Grand Chamber of the European Court of Human Rights asserted the 'special' nature of the marriage status as an argument in itself to justify excluding interdependent sisters from tax benefits.[5] Whereas the correctness of seeing marriage as a 'special' status is assumed by the Grand Chamber, Brake's chapter highlights how philosophical discussion of the extension of state support from different-sex marriage to other relationship forms first considers the normative basis for state support of any relationship and then asks which relationship forms share that characteristic. Especially within a society characterized by diverse religious and ethical views, the 'special status' of marriage must be justified, not merely assumed. Whilst Brake presents an argument for reform, the larger aim is to ensure that the law consistently recognizes the value of care.

B. Social constructs and social life

Lawyers also work within and without the social construct of law in a way less often practised by philosophers. Whilst philosophical theory may criticize existing social practices (for example, as unjust) or argue for a particular legal norm in light of its social effects (for example, promoting certain virtues), lawyers tend to accept that law should reflect and respond to existing social practices to a greater degree. This is particularly evident in the context of family and children's law, where the relationship between familial life and law is porous and the socially constructed nature of law is at the forefront and ever-present. The social constructs of 'family law' speak directly to those constructs that have made meaning of social life. But law's own internal normativity means that lack of fit with social life is not necessarily unjustifiable.

To take a very simple example, when seeking to understand the nature of 'modern' marriage, how much weight should we place on individual pieces of evidence about how couples structure their intimate lives? Should the fact that both parties to

---

[5] *Burden and Burden v United Kingdom* (App No 13378/05) (Grand Chamber) [2006] ECHR 1064: [63].

a marriage keep individual bank accounts have any significance? Might they see their joint lives differently from those who simply have a joint account? Family law scholars currently do not attach any weight to this evidence, but might there be a threshold percentage of married couples so conducting their affairs that would lead us to think it says something about the nature of 'modern' marriage? If that behaviour were to form part of the broader social meaning-making of modern life, legal scholars would need normative argumentation to the contrary to explain the divergence of the social construction of marriage in law.

Yet, legal argumentation can assume the need for fit between 'family law' and family life. In their contribution to this collection, Bendall and Harding are particularly concerned to highlight the lack of fit between the heteronormativity of constructed marriage and how same-sex couples in civil partnerships understand their relationship.[6] But, rather than immediate law reform, they call for further research to explore how legal recognition may shape same-sex couples' lived experience of law. What form would further empirical evidence need to take to justify reform? Whilst evidence from social life is always relevant to law's social constructs, decisions as to whether to reform and the nature of any reforms require the insertion of a coherent cluster of norms to mediate the interaction between law and lived experience. This is one area where philosophical insights may be particularly valuable.

C. Language and concepts

Language plays significant, but differing roles for both disciplines. Legal analysis can be framed and constrained by particular legal terms of art, such as 'proportionality' in relation to rights arguments, which can risk frustrating deeper philosophical engagement.[7] For philosophers, language is often indicative of whether the underlying concept is 'thin' or 'thick';[8] the former suggests a purely evaluative position, whereas the latter is also substantially descriptive. For example, a thin ethical evaluation might be that an act is 'wrong', but a thick evaluation such as 'selfish' or 'malicious' or 'sadistic' would give more detailed description. This could be particularly illuminating for lawyers working with difficult concepts in the family context, such as 'fairness' in financial provision upon relationship breakdown. Might at least some of the difficulty with 'fairness' be explained by the fact that, even in ethics, it is arguably 'impossible confidently to classify' 'fairness' as either 'thick' or 'thin'?[9]

Recognizing the difficulties posed by 'thin' concepts, which lack substantive non-evaluative description, also highlights why reference to norms without specifying the

---

[6] See C Bendall and R Harding's chapter.

[7] It should be noted that 'proportionality' is used too within certain philosophical ethical frameworks; philosophy too has its terms of art.

[8] See, B Williams, *Ethics and the Limits of Philosophy* (Harvard UP 1985). Though it should be noted that Williams cast doubt on the ease of distinguishing between the two different types of concept: B Williams, 'Truth in Ethics' (1996) 8 Ratio 227, 234.

[9] S Scheffler, 'Morality Through Thick and Thin: A Critical Note of Ethics and the Limits of Philosophy' (1987) 96 The Philosophical Review 411, 417.

content may be an inadequate lens through which to relate social life to family and children's law. The Commission on European Family Law, for example, reasons that

> As regards the substance of the Principles regarding Property Relations between Spouses, *equality* between the spouses is the primary but by no means the only consideration.... Principles of *sharing* and *fairness, solidarity, flexibility, legal certainty, protection of the weaker spouse*, and the promotion of *party autonomy* are likewise of fundamental importance in this area of law.[10]

Whilst they note the critical difficulty of balancing these norms,[11] they do not suggest how this balance should be struck in particular instances. Can philosophical insight avoid the risk of arbitrariness that may result from balancing normative labels without content?

For lawyers and non-lawyers alike, the lack of correspondence between some legal terms of art and their plain meaning can problematically affect argumentation. 'Private ordering' in the family law context, for example, and as Bix notes,[12] is not truly private at all. The 'paramountcy' of a child's 'best interests' in law, as Ferguson discusses in her chapter, does not mean that children's interests are prioritized over those of other parties. Inconsistent concern that the term's content, when used as a term of art, corresponds to the term's plain meaning undermines the ability to both critique the nature of the legal term as well as engage with the justifiability of any lack of correspondence between the legal and broader social constructs at stake. Legalistic interpretations of statutory tests, such as the threshold for compulsory child protective intervention,[13] can also serve to further distance the law from its normative underpinnings.

Legal commentators are often more attuned to the expressive aspects of law's effects,[14] since arguments both for and against legal reform can lie in the signals sent by the language employed in the law. When same-sex couples are granted access to the different-sex institution of marriage, for example, does the message sent change if we talk in terms of 'same-sex marriage' or the 'extension of marriage to same-sex couples'? Ferguson takes the view that it does and, preferring the latter view, adopts the language of 'extended marriage'[15] despite the persistent unequal treatment of same-sex couples within marriage.[16] Yet, in their chapter on same-sex relationship breakdown, Bendall and Harding use both framings interchangeably, suggesting the contrary view. Whilst

---

[10] K Boele-Woelki, F Ferrand, CG Beilfuss, M Jäntera-Järeborg, N Lowe, D Martiny, W Pintens, *Principles of European Family Law Regarding Property Relations between Spouses* (Intersentia 2013) 33 (emphasis in original).

[11] ibid 33–34.

[12] BH Bix, 'Private Ordering and Family Law' (2010) 23 Journal of the American Academy of Matrimonial Lawyers 249, 250.

[13] In England and Wales, see *Newham London Borough Council v AG* [1993] 1 FLR 281, 289 (Sir Stephen Brown P) and compare reasoning in decisions such as *Re J (Children)* [2013] UKSC 9.

[14] C Sunstein, 'On the Expressive Function of Law' (1995–1996) 144 University of Pennsylvania Law Review 2021. For an interesting discussion of the range of expressive claims made about law, see RH McAdams, *The Expressive Powers of Law* (Harvard UP 2015) ch 1, especially 13–21.

[15] L Ferguson, 'The Curious Case of Civil Partnership: The Extension of Marriage to Same-Sex Couples and the Status-Altering Consequences of a Wait-And-See Approach' (2016) 28 Child and Family Law Quarterly 347, 354–55.

[16] ibid 354.

the legislators' intention is important, public reception can also change the symbolic significance of language.

By contrast, consider parental time with children, the legal framing of which has changed from dual order terms such as 'custody' and 'access' or 'residence' and 'contact' to single order terms such as 'parenting'[17] or 'child arrangements'.[18] These legal devices have been subject to common reformulation as public reception has undermined legislative intention; the language of winners and losers has been understood as recast despite the legislative attempts to neutralize terminology. With a different direction of justification than typical philosophical argumentation, legal scholars also inconsistently treat public misunderstanding as a justifiable basis to argue for reform, such as in relation to the myth of the 'common law marriage'.[19]

Law reform for expressive, not substantive reasons, is more frequently pressed in the family context in philosophy as in law. This is clearly seen in philosophical debate over the nomenclature of 'marriage' vs 'civil unions' for instance; the expressive power of the name, and not simply the bundle of accompanying rights and obligations, matters. In relation to the English law on divorce, for example, parties very often adduce 'behaviour' within the terms of s1(2)(b) of the Matrimonial Causes Act 1973 to prove that their marriage has 'broken down irretrievably' as required by s1(1). In the recent case of *Owens v Owens*,[20] the trial judge refused to grant the wife a decree nisi on the grounds that her petition had not met the threshold for s1(2)(b). The Court of Appeal dismissed her appeal. In his lead judgment, Munby P recognized '[t]he hypocrisy and lack of intellectual honesty which is so characteristic a feature of the current law and procedure'[21] since it was widely known that so many divorcing couples engaged in the 'consensual, collusive, manipulation'[22] of s1(2)(b).

Whilst taking the threshold seriously could rectify this abuse of the statute, where does the public interest lie in refusing petitions? Any public policy argument here must be expressive, not substantive.[23] If it were substantive, we could not explain our modern history of overlooking collusive divorce by consent. In expressive terms, there is no obvious reason why we should assume that the difficulty of access to divorce is in a linear relationship with the significance of marriage as an institution.[24] These doubts are supported by Trinder finding no evidence that the current law protects marriage.[25] Such fluctuating tolerance and intolerance for undermining legislative provisions is at odds with philosophical reasoning, which seeks consistency in argumentation.

---

[17] See, eg, Alberta's Family Law Act 2003 C F-4.5, s 32.
[18] Children Act 1989 c. 41, s 8 (England and Wales).
[19] A Barlow, C Burgoyne, E Clery, and J Smithson, 'Cohabitation and the Law: Myths, Money and the Media' in A Park, J Curtice, K Thomson, M Phillips, M Johnson and E Clery (eds), *British Social Attitudes – the 24th Report* (Sage 2008) (discussed in C Bendall and R Harding's chapter).
[20] [2017] EWCA Civ 182.   [21] ibid [94] (Munby P).   [22] ibid.
[23] L Ferguson, 'Hard Divorces Make Bad Law' (2017) 51(3) Journal of Social Welfare and Family Law 364.
[24] ibid.
[25] L Trinder, 'Finding Fault?' Interim Research Findings, University of Exeter, online: <findingfault.org.uk/wp-content/uploads/2017/03/Finding-Fault-interim-research-findings.pdf> accessed 24 March 2017 1.

D. The relevance of practice

The realities of, and potential implications for, legal practice vary in their relevance to academic lawyers' and philosophers' work in this area. Much philosophical ink has been spilled lately on the contested[26] notions of ideal and non-ideal theory. At its best, ideal theory in normative political philosophy approaches questions of law, policy, and procedure by asking what structures there should be, in light of certain theoretical commitments such as liberty and equality.[27] For example, one might start from the position of equal respect[28] for individuals in different types of adult intimate relationships, and use that to argue for who should be able to legally adopt a child. Non-ideal theory, by contrast, would take into account specific injustices that systematically differentiate groups of people, and consider how equality is best implemented between groups in—unjustly—unequal starting positions. Through such a lens, for example, historical discrimination against and unjust treatment of women, racial minorities, or same-sex couples could not be ignored in the question of justice in the adoption process, with perhaps heightened scrutiny of norms that would further disadvantage these groups. Rawls defines ideal theory as assuming compliance,[29] hence it mostly ignores remedies (or rectification of injustice). It has been charged that this focus makes it useless in addressing systematic injustice;[30] its defenders argue that we can only measure wrongs by focusing on what should be the case, and ideal theory describes that.[31] In this form, ideal theory does not assume humans are ideal or that they will comply with principles of justice; in fact, such idealizing assumptions tend to characterize ideal theory in its worst form.

One way to encapsulate the differing approaches of lawyers and philosophers could be in terms of non-ideal vs ideal theorizing (although this contrast should not be overdrawn, as many philosophers, particularly those who work on issues such as gender and race, aim to practice non-ideal theory). Concretely, the lawyers in this book focus more on non-intact families, unintended effects of legislation, and gaps in policy—areas where things have gone wrong and need to be put right. The philosophers tend to focus more on values such as love and equality and propose new legal structures that would reflect those values. In short, the philosophers focus on normative justification, the lawyers on making the law fit for purpose, whatever that purpose might be understood to be. This is all a matter of emphasis, of course—the lawyers' essays do reflect values, the philosophers are sensitive to past injustice. For example, Altman's chapter focuses on the justification for 'parental control rights', rather than the need for law reform to accommodate them, and Dwyer's case is centred on articulating a more justifiable basis for current state decision-making on clashes between minority and majority cultures rather than necessarily arguing for different outcomes. Likewise, Brake's chapter

---

[26] See, eg, C Mills, ' "Ideal Theory" as Ideology' (2009) 20 Hypatia 165.
[27] For a valuable overview, see Z Stemplowska and A Swift, 'Ideal and Nonideal Theory' in D Estlund (ed), *The Oxford Handbook of Political Philosophy* (OUP 2012).
[28] See L Ferguson's chapter for a discussion of equal moral consideration.
[29] J Rawls, *Justice as Fairness: A Restatement* (Harvard UP 2001) 13.
[30] See, eg, A Sen, 'What Do We Want from a Theory of Justice?' (2006) 103 Journal of Philosophy 215.
[31] See, eg, Z Stemplowska, 'What's Ideal about Ideal Theory?' (2008) 34 Social Theory and Practice 319, 326–29.

adduces the systematic disadvantages of domestic workers—often immigrants and women of colour—in considering how an ideally just family law should protect them, and political theorist Shanley considers the vulnerability of disadvantaged women in surrogacy arrangements when applying concepts such as 'autonomy' and 'consent'.

Both disciplines seek to appeal to foundational principles or values in their arguments; but here too their methods reflect their differences in training. Whilst philosophers tend to seek *the* correct principle or justificatory framework and trace its implications, lawyers may be more comfortable with a plurality of justification—as might be found in law. For example, one might contrast the approach taken to justifying the financial consequences of relationship breakdown. Whereas Jeske in her chapter searches for one normative basis for spousal support, academic lawyers are more often content with the suggestion of a plurality of interpersonal and social bases.[32] We might wonder if lawyers, more exposed to practice, are more likely to respond to the 'normal chaos of family law'[33] as well as the institutional constraints in the practice of law (as Leckey emphasizes in his chapter). A measure of pragmatism underpins such an approach. In the context of extending end-of-marriage obligations to same-sex couples, as Bendall and Harding discuss in their chapter, how normatively 'thick' could a single basis for spousal support be? Might such a 'thinner' theoretical basis lose value for lawyers before it would for philosophers because lawyers may be more interested in seeking to predict future legal outcomes based on the current conceptual account?

E. Cases and generalizability

Philosophers' and lawyers' use of cases is typically different. Whilst philosophers will sometimes use a case as a clinching counter-example, they are also prone to give them as examples, not—in themselves—reasons for legislation or judicial development. Cases typically exemplify the general principles which serve as reasons, rather than themselves providing reasons for those principles. In legal argumentation, cases are necessarily often binding precedent with their own reason-giving authority, which can include being a reason for reform. But lawyers are also inclined to parse reasoning and outcomes, to criticize one for not being reflected in the other, and to search for policy-based underpinnings ahead of any available, even articulated, normative basis. The likely outcome of a hypothetical future case, whether determined by legislation or the application of judicial precedent, may also be seen as reason-giving, whereas philosophers are trained to follow the argument where it leads (a practice attributed to Socrates)—even if that is someplace surprising.

Recent judicial interpretation of the requirements for a parental order in the surrogacy context provides a ready example. Section 54(3) of the Human Fertilisation and Embryology Act 2008[34] imposes a six-month time limit for applications. Without a parental order, the commissioning couple can only become the child's legal parents via the more

---

[32] See, eg, J Herring, 'Why Financial Orders on Divorce Should Be Unfair' (2005) 19 International Journal of Law, Policy and Family 218. But contrast L Ferguson, 'Family, Social Inequalities, and the Persuasive Force of Interpersonal Obligation' (2008) 22 International Journal of Law, Policy & the Family 61.

[33] J Dewar, 'The Normal Chaos of Family Law' (1998) 61 Modern Law Review 467.

[34] Human Fertilisation and Embryology Act 2008, c 22.

onerous process of adoption. In *Re X (A Child) (Surrogacy: Time limit)*,[35] Sir James Munby P rejected the literal interpretation of the time limit to allow an application made two years and two months after the child's birth. He reasoned that the court needed to assume that Parliament intended a 'sensible' result;[36] that statutory interpretation was informed by the purpose of s 54, which was to have a 'transformative effect' on the child's reality in the context of the paramountcy of the child's life-long 'best interests';[37] and that it could not sensibly be thought that Parliament intended the difference between six months and six months and one day to be determinative, with one day's delay as fatal;[38] and that this result was not 'precluded by the linguistic structure' of s 54.[39]

Whilst the granting of the order is certainly in both the child's 'best interests' and the commissioning couple's interests, it is not clear how, despite Sir James Munby P's assertion to the contrary, this outcome can be seen as other than doing violence to the language of the governing statute. Might it exemplify Dworkin's theory of 'constructive interpretation'?[40] Beyond legal philosophy, how should philosophical analysis interact with the norms of statutory interpretation?

Philosophers may be more inclined to state their arguments in more general terms, using examples that are not intended to be treated as cases, but mere exemplars. Yet lawyers are often concerned with resolving particularly problematic cases, and can sometimes need to be jurisdictionally specific, but can (unintentionally) also assume the ability to generalize from particular jurisdictions. Leckey directly considers this difficulty in his chapter on the Anglo-Canadian judicial adaptation of the common law to the consequences of cohabitation. His argument seeks to inhabit an 'intermediate zone' between the philosophical unpacking of overarching values and the legalistic focus on the detail of jurisdiction-specific case law developments.[41] For some matters, however, the jurisdictional context fundamentally constrains the possibilities for theoretical argumentation in a way that forestalls any such mediating role. In his chapter on family-based immigration, for example, Lister pragmatically appeals to 'common conceptions' of the 'family' in the particular states in question.

But legal specificity can also be contextualized within broader theoretical arguments. The notion of 'parental control rights' with which Altman's chapter is concerned, for example, arguably owes much to the constitutional status of the parental rights doctrine in the United States. The very different perspective on the extent of parents' entitlement to control children's lives presented in Dwyer's chapter is grounded in an American understanding of the state's *parens patriae* powers, which is not constrained to judicial exercise as in England and Wales. While sensitive to that context, however, both chapters offer critical insight into the nature and viability of broader arguments over the justification of parents' rights. Similarly, there is a necessary specificity to 'private ordering' in its various forms, which Bix discusses in his chapter. It is critically important, for example, whether parties are simply *opting between* the state's default and alternative regimes as in some jurisdictions' approaches to matrimonial property,

---

[35] [2014] EWHC 3135 (Fam). [36] ibid [52] (Sir James Munby P).
[37] ibid [54] (Sir James Munby P). [38] ibid [55] (Sir James Munby P). [39] ibid.
[40] R Dworkin, *Law's Empire* (Harvard UP 1986). [41] See R Leckey's chapter.

or entitled to *opt out* of the state's default. But, as Bix contends, 'the argument for private ordering is a general one', often grounded in the notion that competent parties are best placed to protect their own interests.[42]

F. The limits to arguments

Variations in purpose, use of cases, and generalizability also tell in the fact that philosophers and lawyers writing in this field tend to draw limits to their arguments differently. At least some legal scholars limit the reach of their arguments by pragmatic or policy concerns. Often, this is implicit: the logic of the theoretical arguments used to ground the case for reform is not explored, but the arguments are used to underpin the case for incremental reform. One example might be found in how the autonomy-based case for extending different-sex marriage to same-sex couples[43] or, indeed, extending same-sex civil partnership to different-sex couples,[44] is often put. Sometimes legal scholars' pragmatic or policy limits on their arguments are explicit, such as Lister's focus on 'typical cases, not unusual ones'[45] in his examination of family-based immigration in this book (though Lister is also a philosopher).

By contrast, in Brake's chapter on extending state support and protection to all adult caring relationships, she explicitly accepts that the inclusion of paid caring relationships may be seen to entail a *reductio ad absurdum* of her argument for 'minimal marriage',[46] a radical reform of marriage law entailed (she argues) by principles of neutrality and equal treatment; Brake embraces this logical conclusion to her argument. Similarly, in Jeske's chapter on moral and legal obligations to support 'family', she focuses on the functional features of interpersonal relationships to determine both whether a relationship qualifies as 'intimate' and what those intimates owe to one another, and not on a set of desired outcomes. Chambers has recently argued that, rather than an argument from liberty or equality underpinning the extension of marriage to same-sex couples, these liberal values undermine any notion of state-recognized marriage and necessitate the shift to a 'marriage-free state'.[47]

These philosophical arguments echo the Law Commission of Canada's 2001 proposals to move 'beyond conjugality'[48] and adopt a 'more principled and comprehensive approach to encompass the full range of ... close personal adult relationships',[49] which would not simply extend relationship statuses but adopt a new methodology for legally responding to personal relationships. Whilst the Commission's proposals remain exceptionally innovative and continue to be embraced by scholars,[50] they did not find favour with the legislature. Transformation to family life can be rapid, especially when

---

[42] See BH Bix's chapter.
[43] See, eg, Kennedy J's judgment for the majority in *Obergefell v Hodges*, 576 US _ (2015).
[44] See, eg, the arguments by the applicants in *Steinfeld and Keidan v Secretary of State for Education* [2016] EWHC 128 (Admin); [2017] EWCA Civ 81.
[45] See M Lister's chapter.
[46] See, also E Brake, *Minimizing Marriage: Marriage, Morality, and the Law* (OUP 2012).
[47] C Chambers, *Against Marriage: An Egalitarian Defense of the Marriage-Free State* (OUP 2017).
[48] Law Commission of Canada, *Beyond Conjugality: Recognising and Supporting Close Personal Adult Relationships* (Law Commission of Canada 2001) xxvi.
[49] ibid, xi.   [50] See, eg, N Barker, *Not the Marrying Kind* (Palgrave Macmillan 2013) 203–04.

hastened by technological developments, but reform to the governing legal framework is commonly alluvial, casuistic, and piecemeal.

This is, of course, all a matter of emphasis. In her chapter on the justifications for the legal relationships created by surrogacy arrangements, Shanley sees theories of care and relational rights as at the core of the legal and social relationships created between the commissioning couple, surrogates, and the resultant child. Her conclusion on legal-parental status following birth, however, implicitly recognizes the practical limits of surrogacy's socially enlarged understanding of what it means to be a parent. Whilst surrogacy contracts 'create intrinsic and on-going relationships',[51] the 'very small' number of disputes over surrogacy outcomes tells against denying the gestational mother legal parental status immediately following birth.[52]

What can we learn from this interdisciplinary analysis about the justifiable role of policy concerns in limiting the scope of legal rules and principles? Is it simply a matter of perspective? Or is the best understanding of the relationship between theory and policy limits necessarily contextualized to the issue at stake within children's or family law? Might this suggest the need for more careful consideration of the nature of the policy arguments in play?

III. Themes

The chapters in this book are organized by four themes: definitions; relationships; rights and obligations; and regulation and intervention. These themes reflect the core debate with which each chapter engages, rather than the substantive legal context in which the discussion takes place. Through this arrangement, we hope to draw together the contrasting and converging arguments and solutions typically seen as concerned exclusively with either adult relationships or regulating children. But we do not arbitrarily limit discussion of each contributor's arguments to one theme where their points clearly have resonance elsewhere.

A. Definitions

We focus here on the two critical, interwoven issues of the nature of the 'family' and 'family law'. Exploring the 'family law' concept also invites consideration of the place of 'private ordering', which lies at the heart of both determining the limits of 'family law' and the question whether there should be legal intervention in family life at all. Thus 'private ordering' will be discussed in relation to our final theme, which focuses on regulation and intervention, but remains critically relevant here.

1. The concept of 'family'

How necessary is it for philosophers or lawyers to define 'family'? Can we sensibly talk of 'family law' without a clear understanding of the 'family' concept? How should we

---

[51] See ML Shanley's chapter. [52] See ML Shanley's chapter.

understand the nature of the 'family'? Should talk of 'family' be replaced by discussion of 'families'? Whilst the notion of 'families' may be initially attractive as it explicitly signals the diversity of family forms, it is arguably unnecessary. The 'family' concept does not of itself require that only one arrangement be accepted as familial. It does not require us to ask *who* is correctly seen as belonging to *the* family. We can justifiably ask *what* are the characteristics of *a* family, which can be shared by multiple family forms. Indeed, rather than such characteristics comprising the minimum content of a 'family', it may be that multiple, equally valid familial forms possess different combinations of those characteristics.

Philosophers see some concepts, such as 'justice' and 'fairness', as 'essentially contested': their general meaning is agreed, but there is disagreement over what they require in any particular instance.[53] But in relation to law, it is the particular applications that are critical. Consider, for example, the concept of 'fairness' in the family law context. The debate is not about the *application* of a general notion of 'fairness', but what 'fairness' actually *means*: whilst that debate aims to determine the content of 'fairness' as the basis for justifiable distribution of assets and income upon divorce and dissolution, there is no agreed broader concept to be instantiated.

Writing from a philosophical perspective, Archard reasons that 'family' is not such a contested concept.[54] Whilst its meaning is not generally agreed, it is settled that it is 'a distinctively different institution'.[55] This may explain why Okin, in her landmark work in feminist political philosophy, does not focus directly on the definition of 'family' but on its role as the 'linchpin of the gender structure'.[56] In her analysis of the gender injustices within the family, Okin highlights the centrality of the family to children's and women's vulnerability in society.[57] The lack of examination of the 'family' may also simply be due to the liberal tradition—which, Okin contends, for the most part ignored the family while treating it as the protected private sphere, relegating injustices within it outside the scope of political justice. As Eichner notes in respect of Rawls,

> In paying little attention to the issue of families, Rawls's work is hardly atypical; except when families were used as a foil to develop contrasting principles that should apply to the political realm (which was deemed not to include the family), there has been little attention to families in this tradition.[58]

Diduck proposes that

> 'family' is one way to describe forms or expressions of intimate or private living based upon care and interdependence.... What makes a relationship familial ... is not necessarily a biological, legal, or conjugal connection, rather it is what people do in it ....[59]

But Diduck's positioning of legal connections as equivalent to, rather than a potential means of recognition of those non-legal connections, may be problematic. The very persistence of the 'family law' field requires that 'family' be defined, coherently

---

[53] D Archard, *The Family: A Liberal Defence* (Palgrave Macmillan 2010) 1–2 (citing Gallie).
[54] ibid 1.   [55] ibid 5.   [56] SM Okin, *Justice, Gender, and the Family* (Basic Books 1989) 14.
[57] ibid 172.
[58] M Eichner, *The Supportive State: Families, Government, and America's Political Ideals* (OUP 2010) 45.
[59] A Diduck, 'What is Family Law For?' (2011) Current Legal Problems 1, 3.

or otherwise, at least at its core. Lawyers must proceed on the basis that 'family' is an essentially contested concept, the meaning of which is generally agreed, even when discussion suggests that it is not. The need to resolve individual disputes, and regulate society more generally, requires a working legal definition or context-specific definitions. This contrast both opens the opportunity for and immediately complicates cross-fertilization between philosophical and legal writings on the nature of 'family'.

In his chapter, Archard explores three types of definition of 'family': functional; formal, drawing on shared social meanings; and definition based on overlapping similarities or 'family resemblances'.[60] Preferring a functional account, Archard suggests that it has one distinct advantage—it 'allows for a separation of the conceptual and the normative'.[61] But is that sufficient to merit its adoption? There may be further difficulty created by the fact that, once we recognize any non-normative concept of 'family' as a legal concept, it thereby becomes normative. Whilst it may be possible to define 'family' in non-normative terms, how useful is that for the law's purposes?

Further, even if we accept a functional perspective, we still need to draw limits to the functional 'family'. That exercise arguably requires a conceptual account to ground limits to the functional. In his case for family-based immigration, Lister reasons that there seems to be a 'common core'[62] shared across multiple jurisdictions' conceptions of 'family' '... without which the notion of a family hardly makes sense'.[63] This suggests a pre-legal social or natural understanding of 'family', which corresponds to the second type of definition suggested by Archard. But justification is required for this to be replicated as a legal norm, and a conceptual account is required to draw limits beyond any 'common core'. Indeed, the posited inclusion of same-sex relationships as within the 'family'[64] suggests such an account may already implicitly underpin this approach.

The nature of the 'family' has always been more complex than the form-function binary, yet how the two should interrelate remains an open question. This issue was recently before the European Court of Human Rights in *Paradiso and Campanelli v Italy*.[65] An Italian couple had registered themselves as the legal parents of a child born via surrogacy in Russia, despite the fact that surrogacy was illegal in Italy. Further, neither of the commissioning couple were genetically related to the child. By a majority of eleven to six, the Grand Chamber held that no 'family life' within the terms of Article 8 of the European Convention on Human Rights[66] had been established between the commissioning couple and the child. The majority summarized their view as follows:

> Having regard to ... the absence of any biological tie between the child and the intentional parents, the short duration of the relationship with the child and the uncertainty of the ties from a legal perspective, and in spite of the existence of a parental project and the quality of the emotional bounds, the Court considers that the conditions enabling it to conclude that there existed a *de facto* family life have not been met.[67]

---

[60] See D Archard's chapter (citing Wittgenstein in respect of 'family resemblances').
[61] See D Archard's chapter.   [62] See M Lister's chapter.   [63] See M Lister's chapter.
[64] See M Lister's chapter.   [65] (App No 25358/12) (24 Jan 2017) (ECtHR (Grand Chamber)).
[66] Convention for the Protection of Human Rights and Fundamental Freedoms (European Convention on Human Rights, as amended) (1950).
[67] *Paradiso* (n 65) [157] (majority).

Intention, emotional bonds, and short-term physical care were insufficient to form a functional 'family' for the purpose of establishing 'family life'. Whilst the outer limits of 'family' are assessed in practical terms, they are implicitly informed by an unarticulated concept of 'family'. The theoretical debate over the nature of the 'family' becomes unavoidable and critically in need of resolution.

In any event, in the legal context, the disputed term is often not 'family' but one commonly understood to be familial, such as 'parent', 'mother', or 'father'. This creates a further layer of difficulty for the theorist since the multifarious ways in which an individual might acquire any one of those legal statuses risk undermining any potential for coherence within the larger 'family' concept. We should not be too quick to assume that the gestational route to the legal 'mother' status is valued for the same reasons as the genetic route to legal 'father' status. Rather than devaluing the enquiry into the nature of 'family', however, might this multiplicity suggest an alternative path to explore?

2. Defining 'Family Law'

Family Law is a comparatively new field, hence in his foreword to Graveson and Crane's edited collection, *A Century of Family Law: 1857–1957*, Lord Evershed MR reasons that '"Family Law" is not a term of art ...' but '... rather a convenient means of reference to so much of our law ... as directly affects ... the family'.[68] What is at stake when we question the nature of 'family law'? How necessary is it that the aim or aims of 'family law' correspond to that or those of familial forms, whether external or intrinsic?

Why might it matter whether 'family law' is distinctive from other areas of law and, if so, how we should understand its uniqueness? One answer lies in the roles played by 'family law': it can serve as crucial state endorsement to individuals' relationships through permitting individuals to enter into a formal legal 'status' such as marriage or parenthood; it can serve as a mechanism for the enforcement of rights and obligations between and against 'family' members, as well as signalling the justifiability of such enforcement; and it can serve as a mechanism for privileging 'familial' above 'non-familial' relationships (whether in terms of enforcing rights and obligations within the family, protecting 'familial' relationships against state interference, or justifying access to limited state resources), as well as suggesting the justifiability of such privileging. On this view, 'family law' and the 'family' are inter-defined. Diduck, for example, reasons that 'if family is the environment that we live in and what we do as a parent, child, or former or current partner, family law ... is any form or means of regulating, supporting, or governing that environment, those actions, and their consequences'.[69] But does this mean that any uniqueness to 'family law' is contingent upon our understanding of the 'family'?

Archard explores an alternative possible relationship between 'family law' and 'family' in his complication of the truism that 'Family law is the law of the family'[70] on the basis that the former is normative and the latter conceptual.[71] As a result, the conceptual

---

[68] Lord Evershed MR, 'Foreword' in RH Graveson and FR Crane (eds), *A Century of Family Law: 1857–1957* (Sweet & Maxwell 1957) vii–xvi, vii.
[69] Diduck (n 59) 3.   [70] See D Archard's chapter.   [71] See D Archard's chapter.

'family' can be used to evaluate the success of normative 'family law'.[72] Drawing a parallel conclusion that the 'nitty gritty' empirical details of actual families can be used to evaluate normative 'family law', Leckey's comparative study of the regulation of the financial consequences of the breakdown of cohabiting relationships suggests that the boundaries of 'family law' need to be drawn to reflect how the majority arrange their lives.[73]

But, as discussed above, the legal concept of 'family' may itself be considered normative. This means that whether a relationship qualifies as 'familial' in law, hence within the scope of 'family law', can have significant consequences for both affected individuals and the broader social interest. This also gives rise to philosophical argument suggesting that the legal definition of 'family' should be guided by broader normative considerations such as justice and equal treatment, as Brake explores in her discussion of paid caregivers.[74] By contrast, den Otter's consideration of polyamorous relationships demonstrates the political significance of the formal legal status itself as he argues for 'marriage' to be extended to relationships that lack one of the traditional hallmarks—the requirement that there are only two parties to the relationship.[75] Might the range of differing perspectives suggest that 'family law' is ambivalent and, possibly, empty of content?

Eekelaar's account seeks to counter such concerns by setting out the contextualized interactions between legal and social norms within 'family law'.[76] He argues that, in performing its various roles, 'family law' interacts with social norms; it both reflects others as well as seeks to create its own.[77] But, beyond focusing on the detail of the content of 'family law', Eekelaar suggests that 'the most important issue' is to ask 'what is the point of having family law at all?'[78] Diduck suggests that

> [F]amily law is about determining responsibility for responsibility. Family law determines the responsibilities of individuals to each other and by extension, the responsibilities of families and the state and the community to each other. Whether it is about money, care of children, employment, income support, or housing, the purpose of family law is to allocate and enforce responsibility for those responsibilities'.[79]

Eekelaar concludes that the purpose of 'family law' lies in regulation of the exercise of power so as 'to uphold the view of the "common good" taken by those in power',[80] as limited by Finnis' qualification of 'respect for the equal right of all to respectful consideration'.[81] His account of the content of 'family law' is borne out of a need to respond to the expanding range of family forms, which 'scientific advances … still further stretched'.[82]

An alternative response to the difficulty in defining the contours of the 'family law' field might be to conclude that the reference to 'family' should be rejected and the domain otherwise conceived. Elsewhere, Eekelaar proposes adopting the model of 'personal law' to 'refer to laws, whether applicable on the basis of an individual's communal

---

[72] See D Archard's chapter. [73] See R Leckey's chapter. [74] See E Brake's chapter.
[75] See RC Den Otter's chapter. [76] See D Eekelaar's chapter. [77] See J Eekelaar's chapter.
[78] See J Eekelaar's chapter. [79] Diduck (n 59) 6. [80] See J Eekelaar's chapter.
[81] See J Eekelaar's chapter. [82] See J Eekelaar's chapter.

allegiance or not, which purport directly to regulate their private life'.[83] Whilst this response captures the increasingly illusive nature of the field, it may risk creating similar difficulties for defining the scope of the domain in practice. What if we abandon the search for the substantive domain of family life? Might the breadth of accounts instead be seen to reveal the flexibility of 'family law' as a discursive, interpretive, and persuasive tool? In other words, might 'family law' be distinctive for the attitude it requires to be taken to regulating individuals' lives, both in terms of the norms at stake and the way in which those norms interrelate?

But, alongside academic suggestions of the distinctiveness of 'family law', the judicial attitude is more inconsistent. In *Prest v Petrodel*,[84] the UK's Supreme Court had to decide the court's jurisdiction in proceedings concerning financial remedies upon divorce to be able to order properties owned by companies to be transferred to an applicant spouse to satisfy their claim. The companies in question were owned by a group, which was wholly owned and controlled by the husband. Whilst the panel of seven adopted a resulting trusts analysis to justify making the property available to meet the wife's claim, they roundly rejected any suggestion that the 'family law' context provided any special justification for 'piercing the corporate veil'. Lord Sumption reasoned:

> If there is no justification as a matter of general legal principle for piercing the corporate veil, I find it impossible to say that a special and wider principle applies in matrimonial proceedings by virtue of section 24(1)(a) of the Matrimonial Causes Act 1973.... This section is invoking concepts with an established legal meaning and recognised legal incidents under the general law. Courts exercising family jurisdiction do not occupy a desert island in which general legal concepts are suspended or mean something different.[85]

By contrast, the approach to statutory interpretation evidenced in cases such as the surrogacy decision of *Re X*, discussed above,[86] may be said to suggest a distinctive 'family law' approach. But how should we decide whether 'family law'—the substantive domain, the norms, or the interrelation of those norms—is a unique legal field; whether it is in some sense 'special'? This requires agreement about the governing evaluative criteria.

Without consensus on the question of distinctiveness, including its nature, we do not know the full terms of what is at stake when considering whether to extend the benefits of marriage to cohabitants on functional grounds;[87] or whether an intimacy-based argument for financial provision that cuts across formal legal categories of relationship[88] can be sustained within 'family law' or must be understood to cut across the boundaries of 'family law'; or whether we can simply transpose concepts from other areas of law, such as the fiduciary relationship,[89] into 'family law'. Moreover, settling the

---

[83] J Eekelaar, *Family Law and Personal Life* (OUP 2006) 31.   [84] [2013] UKSC 4.
[85] ibid [37] (L'Sumption).
[86] *Re X (A Child) (Surrogacy: Time limit)* (n 35) and corresponding main text.
[87] As Leckey posits in his chapter.   [88] As Jeske proposes in her chapter.
[89] S Altman's chapter explores and rejects this possibility in relation to 'parental control rights'. For a recent argument in favour of the fiduciary characterization, see L Smith, 'Parenthood is a Fiduciary Relationship' (working paper, 24 July 2017) online: <https://papers.ssrn.com/sol3/papers.cfm?abstract_id=3007812> accessed 20 Aug 2017.

issue of distinctiveness has significant consequences for both the nature of the relationship between 'family law' and 'children's law', as well as the possible scope and theoretical basis of 'private ordering' within 'family law'. As a result, it is perhaps surprising that this debate remains unsettled. Has the unavoidable need to interpret and apply 'family law' to resolve individuals' problems led to lawyers being too ready to proceed on the basis that disputed concepts such as the 'family' are valid and with settled content, despite the evidence to the contrary?

B. Relationships

Within this theme, we focus on the legal and moral significance of adult intimate relationships, both those to which a formal legal status has been assigned, such as 'marriage', and those to which it has not, such as cohabitation. We also consider the nature of the adult-child relationship, particularly in terms of the award of parental legal status and legal recognition of more functional parenting through concepts such as 'parental responsibility'.[90] These horizontal and vertical interpersonal ties are united by the importance of status and functional perspectives on relationships more generally. As rights and obligations can flow from relationships or their content, this theme necessarily overlaps with the third.

1. Status

What moral or legal significance, if any, should we attach to the form of individuals' relationships? Should there be legal status relationships, where legal consequences attach to their form as opposed to their function? If so, should identical legal consequences attach to all adult intimate status relationships? Answering these questions, of course, depends on the normative considerations taken to guide 'family law', as well as the pragmatics of legal procedure and desired outcomes.

Currently, 'family' is recognized as a legal status relationship in only some contexts (such as immigration); in other contexts (such as certain instances of tort liability),[91] status is attributed to more particular relationships (such as 'marriage' or 'parent') which are familial in character.[92] Within the conventional confines of 'family law', the use of statuses more particular than 'family' generally prevails though one could argue, of course, that all instances of recognizing the 'family' as a legal status should be seen to thereby constitute 'family law'.[93]

---

[90] See, eg, Children Act 1989 (n 18), s 3(1).

[91] cf liability for negligently inflicted psychiatric injury and presumed categories of close love and affection (*Alcock v Chief Constable of South Yorkshire* [1991] UKHL 5); status-based duty of care in negligence presumed owed by parents to children (*Marc Rich & Co AG v Bishop Rock Marine Co Ltd (The Nicholas H)* [1994] 1 WLR 1071, 1077 (Saville LJ)) (dicta on adults *in loco parentis*, resting on an assumed parent-child status-based duty of care).

[92] The elevation of the family founded on marriage to constitutional status in Ireland is particularly noteworthy in this context: Constitution of Ireland, Art 41 (1 July 1937; as revised October 2015).

[93] For an interesting attempt to bring together a wide range of such contexts, see R Probert (ed), *Family Life and the Law: Under One Roof* (Ashgate 2006).

Varying perspectives on three related issues reveal how arguments engage with status. First, in terms of already-established statuses, arguments involving status either assume their validity or question the justifiability of their persistence as legal statuses from which consequences automatically flow. This dialectical shift dramatically changes the nature of arguments made available. Chapters within our collection illustrate this divergence in approach. Lister's case for family-based immigration assumes the justifiability of the 'family' status based on the 'common understanding'[94] between jurisdictions of its existence and contents. Lister starts from a position that assumes the justifiability of what the law currently is—how 'family' is defined for immigration purposes—but then posits the extension from different-sex to same-sex relationships within that definition.[95] By contrast, Jeske starts by 'dislodge[ing] "family" as a term of fundamental moral significance' for the purpose of determining the moral obligations that intimates owe to each other,[96] particularly as expressed through spousal support or maintenance—her arguments then generating a basis for moral critique of existing law.

Secondly, in terms of the consequences of legal status relationships, approaches vary from a strict binary view that distinguishes status from non-status relationships on the basis of formalities and sees only the former as justifying relationship-specific legal consequences; to a range of moderate views, which blend the formal and the functional, and see non-status relationships as potentially grounding legal consequences, albeit not as significant as those that attach to status relationships; to a fully functional view, which does not distinguish between the legal consequences that can be attached to status and non-status relationships. This final perspective renders the consequences of formalities nothing more than the creation of a 'bare' status.

In his analysis of judicial developments to respond to the financial consequences of the breakdown of cohabitants' relationships, Leckey questions the underlying basis of the financial obligations that flow from the breakdown of the 'marriage' status relationship. He reasons that at least some of the 'robust public interests' that underpin the response to 'marriage' also apply to cohabitants,[97] and suggests that 'family law's' default regime should extend to cohabitation so as to respond to the reality of individuals' lives.[98] This perspective undermines the validity of the existing status, assuming that it is a proxy for relationships with particular functional features such that regulation should focus on the functional content alone. But might positing marriage and cohabitation as meriting a 'family law' response nevertheless be seen as embracing a status perspective? Insofar as the notion of the 'family law' default regime might be seen to embody a cluster of rights and obligations such as conventionally attach to a status, the 'family law' default appears to evoke status.

Thirdly, in terms of responding to relationships not recognized within formal legal status categories, approaches vary from calling for the *expansion* of a particular status; to creating an *additional* status with identical legal consequences; to *substituting* the current status with another, which may also be expanded to accommodate specific non-status relationships; to seeing the logic of the need to respond to the non-status

---

[94] See M Lister's chapter.
[95] See M Lister's chapter.
[96] See D Jeske's chapter.
[97] See R Leckey's chapter.
[98] See R Leckey's chapter.

relationship as requiring the abandonment of any distinction between, and the *convergence* of the treatment of (particular) status and non-status relationships.

Expansion arguments can entail either assuming the justifiability of the current status's normativity and arguing that the new relationship form shares that recognized normative basis, or arguing for extension on the grounds of a different normative basis. The most obvious example of the latter is arguably that of an equality-based discrimination argument for extension regardless of the normative basis for the core status relationship, such as might be made in the context of same-sex couples access to marriage.[99] In his case for better legal treatment of polyamory, Den Otter challenges the unquestioned privileging of different and same-sex marriage on the grounds of 'mono-normativity'.[100] He seems to suggest the justifiability of both the substitution of a more inclusive status of 'plural marriage'[101] and the creation of an additional status 'legal[ly] equivalent' to a two-person marriage.[102]

In relation to convergence-led arguments, functional convergence can sometimes collapse into assumed normative convergence. Herring, for example, draws on the socially constructed nature of the man–woman sex dyad to make the case for sexless family law;[103] in doing so, however, the argument shifts between focus on sex and gender, the latter of which is much more conventionally seen as a social construct. Even if sex is understood as socially constructed, it is not clear that the way that it interacts with aspects of biology should be assumed to have the same normative significance as gender.[104]

The option of creating an additional status relationship highlights how the issue of status is more complicated than categorization as 'status' or 'non-status'. In English law, for example, there is more than one status relationship within both the adult intimate ('marriage', 'civil partnership') and the parenthood categories ('mother',[105] 'father',[106] 'other parent'[107]). Whilst 'marriage' and 'civil partnership' were posited as separate-but-equal, the distinctive labels and persistent substantive differences undermined that impression.[108] The relative status of the 'other parent' compared to the 'mother' and the 'father' remains unclear. Labels have meaning; different labels are assumed to have distinctive meanings. Hierarchies of status relationships—in terms of their legal or moral significance—may be intended or unintended. The need to justify any hierarchy

---

[99] cf Ferguson (n 15). [100] See start of RC Den Otter's chapter.
[101] See end of RC Den Otter's chapter. [102] See end of RC Den Otter's chapter.
[103] J Herring, 'Sexless Family Law' (2010) 11 Lex Familiae 3.
[104] For an overview of the sex/gender distinction within contemporary feminist philosophy, including problems with the distinction itself, see M Mikkola, 'Feminist Perspectives on Sex and Gender' (2016) *The Stanford Encyclopedia of Philosophy* <https://plato.stanford.edu/entries/feminism-gender/#SexDis> accessed 24 August 2017.
[105] The common law award of status is grounded in parturition (*Ampthill Peerage Case* [1977] AC 547, 577 (Lord Simon)). The statutory rule in the assisted-reproduction context is based on gestation (HFEA 2008 (n 34), s 33).
[106] The common law presumptive award of status is grounded in marriage to the gestational mother (*Ampthill Peerage*, ibid 577 (Lord Simon)). The statutory rule in the assisted-reproduction context is grounded in marriage (s 35), consent in the absence of marriage (ss 36–37), with genetic connection as a default in the absence of compliance with the statutory requirements (s 41).
[107] This term refers to the second female parent in the context of fertility treatment: HFEA 2008 (n 34), ss 42–44.
[108] Ferguson (n 15) 354.

requires specific normative argumentation, which is often overlooked or minimized. These difficulties militate against adopting additional status categories in favour of expanding existing categories, yet the former remains a desirable political solution.

Only with attention to the choices entailed by engaging with status can we understand how any one account views the role of status. Each lawyer or philosopher's normative response to existing statuses; preferred accommodation of non-status relationships; and conclusion regarding the consequences of status and non-status relationships rests on a particular view as to the significance of status. In the context of both adult intimate and adult-child relationships, status tends to be valued for the role it plays in structuring social life, which focuses state resources on certain types of relationships. In respect of marriage, for example, the former Secretary of State for Children, Schools and Families, Ed Balls, reasoned that:

> Marriage is an important and well-established institution that plays a fundamental role in family life in our society. However, marriage is a personal and private decision for responsible adults, with which politicians should not interfere. The Government supports couples who choose to get married: for many families marriage offers the best environment in which to raise children, and remains the choice of the majority of people in Britain.[109]

The concept of status relationships does not of itself offer certainty since status could be acquired, for example, through decisions grounded in assessment of the functional content of relationships. The particular conceptions of status employed in practice, however, are either triggered by the satisfaction of formalities or in recognition of a single fact (such as proof of genetic parental connection to a child), hence do achieve valued certainty. But these public policy concerns only explain, and do not justify the existence and persistence of status relationships.

Yet, how individuals value status may be reason-giving. In relation to marriage, for example, Den Otter argues that reforming legal marriage to recognize plural marriage would 'be a step toward removing its social stigma'.[110] The expressive aspect of status may be important to how valued and accepted individuals feel in their life choices. Whether this could be accomplished via bare legal status is open to debate, given that the aspiration to marry currently remains strong[111] despite declining marriage rates.[112] Could status suggest a 'different moral significance' to the relationship if the status concept were empty? The significance of status to individuals' meaning-making supports ascribing substantive legal consequences to status relationships.

---

[109] Department for Children, Schools and Families, *Support for All* (Green Paper, Cm 7787, 2010) 1 (Ed Balls, 'Ministerial Foreword').

[110] See RC Den Otter's chapter.

[111] F Newport and J Wilke, 'Most in U.S. Want Marriage, but Its Importance Has Dropped' *Gallup Polling* (2 August 2013) <http://www.gallup.com/poll/163802/marriage-importance-dropped.aspx> accessed 6 November 2017.

[112] R Fry, 'New Census Data Show More Americans are Tying the Knot, but Mostly It's the College Educated' (*Pew Research Center*, 6 February 2014) online: < http://www.pewresearch.org/fact-tank/2014/02/06/new-census-data-show-more-americans-are-tying-the-knot-but-mostly-its-the-college-educated/> accessed 20 August 2017.

But what of the role that status plays as a proxy for function? Can we justifiably ignore any state interest in prioritizing relationships with particular functional content, via sufficiently accurate status proxies, and rest the normative case for status exclusively on individual flourishing? Even if we sought to move to a fully functional approach, could we do so? Taking the adult intimate and adult-child contexts together may offer some insight. In particular, the English legal concept of 'parental responsibility'[113] repays attention.

Within parenthood, 'parental responsibility' contrasts with legal parental status, and is defined through its content. Section 3(1) of the Children Act 1989 states that it means '[a]ll the rights, duties, powers, responsibilities and authority which by law a parent of a child has in relation to the child and his property'.[114] The breadth and parasitic nature of this definition immediately hints that this might not be the useful starting-point most definitions form.[115] The reference to rights, as well as the bundling and collective label for functional content, is immediately suggestive of status. Moreover, at least in part because there is much functional overlap with legal parental status and the vast majority of those with 'parental responsibility' will also have legal parental status, it is not clear that the mainstay of those with and aspiring to be awarded parental responsibility view it in functional terms. Indeed, much of the difficulty in retaining the functional intention of the concept may be due to the difficulty in sustaining that normative value based on the limited numbers of individuals who hold 'parental responsibility' alone.

As a result of this comparison with the adult–child context, one might wonder if we can make the case for the functional basis of adult intimate relationships such as 'marriage' only because of the broader status-bounded context. If attempts at a purely functional approach inevitably create status, the separability of function is contingent on the persistence of status. This complex relationship within particular legal relationships carries through into the umbrella definition of 'family'. How does the issue of status relate to the issue of the distinctiveness of 'family law'? Does the existence of status relationships of itself suggest 'family law' is distinctive? Or does any distinctiveness more readily or more significantly lie in the consequences of status via discretionary decision-making underpinned by the interrelation of particular norms? If it is the response to relationships that may be a hallmark of 'family law's' distinctiveness, this could equally incorporate the normative recognition of the functional content of relationships. Whilst no debates are resolved through taking these issues together, it does

---

[113] Children Act 1989 (n 90).   [114] ibid.

[115] Probert et al remark that '[i]t has often been noted that the broad definition of parental responsibility set out in the Children Act 1989 is in fact no definition at all': R Probert, S Gilmore, and J Herring, 'A More Principled Approach to Parental Responsibility in England and Wales?' in J Mair and E Örücü (eds), *Juxtaposing Legal Systems and the Principles of European Family Law on Parental Responsibilities* (Intersentia 2010) 213. Bridgeman similarly describes parental responsibility as 'a confused, contradictory yet essentially empty concept': J Bridgeman, 'Parental Responsibility, Responsible Parenting and Legal Regulation' in J Bridgeman, H Keating, and C Lind (eds), *Responsibility, Law and the Family* (Ashgate 2008) 242. Freeman likewise describes the concept as 'clumsy and inchoate' and Wallbank, citing Herring, notes that it has an 'uncertain meaning': M Freeman, 'The Right to Responsible Parents' in J Bridgeman, H Keating, and C Lind (eds), *Responsibility, Law and the Family* (Ashgate 2008) 22 and J Wallbank, 'Parental Responsibility and the Responsible Parent: Managing the "Problem" of Contact' in R Probert, S Gilmore, and J Herring (eds), *Responsible Parents and Parental Responsibility* (Hart Publishing 2009) 296.

highlight the deeply theoretical nature of the significance of the empirical content of relationships.

2. Intimacy and the functional family

The preceding discussion highlights that the functional content of family life is relevant, albeit in uncertain terms, to defining the notions of 'family' and 'family law' and their normative moral and legal significance. Beyond definitions and the award of legal status relationships, how sensitive should the legal regulation of individuals' lives be to either specific functional aspects or any core functional character of their intimate relationships? Does the moral view of the significance of function, as opposed to form, assist the legal debate? How should 'family law' respond to changing functional families?

How can we best encapsulate what is normatively significant about functional families? Here, insight from philosophy may be particularly valuable. When thinking about the place of individuals within families, discussion has focused on redefining the individual's relationships with others through notions such as 'relational'[116] or contextualized[117] autonomy and (welfare) interests. When conceiving of the relationships themselves as normative, discussion has centred on the broader notions of 'care',[118] 'vulnerability',[119] and 'intimacy'.[120]

How can we decide on which of these (or other) concepts, to focus? Which represents the most relevant functional aspects of relationships for legal focus? Dwyer highlights the 'moral hazard' of typical contextualized and relational approaches if parents know that, all else being equal, it is in the child's 'best interests' that their parents are both happy in themselves and in their parenting role.[121] Care can comprise the response to vulnerability, but also create new vulnerabilities.[122] Is there one right end to the conceptual and normative telescope for 'family law'? In her argument for the legal protection of the relationship between paid caregivers and care recipients, Brake focuses on caring. She argues that 'the state should support caring relationships, in which partners are non-fungible and the relationship is itself the primary purpose of the association',[123] limited only by the requirement that the parties should want the state to support their

---

[116] See, eg, J Nedelsky, *Law's Relations: A Relational Theory of Self, Autonomy, and Law* (OUP 2011) (on relational autonomy). In her chapter in this book, Shanley grounds her argument for the consequences of surrogacy in a 'relational analysis'.

[117] This is perhaps best explained in the contrast between a 'contextualized' and a 'relational' approach to welfare. Contrast L Ferguson, 'The Jurisprudence of Making Decisions Affecting Children: An Argument to Prefer Duty to Children's Rights and Welfare' in A Diduck, N Peleg, and H Reece (eds), *Law in Society: Reflections on Children, Family, Culture and Philosophy—Essays in Honour of Michael Freeman* (Brill 2015) 158–59 to J Herring, 'Farewell Welfare?' (2005) 27 Journal of Social Welfare and Family Law 159; J Herring and C Foster, 'Welfare Means Relationality, Virtue and Altruism' (2012) 32 Legal Studies 480.

[118] See, eg, Brake (n 46) 82–88. On the relationship between 'care' and 'vulnerability', see S Dodds, 'Dependence, Care, and Vulnerability' in C Mackenzie, W Rogers, and S Dodds (eds), *Vulnerability: New Essays in Ethics and Feminist Philosophy* (OUP 2014) 181.

[119] See, eg, MA Fineman, 'Equality, Autonomy, and the Vulnerable Subject in Law and Politics' in MA Fineman and A Grear (eds), *Vulnerability: Reflections on a New Ethical Foundation for Law and Politics* (Ashgate 2013) 13.

[120] See, eg, D Jeske, *Rationality and Moral Theory: How Intimacy Generates Reasons* (Routledge 2008).

[121] See JG Dwyer's chapter.   [122] Dodds (n 118) 201.   [123] See E Brake's chapter.

relationship of caring.[124] Jeske reasons that the moral and legal obligations that underpin spousal support are grounded in intimacy, which she defines as characterizing a relationship in which both parties:

> (a) have mutual positive attitudes toward one another that can be described as liking, loving, etc., (b) have a concern for each other that exceeds that which they have for any person merely in virtue of being a person, and their history with each other exhibits that concern, (c) have desires to spend time with each other and have already causally interacted with each other in some relevant manner, and (d) have or are in the process of acquiring knowledge about each other that goes beyond what a stranger or mere acquaintance would have.[125]

Whereas Jeske focuses on the intimate nature of the relationship, Brake's caring argument arguably centres on an aspect of intimate relationships. How many more relationships would be caught by Jeske's argument? Could the criteria for intimacy be satisfied without caring being a feature of the relationship? Could parties who wish their relationship to be seen as a caring one not also be intimate? Whichever frame we use to revalue our connections, it creates difficulties for the ongoing normative significance of the 'family' label. For the organizing notion of 'family' to continue to accurately capture the types of relationship with which the law should be concerned, must it be reformulated to embrace the wider class? Or can it find a new role as part of a larger structure of valued relationships? Writing in sociology, Smart concludes in favour of the latter approach:

> [I]t is now time to ... develop a broader conceptualization, one that can keep the term 'family' in the lexicon, but which puts it alongside other forms of intimacy and relationships without already prioritizing biological or married forms of relationship and/or intimacy.[126]

Does the approach we adopt affect our ability to accommodate new relationship forms as deserving of legal recognition? Should all 'intimate' or 'caring' relationships necessitate the same legal response? In particular, should only some benefit from the recognition and protection of 'family law'? For example, should this protection be restricted to only those caring relationships in which caregiving creates vulnerability (particularly, economic dependence) for the caregiver?[127] If 'intimacy' or 'caring' are taken as the focus of family law, is this because care and intimacy are values which the law should protect and promote—or because care and intimacy create vulnerabilities against which the law should protect?

In his discussion of the nature and scope of 'family law', Archard contends that 'if the value of "intimate relations" lies in something other than serving the proper end of "the family" then any justification of their legal recognition lies beyond that which fixes the proper scope of family law'.[128] Of course, if we move away from bringing together

---

[124] See E Brake's chapter.   [125] D Jeske's chapter; compare Jeske (n 120) 46–47.
[126] C Smart, *Personal Life: New Directions in Sociological Thinking* (Polity Press 2007) 187–88.
[127] T Metz, *Untying the Knot: Marriage, the State, and the Case for their Divorce* (Princeton UP 2010) 126, 138.
[128] See D Archard's chapter.

qualifying relationships under the head of 'family', it becomes more difficult to treat all such relationships as justifiably within the scope of 'family law'. Hence, rather than presenting a way forward, reframing in terms of 'intimacy' or 'care' arguably simply shifts the critical definitional question for 'family law' as outwith the 'family' and within the framing concept of choice, whether 'intimacy', 'care', or something else.

The case for polyamorous or plural marriage, which both Den Otter and Brake discuss in their chapters, highlights what is at stake in determining the limits of recognition. Eekelaar notes that '[t]he fact that areas of people's personal lives are legally unregulated does not mean that they are "norm-free". In many respects, it will make little difference whether the norms are legal or social'.[129] But there are certain aspects of the recognition and enforcement of norms that need to be legal to be effective, both in terms of their expressive and coercive aspects. In the absence of shared, comprehensive definitions, the persuasiveness of the need to look to functional aspects of relationships such as 'intimacy' and 'caring' creates a further difficulty. How should the law respond, if at all, when our understanding of the functional core changes? In respect of surrogacy, for example, Shanley argues that

> surrogacy stretches our understanding of what constitutes a 'family'. Debates and discussions about surrogacy, therefore, are important not only for refining medical practice, legal regulations, and cultural understandings of contract pregnancy and the families created by surrogacy contracts, but also for prompting us to consider the grounding of parent-child relationships in general.[130]

As we develop a more nuanced understanding of the nature of surrogacy, particularly in terms of how we conceptualize the relationships it creates, this can have significant consequences for legal regulation, including beyond the surrogacy context.

But matters may be more complex. In his discussion of judicial attempts to adequately respond to the financial consequences of cohabitation, Leckey highlights that desirable default rules may differ from what would be indicated by the fact-based content of parties' relationships.[131] More broadly, Jeske explains how normative argumentation is vulnerable to functional transformations in social life:

> The normative occupies an unusual space, sharing as it does features with the mathematical realm, and yet so much more at the mercy of the empirical insofar as it relates to human beings with all of their empirical and contingent flaws, hopes, loves, commitments, and needs.[132]

If any broader conceptualization of relationships we value operates outwith the notion of 'family', a transformation in our understanding of the functional value of relationships may require complete reformulation of the system of regulation. If we were able to accommodate values such as 'intimacy' or 'caring' within the 'family' definition, however, this would seem to enable such developments to be more straightforwardly reflected in the legal framework. Of course, this second alternative is available only if we conclude that 'family' can accommodate the wider range of valued relationships

---

[129] See J Eekelaar's chapter.   [130] See ML Shanley's chapter.   [131] See R Leckey's chapter.
[132] Jeske (n 120) 151.

such as friendship and plural marriage from the outset. Serious engagement with the nature of relationships seems to raise many more questions for 'family' and 'family law' than it can answer.

C. Rights and obligations

Within this theme, we bring together discussion of the rights held by and obligations owed to individuals within intimate relationships, both as between adults and as centred around any children. At a conceptual level, rights and obligations are often understood correlatively; X's right against Y to financial orders (particularly spousal support, maintenance, or alimony) corresponds to Y's obligation to pay.[133] But any such correlativity does not extend across contexts: separating couples with children often mistakenly conflate the financial obligations that arise between each other with any right to spend time with and make decisions about their shared children's upbringing. Relationship recognition is one factor that underpins discussion in both areas, so examination of this theme highlights some of the consequences of the debates explored in the second theme, over familial status. As public justifications are important to both the financial obligations owed between adults in intimate relationships and the restrictions that may be imposed on decision-making by and about children, there is also some overlap with the final theme: regulation and intervention.

1. Justifying obligations

What is the nature of any financial obligation owed to one's former spouse once the relationship has broken down? Should there be identical obligations for same-sex couples who have entered into a civil partnership or marriage, where available? What if the parties did not marry but were only cohabitants? Should the same rationale underpin property division and maintenance or spousal support?

With the advent of no-fault divorce to terminate the legal consequences of marriage, any preceding justification for enduring financial consequences fell away. Writing in the US context, Ellman reasoned that 'alimony [is] a remedy to a problem that ha[s] not been clearly identified. We cannot explain how alimony claims should be measured or why former spouses should even be liable to pay them, until we specify why we allow them at all'.[134] The inconsistent description of financial provision regimes as 'redistributive'[135] and 'distributive'[136] highlights the lack of attention to the finances problem. Only a 'distributive' regime denotes entitlement on the part of the applicant; a 'redistributive' regime positions the applicant as supplicant.

---

[133] Eg, JS Mill, *Utilitarianism* (G Sher ed, Hackett Publishing 1979) 48.
[134] I Ellman, 'The Theory of Alimony' (1989) 77 California Law Review 1, 49.
[135] In the English context, see, eg, J Herring, *Family Law* (8th edn, Pearson 2017) 218; *Miller v Miller; McFarlane v McFarlane* [2006] UKHL 24 [137] (Baroness Hale, referring to the 'rationale for redistribution').
[136] In the English context, see, eg, S Gilmore and L Glennon, *Hayes and Williams' Family Law* (4th edn, OUP 2014) 153; *Charman v Charman* [2007] EWCA Civ 503 [29], [69] (Potter P, including reference to the 'three distributive principles').

The absence of consensus over theoretical basis has contributed to the failure to introduce greater certainty by law reform. The American Law Institute's *Principles of the Law of Family Dissolution*,[137] which sought to develop reform out of existing practice, have only had an 'anemic impact'[138] in practice. English law reform has avoided the larger issue of the normative basis for imposing any financial obligation and has instead focused on whether nuptial agreements should be made legally binding and, since the majority of separating couples have limited means only, how best to understand 'needs'.[139] The latter has been implemented via non-statutory guidelines,[140] which follow the Canadian advisory guidelines on spousal support in seeking to encapsulate best practice, rather than explicitly reform the law.[141] In comparison to the ALI Principles, the Canadian guidelines have been 'very successful' and 'widely used'.[142] It is notable that the Canadian approach is explicitly 'not directed at a theoretical reordering' of the law.[143] Thus, in neither the US, England and Wales, nor Canada have reform proposals brought theoretical clarity to financial orders. This is further complicated by the fact that it remains unsettled whether the same normative basis needs to underpin all forms of financial orders, such as division of property and maintenance, or whether the normative basis can be 'pillarised'.[144]

Jeske's chapter brings philosophical insight to this legal quandary, noting the distinction between 'special obligations of intimacy' and obligations in relation to which the intimate relationship has played only an instrumental role in both providing a 'fertile arena' for the generation of obligations and providing to the parties a 'privileged position for promoting value'.[145] Jeske distinguishes between the justifying nature of moral obligation and the non-justificatory existence of legal obligation. Yet the availability of financial orders assumes justification.

Whilst Jeske explores the possibility of a single normative basis for spousal support, academic lawyers tend to ground the obligation in a plurality of bases. It is noteworthy that those multiple bases include both interpersonal[146] and social or public justifications.[147] Jeske critiques three of the leading models of spousal support that form the basis of judicial reasoning—reimbursement/compensation; rehabilitation; and income security.[148] She concludes that, because of the way in which broader social policy is implemented via spousal support, analysis of the prevalent models evidences that

---

[137] American Law Institute, *Principles of the Law of Family Dissolution: Analysis and Recommendations* (ALI 2002).

[138] MR Clisham and RF Wilson, 'American Law Institute's *Principles of the Law of Family Dissolution*, Eight Years after Adoption: Guiding Principles or Obligatory Footnote?' (2008) 42(3) Family Law Quarterly 573, 577.

[139] Law Commission, *Matrimonial Property, Needs and Agreements*, Report No 343 (HMSO 2014).

[140] Family Justice Council, *Sorting out Finances on Divorce* (Family Justice Council 2016).

[141] C Rogerson and R Thompson, 'Spousal Support Advisory Guidelines', (*Department of Justice Canada*, July 2008) < http://www.justice.gc.ca/eng/rp-pr/fl-lf/spousal-epoux/spag/index.html > accessed 6 November, 2017. For a summary, see M Maclean, R Hunter, F Wasoff, L Ferguson, B Bastard, and E Ryrstedt, 'Family Justice in Hard Times: Can We Learn from Other Jurisdictions?' (2011) 33(4) Journal of Social Welfare and Family Law 319, 326–27.

[142] Law Commission 343 (n 139) [3.125].   [143] Rogerson and Thompson (n 141) 1.

[144] Scherpe, 'Towards a Matrimonial Property Regime' (n 2).   [145] See D Jeske's chapter.

[146] For an argument that only interpersonal bases should ground financial orders, see Ferguson, 'Family, Social Inequalities' (n 32).

[147] See, eg, Herring, 'Why Financial Orders' (n 32).   [148] See D Jeske's chapter.

the state 'is approaching [marriage] as an economic institution, not as an intimate relationship'.[149]

Jeske's conclusion poses a significant challenge for academic lawyers: it suggests that any role for public justification undermines the intimacy-oriented case for recognizing and privileging marriage and that, if marriage is privileged, it can only be as an economic institution. If marriage needs to be understood in those terms at breakdown, however, that implies a disconnect between the reasons for relationship recognition and the response to breakdown. The debate over the normative basis of financial orders upon marriage breakdown thus risks undermining the justifiability of both the extension of the legal regime on financial orders to civil partnership[150] and the extension of marriage to same-sex couples.

What if the parties did not enter into a status relationship but were cohabitants? Leckey's discussion of judicial responses to the breakdown of cohabitation highlights 'the significant state interests in the economic regulation of adult intimacy'.[151] This expression of the public interest reflects Jeske's analysis of marriage, hence both supports the adoption of the same default rules on the financial consequences of relationship breakdown and the rejection of the recognition of any of these relationships as deserving prioritization over other relationship forms. But what if we can reconcile the apparently opposed public justification and interpersonal or intimacy-based grounds? Might the public justification for financial orders also underpin the normative basis for recognition, where individuals' relationship recognition is motivated by intimacy? Given the significant impact of financial distribution on individuals' lives, including weighty consequences for couples outside of recognized relationship categories, it is difficult to justify the current Anglo-American focus on developing consistent best practice without also seeking to progress the theoretical debate.

2. Framing the legal regulation of children

Does it matter how we frame children's legal relationships with others? This task is currently fulfilled by various notions: 'children's rights', 'rights for children', 'best interests', obligations, and duties. What, if anything, might make one approach preferable to others? How relevant is the place of these concepts in moral theory to the roles they play in legal regulation?

In contrast to the justification for financial orders, there has been significantly more discussion of the normative basis of the legal devices through which we regulate children. In both cases, however, lawyers—academics and practitioners—have tended to overlook theoretical uncertainties and focus on legal practicalities,[152] whilst assuming

---

[149] See D Jeske's chapter.
[150] Civil Partnership Act 2004 c. 33, s 72; *Lawrence v Gallagher* [2012] EWCA Civ 394.
[151] See R Leckey's chapter.
[152] In the financial orders case of *McFarlane v McFarlane; Parlour v Parlour* [2004] EWCA Civ 872, eg, Thorpe LJ reasoned that, 'in this jurisdiction we should not flirt with, still less embrace, any of the categorizations of the defining purposes of periodical payments advanced by academic authors. The judges must remain focused on the statutory language, albeit recognizing the need for evolutionary construction to reflect social and economic change.... [T]o adopt one model or another or a combination of more than one is to don a strait-jacket and to deflect concentration from the statutory language' ([106]).

normative justification. For example, in discussing whether there is a case for children not having rights, Herring notes the theoretical debate over the applicability of the 'will theory' and 'interest theory' of rights to children; however, reasoning that the issue is 'discussed in detail in books on jurisprudence',[153] he does not express a preference for one theoretical account. This common perspective means that the surrounding legal discussion of the rights that children (are said to) have assumes theoretical justification where there may be none.

In the legal arena, the lack of shared normative understanding, or even significant ongoing discussion thereof, may contribute to the damage done by inaccurate 'children's rights' argumentation, which Alderson describes:

> NGOs are among the foremost child rights advocates. Yet when NGO members present rights as simplistic uniform rules, instead of complex universal principles that are open to local interpretations, such as when NGOs claim that the UNCRC bans child labour (it does not), then they can unfortunately increase opposition to children's rights and so offer the critics strong, albeit misinformed, anti-rights arguments.[154]

Treating 'children's rights' as simple legal rules without understanding their conceptual nature risks undermining the value of 'children's rights'. But, as Macleod argues in his contribution to this collection, avoiding that situation may not need to ' ... turn on defending a determinate position about the deep philosophical foundations of moral rights',[155] so that 'children's rights can be vindicated as important even if they are incompletely theorized'.[156] For the purposes of legal practice, however, can this strategy be successful? Or can legal coherence and consistency only be grounded in a comprehensive theoretical account? Macleod's case for incomplete theorization offers an interesting way forward for lawyers.

Macleod examines various types of scepticism about 'children's rights' in moral theory and concludes that reluctance to recognize 'children's rights' in that context is unjustified.[157] Two broader aspects of Macleod's discussion are particularly valuable in contrast to the legal literature. Firstly, in relation to the categories of rights children might have, Macleod outlines Feinberg's three categories of rights; 'A-rights', 'A-C rights', and 'C-rights'. Only the final type is held by children exclusively; Macleod suggests the right to be loved[158] and the right to play[159] as examples of such moral rights. For the lawyer, however, these are not typically the types of rights discussed as 'children's rights'. Moreover, the language of 'children's rights' tends to be used quite imprecisely in the legal context: it can refer to 'A-C rights', such as the right to life;[160] 'A-rights', such as liberty rights to exercise autonomy and make determinative decisions (eg, freedom of religion);[161] and 'C-rights', though these are less frequently recognized in law, and rights are posited as 'C-rights' that are better understood as 'A-C rights' such as the

---

[153] Herring (n 135) 482.
[154] P Alderson, 'Common Criticisms of Children's Rights and 25 Years of the IJCR' (2017) 25 International Journal of Children's Rights 307, 311.
[155] See CM Macleod's chapter.   [156] See CM Macleod's chapter (setting out his case).
[157] See CM Macleod's chapter.   [158] See CM Macleod's chapter.   [159] See CM Macleod's chapter.
[160] See, eg, *Re A (Children) (Conjoined Twins: Surgical Separation)* [2001] Fam 147.
[161] See, eg, *R (on the application of Begum) v Headteacher and Governors of Denbigh High School* [2006] UKHL 15.

right to education.[162] Both 'A-C rights' and 'A-rights' can be expressed as fundamental human rights in law. Macleod understands 'children's rights as the set of rights comprised by both "A-C rights" and "C-rights"'.[163] Were this to be transplanted directly into the legal context, might it make the use of the language of 'children's rights' more confusing since it suggests that 'children's rights' are both distinct from and blended with fundamental human rights?

In the legal arena, Ferguson distinguishes between 'children's rights' and 'rights for children',[164] where the former encapsulates one means of prioritizing children's interests over those of other parties and comprises both additional rights given to children ('C-rights') as well as fundamental human rights, where the application of the content of the right is critically affected by the fact that the rightsholder is a child. The latter rights are not straightforwardly expressed as 'A-C rights' but might be usefully considered as a C-specific gloss on 'A-C rights'. Whilst Ferguson seeks to highlight the way in which children's unique status, capacities, and interests mean that regulation with fundamental human rights can become more than the mere application of 'A-C rights' to the facts, how workable is this as a normative account for lawyers? Overlaying the categorization of adult and children's rights in moral theory serves to highlight the need for increased precision in legal reasoning and analysis.

Secondly, Macleod posits three features of moral rights that might justify 'children's rights': signalling, normative weight, and enforcement.[165] This can be neatly contrasted with the features of legal rights that might justify 'children's rights': aspirational or expressive value, procedural protections and recognition, and substantive aspects.[166] The first legal aspect straightforwardly corresponds to the equivalent in moral theory. Normative weight in the context of moral theory means that rights are typically given priority over competing interests,[167] which can also often justify enforcement. There is a sense in which normative weight underpins all three features of legal rights since law is itself a normative exercise. Understood in terms of the consequences for competing interests, however, it is better related to the substantive aspects of legal rights in practice. Whilst enforceability is not a requirement for recognition as a moral or legal right, the long-term value of unenforceable rights is open to question, particularly in the case of children, who are less likely to be in a position to independently protect their own interests by other means.

Beyond the non-instrumental desire for normative coherence, it is critical to resolve the theoretical debate for instrumental reasons: there are many ways in which we fall short in our treatment of children, yet it is possible that a better understanding of one or more of these concepts could improve that situation. Ferguson argues that 'it is the potential for ensuring a better outcome from the child's perspective that should determine which approach or approaches we prefer'.[168] Even if correct, of course, that might

---

[162] See, eg, Herring (n 135) 486. [163] See CM Macleod's chapter.
[164] L Ferguson, 'Not Merely Rights for Children but Children's Rights: The Theory Gap and the Assumption of the Importance of Children's Rights' (2013) 21 International Journal of Children's Rights 177, 179–82.
[165] See CM Macleod's chapter. [166] Ferguson, 'Not Merely' (n 164) 183–90.
[167] See CM Macleod's chapter. [168] Ferguson, 'The Jurisprudence' (n 117) 152.

simply prompt the question: what are better outcomes from the (affected) child's perspective? How straightforwardly can such a question be answered?

This shifts the discussion from focus on the correct frame to directly targeting the relationship between children's interests and the interests of other parties and the community. It is in this context that Ferguson's contribution to this collection presents a case for the prioritization of children's interests. Rather than positively arguing for prioritization, she outlines and tests the case that would need to be made if the current legal language governing the regulation of children, such as 'best interests' and 'children's rights', were to speak for itself. Approaching the issue as whether children are a 'special case' to be prioritized enables us to avoid the debate over the precise theoretical basis of 'children's rights' or 'best interests'. Macleod's incomplete theorization thus shares a strategic aim with Ferguson, though the two authors adopt very different means to achieve that end.

Ferguson's prioritization argument stands in direct contrast to Altman's case for 'parental control rights', which he sets out in his contribution to this collection. Rather than the term 'parental rights', Altman uses the language of 'parental control rights'

> to distinguish parental entitlements to control their children's lives from other moral claims asserted by parents, such as the right to become a parent, and the right to associate with one's children, including claims for child custody, for visitations, and for limits on relocation by the child and custodial parent.[169]

He reasons that '[p]arental control … benefits children and society by enticing people to become parents or to carry out their parenting duties well'.[170] This may be correct from the parent's perspective, but how desirable are parents who require such incentives? The recasting of the parent–child relationship as primarily grounded in 'parental responsibility' in English law[171] suggests indirect justification for the parental role. Altman posits that to adopt the indirect approach, to ground 'parental control rights' in the interests of their children and broader society is to treat them as a means only. The value of a directly justified right, Altman argues, lies in the ability for parents to resist the state overriding decisions 'deemed unwise'.[172] Dwyer counters in his chapter, reasoning that the independent interest account 'conflates caring greatly about something and having a fundamental interest at stake'.[173]

The definitional limits of Altman's argument are particularly interesting for lawyers. He suggests that each type of parental rights is grounded in distinct parental interests; but one could also accept the relatedness of the contexts whilst seeing parents as having independent rights in some contexts but not others. This highlights the need to further examine the relationship between concepts such as 'parental responsibility' and contexts such as parental disputes over spending time with their children and relocation.

Altman examines and rejects two potential bases for 'parental control rights'— intimacy and the fiduciary nature of the parent-child relationship. Whilst Altman does not seek to alter outcomes in practice, but only to propose a better understanding of the basis of parental control rights, it is an interesting question whether the expressive

---

[169] See S Altman's chapter.   [170] See S Altman's chapter.   [171] Children Act 1989 (n 90).
[172] See S Altman's chapter.   [173] See JG Dwyer's chapter.

aspect of drawing on parent-centred interests could have the unintended consequence of extending protection of parents' non-ideal decisions in practice. Might this be a reason to reconsider a parent-oriented expression of the parent–child relationship?

In respect of intimacy, Altman argues that realistic state intervention in families would not undermine the parental interest in intimacy,[174] and the minimum degree of privacy and autonomy it requires.[175] Without the parental interest in intimacy being in conflict with state intervention, this interest is unable to protect parents' unwise decisions from being overridden. This can be compared with Jeske's argument that the moral and legal obligations that underpin spousal support are grounded in intimacy.[176] For Jeske, intimacy enables a more expansive understanding of morally and legally valuable relationships. Similarly, Altman's rejection of the parental interest in intimacy rests on intimacy being insufficiently narrow to conflict with most exercises of state intervention. Whereas Jeske grounds her case in intimacy directly, however, Altman focuses on the parental interest in intimacy. Do we need to distinguish between these references to intimacy, especially given that the parental interest lacks the mutuality contemplated by intimacy itself?

Altman also rejects the case for treating 'parental control rights' as grounded in the parental interest in 'fiduciarity'. He argues that the Brighouse-Swift account incorrectly requires the interest in acting to further children's welfare to include determining the child's moral instruction.[177] He further contends that the narrower Hannan–Vernon account, which distinguishes the parental interest in becoming a fiduciary from the exclusively child-oriented exercise of the fiduciary role, is unworkable.[178] Altman's rejection of the fiduciary account is particularly thought-provoking for lawyers since, within the legal literature, this understanding of the parent–child relationship has been presented in various forms since the 1970s and has recently begun to gain more traction.[179] A careful assessment requires us to determine whether 'fiduciary' must bear the same meaning as in other contexts, or whether—to return to the unsettled debate—the 'family law' conceptualization can and should be distinctive.

The political impact of legal arguments cannot be underestimated, and how we assess Altman's proposal for an independent basis for 'parental control rights' is at least in part political. When might we prefer Appell's account, which sees 'parental rights [as] a woman-centred and empowering doctrine that serves important social and political interests and acts as one of the only barriers to dismissing mothers who do not meet dominant norms'?[180] The political signal of repealing legal language that 'prioritises' children's interests, by contrast, might explain why, as Ferguson considers, that language persists despite academic convergence on equal treatment with adults.

Moreover, might the political appeal of concepts such as 'parental control rights' in the US context be grounded in excessive concern over children's rights? This should be

---

[174] See JG Dwyer's chapter. [175] See JG Dwyer's chapter.
[176] Jeske (n 125) and corresponding main text. [177] See S Altman's chapter.
[178] See S Altman's chapter.
[179] See, eg, Smith, 'Parenthood' (n 89), especially n 4 for references to earlier arguments that the parent–child relationship is best understood as fiduciary.
[180] AR Appell, 'Parental Rights Doctrine: Creating and Maintaining Maternal Value' in MA Fineman and K Worthington (eds), *What is Right for Children?* (Ashgate 2009) 123.

considered against the backdrop of the constitutional protection of parents' rights in the United States. In *Troxel v Granville*,[181] Justice Scalia reasoned that 'the interest of parents in the care, custody and control of their children—is perhaps the oldest of the fundamental liberty interests recognized by this Court'.[182] Further informing an understanding of the US context is its failure to ratify the United Nations' Convention on the Rights of the Child[183] despite the fact that, as Tobin explains, '[f]ar from seeking to drive a wedge between children and their parents, the CRC makes it clear that children's interests are best served when they enjoy a strong and supportive relationship with their parents'.[184]

The possibility and nature of independent parental rights critically affects any conclusions we can reach on whether parents have rights that can conflict with children's rights or interests, or whether, properly understood, they can never conflict. This is particularly important given Eekelaar and George's argument that jurisdictions are moving away from a 'possessory rights' understanding of the parent–child relationship to one grounded in 'parental responsibility' and similar concepts.[185] Due to the nature of the public interest in resolving any conflict of rights, this issue is discussed within the final theme.

D. Regulation and intervention

We focus our final theme on the interface between the 'family', 'family life', and the state. Of course, as Dwyer argues in his contribution to this collection, there exists no practical alternative to 'state intervention into the family' of 'leaving families alone'.[186] The socially constructed nature of law means that the state is necessarily involved in every area under discussion, such as the definition of 'family' and the recognition of particular relationships through the award of a legal status. Here we discuss situations in which the question of whether and how the state should intervene or regulate is the central issue: firstly, the justifiable threshold for, and nature of intervention in 'family' formation and 'family life', including conflicts between 'family' members; secondly, the place for 'private ordering' more generally.

1. Public policy and intervention in the 'family'

Is the state justified in restricting or burdening recognition of 'families' in which children are created with external support, such as via fertility treatment, surrogacy, and adoption? What model of the 'family', if any, should be reflected in such contexts? When is the state justified in removing children from parental care? Is the state justified in criminalizing the physical punishment of children by their parents or in overriding decisions parents make about their children's medical treatment? Are disputes between

---

[181] 530 US 57 (2000) (US Sup Ct).   [182] ibid.   [183] 20 November 1989, 1577 UNTS 3.
[184] J Tobin, 'Fixed Concepts but Changing Conceptions: Understanding the Relationship Between Children and Parents under the CRC' in MD Ruck, M Peterson-Badali, and M Freeman (eds), *Handbook of Children's Rights: Global and Multidisciplinary Perspectives* (Routledge 2017) 58.
[185] J Eekelaar and R George, 'Children's Rights: The Wider Context' in J Eekelaar and R George (eds), *Routledge Handbook of Family Law and Policy* (Routledge 2014) 288.
[186] See JG Dwyer's chapter.

'family' members ever truly private? Should such disagreements involving children be resolved differently from those concerned only with adults?

'Family' formation and intervention in 'family life' are taken together here because both contexts evidence an underlying priority for parent–child relationships created through genetic and gestational connection. The surrogacy process raises moral and legal quandaries and, when children are born as a result of surrogacy, the question of who should be granted legal parental status is a complex one. Surrogacy is often discussed as an exception to the general approach to procreation and parenthood but, as Shanley argues in her contribution to this collection, an examination of surrogacy prompts reconsideration of the basis of the parent–child relationship more generally.[187]

Shanley contends that a shift from focusing on individual rights to the complexity of the affected relationships is overdue, with increased recognition and role for gamete donors and surrogates post-birth. In this regard, she highlights the potential for increased, regulated non-anonymity; pre-birth meetings between the surrogate and the commissioning parent or parents; and post-birth contact between the surrogate and commissioning parent or parents, and between the surrogate and the child. Shanley recognizes the risk that entitlement to information about donors or surrogates might further entrench a biologized concept of 'family', though suggests that is forestalled by practical safeguards.[188] Given the binary nature of the award of status, it is an interesting question whether the legal framework would be able to embody the moral complexity, particularly in the expressive aspects of the award of legal parental status.

The normative view we take of preferable 'family' forms is reflected in the threshold we set for justifiable intervention in 'family life' and the decision to adopt a 'best interests' or a 'threshold' model of child protection. As the latter requires family dysfunction beyond merely not acting in the child's 'best interests', it suggests a privileging of (birth) parents over children—that parents and not the state bear the primary responsibility, hence a concomitant right to raise their children as they see fit.[189] But should this be seen as a moral or legal right? Setting the appropriate threshold for intervention in 'family life' requires balancing the interests of the state against those of the 'family' unit. Whether individuals' interests, especially children's interests, fall on the same side as those of the state or the 'family' unit, or both, is vital to determining this threshold.

In the seminal case of *Re H & Ors (Minors) (Sexual Abuse: Standard of Proof)*,[190] for example, Lord Nicholls addressed the various parties' interests that determine the threshold for intervention:

> On one side are the interests of parents in caring for their own child, a course which prima facie is also in the interests of the child. On the other side there will be circumstances in which the interests of the child may dictate a need for his care to be entrusted to others.[191]

---

[187] See ML Shanley's chapter.   [188] See ML Shanley's chapter.
[189] K Swift, 'Child Abuse Reporting Systems in Canada' in N Gilbert (ed), *Combatting Child Abuse: An International Perspective on Reporting Systems* (OUP 1997) 38.
[190] [1996] AC 563.   [191] ibid 584–85 (Lord Nicholls).

This suggests that it is the connection between parents and their children which sustains the parental interest and justifies the threshold for intervention requiring greater dysfunction than merely not acting in the child's 'best interests'. Is this a justifiable characterization of the child's interests at stake?

Previous discussion of Altman's chapter sets out his view of 'parental control rights', which favours an independent parent-oriented perspective that supports the current deferral to parental behaviour. By contrast, Shanley's analysis of the relationships created by surrogacy prefers a relational rights perspective. Understanding parental relationships in this way forestalls the possibility of a parent-oriented perspective on freedom from state intervention, but this does not mean that there could not be a 'family' unit for such protection. By contrast, on Dwyer's view, any notion of parental rights, howsoever grounded, 'is an affront to the equal moral personhood of children'.[192] Moreover, the state acts in a fiduciary role when it recognizes a child's legal parents, hence is 'bound to choose the best parents from among adults willing to serve'.[193] This justifies greater intervention in 'family life', though the state should continue to respect parental decisions that do not significantly impact on the child's welfare.[194]

There are two contexts in which the connection between the nature of the parent–child relationship, hence parental rights, and intervention in 'family life' is especially critical: the resolution of conflicts of rights and interests between parents and children, and cultural and religiously-grounded arguments for freedom from state intervention.

When individuals' rights and interests appear to be at odds with those of other family members, the community, or the state, there are two basic approaches to framing the issue for resolution. On the one hand, properly understood, there may be no conflict, hence the outcome that favours one party's rights or interests can straightforwardly be preferred. Alternatively, whilst such a conflict exists, one party's rights or interests, or a particular right or interest may be seen to outweigh those of others or other rights or interests.

Where it is understood that there is a genuine conflict, it is critical whether the conflict is resolved as a matter of law or as a matter of fact. The latter suggests that the particular circumstances of the dispute justify more weight being placed on one party's rights or interests, or a particular right or interest, in the final balancing exercise. The former suggests that the nature of one party's rights or interests, or a particular right or interest, requires privileging from the outset before application to the facts. Whether we conclude that there is a conflict and, if so, how it should be resolved is shaped by how we construct and understand the nature of children's and parents' interests.

A proper understanding of the nature of a particular statutory, judicial, or academic approach to the relationship between the interests of children and others thus requires precise reasoning. But language and analysis can seem insufficiently clear on this point. In his contribution to this collection, Macleod argues that 'it seems extremely difficult to deny that children have distinct (though complex) claims or interests that merit

---

[192] See JG Dwyer's chapter.
[193] JG Dwyer, 'The Moral Basis of Children's Relational Rights' in J Eekelaar and R George (eds), *Routledge Handbook of Family Law and Policy* (Routledge 2014) 279; see also JG Dwyer's chapter.
[194] Dwyer, 'The Moral Basis', 279.

recognition as especially important'[195] and that 'protection of some of these claims or interests has a kind of normative priority or urgency over other considerations'.[196] When might this occur? Would such priority be as a matter of law or fact? How might this be affected by the nature of any conflict of interests or rights?

Ferguson is unusually explicit as to the nature of her claim: that children's interests should be prioritized as a matter of law over those of others, including their parents'. The controversial nature of her position perhaps suggests why reasoning is typically less precise. But can we improve the treatment of children without such unequivocal analysis? Consider the European context: the ECHR does not itself describe the relative position of the child and the European Court of Human Rights has variously articulated it. Children's 'best interests' have been said to be 'of particular importance',[197] 'the primary consideration',[198] 'the paramount consideration'[199] and to 'prevail';[200] 'consideration' of children's interests has also been described as 'of crucial importance'.[201] Academic debate assumes these different terms represent different ways of preferring children's interests; discussion centres on which view to prefer. The two most commonly contrasted formulations are those in *Johansen v Norway* and *Yousef v The Netherlands*. The Court in *Johansen* contends that:

> [A] fair balance has to be struck between the interests of the child ... and those of the parent.... In carrying out this balancing exercise, the Court will attach particular importance to the best interests of the child, which, depending on their nature and seriousness, may override those of the parent.[202]

Whereas, in *Yousef*, the Court reasons that:

> in judicial decisions where the rights under Art.8 of parents and those of a child are at stake, the child's rights must be the paramount consideration. If any balancing of interests is necessary, the interests of the child must prevail.[203]

Academic preference has been expressed for the *Johansen* formulation over the *Yousef* formulation.[204] Such expression of preference assumes that the language is significant.

---

[195] See CM MacLeod's chapter.   [196] See CM MacLeod's chapter.

[197] Eg, *Johansen v Norway* (1997) 23 EHRR 33 [78] [*Johansen*]; *Hoppe v Germany* (2004) 38 EHRR 15 [49]; *Görgülü v Germany* [2004] 1 FLR 894 (ECtHR) [43]; *Süss v Germany* [2006] 1 FLR 522 (ECtHR) [88]. Similarly, in *Hokkanen v Finland* (1995) 15 EHRR 139 [58], the ECtHR reasons that, when considering the rights and freedoms of all concerned parties, the child's best interests and rights are 'more particularly' to be taken into account.

[198] Eg, *Neulinger v Switzerland* (2012) 54 EHRR 31 [134] (though this is mentioned in the context of the need to strike a 'fair balance' between the parties' competing interests; the ECtHR referred to the Preamble to The Hague Convention on the Civil Aspects of International Child Abduction (25 Oct 1980) in which children's interests are described as being of 'paramount importance').

[199] Eg, *Yousef v The Netherlands* (2003) 36 EHRR 20 [73].   [200] ibid [73].

[201] Eg, *Elsholz v Germany* (2002) 34 EHRR 58 [48]; *TP and KM v United Kingdom* (2002) 34 EHRR 2 [70]; *Scott v United Kingdom* [2000] Fam LR 102 (ECtHR) [18–94]. In *Süss*, in addition to the standard recitation of the *Johansen* 'particular importance' formulation, the ECtHR also describes the child's best interests as of 'crucial importance' ([86]).

[202] *Johansen* (n 197) [78].   [203] *Yousef* (n 199) [73].

[204] See, eg, S Choudhry and H Fenwick, 'Taking the Rights of Parents and Children Seriously: Confronting the Welfare Principle under the Human Rights Act' (2005) 25 Oxford Journal of Legal Studies 453, 478.

Even if language *should* matter, as Ferguson argues, *does* it in fact matter here? This remains to be settled.

How, if at all, are these arguments affected by the addition of cultural or religious considerations? This turns on whether the basis of any parental interests should be relevant when weighed against the child's, as well as how we should evaluate the child's place within a community or culture. In his contribution to this collection, Dwyer argues that the child's interests alone are relevant to decision-making about fundamental aspects of their welfare and others' interests are relevant only indirectly.[205] Whilst religiously or culturally-grounded decisions can have 'intense significance' for parents and other caregivers, Dwyer reasons that it is mistaken to see those as the only justifications for attaching such importance to decisions.[206] On his account, therefore, there are no rights or interests to be balanced against the child's, nor is any special weight to be given to religious and cultural concerns.

Dwyer contends that ascribing legal rights to parents, which recognize parents' independent interests, would be 'in derogation of the state's *parens patriae* role'.[207] We might understand this as a theoretical case for the 'no conflict' option discussed above being the only permissible interpretation of any apparent conflict of rights or interests. This can be directly contrasted to Altman's argument for an independent basis for parental rights. The centrality of the state interest to Dwyer's account is particularly significant. How can we decide whether the state interest lies in recognizing only children's rights and interests directly or also recognizing that there are other rights and interests with which they may conflict?

2. Private ordering

There is a sense in which the issue of 'private ordering' is the first question to be asked in interrogating family law and children's law. Just because a legal regime exists, which already recognizes and regulates particular relationships as 'familial', does not mean it should be assumed to be the starting-point from which analysis begins. Does 'private ordering' move relationships outside of 'family law', or do they necessarily remain within 'family law'? Why might it matter? Are there compelling reasons of liberty, state neutrality, or choice for adult relationships to be treated as a matter of 'private ordering', and not pre-defined status? Yet could relationships involving children be consigned to 'private ordering' (in any meaningful sense) without unacceptable conflict with children's interests? And would relegating adult relationships to 'private ordering' fail to protect those made vulnerable by caregiving or in gender-structured relationships?

In the legal context, 'private ordering' is conventionally associated with protection of autonomy in the form of express agreements reached between the parties, as Bix discusses in his contribution to this collection. But, as his analysis of possible justifications for recognizing and, possibly, enforcing such agreements highlights, matters are more complex. In addition to autonomy, he examines arguments from social utility,

---

[205] See JG Dwyer's chapter. [206] See JG Dwyer's chapter. [207] See JG Dwyer's chapter.

Eekelaar's 'privileged sphere' of personal interactions,[208] the protection of dignity and against exploitation, and broader public policy arguments.

Current attempts to better understand the nature of the debate over 'private ordering' face two critical difficulties: firstly, in practice, justifications for restrictions have been inadequately articulated; and, secondly, its expansion has often occurred in procedural terms, such as with the introduction of family law arbitration in England and Wales.

Consider nuptial agreements. Until recently, nuptial agreements were deemed void at common law in England and Wales as contrary to public policy for 'undermin[ing] the concept of marriage as a life-long union'.[209] In 2014, the Law Commission opined that 'the evolution of the law and changed social attitudes have rendered this public policy rule obsolete'[210] but did not clearly articulate why binding nuptial agreements do not undermine marriage. Yet, as discussed above, the meaning of marriage in society both informs and is informed by its conceptualization in 'family law'. The default statutory regime provides the law's understanding of the meaning of marriage at its breakdown and, to an extent, more generally. In her dissent in *Radmacher v Granatino*,[211] Lady Hale recognizes that the debate over the status of nuptial agreements raises 'some profound questions about the nature of marriage in the modern law',[212] though reaches no conclusion on the extent to which, if at all, nuptial agreements should be able to alter the 'irreducible minimum' of marriage.[213] The public policy debate has

> shift[ed] from moralist concerns to protect the institution of marriage from spouses and others who make agreements liable to destabilise an individual marriage to more benevolent, paternalist concerns to protect individual contracting spouses (or would-be spouses) from agreeing terms which, with the benefit of hindsight, might be judged imprudent.[214]

Yet, it remains unsettled how 'private ordering' outside of the default regime should relate to the meaning of 'marriage'. Further, any case for maintaining or even reinforcing legal regulation of intimate relationships should be set against Jeske's suggestion that state intervention may be more likely to destroy intimacy than promote it,[215] and Eekelaar's discussion of contexts in which the legalization of social norms may risk undermining them.[216]

This analysis highlights the key dilemma created by the increasing pace of 'private ordering' in domestic and international family and children's law regimes, such as through the recent launch of the International Family Law arbitration scheme: there is no shared understanding of the justifiable public interest in regulating and intervening explicitly in individuals' intimate lives by the creation of default regimes rather than implicitly by creating or leaving space for private ordering. What is required for individuals to be '(part) author of [their] own li[ves]'?[217]

---

[208] Eekelaar (n 83) 82. [209] *N v N* [1999] 2 FLR 745, 752 (Wall J).
[210] Law Commission 343 (n 139) [4.28]. [211] [2010] UKSC 42.
[212] ibid [132] (Lady Hale). [213] ibid (Lady Hale).
[214] J Miles, 'Marital Agreements: "The More Radical Solution"' in R Probert and C Barton (eds), *Fifty Years in Family Law: Essays for Stephen Cretney* (Intersentia 2012) 99–100.
[215] See D Jeske's chapter. [216] See J Eekelaar's chapter.
[217] J Raz, *The Morality of Freedom* (Clarendon 1986) 369.

PART I
DEFINITIONS

1
Family Law and Legal Theory

John Eekelaar

I. Introduction: Definitions and Theories

Can there be a theory of family law? The subject matter is elusive. What is a family? What is law? Historically, strands of legal activity that were later collected together into what is usually understood as 'family law' were in England treated independently: eg, divorce,[1] marriage,[2] 'infants', and children.[3] Roman law also failed to develop a unified concept of family law. Ironically, the concept of family law as a unified field of study and practice emerged in western countries[4] just when a significant relaxation of family forms began to occur in those jurisdictions, to be followed, in the early twenty-first century, by scientific advances which still further stretched the concept.

But it is necessary to ask for what purpose a definition of 'family' or 'family law' is sought. In the abstract, few practical consequences seem to turn on it, except perhaps in jurisdictions which assign 'family law' to a distinct branch of the court system, or when designing a law syllabus or determining the remit of a book or journal, though (as will be seen) it could have important consequences in applying legal instruments. But then the nature and purpose of the instrument could be determinative. When issues as diverse as married and unmarried cohabitation (same-sex or opposite sex, with or without children), religious practice, personal identity, and the regulation of in vitro fertilization and embryo transplantation (including 'ownership' and disposition of embryos) fall for consideration, it may help to think of these as matters pertaining to the personal or 'private' lives of individuals. The fact that 'private' life is to be respected as well as 'family' life under Article 8 of the European Convention on Human Rights has enabled decisions under the Convention to respond to this feature.[5] So it might be

---

[1] See the many editions of *Rayden on Divorce* (Butterworths, 17th edn, 1998).
[2] See J Arnold, *The Marriage Law of England* (Staples Press 1951); J Jackson, *The Law Relating to the Formation and Annulment of Marriage and Allied Matters in English Domestic and Private International Law* (Sweet & Maxwell 1951).
[3] See A Simpson, *A Treatise on the Law and Practice Relating to Infants* (Stevens and Haynes 1875); Clarke Hall and Morrison's *Law Relating to Children and Young Persons* (Butterworths 1967).
[4] See the discussion by W Müller-Freienfels, 'The Emergence of Droit de Famille and Familienrecht in Continental Europe and the Introduction of Family Law in England' (2003) 28 Journal of Family History 31. The textbook *Family Law* by PM Bromley first appeared in 1957.
[5] See eg, *Evans v United Kingdom* (2006) 43 EHRR 21 (right to become parent or not in context of use of frozen embryos); *Mikulić v Croatia* (App No 53176/99) [2002] 1 FCR 720 (right to establish identity of parent). In *Schalk and Kopf v Austria* (App No 30141/04) [2011] 2 FCR 650 the ECtHR accepted that discrimination against same-sex partners might now be held to infringe their right to 'family' life rather than, as previously, their 'private' life, though it did not (yet) require states to introduce same-sex marriage.

better to describe the subject matter of family law as 'personal' law[6] in the sense of the constellation of issues that arise in the context of people's intimate relationships and reproductive behaviour, but extending to social and blood relationships which follow from these.[7] Nevertheless, the conventional term 'family law' will be used here.

Given this diversity of subject matter, it is understandable that Brian Bix baulked at the idea that a single theory of family law could be constructed, at least for the US.[8] There is a danger that any purported overarching theory would be more in the nature of an ideology than an attempted explanation of the phenomenon observed. Nevertheless, it will be argued that there is a pervasive feature which is central to understanding both how family law operates and how it should operate. This is so because individuals do not lead their 'private' lives in a social vacuum, but in a universe of social and legal norms. It arises immediately with respect to the question of what a family is. The anthropologist Robin Fox[9] reduced the concept to the mother–baby unit, but in *Fitzpatrick v Sterling Housing Ltd* the majority of the House of Lords was persuaded that membership of a 'family' for the purposes of succession to a tenancy under the Rent Act 1977, considering the general objectives of the legislation, required that 'there should be a degree of mutual inter-dependence, of the sharing of lives, of caring and love, of commitment and support', which, in view of changes in the public's 'attitude', could include same-sex couples, even if no children are involved.[10] The fact that the conclusion was attributed also to Parliament's intentions does not lessen the fact that it was based on a perception of social norms about what could be considered such a relationship, and how the parties in it behave. Nor is it lessened by the conflicting judicial opinions about what those social norms were, since social norms frequently conflict.

It will be argued that understanding the way legal and social norms interact should be central to theorizing about family law. In fact, there may need to be a number of theories explaining, or justifying, the specific interactions in the various circumstances in which they occur. One reason for this is that family law operates very closely alongside social practices, so much so that it can sometimes be overwhelmed by them, as happened to the English divorce law before it was reformed as from 1971.[11] It is arguable that a similar process is occurring now regarding the inception of relationships, with the institution of marriage becoming more flexible (eg, extension to same-sex couples, the use of prenuptial agreements), and for many people, being abandoned altogether.

Of course, these issues are not unique to family law. They will be found in all areas of law. But, as Ira Ellman[12] has observed, the salience of the interaction between legal and social norms is heightened in family law because of the intimate and personal nature

---

[6] See J Eekelaar, *Family Law and Personal Life* (OUP 2nd edn, 2017) 28.
[7] But see the discussion by David Archard in Chapter 2 of this book.
[8] BH Bix, *The Oxford Introductions to US Law: Family Law* (OUP 2013) 3.
[9] R Fox, *Kinship and Marriage: An Anthropological Perspective* (CUP 1983) 37. See also M Fineman, *The Neutered Mother, the Sexual Family, and other Twentieth Century Tragedies* (Routledge 1995), proposing that only the mother–child dyad be especially protected by the law.
[10] [1999] UKHL 42, [23].
[11] See C Smart, 'Divorce in England 1950–2000: A Moral Tale?' in SN Katz, J Eekelaar, and M Maclean (eds), *Cross Currents: Family Law and Policy in the US and England* (OUP 2000) ch 16; J Eekelaar, 'The Place of Divorce in Family Law's New Role' (1975) 38 Modern Law Review 241.
[12] I Ellman, 'Why Making Family Law is Hard' (2003) 35 Arizona State Law Journal 699.

of much of its content, and the problem of power is particularly challenging because its exercise may be subtle and hidden, and, perhaps more importantly, gender-based, thus engaging the complex of social norms that affect gender relationships. By reinforcing social norms operating within the 'intimate' sphere, the law can enhance predictability and security in intimate relationships which can be important to people, but at the same time enhance the use of such power. Yet the law can also provide a counterbalance in favour of those who are subject to such power.

It will be argued that appreciation of the interaction between all these forces should be central to an understanding of family law. This falls short of a general theory, but in conclusion, however, a suggestion will be made about what now is, and should be, the main (but not the only) point of having family law at all.

A. Social and legal norms

For present purposes, norms will be considered to be legal norms if they are recognized as such by officials within a legal system with authority to do so, and all norms not so recognized (including moral norms) will be seen as social norms. HLA Hart identified social norms as the social practices of most members of a society which those members saw as guides to behaviour and which occasioned criticism if broken. Ronald Dworkin, however, argued that this ignored the importance of society's members having reasons for following the rules beyond just doing what other people did. Hart later accepted that Dworkin's qualification was necessary in an account of *moral* rules, but did not accept it with respect to social ('conventional') rules, writing: 'some rules may be accepted simply out of deference to tradition or the wish to identify with others or in the belief that society knows best what is to the advantage of individuals'.[13] In practice however it may be difficult to distinguish whether people do certain things because they think they ought to conform to what other people do, or whether they happen to do the same things for different reasons. The distinction is not important for present purposes, however. What is important is that these are norms that are not applied as law by legal officials.

This is a fairly orthodox positivist position. In their introductory chapter to the volume on family law in the *International Encyclopedia of Comparative Law*,[14] Max Rheinstein and René Konig made it clear that, while family *behaviour* was determined by 'religious and ethical beliefs, conventions and habits' (which they termed *mores*), for them, family *law* comprised only 'norms sanctioned by governmental action'.[15] In 1997 Brian Tamanaha put it slightly differently: '[law] includes only those norms that are actually enforced by publicly approved coercive institutions'.[16] Yet this view has been famously challenged by Ronald Dworkin,[17] who claimed that certain 'principles' could be part of the law without (in John Gardner's words) 'anyone ever having made it'.[18] But

---

[13] HLA Hart, *The Concept of Law* (2nd edn, Clarendon Press 1994) 255–59, 257.
[14] *International Encyclopedia of Comparative Law*, vol IV (Mohr Siebeck 1971, 2007).
[15] ibid s 1: 4–5.   [16] B Tamanaha, *Realistic Socio-Legal Theory* (Clarendon Press 1997) 122.
[17] R Dworkin, 'The Model of Rules' (1967) 35 University of Chicago Law Review 14.
[18] J Gardner, *Law as a Leap of Faith* (OUP 2012) 85. Gardner rejects Dworkin's position.

Joseph Raz has insisted that, while courts may pay regard to moral and social norms (that is, norms without a 'pedigree' from a social source) in making their decisions, such norms are not legal norms.[19]

Yet if a court incorporates a social norm into its decision, as in the *Fitzpatrick* case mentioned earlier (other examples will be given later), should the norm be seen as having been part of the legal system, and therefore as being in some sense 'law', prior to its incorporation? It is institutionally important that law-applying institutions (courts) should regard themselves, and be regarded, as applying law that already exists rather than inventing law to suit the case in hand. The fabric of law surely includes values and it is surely not fanciful to see these as seeping into that fabric as social norms change without being expressly adopted by a legal official, and therefore as capable of being applied by a court as law. Even if it is not known before the decision whether the court will do this, the fact that the norm exists puts its violator on notice that a court might hold that violation of the norm is a legal transgression. This suggests that norms outside the boundary demarcated by Rheinstein and Konig may have legal consequences, and are therefore in some sense 'law'.[20]

However for an understanding of family law it is unnecessary to take a position on these issues. Rather, the lesson to be drawn is of the relevance of all these norms, and the interaction between them, for people's personal lives. This follows Tamanaha's more recent conclusion, where, having set out a wide range of contexts in which norms affect people's lives, he concludes that resolving conceptual issues about their nature or definition is not essential, for 'what matters most is framing situations that facilitate the observation and analysis of what appears to be interesting and important'.[21] What is important in this context is the practical issue of whether norms that are not enforced as law later receive such enforcement, why that does or does not occur and what justifications exist for these outcomes.

II. The Interdependence of Legal and Social Norms

A. Parent–child relationships

The fact that areas of people's personal lives are legally unregulated does not mean that they are 'norm-free'. In many respects, it will make little difference whether the norms are legal or social. For example, in 1971 SJ Stoljar wrote, regarding European codes, that there was a 'further requirement, now recognized universally, that children must obey their parents and do what they say'.[22] Legal codes do contain provisions

---

[19] J Raz, *Between Authority and Interpretation: On the Theory of Law and Practical Reason* (OUP 2009) 191 ff.

[20] In J Eekelaar, 'Judges and Citizens: Two Conceptions of Law' (2002) 22 Oxford Journal of Legal Studies 497, I suggested that it is reasonable to hold that judges can regard a social norm as having become part of the law prior to their decision confirming this, while citizens may not do so and can argue accordingly prior to the court's decision, though the decision is necessary to determine the matter with finality.

[21] BZ Tamanaha, 'Understanding Legal Pluralism: Past to Present, Local to Global' (2008) 30 Sydney Law Review 375.

[22] *International Encyclopedia of Comparative Law* (n 15) s 7, 23–24. Stoljar does not provide any examples.

regarding children's duties towards their parents. Article 91(1) of the Polish Family and Guardianship Code sets out the child's obligations to help meet the needs of the family if the child has income from work and lives with the parents or to help the parents in the household if the child is maintained by the parents and lives with them. The French Civil Code proclaims that a 'child, at any age, owes honour and respect to his father and mother', and 'may not, without the permission of the father and mother, leave the family home'.[23] Section 1618a of the German Civil Code states: 'Parents and children owe each other assistance and respect' and section 1619 adds: 'As long as the child belongs to the household of its parents and is brought up or maintained by its parents, it has a duty to perform services for its parents in their household and business in a manner appropriate for its strength and its position in life.' While such duties potentially invite the apparatus of the state bureaucracy into the household, the likelihood is that the social norm is more important, and the prospect of institutional enforcement where it is legalized insignificant. It is more likely to support a derivative action, such as a claim against a third party who injures the child, depriving the father of those services. There are, it seems, no equivalent legal duties on children in English law, but few would deny the existence of social norms to similar effect. In the English perception, a disobedient child, or one who leaves home, is less likely to be seen as violating legal duties towards their parents than as a sign of failure of the relationship between the parents and child, leading to state intervention if the child becomes socially disruptive or endangered.

As regards parents' duties towards their children, historically, in England, as elsewhere, the legal structure of the parent–child relationship was designed to protect a father's interests in his children and their property as potential sources of income and support.[24] However, there is much evidence that from medieval times parents considered themselves, and were considered, to have an obligation to nurture and educate their children (although how this was interpreted could be different from contemporary ideas).[25] In 1765, William Blackstone observed that a parent's duty to support his children was 'a principle of natural law' (in effect, a social norm), but went on to state that 'the principle of law that there is an obligation on every parent to provide for those descended from his loins' was 'thus pointed out', and proceeded to set out the content of section 7 of the Poor Relief Act 1601. This allowed a Court of Quarter Sessions to order the 'father and mother, grandfather or grandmother' of 'poor, impotent, persons' (who would have been supported by parish funds) to maintain such persons, but only for necessaries, with a penalty for non-compliance of 20 shillings a month.[26] The policy was reinvigorated in the unsettled early nineteenth century in the Poor Law Amendment Act 1834. The law therefore enforced the social (or moral) obligation only when failure to perform it threw the cost on the community.

---

[23] Code Civil, arts 371 and 371.3.
[24] This is set out in J Eekelaar, 'The Emergence of Children's Rights' (1986) 6 Oxford Journal of Legal Studies 161.
[25] See S Shaher, *Childhood in the Middle Ages* (Routledge 1990); L Pollock, *Forgotten Children: Parent–Child Relations from 1500 to 1900* (CUP 1983).
[26] *Blackstone's Commentaries on the Laws of England* (HW Ballantine ed, Blackstone Institute 1915) 310.

B. Husbands and wives

This interdependence between the norms occurs also when a social norm such as the husband's duty to support his wife in earlier English law became directly enforceable only when certain other conditions were present. This obligation was not directly enforceable while the parties were living together,[27] but could become so if they separated, or if the husband assaulted the wife.[28] In more modern times, social security law as introduced after the Second World War was premised on the assumption, not legally prescribed, that a husband would hand the benefits he received on to his wife and children, since a married man who had paid his contributions would receive additional benefits for his wife and children.[29] In such cases the successful operation of the law depended on the underlying social norms.

III. Family Law and the Exercise of Power

We now need to look in more detail at the dynamics underlying the interaction between legal norms and social norms in family matters. Legal norms may sometimes protect and reinforce existing social structures, and sometimes discard such structures or attempt to perpetuate them into the future, often through the exercise of power by male groups over women.

Jack Goody has described how the medieval church overturned a range of former family practices, for example, by extending the scope of relationships prohibited for marriage and refusing to recognize forms of adoption and concubinage, so as to exercise 'a large measure of control in the domestic domain',[30] thereby increasing its landholdings and authority. Maria Antokolskaia noted that all European 'family law' before the reformation was canon (church) law, Catholic in the west and Orthodox in the east. Under this law 'the concubine became no more than a mistress and her children were bastardized'. Divorce became increasingly restrictive, although nullity provided some ways around it.[31] Guardianship law protected a parent's interests in the marriage of an heir; legitimacy ensured orderly devolution of family status and wealth; marriage, property, and succession law secured the property interests of landed families. These types of law sustained the whole social structure.

Customary legal systems also set a framework within which people live their lives, particularly, but not exclusively, with regard to their family relationships. A key concern in these systems, as indeed in all systems of family law, from the earliest times,

---

[27] If she lacked the means to purchase 'necessities' a wife could be treated as her husband's agent. But the effectiveness of this tactic depended on the willingness of the third party to grant credit and enforce against the husband.

[28] For example in separation orders in the ecclesiastical courts. From 1878 a support order could be made in a magistrates' court, but only if the husband assaulted the wife: Matrimonial Causes Act 1878.

[29] Social Security Act 1975, ss 44–47, 66.

[30] J Goody, *The Development of the Family and Marriage in Europe* (CUP 1983) 59.

[31] MV Antokolskaia, 'Development of Family Law in Western and Eastern Europe: Common Origins, Common Driving Forces, Common Tendencies' (2003) 28 Journal of Family History 52, 55.

is the regulation of human reproduction, for this determines the allocation of human resources (children). An example is provided by Tom Bennett:

> As fieldwork on the Tshidi people in Botswana showed, customary marriages are not defined by the performance of single acts or ceremonies. Instead, the Tshidi regard marriage as a process. It begins with a series of meetings between senior representatives of the bride and groom's families, at which the parties settle the terms and conditions of the union. When agreement is reached on the amount of livestock or cash to be paid, the Tshidi allow the future husband to take up residence with the bride's family, where he may start cohabiting with his wife. After a period of time, the couple moves to the husband's homestead, and the bridewealth is formally handed over. Although payment of the full amount is usually delayed, the wife's guardian has justification for demanding more with the birth of each child. Not until all marital obligations are fulfilled, however, can a couple be considered fully married.[32]

IV. Restraints on Power: Countervailing Rights

After the 1960s, in western jurisdictions, the social institutions that family law was previously designed to sustain (in particular, marriage, legitimacy and male superiority) were undermined and replaced by a form of law that recognized individual self-determination and sought to protect individual well-being.[33] An important means by which this was brought about was through the rhetoric of 'rights' of individuals, both of adults and children, and human rights. The examples are legion. They include a realistic right to divorce, on a gender-neutral basis, including safeguarding the vulnerable spouse's property and economic interests; protection against violence and abuse, including a widening perception of the way power may be abused within the family;[34] equal parental rights respecting children; abolition of the status of illegitimacy and discrimination against fathers of non-marital children; gay (equal) marriage; focus on the best interests of children and an enhanced voice for children. We will consider some specific instances.

A. Parents and children

As James Dwyer shows in Chapter 13 of this book, by granting parental status, the state confers considerable power on parents. The way it is exercised is determined mainly by social norms. However, when the physical or emotional health of children is at risk, intervention should be justifiable under the 'harm' principle, which allows 'coercive' intervention to prevent the infliction of harm on others.[35] This is one of the points

---

[32] TW Bennett, 'Comparative Law and African Customary Law' in M Reimann and R Zimmermann (eds), *Oxford Handbook of Comparative Law* (OUP 2006) 647.

[33] See Eekelaar (n 6) ch 2 and J Eekelaar, 'Then and Now: Family Law's Direction of Travel' (2013) 35 Journal of Social Welfare and Family Law 415. C Smart, 'Law and Family Life: Insights from 25 Years of Empirical Research' (2014) 26 Child & Family Law Quarterly 14, describes changes in family living and attitudes over a similar period.

[34] Creating awareness of this issue has been said to have been one of the major successes of feminism in family law: KT Bartlett, 'Feminism and Family Law: Family Law and American Culture' (1999) 33 Family Law Quarterly 475, 495.

[35] JS Mill, *Utilitarianism, On Liberty and Considerations on Representative Government* (1859).

at which family law encounters wider theoretical discussion, for the harm principle has been extensively debated.[36] But while intervention to prevent serious damage to a child's health is not within an area of controversy, particular difficulties may arise when parents seek to bring up their children according to norms of a belief system of which the state disapproves, but which may be given legal protection by instruments such as the First Amendment to the US Constitution[37] and Article 2 of the First Protocol of the European Convention on Human Rights.[38] Despite fears that have arisen over possible fundamentalist religious teachings which are thought to be at variance with 'national' values, intervention (in the United Kingdom) has been largely in the area of education outside the home, unless an opening is found to influence home teaching, such as if the parents are in dispute with one another.[39] It took a decision of the European Court of Human Rights for the UK Parliament to confine the defence of 'reasonable chastisement' (which incorporates social values) when parents apply corporal punishment to their children to prosecutions for common assault.[40]

B. Adult relationships

Feminist scholarship has famously demonstrated that legal norms sustain power relationships in many ways, so that merely by underwriting a power structure, they can protect the social norms generated by that structure.[41] In western jurisdictions, the power given to husbands over their wives by the law was, until the second half of the twentieth century, immense. He could determine their standard of living, where they lived, the terms of their separation (should he agree to it), control the property, claim damages from someone with whom she had committed adultery and even compel her to have sexual relations with him.[42] However, social norms may also have generated certain constraints on the way that power was exercised. Thus, despite their legally underwritten power, husbands and fathers were expected to behave benevolently, and to provide sustenance for their families. These social norms provided some balance or redress against the legally reinforced social norms that sustained patriarchy, but they received scant attention from the law. Hence, at least in the English context, apart from

---

[36] For example HLA Hart, 'Social Solidarity and the Enforcement of Morality' in *Essays in Jurisprudence and Philosophy* (OUP 1983) 248–62; J Feinberg, *Harm to Self* (OUP 1986); J Feinberg, *Harmless Wrongdoing* (OUP 1990); J Raz, *The Morality of Freedom* (OUP 1986).

[37] 'Congress shall make no law respecting an establishment of religion, or prohibiting the free exercise thereof'.

[38] This requires that 'no person shall be denied the right to education. In the exercise of any functions which it assumes in relation to education and teaching, the State shall respect the right of parents to ensure such education and teaching in conformity with their own religious and philosophical convictions'.

[39] See R Taylor, 'Responsibility for the Soul of the Child: The Role of the State and Parents in Determining Religious Upbringing and Education' (2015) 29 International Journal of Law, Policy & the Family 15.

[40] *A v The United Kingdom* (1999) 27 EHRR 611. Children Act 2004, s 58.

[41] See F Olsen, 'The Myth of State Intervention in the Family' (1984–5) 18 Michigan University Journal of Law Reform 835; R Gavison, 'Feminism and the Public–Private Distinction' (1992) 45 Stanford Law Review 1, 14–18 (accepting the points but also arguing that there can be good reasons for restraint in legal intervention in those structures); C Smart, 'Regulating Families or Legitimating Patriarchy? Family Law in Britain' (1982) 10 International Journal of the Sociology of Law 129.

[42] See J Eekelaar, 'Families and Children: From Welfarism to Rights' in C McCrudden and G Chambers (eds), Individual Rights and the Law in Britain (OUP 1994) 302–09.

the general criminal law, there were hardly any institutional constraints on the way parents treated their children until the late nineteenth century, and how husbands treated their wives until the late twentieth century; however, many social norms may have demanded restraint (and they were by no means clear even on that). But more recently the norms became clearer, and they were eventually picked up by the courts. Consider a husband's former immunity from prosecution for marital rape. The original legal position was stated with clarity by the Scottish High Court of Judiciary in *S. v H.M. Advocate*.[43]

> Then, no doubt, a married woman could be said to have subjected herself to her husband's dominion in all things. She was required to obey him in all things. Leaving out of account the absence of rights of property, a wife's freedoms were virtually non-existent, and she had in particular no right whatever to interfere in her husband's control over the lives and upbringing of any children of the marriage.

Things have since changed:

> By the second half of the 20th century, however, the status of women, and the status of a married woman, in our law have changed quite dramatically. ... A live system of law will always have regard to changing circumstances to test the justification for any exception to the application of a general rule. ... It cannot be affirmed nowadays, whatever the position may have been in earlier centuries, that it is an incident of modern marriage that a wife consents to intercourse in all circumstances, including sexual intercourse obtained only by force.

Here changes in social norms allowed the courts to hold *that the law too had changed*, although such changes could not be traced to a recognized social source of law creation. An analogous process occurs when the European Court of Human Rights makes the application of the European Convention on Human Rights contingent on 'European' or even 'international' developments on issues such as the right of transgender persons to legal recognition,[44] and the right of homosexuals to adopt,[45] and perhaps eventually to marry,[46] though, given its international character, the Court relies mainly on domestic legislation (legal norms) of member (and sometimes other) states as indicators of opinion.

C. Rights and responsibility

The relaxation of the legal and social structures within which personal relationships are supposed to take place has raised new concerns that the predictability and security those structures created have been threatened. The response has been to try to encourage individuals to exercise their rights responsibly. So the law may seek to *build up* a social norm. An early example was the interference by courts in freedom of testation (another form of power), first allowed in the common law world in New Zealand's Testator's Family

---

[43] 1989 SLT 469, 473. This was cited, and followed, by the House of Lords in *R v R* [1991] UKHL 12.
[44] *Christine Goodwin v The United Kingdom* (2002) 35 EHRR 447.
[45] *EB v France* (2008) 47 EHRR 21, [92].
[46] *Schalk and Kopf v Austria* Application no 30141/04 judgment 24 June 2010 [2011] 2 FCR 650.

Maintenance Act 1900, permitting a court to override testamentary provisions by ordering such provision as it deemed fit out of the estate in favour of the testator's wife, or husband, and children. This model was followed in England in 1938 (on testacy) and 1952 (on intestacy).[47] Here the courts are endeavouring to instil a form of responsible behaviour by conferring rights on the protected individuals to make legal challenges against those who do not follow them. In the context of divorce, in *Piglowska v Piglowski*[48] Lord Hoffmann said of judicial guidelines regarding the way property and financial orders after divorce should be made: 'These guidelines, not expressly stated by Parliament, are derived by the courts from values about family life which it (sic) considers would be widely accepted in the community.'[49] The wider hope is that divorcing parties will follow these principles in negotiating their own arrangements.[50] So in that case the courts drew on social values in formulating legal principles which it was hoped would, in turn, further reinforce those values. Similarly, legislation proclaiming that, when parents separate, 'a court ... is as respects each parent ... to presume, unless the contrary is shown, that involvement of that parent in the life of the child concerned will further the child's welfare'[51] is designed to develop an existing social norm of shared parenting after parental separation.

Governments might attempt to manipulate social norms in other ways. They could try to reconcile an ideology of promoting individual choice with government policies by persuading people to internalize the norms fashioned by such policies.[52] An example is found in attempts in England in the 1990s to compel people initiating divorce to attend meetings which would provide information that was heavily loaded to induce certain types of behaviour deemed desirable by government (such as reconciling with the other party)[53] and has continued in efforts to promote resort to mediation rather than to legal advice.[54] But using legislation to replace, reinforce, or generate social norms in the complex sphere of family relationships carries risks. The encouragement of shared parenting in Australia has led to overly complex legislation[55] and does not seem to have brought about more shared parenting agreements. Instead, it seems to have led to courts imposing such an outcome more frequently in disputed cases, where it is probably least appropriate.[56]

---

[47] Inheritance (Family Provision) Act 1938; Intestates' Estate Act 1952.
[48] [1999] 3 All ER 632, 644.
[49] For an excellent summary, see J Miles and J Scherpe, 'The Legal Consequences of Dissolution: Property and Financial Support Between Spouses', in J Eekelaar and R George (eds), *Routledge Handbook of Family Law and Policy* (Routledge 2014) ch 2.6.
[50] This strategy has been particularly successful in Canada: see C Rogerson, 'Child Support, Spousal Support and the Turn to Guidelines' in J Eekelaar and R George (eds), (n 49) ch 2.7.
[51] Children and Families Act 2014, s 11(2) (for England and Wales).
[52] For such a strategy, see RH Thaler and CR Sunstein, *Nudge: Improving Decisions About Health, Wealth and Happiness* (Yale UP 2008).
[53] See J Eekelaar, 'Family Law: Keeping us "On Message"' (1999) 11 Child & Family Law Quarterly 387; H Reece, *Divorcing Responsibly* (Hart Publishing 2003).
[54] In doing this, the 'information' seeks to shape preferences by extolling appealing features (eg voluntariness) and contrasting it with 'expensive' lawyers: see R Baldwin, 'From Regulation to Behaviour Change: Giving Nudge the Third Degree' (2014) 77 Modern Law Review 83, 836.
[55] See J Dewar, 'Can the Centre Hold? Reflections on Two Decades of Family Law Reform in Australia' (2010) 22 Child and Family Law Quarterly 377.
[56] See B Fehlberg and B Smyth, with L Trinder, 'Parenting Issues After Separation: Developments in Common Law Countries' in J Eekelaar and R George (eds), (n 49) ch 3.3. For similar evidence from Sweden,

D. Agreements

One approach to reconciling autonomy with a form of regulation is through the promotion of agreed terms between individuals. As emphasized by Brian Bix in Chapter 12 of this book, this refers to agreements that the state will enforce. There is now considerably more scope than formerly for people to set the terms of relationships between adults, and even (as mentioned earlier) of parental relationships. Some have gone as far as to advocate that marriage should be abolished and replaced by an extensive use of contracts,[57] as perhaps foreshadowed by enforceable pre-nuptial agreements. It has been argued that to operate fairly within intimate, gendered, long-lasting relationships, contracts should be viewed as *relational* so that not only are all the circumstances at the time of entry into the contract relevant to its interpretation, but also that the interpretation should be affected by the way the relationship evolves.[58]

But the resulting situation would be little different from that presently reached in many systems, where the legal effect of any such contracts will be subject to an assessment of factors relevant in the exercise of the adjustive jurisdiction on divorce. But fully contractualizing the relationship between adults could also reduce the room for the operation of social norms of altruistic, loving, behaviour. The same result could follow if moral obligations between intimates were generally transformed into legal obligations, as discussed by Diane Jeske in Chapter 8 of this book. Allowing compensation claims to be made by spouses against partners for breaches of a variety of 'family obligations' including infidelity, failures in sexual relationships, homosexuality and other forms of marital disharmony[59] introduces the mechanisms of the law into delicate social and personal relationships, sometimes affording a party with greater access to such services additional opportunities to exert power over the other. It is for reasons such as these that in many countries the law withdrew from making judgments about fault in the context of divorce, even though social and moral norms exist in that context.

In exploring some feminist calls for dissolving the divide between the public and private, Ruth Gavison observes that, 'Generally, we want to afford immunity for voluntary consensual associations where consent and freedom are not illusory.'[60] I have called this the 'privileged' sphere where the value protected lies in the location where activities occur rather than the activities themselves.[61] But since this is also the sphere in which 'hidden' power may be exploited, it is one of the most difficult contexts in which decisions about whether legal norms should encroach upon social norms are made. And

---

see L Bruno, 'Contact and Evaluations of Violence: An Intersectional Analysis of Swedish Court Orders' (2015) 29 International Journal of Law, Policy & the Family 167.

[57] Eg, M Fineman in A Bernstein (ed), *Marriage Proposals: Questioning a Legal Status* (NYU Press 2006), especially at 58.

[58] See S Thompson, *Prenuptial Agreements and the Presumption of Free Choice: Issues of Power in Theory and Practice* (Hart Publishing 2015), especially ch 5.

[59] See M Martin-Casals and J Ribot, 'Damages in Family Matters in Spain: Exploring Uncharted New Land or Backsliding?' in B Atkin (ed), *International Survey of Family Law 2010* (Jordans, Family Law) 337.

[60] R Gavison, 'Feminism and the Public-Private Distinction' (1992) 45 Stanford Law Rev 1, 37.

[61] Eekelaar (n 6) 68–89.

V. Rights and Care

Concerns about lack of responsibility and the rhetoric of individual rights has caused a number of commentators to lament their apparently 'self-centred' nature, and to stress the need to remember that individuals operate in communities, including personal relationships, to which they have obligations.[62] Most notably, it was argued that, in family contexts, rights should be seen as 'relational' rather than 'individualistic'. Developing this idea, Martha Minow and Mary Lyndon Shanley drew on feminist literature extolling the 'ethic of care', and argued that family law must value 'the efforts of continuous attention and help', such as the continuing obligations of each parent to their children should they exercise their individual 'right' to divorce.[63] These perspectives have found full expression in the view that 'each individual is in basic ways constituted by networks of relationships of which they are a part'.[64]

Such arguments are a useful corrective to extreme claims about rights (for example, against any intrusion into the family). They draw attention to strong social norms related to care and support, and the way people influence one another and can be affected by the experiences of others. But, rather than being seen in opposition to the idea that individual rights are important protections against the exercise of power, they simply make vivid two features that are inherent in conceptualizations of rights. The first is that any right holder will be surrounded by other right holders, some of whom will have rights against her or him, with which that person's rights need to be reconciled. Within a family, these others will be family members. There is evidence that some family members appear more comfortable in thinking that their partners have rights against them rather than about their own rights.[65] The second is that rights come, as it were, encased in social norms. These norms create an expectation that the rights should be exercised responsibly, that is, with proper regard to such norms. 'Proper regard' may imply refraining from exercising a right if this would injure someone else's interests. A married person may have a right to end a marriage, but attention to the interests of children, or the other spouse, may counsel against its exercise, or influence the way it is exercised.

In this sense it can be said that all rights are 'relational', and that the dominant goal of family law is, or should be, an 'ethic of care'.[66] It is important, however, that at least the core of this ethic is perceived as being what its beneficiaries are entitled to, rather than

---

[62] See eg, MA Glendon, *Rights Talk: The Impoverishment of Political Discourse* (The Free Press 1991); E Etzioni, *The Spirit of Community: Rights, Responsibilities and the Communitarian Agenda* (Crown 1993); MC Regan Jr, *Alone Together: Law and the Meaning of Marriage* (OUP 1999).
[63] M Minow and ML Shanley, 'Relational Rights and Responsibilities: Revisioning the Family in Liberal Political Theory and Law' (1996) 11 Hypatia 4.
[64] J Nedelsky, *Law's Relations: A Relational Theory of Self, Autonomy, and Law* (OUP 2011) 19.
[65] J Eekelaar and M Maclean, 'Marriage and the Moral Bases of Personal Relationships' (2004) Journal of Law and Society 510.
[66] See eg, J Herring, *Older People in Law and Society* (OUP 2009) 124–31; *Caring and the Law* (Hart Publishing 2013) especially ch 6.

simply as aspects of virtuous behaviour by others (though that is important too). Here again, the boundaries between what the law requires and what social or moral norms further expect are hard to draw. For example, could one conclude that the social norm favouring kind and altruistic behaviour could modify the nature of the right? Property holders who have a right to occupy premises have this whether or not they intend to act kindly to their neighbours (though they must of course respect the neighbour's legal rights, and should exercise their right responsibly). Could one say that family members have a legal duty to act altruistically towards one another, so that, eg, a spouse could be required to forgo part of the assets to which he or she is entitled in order to give additional assistance to the other to which that other would not otherwise have been entitled?

If one did, altruism would no longer be possible. The duty of parents to care for their child arises from their position as parents: it is not altruism (though parents may act altruistically towards their children). Nor could parents make their care for the child conditional on the child acting altruistically towards themselves. It is however well recognized that enjoyment of good relationships is essential to individual well-being, and maintaining them must be an important element in the application of the 'best interests' principle.[67] Insofar as the determination of a child's best interests is based on an assessment of a child's hypothetical wishes, there could be some room to assume a child might wish to act altruistically. But, as Dwyer has argued,[68] this should not be given much weight, because modifying an outcome indicated by the best interests (for example, by requiring visits to a parent against a child's wishes when this impinges adversely on the child's best interests) essentially assumes that children have a duty to act altruistically. Doubt was expressed earlier over translating a child's social duty to assist other family members into a legal obligation, and the virtue of behaving altruistically lies in its voluntariness. So, while parents might well encourage altruism in their children as an important element in the child's future well-being, it seems unnecessary to regard a duty to behave altruistically as part of the best-interests principle (to which the child has a right).

Although the benefits of maintaining relationships are important, there is a danger that this could equate a child's interests with conformity to accepted social practice, as in the Victorian view that:

> it is for the general interest of families, and for the general interest of children, and really for the interest of the particular infant, that the court should not, except in very extreme cases, interfere with the discretion of the father but leave him the responsibility of exercising the power which nature has given him by the birth of the child.[69]

Recent legislative attempts to create presumptions of shared care after parental separation,[70] and some decisions enforcing such care against a child's strong

---

[67] See J Herring and C Foster, 'Welfare Means Relationality, Virtue and Altruism' (2012) 32 Legal Studies 480, arguing that the virtue of acting altruistically should form part of the 'best interests' principle.

[68] JG Dwyer, *The Relationship Rights of Children* (CUP 2006) 240. Dwyer's reasons centre on the uncertainties inherent in imputing hypothetical choices.

[69] *Re Agar-Ellis* (1883) 24 Ch D 317, 334.

[70] R Kaspiew, M Gray, I Qu and R Weston, 'Legislative Aspirations and Social Realities: Empirical Reflections on Australia's 2006 Family Law Reforms' (2011) 33 Journal of Social Welfare and Family Law 397.

wishes,[71] have the same character. Approaching the matter from the point of view of a child's legal rights, however, seeks to assess the child's interests as far as possible through the child's perception and experience of its well-being. This does not, of course, mean that everything the child wants is to be indulged. Their wants are to be reconciled with those of others, practicality and their own competence. Given a supportive environment, they are likely to include altruistic elements.

VI. The Resolution of Family Conflicts

Susan Boyd has expressed concern that the emphasis on children's relationships with each parent subordinates issues concerning the nature of the mother's relationship with the father, which itself must be seen in its total social context (such as the relative economic and social positions of each of them).[72] On this view, 'relational' is taken to mean being aware of every implication of the decision to be made on *all* affected parties, especially over time. This is an important warning that law and policy makers should always be aware of the social context in which law and policy operates, including the opportunities for exploitation of relationships.

But Boyd's admonition has particular force in the context of dispute resolution. It may be salutary to refer to the approach of a customary law system discussed by John Comaroff and Simon Roberts.[73] From their research in Botswana, they distinguished disputes over a specific value—which could be decided by the application of rules—from disputes over the nature or quality of the disputants' relationship, where resolutions—which might involve transforming the linkage or terminating it—that were not disposed of by straightforward application of rules but involved consideration of the history of the relationship, had a flexible approach to the relevant rules (which they called 'normative manipulation'). In these circumstances the norms were not valued 'hierarchically' but viewed relative to each other depending on context. This process was, and appeared to be, norm governed, but the norms were used as a basis for argument and justification rather than the imposition of an outcome. This is not unlike the process of negotiation by lawyers or facilitation of agreement by judges in family courts.[74]

A dominant theme in family mediation however is that the parties should be assisted to fashion their own solutions, uninfluenced by the mediator.[75] It has become common to observe, especially in the mediation literature, that resolving family disputes through mediation is better than through adjudication because a mediated solution represents the parties' own agreement rather than one imposed from without. This view probably

---

[71] *Re S (Transfer of Residence)* [2010] EWHC 192 (Fam); *Re S (Transfer of Residence)* [2011] 1 FLR 1789. J Eekelaar, 'Family Justice on Trial: re A' (2014) 44 Family Law 543.
[72] SB Boyd, 'Autonomy for Mothers? Relational Theory and Parenting Apart' (2010) 18 Feminist Legal Studies 137.
[73] J Comaroff and S Roberts, *Rules and Processes: The Cultural Logic of Dispute in an African Context* (University of Chicago Press 1981) 219–36.
[74] See J Eekelaar and M Maclean, *Family Justice: The Work of Family Judges in Uncertain Times* (Hart Publishing 2013).
[75] In the English context, see eg, M Roberts, *Mediation in Family Disputes: Principles and Practice* (4th edn, Ashgate 2014) 70; M Stevenson, 'Mediation and Settlement-Broking' (2015) 45 Family Law 575.

rests on an exaggerated understanding of individual autonomy. Without the constraints, however exercised, of legal norms, they will be exposed to power imbalances and the uncertainties of social norms. Yet they could make informed departures from, or compromises over, the direct application of legal norms. So, as in the Botswana case, legal norms (especially the primacy of children's interests) should play an important part in this process, but could be responsibly adapted and modified so as to minimize damage to the well-being of everyone affected.

VII. What Then is the Point of Family Law?

The account above runs the risk inherent in all analytic jurisprudence of engaging in the limited exercise of attempting to clarify the interaction between legal and social norms that constitute 'family law', and of neglecting the most important issue: what is the point of having family law at all? This is not quite the same question as that asked by Alison Diduck in 2011 when she analysed the values revealed in ancillary-relief judgments across a number of years.[76] This certainly shows what judges were seeking to achieve when dealing with separating parties. Earlier they had sought to identify responsible parties within a paternalistic/patriarchal social structure: more recently they encouraged a more individualized ethic. But the deeper question is why the law should be concerned with any of this at all.

It might be said that, from the earliest times, the point of family law was to uphold social power structures, in particular, patriarchy. We have observed that these have been diminished by the growth of countervailing legal rights. That does not mean that family law no longer constructs frameworks. Elizabeth Brake, in Chapter 3 of this book, considers how these may be developed. Civil partnership regimes (in France, the *pacte civil de solidarité*), introduced by many states before accepting gay marriage, provided structures with varying content which affected the allocation of some state and private benefits and the distribution and devolution of property.[77] Despite the well-known, steep and widespread decline in marriage rates,[78] the United States Supreme Court has recently referred to marriage as the 'keystone of our social order' and referred to an 'expanding list of government rights, benefits and responsibilities' attached to it.[79] But in Europe marriage (or some equivalent institutions) may be more important in their symbolic than legal effect, both as a means by which individuals, or a couple, manifest their perception of their own identities, and as providing an occasion for kin and

---

[76] A Diduck, 'What is Family Law for?' (2011) 64 Current Legal Problems 287.
[77] See A Boele-Woelki and A Fuchs (eds), *Legal Recognition of Same-Sex Relationships in Europe* (Intersentia 2012).
[78] As examples, between 1970 and 2012 crude marriage rates (per 1000 inhabitants) fell from 7.4 to 5.1 (Denmark), 7.4 to 4.8 (Germany), 7.3 to 3.5 (Spain), 7.8 to 3.7 (France), 9.5 to 4.2 (Netherlands), 8.5 to 4.4 (UK): <http://ec.europa.eu/eurostat/statistics-explained/index.php/File:Crude_marriage_rate,_selected_years,_1960%E2%80%932012_(per_1_000_inhabitants)_YB14.png> accessed 8 July 2015, and between 2000 and 2012 from 8.2 to 6.8 (USA): <http://www.cdc.gov/nchs/nvss/marriage_divorce_tables.htm> (accessed 27 October 2017). For a detailed analysis see John Haskey, 'Marriage Rites — Trends in Marriages by Manner of Solemnisation and Denomination in England and Wales, 1841–2012' in J Miles, P Mody, and R Probert (eds), *Marriage Rites and Rights* (Hart Publishing 2015) ch 2.
[79] *Obergefell et al v Hodges et al* [2015] WL 2473451 [15].

community approval of the relationship and reinforcement of peer support for the couple.[80] Once again, social norms, including social-media usage, may interact with legal institutions in important and complex ways.

The legal significance of these frameworks is probably strongest if the relationship breaks up, when it becomes necessary to decide on the fairest way to treat the couple and any children involved. But usually the issues that arise on relationship breakdown are the same whether the individuals involved have lived under one of these frameworks or not. So while, as Robert Leckey points out in Chapter 5 of this book, jurisdictions have generally been slow to apply the same legal provisions to breakdowns in unmarried, or unregistered, relationships as apply where the parties are married or civilly partnered, there is pressure to bring them closer together, reflecting an approach to the objectives of family law that rests more on function than form.[81] This suggests that the role of family law in protecting individual interests against the economically more powerful, and children's interests when they conflict with those of adults, is as important as, or even more important than, seeking to ensure conformity to institutional frameworks.

There can be no greater exercise of power than in the use of assisted reproduction to create a child, so rules that determine who are, or can be, such a child's parents, or have parental responsibility for the child, have profound implications for the exercise of power over newly born members of society (see also Mary Lyndon Shanley's discussion of surrogacy in Chapter 14 of this volume). Here again, legal rules that attempt to confine such procedures within replications of the marital family, for example by banning or severely restricting surrogacy, channel that power into pre-existing social and legal frameworks.[82] But new frameworks are emerging, such as when parental responsibility for such children may be acquired by someone not biologically related to the child, but who is a partner of the biological parent,[83] or even who is in an 'enduring family relationship' with that parent, suggesting a more functional perspective.[84] Adoption too is a formidable exercise of power over children, especially intercountry adoption, which, like international surrogacy, can remove children not only from their natural parents, but from their families and communities. In all these cases there is a danger that the framework into which children are introduced consists of people with economic power who can effectively pay for children either to be delivered to them or even to be created and then placed with them.

In all these cases, family law is still in the process of developing countervailing rights to protect the interests of individuals, whether adults or children, against the way power is exercised within these new frameworks. But in general the diminution of the role of

---

[80] See J Miles, P Mody, and R Probert (eds), *Marriage Rites and Rights* (n 78).

[81] For excellent analyses see W Schrama, 'Marriage and Alternative Relationships in the Netherlands' and EE Sutherland, 'Unmarried Cohabitation' in J Eekelaar and R George (eds), (n 49) chs 1.2 and 1.5, and also K Boele-Woelki, C Mol and E van Gelder (eds), *European Family Law in Action. Vol V – Informal Relationships* (Intersentia 2015).

[82] For France, see K Parizer-Krief, 'Gender Equality in Legislation on Medically Assisted Procreation in France' (2015) 29 International Journal of Law, Policy & the Family 205.

[83] For the UK, see Human Fertilisation and Embryology Act 2008, s 42(1).

[84] Human Fertilisation and Embryology Act 1990, s 30; Human Fertilisation and Embryology Act 2008, s 54.

family law in upholding institutional structures has directed its primary functioning towards grappling with the consequences of casualties of damaged personal relationships. It manages people as they navigate the process of readjustment, and seeks to provide protective measures for those whose welfare is threatened by these failures. In doing all these things, family law needs to be aware of, and sensitive to, the network of social norms that exists in the society within which it operates. Some of these will supplement the legal norms, others may oppose them. These may also have a bearing on the role of institutional frameworks.

In diverse societies, the law confronts power structures created by cultural or religious norms of minority groups that may differ from those of a state's family law. This raises one of the most difficult issues for family law in some modern societies. Can concurrent, possibly conflicting, systems operate alongside one another? It is quite possible that they can, and a number of states officially recognize discrete legal systems for specified sections of their populations which co-exist with state law.[85] Others may accept that certain groups will follow norms of family living that are distinct from those of the wider society, but leave these to be regulated through the institutions of those groups, selecting only certain practices (such as solemnizing marriages) to which they will give recognition for state purposes. The choice between strategies reflects theories of the state rather than of law. Is the nation state to be seen as ultimately responsible for the well-being of all the citizens over whom it exercises jurisdiction, and accountable to international bodies for the observance within its jurisdiction of human-rights norms? If it is, it seems hard to accept that the state might authorize groups to exercise exclusive jurisdiction to which it lends it authority over the family lives of their members, though forms of this strategy are used in some countries. Yet individual group members might place great store in being able to identify with their normative system. Family law can help to integrate diverse groups into the larger social structure by strategies such as giving official recognition to marriages solemnized according to group norms (and thereby showing approval, or at least acceptance, of the group practice, and making available the civil law of marriage to people so married), provided they comply with certain standards, and by allowing the group's members access to state (legal) norms at all times.[86] Once again, the interaction between legal and social norms becomes a key issue in the application and understanding of family law.

Against the view that the 'point' of law in general is solely to aid the exercise of power, John Finnis has replied that those concerned only with exercising power (he calls them 'tyrannical') could sustain their power in ways other than through the use of law, or if they use law, they do so cynically, for their own ends,[87] whereas the true purpose of having law (the rule of law) is to hold rulers 'to their side of a relationship of reciprocity in which the claims of authority are respected on condition that authority respects the claims of the common good (of which a fundamental component is respect for the equal right of all to respectful consideration)'.[88]

---

[85] See Y Sezgin, *Human Rights under State Enforced Religious Family Laws in Israel, Egypt and India* (CUP 2013); M Maclean and J Eekelaar (eds), *Managing Family Justice in Diverse Societies* (Hart Publishing 2013).
[86] See M Malik, 'Family Law in Diverse Societies' in J Eekelaar and R George (eds), (n 49) ch 7.4.
[87] See J Finnis, *Natural Law and Natural Rights* (2nd edn, OUP 2011) 274.   [88] ibid 272–73.

On the basis of this perception of law, how would family law be viewed? It might be possible to see its purpose as to uphold the view of the 'common good' taken by those in power. But Finnis adds a crucial qualification: that a fundamental component of the common good is 'respect for the equal right of all to respectful consideration'.[89] While that qualification does not necessarily yield determinate conclusions, it cannot be plausibly claimed that family law has always observed it. However, the countervailing rhetoric of rights described earlier could be said to be an attempt to promote such 'respectful consideration', or, if one prefers, care. While social and political processes that uphold such structures can *benefit* by their reinforcement through law, law is *necessary* (if not sufficient) if power is to be constrained to respect the well-being of individuals. That could now be said to be its primary purpose. Is this perhaps a theory?

---

[89] ibid.

2
Family and Family Law
Concepts and Norms

David Archard

I. Introduction

Let me start with what seems like an evident truism: Family law is the law of the family. Areas of the law are defined by their subject matter. So property law is that branch of the law that deals with ownership; contract law is that branch of the law that defines and enforces contracts. And so on. This much sounds unproblematic. However in the case of the family and family law there are at least two complications, one essentially conceptual and the other essentially normative. The first is an uncertainty brought on by massive changes of various kinds over the last hundred or so years as to whether there is any one kind of thing that merits the name 'family'. The second flows from this lack of conceptual clarity and from the fact that the law defines and changes the status of individuals, ascribes rights and responsibilities, and offers forms of protection to designated persons. This—in respect of the family—needs justification. What exactly *should* family law look like?

In what follows I want to resist the pressure to give up on the idea that there is something distinctive meriting the title 'family law'. However I will suggest that we need to think about two rather different elements of family law. To that end I will make a series of claims that are both conceptual and normative.

II. 'Everything is Changed'

I start with the factual observation that is denied by no-one who writes in this area. This is that what we once found it relatively uncontentious to characterize as 'the family' has been subject to massive changes of various kinds: social, cultural, biological, scientific, political, and legal. Indeed the law has played its part in these changes by recognizing relationships that were previously not tolerated or were at least denied formal recognition.

The result has been a kaleidoscope of family forms in which—to summarize crudely and simply—parents can be single or many; children can be biologically related or unrelated to those who act as their guardians; adults and children can occupy one or several households; adults can be married or unmarried, single sex, or heterosexual.

At one time—as Raymond Williams observes in his classic dictionary of key cultural concepts—'family' united two elements, 'kin' and 'household'. A family was the social group whose members occupied a shared living space and who were united by blood relationships.[1] This is no longer the case.

I want to deny two claims that are often made in conjunction with an acknowledgement of this extensive change. I will term these the 'moral decline' and the 'disappearance' theses. The first claim—that of 'moral decline'—is that such changes as are widely recognized betoken—are evidence of—or are in themselves a kind of societal degeneration. Thus, most obviously, various writers, ranging from philosophers through social historians to public essayists, bemoan the disappearance of the 'traditional' family. This is one whose adults form a married, heterosexual couple, and whose dependent children are their biological offspring. Brenda Almond is a good example of an applied moral philosopher who thinks the traditional family ought to be protected inasmuch as non-traditional forms have deleterious social consequences;[2] Patricia Morgan is a leading policy advocate of the virtues of the traditional marriage and of the terrible social consequences of its erosion or disappearance.[3]

I do not intend to spend time here responding at any great length to the 'moral decline' thesis. I will say only two things in summary.[4] First, worries about the decline of 'the family' are recurrent and can be found repeated over the last two-hundred years.[5] Their longevity and repetition are not evidence of their likely truth or plausibility. For in fact subsequent history has tended to show that each reiteration of the basic worry was mistaken. Moreover, these worries nearly always take the form of signalling an imminent, final, and catastrophic change for the worse. Thus their reprise—even in different forms—over a long period of time that has not seen the threatened disaster eventuate suggests that they are akin to other forecasts of doom whose prophets survive their worst warnings.

Second, the thesis understood as a serious claim rather than an expression of cultural pessimism either takes an intrinsic or instrumental form. That is to say that it asserts either that there is something inherently wrong with the new family forms; or it asserts that these forms are wrong for what they lead to. The first form of the claim—as in, for example, the assertion that it is just wrong for a gay couple to be parents—is open to reasoned moral criticism and, if used as the basis for law and policy, violates a familiar principle of liberal neutrality.

The instrumental claim—expressed as, for example, the contention that the growth of non-traditional family forms is responsible for a range of social and economic problems such as mental illness, crime, etc—is empirically contentious and widely contested. Moreover, such a claim can only inform law and policy at a significant moral cost, namely that of enforcing family forms against the grain both of individuals' choices and of broader, irreversible social developments.

---

[1] R Williams, *Keywords* (Fontana Communications Series, Collins 1976).
[2] B Almond, *The Fragmenting Family* (OUP 2008).
[3] P Morgan, *Family Policy, Family Changes: Sweden, Italy and Britain Compared* (Civitas 2006).
[4] See D Archard, *The Family: A Liberal Defence* (Palgrave 2010), Introduction.
[5] L Gordon, *Heroes of Their Own Lives* (Viking 1988) 3.

III. The Family is No More

What I have termed the 'disappearance' claim is essentially the conceptual assertion that there is no longer anything or any one thing that can be called 'the family'. I shall provide some examples of this basic claim, and variants of it, that can be found extensively repeated in sociological and socio-legal writing on the family. I shall then subject the 'disappearance' claim to criticism. The disappearance claim is expressed either as a refusal to use the definite article ('*the* family is no more'); or as a preference for an adjectival qualification of the concept ('*the* family is dead; long live the new family (however that is characterized)').

Examples of those who resist the definite article include Diana Gittins who defines her first task as questioning 'the assumption that there is, and has been, one single phenomenon that we can call *the* family.... Thus, it is essential to start thinking of *families* rather than the family.'[6] Lorraine Fox Harding invokes the diversity of modern family forms and normative differences about what the family should be like to conclude, 'The term, "*the* family" is on the whole avoided in this book.'[7] Jon Bernardes states that 'family situations in contemporary society are so varied and diverse that it simply makes no sociological sense to speak of a single ideal-type model of "the Family" at all.'[8]

Those opting for an adjectival qualification of any use of the term 'family' include Judith Stacey who writes that, 'It is not possible to characterize with a single term the competing sets of family cultures that coexist at present.' She thus opts for the 'postmodern' family, not as a new model of the family but as something beyond and different from whatever has come before.[9] Elisabeth Beck-Gernsheim concludes from all the changes 'that it is difficult to speak of the family' and entitles a subsequent section of her book, The Contours of the Post-Familial Family.[10]

There are two interestingly different defences of this 'disappearance' claim. The first is that there is somehow something problematic in using a single concept and definite article when there are so many different kinds of family. This is straightforwardly to misunderstand the distinction between the use of a kind or type of term and an acknowledgement of a plurality of different instances that fall under a single term. Thus a book entitled 'The History of the Car' that outlines the development of the automobile does not tell the story of a single vehicle nor that of a particular style or design of vehicle nor that again of only one manufacturer's product. One can similarly speak quite sensibly of 'the family'—understood as a distinctive social unit—whilst recognizing that this type of social organization can take many different forms. Think—if one still needs persuasion—of other social-kind terms, such as 'neighbourhood', 'tribe', and 'class'.

---

[6] D Gittins, *The Family in Question* (Macmillan 1985) 1–2.
[7] LF Harding, *Family, State and Society Policy* (Macmillan 1996) xi–xii.
[8] J Bernardes, 'Do We Really Know What "the Family" Is?' in P Close and R Collins (eds), *Family and Economy in Modern Society* (Macmillan 1985) 209.
[9] J Stacey, *Brave New Families: Stories of Domestic Upheaval in Late-Twentieth-Century America* (with a new Preface, University of California Press 1998) 18.
[10] E Beck-Gernsheim, *Reinventing the Family: In Search of New Lifestyles* (P Camiller tr, Polity Press 2002) 2, 7–10.

The second defence of the 'disappearance' claim is that continued use of the definite article presumes that one kind of family is to be favoured. Thus, it will be suggested that talk of 'the family' in effect means only the traditional family. I will select one example of the kind of reasoning involved in this sort of defence of the 'disappearance' claim and consider it at length. Gillian Douglas writes that,

> Even within one society, the 'family' may be a concept open to numerous interpretations, each with a baggage of competing values. Using the definite article, referring to *the* family, suggests a commonly understood notion embodying a certain set of norm ...
>
> The family, then, is not a naturally occurring fixed phenomenon but a concept which is constructed in a multiplicity of ways and for a variety of purposes.[11]

To make better sense of Douglas' final sentence it helps to introduce and define some terms employed by philosophers of science. In the first instance, there are 'natural kinds'. These describe those basic groupings of objects within nature that the physical sciences disclose as sharing key properties in common. The scientific discovery of these kinds and of their essential properties is said, in a frequently employed metaphor due to Plato, to 'carve nature at its joints'.[12] So Douglas is right to assert that 'family' is not a natural-kind term as is, for instance, 'genome' or 'haplogroup'.

By contrast with 'natural kind' are 'artefact kinds' which group together those objects that are the product of human activity: they may share something in common but this is not an essential, natural property. Examples would be tables, cutlery and pens. There are also entirely arbitrary groupings of random objects such as 'those queueing every morning for the Number 19 bus.'

Of interest here is the idea of 'social kinds'. These gather together objects, most notably persons, whose existence as a group is to be explained by social causes. Examples would be 'voters' or 'consumers'.[13] 'Family' is, then, a social-kind term.

Now of social kinds various different things can be and are said. One is that their existence is entirely a matter of their being regarded as constituting a kind. That one is thought of as a member of kind, K, is sufficient to be a member of K. It will also be said that social kinds are fundamentally normative and not neutral, descriptive terms. Another thing that will be said is that there are no natural facts that underlie membership of a social kind. A social kind is not, in other words, a natural kind, or even a set of natural kinds. It may also be said—and this constitutes the most radical of claims—that a social kind has no real existence.

What can be said of the social-kind term 'family' is that it is not sufficient to regard oneself as a family for one's group to count as a family. The Cosa Nostra calls itself a 'family'; those who constituted the murderous late 1960s Californian commune led by Charles Manson called themselves a 'family'. In neither case is the use of the term

---

[11] Douglas, *An Introduction to Family Law* (OUP 2001) 1–2.
[12] A Bird and E Tobin, 'Natural Kinds', *Stanford Encyclopedia of Philosophy* (Spring edn, 2016) <http://plato.stanford.edu/entries/natural-kinds/> accessed 26 May 2016.
[13] MA Khalidi, 'Kinds (Natural Kinds vs. Human Kinds)' in B. Kaldis (ed), *Encyclopedia of Philosophy and the Social Sciences* (Sage 2013).

anything other than metaphorical. Both groups are analogous to families; they are like but are not proper instances of families.

No natural facts underlie membership of the social kind 'family'. The members of a family may but need not display any biological or genetic relations to one another.

Is the social kind 'family' fundamentally normative? I will later suggest that a morally neutral definition of 'family' can be offered. This is perfectly consistent, as I will also argue, with two views: first, that the family is a morally desirable form of social organization; second, that some forms of the family are morally preferable to others. However, both of these claims need to be defended and the truth of neither follows from agreement on what constitutes a family.

Douglas is right if she is taken to mean that people may use the term 'family' in such a way as to mean only one particular form of family; moreover they may intend by 'family' that form of it which is thought by them to be the best. However, this is simply to use the term in a mistaken and normatively question-begging fashion. There is nothing in the use of the term 'the family' that commits the speaker to meaning, by that usage, only one kind. Still less is the speaker committed to endorsing that one kind as best or preferable to others. Douglas is thus mistaken in saying that any reference to 'the family' entails a normative commitment to one form of the family.

This is not to deny that 'the family' can be, and is, deployed rhetorically in some contexts in such a way as to make it clear that the speaker does endorse a particular familial form. It is also true that the family, its future, its social role and its changing character is one of those disputed and controversial matters that encourages such rhetorical usage. That, of course, makes it all the more important to distinguish rhetoric from reasoned argument, and loaded definitions from conceptual clarification of a key term. Thus, it is appropriate not to abandon the use of the term 'the family' but to resist that use of it, whether rhetorical or otherwise, that commits the hearer to endorse the speaker's own preferences for one family form. Indeed it should be possible for those who understand, and value, the plurality of family forms to celebrate the variegated nature of this single social institution. Rather than give up on the use of the phrase 'the family' one should continue to use it as an umbrella term under whose broad canopy a welcome plurality of familial types can be gathered.

There are, it should be noted, two ways in which we might mistakenly make a normative commitment to one preferred family form. The first is by confusing 'concept' with 'conception'. The distinction was famously used by John Rawls, who in turn borrowed it from HLA Hart, in order to argue that, whilst all can agree what is meant and required by the concept of 'justice'—something like the 'fair and non-arbitrary treatment of all persons'—it is nevertheless controversial what exactly this requires by way of specific rules of social distribution. Thus, whilst there may be a single, univocal concept of justice, there are different and competing 'conceptions' of justice.[14] Similarly one might argue that there is a single, univocal concept of 'family' but various different and competing conceptions.

---

[14] J Rawls, *A Theory of Justice* (rev edn, OUP 1999) 5; Rawls cites HLA. Hart, *The Concept of Law* (Clarendon Press 1961) 155–59.

Second, some may use the term 'family' in a manner that has been described as 'persuasive definition'.[15] Essentially, a persuasive definition offers a statement of what a term means that is done with the purpose of changing people's attitudes towards what is covered by the term. Frequently it trades on people's favourable regard for what is picked out and seeks to have them share the persuasive definer's understanding of the term. This may be reinforced by the use of qualifications such as 'true' or 'real' or 'genuine'.[16] Thus, rather than saying 'This is the best kind of X', someone says, 'A real or genuine X is this' such that what X then looks like is how the speaker wants everyone to think an X should be.

So consider someone who says, 'Real freedom is being able to do what you really want to do'; or 'real democracy is one in which all views are rationally deliberated'. In exactly this fashion, someone might say, 'A real family is one whose adults are married and the biological parents of the offspring'. Persuasive definitions of 'the family' should be recognized for what they are and resisted.

In sum, the 'disappearance thesis' is without good foundation and there are no reasons not to continue to use the term 'the family'. We can distinguish between the family as a distinctive social entity or unit or institution and the various forms of the family. In turn, we can then—as an entirely separate matter—evaluate those various forms.

IV. The Family and Family Law

I began by asserting that 'family law' is the law of families. Thus far, I have only provided reasons not to conclude—from the enormous changes undergone by the family and by the wide variety of contemporary forms of family life—that we should abandon the use of the term 'the family'.

However, it does not follow that 'family law' is simply and straightforwardly the law of 'the family'. Indeed we should start this part of my analysis by distinguishing two claims. The first is that the family can be defined independently of the law and is that which the law should regulate. The family of family law is the very same family as exists outside the law. So we can first define the family and then proceed to agree what the law should have to do with this social entity. The concept of the family is prior to the delineation of family law.

The second and very different claim is that the family about which the law speaks is distinct from the extra-legal concept of the family. There is 'the family' of 'family law' and there is 'the family' of non-legal academic discourse and popular usage. The family of family law is a construct of the law. So we can only understand what *that*—the legal family—is like by understanding how the law—in its statutes, cases, adjudications, juridical clarifications—defines a family and its constituent members.

Moreover, the law's 'family' could be more or less similar or related to the 'family' as it is understood outside the law.

These are two very different claims about the relationship between 'the family' and 'family law'. However, the second claim cannot be so radical as to insist upon significant

---

[15] C Stevenson, 'Persuasive Definitions' (1938) 47 Mind 331.
[16] T Govier, *A Practical Study of Argument* (3rd edn, Wadsworth 1992) 96.

differences between the two understandings of family. These understandings cannot be or come too far apart. For what the law seeks to recognize and regulate must itself be recognizable as that institution which, outside the law, is a distinctively different kind of social unit. Family law is the law of the family and not that of the tribe or nation or neighbourhood. There may be some differences between the idea of the family as it is understood outside and prior to the construction of family law and what the law construes as the object of its regulation. However, these differences cannot be such as to make what the law regulates unrecognizable as familial.

Nevertheless, the opportunity for a gap of sorts between the two concepts of the family derives from the following: the law is a fundamentally normative enterprise. By this I do not mean to beg the question against a positivist view of law. Such a view seeks to distinguish the matter of whether or not some system of rules counts as 'law' from that of whether or not some law or legal system is good.[17] Rather I mean that what law does is afford to individuals a certain status, and ascribe to them particular rights and duties. To the extent that it does this, any system of law can be subject to questions such as, 'Should individuals be accorded the entitlements and responsibilities that they are accorded?' and 'Is it a good thing that individuals are given the status that they are given?'

We should note that family law directly affords a certain status to some individuals and groups and not others. There is benefit in being recognized as a 'parent' or as a 'family'. There are also other benefits that indirectly accrue to individuals and groups thus recognized in family law, but which derive from other areas of the law. Thus, the distribution of welfare benefits, public housing entitlements, immigration rights, taxation, and inheritance liabilities will normally depend on this prior identification of families and family members. These goods are not insignificant.

Family law shares the general normative feature of law as a whole. Thus, family law is said to be concerned with status, rights and responsibilities, and the protection of its weaker members.[18] Moreover, it does this, and is justified in doing so, to the extent that valuable social ends are thereby served. For example, Frances Burton asserts that 'Family law defines and alters status, protects individuals, and groups, provides machinery to divide and manage property, and attempts to support the family as a desirable social unit.'[19]

As a result there is a potential gap between some neutral conceptual definition of 'the family' and that conception of the family that the law ought to and does support. There is the non-normative definition of the family and then there is the normative appraisal of the family that the law engages in when it selectively affords status, rights, and duties to some individuals and groups, and not to others. Consider the following analogy. We can agree what counts as a 'car'. Perhaps we will do so by means of an account of what distinguishes this form of vehicular transport from others: what makes something a 'car' and not a 'bicycle', or a 'lorry'. The law allows some cars to be registered for

---

[17] The seminal contemporary statement of legal positivism is HLA Hart, *The Concept of Law* (2nd edn, Clarendon Press 1997).

[18] J Masson, R Bailey-Harris, and R Probert, *Cretney Principles of Family Law* (8th edn, Sweet & Maxwell 2008) 2–3.

[19] F Burton, *Family Law* (Cavendish Publishing Ltd 2003) 11.

road usage and others not. To that extent it affords the legal status of a 'car' (one whose owner is legally recognized, which can be formally registered, permissibly driven on the public roads, and which is taxed) to some set of vehicles within the agreed category of 'cars'. Stock cars and self-driven cars cannot at present be driven on public roads. The making of this distinction between cars in general and legally recognized cars is, in turn, justified by social ends such as, in this case, public safety and health.

V. Concepts, Functions, and Norms

Let me try then to offer a morally neutral definition of 'the family' but one which points the way to the manner in which important normative questions—and precisely those that should preoccupy the formulators and critics of family law—might be addressed. I shall first motivate the use of a morally neutral functional definition of the family and defend its deployment against various criticisms, and then spell out what my preferred functional definition is before indicating what normative questions are broached but whose answers are not presumed by such a definition.

It has been suggested that there are three possibilities for providing a definition of the family.[20] These are, first, a 'functional' definition of a family in terms of what it does, its ends and purposes; second a 'formal' definition of what counts as a family that is rooted in shared social meanings; and, third, a 'family resemblances' account that views families not as all sharing a single set of features but rather as having overlapping similarities.[21]

The problem of a 'formal' definition is the lack of any clear consensus of meaning. Moreover, such differences as there are about what counts as an instance of a family are frequently morally loaded ones that presume that certain kinds of family are ideal or preferable to others. The problem of a 'resemblances' account is that it turns on an agreement as to what counts as sufficiently similar to what, further, can be agreed is a paradigmatic or baseline instance of 'family'. Just as it may be hard to agree who counts as a member of a 'family' (a second cousin twice removed?) it may be hard to agree whether something does sufficiently resemble what we may agree does count as a family.

A functional definition of the family need not presume any normative view of what makes for a better or worse kind of family; nor, indeed, does it presume any view as to the value of the family in the service of those ends that define it. I am going to offer a functional definition that sees the family as serving a custodial or guardianship role for children. The advantages of a functional definition are precisely that it can illuminate key normative questions without presuming their answers. In this manner we can also best address juridical and indeed political philosophical questions about the role of the family within society.

---

[20] 'Looking for a Family Resemblance: The Limits of the Functional Approach to the Legal Definition of Family' (1991) 104 Harvard Law Review 1640.
[21] This influential idea of conceptual categorization is famously due to Ludwig Wittgenstein in his posthumously published *Philosophical Investigations* (1953) who himself uses the example of 'games' to illustrate its utility.

The immediately apparent disadvantage of such a functional definition is that it seems in tension with three characterizations of the 'familial' that are widely shared. The first views the family approvingly as displaying a certain quality of relationship between its members. Carol Levine, for instance, defines family members as those 'individuals who by birth, adoption, marriage, or declared commitment share deep, personal connections and are mutually entitled to receive and obligated to provide support of various kinds to the extent possible'.[22] Understandings of the 'familial' that insist upon the affective character of certain possible relationships invoke social understandings that need not be shared and may indeed be contested. They thus run afoul of the problem of any 'formal' definition of the family in the absence of a clear consensus of meaning.

Yet even if we do share an understanding of what might make the family ideal or morally valuable in this affective sense, we can surely envisage many instances of family that do not display those 'deep, personal commitments' of which Levine speaks. Moreover, what obligations family members owe to one another is an important normative question, but it is one whose answer should not simply be presumed by defining the family in a certain moralized fashion.

Others speak of the familial in terms of the 'intimate'. But, as Diane Jeske points out in her chapter, intimacy is not present in all relationships understood to be familial, and it is present in many relationships regarded as 'non-familial'. She sees this as reason to 'dislodge' the concept of the family 'as a term of fundamental moral significance' and attend instead to what *is* morally important and valuable, namely intimate relationships.[23] But the choice here need not be exclusive. We can *both* recognize those relationships that are valued for their intimacy (as I suggest at the end of this chapter) *and* acknowledge those normative questions that arise from attending to the morally neutral functional definition of the family.

The second characterization of the family that is widely shared and yet in tension with a functional definition is one that sees it as comprising all those people to whom one is related by marriage, declared commitment, and blood. Yet my sister-in-law and my great grandparents whom I may happily call part of my 'family' played no part in my upbringing or in my parenting of my children. However this shows no more than that the English-language use of family can mean one of two things: the distinctive social unit in which children are reared, and the broad set of persons one counts as 'kin'.[24]

Consider—by way of a relevant parallel—how an adopted child may appear to be contradicting herself and yet reasonably say both to her adoptive father and to her biological father, 'You are not my father'. Of the former she means that he is not the man who procreated her; of the latter she means that he is not the person who has discharged the custodial role of bringing her up.

The third challenge to the functional definition takes the form of an assertion that families need not have children. Tamara Metz asks, rhetorically, 'Why, for instance,

---

[22] C Levine, 'AIDS and Changing Concepts of Family' (1990) 68 The Millbank Quarterly 33, 36.
[23] D Jeske's chapter, 'Moral and Legal Obligations to Support "Family"'.
[24] L Nicholson, 'The Myth of the Traditional Family' in HL Nelson (ed), *Feminism and Families* (Routledge 1997) 28–29.

must family involve care of children? Why not families of adults?'[25] The answer to that challenge is that concepts are not infinitely malleable. They have boundaries that limit their extension. A line should be drawn between families and other kinds of social institution, such as clans, friendships, households, and adult communes. This is not to deny that some adults might not live with and look after some other group of dependent adults in need of care. This could merit the title of 'family' but only in scare quotes and in a metaphorical way or one that is clearly parasitic upon the primary definition that necessarily involves children. Essentially, the family as a distinctive social institution is one whose members are adults caring for children.

Finally, I want to resist the concern that a functional definition is inherently conservative. Nothing in the claim that a family is essentially defined in terms of the custodial role that some adults play in respect of some children presumes, entails, or requires a particular understanding of which adults discharge that role, how they discharge that role, their biological relatedness one to another, living arrangements, or indeed anything else that is normatively traditional or conformist.

I will now formally define my functional definition of the family, before turning to normative matters. A family is that group of individuals whose adults take primary custodial roles in respect of its dependent children.[26] Similar definitions can be found defended by Margaret Mead ('the permanent group which rears the children'[27]) and Veronique Munoz-Dardé ('any social unit in which a group of elders are primarily responsible and have primary authority over a *particular* group of children'[28]).

Such a definition takes the form of asserting that an X is what characteristically does Φ.[29] Its employment does not presume the answers that might be given to two importantly distinct but individually significant normative questions: Does X do Φ better or worse than anything else? And, which instances or kinds of X do Φ better or worse than others? Thus, we can ask whether the family is the best social unit for raising children, and we can ask which familial forms are better or worse for raising children. Nevertheless, the functional definition of the family does not of itself indicate what the answers to these questions will be. Hence a functional definition of the family allows for a separation of the conceptual and normative, but also indicates what would be the basis of an evaluation both of the family and of familial forms.

Such evaluations will combine both empirical and normative argument. Thus, in answer to the first question, some will maintain that the family is to be deprecated by comparison with collectivist alternatives in which society, to varying degrees, assumes responsibility for the rearing of its young.[30] Others will defend the family as an institution by appeal to the important goods realized in and through the parenting

---

[25] T Metz, 'Review: The Family, A Liberal Defence' (2011) Notre Dame Philosophical Reviews <http://ndpr.nd.edu/news/24762-the-family-a-liberal-defence/> accessed 26 May 2016.

[26] For a fuller and more formal account of this preferred functional definition, see Archard (n 4) 10 ff.

[27] M Mead, 'Constraints and Comparisons from Primitive Society' in BJ Stern (ed), *The Family, Past and Present* (LD Appleton-Century Co 1938) 5–6.

[28] V Munoz-Dardé, 'Is the Family then to be Abolished?' (1999) 94 Proceedings of the Aristotelian Society 37, 44.

[29] This manner of defining things goes back to Plato, *Republic* 353a. Translated by P Shorey in E Hamilton and H Cairns (eds), *The Collected Dialogues of Plato* (Princeton University Press 1961) 575–844 at 603.

[30] M Barrett and M McIntosh, *The Anti-Social Family* (2nd edn, Verso 1991).

of children.[31] Still others may adopt a 'Churchillian' defence of the family as a flawed social institution that is, nevertheless, better than the alternatives.[32]

Answers to the second question (What family forms are better or worse at realizing its basic end, namely that of rearing children?) will evidently range from a defence of the traditional family to a refusal to give normative priority to anything other than unconstrained individual choice of family form. As noted at the outset it is important to be clear as to whether the defence of some particular family form is on intrinsic or instrumental grounds. The assertion that there is something inherently wrong with certain family forms is morally contentious; the assertion that certain family forms have deleterious consequences is empirically contentious (and widely contested). The key point—which it is worth repeating—is that there is no reason to abandon conceptual clarity as to what counts as a family for fear of prejudicing debate either as to the value of the family or as to the evaluation of familial forms.

VI. Law and Function

In regard to family law, the functional definition of the family provides the maximum opportunity for the inclusion of difference within the scope of legal regulation. Nothing need fall outside the umbrella of family law on the grounds that some custodial practices are not proper, real, or genuine families. Nevertheless, critics of this definition may insist that some kinds of relationships between adults—independently of and separate from their relations to dependent children—merit legal recognition. They can look to my concluding comments on the category of the 'intimate' for reassurance as to what might otherwise be excluded.

The two normative questions identified in the previous section also have equivalent forms when it comes to considering the nature and scope of family law: Should the law extend recognition and protection to the family? Which of the possible family forms should the law recognize and protect? The answer to the first question—at least in modern liberal democratic jurisdictions—has been a fairly unambiguous 'yes'. Attempts to legislate against the family have been the hallmark of authoritarian regimes of both the left and the right. Conversely, defences of the family as an institution have appealed to the idea that its existence is one of the best guarantees of individual liberty and supplies an estimable obstacle to the unconstrained exercise of state authority.[33]

However, it seems enough to acknowledge that the family's purpose—the rearing of children—is sufficiently important that the law should recognize the family and give the discharge of that purpose adequate protection. This, for instance, means according parents certain rights and responsibilities. It means ensuring that children are protected when parents fail to discharge those custodial duties. This latter duty exemplifies

---

[31] An important and influential example of such an approach is to be found in A Swift and H Brighouse, *Family Values: The Ethics of Parent–Child Relationships* (Princeton UP 2014).
[32] See Archard (n 4) Ch 4.
[33] A classic conservative defence of this kind is F Mount, *The Subversive Family: An Alternative History of Love and Marriage* (The Free Press 1992).

the doctrine of *parens patriae* whereby a state is obligated to protect and care for those who are unable to do so for themselves.

Should the law discriminate between different family forms in the light of a judgment as to which of those forms best serves the end of family? If some familial forms do worse at raising children than others, should the law discriminate by, for instance, refusing familial or parental status to certain groups and individuals? We should distinguish the question of whether the state should encourage some familial forms, and discourage others, from that of whether the law is an appropriate and suitable means of doing this.

The state might reasonably seek to encourage the formation of certain kinds of family. Were it to do so on the grounds that some forms are intrinsically morally better than others (two-parent families accord with the demands of scripture; unmarried cohabitation is living in sin) then it would violate the demands of liberal neutrality.[34]

If the state appealed to what I have called instrumental criticisms of some familial forms—essentially their poorer outcomes for dependent children and socially deleterious consequences—then it would be exempt from a criticism on anti-perfectionist grounds. Yet, as argued earlier, such instrumental critiques are notoriously contentious and openly contested.

The law could in principle criminalize those who procreate and seek to form family units of the putatively wrong kind. However it is very hard to see how exactly we might define the crime of 'unlicensed family formation'; nor is it easy imaginatively to construct the forms of policing that would detect such a crime. The moral costs both of policing and punishing the crime are egregious. It is probable that something less than criminalization—such as a refusal of status (and associated rights) together with those benefits and goods that follow from recognition—might serve as powerful disincentives to the creation of certain kinds of family. Yet we should be fully aware of the possible enormous moral costs of even this strategy. Most of these would fall on those—the children—who would very likely be already disadvantaged by the circumstances of their birth and upbringing.

The law certainly can seek to prevent the creation of 'artificial' families that do not conform to a desired template. This is most obviously the case when the state regulates the use of fertility treatment. Thus those who would be unable to have children other than by the use of regulated methods of artificial reproduction can be subject to constraints as to familial form. These might include the marital status of the custodial adults, and the exclusion from fertility treatment of same-sex or single parents. Even a simple requirement that fertility treatment take proper account of the 'welfare of the child' could be construed in law to exclude certain familial possibilities.[35]

---

[34] For an account of the principle of liberal neutrality and the contrasted ideal of perfectionism see the entry on 'Perfectionism' in the *Stanford Encyclopedia of Philosophy*: S Wall, 'Perfectionism in Moral and Political Philosophy', *The Stanford Encyclopedia of Philosophy* (Winter edn, 2012) <http://plato.stanford.edu/entries/perfectionism-moral/> accessed 26 May 2016.

[35] Notoriously, the UK's Human Fertilisation and Embryology Act 1990 stipulated in Section 13(5): A woman shall not be provided with treatment services unless account has been taken of the welfare of any child who may be born as a result of the treatment (including the need of that child for supportive parenting), and of any other child who may be affected by the birth. This provision was removed from the amended HFEA 2008.

The law can also determine who may adopt or foster children; it can specify the criteria for the allocation of custodial rights in the event of familial breakdown. In all of these ways law can shape and influence family form. However, in the normal course of events individuals procreate, begin and sustain close relationships, and assume responsibility for the care of dependent children. We do not have to accord individuals a fundamental right to do this. It is enough to acknowledge the significant moral costs of interfering with their freely chosen actions. In this manner, the law's space for influencing family form is severely limited.

VII. Family and Intimate Relations

As stated earlier, the once apparently necessary yoking together of 'kin' and 'household' to define the family has been overtaken by developments. The relations of custodial adults to their dependent children need no longer be biological; family units need not share a single domestic space. Nevertheless, some of those who celebrate the diversity of familial forms also often celebrate something that is not captured within the minimal functional definition of family already given. This—as mentioned earlier—is expressed in terms of intimacy and exclusive affectivity. For now I grant the presumption that the familial is a sphere of intimate relations. Those who form a family share an emotional life that those who are outside the family do not. The ties of family love are not simply those that are formally defined in terms of enforceable rights and duties. They are those of mutual interdependence, shared lives, sustained care and love, reciprocal commitment, and support.

Indeed there is evidence that a right to 'family life' (as protected by Article 8 of the European Convention on Human Rights) is increasingly understood in terms of family 'ties' construed precisely in terms of shared, interdependent, committed, mutually supportive lives.[36]

These comments permit us to distinguish between two elements of the family once we strip our concept of it free from presumptions of a shared household, kin relationships, and size of group. First, it is a multi-generational social unit in which some adults are charged with care and custody of children to the exclusion (but not total) of others; second, it is a sphere of intimate relations of mutual care and support between persons. Now those persons need not be married; their relationships need not be sexual, or, if so, not necessarily monogamous or exclusive; nor necessarily heterosexual; and not restricted to couples.

There may well be reasons why the law should support what I will call 'intimate relations'. Such support would go beyond the recognition and enforcement of a right of privacy that simply protects the enjoyment of those relations from certain kinds of external interference. The law would do more. It would accord status to those relations. However, it is important to recognize the reasons why it might do so. Inasmuch as 'intimate relations' are conducive to the efficacious, indeed optimal, discharge of

---

[36] H Stalford, 'Concepts of Family under EU Law—Lessons from the ECHR' (2002) 16 International Journal of Law, Policy & the Family 410.

custodial duties then the law has a reason grounded in its general recognition and protection of the family.

Yet, if the value of 'intimate relations' lies in something other than serving the proper end of 'the family' then any justification of their legal recognition lies beyond that which fixes the scope of family law. Anne Bottomley and Simone Wong, for instance, argue that the privileges of legal recognition, currently accorded to the family, should be extended to the 'shared household'. Such a household, they maintain, is 'not defined by either sexual partners or familial relationships, but rather by a shared emotional economy'.[37]

Thus, it is perfectly possible that the law should accord to certain forms of intimate relation the same recognition and privileges as the family. However, this does not mean that these intimate relations *are* familial, that is to say that they are properly included within the category of the family. We should restrict the scope of family law to that which governs 'the family' and in doing so acknowledge why it is important for the law to recognize the family as a particular social institution. This is perfectly consistent with a demand that the law also recognizes what is distinctive and valuable in non-familial social relations. The fact that what is valuable can be found exhibited in families does not justify extending *family* law as opposed to other domains of the law. To speak of a shift from the 'family' to 'familiarity'[38] is unnecessary.

In sum, we can still talk of 'the family' in ways that allow us to evaluate the best forms of family law, and do so in ways that neither prejudge what counts as the best kind of family, nor deny ourselves the opportunities to explore what other kinds of relationship the law might recognize.

---

[37] A Bottomley and S Wong, 'Shared Household: A New Paradigm for Thinking about the Reform of Domestic Property Relations' in A Diduck and K O'Donovan (eds), *Feminist Perspectives on Family Law* (Routledge 2006) 43.

[38] A Diduck, 'Shifting Familiarity' (2005) 58 Current Legal Problems 235.

PART II
RELATIONSHIPS

3
Paid and Unpaid Care
Marriage, Equality, and Domestic Workers

Elizabeth Brake

I. Introduction

Modern states support and protect certain adult relationships, primarily through marriage law (and civil unions, domestic partnerships, and so on). This apparently simple point raises many questions. Which relationships currently receive support and protection—and which should? Through what legal measures do states support and protect relationships—and how should they? These questions have a descriptive component, asking what different states actually do, and a normative component, asking what an ideally just state would do. Answering the normative questions—which relationships should the state support and how—requires answering a third, more fundamental, question: should a just state support and protect relationships at all? An answer is needed to respond to marriage abolitionists, who argue that the state should not be involved at all in marriage, or regulating and privileging certain intimate adult relationships.[1]

In this chapter, I address these three questions—*why* the state should support relationships, *which* relationships it should support, and *how* it should—then extend the arguments to a surprising category: paid caregivers. I argue that family law, or law regarding intimate relationships, should extend protections to paid caregivers or care workers, or, more broadly, domestic workers, whose intimate involvement in family life may lead to caring relationships. Such workers are profoundly vulnerable. In US law, they have been seen as too much like family ('companions') to be fully protected as workers by provisions such as overtime, minimum wage, and protection against retaliation and discrimination—yet they have no protections as family members.[2] I argue that justice requires recognizing their claims both as workers and as members of caring relationships—that is, as legal members of the family. Their claims as workers are a matter of labour law; here I focus on their claims in the distinct area of family law.

Relationships between paid caregivers and their care recipients can be intimate and caring, yet they are not typically eligible for state support and protection. These relationships typically lack the relationship protections of family law. Further, the material

---

[1] Among others, C Chambers, 'The Marriage-Free State' (2013) 113 *Proceedings of the Aristotelian Society* 123; C Card, 'Against Marriage and Motherhood' (1996) 11 *Hypatia* 1.

[2] N Schoenbaum, 'The Law of Intimate Work' (2015) 90 *Washington Law Review* 1167, 1185. Paid caring relationships are also subjected to unique burdens, as in Illinois' Presumptively Void Transfers Act (Pub Act 98-1093), which enacts a rebuttable presumption that a transfer of more than $20,000 to a caregiver is void.

conditions of care work can threaten care workers' prior relationships—especially when their work requires them to relocate.

State support and protection of adult intimate relationships has significant implications for those affected, as we have seen with same-sex couples and can see in the cases of polygamists, polyamorists, and 'mere' friends. Due to these implications, protecting the caring relationships of paid caregivers is one aspect of achieving social justice for them. Paid caregivers are too much like family, in the eyes of law, to receive full protection as workers—yet they are also categorically excluded from the protections of family law. This in-between status makes them vulnerable to a range of injustices. Justice within the family should include justice for domestic workers, and support and protection for their caring relationships is one aspect of that.

The arguments of this chapter proceed within normative political philosophy, asking what laws and policies a state guided by liberal egalitarian principles of justice should adopt. In *Minimizing Marriage,* I pursued the logical implications of a liberal egalitarian principle of equal treatment applied to marriage law: if marriage equality applies to same-sex couples, it should, by parity of reasoning, apply to other caring relationships currently excluded from marriage—small polyamorous groups or networks and non-sexual friendships.[3] I argued that all caring relationships merit legal support, and their members have claims to such support—although equal treatment for the unmarried requires that such legal entitlements be less than the current norm. But if all caring relationships equally merit state support and protection, this extends to caring relationships which involve payment. This might be thought to be a reduction to absurdity of my view that all caring relationships deserve state support and protection; I will argue instead that we should accept this implication. Doing so would benefit, symbolically and practically, a class of vulnerable workers currently excluded from equal treatment.

My arguments are guided by feminist analysis of gender inequality and feminist care ethics.[4] As Nancy Folbre and Julie Nelson write, '[n]eglecting the "connected" aspects of human life—including physical need, responsibility for others, and altruism—is a form of gender bias, in that aspects of human life traditionally associated with femininity are being irrationally downplayed.'[5] Care and legal rights are not oppositional; law can protect and support care. The state should protect caring relationships, just as it should protect liberties and equal opportunity. Subsuming care, paid and unpaid, under norms of justice protects the vulnerable, especially women who perform care, women of colour and migrant women, and people with disabilities who rely on care workers. (Those familiar with *Minimizing Marriage* may wish to skip to section 5.)

---

[3] For these arguments, see E Brake, *Minimizing Marriage: Marriage, Morality, and the Law* (OUP 2012). For an influential statement of liberal egalitarianism, see J Rawls, *A Theory of Justice* (Harvard UP 1971); J Rawls, *Political Liberalism* (Columbia UP 1993).

[4] See, eg, SM Okin, *Justice, Gender, and the Family* (Basic Books 1989) and V Held, *The Ethics of Care: Personal, Political, and Global* (OUP 2006).

[5] N Folbre and J Nelson, 'For Love or Money – Or Both?' (2000) 14:4 The Journal of Economic Perspectives 123; see 131–40.

II. How Does the State Support Relationships?

Modern liberal states protect and support certain relationships between adults. We can distinguish two mechanisms by which they do so within marriage, civil unions, domestic partnerships, and recognition for implied or express agreements in marriage-like relationships: legal entitlements which have functional consequences and the formal legal status or pure recognition (for example, as 'marriage').

Functional consequences and legal status can make entering and maintaining a relationship more desirable *for reasons external to the relationship*, by providing direct economic benefits or other entitlements, such as special tax status, inheritance rights, or entitlement to be on one's spouse's health insurance or pension plan. Access to health insurance, for example, is an incentive to marry and to stay married. Such benefits are so pervasive that Mary Anne Case suggests that determining eligibility for third-party benefits may be the most important function of marriage law.[6] Likewise, the legal (and corresponding social) status attached to marriage can provide incentive to marry. The value of such benefits does not depend on spouses' valuing the relationship. Of course, there may also be costs; for example, marriage in the US can bring either a tax bonus or penalty. Law can be framed to incentivize or dis-incentivize marriage by altering its costs and benefits.

But functional entitlements and legal status can also protect relationships directly, rather than simply incentivizing them; some functional entitlements enable members to continue a relationship and maintain intimacy when this would otherwise be difficult or impracticable, usually by securing proximity or privacy. These include special immigration eligibility, evidentiary privilege, in-state residence, hospital or prison visiting rights, eligibility for spousal relocation policies, bereavement or caretaking leave, or inheritance tax provisions for a family home. These entitlements have a close connection to protecting the proximity and privacy of parties to a relationship. For example, there is a close connection between hospital visiting and intimacy and care. Status can also protect a relationship directly: in a society which prohibited unmarried cohabitation, the legal status of marriage would allow intimacy without legal penalty.

In my view, only those legal entitlements which directly support and protect relationships in this second way have a clear legal rationale and justification. Indeed, it may be unjust to distribute benefits which do not directly protect relationships (such as health insurance) through marriage; the unmarried are treated unfairly by being denied such benefits yet being forced to subsidize them for others. There is no reason why marriage should bring an entitlement to health insurance—and this appears particularly unjust if one thinks there is a universal entitlement to health insurance.[7] An ideally just marriage reform—what I call 'minimal marriage'—would support only a subset of current marital benefits, those which directly support relationships.

Pure recognition, like functional consequences, can support relationships—in this case, by providing a basis for social recognition, affecting how others respond,

---

[6] See MA Case, 'Marriage Licenses' (2004–2005) 89 Minnesota Law Review 1758.
[7] Card, 'Against Marriage and Motherhood' (n 1), eg, argues that marriage is unjust on these grounds.

generally by affording privacy and discouraging exit. Conservatives have made this point in defence of marriage, as have advocates for same-sex marriage who point out that a civil union is not equivalent to marriage.[8] But such social recognition may also disadvantage the unmarried. For example, it is often considered rude to invite only one spouse, but acceptable to invite only one partner in an unmarried couple. Such social discrimination is problematic when it results in worse treatment of the unmarried; law should refrain from underwriting such discrimination by providing a single, rather than two-tier status, for all caring relationships.[9]

Finally, the state can support the formation of relationships more broadly (as opposed to supporting particular relationships), through education, advertising, or even urban planning. For example, the US government promotes marriage; similar promotion policies could encourage caring relationships other than monogamous sexual relationships.[10] The ideal content of such policies depends on the more fundamental normative question: why should the state support relationships at all?

Before proceeding, I should note that marriage law serves functions other than protecting relationships: it imposes obligations and property division on dissolution and organizes parental rights and obligations. I have focused on entitlements for two reasons. First, I argue that citizens have a claim of justice to the entitlements which enable them to maintain relationships ('minimal marriage rights'). Second, while members of all caring relationships have a claim to these entitlements, not all have a claim to support and property; the plausible rationale for support and property division (economic inequality created through mutual reliance) does not apply to all caring relationships. This rationale does apply to relationships not formalized in law; arguably, support and property obligations can arise without formal voluntary undertaking.[11] Minimal marriage rights require formal legal registration (although this does not foreclose the possibility of provisions regarding intestacy or next-of-kin rules where there is no formal arrangement).[12] Minimal marriage is an idealized scheme for an ideally just society; my claim that domestic workers should be eligible for minimal marriage rights implies, in actual societies, that they have a claim to certain protections of family law.

III. Which Relationships Should the State Support?

My simple answer is that the state should support caring relationships, in which partners are non-fungible and the relationship is itself the primary purpose of the association. An even simpler—and even more surprising—answer is this: the state should

---

[8] Eg, see R Scruton, *Sexual Desire* (The Free Press 1986), 356–59 and S Macedo, *Just Married: Same-Sex Couples, Monogamy, and the Future of Marriage* (Princeton UP 2015).

[9] The nomenclature of this status is considered in *Brake* (n 3) 185–88 and E Brake, 'Recognizing Care: The Case for Friendship and Polyamory' (2014) 1 Syracuse Law and Civic Engagement Journal <http://slace.syr.edu/issue-1-2013-14-on-equality/> accessed 27 May 2016.

[10] Eg, the Healthy Marriage Initiative of the US Dept of Health and Human Services.

[11] Brake (n 3) 193–97 examines this closely. See also discussion of support obligations by R Leckey, C Bendall and R Harding, and D Jeske in chs 5, 6, and 8.

[12] For one approach, see the piecemeal regulation scheme in C Chambers, 'The Limitations of Contract: Regulating Personal Relationships in A Marriage-Free State' in E Brake (ed), *After Marriage: Rethinking Marital Relationships* (OUP 2016).

support just those caring relationships which the parties want it to. While this may seem like the undesirable slippery slope allegedly following legalization of same-sex marriage, I will try to make the view plausible.

A compelling liberal argument for same-sex marriage points out that the state provides benefits through marriage to members of relationships possessing certain features, such as being loving, intimate, and committed.[13] Because many same-sex relationships share these features, equal treatment requires that justification be given for excluding their members from marital benefits. Excluding citizens from state benefits without justification is a form of unequal treatment which amounts to unjust discrimination. But according to the influential theory of political liberalism, the legitimate justifications for unequal treatment are constrained; within political liberalism, justifications for law, at least in important matters, should not depend wholly on contested 'comprehensive' ethical or religious views (views concerning the whole conduct of life).[14] Moreover, equal treatment requires that justification for excluding a group from certain benefits provides good reason for their exclusion: for example, legal blindness is a justification for excluding applicants from getting a driver's licence, whereas race or sex are not.[15] These constraints rule out many justifications often proffered for excluding same-sex couples from marriage; without a legitimate, relevant justification, their exclusion is a form of unjust discrimination.[16]

This argument for same-sex marriage has implications for other relationships. Just as loving, intimate, committed same-sex relationships are relevantly similar to different-sex marriages, there are also loving, intimate, committed relationships which are not sexual and which involve more than two people. If the rationale for marriage law is to protect loving, intimate, and committed relationships against certain institutional threats, requiring sexual intimacy and only two partners seems as arbitrary as requiring sexual difference, as the following examples of non-sexual or non-dyadic relationships suggest.

Two close friends of three decades who take care of each other, or two 80-year-old sisters cohabiting for life, are in a loving, intimate, committed relationship even if there is no sexual component. But such couples have been denied legal protections—such as exemption from inheritance tax on a family home and special immigration eligibility—which are available through marriage.[17] Requirements of sexual consummation exclude 'mere' friends or adult siblings from legal marital entitlements which would protect

---

[13] The set of features is characterized differently by different authors. Particularly clear versions are found in A Rajczi, 'A Populist Argument for Same-Sex Marriage' (2008) 91:3–4 The Monist 475; R Wedgwood, 'The Fundamental Argument for Same-Sex Marriage' (1999) 7 Journal of Political Philosophy 225; AA Wellington, 'Why Liberals Should Support Same Sex Marriage' (1995) 26 Journal of Social Philosophy 5.
[14] See Rawls, *Political Liberalism* (n 3). For reasons for accepting political liberalism see Brake (n 3) 134–39. For a divergent view of what neutrality requires, see M Lister's chapter.
[15] Rajczi, 'A Populist Argument for Same-Sex Marriage' (n 13) 476.
[16] For detailed arguments see Brake (n 3) 139–45.
[17] In Brake, 'Recognizing Care' (n 9) I discuss a case in which an elderly woman was deported because her cohabiting friendship of three decades had no legal status under Canadian law. In the UK, the two elderly Burden sisters, lifelong cohabitants, challenged the restriction of inheritance tax exemption to married couples and partners; they pointed out that this tax would force one to leave the family home if the other died. *Burden and Burden v United Kingdom* (13378/05) [2008] STC 1305 (ECtHR (Grand Chamber)).

their relationships. In the absence of a legitimate justification for excluding members of such relationships from legal protections, failure to do so is unjust.

Of course, such friends (or, *a fortiori*, siblings) might not want to be considered married. This is a reason for calling the legal status protecting relationships something other than 'marriage'. But it is not a reason to exclude them from entitlements such as special immigration eligibility or inheritance tax status. In the absence of a legitimate justification for preferential treatment for sexual partners, excluding people who do not identify as romantic or sexual partners is a form of unjust unequal treatment.

The same reasoning extends to small groups, whether polyamorous (involving multiple romantic love and sex relationships) or care networks of friends. Three lesbians living in polyfidelity are in a loving, intimate, committed relationship—as would be three friends, or three sisters, in a relationship of mutual caring.[18] A law protecting all relationships equally—what I call minimal marriage—would allow parties to share marital entitlements with multiple partners.

This argument is based on a general principle of equal treatment, not particular cases. However, it might be thought that such cases are too rare to deserve recognition. But while such arrangements may be unfamiliar to some, they are not rare: as the percentage of people living outside marriage has increased (to more than 50% of adult women in the US), people have moved into new forms of relationship, including 'urban tribes', networks of friends, cohabiting single parents, and extended families.[19] Non-romantic relationships are the primary relationships in many peoples' lives, but this reality is often obscured by the legal and social privileging of romantic couples.

There might seem to be legitimate justifications for excluding groups from legal relationship protections. Some theorists argue that such relationships lack a valuable emotional dimension which dyads have, such as intimacy, reciprocity, or a sense of specialness. But as an empirical claim, this denies the testimony of polyamorists and friends who claim their small groups provide the love and intimacy which others get from monogamous sexual relationships.[20] When such testimony comes from adults who have freely entered polyamory or friend networks, with experience for comparison, and against the monogamous promptings of the wider culture, dismissing their experience seems paternalistic.[21] Additionally, a judgment that monogamy is more valuable is inadmissible as a reason for legal discrimination within political liberalism, because it is a contested comprehensive ethical view. Such objections lack the proof of harm which would be good reason for policy.

---

[18] On polyamory, see RD Otter's chapter, see also EF Emens, 'Monogamy's Law: Compulsory Monogamy and Polyamorous Existence' (2004) 29 New York University Review of Law and Social Change 277.

[19] See Brake (n 3) 169–70.

[20] See Emens, 'Monogamy's Law: Compulsory Monogamy and Polyamorous Existence' (n 18) 312–17; E Sheff, *The Polyamorists Next Door: Inside Multiple-Partner Relationships and Families* (Rowman & Littlefield Publishers 2013).

[21] On polyamorist demographics, see M Goldfeder and E Sheff, 'Children of Polyamorous Families: A First Empirical Look' (2013) 5 Journal of Law and Social Deviance 150. Sheff's empirical research in this under-studied area found that polyamorists tended to be 'very highly educated, middle or upper middle-class people living in urban or suburban areas of large cities and working in professional occupations,' 193. Goldfeder and Sheff also report that the polyamorous families studied resemble stepfamilies in their stability as child-rearing units.

Second, some argue that group sexual relationships are mostly inegalitarian and harmful male-headed polygamy and hence should be legally discouraged. There is evidence that polygamy—as it is often practised—is correlated with certain harms, such as child sexual abuse, lack of access to education and to exit, 'grooming' young girls for entry, and expelling young boys from the community. Thom Brooks, surveying the empirical literature attributing harm to polygamous marriages, argues against legal polygamy on grounds of harm. Indeed, if polygamy is demonstrably significantly harmful to the vulnerable (particularly children), this provides a reason for treating it differently.[22]

But polyamory—the practice of multiple sex and love relationships—differs from polygamy, which typically involves rigid gender and marital roles. Polyamory tends to be more egalitarian and lack the harmful background conditions of polygamy. While there is, so far, little research on polyamory, Elisabeth Sheff's fifteen-year longitudinal study of polyamorous families found no developmental problems in the twenty-five children studied.[23] Even if the harms associated with polygamy justify treating it differently in law, this does not provide reason against equal treatment for polyamory.[24]

Finally, it may seem that designing marriage law for groups creates insuperable practical problems for policy-making.[25] Consider, for example, rules for evidentiary privilege or benefit entitlements within group marriage. Practical concerns such as potential abuse and limited resources should inform policy. But if there is no principled reason to discriminate against group relationships, equal treatment requires at least extending protections which do not create practical difficulties. For example, members of a triad might have to take turns exercising conjugal visiting rights to the third, incarcerated member. This would not interfere with the aims of punishment by increasing the number of conjugal visits, but it would acknowledge that the prisoner has two significant relationships. On the other hand, added complications in the tax code might be reason against recognizing large units in that context.

So far, I have argued that non-romantic friendships and small groups should have equal access to the same functional entitlements and legal status as dyadic couples (as practical). This can be understood as a conditional: *if* the state supports any relationships, it ought to treat them equally. But this prompts a question: why should the state support relationships at all? Without justification, any benefits for marriage, civil unions, or domestic partnerships might be a form of unjust unequal treatment; they exclude the unmarried and un-partnered—anyone not in a caring relationship. My own arguments might seem to imply that special treatment for any relationships is unjust.

---

[22] T Brooks, 'The Problem with Polygamy' (2009) 37:2 Philosophical Topics 109. See also Macedo (n 8).
[23] See Goldfeder and Sheff, 'Children of Polyamorous Families: A First Empirical Look' (n 21); Sheff (n 20).
[24] Some argue that recognizing polygamy might alleviate its harms: see C Calhoun, 'Who's Afraid of Polygamous Marriage? Lessons for Same-Sex Marriage Advocacy from the History of Polygamy' (2005) 42 San Diego Law Review 1023. See also Brake (n 3) 197–200.
[25] See Macedo (n 8), Part III, for a sustained discussion of these points. On the emotional aspect, see also C Bennett, 'Liberalism, Autonomy, and Conjugal Love' (2003) 9 *Res Publica* 285.

IV. Why Should the State Protect and Support Caring Relationships?

In my view, the state should protect and support caring relationships, thus discriminating between caring and non-caring relationships. As noted above, political liberalism prohibits a liberal state from justifying such discrimination, or differential treatment, only by appeal to contested ethical or religious beliefs, such as a belief that caring relationships are especially valuable. The legitimacy of such differential treatment depends on whether there is a broadly shared political reason for supporting caring relationships.

Certainly, the view that caring relationships are valuable is not widely contested in the way that similar views about heterosexuality, for example, are contested. Caring relationships are widely valued. Contesting the view that they are valuable would require arguing that friendships have no greater value than superficial encounters. There are simply very few arguments of this sort.

Some reasons which might at first appear to justify supporting adult caring relationships weaken under scrutiny. One such reason is protecting children. To the claim that marriage protects children, Samantha Brennan and Bill Cameron respond that, as many marriages end in divorce, treating the parent–child relation separately in law would better protect children.[26] In any case, such a reason would only justify supporting adult relationships which include children. Another rationale is protecting adult caregivers financially. As Tamara Metz has argued, caregivers can sacrifice their own interests, coming to depend financially on their partner; she proposes an intimate caregiving union (ICGU) status to protect them by requiring financial support.[27] Metz's ICGU might apply to a full-time housewife whose ability to compete for high-paying jobs has diminished. ICGUs would protect equal opportunity as well as financial interests of caregivers: as feminists have pointed out, the division of labour within gender-structured marriage threatens women's equal opportunity.[28] But these reasons apply only to relationships in which inequalities develop, and perhaps only to gender-structured relationships. Also, this rationale justifies property division and spousal support—not minimal marriage entitlements. After all, if relationships are sites of economic vulnerability for women and caregivers, why should the state protect them as opposed to simply dividing resources when they end? Feminist marriage abolitionists have argued against marriage for precisely this reason. The benefits obtained through marriage can provide powerful inducements for vulnerable parties to stay in abusive or unloving relationships.[29]

A justification for state protection of relationships should show why caring relationships are themselves valuable from the political point of view. I argue that caring

---

[26] S Brennan and B Cameron, 'Is Marriage Bad for Children? Rethinking the Connection between Having Children, Romantic Love, and Marriage' in Brake (ed), (n 12); see also Brake (n 3) 145–51.

[27] T Metz, *Untying the Knot: Marriage, the State, and the Case for their Divorce* (Princeton UP 2010) 126, 138, ch 5.

[28] See Okin (n 4). For updated statistics, see my 'Equality and Non-Hierarchy in Marriage: What Do Feminists Really Want?' in Brake (ed), (n 12).

[29] See Card (n 1).

relationships are 'primary goods', goods of the kind which the state can recognize without appealing to a contested doctrine; these are goods 'normally needed' for citizens' varying life plans and for the development and exercise of the moral powers.[30] Caring relationships have a close, irreplaceable connection to mental health goods such as self-respect, goods normally needed in the pursuit of life plans and not simply good within contested moral or religious doctrines. Thus, state support of such relationships need not depend on contested doctrines.

Once relationships are understood as the kind of good which the state should support, equal access to them becomes a matter of justice. Of course, the state can only distribute the legal and social bases of relationships, not relationships themselves; these legal and social bases of caring relationships simply are minimal marriage rights. It might be thought that caring relationships do not need legal protection. But sometimes they do, when relationships are threatened by illness, national boundaries, or employment (such as job relocation). Because minimal marriage rights are those needed to protect relationships, they will depend on background legal and social institutions; for example, if there were open borders, special immigration eligibility would be unnecessary.

In sum, caring relationships of all types—so long as they are between consenting adults—should, in principle, all be eligible for the same legal protections and supports. This presupposes ongoing commitment, because legal protections would not apply to a brief encounter. But the duration of commitment could reasonably vary, as in renewable or temporary marriage contracts.[31] The state should only discriminate among reciprocal, committed caring relationships on grounds of criminality, harm to the incompetent, and coercion.

Thus, my simple answer to the question of which relationships the state should support is that it should support caring relationships which parties want supported. Such support could, like legal marriage, be abused—for example, if partners sought special immigration eligibility only because they wanted to immigrate and not because they valued the relationship. How to prevent such abuse, and weigh the financial costs of recognition to the state and third parties, are important practical questions. But setting these aside, the fact that parties want a relationship protected for its own sake is evidence that it is the kind of relationship which the state should protect.[32] Now, I turn to the question of whether paid caring relationships should be eligible for such protections.

V. Paid and Unpaid Care

A. Theory

My arguments seem to imply that paid caregiving relationships should be eligible for minimal marriage, but this may be taken as a reduction to absurdity. By paid caregiving

---

[30] For details, see Brake (n 3) 171–85. The phrase 'normally needed' is taken from Rawls' definition of primary goods. See Rawls, *Political Liberalism* (n 3) 76.
[31] See Daniel Nolan, 'Temporary Marriage' in Brake (ed), (n 12).
[32] I discuss very large groups, teams, and acquaintances in Brake, 'Recognizing Care' (n 9).

I mean paid material caregiving, tending to material needs, not merely the emotional, attitudinal caring of caring relationships. Some care workers prefer the term 'care work', as 'care*giving*' can obscure 'class exploitation', but some 'home care workers describe themselves as caregivers', seeing their work as a vocation to respond to others' needs.[33] I will use both terms interchangeably. Such workers may include nurses or aides in institutional settings, as well as home-care workers; my focus on domestic care workers should not be taken to exclude care workers outside the home.

Relationships between paid caregivers and their care recipients can develop into attitudinally caring relationships while continuing on a paid basis. When this happens, should the relationship be eligible for legal protections as a caring relationship? Do such relationships merit equal treatment with unpaid relationships, or should payment affect the eligibility of reciprocal caring relationships for protections? I will argue that it should not—and that this is neither absurd nor merely academic; it suggests policies which would promote social justice for a large group of people—people, moreover, who tend to be especially vulnerable.

The cases I have in mind are those in which a long-term paid caregiver becomes close with a client, mutual care develops, there are reciprocal expressions of friendship and affection, the parties share much of life, and they become non-fungible to one another. Paradigmatic cases would include a paid companion cohabiting as an intimate friend with her employer or long-standing domestic workers and home health aides. The caregiver might be employed directly by the cared-for or her family or by a third-party employer. These are cases in which a paid professional relationship continues alongside the caring relationship, not in which the professional relationship ceases (as when, eg, someone marries a paid service provider and ceases to employ them in a professional capacity).

There are two related cases I cannot consider here, due to their complexity. First, sex workers and their clients—if a caring relationship develops between them, but sex continues on a paid basis, should their relationship be eligible for equal treatment? Why is it relevantly different, in the eyes of the state? Part of the complexity here is the background debate over whether sex work should be legal at all and associated concerns about harms to women. But if we bracket these concerns, it seems to me that the case should be treated similarly with that of paid caregivers. Second is that of paid childcare. Parent's and children's rights are beyond the scope of this essay, but there is a parallel case here to that of paid caregivers for adults: does a caring relationship between a nanny and a child merit legal support and protection, in both their interests? The answer to the central question concerning paid caregivers for adults should guide thinking about these other professional relationships. The case of paid caregivers for adults, however, lacks their inherent complications (although conflicts with other family members could arise in the case of adult care recipients, as they could with parents and children; this increases the need to verify competence, which I discuss below).

It might be thought that legal protection for caring relationships should categorically exclude professional relationships. But I am asking whether professional relationships

---

[33] E Boris and J Klein, *Caring for America: Home Health Workers in the Shadow of the Welfare State* (OUP 2012) 8–9.

can be eligible for support as caring relationships; it would beg the question to take professional relationships as categorically excluded from state support. Again, a relevant distinction must be found to justify differential treatment. But while there is an intuitive distinction between personal caring relationships, such as friendships and romantic relationships, and professional relationships, considerable overlap occurs. It might be thought that the distinction is simple: professional relationships are those in which one party pays another for services or the parties interact as part of work. However, this will not do. Friends and spouses can pay one another for services (note the 'wife bonus' and—likely unenforceable—'push bonus' described in Wednesday Martin's *Primates of Park Avenue*[34]). Professional relationships, like non-professional caring relationships, can involve economic or physical dependency and vulnerability, affectionate bonds, intimacy, and considerable time together, and they can be intended to be temporary or permanent. None of these characteristics clearly distinguish professional from non-professional relationships. Co-workers may have considerable affection and intimacy, for instance, while some spouses do not.

The most important distinguishing criterion may be the purpose of the relationship. A professional relationship tends to be primarily concerned with a goal extrinsic to the relationship, so that the relationship is instrumentally valuable to its members and they are fungible to one another. That is, parties could be replaced with another equally competent lawyer or nurse with no loss (except transition costs). By contrast, in caring relationships, the relationship itself is a primary purpose, and the friend or spouse could not be switched for another person (not even the other's identical twin).[35] Being with that particular, non-fungible individual is an object of the relationship. Of course, people can pursue external goals through caring relationships: building a home or family. One can value one's relationship with one's spouse for its own sake, while also valuing the financial security and material care the relationship makes possible. While we can imagine marriages and friendships in which the relationship is not a primary goal, in which unscrupulous opportunists seek out whomever is available, these are intuitively 'sham' marriages or friendships, not true caring relationships.[36]

A relationship which begins to serve a goal external to the relationship—such as work for the care worker and care for the recipient—can develop into a caring relationship which is valued for its own sake and in which parties are non-fungible. One way of determining whether the relationship is valued primarily for its own sake is asking whether both parties would choose to continue it absent the paid relationship—if possible. The fact that a continuing relationship might not be possible without the work relationship suggests why there is a need for legal protections for such relationships. They might be vulnerable to decisions by family members or the caregiver's employer about the caregiver's continued employment. Precisely because the care recipient is to some degree dependent, continuing the relationship might face obstacles such as

---

[34] W Martin, *Primates of Park Avenue: A Memoir* (Simon and Schuster 2015).

[35] This raises questions in philosophy of love which I cannot discuss here; for critical discussion, see C Johnson, 'Against the Substitution Argument'(unpublished).

[36] One further condition for such relationships to be *caring* relationships is that partners are valued positively. This rules out feuds or revenge fixations, in which the relationship is a primary purpose and the other seen as non-fungible—but negatively. See also Brake (n 3) 174.

difficulties with mobility, communication, time, and travel costs. But minimal marriage rights—the social and legal bases of caring relationships—are to protect caring relationships in the face of such external, institutional threats. This is not to say that the state should provide whatever is needed to maintain relationships, but that when their social and legal bases fall under institutional rules, the state should shape those rules for their protection.

When paid care relationships become reciprocal caring relationships to which both parties consent, they should be eligible for minimal marriage as a matter of equal treatment. This would require parties to register formally for these relationship protections. Paid care relationships may be threatened in ways against which minimal marriage rights protect: hospital visitation rights, special immigration eligibility, in-state residency, eligibility for spousal relocation policies, special tax status for inheritance of a shared home. But given the special features of such relationships—physical dependency on one hand, economic dependency on the other—different provisions may be appropriate to protect these relationships. These might include, for example, protections against the employee's arbitrary reassignment, visitation rights, a role for the care worker in end-of-life decision making, and a symbolic or expressive shift in the law's regard for such workers as family members.

Denying equal access to relationship protections to such relationships requires providing a reason to distinguish them. There are several possible reasons why payment might seem a distinguishing factor, but none—I believe—succeeds.

A first objection is that paid relationships involve inequality and power imbalance. Of course, caregiving can be performed with dignity—a spouse caring for her sick partner does not thereby become servile. But there is a structural inequality: the client can hire or fire the caregiver, and the caregiver depends on the client for her livelihood. Minimal marriage benefits—such as special immigration eligibility—might increase the employer or client's power over the care worker.

But such economic dependence exists in many marriages, and under liberal divorce law either party can end the marriage unilaterally. Economic dependence in either case may be unjust when it affects equal opportunity or the dependent's autonomy. Worker protections under a just labour law are needed to protect care workers' autonomy and equal opportunity. The justice of minimal marriage entitlements which might exacerbate unequal power relations is contingent on such labour law protections.

We should not underestimate the extent to which economically dependent caregivers, particularly immigrants, are liable to abuse:

> The power imbalance between domestic workers and employers is severe. The employers are commonly of a privileged class, race, and immigration status with respect to the women they hire to care for their homes and families.... The workplace is their employers' private homes ... a place where the government has no business or authority. Advocates often compare the industry to the 'Wild West' because it seems to function above the law. Employers can utilize sexual and gender-based harassment to instill fear, as well as exploit workers' immigration status to establish control in the workplace.[37]

---

[37] AJ Poo, 'Domestic Workers Bill of Rights: A Feminist Approach for a New Economy' (2009) 8:1 The Scholar and Feminist Online <http://sfonline.barnard.edu/work/poo_01.htm> accessed 3 June 2016. On

The appropriate response is to bring such relationships under the auspices of justice under labour law, with full worker protections. Moreover, whatever regulations should protect economically vulnerable caregivers (such as Metz's ICGUs) also apply here. Rather than being excluded both from full protection as workers and family members, care workers should have both sets of protections. But because minimal marriage protects caring relationships, it would not be appropriate in cases where care workers and clients do not form caring relationships (as is presumably the case when abuse and exploitation is present).

Care recipients, especially those with diminished mental or physical capacity, are also vulnerable to abuse or manipulation. Again, abuse is possible in other relationships (and widespread in marriages and cohabitation in the US).[38] Vulnerability is not a reason to exclude care worker relationships from minimal marriage protections. However, it suggests a need for oversight to protect against undue influence.

This suggests a second reason for excluding paid relationships from minimal marriage. Paid caregiver relationships should be regulated independently by labour law and standards of care. There should be oversight to detect abuse and ensure that the client receives adequate care and that the caregiver has decent working conditions and fair wages. But these independent regulatory frameworks might conflict with relationship-protecting entitlements. (For example, Canada's special immigration provisions for caregivers differ from its provisions for spouses.) Further, the intrusiveness of oversight might seem to impinge inappropriately on family privacy. However, these concerns are not decisive. Labour law does not generally provide minimal-marriage-like protections. Where frameworks do conflict, one set of rules might be more appropriate (for example, that a caring relationship has developed would be reason to upgrade the caregiver's immigration eligibility). And oversight could be appropriate given the special nature of the relationship—just as oversight of foster and adoptive parents is not thought to interfere illegitimately with family privacy.

Third, it might seem that the contractual basis of care work is incompatible with the altruism of loving relationships. But exchange of money for services does not distinguish care work from some marriages. Psychologically, the dichotomy between caring for love or for money is a false one; as the next section will elaborate, many caregivers claim both motivations.[39] Conceptually and empirically, the fact '[t]hat most people enter caring occupations in order to earn a living ... does not diminish the importance of the moral values, caring norms, and personal attachments that often infuse their performance on the job.'[40] Finally, contractual terms of employment might protect the

---

the separation between the two sides of care, and the potential asymmetry of dependency care, see A Bhandary, 'Liberal Dependency Care' (2016) 41 Journal of Philosophical Research 43.

[38] See Brake, 'Equality and Non-Hierarchy' (n 28).

[39] Folbre and Nelson, 'For Love or Money – Or Both?' (n 5). For a summary of the critique of the 'separate-spheres' view that altruism is incompatible with contract, see K Matsumura, 'Public Policing of Intimate Agreements' (2013) 25 Yale Journal of Law & Feminism 159, 177–80.

[40] C Howes, C Leana, and K Smith, 'Paid Care Work' in N Folbre (ed), *For Love and Money: Care Provision in the United States* (Russell Sage Foundation 2012) 65.

caregiver's interests (including pride and a sense of professionalism)—especially when the employer is a third party.

Fourth, it might be thought these arguments, absurdly, require equality for corporations (or robots!) which provide care. After all, in the US, corporations are in many contexts considered legal persons.[41] This would indeed be a reduction to absurdity, if it meant someone could 'marry', even minimally, a corporation or robot. The difference, of course, is that a corporation or robot cannot experience the attitudinal care which minimal marriage protects. Even if a corporation is a person legally, it is not psychologically.

One further concern is not, I think, sufficient reason to exclude paid caregivers from minimal marriage, but it suggests practical problems. Care recipients may sometimes lack legal capacity to consent, or it may be difficult to tell whether they have it. This might be the case if the client had dementia or a cognitive disability. (Similar situations between nannies and children, and between people who both lack legal capacity, are beyond the scope of this chapter.) Minimal marriage rights must be the subject of mutual, competent consent.[42] Yet there is some intuitive pull to cases in which parties enjoyed a reciprocal relationship when both parties were competent, yet neglected to formalize it before a sudden loss in capacity. If the client continues to reciprocate attitudinal care, and would have consented to a legal relationship just prior to the diminished capacity, minimal marriage rights could protect both their interests. This is not merely academic; a care recipient's closest relationship could be with her caregiver, yet on losing capacity she might lose power to continue the relationship.

The state should extend some protections of family law to caring relationships between care workers and their clients. This extends the legal categories of family and work to recognize how people actually live. As Naomi Schoenbaum suggests, categorically separating family and work obscures the real work, paid and unpaid, done in the family as well as the caring relationships overlapping with paid work.[43]

B. Practice

Empirical data about care workers shows the relevance and importance of such protections. While my argument is principled, not case-based, it might be thought that there are so few cases of such relationships that they do not merit legal reform. Of course, justice can require legal reform even if the cases affected are not typical—for example, legislation permitting interracial marriage could not have emerged under this constraint, as when such relationships were prohibited they could not become typical. However, in the case of care work, there is evidence that such relationships are already typical of many people's lives.

Demographic shifts explain why paid caregiver relationships have become widespread. As middle-class women increasingly work outside the home, their unpaid care work for children and elders must be replaced, and the 'fertility decline' and

---

[41] Eg, see 1 USC s 1.   [42] On this point see Brake (n 3) 164.
[43] Schoenbaum, 'The Law of Intimate Work' (n 2) 1219–23.

'increased longevity' increase the need for paid eldercare.[44] Eileen Boris and Jennifer Klein note that this 'vast workforce' of paid caregivers is 'among the fastest growing occupations' in the US.[45] According to the 2012 Census, '[h]ome health care and services for the elderly and persons with disabilities … are now the industries with the first and second-fastest rate of growth of employment in the United States.'[46]

Empirical research suggests that this work is often combined with reciprocal affection. Folbre and Nelson, documenting the shift into market-based care, suggest that love and money are increasingly 'intertwining'.[47] Schoenbaum reports that intimate work produces reciprocal intimacy and that such 'work ties are pervasively referred to as "like family"'.[48] One of Boris and Klein's 'faces' of care work is Rosa, who 'treated the 93-year-old [client] as if he were a member of her own family: 'I've grown so attached to him I sometimes take him home with me'. [Her client] returned the affection: 'I love Rosa … like I loved my own mother.'[49]

In some cases, such deep emotions may emerge from a tragic emotional displacement, yet the emotions are no less real. Arlie Hochschild quotes such a worker: 'The only thing you can do is give all your love to [the two-year-old American child]. In my absence from my children, the most I could do with my situation is give all my love to that child.'[50] While I have bracketed cases involving children, care workers' reports suggest that such transferences take place with adults too.

Of course, this transference simultaneously creates a caring relationship and issues from a harm—one which could be exacerbated by redefining family to include paid relationships. In such cases, care for a client replaces care in a relationship which has been painfully severed by economic privation. This reality can be obscured by the caring bonds which develop with clients. Arlie Hochschild, quoting a nursery director, reports a widespread view that caregivers from supposedly warm and close-knit 'Third World' cultures are more patient and loving than professional American women: 'the teacher's aides we hire from Mexico and Guatemala know how to love a child better than the middle-class white parents.' Ironically, the reality elicited from interviews with Filipina nannies is that such 'maternal' love is 'informed by an American ideology of mother-child bonding and fostered by intense loneliness and longing for their own children.'[51] Encouraging workers to see clients as family could detract from their pre-existing relationships, as can the temporal and emotional pressures on care workers. Threats to pre-existing relationships give reason to address the background economic circumstances which create these difficult choices. Support for caring relationships should extend to protecting care workers' non-work relationships (as through immigration law enabling family reunification). But while such policies are required by justice, it remains true

---

[44] See Howes et al, 'Paid Care Work' (n 40) 70 and A Hochschild, 'Love and Gold' (2009) 8:1 The Scholar and Feminist Online <http://sfonline.barnard.edu/work/hochschild_01.htm> accessed 3 June 2016.

[45] Boris and Klein (n 33) 5–6.   [46] Howes et al, 'Paid Care Work' (n 40) 82.

[47] Folbre and Nelson, 'For Love or Money – Or Both?' (n 5) 138.

[48] Schoenbaum, 'The Law of Intimate Work' (n 2) 1180, 1177. Such feelings are sometimes reported by gestational surrogates; ML Shanley discusses contractual pregnancy and care in her chapter.

[49] Boris and Klein (n 33) 4.

[50] R Parreñas, *Servants of Globalization: Women, Migration, and Domestic Work* (Stanford UP 2001) 87, cited by Hochschild, 'Love and Gold' (n 44), 1 (interpolated text in Hochschild).

[51] Hochschild, 'Love and Gold' (n 44), 3.

that caring relationships do develop in the context of paid care, and these relationships in some cases need legal protection. Also, as I will discuss below, minimal marriage can distinguish between care workers' primary and secondary relationships.

A repeated theme in work on organizing domestic labour are the opportunities and challenges of organizing workers with such close relationships with their clients or employers. Jennifer Fish reports that negotiations in the 2011 International Labour Organization conference over Convention 189, 'Decent Work for Domestic Workers' (near-unanimously adopted) drew on relationships between workers and employers—rather than opposing them. The International Domestic Workers Network used 'affective techniques that asked [representatives] to "think of your domestic worker when casting your vote" '.[52] Care workers are even vulnerable to exploitation due to their 'willingness to act altruistically'.[53] In an article on organizing domestic labour in South Asia, the author notes that a loving relationship with the client often 'sustains the domestic worker' but can be abused by employers and complicates organizing labour.[54] This literature speaks to the widespread existence of close relationships between care workers and their clients.

However, these caring relationships are not always recognized as such; their paid status may trigger suspicion. Baseball player Ernie Banks' will made headlines because he left his estate to his caregiver of twelve years.[55] His estranged wife disputed this; yet if the caregiver—of twelve years!—had been an unpaid companion, there would likely have been less of a sense of incongruity. The intuitive tendency to distinguish caring and professional relationships can obscure the caring relationships in such contexts.

Giving paid care relationships access to legal protections as family would be a step towards what Melissa Murray describes as 'reconciling the legal construction of the family as a nuclear entity with the reality of nonconforming family arrangements', including how families provide care.[56] In the context of child care, Murray makes the point that existing legal classifications obscure the existence of non-parental caregivers, as law has no category for them. Indeed, she compares aspects of this legal situation to the doctrine of coverture—non-parental caregivers are hidden within the family zone of privacy just as wives were under coverture—and similarly deprived of rights.[57] This legal invisibility also applies to paid caregivers for adults.

Of course, not everyone views the shift to market-based care as a good thing. For critics, extending minimal marriage rights to care workers and their clients would have the

---

[52] J Fish, 'Making History through Policy: A Field Report on the International Domestic Workers Movement' (2015) 88 International Labor and Working-Class History 160.
[53] Schoenbaum, 'The Law of Intimate Work' (n 2) 1172.
[54] M Batra, 'Organizing in the South Asian Domestic Worker Community: Pushing the Boundaries of the Law and Organizing Project' in S Jayaraman and I Ness (eds), *The New Urban Immigrant Workforce: Innovative Models for Labor Organizing* (ME Sharpe Inc 2005), 124–25.
[55] J Meisner, 'Ernie Banks' Contested Will Cuts out Family, Leaves Assets to Caretaker' *The Chicago Tribune* (18 February 2015) <http://www.chicagotribune.com/news/local/breaking/ct-ernie-banks-will-met-20150217-story.html> accessed 3 June 2016. Banks may indeed not have been competent when he made the will; my point is that in media reports, suspicion about the will was connected to the fact that the heir was a paid caregiver.
[56] M Murray, 'The Networked Family: Reframing the Legal Understanding of Caregiving and Caregivers' (2008) 94 Virginia Law Review 385, 386.
[57] ibid. 396–98.

bad effect of decreasing authentic caring relationships. On one such critique, market-based care is part of a trend of outsourcing aspects of intimate life and sacrificing non-fungible relationships to the worst aspects of consumerist culture. Middle-class and wealthy people can 'outsource' not only childcare and eldercare, but domestic activities, dating, and gestation.[58] There are even services named 'rent-a-friend' or 'rent-a-mom.' Yet both clients and care workers might feel cheated by work of their own most valued relationships. Describing 'care chains' in which nannies leave their own children to devote themselves to the children of other mothers, Hochschild writes: 'two working mothers giving their all to work is a good idea gone haywire.'[59] The concern is that commodifying care comes at the cost of emotional depth and authenticity.[60] The point does not only apply to mothers: outsourcing care costs the left-behind adult loved ones of care workers, and some family members who pay for care might prefer to care for adult relatives themselves but be constrained by their own work. From this perspective, treating paid and unpaid caring relationships equally might further displace the emotions of those in the care chain from their prior relationships.

In response, the aim of minimal marriage rights is to protect truly caring relationships which do develop. They provide a buttress against the market by demanding that certain relationships be recognized as valuable and so entitled to certain protections (such as bereavement leave). This is a pragmatic point: paid caregiving is widespread and likely to remain so. Even if state action to change this were justified (for example, by encouraging unpaid caregiving), liberties such as free choice of occupation sharply limit means to do so (although policies such as extended parental leave and flexible working hours could have some effect).

However, there is also a less pragmatic, more principled, response. While it is true that 'care chains' can be tragic, they do not characterize all cases: some working women prefer non-caregiving work to full-time caregiving, and some care workers do not sacrifice other relationships to their work. Also, the point that relationships in the context of work are somehow less 'authentic' is dubious. Caring relationships in the context of paid care can be just as caring as those outside this context. By recognizing this, law performs a symbolic or expressive function, shaping perceptions of the existence and worth of caring relationships in different contexts.

Our sense of what is typical is shaped by the existing legal *status quo*. Law makes certain life choices visible—the way law constructs marital status, for example, makes a certain kind of relationship more socially salient. Contrasted with legal marriage, friendships can seem formless and uncommitted. But one reason for this appearance is that they lack access to a legal status. Further, because law shapes choices by providing incentives and disincentives, it reinforces its framers' assumptions about which relationships are prevalent. These points also apply to care work: relationships between care workers and their clients may seem less caring because they are treated differently in law. But if care workers were considered as family under law, this perception would

---

[58] See A Hochschild, *The Outsourced Self: What Happens When We Pay Others to Live Our Lives for Us* (Picador 2013). Gestational surrogacy is discussed by ML Shanley in her chapter.
[59] Hochschild, 'Love and Gold' (n 44).
[60] Folbre and Nelson, 'For Love or Money – Or Both?' (n 5) 131.

shift. Equal treatment for paid and unpaid caring relationships, in itself required by justice, would have the good consequences of making visible the caring relationships often involved in care work.

A second practical objection is that the broader social effects of treating care workers as family would have undesirable consequences for care workers themselves. We have briefly discussed the concern that it might detract from care workers' relationships with their non-work families, to which I will return. Another concern is that subsuming care workers under the family paradigm in law might entrench the perception that they are not 'real workers'. Care workers are already not afforded equal protection as workers. Care work is undervalued, likely due to race and gender bias, and lacks basic worker protections because of the intimacy and altruism involved.[61] And care workers are largely vulnerable—women, migrants, and people of colour.[62]

Ai-Jen Poo writes that 'domestic workers have been explicitly excluded from labor laws since the New Deal. The exclusion of domestic workers—most of whom were African American women in the South at the time those labor laws were passed—is rooted in the legacy of slavery.'[63] Schoenbaum notes that US law exempts 'babysitters and companions for the elderly from overtime and minimum wage' and 'live-in domestic workers from overtime'.[64] Intimate workers are also exempted from worker protections against retaliation and discrimination, while as workers they are categorically excluded from family law protections.[65]

Like Schoenbaum, I think it is important to challenge the dichotomy between work and intimacy, or care; overcoming this dichotomy would mean undermining the tension between being family and a 'real worker', being a caregiver and protected under labour law. This could extend to protecting unpaid caregivers within families too. Schoenbaum writes that 'law's separate regulation of intimacy and work creates a blind spot to a social reality—like intimate work—that combines the two. Law thus fails to protect the value and guard against the vulnerability of intimate work.'[66] While she focuses on protecting intimate workers as workers, I focus on protecting them as members of caring relationships.

Schoenbaum identifies lost investments in relationships as a vulnerability specific to intimate workers: 'Because the value of intimate work derives from relationship-specific investments, it is largely lost when the intimate work relationship ends, either through termination or reassignment of the worker, or the worker's or consumer's departure.'[67] She suggests these relationships are valuable in themselves as well as instrumentally valuable in helping the worker do her job. However, 'work law leaves intimate workers and consumers perpetually vulnerable to these relationships being ruptured.'[68]

---

[61] Schoenbaum, 'The Law of Intimate Work' (n 2) 1185–1218, 1218–23; see also Howes et al, 'Paid Care Work' (n 40) 71–73, Boris and Klein (n 33) and Fish, 'Making History through Policy' (n 52).

[62] See Howes et al, 'Paid Care Work' (n 40) 66, 68–71, 73, 83, for demographic statistics.

[63] Poo, 'Domestic Workers Bill of Rights' (n 37); see also Boris and Klein (n 33).

[64] Schoenbaum, 'The Law of Intimate Work' (n 2) cites 29 USC s 213(a)(15) and s 213(b)(21), fn 21. At the time of writing, some US home care workers are now entitled to overtime and minimum wage, since 2015; see The Editorial Board, 'Home Care Workers Can Finally Claim Victory' *The New York Times* 2 July 2016 <http://www.nytimes.com/2016/07/03/opinion/sunday/home-care-workers-can-finally-claim-victory.html> accessed 6 July 2016.

[65] ibid. 1202–05, 1187–98, 1186. [66] ibid. 1171. [67] ibid. 1210. [68] ibid. 1210.

Although such workers and clients are not fungible, this non-fungibility is not recognized in the US law of non-compete agreements, duty of loyalty, trade secrets, and termination and transfer. The loss of a relationship is not seen as a cost to be remedied in the law of unjust termination. Legal protections could protect relationships in some situations (for example, special eligibility for immigration could protect a relationship in the case of the threatened deportation of the care worker) and would be consistent with law recognizing the instrumental value of intimate work relationships.

Once again writing in the context of parenting, Murray points out that law constructs caregiving for children as 'all-or-nothing', with no steps between being a legal parent and a legal stranger to a child, excluding non-parental caregivers from rights and benefits.[69] Murray describes an in-between status which would recognize caregiving but be distinct from legal parenthood, with limited entitlements. Minimal marriage allows for such a continuum in the case of adult relationships, as parties could exchange all entitlements reciprocally, or only one; minimal marriage rights need not be bundled and exchanged reciprocally. In this respect, it is not 'all-or-nothing', nor is it exclusive. This goes some way to addressing the concern that treating clients as family may weaken care workers' attachments to their non-work families: an in-between status could recognize relevant differences.

In sum, care workers (and domestic workers generally) need more legal protections. They need protections for fair pay and against abuse. Legal protections for their relationships under family law would protect another aspect of their lives—the relationships with clients which become valuable to them.

Family law protections for care workers would also move, symbolically, beyond the work-care dichotomy. This dichotomy is harmful to unpaid caregivers (usually women), whose domestic care work is not seen as work but as altruism which justly goes uncompensated, and to paid care workers who have legal protections neither as workers nor as family and whose work is seen as less valuable by analogy with women's unpaid work in the home. Thus Schoenbaum writes that 'legal recognition of intimate work ... would begin to break down the categorical regulation of intimacy and work, generating a law that better reflects the reality of our lives, with benefits for gender equality.'[70]

Finally, it might be thought impracticable to test whether people in such relationships truly care, as opposed to feigning care to gain entitlements. Evidence that both parties freely value their relationship, seeing it as family and seeking legal protections for it, seems adequate. (Again, tests for competence may be necessary.) My arguments, as Schoenbaum writes in another context, 'support a case for recognition if [the relationship] can be proven to warrant it'.[71]

VI. Conclusion

Justice requires the state to support caring relationships and access to them. The background culture can support their formation or nudge us towards solitary pursuits.

---

[69] Murray, 'The Networked Family' (n 56) 398; see 398–409, 447–52. Grandparents are an exception in some jurisdictions.
[70] Schoenbaum, 'The Law of Intimate Work' (n 2) 1219.   [71] ibid. 1235.

Background institutions can make forming and maintaining relationships extremely costly for some people, as evidenced by 'the other marriage equality problem', the increasing gap in marriage rates between wealthy and poor in the US,[72] as well as the 'care chains' from rich to poor countries. Numerous policies can address this, among them care-leave and flex-time provisions so that those who choose can rely less on paid care, and protecting existing relationships between care workers and their loved ones through family reunification. However law supports caring relationships, it should not exclude relationships with care workers from its scope.[73]

---

[72] See L McClain, 'The Other Marriage Equality Problem' (2013) 93 Boston University Law Review 921.
[73] I am indebted to the helpful comments of participants in the workshop on this volume at Oriel College, Oxford and to Asha Bhandary, Lucinda Ferguson, Kaiponanea Matsumura, Mary Lyndon Shanley, Janet Jakobson, Mary Margaret Fonow, and members of the Philosophy Department at Umeå University, Sweden.

4
A Perfectionist Argument for Legal Recognition of Polyamorous Relationships

Ronald C. Den Otter[1]

I. Introduction

Although several American legal scholars have defended the constitutional right to marry more than one person at the same time or have advocated the decriminalization of polygamy on substantive due process, equal protection, or free exercise grounds, none of them have fully articulated the ways in which plural marriage could be beneficial.[2] Their silence is far from surprising when so many Americans have internalized beliefs about the superiority of monogamy.[3] For now, this approach to defending the option of plural marriage is not only legally wise but rhetorically shrewd. In the eyes of an increasing number of Americans, the state does not have the constitutional authority to interfere unnecessarily with the most personal of personal choices, including whom one may marry, or to treat minorities unequally without adequate justification. Someday, the American public may come to see plural marriage as sufficiently similar to same-sex marriage to warrant the same legal treatment.

In what follows, 'plural marriage' covers all possible multi-person marital arrangements among consenting adults, including polygyny, incestuous intimate relationships between (or among) consenting adults, close but platonic friendships, caregiving networks, and so on. The term refers to other marriage-like legal statuses as well, whatever they are called, like domestic partnerships or civil unions. In this chapter, I limit my discussion to 'polyamory', defined as 'consensual openly-conducted, multi-partner relationships in which both men and women have negotiated access to additional partners outside of the traditional committed couple'.[4] I put polyamory, as opposed to polygyny,

---

[1] Professor, Political Science Department, California Polytechnic State University, San Luis Obispo, denotter@calpoly.edu. I would like to thank Lata Murti, Martin Battle, Joe Fischel, Sonu Bedi, Steve Macedo, Maxine Eichner, William Galston, Andrew Sabl, Emma Scott, and Matt Moore for their help with this chapter. In particular, I am grateful to Elizabeth Brake for her thoughtful comments.

[2] See, eg, RC Den Otter, *In Defense of Plural Marriage* (CUP 2015); S Bedi, *Beyond Race, Sex, and Sexual Orientation: Legal Equality Without Identity* (CUP 2013) 208–47; EF Emens, 'Monogamy's Law: Compulsory Monogamy and Polyamorous Existence' (2004) 29 New York University Review of Law and Social Change 277; S Levinson, 'The Meaning of Marriage: Thinking About Polygamy' (2005) 42 San Diego Law Review 1049; LH Tribe, *American Constitutional Law* (2nd edn, Foundation Press 1988); J Turley, 'The Loadstone Rock: The Role of Harm in the Criminalization of Plural Unions' (2015) 64 Emory Law Journal 1905.

[3] While I focus on the American context and refer to American constitutional law and doctrine, my perfectionist arguments can be easily transposed to any liberal state that promotes certain intrinsic goods.

[4] E Sheff, *The Polyamorists Next Door: Inside Multi-Partner Relationships and Families* (Rowman & Littlefield 2013) 1.

front and centre, to avoid an obvious objection: that plural marriage is tainted by too much gender inequality for the state to accord it legal status. Polyamorists value such equality, as much as the most progressive monogamists do, and polyamorists are more dedicated to living up to the principle than many opposite-sex couples, especially those that adhere to traditional gender norms. While the concern about how women are treated in plural relationships is important, it should not overshadow the possibility that polyamory, as a way of living, can be superior to monogamous alternatives, at least for some persons in some circumstances.

Those political philosophers and theorists who defend plural intimate relationships eschew perfectionism.[5] As an alternative, they invoke some kind of anti-perfectionist, or neutral, liberalism. Such liberalism can be defined as liberalism which holds that state actions should not be justified by beliefs about what is most worthwhile in human life; such neutrality can be defended as a means of insuring the equal treatment of persons with different conceptions of the good. The flaw in the standard anti-perfectionist liberal approach, which avoids comparative judgments between monogamy and polyamory, is that those who employ it appear to be conceding the superiority of monogamous marriage. In my view, they should not be so willing to make this concession. Polyamory could have distinct benefits, like more sex, more love, more caring, more compersion (less jealousy), more honesty, and more self-reflection.

The reluctance of those who support polyamorous marriage to work its potential merits into the conversation about the future meaning of marriage in the United States, enables states to continue putting their imprimatur on monogamous intimate relationships.[6] This state of affairs remains problematic for anyone who endorses some kind of liberal neutrality, is sympathetic to political liberalism, or cares about everyone's having a wider range of marital options to select from in the name of marital choice or equality. However, in what follows, I do not resort to neutrality or the value of personal choice as an exercise of one's autonomous capacities. Rather, in the spirit of John Stuart Mill, I explain why a liberal society must help individuals to find a mode of living that is best for them. As such, the state must allow polyamorists to marry one another. My defence of the legal recognition of plural marriage is perfectionist in that it is predicated upon more than a thin theory of the good. I highlight the distinct benefits that polyamory can generate. As I shall argue, constitutionally requiring states to allow polyamorists to marry one another is not only about respecting their marital choice or treating them equally; it also involves giving polyamorists, and anyone else who wants to experiment, the opportunity to experience these distinct benefits.

This chapter will be divided into the following sections. First, I describe the place of liberal principles, like freedom and equality, in American constitutional doctrine and

---

[5] '[A]ll perfectionists defend an account of the good that is objective in the sense that it identifies states of affairs, activities, and/or relationships as good in themselves and not good in virtue of the fact that they are desired or enjoyed by human beings.' S Wall, 'Perfectionism in Moral and Political Philosophy', *The Stanford Encyclopedia of Philosophy* (Winter edn, 2012) <http://plato.stanford.edu/entries/perfectionism-moral/> accessed 26 May 2016.

[6] There is a long tradition of philosophical thinking about marriage and the family. See E Brake, 'Marriage and Domestic Partnership', *The Stanford Encyclopedia of Philosophy* (Fall edn, 2012) <http://plato.stanford.edu/archives/fall2012/entries/marriage/> accessed 27 May 2016.

their role in the recent debate over same-sex marriage, to set the stage for the perfectionist argument on behalf of polyamory that follows. Second, I introduce the general idea of Millian experiments in living to explain why liberal states should protect and promote unconventional lives. Third, I give an overview of polyamory. Fourth, I elaborate on some of the distinct benefits of an ideal polyamorous relationship and ponder what could happen if the state were to cease favouring two-person marriages. I conclude with some thoughts on how a society could benefit from marital experimentation.

II. Marital Choice

A. American constitutional law

Almost by definition, in the United States these days, to be a progressive is to be in favour of the legal recognition of same-sex marriage and the enactment of a federal law that would end all forms of private discrimination on the basis of sexual orientation or identity. Heterosexism, the idea that opposite-sex attractions are the norm and therefore are better than the alternatives, is much less socially acceptable than it used to be in the United States. When it comes to gays' and lesbians' right to marry, the burden of proof now falls on the state to justify unequal legal treatment.[7] Even under the most deferential standard of review, rational basis, the state must have at least a legitimate interest in restricting the legal status of marriage to couples.[8] Before 2015, United States Supreme Court decisions such as *Romer, Lawrence*, and *Windsor* put into some doubt the extent to which states may classify on the basis of sexual orientation.[9] *Obergefell* resolved any lingering uncertainty about whether states which limited marriage to opposite-sex couples were acting unconstitutionally.[10]

Not that long ago, the claim that the United States Constitution compels states to allow a man to marry another man or a woman to marry another woman only might have appeared in a hypothetical fact pattern on a law professor's exam. The debate over same-sex marriage raises the deeper question of why a state may continue to deny marriage licences to plural marriage enthusiasts, including polyamorists, who meet all of the other valid eligibility requirements.[11] While public opinion in the United States has changed rapidly with respect to same-sex marriage, mononormativity, as a rationale for laws that privilege monogamy, has not yet received the same scrutiny.[12] Just like the

---

[7] In American equal protection doctrine, in some instances, this requirement means that a heightened standard of review is triggered. The state then has the burden of proof in trying to rebut the presumptive unconstitutionality of the legislative classification in question. A court is supposed to invalidate it unless the state can prove that (a) its interest is sufficiently strong and (b) the legislative means, which the state employed, clearly serves the state's interest.

[8] Under rational basis standard of review, judges are supposed to view the legislation in question with a strong presumption of its constitutionality. However, if the person(s) challenging the law can rebut the presumption, by showing that either the state lacks a legitimate interest or the legislation is not rationally related to the legislative goal, then the court can invalidate the law.

[9] See *Romer v Evans* 517 US 620 (1996); *Lawrence v Texas* 539 US 558 (2003); *US v Windsor* 570 US _ (2013).

[10] *Obergefell v Hodges* 576 US _ (2015).

[11] Sonu Bedi coined the term 'plural marriage enthusiasts'. See Bedi (n 2) 244.

[12] The term 'mononormativity' is found in D Anapol, *Polyamory in the Twenty-First Century: Love and Intimacy with Multiple Partners* (Rowman & Littlefield 2010) 169.

reasons that American lawmakers used for years to discriminate against gays and lesbians, the reasons that lawmakers utilize to prevent polyamorists from forming their own marriages may turn out to be unsatisfactory. An increasing number of political philosophers and theorists doubt that a marriage must be limited to two, and only two, persons.[13]

B. Liberalism

The creation of an equal legal status for polyamorists would signal to the public that multiplicity may be an optimal marital arrangement in some circumstances. Elsewhere, I have advanced the view that the US Constitution requires states to end all forms of marital discrimination.[14] The most straightforward, recognizably liberal way of arguing for the legal recognition of same-sex marriage is to prove that a liberal state committed to some form of neutrality between conceptions of the good cannot endorse and promote a conception of the good that incorporates only opposite-sex marriage. For similar reasons, one could be sceptical that a numerical restriction on marriage is consistent with the principles of freedom and equality that Americans subscribe to in the abstract. Neutrality may entail that the state should disestablish marriage and either replace it with a more inclusive legal status or privatize it.[15] The point is that legal recognition of only one kind of marriage raises concerns about how the state is using its authority to favour some ways of life over others. Few human beings would be indifferent to how they arrange their intimate relationships or family lives, and the existence of a legal status of marriage, or something like it, is bound to affect them.[16]

The debate in America over whether states may limit marriage to opposite-sex couples nicely illustrates the implicit liberal commitments of American constitutional doctrine to equal treatment.[17] Early on, progressive law professors called attention to the unjustifiable inequality that characterized laws that would only allow a man to marry a woman long before judges started to take such a point of view seriously.[18] Likewise, the first philosophers who defended a right to same-sex marriage underscored the importance of avoiding discriminatory treatment.[19] Constitutionally and philosophically, the

---

[13] See, eg, C Calhoun, 'Who's Afraid of Polygamy? Lessons for Same-Sex Marriage from the History of Polygamy' (2005) 42 San Diego Law Review 42 1023; AF March, 'Is There a Right to Polygamy? Marriage, Equality and Subsidizing Families in Liberal Public Justification' (2011) 8 Journal of Moral Philosophy 244; T Metz, 'The Liberal Case for Disestablishing Marriage' (2007) 6 Contemporary Political Theory 196; T Metz, *Untying the Knot: Marriage, the State, and the Case for their Divorce* (Princeton UP 2010); E Brake, 'Minimal Marriage: What Political Liberalism Implies for Marriage Law' (2010) 120 Ethics 302; E Brake, *Minimizing Marriage: Marriage, Morality, and the Law* (OUP 2012).

[14] See Den Otter (n 2); RC Den Otter, 'Three May Not be a Crowd: The Case for a Constitutional Right to Plural Marriage' (2015) 64 Emory Law Journal 1977.

[15] For an early argument defending the abolition of civil marriage, see C Card, 'Against Marriage and Motherhood' (1996) 11 Hypatia 1. For more on neutrality and the family, see M Lister's chapter.

[16] MC Nussbaum, 'A Right to Marry?' (2010) 98 California Law Review 668.

[17] Liberalism takes many forms and manifests itself in many ways. See S Wall, 'Introduction' in S Wall (ed), *The Cambridge Companion to Liberalism* (CUP 2015).

[18] See, eg, A Koppelman, *The Gay Rights Question in Contemporary American Law* (University of Chicago Press 2002); E Gerstman, *Same-Sex Marriage and the Constitution* (CUP 2004).

[19] See, eg, R Wedgwood, 'The Fundamental Argument for Same-Sex Marriage' (1999) 7 Journal of Political Philosophy 225.

problem with unequal treatment can be broken into two related concerns: (a) same-sex couples that would like to marry but are not allowed to do so are denied the tangible benefits that typically accompany the legal status of being married, and (b) state endorsement of only opposite-sex marriage announces to the public that same-sex relationships are inferior.[20]

C. Anti-polygamist critiques

1. Allegations of harm

A number of those who advocated for the legal recognition of same-sex marriage still do not think that the state must do away with numerical restrictions. Almost always, critics of polygamy have polygyny in their sights. They then argue against legal recognition of such relationships—even in the absence of any signs of coercion, fraud, or undue influence that might negate consent—by identifying the harms that are supposed to be associated with polygyny.[21] In particular, they try to corroborate the allegation that polygyny directly harms women in such relationships.[22]

This general approach has at least three noticeable flaws. First, anti-polygamists only have polygyny in mind, and not polyamory. Even if the harms that they allege appear in all polygynous relationships, those harms may be absent in polyamorous ones, which have different dynamics, moral commitments, and shared goals. At most, both polygyny and polyamory may have (but will not always have) the same structure, for instance, when one man 'marries' two women, forming what is known as a 'vee'.[23] To establish that polygyny is harmful, then, is not to prove that polyamorous relationships are harmful. Second, critics target certain kinds of polygynist relationships, namely ones associated with the awful crimes of Warren Jeffs and Winston Blackmore, while neglecting those that are more progressive, like that of Kody Brown on TLC's popular reality television programme, *Sister Wives*.[24] In doing so, they single out polygynous Fundamentalist Latter-Day Saint (FLDS) cult-like, insular communities.[25] Stephen Macedo calls such situations 'problem cases'.[26] While FLDS receive almost all of the media attention, other sorts of polygynous practices take place in the United States as well.[27] None of these communities have been studied in sufficient depth to generalize so much from them.

---

[20] On both these points, see Nussbaum, 'A Right to Marry?' (n 16) 669.

[21] See, eg, MI Strassberg, 'Scrutinizing Polygamy: Utah's *Brown v. Buhman* and British Columbia's *Reference Re: Section 293*' (2015) 64 Emory Law Journal 1815; S Macedo, *Just Married: Same-Sex Couples, Monogamy, and the Future of Marriage* (Princeton UP 2015).

[22] When they extend their critique to polyamory, though, they admit how it differs 'in important ways' from polygyny. See, eg, MI Strassberg, 'The Challenge of Post-Modern Polygamy: Considering Polyamory' (2003) 31 Capital University Law Review 440.

[23] In a 'vee', the two women are not romantically involved with each other but both of them are so involved with the male. One could respond that this arrangement is not a genuine form of polyamory.

[24] J Bennion, *Polygamy in Primetime: Media, Gender, and Politics in Mormon Fundamentalism* (Brandeis UP 2012).

[25] See LG Beaman, 'Introduction' in G Calder and LG Beaman (eds), *Polygamy's Rights and Wrongs: Perspectives on Harm, Family, and Law* (University of British Columbia Press 2014) 6.

[26] Macedo (n 21) 159.

[27] See, eg, PL Kilbride, *Plural Marriage for Our Times: A Reinvented Option?* (Bergin & Garvey 1994) 93–104.

Equally importantly, FLDS groups are diverse, and some of their members are more progressive than others.[28] There have been independent FLDS polygamists for a long time as well.[29] Third, and related to the second point, the data that critics rest their case on is not beyond dispute, especially when they rely on biased samples. If it turns out that they are more wrong than they are right about evidence that purportedly demonstrates the causal relationship between the structure of a polygamous relationship and serious harm, then their position will be even weaker.

2. Allegations of gender inequality

Granted, if such harms are not only serious but widespread, then that could be *pro tanto* justification for not according them legal status and maybe even keeping such relationships illegal. Along similar lines, some feminist critics maintain that plural marriage manifests the most extreme kind of gender inequality.[30] A woman in a polygynous relationship who is not harmed physically or emotionally by being in such an arrangement still could suffer from the adverse consequences of being treated so unequally, like being deprived of the opportunity to have the kind of life in which she is not simply a wife or a mother but can work outside of the home, pursue other ends, and share equally in joint decisions regarding finances, children, and so on.

This general line of critique also suffers from some non-trivial difficulties. First, irrespective of what is called the hub-and-wheel structure of a typical polygynous marriage, many real monogamous marriages exhibit different kinds and degrees of gender inequality. One cannot gesture to the structure of a plural relationship and then conveniently overlook its interpersonal dynamics when polyamory is being discussed. After all, the two-person structure of a traditional opposite-sex marriage never has and never will guarantee that women will be treated as equals. At most, its structure may be more conducive to such treatment. Mill once famously referred to the family as a 'school of despotism'.[31] And he was not referring to plural families. Second, in making comparative judgments between monogamy and polygamy, critics frequently compare ideal monogamist relationships to the worst kinds of polygamist ones. By the same token, it would be unfair to discredit monogamy by using Ray Rice or John Edwards' marriages, involving abuse and infidelity, as if either of them was the norm.[32] It is not terribly difficult to find egregiously bad examples of dysfunctional monogamous marriages. Nobody, though, believes that the couple should be automatically divorced or should not have been permitted to marry in the first place. Third, and most importantly, a polyamorous union is considerably more likely to be egalitarian than

---

[28] Bennion (n 24) 287.   [29] MK Zeitzen, *Polygamy: A Cross-Cultural Analysis* (Berg 2008) 94.

[30] See, eg, SM Okin, 'Introduction' in SM Okin (ed), *Is Multiculturalism Bad for Women?* (Princeton UP 1999) 14.

[31] JS Mill, 'The Subjection of Women' in S Collini (ed), *On Liberty and Other Writings* (CUP 1989) 160.

[32] Ray Rice was a running back for the Baltimore Ravens. In 2014, he was arrested and charged with aggravated assault for knocking unconscious his then fiancée, Janay Palmer, in an elevator. The couple later married. John Edwards was John Kerry's running mate in 2004 and ran as a candidate in the Democratic presidential primary in 2008. During the primary, while his wife, Elizabeth Edwards, was undergoing treatment for breast cancer, Edwards had an affair with one of his campaign photographers, Rielle Hunter, who subsequently had his child. Elizabeth Edwards died of breast cancer in 2010.

a traditional, opposite-sex marriage that incorporates a gendered division of labour and other patriarchal behaviours. Few critics would respond that a promise of at least minimal equality in their daily interactions ought to become a legal requirement for a couple to obtain a marriage licence.[33] Just because someone has been able to establish that one kind of plural marriage is morally suspect does not mean that she has come close to proving that all kinds are equally troubling as long as relevant differences between or among them exist.

Because polyamory differs from polygyny in important respects, an argument that supports the conclusion that the state should not recognize or support the latter does not necessarily pertain to the former. As noted, if one is committed to some version of liberal neutrality, then defending the state's privileging monogamy will not be easy; that is, if there is no state interest in privileging monogamy over polyamory in marriage, equal treatment seems to be required. In the rest of this chapter, my plan is not to dwell on the unfairness of this unequal marital treatment in which all prospective monogamous marriages are assumed to be harmless or equal enough but plural ones, due to the risks that are supposed to come with them, never cross the threshold of acceptability. Notwithstanding the temptation for anti-polygamists to treat polyamory as if it did not differ from polygyny, polyamory does not raise the kinds of worries that traditionally have been voiced against polygyny, such as the abuse of women and the denial of their equality.

If anti-polygamists cease reducing all plural relationships to the worst types of patriarchal polygyny, then they, and those who are on the fence, might become receptive to the possible merits of the view that states should not be able to continue to discriminate against polyamorists and that polyamorists deserve legal protection against certain kinds of discrimination. Polyamorist relationships exhibit considerable variance.[34] Yet, apart from their not being able to have the kind of marriage that they may desire, polyamorists have no legal protection against job and housing discrimination and loss of children in custody battles.[35]

True, in the non-ideal case, one could object that the worst case of polyamory would be worse than the worst case of monogamy. Imagine that a man pressures his financially dependent wife to allow a new woman into their marriage and neither woman desires this situation but acquiesces to it due to concerns about financial security. If this turns out to be the likely scenario, then the resulting marital situation would be much worse than a merely unhappy marriage would have been.

There are two responses, which, together, may not rebut this objection but take some of the sting out of it. First, advocates for the inclusion of plural relationships in the legal definition of marriage or a marriage-like status maintain that the state should regulate them. In fact, without legalization or legal recognition, the problem of women being exploited, without viable exit options, is likely to be worse than it would be if women had a legal right, for example, to a fair share of the community property that

---

[33] They still could be committed to fostering such equality in less intrusive ways, such as ensuring that exit is a financially viable option through community property and spousal-support laws.

[34] See C Klesse, 'Polyamory and Its "Others": Contesting the Terms of Non-Monogamy' (2006) 9 Sexualities 565.

[35] Emens, 'Monogamy's Law' (n 2) 277–359.

accumulated during the relationship. There is no good reason why the state could not provide rules with respect to entry and exit, as it already does for monogamous marriage, to minimize the likelihood that women are being taken advantage of or financially pressured to stay in an unhealthy or even dangerous relationship. By falsely assuming that plural marriage would not be regulated, anti-polygamists have set up a straw person. Without knowing what kinds of regulation of plural marriage would be in place, the above objection does not have much force. There also is no good reason why the consent of the first wife could not be legally required for a second (or a third) woman to enter the marriage. And if the anti-polygamist replies that this safeguard still is insufficient, the counter is that as long as her consent is as informed as it could be in non-ideal conditions of the real world, then she should be allowed to do what she wants to do, especially when she can subsequently leave the marriage without losing her standard of living or her custody and/or visitation rights with regard to her children.[36]

Second, any of the aforementioned problems can (and do) occur in a monogamous relationship as well. This is yet another example of anti-polygamists' giving monogamy the benefit of the doubt by presupposing that it is less morally problematic than it really is. After all, coercion, exploitation, and abuse characterize some, and perhaps many, monogamous relationships as well. If there is anything that everyone should have learned from feminist critiques of the nuclear family long ago, it is that the family should not be romanticized.

Nevertheless, when it comes to monogamous marriage, the state does not vet the person that anyone plans to marry or assess the quality of the reasoning that leads to the decision, despite the possibility or even likelihood of adverse consequences. It is not hard to conceive of how one party, in a monogamous relationship, can use the power that she or he has in the relationship, financial or otherwise, to manipulate the other person to get what he or she wants or to dominate the decision-making process.[37] When this sort of behaviour occurs, nobody concludes that the state should cease supporting monogamous marriage.

Once one looks beyond their form, almost any polyamorist relationship would be considerably better, in terms of gender equality, than the monogamous marriage of those who identify with any conservative religious group. The primary causes of gender inequality in any personal relationship are likely to stem from the convictions that the participants endorse and the behaviours that follow from them. An evangelical Christian or Orthodox Jewish family, which incorporates a traditional, gendered division of labour into its daily life, would not score high on any equality scale. Additionally, a family like this one would do poorly if the basis of comparison were a polyamorous family that lives up to its ideal of gender equality.

---

[36] See DJ Klein, 'Plural Marriage and Community Property Law' (2010) 41 Golden Gate University Law Review 33, 48–53; AD Davis, 'Regulating Polygamy: Intimacy, Default Rules, and Bargaining for Equality' (2010) 110 Columbia Law Review 1955; M Goldfeder, *Legalizing Plural Marriage: The Next Frontier in Family Law* (Brandeis UP 2016).

[37] For insight into the specifics of the problem of gender inequality in intimate relationships, see E Brake, 'Equality and Non-Hierarchy in Marriage: What Do Feminists Really Want?' in E Brake (ed), *After Marriage: Rethinking Marital Relationships* (OUP 2016) 100.

Even if monogamous marriages work better for most people most of the time, it does not follow that they work better for all people all of the time. Not only do people pursue different ends under conditions of moral pluralism, they can (and do) love and care for each other differently. For the most part, in liberal societies, how they decide to do so is left up to them. Under American family law, couples have considerable freedom to tailor their marriage to their particular ends. A person who is convinced of the intrinsic superiority of monogamy still would have to concede that the members of a polyamorist moresome could be happy or flourish, even if it is inferior, unless she wilfully ignores contrary evidence. Even the most radical of gender egalitarians would have to draw a line somewhere when it comes to what a liberal state may permissibly do in trying to ensure equality between men and woman in intimate relationships.

The moment that one can no longer object to polyamorist marriage by citing purported state interests in preventing other crimes, ensuring gender equality, and promoting child welfare, it is much harder to articulate why the state may continue to make such an option unavailable, particularly to polyamorists. Even the most vocal anti-polygamists do not claim that polyamorist relationships carry such risks. Put in American constitutional terminology, none of the state's interests in disallowing polyamorists to marry one another appear to be either compelling or important, which is what a heightened standard of review would require under fundamental rights or equal protection analysis. The dubiousness of the countervailing state interests against permitting polyamorists to marry one another, coupled with a strong presumption in favour of marital choice and equal treatment, establishes more than the plausibility of the view that states must give polyamorists the same rights that married American couples already enjoy.

III. Millian Experiments in Living

A. Overview

In this section, I make three value-pluralist assumptions that most liberals, despite their differences, can concur with or at least accept as plausible: (a) there is not a single good life but many kinds of good lives; (b) there are many individual goods that cannot be reduced to a single good; and (c) individuals can arrange and re-arrange these goods in multiple ways as they form, revise, and pursue their respective conceptions of the good.[38] Liberal societies are committed to allowing a wide variety of lives, and such societies also concern themselves with protecting the liberty to choose one's own life plan from the start. Grounded in the state's role in actively promoting (not just allowing) such pluralistic values, my perfectionist argument differs importantly from neutralist, and standard choice or equal treatment, arguments for plural marriage. As noted, some proponents of the right to plural marriage in the American context treat marital choice as a trump card. In American constitutional theory, the defence of the importance of personal choice in many areas, ranging from reproduction to freedom of religion, is rarely consequentialist or perfectionist. The neutralist strategy of avoidance

[38] T Hurka, *The Best Things in Life* (OUP 2011) 6.

of the prospective merits of polyamory has a hidden cost: it reinforces the marital norm of monogamy that everyone is supposed to follow by obscuring how the state's privileging certain intimate relationships marginalizes others that may be equally or more worthwhile. But there is an alternative perfectionist argument for the legal recognition of plural marriages: it would be a step towards removing its social stigma and inducing more people more often to try unconventional marriages as part of deciding what kind of life best suits them.

In putting forth a broadly perfectionist liberal case for plural marriage, inspired by Mill's famous idea of experiments in living, I underscore the benefits of marital nonconformity both to the individual and the society in which she lives. For Mill, the best kind of human life contains both the exercise of autonomy and happiness. I emphasize the perfectionist side of Mill by maintaining that the state should recognize plural marriages even when they do not maximize happiness, however it might be defined. Polyamorous relationships are in themselves valuable; they can have goods that differ both in quality and quantity from those that exist in monogamous ones. For polyamorists, legal recognition of their relationships could provide them with an invaluable opportunity to have better lives, due to the presence of goods like more sex, more love, more caring, more honesty, and more compersion (less jealousy). Moreover, the willingness on the part of lawmakers and/or judges to let polyamorists experiment with various marital arrangements in the absence of legal disadvantages could prompt monogamists to be more reflective about their own intimate relationships. While it is impossible to predict exactly how beneficial the legal recognition of polyamorous marriage could be, it is reasonable to keep in mind that the possible risks should not be overstated and the possible rewards should not be understated.

B. Mill's 'On Liberty'

Polyamory was not what Mill had in mind when he proposed his famous idea of experiments in living.[39] Nonetheless, he identifies a problem that has not disappeared from contemporary liberal democracies: the most serious threat to individuality is found in the tyranny of public opinion, which pressures people to conform to widely accepted social norms, thereby depriving them of the goods that could come from a different way of living. In Mill's eyes, unconventional ways of life must be not only tolerated but supported as well because they yield examples of what could be better, making social progress possible.[40] While most Americans think of themselves as open to difference, they have a history of fearing the other, making rash judgments, and condemning what is unfamiliar to them. This phenomenon can provide the impetus for legislative majorities to enact prejudices into laws that interfere with the most important aspects of some persons' lives.

For Mill, public opinion can effectively suppress dissent and difference.[41] In the end, he seems to be mostly pessimistic about the prospects of successfully resisting the

---

[39] Mill expresses ambivalence towards Mormon polygyny. Mill, 'On Liberty' (n 31) 91–92.
[40] ibid 57.
[41] A Zakaras, *Individuality and Mass Democracy: Mill, Emerson, and the Burdens of Citizenship* (OUP 2009) 127.

forces of conformity. Majorities tend to marginalize minorities because of their difference, and nobody wants to be treated in that way if she can avoid it, making assimilation more attractive than it otherwise would be. Mill is fully aware that most people care too much about what others think. They are afraid to be different and risk the disapproval of their families, friends, colleagues, and neighbours. In his eyes, some hope persists, insofar as some people remain willing to engage in acts of nonconformity.[42] To follow custom uncritically is to fail to fulfil the ethical duty of developing one's own identity. The unwillingness or inability to do so is a tragedy because it also has the cumulative effect of impeding human development. As Mill sees it, the nature of a good human life cannot be known a priori; it has to be determined by experience. The 'experiments' part of 'experiments in living' is Mill's suggestion that the kinds of lives most people take for granted are not necessarily the best. Essentially, a life is not best because it is 'the best in itself, but because it is his own mode [of living]'.[43] Above all, people have to do it themselves.[44]

If that were not the case, then it would be less morally troubling for the state to coerce or nudge people to conform to what it takes to be the best human life. In stark contrast, Mill highlights just how personal this experimentation must be. The implication is not that a particular conception of the good that meets this test is necessarily better than every conceivable alternative. Instead, persons are supposed to formulate their own hypotheses, test them against the world, and adjust their behaviours accordingly.[45] In this respect, one's life always is a work in progress. As hard as it might be to do, people must entertain the possibility that they may have to alter the way in which they think and behave to find the best possible life for themselves *qua* individuals.

IV. Polyamory

A. Overview

In the preceding section, my purpose was not to channel Mill to discern what he might have thought about polyamory or prospective contemporary examples of experiments in living more generally. Instead, I put forth some preliminary thoughts on how Americans could think about unconventional marriages without the dubious assumption that monogamy is the only legitimate kind of marriage. The willingness of states to give marriage licences to polyamorists not only would end a particularly invidious kind of marital discrimination, it also could stimulate a discussion about the unique benefits of polyamory for polyamorists and everyone else. Their possible benefits cannot be summarily dismissed without first giving individuals a chance to engage in such marital experiments.

The exact number of polyamorous people, defined loosely as people in open sexual and emotional non-monogamy, is unknown.[46] Nobody could know in advance how many people would be interested in trying a version of it under circumstances that are

---

[42] Mill, 'On Liberty' (n 31) 67.   [43] ibid.
[44] J Skorupski, *Why Read Mill Today?* (Routledge 2007) 25.
[45] ES Anderson, 'John Stuart Mill and Experiments in Living' (1991) 102 Ethics 26.
[46] Sheff (n 4) 2–3.

less hostile to unconventional intimate relationships. For the time being, individuals who describe themselves as polyamorous tend to be white, straight, well-educated, and socioeconomically privileged.[47] There are fewer bisexual men than bisexual women in polyamorous relationships.[48] In a polyamorous arrangement, almost any combination of numbers, gender, and sexual orientation could come about.

Because many Americans continue to associate polyamory with promiscuity and frequently are under the impression that unconventional sexual behaviour is not something to be proud of, they too often confuse polyamory with something else.[49] Polyamory is not synonymous with swinging, group sex, or an open marriage. It is inherently more complex than monogamy.[50] For this reason, as a relationship form, it is likely to be prone to certain interpersonal challenges involving coordination, collective action, and communication.[51] Furthermore, it may be very difficult to find the time and energy to establish a close emotional connection with more than one intimate partner. As Oscar Wilde might have put it, the trouble with a multi-person marriage is that it might take up too many evenings. For some or even most persons, then, monogamy is preferable. According to one scholar, 'Polyamory is not for everyone. Complex, time-consuming, and potentially fraught with emotional booby traps, polyamory is tremendously rewarding for some people and a complete disaster for others.'[52]

My aim is not to romanticize polyamorous relationships. After all, a real plural marriage, predicated upon polyamory, could be ruined by the same kinds of dysfunctional behaviour that would ruin a monogamous marriage: selfishness, dishonesty, insensitivity, stupidity, laziness, manipulation, jealousy, exploitation, and physical and emotional abuse. The point is that one should not assume that such behaviour would be more prevalent in a polyamorous marriage, unless its structure predisposes it to such problems.[53] The most recent empirical evidence indicates the contrary for actual polyamorous relationships.[54] Obviously, not all of them will embody the ideal, yet the same could be said about all monogamous ones as well. The appropriate basis of comparison, then, is either ideal versus ideal or non-ideal versus non-ideal.

For polyamorists, the multi-person structure of a plural relationship is to be celebrated. Without pre-fabricated notions about what intimacy is supposed to be like, adults have the freedom to let their feelings for others take them wherever they lead.[55] In their view, it is natural to want to spend quality time with more than one partner, just as it is natural to want to have multiple friends, and some people will be more sexually and/or emotionally satisfied in plural marriages, with everyone being subject to the principle of full disclosure. That does not guarantee, of course, that polyamorists

---

[47] E Sheff and C Hammers, 'The Privilege of Perversities: Race, Class, and Education Among Polyamorists and Kinksters' (2011) 2 Sexuality and Psychology 198.

[48] E Sheff, 'Polyamorous Families, Same-Sex Marriage, and the Slippery Slope' (2011) 40 Journal of Contemporary Ethnography 487, 497.

[49] M Warner, *The Trouble with Normal: Sex, Politics, and the Ethics of Queer Life* (Harvard UP 1999) 21.

[50] Anapol (n 12) 65.   [51] Sheff (n 4) 69.   [52] ibid ix.

[53] For such an argument, see T Brooks, 'The Problem with Polygamy' (2009) 37 Philosophical Topics 109.

[54] Sheff, 'Polyamorous Families' (n 48) 487–520.

[55] Anapol (n 12) 4–5. On the moral significance of intimacy in relationships, see D Jeske's chapter, 'Moral and Legal Obligations to Support "Family"'.

will not lie to their intimate partners or treat them poorly. Yet there is no reason to think that polyamorist relationships are more likely to be dishonest or morally flawed in other respects than their monogamous counterparts. As I shall explain shortly, an ideal polyamorous relationship may compare favourably to an ideal monogamous one. The implication of the presence of high risks and high rewards in the former is not that informed, consenting adults should be denied the option of a plural marriage. What is implicit in anti-polyamorists' critique is that persons, especially women, ought to be risk-averse. Apart from how paternalistic this rationale is, the option of no-fault divorce, coupled with other aforementioned legal rights, would mean that they could end their experiment in living if it was not functioning as they had anticipated.

Certainly no one thinks that monogamists must become polyamorous if they prefer monogamy, even when their monogamous relationship is not working. Oddly enough, the reverse seems to be true for anti-polyamorists: everyone should be monogamist if they want the highest form of intimacy. For them, one size fits all, and polyamorists are simply mistaken about the type of marital relationship that is best for them. A given polyamorous relationship could be worse than a given monogamous relationship, but it is not inherently worse, as far too many people assume. Those who draw the line at monogamy, quite frankly, do not want others to take seriously non-monogamous alternatives because they fear others may adopt those forms someday, which amounts to saying that competent adults are better kept in ignorance for their own good. From a polyamorist perspective, if a person loves more than one person or loves a person who already loves someone else, then they should not be dissuaded from seeing what happens provided that all of them are transparent with one another about the absence of sexual and emotional exclusivity.

V. Individual Benefits

A. Overview

In this section, I begin to spell out the distinct benefits that polyamorist relationships could generate for those who partake in them. For the most part, the literature offers practical advice for those who are practising polyamory or thinking about doing so.[56] Although that focus is understandable due to the continuing marginalization of polyamorists and the dangers of not being sufficiently secretive about how they live, the need for more conceptual, normative, and empirical analysis of polyamory could not be more pressing. My belief is that perfectionist arguments, which so far have received little attention, deserve a closer look. Not only could a perfectionist argument stand on its own, but it also could supplement legal arguments designed to call into question the constitutionality of laws that limit marriage to couples, opposite-sex or same-sex.

A perfectionist argument could do so by undermining the anti-polygamist claim that all plural relationships are intrinsically worse. As I explained earlier, while requiring states to give marriage licences to polyamorist threesomes, quads, moresomes, and

---

[56] See, eg, R Nearing, *Loving More: The Polyfidelity Primer* (PEP Publishing 1992). For another list of polyamorous values, see Emens, 'Monogamy's Law' (n 2).

so on, can more easily be defended on constitutional grounds of marital choice and equal treatment, it is imperative to formulate perfectionist arguments as well. Their formulation would enable more Americans to appreciate why the denial of the right to marry more than one person at the same time also prevents some, and perhaps, many individuals, from having a better life. At minimum, those who maintain that polyamorists should be able to marry and form a plural marriage must not concede that such a marriage is necessarily inferior. Like everyone else, polyamorists have lives to lead and the quality of their lives count as much as any other life. As American society becomes more tolerant of sexual minorities, polyamorists no longer will have to be so reticent about how their intimate lives can be better than those of monogamists.

B. More sex, more love, and more caring

Here, I sketch the types of goods that a polyamorous relationship makes possible, fully aware that whether any such relationship, as a matter of fact, has such goods is contingent upon its particulars. I have proceeded in this manner because as part of their defence of monogamy, anti-polygamists either claim that monogamy is intrinsically superior or they publicize the harms associated with the worst manifestations of polygamy. I now want to stop playing defence and begin playing offence. One of the themes in the small literature on polyamory is that it is unlikely that one partner will meet all of the other partner's needs and that one (or both) of them may want (and seek) different types of intimacy with others.[57] Normally, social pressures move would-be polyamorists to adopt norms that do not suit them, may frustrate them, and may make them miserable. For example, they may want to have much closer friendships with others or spend more time with them engaging in different activities. They may want to have sex with other people as well, because they prefer variety, but know that an open marriage is out of the question with their current partner. As a result, they may have an affair. Such behaviour is not only wrong because of the deception that it entails, but its disclosure is likely to bring about trauma for third parties inasmuch as they are emotionally devastated by the betrayal and never will be able to trust their partner (and perhaps anyone else) again.

From a polyamorist standpoint, people who find themselves in such situations do not have to lie to their partners or remain miserable. Even couples that have healthy relationships are unlikely to be compatible in all ways. Thus, no one can meet all of her partner's needs, even under the best of conditions. Unless the participants can communicate effectively, are willing to consider accommodating what the other wants, and can be transparent, marital troubles are inescapable. In other words, the two-person structure of an intimate relationship or marriage may cause or contribute to serious problems that a multi-person structure could mitigate.

Take the importance of sexual experimentation for some individuals. When it comes to sex acts, people, unless they are inclined to a religious view, do not immediately think of reproduction. And even when they do, most of them do not simply reduce

---

[57] T Taormino, *Opening Up: A Guide to Creating and Sustaining Open Relationships* (Cleis Press Inc 2008) xix.

sex to a physical act that may result in the fertilization of an egg.[58] Most sexually active opposite-sex couples are not sexually active just to reproduce. The widespread use of various kinds of contraception also substantiates this claim. Pleasure is more likely to come to mind, but to conceive of every sex act as merely a bodily pleasure, is to miss how it can enhance the quality of an intimate relationship by making the participants emotionally closer than they already are. In some instances, physical intimacy can assist them in becoming more open and more understanding of their respective flaws.

Polyamorists have more of this good because a polyamorist does not have to go outside of his or her committed relationship to seek sexual variety or experimentation or feel guilty about having such desires. Whereas some polyamorist relationships are closed to outsiders, others may be open, depending upon the rules that the participants have agreed upon. They may be able to have (safe) sex with others outside of the primary relationship with the expectation that each of them has informed the others about the prospective behaviour and has received their permission to proceed. What should be noted is that for the vast majority of monogamous couples, sex with someone else is adultery, and normally carries with it the risk of serious harms. In essence, to promise sexual exclusivity is to agree to a vow of celibacy with respect to anyone else for the duration of the intimate relationship or marriage. While most Americans believe that they can keep that promise, it is evident that many of them cannot.

Whereas sexual gratification may strike many readers as a lesser human good, due to its association with hedonism, love usually occupies a higher place in the hierarchy of human goods. There are various kinds of love, like *philia, storge, agape,* and *eros*.[59] Each kind of love can manifest itself in multiple ways depending upon the specifics of the circumstances and none of them is obviously lesser than the others. On the assumption that pluralism about love is defensible, and different people will value different kinds of love differently, it stands to reason that they will love differently as well. Without argument, then, I will proceed on the assumption that a human life would be better, other things equal, if it had more *eros*, although there may be exceptions to this general rule. The vast majority of people want to love and be loved.

As such, love can be seen as a good that is conducive to human flourishing. Mere sexual attraction may be overrated, and it is certainly possible that a marriage—involving close but platonic friends—could have the kind of love, understood as a deep concern for each other's well-being, that most romantically involved couples may never have because they are distracted by physical appearance. Sex also could complement love, as noted, bringing two people emotionally closer together. The advantage of polyamory is that love is not limited to one partner but rather can extend to everyone in the network and each person can relate to (and love) the others in different ways. Indeed, a parent is fully capable of loving more than one child, a child more than one parent, a sibling more than one sibling, and so on. Yet most Americans cannot see how this line of reasoning could possibly apply to, say, a polyamorist triad, notwithstanding what polyamorists have to say about their own intimate lives.

---

[58] Even the New Natural Law thinkers do not do so. See, eg, S Girgis, RT Anderson, and RP George, *What is Marriage? Man and Woman: A Defense* (Encounter Books 2012) 51.
[59] See R de Sousa, *Love: A Very Short Introduction* (OUP 2015) 1–4.

In practice, it may be hard to separate love from care, and normally, one who loves another wants to care for that person, which is not to suggest that one has to love someone to care for him or her. In the growing literature on care in the last few years, liberal feminists, like Elizabeth Brake and Tamara Metz, have connected its value to marriage and marriage-like relationships.[60] While I am not going to attempt to rehearse their respective arguments, it does not require much imagination to grasp just how important the giving and receiving of different kinds of care is to most persons, even when they are adults without a disability. The kind of care that they need or want may differ, but people can care for others, included their loved ones, in multiple ways. Other things equal, family members, and not-paid strangers, should care for one another, which is one of the advantages of extended families more generally. When polyamorists have more partners to care for and to care for them, as the need arises, they have the opportunity to have more of this good in their lives.

C. Less jealousy, more compersion

For a polyamorist triad, having a shared intimate life with more sex, more love, and more care is not only desirable but probably more likely to be fulfilling, despite the extra work that it demands. Perhaps the most challenging aspect of being part of such a group is dealing with the feelings that most people would experience if their significant other were physically intimate with someone else, even without deception. A monogamist might see this sort of reaction as not only understandable but completely justified insofar as a healthy relationship must be premised upon sexual and emotional exclusivity. Polyamorists unapologetically reject this claim and also stress the importance of overcoming jealousy.[61] As they see it, jealousy is not an expression of love for another but a vice, manifesting the selfishness that prevents an intimate relationship from reaching its full potential. 'Compersion', which is taking joy in one's partner(s)' pleasure or happiness with someone else, captures a more appropriate reaction.[62]

Granted, it is one thing for a man, who is married, to go golfing with his buddies and quite another for him to have sex with another woman, as far as most Americans are concerned. A polyamorist would insist that upon closer examination, these two situations are not as dissimilar as they initially appear to be. For most adults, to be jealous of a friend's friends is to be immature. After all, having multiple friends is not only normal but usually desirable when each of them has admirable qualities. By contrast, having multiple husbands or wives strikes most Americans as not being in the same ballpark. Polyamorists challenge the double standard by asking why the latter remains socially unacceptable provided that the arrangement is fully transparent. For them, the cure for jealousy involves introspection. A person who feels this way ought to investigate why he or she feels the way that he or she does. When someone examines the deeper reasons why he or she experiences jealousy, that individual can begin to overcome certain

---

[60] See Metz (n 13); Brake (n 13).
[61] See, eg, Anapol (n 12) 105–26; D Easton and JW Hardy, *The Ethical Slut: A Practical Guide to Polyamory, Open Relationships, and Other Adventures* (2nd edn, Celestial Arts 2009), 108–30; Taormino (n 57) 153–81.
[62] Anapol (n 12) 22.

fears and insecurities, like not being everything to her partner, feeling inadequate, and being abandoned.

D. Radical honesty

The importance of compersion to polyamorists ties into their commitment to radical honesty, understood as complete openness about everything with their partners. One does not have to look very far in philosophical writings, or even admire Kant, to notice the place of honesty in a good human life. As Seana Shiffrin observes, nobody has direct access to others' minds.[63] Consequently, to a greater or lesser extent, everyone has to trust their intimate partner by believing that what he or she is telling them can be taken at face value.

That is not to say that risks are absent. The more intimate one is with another, the more likely it is that one or both of the participants have the knowledge they need to take advantage of the other's vulnerability.[64] It is hard to imagine that any human relationship could be healthy if it were fundamentally dishonest. Few people want to live in a fool's paradise yet that does not entail that being fully honest with themselves or others comes easily. No doubt, at times, the temptation to manipulate others to reach the outcomes that that they prefer will be too great for them to resist. While intimate relationships can be ruined by such behaviour, they also are particularly well-suited for the kind of interactions that compel people to be less self-involved. Any kind of successful intimate relationship, including close friendships, calls for a firm commitment not only not to lie but also not to mislead on the part of all of those who are part of it. Dishonesty, and the lack of trustworthiness that is produced by it, is the enemy of genuine intimacy.

Above all, then, polyamorists begin by attempting to put their commitment to radical honesty into practice.[65] The meaning of the 'radical' part is that they must learn to be fully transparent to their intimate partners, and not only when it is convenient or comfortable. All of the participants in a polyamorist relationship are expected to listen carefully and articulate what they prefer in group discussions and decision making. Effective communication only occurs when a person does not filter how she feels and what she thinks because she is convinced that her partner(s) could not possibly understand where she is coming from. Likewise, when she suspends judgment and just listens, the odds go up that the members of the group will not make unwarranted assumptions about what she is thinking or feeling.[66]

The ability and willingness to understand another's perspective is only a part of the long and often painful process of developing the interpersonal skills that enable people to have more fulfilling lives. For some polyamorists, their intimate relationships tend to be better simply by virtue of the fact that they are more honest.[67] The only way in which anyone can really get to know anyone else is for each partner to feel comfortable enough to be willing to share the most personal of personal information. This

---

[63] See SV Shiffrin, *Speech Matters: On Lying, Morality, and the Law* (Princeton UP 2014).
[64] See O O'Neill, 'Between Consenting Adults' (1985) 14 Philosophy and Public Affairs 252.
[65] Easton and Hardy (n 61) 21.   [66] Sheff (n 4) 91.
[67] Sheff, 'Polyamorous Families' (n 48) 503.

willingness not to hold back is what makes greater intimacy possible. The vast majority of intimate relationships probably are not as honest as they could be. Partners do not share everything with each other and will rationalize their dishonesty and conceal the kind of person that they really are because they fear that their partner will no longer love them or stay with them when they learn the unpleasant truth.

For polyamorists, though, this all-too-human way of being in a monogamous relationship can be avoided. Expectations of sexual and emotional monogamy, especially unrealistic ones, cause misery by almost forcing people to be more dishonest than they otherwise would be and precipitating feelings of guilt and shame. The polyamorist commitment to radical honesty is intended to avoid this foreseeable situation. If a woman wants to have other sexual partners, then she does not have to hide that fact from her partner(s), creating a more authentic relationship in which neither person has to deceive the other about what he or she really wants, thereby minimizing hypocrisy. Anyone who claims that he or she is always completely honest in every situation is probably lying or is not self-aware. It is far too easy to slip into the habit of exaggerating, not disclosing when disclosing is called for, or telling so-called white lies in an attempt to present oneself in the best possible light and avoid antagonizing others. Not respecting others' autonomy by not being as honest as one could be with them and to rationalize it is bad enough. But for a person to lie to themselves about what they are really like and be in denial about the need to change is a tragedy.

To their credit, polyamorists do not shy away from human faults. If anything, they are considerably more cognizant of the kinds of problems that tend to appear in real intimate relationships. At the same time, perhaps counterintuitively, polyamorists have an optimistic vision of what human beings, at their best, are capable of. These interpersonal challenges, which come with any multi-person relationship, may make polyamory less appealing to most people. What needs to remembered is that such a relationship presents an opportunity for the participants to have an even better intimate relationship if they are able to come to terms with their fears, insecurities, and unhealthy desire to control others.

VI. Social Benefits and Costs

A. Benefits

Apart from any distinct benefits for individuals, like those spelled out above, the existence of a variety of plural marriages could induce more Americans to move beyond marital norms, some of which may no longer be suitable at a given historical moment. Polyamorists customize their relationship.[68] In doing so, like ideal same-sex couples, they may provide an example for others to emulate. Even if the interpersonal dynamics of a given multi-person relationship are more difficult to manage, which polyamorists do not deny, more people would reflect more deeply about what they want from their intimate relationships. As a consequence, monogamists, who do not believe that polyamory is for them, still might make more informed marital decisions and improve

---

[68] Sheff (n 4) 21, 61.

the quality of their intimate relationships. Following Mill, real examples of unconventional ways of life have no substitutes. If more polyamorists were out, then monogamists could learn something from their unconventional lives and take a hard look at their own intimate relationships. At the very least, monogamists might come to have less unrealistic expectations about themselves and their partners.

B. Costs

Polyamorists continue to suffer from the tyranny of public opinion, the anxiety that comes with the possibility of being outed, the fear of being ostracized by others due to their difference, and the risk that their lifestyle could be used against them. Society can emotionally blackmail those who are unconventional by telling them that they are 'morally deficient, psychologically disturbed, and going against nature'.[69] These same kinds of accusations were once levelled, without a hint of irony, against gays and lesbians. Most Americans internalize a norm of monogamy early in life and conclude that the only choice is monogamy or infidelity if they are going to have a romantic relationship.[70] Nobody should have to lead a secret life, when she is not doing anything wrong, and constantly have to worry about being exposed.

On the surface, a polyamorous intimate relationship differs from a monogamous one, and that fact can distract Americans from what really matters when it comes to assessing marital quality: how the participants treat one another. As Elizabeth Brake puts it, 'One of the most common responses to minimal marriage is that polyamorous groupings or care networks are too different in some important respect from dyadic caring relationships to deserve equal recognition in law.'[71] The point that I have been trying to develop in this chapter is that whereas they are different in some respects, the difference can be advantageous. Like a monogamous marriage, the success of any given polyamorous marriage, however it is measured, will be a function of its specifics.[72] In the wake of legal recognition of plural intimate relationships, the measure of a successful marriage could become less about its form—whether it is two-person or opposite sex—and more about its quality. Just because two marriages have the same structure (or number of persons) hardly means that they resemble each other. Any plural marriage would not be the sum of its parts. Rather, only a more holistic understanding would account for how three or more polyamorists love and care for one another and how their daily interactions create an intimate relationship that for them is better than being monogamous or staying single.

VII. Conclusion

In ceasing to reinforce the common belief that monogamy is intrinsically superior, the state would level the playing field by making it more acceptable for competent adults

---

[69] Easton and Hardy (n 61) 9.   [70] Anapol (n 12) x.
[71] E Brake, 'Recognizing Care: The Case for Friendship and Polyamory' (2014) 1 Syracuse Law and Civic Engagement Journal < http://slace.syr.edu/issue-1-2013-14-on-equality/> accessed 27 May 2016. See also E Brake's chapter 'Paid and Unpaid Care: Marriage, Equality, and Domestic Workers'.
[72] See J Mahoney, 'Liberalism and the Polygamy Question' (2008) 23 Social Philosophy Today 161.

to experiment with different kinds of marital arrangements, including polyamory. It is impossible to know in advance exactly what such a marital regime, without legal disadvantages and social stigmas for polyamorists, would be like, but it stands to reason that all persons could gain something from the increased visibility of marital experiments, even when they do not directly partake in them, to improve their intimate lives.

My aim in this chapter has not been to displace conventional anti-perfectionist arguments in support of plural marriage. Those kinds of arguments continue to be more promising in American law inasmuch as they are more firmly rooted in the implicit liberal commitments of American constitutional doctrine. Alternatively, I have given a distinct perfectionist argument by elaborating on why polyamory, because of its distinct goods, can be a superior marital arrangement for at least some people in some circumstances. In doing so, I may have established the plausibility of shifting the burden of proof to anti-polygamists to justify their belief that the legal definition of marriage should exclude polyamory. Americans still live in a society in which social pressures and legal incentives push them in a monogamous direction.[73] In a new marital regime that leaves enough room for polyamorous marriages, some people might not choose monogamy if other options were available.

We must cease viewing polyamorists and their way of life through preconceptions that have little basis in reality. This much, I believe, anyone can state with confidence: the claim that monogamous marriage is intrinsically superior calls for a much better defence than anti-polygamists have given it so far—particularly when polyamory, as opposed to polygyny, serves as the basis of comparison—and that they stop comparing ideal monogamous relationships to non-ideal polygamous ones. When we refuse to take plural alternatives seriously, we are less likely to consider how marital experimentation could have positive effects in some people's lives, including our own. The very notion of polyamory unsettles many people because it directly challenges the widely-held belief that it is always morally inappropriate to have more than one intimate partner simultaneously. The state can play an instrumental role in ending discrimination against polyamorists, who otherwise meet all of the other valid eligibility requirements for marriage licences, by treating their intimate relationships as if they were the legal equivalent of a two-person marriage. When all is said and done, the state should not be enacting laws that contribute to depriving polyamorists of the kind of life that they believe, and may be, best for them.

---

[73] Emens, 'Monogamy's Law' (n 2) 284.

5
Cohabitants, Choice, and the Public Interest

Robert Leckey[1]

I. Introduction

Through the narrow entry of property disputes between former cohabitants, this chapter aims to clarify thinking on issues crucial to philosophical examination of family law. It refracts big questions—such as what people who live together should owe one another and the balance between choice and protection—through a lens of legal attention to institutional matters such as legal sources and the respective roles of judges and legislatures. A major theme will be the limits on judicial law reform in the face of social change, both in substantive scope and in the capacity to acknowledge the state's interest in intimate relationships. The chapter aims to relativize the focus on choice so prominent in academic and policy discussions of cohabitation, and to highlight the character of family law, entwined with the general private law of property and obligations, as a regulatory system.

Is the question of cohabiting conjugal couples relative to married spouses far from the scholarly cutting edge? Many researchers in the social sciences have moved on, notably to partners 'living apart together' and to the uncoupled or single. A number of philosophers now focus on appropriate recognition of enduring non-conjugal unions and of polyamorous configurations.[2] Still, the staid, cohabiting couple—in the majority of cases, a union of different sexes—generates a substantial portion of the family disputes before lawyers and judges. The vicissitudes of academic fashion should not relegate it to the past when in many jurisdictions it remains an ongoing 'problem'. Nor, for that matter, should critical scholars neglect the processes that frame cohabitation as such, embedding instrumental assumptions about law's vocation and relationship with social life.

This chapter refers to a range of Anglo-Canadian legal sources, drawing out their underlying policies and justifications. It takes the past and present legal ordering of the family as a repository of values and aims relevant to contemporary debate, perhaps invoking Dworkin's interpretive idea of law as integrity.[3] Readers will quickly

---

[1] Dean and Samuel Gale Professor, Faculty of Law, McGill University. This research was supported by the Social Sciences and Humanities Research Council. I acknowledge the excellent research assistance provided by Jacob Schweda. For comments on earlier versions, I am grateful to Nicholas Bala, Benjamin Berger, Susan Boyd, Elizabeth Brake, Lucinda Ferguson, Andrew Hayward, Daniel Monk, Mary Jane Mossman, Nick Piska, Carol Rogerson, Jacob Schweda, and Lionel Smith. Earlier drafts benefited from the feedback of audiences at the volume's workshop; at the Fourth Worldwide Congress of The World Society of Mixed Jurisdiction Jurists, McGill University; at the workshop Comparative Unjust Enrichment, Gault Nature Reserve, Mont St-Hilaire, Quebec; and at the Durham Law School.

[2] See RC Den Otter's and E Brake's chapters.

[3] R Dworkin, *Law's Empire* (Belknap Press 1986).

grasp that the chapter occupies an intermediate zone. Consequently, it courts the risk of disappointing both those who, ready to fly higher, would press further philosophical reflections on autonomy, commitment, love, and the state, and those who, closer to the ground of a national legal system, would multiply the doctrinal details and burrow into the latest case law. The hope is that the chapter nevertheless elucidates readers' thinking on how family law addresses the cohabitation question and many others.

The first section presents four judgments in which English and Canadian judges respond to cohabitation by adapting the common law. Consistent with the logic of property law, the judges purport to give effect to parties' intentions via fact-based rulings. Arguably, though, they allocate assets in the light of the partners' lived relationship, consistent with a logic of family law. In contrast, the second section sketches the unapologetic override of spouses' intentions when judges apply enactments that regulate marriage and its breakdown. Beyond individuals' intentions, such law rests on state interests in economically interdependent relationships, which are not limited to marriage. Raising institutional questions, the third section exposes assumptions that underlie critical and approving views of judicial recognition of cohabitation. Together, these sections highlight the limits of judicial responses to social change in the form of cohabitation. The final sections offer alternative lenses to the fact-based focus on individual parties' intentions. The fourth section relativizes choice in marriage, which is often a justification for that institution's obligations and for abstaining from regulating cohabitants. The fifth section proposes the lens of default rules, which shifts the focus from individuals' intentions and choices to family law as a system of regulation. The overall message may be that considering the cohabitation question, and by implication others in family law, requires integrating attention to choice and intention, to public interests in intimate relationships, to protection and compensation, and to family law as regulation.

II. Addressing Cohabitation Under the Common Law

A significant shift is underway to recognize cohabitants by modifying the general private law. This section studies four judgments that do so as embodying judges' institutional limits in responding to social change. The first subsection introduces two leading cases from Canada regarding unjust enrichment and two from England and Wales addressing beneficial shares in the family home. The second subsection highlights the judges' depictions—at times contrived—of their initiatives as giving effect to the parties' intentions, rather than imposing a vision of justice in cohabitation relationships. The third exposes the judges' stated reasons for adapting the law, ranging from responding to cohabitation's specificity to picking up parliamentary slack.

A. Four adaptive efforts

The four judgments recognize that cohabitation generates risks of economic exploitation and they aim to loosen evidentiary requirements when an economically weaker partner claims a share of wealth, at least in some circumstances. Subsequent trial judges have given effect to this aim to varying degrees. Reading the judgments together brings into view the judges' effort to reconcile their activity with a logic of property law or the law of obligations. Nevertheless, clustering them risks eliding differences. For instance, the Canadian cases, applicable whatever the form of accumulated wealth, are arguably bolder and more transformative than the English cases. The latter apply directly only to cohabitants who are owner-occupiers and have joint legal ownership.[4]

The Canadian cases develop the law of unjust enrichment. Unjust enrichment is a judge-made doctrine that reverses a transfer where, without good reason, a person impoverishes themself by enriching another. Over decades, Canadian litigants and judges have used it to palliate the economic fallout of unmarried cohabitation. Building on its earlier cases,[5] the Supreme Court of Canada in *Peter v Beblow* allowed a claim in unjust enrichment arising from domestic labour and improvements to property.[6] The Court upheld a remedial constructive trust—a proprietary stake for the plaintiff in property legally owned by the defendant. The judgment eased claims by presuming a correlation between a claimant's impoverishment and the defendant's enrichment and that a transfer in the form of unpaid household labour is unjustified. The judges rejected the ideas that it was immoral to view household labour through the lens of unjust enrichment and that 'love' justified an unremunerated transfer.

In *Kerr v Baranow*,[7] the Supreme Court of Canada injected the spirit of the constructive trust into its approach to monetary orders reversing unjust enrichment. Instead of improving an identifiable property, the claimant had contributed indirectly to the success of her partner's business by running the household. The Court held that, in circumstances of a 'joint family venture' where the parties' efforts had led to wealth accumulation, the doctrine of unjust enrichment could prevent a party from exiting the relationship with a 'disproportionate share of the jointly earned assets'.[8] The award far exceeded the replacement cost of the claimant's housekeeping and childcare services.

The English cases quantified shares in a jointly owned home where the parties had not declared their respective beneficial interests. *Stack v Dowden* ruled that where cohabitants jointly held a domestic property, with no declaration of trust specifying the beneficial title, there was a prima facie case that both the legal and the beneficial interests were joint and equal.[9] Where one contends that equity should not follow the law in this way, the court should examine the parties' whole course of conduct in relation to the property. Factors other than the parties' respective financial contributions might indicate 'their true intentions'.[10] That judgment's meaning proved contentious,[11] leading the judges to revisit the issues in *Jones v Kernott*.[12] In the latter, the judges repeated that the primary search was for the parties' actual intent, objectively deducible from their words and conduct. Only where the parties had intended to depart from a beneficial joint tenancy, but a search for actual or inferred intentions failed to indicate their

---

[4] A Hayward, 'Finding a Home for "Family Property"' in N Gravells (ed), *Landmark Cases in Land Law* (Hart 2013) 236.
[5] Eg, *Pettkus v Becker* [1980] 2 SCR 834.   [6] [1993] 1 SCR 980.
[7] 2011 SCC 10, [2011] 1 SCR 269.   [8] ibid [60] (Cromwell J).
[9] [2007] UKHL 17, [2007] 2 AC 432.   [10] ibid [69] (Baroness Hale).
[11] On matters 'undecided or unclear', see Law Commission, *Cohabitation: The Financial Consequences of Relationship Breakdown* (2007) [2.13].
[12] [2011] UKSC 53, [2012] 1 AC 776.

respective shares, could the court review the parties' course of dealings to reach a 'fair' outcome.

B. Respecting parties' intentions?

Judicial technique in the cohabitation cases telegraphs that the judges perceive a need to follow principles of property law rather than of family law. Instead of openly allocating assets to render just the consequences of the parties' shared life, the judges purport to observe a constraint against imposing obligations to which the debtors have not consented *ex ante* or at least foreseen.[13] Arguably, though, the cases go beyond realizing the parties' individual choices and subjective intentions or expectations. The upshot is that the judgments are oblique, at times opaque. However many judgments in other fields fail the highest standards of transparency, these cases manifest tension between the impulse to redress perceived injustices arising from an increasingly widespread, socially acceptable form of family life, and the idea of choice and consent as the triggers for transfers under the law of property and obligations.

The judges show ambivalence about the idea of devising special principles for cohabitants within private law. The Canadian judges reject the notion of distinguishing commercial and family categories of unjust enrichment. McLachlin J insists in *Peter* that the same principles of unjust enrichment govern all cases, but she affirms that 'the courts should exercise flexibility and common sense when applying equitable principles to family law issues with due sensitivity to the special circumstances that can arise in such cases'.[14] In the House of Lords, the ambivalence about an approach specific to family life manifests itself in the opposition between Baroness Hale's attention to 'the domestic consumer context'[15] and Lord Neuberger's 'spirited defence' of the context-neutral resulting trust.[16]

The judges perform adjudicative acrobatics around the question of whether they are giving effect to the parties' actual mutual intentions or imposing what they conclude to be fair. They signal that their mission is to search out and vindicate the parties' actual intentions. Such an approach should respect parties' autonomy and lead to a range of outcomes respectful of the pluralism of cohabitation relationships. Yet the judges preserve room to impose an outcome that they determine to be fair. Whether she intended it or not, ambivalence about the judge's margin of manoeuvre marks Baroness Hale's piling together of terms as if interchangeable. In *Stack*, she refers to the search 'to ascertain the parties' shared intentions, actual, inferred or imputed',[17] whereas those terms have conceptual (and arguably important practical) distinctions.[18] Moreover, although

---

[13] J Miles, 'Property Law v Family Law: Resolving the Problems of Family Property' (2003) 23 Legal Studies 624; see also R Probert, 'Family Law and Property Law: Competing Spheres in the Regulation of the Family Home' in A Hudson (ed), *New Perspectives on Property Law, Human Rights and the Home* (Cavendish Publishing 2004).
[14] *Peter* (n 6) 997 (McLachlin J); see similarly *Kerr* (n 7) [33]–[34] (Cromwell J).
[15] *Stack* (n 9) [58] (Baroness Hale).
[16] KJ Gray and SF Gray, *Elements of Land Law* (5th edn, OUP 2009) 851 [7.2.27].
[17] *Stack* (n 9) [60] (Baroness Hale).
[18] The chief distinction between inferred and imputed intention may lie in the degree of judicial candour: imputed intention makes plain its 'direct confrontation with the property paradigm'. N Piska,

Stack insists that '[e]ach case will turn on its own facts',[19] Baroness Hale prejudges the multi-factored inquiry. She states that 'it will be very unusual' for joint legal owners to have intended their beneficial interests to differ from their legal interests.[20] Such a statement purports to direct trial judges to make such circumstances rare, although subsequent case law may indicate 'a trend towards "exceptional" cases'.[21] Cromwell J undermines his insistence on the parties' wishes by saying that the parties' expressed or inferred 'actual intentions' receive 'considerable weight'.[22] If the parties' intentions were truly the heart of the inquiry, they would be determinative, not a factor on the metaphorical scales.

Finally, the judges sometimes indicate that it is not any expectation of the parties that is relevant, but only that which is 'legitimate'[23] or 'reasonable'.[24] These adjectives shift the judicial task from excavating whatever the parties had worked out for themselves. They overlay the search for actual expectations with an evaluative gloss, inviting the judge to exclude some expectations as illegitimate or unreasonable. The enterprise's normative dimension is plain in the idea that it would be 'difficult (and, perhaps, absurd)' to suppose that a court would infer an unfair shared or common intention.[25] Signs that the judges are not, after all, giving effect to parties' intentions invite scrutiny of their stated reasons for adjusting the law.

C. Reasons for judicial law reform

The judges indicate several reasons as prompting them to modify the private law for cohabitants. Some bear on justice for the parties in a private sense; others acknowledge broader, more public matters. Two related considerations focus on how the partners lived together. One justification for adjusting the private law is cohabitation's distinctiveness. The judges offer their—perhaps idealized—understanding of such relationships. The latter must be 'much closer and trusting' than commercial relationships.[26] Living together is 'an exercise in give and take'.[27] Cohabitants 'do not hold each other to account financially'[28]—except, of course, when the relationship unravels.

A second reason for adapting legal mechanisms comes from evidentiary concerns. Under the applicable doctrines, the claimant must ordinarily prove her contributions. The judges observe, and apparently take as unobjectionable, the frequent lack of detailed financial records within cohabitation.[29] Recordkeeping aside, a cohabitant may make contributions to which assigning a value is difficult, such as the intangible efforts 'of making a house a home'.[30]

'Constructive Trusts and Constructing Intention' in M Dixon (ed), *Modern Studies in Property Law* (Hart 2009) 222.

[19] *Stack* (n 9) [69] (Baroness Hale).   [20] ibid.   [21] Hayward, 'Finding a Home' (n 4) 243.
[22] *Kerr* (n 7) [94] (Cromwell J).   [23] *Peter* (n 6) 990 (McLachlin J).
[24] ibid 1014 (Cory J) (concurring as to the result).   [25] *Jones* (n 12) [66] (Lord Collins).
[26] *Peter* (n 6) 1013 (Cory J) (concurring as to the result).   [27] *Stack* (n 9) [3] (Lord Hope).
[28] *Jones* (n 12) [20] (Lord Walker and Baroness Hale).
[29] *Peter* (n 6) at 1014 (Cory J) (concurring as to the result); ibid at 1000 (McLachlin J); *Jones* (n 12) [20] (Lord Walker and Baroness Hale).
[30] *Peter* (n 6) at 1014 (Cory J) (concurring as to the result).

These reasons—a mix of the empirical and the normative—seem to do significant justificatory work. Cromwell J states that '[t]he goal is for the law of unjust enrichment to attach just consequences to the way the parties have lived their lives'.³¹ He does not explicate, however, how the existing law fails to do so. Absent a substantive justification for the good of informal, long-term relationships of trust and mutual care, one judicial response to these relationships' recurring features might be to enjoin people to get married, to keep their receipts, or to avoid investing in family life at the expense of a career.

Other reasons go further towards justifying judicial law reform, although they, too, rest on unexposed premises. One reason reaching beyond the justice for individual parties relates to cohabitations' impact on the justice system. In *Stack*, Lord Hope indicates that the rise in house prices and the increasing numbers of cohabitants have made their property disputes 'a matter of general public interest'.³² Taking him at his word, his avowed focus on the need for a law that is 'simple' and 'accessible' suggests the problem to be primarily that too many disputes burden the justice system.³³ With the problem framed as one of access to justice, rather than of substantive justice, any clear solution that facilitated negotiation and settlement might be an improvement.

By invoking matrimonial law, the Canadian judges reach beyond the pursuit of justice for individual parties. In *Peter*, McLachlin J answers arguments against allowing domestic labour to generate a claim in unjust enrichment. She notes that, without damage to society, federal divorce legislation and provincial matrimonial-property acts have recognized and compensated such labour for some time.³⁴ In *Kerr*, Cromwell J connects the notion of a joint family venture to the reform of matrimonial-property legislation in the late 1970s and early 1980s.³⁵ Despite the different legal positions of married and unmarried partners, the implication is that the compensatory impulse underlying those legislative reforms prompts judges to adapt the common law for cohabitants. Significantly, in the Canadian context, the judicial development of ancillary relief for divorcing spouses rests on articulated public interests, including human-rights values, and reflects sensitivity to systemic gender discrimination.³⁶ These interests thus enter the Canadian common law of unjust enrichment.

In the English cases, Parliament's inertia provides a further reason for adapting the law. For Baroness Hale in *Stack*, 'the evolution of the law of property to take account of changing social and economic circumstances will have to come from the courts rather than Parliament'.³⁷ For Lord Collins in *Jones*, Parliament's inaction, 'despite the Law Commission Report', obliged judges to 'adapt[] old principles to new situations'.³⁸ This 'strong sense'³⁹ that the absence of statutory reform is galvanizing the judicially creative use of equity coexists uneasily with the insistence that the judgments merely give

---

³¹ *Kerr* (n 7) [88] (Cromwell J).   ³² *Stack* (n 9) [2] (Lord Hope).   ³³ ibid [3] (Lord Hope).
³⁴ *Peter* (n 6) [994] (McLachlin J).   ³⁵ *Kerr* (n 7) [61] (Cromwell J).
³⁶ *Moge v Moge* [1992] 3 SCR 813; Alison Diduck and Helena Orton, 'Equality and Support for Spouses' (1994) 57 Modern Law Review 681; on English law in the era of the Human Rights Act, cf Alison Diduck, 'Ancillary Relief: Complicating the Search for Principle' (2011) 38 Journal of Law and Society 272.
³⁷ *Stack* (n 9) [46] (Baroness Hale).
³⁸ *Jones* (n 12) [57] (Lord Collins). See further ibid [35] [36] (Lord Walker and Baroness Hale); *Gow v Grant* [2012] UKSC 29 [45]–[56] (Baroness Hale) (concurring).
³⁹ A Hayward, 'Family Property and the Process of Familialisation of Property Law' (2012) 24 Child and Family Law Quarterly 284, 299.

effect to the parties' intentions. This chapter's third section will unpack assumptions underpinning the idea that cohabitation merits law reform and that courts are fit surrogates for parliamentary action. Before doing so, though, it will be helpful to identify the public interests justifying legislation that can override married spouses' expressed intentions.

III. An Avowed Public Interest in Adult Intimacy

Judges acknowledge robust public interests in the economic regulation of intimate partners, at least married ones. This section will suggest that marital status does not delimit those interests' field of application: at least some of them appear to apply to cohabitants. Countermanding reasons may justify operationalizing those interests in law differently as between married and unmarried spouses. Still, at first blush, the relevance of public interests in adult intimacy and economic interdependence to cohabitants poses a counterweight to the logic of property law's focus on individual intentions.

When looking to the judicial application of legislation that overrides married spouses' expressed wishes, *Hyman v Hyman* remains a starting point.[40] That dispute turned on whether a separation agreement, by which a wife undertook never to claim additional maintenance from her husband, precluded her from seeking permanent maintenance when the parties eventually divorced. The House of Lords held that spouses' agreement could not oust the court's statutory jurisdiction to award maintenance in connection with a divorce. A justification was that the husband's provision for the support of his wife was 'a public obligation',[41] made in the wife's interests and those of the third parties who might otherwise become responsible for her sustenance.[42] The effect was to limit freedom of contract without reference to the spouses' choices or shared expectations.

Judicial scrutiny of prenuptial agreements under statutes providing for ancillary relief on marriage breakdown offers another occasion where contractual expressions of intention may receive less than full effect.[43] On some views, contemporary courts have accorded such agreements too much weight and, indeed, have come close to making such agreements binding. The leading English and Canadian cases prompted robust dissents that caution against prenuptial agreements.[44] Even if judges in these jurisdictions will rarely disturb such an agreement, they acknowledge their jurisdiction to do so in appropriate cases, backed by public interests.

Preventing a former spouse from becoming a public charge is just one of the 'important wider social interests'[45] in financial provision on marriage breakdown. Herring offers a list that includes care for dependants, the symbolic value of childcare, children and other dependants, encouraging the stability of marriage, and gender equality.

---

[40] [1929] AC 601.   [41] ibid 628 (Lord Atkin).   [42] ibid 608 (Lord Hailsham).
[43] Eg, A Sanders, 'Nuptial Agreements, Comparative Law and the Notion of Contract' in A Popovici, L Smith and R Tremblay (eds), *Les intraduisibles en droit civil* (Thémis 2014); JM Scherpe (ed), *Marital Agreements and Private Autonomy in Comparative Perspective* (Hart 2012).
[44] *Radmacher v Granatino* [2010] UKSC 42, Baroness Hale, dissenting; *Hartshorne v Hartshorne* 2004 SCC 22, [2004] 1 SCR 550, Deschamps J, dissenting.
[45] J Herring, 'Why Financial Orders on Divorce Should Be Unfair' (2005) 19 International Journal of Law, Policy & the Family 218, 219.

Other scholars agree that the state's economic regulation of intimate relationships appropriately promotes the same or similar interests and public goods. Like Herring, Eichner emphasizes the imperative of ensuring that children and adults receive caretaking.[46] She further suggests that the goods implicated in regulating adult intimacy might include equal opportunity for all citizens, sex equality, and civic fellowship.[47] For Fineman, it is a demand of justice 'that society recognize that caretaking labor produces a good for the larger society', while equality demands such labour's valuation, compensation, and accommodation.[48] The general idea is that the state benefits from the stability and caregiving produced when individuals invest in long-term relationships.

These social interests or public goods may help to justify the legal system's override of expressed intentions. They may also help to justify measures aimed at fostering the flourishing of long-term conjugal relationships, such as mechanisms palliating the fallout when such relationships end. Admittedly, connecting such social interests to the economic regulation of divorce is controversial. On some views, redressing social inequalities through the private law of the family overburdens interpersonal obligations.[49] Linking the state's interest in social reproduction and care with obligations enforced by the private law of the family may collude in a neo-liberal project of privatization.[50] Doing so may ally with a particular, and contestable, conception of law's role as regulating families in the service of the market, voracious for stable and productive workers. For Fineman and many other feminists, valuing care does not entail privatizing responsibility within 'the family', a policy move that in many circumstances risks exacerbating women's inequality. Finally, Frantz and Dagan suggest that one need not evoke state or public interests to justify property distribution among spouses, even equal sharing more automatic than English law's discretion. They suggest that, from a perspective internal to the spouses, attractive conceptions of community, autonomy, and equality justify viewing marriage as an egalitarian liberal community.[51]

The point for present purposes is that public interests associated with the legal regulation of marriage are relevant beyond it.[52] Indeed, in her effort to give their due to 'both the private and public interests in intimate relationships', Eichner looks to economically interdependent relationships, whatever their legal status.[53] Concern about preventing someone from falling on state support may be especially strong in motivating reforms that 'recognize' cohabitants. In short, society might, for a number of

---

[46] M Eichner, 'Principles of the Law of Relationships among Adults' (2007) 41 Family Law Quarterly 433, 434.

[47] M Eichner, 'Marriage and the Elephant: The Liberal Democratic State's Regulation of Intimate Relationships between Adults' (2007) 30 Harvard Journal of Law & Gender 25, 48.

[48] MA Fineman, *The Autonomy Myth: A Theory of Dependency* (New Press 2004) 38.

[49] L Ferguson, 'Family, Social Inequalities, and the Persuasive Force of Interpersonal Obligation' (2008) 22 International Journal of Law, Policy & the Family 61.

[50] B Cossman, 'Family Feuds: Neo-Liberal and Neo-Conservative Visions of the Reprivatization Project' in B Cossman and J Fudge (eds), *Privatization, Law, and the Challenge to Feminism* (University of Toronto Press 2002).

[51] CJ Frantz and H Dagan, 'Properties of Marriage' (2004) 104 Columbia Law Review 75, 80.

[52] Marriage does not monopolize constraints on private consent or conduct in the name of public considerations. On sado-masochistic gay sex, cast as producing public or social harms, see *R v Brown* [1994] 1 AC 212.

[53] Eichner, 'Principles of the Law of Relationships among Adults' (n 46) 437.

state and public-regarding reasons, adapt its legal rules to the increasing prevalence of unmarried cohabitation and the upbringing of children within that familial form.[54]

Indeed, the patchwork regulation to which cohabitants are subject hints at legislative acknowledgement of such reasons. In many jurisdictions, social-security law assesses the cohabiting couple as an economic unit: it presumes economic interdependence, whether or not backed by an enforceable private obligation of maintenance. Some recognition may flow from fiscal concerns, on the assumption that economies of scale and pooled resources in a shared household justify reducing state benefits. A broader public interest comes into view where recognizing cohabitants imposes burdens on third parties. For instance, measures permitting a surviving cohabitant to take over a residential lease imply that society benefits from protecting the dwelling of individuals who have made a home together.

The contrast between judges' indirectness when adapting the common law for cohabitants and their direct acknowledgement of the state's interest in regulating intimacy in the marriage cases may stimulate different reactions. Fans of activist judges may infer a charge that the Canadian and English judges should have gone further and acknowledged that they override the parties' intentions in service of a conception of fairness. Others more alert to institutional constraints might approve the judicial initiatives while thinking that a strict duty of candour would hamper judges' ability to redress injustice. Others yet might take legislative inertia on cohabitation as a ground for chiding Parliament, while noting that—unlike modifications of the common law—statutes authorizing ancillary relief after marriage boast a democratic pedigree. Still others might question the prevailing common sense by which current law affecting cohabitants presents a 'policy problem' that requires intervention. This chapter's next section will identify issues underlying these differing reactions, deepening the appreciation of the interaction between philosophical questions of commitment, choice, and obligation and institutional dynamics such as the vocation of private law and the judicial role.

IV. Regulatory Approaches

The chapter's first section illustrated judicial adaptation of the common law in efforts to take account of the frequency of cohabitation and its characteristics, in a context where legislative reform is not forthcoming. Analogies with marital legislation in Canadian cases, and direct reference to Parliament's stasis in the cases from England and Wales, undercut the judgments' avowed concern with giving effect to parties' true intentions. If it is possible to analyse adult intimacy as a matter of moral or political philosophy, thinking about it as a matter of family law necessitates engagement with institutional questions such as the four that follow. The favoured answers may vary by jurisdiction, although scholars within a place will also disagree. When comparing philosophical interventions on family law from different places, then, it is worth being alert to potential differences on such institutional matters.

---

[54] ES Scott, 'Marriage, Cohabitation and Collective Responsibility for Dependency' [2004] University of Chicago Legal Forum 225.

First, what is the place of public-policy argumentation or efforts to advance social interests, beyond justice for parties to a dispute, in the judge-made common law generally? This chapter's preceding sections contrasted common law cases, in which the Canadian and English judges emphasized justice for the parties and respect for their intentions, with marriage cases in which legislation authorizes judges to override expressed intentions. It would be wrong, however, to evoke the much-criticized, but hardy, public–private distinction[55] and to associate public interests with legislation and private justice with the common law. A distinguished comparatist notes that '[d]ifferent legal systems may find it more or less appropriate for judges (or legislators, or regulators, or scholars) to have a normative impact on the content of private law rules'.[56] Private-law purists may object to references to public policy as an unprincipled objectionable 'instrumentalization' of the bilateral relation between plaintiff and defendant.[57] A less absolutist approach towards the relation between private law and public policy takes principle, utility, and policy as 'complementary strands in a single rope, or different dimensions of a single phenomenon'.[58] This chapter's sample prompts mention that conceptions of the judge's role are probably stricter in England than in common-law Canada, a matter of legal culture that likely influenced the cases.

Second, what is the role of family law? Specifically, why and how is it a 'problem' if there is a gap between social practice and the families addressed by family law? In what measures should family law address the empirical reality of family life versus express a normative ideal? How much should law reflect people's expectations as to what it is or should be? Scholars cast this question variously, exploring whether family law deals with 'reality' or concentrates on the 'ideal',[59] whether the aim is to 'support family life' as it unfolds or, through moral regulation, to promote or incentivize particular family structures.[60] A different formulation focuses on family law's 'channelling function', by which it 'creates (or more often) supports social institutions which are thought to serve desirable ends'.[61] The gender question highlights tension between empirical and normative approaches. Some will favour recognition of interdependency and support for it, especially when it leaves women economically vulnerable. Others may prefer rules positing or fostering women's independence and individualism.[62]

The perception of a society's heterogeneity and moral fragmentation may appear to favour regulating families as they are. Even ostensibly empirical approaches, however,

---

[55] For early classics, see FE Olsen, 'The Family and the Market: A Study of Ideology and Legal Reform' (1983) 96 Harvard Law Review 1497; K O'Donovan, *Sexual Divisions in Law* (Weidenfeld & Nicolson 1985).

[56] H Dagan, 'The Limited Autonomy of Private Law' (2008) 56 American Journal of Comparative Law 809, 810.

[57] EJ Weinrib, *The Idea of Private Law* (OUP 2012); but for a circumscribed openness to the possibility that public right and institutional considerations should lead to adjustments to individuals' private-law rights, see EJ Weinrib, 'Private Law and Public Right' (2011) 61 University of Toronto Law Journal 191, 210–11.

[58] S Waddams, *Dimensions of Private Law: Categories and Concepts in Anglo–American Legal Reasoning* (CUP 2003) 191.

[59] E Hasson, 'Setting a Standard or Reflecting Reality? The "Role" of Divorce Law, and the Case of the Family Law Act 1996' (2003) 17 International Journal of Law, Policy & the Family 338, 340.

[60] J Rodger, 'Family Policy or Moral Regulation?' (1995) 15 Critical Social Policy 5, 7.

[61] CE Schneider, 'The Channelling Function in Family Law' (1992) 20 Hofstra Law Review 495, 498.

[62] A Bottomley, 'From Mrs Burns to Mrs Oxley: Do Co-habiting Women (Still) Need Marriage Law?' (2006) 14 Feminist Legal Studies 181, 209.

cannot dispense with normative judgments. That is, even one eager to support efforts to 'reconcile' the law 'with the realities of people's lived experiences'[63] will have at least an implicit standard by which to exclude exploitative, non-consensual, or otherwise pathological situations.[64] Deciding 'how much to preserve and to rearrange' remains, then, a 'normative task'.[65]

Third, is it legitimate for judges to take up law reform where the legislature does not do so? The judgments considered above gesture towards an affirmative answer. On other views, judicial law reform lacks legitimacy. Reluctance to assume an overt law-making power might, then, reflect 'perceptions of the proper constitutional role of judges and of the need for legal continuity'.[66] For example, Mee criticizes the judges in the English cohabitation cases for their attempts 'to short-circuit the democratic process by, in effect, advancing a reform scheme of their own'.[67] This question is significant since one may incline to infer legally relevant commitment from cohabitants' shared life without seeing the drawing of that inference as rightfully a judicial task.

Fourth, how effectively can judges adapt private law, such as family law, to changing social practice? Analogizing with courts' reasons for deference to the legislature in public law, Hopkins highlights the 'practical limits on the courts' law-making role' that call for balancing creativity with restraint.[68] In his dissent in *Stack*, Lord Neuberger warns of the 'particular danger' when a court, rather than the legislature, effects change based on a particular case's facts, uninformed by both public consultation and 'input from the democratically elected legislature'.[69] If it is easy to observe the rise in cohabitation, interpreting demographic evidence, including cohabiting couples' 'intentions and emotions', may be harder.[70] Indeed, Probert observes that empirical researchers dispute the trends to present to policy-makers.[71] More concretely, it is worth signalling the limits of the devices by which judges might pick out cohabitants. While *Stack* addresses beneficial ownership of the home in the 'domestic-consumer context', arguably the domestic and commercial occupy a 'continuum',[72] with people buying homes for multiple reasons. The farm cases, prominent in a number of jurisdictions at family law's

---

[63] Hayward, 'Finding a Home for "Family Property"' (n 4) 251–52.
[64] cf R Leckey, *Contextual Subjects: Family, State, and Relational Theory* (University of Toronto Press 2008) 19–21.
[65] LC McClain, 'Love, Marriage, and the Baby Carriage: Revisiting the Channeling Function of Family Law' (2007) 28 Cardozo Law Review 2133, 2182; on this question of family law's role, see generally J Eekelaar's chapter.
[66] S Waddams, 'Private Right and Public Interest' in M Bryan (ed), *Private Law in Theory and Practice* (Routledge 2007) 17.
[67] J Mee, '*Burns v Burns*: The Villain of the Piece?' in S Gilmore, J Herring and R Probert (eds), *Landmark Cases in Family Law* (Hart 2011) 190.
[68] N Hopkins, 'The Relevance of Context in Property Law: A Case for Judicial Restraint?' (2011) 31 Legal Studies 175, 194–95.
[69] *Stack* (n 9) [102] (Lord Neuberger).
[70] R Probert, *The Changing Legal Regulation of Cohabitation: From Fornicators to Family, 1600–2010* (CUP 2012) 262.
[71] ibid 264.
[72] Hopkins, 'The Relevance of Context' (n 68) 192; see also A Hayward, 'The "Context" of Home: Cohabitation and Ownership Disputes in England and Wales' in M Diamond and TL Turnipseed (eds), *Community, Home, and Identity* (Ashgate 2012) 193–99.

intersection with the general law of property and obligations, crystallize the entwinement of people's work with where they live.[73]

These questions clarify analysis and debate and they illuminate the judiciary's institutional constraints. Each question may inspire nuanced responses. One may conclude, all things considered, that it is right for judges to adapt the private law in furtherance of social interests without ignoring the reasons for hesitation. Distinguishing the questions also brings into light the variety of positions running across them. It is possible to favour a family law that closely reflects current social practice without thinking that achieving that aim is a proper or feasible task for the judiciary. These questions provide a basis for situating the judges in the cases studied above—perhaps most easily Baroness Hale—and some of those judgments' critics. The chapter turns now from the judiciary's efforts to grapple with cohabitation, despite the perceived constraint of parties' intention, to alternative framings of the issues.

V. Moderating Appeals to Choice

This section offers a counterweight to the 'dominance of the language of "choice" in all aspects of marriage—from non-marriage, to cohabitation, ceremony, and rites'.[74] Emphasis on liberal ideas of autonomy and choice are manifest in the reluctance to impose relational obligations on adults who have not formally signalled their consent; the view of marriage as a chosen promise; and the notion of a consequential choice between options of marriage and cohabitation. Here the analysis yields no precise policy outcome on the cohabitation question, but it relativizes the place of choice as a reason against attributing to cohabitants legal effects that they have not 'chosen'.

A strand of philosophical literature focuses on marriage as promise and on the basic good of obligation taken on intentionally.[75] For a legal scholar, the view of marriage as a 'promise-based normative relationship'[76] leads to the idea that 'the kinds of obligation to each other that we embrace' help to constitute and characterize the relationship.[77] A related idea, drawing on Raz, is that differentiating marriage from cohabitation enhances people's autonomy by giving them a meaningful choice.[78]

The recognition of same-sex marriage dovetails with this emphasis on choice. Before same-sex marriage, gay and lesbians 'had no choice' to marry; now they ostensibly have one. Gay men and lesbians may have lost, however, the possibility of passing unrecognized. Legislation that confers the option of a formal civil status may trigger legislated forms of 'deprivative recognition', requiring same-sex cohabitants to declare themselves

---

[73] L Chambers, 'Women's Labour, Relationship Breakdown and Ownership of the Family Farm' (2010) 25 Canadian Journal of Law and Society 75.
[74] R Probert, J Miles, and P Mody, 'Introduction' in J Miles, P Mody and R Probert (eds), *Marriage Rites and Rights* (Hart 2015) 6.
[75] S FitzGibbon, 'Marriage and the Good of Obligation' (2002) 47 American Journal of Jurisprudence 41.
[76] W Chan, 'Cohabitation, Civil Partnership, Marriage and the Equal Sharing Principle' (2013) 33 Legal Studies 46, 53.
[77] ibid.
[78] S Lifshitz, 'Married against Their Will? Toward a Pluralist Regulation of Spousal Relationships' (2009) 66 Washington and Lee Law Review 1565, 1594.

for governmental purposes such as cumulating income and reducing benefits.[79] In any event, choice as the push for same-sex marriage indirectly bolsters the notion that cohabitants have 'chosen not to marry'. It makes it harder to see discrimination based on marital status in the treatment of unmarried different-sex couples.[80]

One might push back at the prominence of 'choice' by challenging the focus on formally expressed voluntary undertakings as the markers of legally significant relationships. Scheffler, a philosopher, opposes the idea that relationships are reducible to voluntary undertakings.[81] His work has inspired an account of cohabitation relationships as 'the source of legal duties, without the need for any assistance from contract'.[82] Empirical research has revealed a sense that obligations derive from the nature of a relationship, its 'normative pull'.[83] From this perspective, the Canadian case of *Kerr*, with its indicia of a 'joint family venture',[84] and *Jones*, interpreting the joint purchase of a home as 'a strong indication of emotional and economic commitment to a joint enterprise',[85] may supplement emphasis on commitment's formal expression.

An alternative approach is to tackle the focus on choice in connection with marriage, the formal act of relational commitment par excellence. Where legislatures amend their regimes of marriage, the amendments often apply to parties already married, without concern for the spouses' common intention at their union's outset. Moreover, even while the legislature does nothing, shifts in judicial interpretation may substantially alter the effects of legislation operative on marriage breakdown.[86] Even if one theorizes marriage as a general consent, with incomplete information, to the possibility of an eventual sharing *ex post*,[87] it is difficult to link major reforms to marriage and divorce with spouses' initial intentions. Recall the English shift from provision for needs to a yardstick of equal sharing, in *White* and successive cases, or many jurisdictions' reduced emphasis on fault or its elimination. Prenuptial agreements' increased weight in English law may be the counterpart of the equality principle on divorce,[88] but *Radmacher* came too late for all couples (or wealthy individuals inclined against sharing) married prior. Reforms applicable to existing marriages manifest, then, a judicial and legislative willingness to trump spouses' mutual intentions or expectations in the

---

[79] E Aloni, 'Deprivative Recognition' (2014) 61 UCLA Law Review 1276. A lawyerly eye on the effects of 'recognizing' new relationship forms may temper philosophical assumptions that recognition is a benefit. cf E Brake's chapter.

[80] L Glennon, 'Obligations between Adult Partners: Moving from Form to Function?' (2008) 22 International Journal of Law, Policy & the Family 22, 29.

[81] S Scheffler, 'Relationships and Responsibilities' (1997) 26 Philosophy & Public Affairs 189.

[82] IM Ellman, '"Contract Thinking" was *Marvin*'s Fatal Flaw' (2001) 76 Notre Dame Law Review 1365, 1375.

[83] J Eekelaar, 'Why People Marry: The Many Faces of an Institution' (2007) 41 Family Law Quarterly 413, 422.

[84] *Kerr* (n 7) [89]–[99] (Cromwell J).   [85] *Jones* (n 12) [19] (Lord Walker and Baroness Hale).

[86] C Rogerson, 'The Canadian Law of Spousal Support' (2004) 38 Family Law Quarterly 69; *White v White* [2000] UKHL 54, [2001] 1 AC 596; *Miller v Miller; McFarlane v McFarlane* [2006] UKHL 24, [2006] 2 AC 618.

[87] D Markovits, 'Sharing *Ex ante* and Sharing *ex post*: The Non-contractual Basis of Fiduciary Relations' in AS Gold and PB Miller (eds), *Philosophical Foundations of Fiduciary Law* (OUP 2014) 221–22.

[88] J Miles, 'Marriage and Divorce in the Supreme Court and the Law Commission: For Love or Money?' (2011) 74 Modern Law Review 430, 441.

name of changing policy objectives and social values regarding intimate relationships, including human-rights values.

Furthermore, if consent and individual choice were the primary goals in the regulation of intimate relationships, there would be more scope for opting out of public-law rules such as those of income tax. One might expect greater efforts to ensure that people knew *ex ante* the obligational content of marriage as codified in the law 'governing marriage and family life' and to ensure its stability during marriages.[89]

The contingency and newness of the 'choice' between marriage and cohabitation offers one more reason for moderating appeals to this idea. It is only recently that 'marriage's monopoly'[90] has receded, making it plausible for individuals to cohabit without risk of social stigma and legally imposed disadvantages—for them and their children.[91] Consequently, it is anachronistic to read England's grant of broad discretion to order ancillary relief or Canadian provinces' presumed equal sharing of gains as based on the 'choice' to assume significant relational obligations. Rather than elaborating a meaningful option between marriage and cohabitation, those measures' drafters understood themselves to be regulating the set of socially acceptable or legitimate families.

Two points emerge. First, protecting the 'choice' to marry or to remain free from relational obligation cannot credibly feature in timeless or abstract debates. Given that it was not historically a preeminent consideration, those who would make it so now bear the burden of justification. Second, the enactment of measures for ancillary relief and property sharing in conditions where marriage was not 'chosen' over viable alternatives indicates values or policy aims other than choice. These values or policy aims include protection of those rendered economically vulnerable by relationships and compensation for domestic labour. Readers of a certain critical bent might add the shoring up of a normative sexual morality rooted in the heteronormative home. Assuring children's protection and security might be another policy aim, with which the regulation of adult intimacy often intersects. Still, focusing on children risks detracting attention from the justice claims and vulnerability arising from childless (or 'childfree')[92] adult relationships. The set of legal sources militates, then, for protection's and compensation's place in current discussions about cohabitation.

Is there an objection that it is attractive to raise the autonomy bar by increasing the weight accorded to choice? Reforms by statute or judicial interpretation have expanded the role for choice regarding a number of matters touching family or intimate life. Think of recognizing married women's right to withhold consent to sex with their husbands, of gay men's and lesbians' space publicly to have a partner of the same sex, and of the expanded scope for prenuptial agreements. It is still appropriate, however, to temper the objective of increasing respect for choice against the other policy aims manifest in family law. The regulation of adult relationships, married or unmarried, is not a zero–sum operation between freedom of choice and oppression. Instead, it represents

---

[89] C Pateman, *The Sexual Contract* (Stanford UP 1988) 164 [footnote omitted].
[90] WN Eskridge, 'Family Law Pluralism: The Guided-Choice Regime of Menus, Default Rules, and Override Rules' (2012) 100 Georgetown Law Journal 1881, 1924.
[91] Probert (n 70) 277.
[92] S Westwood, 'Complicating Kinship and Inheritance: Older Lesbians' and Gay Men's Will-Writing in England' (2015) 23 Feminist Legal Studies 181, 188.

trade-offs between aims including fostering freedom of choice, protecting the vulnerable, and justly compensating caring work. The contemporary focus on choice risks evacuating those legitimate but competing aims. In other conversations, emphasis on the 'individual' who 'chooses' to take up reproductive and care work may lead to holding her responsible for any consequent economic disadvantages, thereby privatizing the costs of welfare and care.[93]

The suggestion is not to dispense with choice, but to exercise care when invoking it, informed by a historically and sociologically informed account of family law's development. Along with 'property' and 'intention', choice may have a place in the liberal 'legal consciousness as an immutable truth'.[94] Revealingly, even the judges who distort the search for cohabitants' 'true intention' in the service of law reform do not jettison a consequential 'choice to marry'. Thus, Baroness Hale's dissent in *Radmacher* concludes: 'Marriage still counts for something in the law of this country and long may it continue to do so'.[95] Parallel to adapting unjust enrichment for cohabitants, the Supreme Court of Canada has emphasized autonomy and choice when dismissing their equality claims under the Canadian Charter of Rights and Freedoms.[96] Whatever choice's extent, partners exercise it not in a vacuum, but against a backdrop of default rules, to which the chapter turns now.

VI. Default Rules and Family Law's Reach

The law-and-economics literature on default rules may provide useful tools for rethinking the regulation of cohabitation. Sunstein emphasizes that there are always default rules and that they shape outcomes. It follows that those designing default rules may as well adopt ones that enhance utility.[97] These propositions—however evident to many lawyers—may be less so to some philosophers. They may trouble the idea that it is plausible to think of adult partners as free from rights and obligations until they consent thereto. Rather, they are subject to one set of default rules laid down and backed by the state—notably the generally applicable regimes of property, contract, and tort—until they move to another. This legal feature troubles the public/private boundary and undermines the idea that the regulatory choice lies between intervention and non-intervention.[98]

---

[93] A Diduck, 'What Is Family Law For?' (2011) 64 Current Legal Problems 287, 313; see also G Calder, 'The Personal *Is* Economic: Unearthing the Rhetoric of Choice in the Canadian Maternity and Parental Leave Benefit Debates' in R Hunter and S Cowan (eds), *Choice and Consent: Feminist Engagements with Law and Subjectivity* (Routledge 2007) 130; R Johnson, *Taxing Choices: The Intersection of Class, Gender, Parenthood, and the Law* (UBC Press 2002) 125.
[94] C Rotherham, 'Proprietary Relief for Enrichment by Wrongs: Some Realism about Property Talk' (1996) 19 University of New South Wales Law Journal 378, 382.
[95] *Radmacher* (n 44) [195] (Baroness Hale) (dissenting).
[96] *Nova Scotia (Attorney General) v Walsh* 2002 SCC 83, [2002] 4 SCR 325; *Quebec (Attorney General) v A* 2013 SCC 5, [2013] 1 SCR 61.
[97] CR Sunstein and RH Thaler, 'Libertarian Paternalism Is Not an Oxymoron' (2003) 70 University of Chicago Law Review 1159.
[98] FE Olsen, 'The Myth of State Intervention in the Family' (1985) 18 University of Michigan Journal of Law Reform 835.

As explored above, judges developing the common law refer frequently to the parties' expectations or intentions. Yet at least some of the time, the judges pursue a fair or just result separable from the parties' common intentions. The research on default rules offers a way of understanding what the judges may be doing in such circumstances. It also offers a partial response to social-science research on cohabitants' expectations, their knowledge of the law, including the 'common law marriage myth', and their reasons for cohabiting. Such research often assumes that legal rules should align better with what ordinary cohabitants expect the law to be or would think fair.[99] The suggestion is that judges—Janus-faced, resolving the concrete dispute from the past and shaping the precedent that will guide conduct and dispute resolution in the future—may have reason to add other considerations.

Ayres proposes that efficient default rules (judge-made or enacted) may diverge from 'what the parties would have contracted for'.[100] They may include 'penalty defaults' that would incentivize one party to contract around the default rule, asserting an affirmative choice for an alternative rule. This proposition is controversial,[101] but for present purposes introducing it will suffice. The penalty default rests on assumptions that the party disadvantaged by the rule will know the law at the appropriate time and will initiate with its contractual partner a contractual derogation of the default rule. What does the idea of the penalty default suggest for cohabiting couples, especially the 'uneven couples'[102] with asymmetrical degrees of commitment or desires for financial sharing? It might lead to adopting a default rule of sharing that would force the party less keen on relational commitment to disclose his intentions to the other partner and attempt to secure an opt-out.[103]

The vocabulary of default rules might structure a franker conversation than the Canadian and English judges' contorted discussions of imputation, intention, and legitimate expectations. Even when the English judges refer to Parliament's inaction, they do not recognize that they are designing a default regime, one that will shape departures from it by the instruments of property acquisition or contract. Alternatively, even if institutional limits on the judicial role make it inappropriate for judges to admit that they are replacing one default rule with another, the work on default rules might lead scholars to be less critical where the legal change may not appear to serve the interests of the entire group of cohabitants. Perhaps the presumption of equal legal and beneficial title in *Stack* and *Jones*, delivered under cover of a search for the parties' intentions, may be an effort to set up a penalty default with an aim of flushing out the party whom it would disadvantage. Rereading the private-law cases as developing default rules, the question is not whether the rules would do justice to their catchment set of cohabitants,

---

[99] A Barlow, S Duncan, G James, and A Park, *Cohabitation, Marriage and the Law: Social Change and Legal Reform in the 21st Century* (Hart 2005).

[100] I Ayres and R Gertner, 'Filling Gaps in Incomplete Contracts: An Economic Theory of Default Rules' (1989) 99 Yale Law Journal 87, 91.

[101] Eg, EA Posner, 'There Are No Penalty Default Rules in Contract Law' (2006) 33 Florida State University Law Review 563; but see I Ayres, 'Ya-HUH: There Are and Should Be Penalty Defaults' (2006) 33 Florida State University Law Review 589.

[102] A Barlow and J Smithson, 'Legal Assumptions, Cohabitants' Talk and the Rocky Road to Reform' (2010) 22 Child and Family Law Quarterly 328, 335, 346, 348.

[103] Scott (n 54) 259–60.

but whether they are likely to prompt action by the partner best placed to know the law and to force a potentially awkward conversation about contracting out.[104]

Since there are always default rules, the cohabitation question is not whether to regulate cohabitants the same ways as married spouses or to leave them unregulated. It is whether to make their default the sharing rules of family law or the background rules of contract, property, trusts, and unjust enrichment, developed largely for arm's-length strangers. The basic question is the following: what proportion of households should be presumptively subject to family law's protective and allocative mechanisms? Rates of cohabitation vary substantially and can affect the persuasiveness of some arguments or the characterization of the social problem and evaluations of its urgency. In the Canadian province of Quebec, more than one-third of census couples are unmarried. The number is higher within subgroups, such as younger people and Francophones. More than three-fifths of children under the age of five were born to unmarried parents and in some census divisions, over half of children fourteen and under live with cohabiting parents.[105] In the UK, cohabiting-couple families are the fastest growing family type, accounting for 16.4 per cent of all families.[106] In Britain, research indicates an inverse relationship between the level of education—presumably closely tied to class—and rates of cohabitation.[107] Such data may help to broaden the focus from the intentions or situation of individual couples.

However persuasive the question of choice on a couple-by-couple basis may be—and the preceding section registered cautions—is it a problem for family law where 10 per cent or 20 per cent of couples fall outside a regime designed for the set of legitimate conjugal couples? Is it a problem where three-fifths of children are born and raised outside marriage, and their parents' relationship persists or runs aground, largely outside family law? Cohabitants who are parents owe support directly to their children, but their home attracts none of the protections of married spouses' family residence and there is no mechanism to compensate for disadvantage flowing from childcare.

Theorists should have an account for the appropriate coverage of family law's default regime. If the economic rules developed for the set of legitimate families, applied through the instrument of marriage, no longer reach that set, it may be appropriate to inquire as to who suffers and in what form. If those rules no longer suit a large number of households, it may be time for reform, preferably by Parliament. Of course, 'family law' and 'matrimonial law' are not fixed bundles. One might extend protective measures allowing a parent with care of children to stay temporarily in the family home without extending a sharing of capital. Arguably, though, it is problematic for family

---

[104] But on the negative effect that lucid contemplation of the relationship's end may have on the optimism that eases it as a going concern, see H Reece, 'Leaping without Looking' in R Leckey (ed), *After Legal Equality: Family, Sex, Kinship* (Routledge 2015) 122–24.

[105] A Milan, *Marital Status: Overview, 2011* (Statistics Canada, Minister of Industry, 2013) 5; Statistics Canada, *Portrait of Families and Living Arrangements in Canada: Families, Households and Marital Status, 2011 Census of Population* (Minister of Industry, 2012) 14; Institut de la statistique du Québec, *Le bilan démographique du Québec* (Gouvernement du Québec, 2014) 48.

[106] Office for National Statistics, *Families and Households, 2014* (2015) 7.

[107] Máire Ní Bhrolcháin and Éva Beaujouan, 'Education and Cohabitation in Britain: A Return to Traditional Patterns?' (2013) 39 Population and Development Review 441.

law's scope of application to have shrunk substantially in virtue of legislative inattention while the locus of family life has shifted.

Such empirical questions about the proportion of households affected distinguish the lens of default rules from the lens of fundamental rights, such as gender equality and freedom from discrimination. Through the latter, the numbers of people affected may be less relevant where a regime's contours appear to violate the equality of women or of vulnerable cohabitants. Proportionality reasoning may give a pass, however, to a law that produces problems in relatively few cases. The law might pass muster as one of the least restrictive means of pursuing the legislative aim or its harms might appear proportionate to its benefits.

A judicial invocation of default rules prompts recognition of that optic's limits. Dissenting in the rights case that rejected cohabitants' discrimination claim, a Canadian judge held that a presumptively applicable default scheme, subject to opting out, would 'protect those spouses for whom the choices are illusory and who are left economically vulnerable at the dissolution of their relationship'.[108] The judge exaggerates the protective effects of shifting the default rule. It does not guarantee protection to the economically vulnerable partner. A reason is that rules subject to opting out still depend on autonomy, knowledge of one's legal rights, and the capacity to enforce them. Shifting the default does not dissolve power imbalances.[109] An exploitative stronger partner might still pressure his partner to opt out. Still, moving the default rule can redistribute the cards. Depending on the regime, a valid opt-out requires receipt of independent legal advice. It takes place via a contract that may be subject to challenge under the common law grounds of undue influence and unconscionability. By contrast, where no protective rules apply by default, there is no contractual basis by which to challenge the ongoing state of never having opted in.

VII. Conclusion

This chapter has studied judicial adaptations of the common law in cohabitation cases with a view to identifying the institutional constraints on such judicial law reform. The imperative of fidelity to parties' intentions limits both the extent of judicial transformation and the transparency of judicial discourse. By contrast, the enactment and application of legislation occasions more candid acknowledgement of the pursuit of aims other than respect for individual intentions, such as protection, compensation, and a range of other social interests. These institutional differences—the courts versus the legislature, the common law versus statute—are integral to a legal–philosophical study of these issues and others in family law. Reading broadly in the law of marriage and divorce, the chapter has cautioned against taking choice and consent to familial duties as an overweening factor when debating policy approaches to cohabitation. It has also proposed a focus on default rules—their omnipresence and the possibility of a default rule that aims otherwise than to capture what parties would have agreed on—as a

---

[108] *Quebec* (n 96) [376] (Abella J) (dissenting).
[109] S Thompson, *Prenuptial Agreements and the Presumption of Free Choice: Issues of Power in Theory and Practice* (Hart 2015) 148–52.

complement. The significant state interests in the economic regulation of adult intimacy, coupled with institutional constraints on judges' ability to deal with those interests, point to a robust role for legislative responsibility in this field.

Before concluding, it is fair to recognize candidly family law's limits at assuring justice, however understood. Class dimensions inflect the devices studied above. The claim in unjust enrichment and the common-intention constructive trust matter only where the parties have substantial assets. They do nothing for parties who were just scraping by during their union—and are perhaps poorer still afterwards. Even alternative measures tied to income rather than to assets, and pegged to need, not contributions—like the maintenance obligation enacted for cohabitants in most Canadian provinces—are nugatory if potential beneficiaries do not know their rights and have the wherewithal to assert them. Cuts to legal aid have exacerbated already serious problems of access to family justice. This chapter's concluding word is a call, then, for integrating attention to family law's philosophical foundations with sensitivity to institutional legal factors and alertness to the nitty gritty of such matters on the ground.

6

Heteronormativity in Dissolution Proceedings

Exploring the Impact of Recourse to Legal Advice in Same-Sex Relationship Breakdown

Charlotte Bendall[1] and Rosie Harding[2]

I. Introduction

As more and more jurisdictions worldwide become accustomed to the practice of formally recognized same-sex relationships, attention must now turn away from arguing for legal change and theorizing about the possible implications of it, and towards exploring the impacts and effects that legal recognition has on lesbians and gay men. This chapter provides an analysis of in-depth semi-structured interview data with solicitors and clients about their experiences of civil partnership dissolution. The aim of the chapter is to examine the extent to which the legal culture surrounding civil partnership dissolution (and, by extension, same-sex divorce)[3] requires lesbians and gay men to conform to heteronormative patterns of relating. Many critical and feminist contributions to the literature on same-sex marriage have suggested that same-sex marriage will have these sorts of effects on lesbians and gay men.[4]

The chapter is in four sections. We begin by exploring some of the arguments that were made before same-sex marriage[5] became a legal and political reality around the potential effects of same-sex relationship recognition. These range from questions about whether it will result in assimilation into or transformation of the institution of marriage,[6] through to those which engage with questions about heteronormativity and the shaping of socially non-normative ways of living and being that can come from

---

[1] Lecturer in Law, Birmingham Law School, University of Birmingham, email: c.l.bendall@bham.ac.uk
[2] Professor of Law and Society, Birmingham Law School, University of Birmingham, email: r.j.harding@bham.ac.uk
[3] We write on the basis that, given that both are types of formalized same-sex relationship recognition, at least some of the observations that can be made about civil partnerships are applicable to same-sex marriage. That said, there is presently a lack of research as to the whether there are differences between those lesbians and gay men that choose to enter into a marriage and those that opt for civil partnership.
[4] See, eg, R Auchmuty, 'Same-Sex Marriage Revived: Feminist Critique and Legal Strategy' (2004) 14 Feminism & Psychology 101; ND Polikoff, 'Why Lesbians and Gay Men Should Read Martha Fineman' (2000) 8 Journal of Gender, Social Policy & Law 167.
[5] Throughout this chapter we use the term same-sex marriage where it is necessary and appropriate to differentiate between same-sex and different-sex relationships. In many jurisdictions there are subtle legal differences between same-sex marriage and different-sex marriage, like the way that legal dimensions of sexual activity (eg, consummation; adultery) are recognized and operationalized.
[6] ND Hunter, 'Marriage, Law and Gender: A Feminist Inquiry' (1991) 1 Law & Sexuality 9; ND Polikoff, '"We Will Get What We Ask For: Why Legalizing Gay Marriage Will Not "Dismantle The Legal Structure of Gender in Every Marriage"' (1993) 79 Virginia Law Review 1535.

incorporation into formal regulatory domains.⁷ We then provide a brief methodological note about the in-depth interviews—with fourteen solicitors and ten clients—we explore in the remainder of the chapter. In section four, we turn to explore these data around two intersecting themes: dissatisfaction with the adversarial nature of the legal process; and navigating heteronormative understandings of relationships. We conclude with a discussion of what these findings mean for the future potential of same-sex relationship recognition to transform the nature of marriage.

II. Same-Sex Marriage: Transformation, Assimilation, and Legal Consciousness

The battle lines between feminist critique of marriage⁸ and lesbian and gay social movements seeking marriage equality⁹ were drawn in the late twentieth century, around the time that the first legal recognition frameworks for same-sex relationships were being introduced in Scandinavian countries.¹⁰ For some scholars, legal recognition of same-sex relationships provided possibilities for transforming the imbalanced gender roles that characterized different sex marriage.¹¹ For others, however, the inclusion of lesbians and gay men in the privatized, state supported institution of marriage could never result in emancipation of LGBT people or of women from oppressive, patriarchal structures that perpetuate gendered inequalities.¹² Since the beginning of the twenty-first century, increasing numbers of jurisdictions have created formal legal recognition frameworks for same-sex relationships, often following the 'stepping-stones' model experienced in jurisdictions like the Netherlands,¹³ introducing 'civil unions' or 'civil partnerships' as 'equality practice' before opening up access to full legal marriage for same-sex couples.¹⁴

Since civil partnerships and same-sex marriage have become a legal reality in many jurisdictions,¹⁵ academic attention must now shift to measuring the social, legal, and discursive impacts of this change. Of particular interest is the mapping of the extent to which legal recognition forces those who decide to engage in it into more heteronormative ways of living. 'Heteronormativity' combines the two ideas of heterosexuality

---

⁷ R Harding, *Regulating Sexuality: Legal Consciousness in Lesbian and Gay Lives* (Routledge 2011).
⁸ Auchmuty, 'Same-Sex Marriage Revived' (n 4).
⁹ C Kitzinger and S Wilkinson, 'The Re-branding of Marriage: Why We Got Married Instead of Registering a Civil Partnership' (2004) 14 Feminism & Psychology 127.
¹⁰ R Wintemute and M Andenaes (eds), *Legal Recognition of Same-Sex Partnerships: A Study of National, European and International Law* (Hart 2001).
¹¹ Hunter, 'Marriage, Law and Gender' (n 6).
¹² PL Ettelbrick, 'Since When is Marriage a Path to Liberation?' in S Sherman (ed), *Lesbian and Gay Marriage* (Temple UP 1992) 20; Polikoff, 'We Will Get' (n 6).
¹³ K Waaldijk, 'Small Change: How the Road to Same-Sex Marriage Got Paved in the Netherlands' in Wintemute and Andenaes (eds), (n 10) 437.
¹⁴ WN Eskridge Jr, *Equality Practice: Civil Unions and the Future of Gay Rights* (Routledge 2002).
¹⁵ The most recent (at time of writing) jurisdiction to legalize same-sex marriage was Germany on 1 October 2017. The pace of change in the legal arena of same-sex marriage is relentless, and it can be difficult to keep up with the numbers of jurisdictions allowing civil partnership and same-sex marriage, such that one of the most reliable sources of information about the status quo at any given date is (unusually) the 'wikipedia' page on the issue, see: <http://en.wikipedia.org/wiki/Same-sex_marriage>.

and normativity to create, 'the idea that society assumes heterosexual identity, practices and behaviour to be normative, and thus law and social structures are organized as if this were the case'.[16] Embedded in heteronormativity are assumptions about gendered normativities, particularly about the complementarity of 'masculinity' and 'femininity' in interpersonal relationships. These gendered assumptions include that the 'man' of the relationship engages in the production and circulation of commodities, and the 'woman' performs work within the home.[17] Post *White v White*,[18] the family courts have tended to base their financial-relief decisions around addressing the scenario where husbands and wives carry out these distinct roles within a marriage. In so doing, they have, arguably, naturalized traits that perpetuate women's oppression, treating their difference from men as inherent. The courts have, in 'big money' matters, maintained the constructed 'breadwinner'/'homemaker' binary through a process of constant repetition, even to the point of implicitly following these norms in *Lawrence v Gallagher*,[19] the only reported civil partnership dissolution case to date.[20]

Judith Butler's work on gender highlights the possibility of disrupting what she terms to be the 'heterosexual matrix' by doing things differently.[21] With that idea in mind, same-sex couples seemed to present an opportunity to challenge the existing 'codes of hierarchical binarisms', and to generate new domains of intelligibility.[22] Yet, Harding has argued that the regulatory effects that accompany formal recognition of same-sex relationships operate to, '[push] lesbians and gay men towards heteronormative lifestyles'.[23] More specifically, normalizing forces, such as the extension of marriage (or quasi-marriage, in the form of civil partnership) rights to same-sex couples, have been employed in order to position gay and lesbian family life so as to be intelligible within the framework of heteronormativity. Same-sex couples are now 'known and knowable to the state', resulting in greater regulation of lesbians and gay men, particularly those who are economically marginalized.[24] Neither law nor society has yet 'completely embrac[ed] non-heterosexual lifestyles' or 'allow[ed] for the growth of non-heteronormative ways of living and being'.[25]

This chapter, focusing on relationship breakdown, considers the extent to which there is still transformative potential amongst those with experience of civil partnership. It does so by exploring empirical data and by drawing on insights from legal consciousness studies, which have examined social constructions of 'legality'.[26] Legal consciousness studies seek to understand how everyday uses of, experiences with, and talk about law serves to construct and enact legality. In other words, how law as it is done in practice produces effects on law as it is written down in books. Legal Consciousness, as a conceptual frame, seeks to interrogate the mechanisms by which everyday experiences of law shape and change law. In the empirical analysis that follows below, we see some

---

[16] Harding (n 7) 40. [17] M Lloyd, *Judith Butler: From Norms to Politics* (Polity Press 2007).
[18] *White v White* [2000] UKHL 54. [19] *Lawrence v Gallagher* [2012] EWCA Civ 394.
[20] C Bendall, 'Some Are More "Equal" Than Others: Heteronormativity in the Post-*White* Era of Financial Remedies' (2014) 36 Journal of Social Welfare & Family Law 260.
[21] J Butler, *Gender Trouble: Feminism and the Subversion of Identity* (2nd edn, Routledge 1999).
[22] ibid 185. [23] Harding (n 7) 40. [24] Harding (n 7). [25] ibid 40.
[26] P Ewick and SS Silbey, *The Common Place of Law: Stories from Everyday Life* (Chicago University Press 1998); Harding (n 7); Kathleen E Hull, 'The Cultural Power of Law and The Cultural Enactment of Legality: The Case of Same-Sex Marriage' (2003) 28 Law & Social Inquiry 629.

examples of engagement 'with the law' which understands law as an 'arena of competitive and tactical manoeuvring where the pursuit of self-interest is expected and the skilful and resourceful can make strategic gains'.[27] As we will demonstrate below, clients from our interview study describe this game of 'law' as having been 'played' by solicitors, who are working to construct their clients' cases to fit with heteronormative ideas about gendered roles in relationships. This is despite Peel and Harding's contention that, in the relative absence of pre-existing models, lesbian and gay relationships may be conducted more creatively than different-sex couples.[28] We argue that early evidence suggests that the balance of power in legal matters relating to same-sex relationship breakdown has shifted towards legal representatives, with assimilation towards the heteronorm as a consequence.

We will also highlight below some discourse that fits more coherently within the 'against the law' legal consciousness schema, through which, 'people exploit the interstices of conventional social practices to forge moments of respite from the power of law. Foot-dragging, omissions, ploys, small deceits, humour, and making scenes are typical forms of resistance for those up against the law'.[29] This was, on occasion, in juxtaposition with a more 'with the law' type of approach, which would seem to fit well with Ewick and Silbey's suggestion that, 'legal consciousness is neither fixed nor necessarily consistent; rather it is plural and variable across contexts, and it often expresses and contains contradiction'.[30] A perhaps surprising finding that we explore in more detail below is that whilst formal legal recognition has brought same-sex partners to 'law' to a greater extent, practitioners have still reported a relative determination by lesbian and gay clients to settle on their own terms. This sits well with Harding's previous finding that lesbian and gay families often work around legal presumptions and create their own rules.[31] Although heteronormative conceptions of gender have been carried over from (different-sex) marriage into civil partnership proceedings, gay and lesbian clients often appear to discursively resist the imposition of heterosexual relational norms on their relationships. In the analysis that follows, we draw on the tools of legal consciousness to interrogate clients' and solicitors' discursive formulations of sameness and difference, assimilation and transformation in civil partnership dissolution proceedings.

A. Methodology

The dataset in this research originates from an in-depth interviewing project that took place between September 2013 and June 2014 with fourteen solicitors and ten clients that had had direct involvement in civil partnership dissolution matters.[32] Ethical approval was granted by the University of Birmingham Research Ethics Committee. Empirical methods were selected because we considered that hearing how things are working 'on the ground' (as opposed to conducting library-based research) would best

---

[27] Ewick and Silbey (n 26) 48.
[28] E Peel and R Harding, 'Divorcing Romance, Rights, and Radicalism: Beyond Pro and Anti in The Lesbian and Gay Marriage Debate' (2004) 4 Feminism & Psychology 584.
[29] Ewick and Silbey (n 26) 48.   [30] ibid 50.   [31] Harding (n 7).
[32] Charlotte Bendall conducted all of the interviews.

enable the gathering of information about how dissolution matters were playing out in practice. Solicitors (rather than barristers or judges) were selected as the most appropriate legal professional informants, because the vast majority of relationship breakdown matters settle out of court. Further, solicitors play a key role in financial relief matters, as part of which they 'translate personal conflicts into legally recognisable categories of dispute'.[33] The decision to interview both solicitors and clients was motivated by a desire to hear the voices of both the 'locally powerful'[34] and the 'dispossessed'.[35]

The empirical approach used in both solicitor and client interviews was the in-depth, semi-structured, qualitative interview, as is increasingly common in socio-legal research. This semi-structured interview approach provided the best opportunity to explore the solicitors' and clients' experiences and thoughts in detail.[36] During the interviews themselves, an interview schedule was used to provide a greater structure for comparability than one would tend to have if conducting a completely unstructured interview.[37] There was, however, also a degree of flexibility in the conduct of the interviews, enabling the researcher to explore the meaning contexts of participants' discourse and to pursue relevant lines of investigation.[38] This flexibility also gave participants the opportunity to develop their ideas and explain their views.[39] In analysing the data from these interviews, we were cognizant of the fact that what people say in the artificial discursive environment of a research interview cannot automatically be assumed to be reflective of the 'truth'.[40] Also, when exploring people's experiences of emotionally charged topics, such as relationship difficulties, Brannen suggests that respondents' accounts tend to be contradictory and filled with emotion.[41]

Such challenges of interviews are not restricted to those with clients in this study. Professional interviews also have limitations in terms of the representativeness of the data gathered. Firstly, as Macauley argues, within the interview scenario, 'people like to entertain you'.[42] As a result, they often choose to tell you, 'the best story that they've got', as opposed to what they consider to be an accurate account of events and experiences.[43] Secondly, interview respondents may feel under pressure to supply answers so as to 'fit in' with what they believe the interviewer 'expects' of them.[44] Likewise, they might tailor their answers so as to comply with what they believe the researcher's point of view to be. Thirdly, it is possible that interview respondents might be made to feel 'under the microscope' whilst being interviewed, as though they are being somehow scrutinized or tested,[45] a problem that came up in some of the solicitor interviews in this

---

[33] C Smart, *The Ties That Bind: Law, Marriage and the Reproduction of Patriarchal Relations* (Routledge & Kegan Paul 1984) 160.
[34] ibid.
[35] D Herman, *Rights of Passage: Struggles for Lesbian and Gay Legal Equality* (University of Toronto Press 1994).
[36] T May, *Social Research: Issues, Methods and Process* (3rd edn, Open UP 2001).   [37] ibid.
[38] RM Lee, *Doing Research on Sensitive Topics* (Sage 1993).
[39] N Gilbert, *Researching Social Life* (3rd edn, Sage 2008).
[40] M Denscombe, *The Good Research Guide for Small-Scale Social Research Projects* (3rd edn, Open UP 2007).
[41] J Brannen, 'The Study of Sensitive Subjects' (1988) 36 Sociological Review 552.
[42] S Macauley, 'Non-contractual Relations in Business' in S Halliday and P Schmidt (eds), *Conducting Law and Society Research: Reflections on Methods and Practices* (CUP 2009).
[43] ibid 22.   [44] Denscombe (n 40).   [45] ibid.

study. Accordingly, interviewees may purposely attempt to answer the questions posed in such a way as to reflect favourably on themselves.[46] Notwithstanding these limitations of empirical qualitative interview research, the recruitment and sampling processes followed in this project were aimed at gaining as broad a range of perspectives as possible, such that the data from the project can be understood, at the very least, to be a reliable snapshot of contemporary discourse around civil partnership dissolution from both clients and solicitors.

B. Recruitment and sampling

As is common in research involving lesbian and gay issues, sampling and recruitment can be challenging because of the difficulties of locating a relatively unknown population.[47] Solicitors' firms were selected by conducting an internet search for the term 'civil partnership dissolution solicitor'. The firms' websites were subsequently examined to establish whether any of the solicitors' individual profiles specified that they had experience of advising on civil partnership and, where this information could not be located, the heads of the firms' family departments were e-mailed. In total, 291 firms were contacted, from which fourteen practitioners from ten different firms agreed to participate in the research. It had been hoped that the solicitors would provide introductions to their clients, with further interview participants being attained in this way, and this did occur twice. However, it soon became clear that many of the firms contacted had not advised on a high number of civil partnership cases, which is understandable considering the very small number of dissolution proceedings that have happened to date. Civil partnerships have only been available in England and Wales since December 2005, and the first dissolutions of recognized civil partnerships happened in quarter two of 2007. From January 2007 to December 2013, there were a total of 3,466 dissolutions of civil partnerships recorded.[48] This figure represents a very small proportion of the overall family law relationship breakdown matters over that period: by way of contrast, there were 719,075 divorces recorded from 1 January 2007 to 31 December 2012.[49] In addition to this, several of the solicitors displayed a reluctance to grant access to their clients. Accordingly, we deployed our (previously approved) 'backup' recruitment plan to access clients, drawing on direct strategic-opportunistic and snowball-sampling approaches. An advertisement was sent to 217 lesbian and gay organizations, mailing lists and publications with a potential interest in the subject in an attempt to recruit people that had sought legal advice. Twitter was also used, with direct 'tweets' being sent to 87 individuals and organizations and relevant 'hash tags' being utilized (such as '#LGBT', '#LGBTQ' and '#LGBTfamilies'), and details of the project featured on the notice boards of two online forums.

---

[46] ibid.   [47] Peel and Harding, 'Divorcing Romance, Rights, and Radicalism' (n 28).
[48] Office of National Statistics, *Statistical Bulletin: Civil Partnerships in the UK, 2013* (2015) <http://www.ons.gov.uk/ons/dcp171778_395000.pdf> accessed 17 October 2017.
[49] Office of National Statistics, *Statistical Bulletin: Divorces in England and Wales, 2012* (2014) <http://www.ons.gov.uk/ons/dcp171778_351693.pdf> accessed 17 October 2017.

Of the solicitors interviewed, five were males and nine females, and eleven identified as heterosexual, two as lesbian and one as gay. They ranged from twenty-eight to fifty-nine years of age and dealt with cases concerning a range of assets, from modest amounts to multi-million pound 'big money' matters. The solicitors were located in the Southwest and Southeast of England, Greater London and the Midlands. In terms of the clients, six of these respondents were men and four were women, and six identified as gay, two as lesbians, one as both, and one as bisexual. They ranged from thirty-eight to fifty-four years of age (mean age = forty-five), and they resided in locations across Greater London and the Midlands. Their assets ranged from very little to significant and, whilst three were in the process of dissolution and asset division, seven had completed this process. The partners' relationships varied in length: although one client had been with her partner for twenty-five years, a further one spent only a week living with their civil partner, with a prior year of cohabitation before the civil partnership ceremony.

III. Approaches to and Perceptions of the Law of Civil Partnership Dissolution

We now turn to discuss these data in depth. Interviews were digitally recorded and transcribed verbatim by the first author. Data from both components of the interview study were analysed using thematic analysis.[50] NVivo software was utilized to assist with the coding process. Two key themes were identified that relate to this chapter. Firstly, many of the client participants blamed the legal practitioners involved for encouraging and fostering an adversarial and inflammatory approach in the matter. Some clients perceived this approach to be for the gain of the solicitors, rather than as a means of resolving the dispute. Others, however, felt that their own legal representatives did not represent their views and positions strongly enough in the process. The second theme coheres around the ways that clients and solicitors both used discourse that we have coded as drawing on heteronormative understandings of relationships, but in different ways. Whereas some solicitors sought to include same-sex matters in their previously developed knowledge base from heterosexual-divorce proceedings and legal precedents, clients found this frustrating, and often wished to emphasize the different nature of same-sex relationships. Other solicitors highlighted the differences in approach that their lesbian and gay clients had to matters, particularly to issues around money and maintenance. Running through both of these themes was an overall view that adversarial dispute processes in same-sex relationship dissolution sat in opposition to common understandings that ex-partners remain important to lesbians and gay men, and that the breakup of an intimate relationship need not mark the end of a friendship. We discuss each of these themes in turn.

---

[50] V Braun and V Clarke, 'Using Thematic Analysis in Psychology' (2006) 3 Qualitative Research in Psychology 77.

A. The adversarial nature of legal process

Several clients in this study suggested that the solicitors involved in their matter (and particularly those on the other side) had adopted an aggressive strategy, encouraging their disputes to become more adversarial than they would have expected, wanted, or needed them to be. Consider this excerpt from Anthony's[51] interview:

> I think my ex thought that I was, in the background, working with legal. So, all of a sudden, he got representation. I didn't have any, I hadn't consulted. I'd thought about it and done a little bit of research, but I hadn't actually engaged. I thought we'd do that together. So, I had to find somebody and I've got a friend who's a barrister and he recommended a website and that's how I found [firm]. But I was left, after that meeting, thinking that this was going to be trickier and perhaps more expensive than I had realised, and longer, and that was a bit of a 'come to Jesus' moment, thinking, 'Oh my goodness, this is really going to be difficult'. We had our first collaborative meeting and the word 'collaboration' had escaped my ex's representation because he went on attack mode. He just started really attacking. […] I believe that his solicitor gave him an outcome that wasn't realistic and between the two of them … ultimately, you appoint a solicitor and they act on your behalf so I can't blame the solicitor per se, but he set unrealistic expectations and then it became a, 'Let's screw this guy', me being the guy, and luckily the judge saw through that. (Anthony)

Here, he suggests that whereas he had hoped to engage in a collaborative process, his partner's legal representative had forced them into a protracted dispute. Indeed, Anthony's case was the only one of the concluded cases in this interview sample that had proceeded through to final hearing. Similarly, Isaac described his partner's solicitors as being 'very aggressive' in contrast to his own, more open solicitors:

> They were very aggressive, there's a term for it. Yeah, umm, so they were … so, whereas my, umm, solicitors were very open and wanted to have a resolution, they were from the outset very aggressive in saying what they wanted, and saying how their client had been hurt. (Isaac)

Bill contrasted his knowledge of his ex-partner's approach to money with the way the dispute between them seemed to be playing out, attributing this to the solicitors on the other side:

> And he never, really, seemed to give any importance to money. And, I'm still, you know, I still think that. Which is why I've still got a problem that his solicitor is putting him up to it … [and] trying to almost drag this thing out … trying to say, 'Actually, you could … you know, you may be entitled to more by law'. You know, if the law allows this. And, I still don't feel that that's him. And, I could be wrong, but I've known him since 1994, err, and I don't think that I'm wrong. (Bill)

These constructions of the 'other side' as being the catalyst for an aggressive or adversarial approach are interesting, because they seem to chime with Day Sclater's[52] contention

---

[51] All names are pseudonyms. Clients have been given first names and solicitors have been allocated surnames in order to easily differentiate between the two groups of interviewees.
[52] S Day Sclater, *The Psychology of Divorce: A Research Report to the ESRC* (University of East London 1998).

that it helps psychologically to 'paint' the other side in a negative light (and oneself in a positive one) in relationship disputes. Yet this seems to sit awkwardly with research that highlights the importance of ex-partners in lesbian and gay 'families of choice' kinship networks.[53]

In fact, some clients were explicitly resistant to the possibility that their dissolution should become adversarial, or that they should push the other side for a better settlement. Consider this excerpt from Edward's interview, which gives an indication of this issue:

> [my solicitor] thought that I was being very generous and that I should go for more. But, that's the nature of solicitors, isn't it? They certainly wanted me to go away and think about the money quite a bit, and discuss it with other people. But, I was ... I went into that very eyes-open, I knew that there'd be a pressure on me to try to change my mind, and I was happy with what I had decided. (Edward)

Similarly, several practitioners indicated that their civil-partner clients had preferred to keep their disputes out of law, and out of court especially, by comparison to different-sex partners. In this respect, it was detailed how:

> I think that, in comparison, we did settle the money issue very fast. If this was an opposite-sex couple, no we wouldn't have. [...] What I did find is that the finances, every time you got the letter, 'Okay'. (Ms Ennis)
>
> I deal with some very acrimonious divorces and, at the moment, I haven't dealt with a terribly [...] acrimonious civil partnership. (Ms Clarke)

In contrast, both Debbie and Bill felt that they had been disadvantaged by the lack of 'fight' on their side of the dispute, and would have preferred their legal representatives to have been more adversarial on their behalf:

> Basically, I just had to abide by her rules, and felt that I'd been bullied again, by the court, and herself, and the solicitor. And, a little bit by mine. I didn't feel like my solicitor was very supportive at all. Like, everything that would come from them, the other side, she'd then sort of say, 'Oh well, they're right'. There was never any—no fight, nothing (Debbie).
>
> I felt that it was going to give me more rights than was indicated. [...] Given the wrong that has been done to me, I would have thought, you know, we should absolutely take him to the cleaners. And then, for the first solicitor to say, 'Well, no, actually ... no, we don't actually take him to the cleaners', it almost seemed a bit too well-mannered and watered down [...]. I think that this whole thing looks a bit—there's no—there doesn't seem, to me, to be any substance or, you know, anything—you know, a punch. And, I think that that was what I was expecting. I was expecting a bit more punch. And, it was all a little bit mumsy, to be honest with you. And, 'Oh, you know, we can't, you know, oh no' and 'They will have these rights and, you know, we mustn't upset anybody'. So yeah, it was ... definitely, I think, a lot more—it doesn't seem a lot like the Nigella Lawson case—obviously, I know that that's a different—but, you know, where it's all insults, and all of the rest of it, being thrown. I expected something a little bit more like that. (Bill)

---

[53] J Weeks, B Heaphy, and C Donovan, *Same Sex Intimacies: Families of Choice and Other Life Experiments* (Routledge 2001).

Importantly, Anthony blamed the conduct of their dissolution matter for the lack of ongoing relationship between him and his ex-partner:

> But the only person that won was the legal representation. I didn't win, I just didn't lose. My ex certainly didn't win; mentally it was stressful, as you can appreciate, frustrating, and it burnt every bridge between us two. Because we were okay. When I bought him a property ... as part of the agreement, we bought a flat in [city] for a new place for him to go to live without a mortgage, and during the purchase process I was ready to go to put the curtains up, wire the wifi up and set everything up, because it was, you know, helping. By the time it actually got to that point, I wouldn't have, you know, got the hose out if he was on fire. And it shouldn't have been that way because we weren't a fight-y couple. And now it's beyond any sort of reconciliation in terms of friendship. But it was purely because of the legal process. (Anthony)

Overall, it appears from these data that lesbian and gay clients are somewhat resistant to the adversarial nature of legal representation in dissolution matters, preferring to engage in private ordering of their affairs. This is perhaps a somewhat surprising finding, given that those that have chosen to enter into a civil partnership may be expected to be committed to a legalized approach. One reason for this resistance to the adversarial nature of legal involvement might be the relative recency of same-sex couples' inclusion in formally recognized relationships,[54] and the consequent lack of understanding of the implications of entering into a civil partnership. Given that aside from the name, civil partnership in England was legally identical to marriage,[55] a further reason might be as a result of a general lack of understanding of the very great similarities between civil partnership and marriage. Solicitor Ms Field commented, in this respect, that there had initially been a 'surprising' level of 'ignorance' amongst civil partners, and she expressed uncertainty as to the level of comprehension, even to date, of the monetary obligations that arise. It is possible that the discourse will shift over time, as same-sex couples become more used to the legal and financial implications of the dissolution of formal relationships. Equally, however, lesbians and gay men do not exist in a social vacuum. As Bill mentioned, understandings of the legal process are shaped, in significant ways, by media representations. Most of the cultural and/or media representations of the financial consequences of relationship breakdown are from heterosexual contexts, so it would be naïve to consider that lesbians and gay men only prefer to settle things themselves because of subcultural 'outside the law' influences from the era before formal legal equality.

B. Heteronormative understandings of relationships

Our second theme, that of heteronormative understandings of relationships, builds on the final point above. Same-sex couples appear to do many things, both during relationships and when they break up, differently from heterosexual couples.[56] Yet this sits

---

[54] See further Harding (n 7).

[55] CF Stychin, '"Las Vegas is Not Where We Are": Queer Readings of The Civil Partnership Act' (2006) 25 Political Geography 899.

[56] C Carrington, *No Place Like Home: Relationships and Family Life Among Lesbians and Gay Men* (University of Chicago Press 1999); LA Kurdek, 'The Allocation of Household Labor by Partners in Gay and Lesbian Couples' (2007) 28 Journal of Family Issues 132; CJ Patterson, EL Sutfin, and M Fulcher, 'Division

in tension with the formal legal frameworks surrounding civil partnership dissolution, and same-sex divorce, both of which are very similar to the legal approach to divorce for different-sex couples.[57]

Many of the solicitors in this study had only acted in a very small number of dissolution proceedings, and one, in fact, had no direct experience of a civil partnership dissolution matter. Their constructions of the legal differences between dissolution and divorce are very interesting:

> I see them as being the same and I very naughtily often refer to 'divorce' when it should be 'dissolution', umm, and refer to "decree nisis" when it should be "conditional orders". Umm, I perceive them as the same because the law currently does. Umm, whether I would change my view in the future, umm, it very much all depends on case law. (Ms Gale)
>
> I don't see the issues being necessarily different, I don't see the dynamics being particularly different. The law is the law, and we kind of have it, and that's it. And it's an area that I wish that there was a way that we could, perhaps, do more of it but we're not, unfortunately. On the flip side, we do get a lot of other work, so we're quite busy. But, it is something that I would like to see more of, because I think that there would be nuances and legal arguments to be had which would actually be quite exciting and quite good. New law and new stuff is always great. It tests you and it takes you out of your comfort zone. (Mr Derrick)
>
> I think that that's probably one of the most important facts, really, to home in on quite early, is to make it clear that, in the majority, the law has sought to almost mirror what has been the position for marriages for some time, and well before civil partnerships were available to be entered into […] you explain it to them and say, 'Well, there is no difference, and the law sees there as being no difference.' (Mr Kennedy)
>
> I would just literally apply all of the principles that I do already. I really don't think that I would do anything differently at all. I wouldn't, because the law is being applied across the board, so I wouldn't look to do anything different at all. (Ms Clarke)
>
> The lack of authority on civil partnership has not stopped me arguing the issues. Because, I will get a divorce case out and say, 'The facts are similar in terms of length of relationship, disparity of wealth, why don't you apply them?' (Ms Irvine)

As is clear across these solicitors' interviews, in practice advising civil partners on dissolution and advising straight married couples about divorce are constructed as identical. That the practitioners should adopt such a view may be understandable, given that the formal legal frameworks surrounding civil partnership dissolution are very similar to the legal approach to (different-sex) divorce, and that the common law is founded on the doctrine of precedent. Yet, we argue that, for all practical purposes, same-sex relationships are being assimilated into the marriage model in the realm of legal recognition. In doing so, the potential for opening up new critical dialogues and new ways of implementing equality and fairness on relationship breakdown may be lost. This is

---

of Labour Among Lesbian and Heterosexual Parenting Couples: Correlates of Specialized Versus Shared Patterns' (2004) 11 Journal of Adult Development 179.

[57] The only substantive difference in English law between civil partnership dissolution and heterosexual divorce is the lack of 'adultery' as a factor in evidencing the irretrievable breakdown of the relationships (s 168 of the Civil Partnership Act 2004). In terms of same-sex divorce, whilst adultery is included as a factor in s 1 of the Matrimonial Causes Act 1973, the common law definition of adultery has been applied to this factor, which only relates to heterosexual penetrative vaginal intercourse *R v R* [1952] 1 All ER 1194. See further: H Brook, 'How to Do Things with Sex' in C Stychin and D Herman (eds), *Sexuality in the Legal Arena* (Bloomsbury 2001) 132.

not only in relation to same sex-partners, but also in the context of different sex matters (given that many opposite-sex relationships are also lived in a way that differs from the law's fixed, homogenous understandings of gendered role division).

The solicitors constructed the issues and the legal frameworks in dissolution matters as being identical to different-sex divorce, except for the lack of adultery grounds in civil partnership dissolution.[58] The lack of adultery as a reason for irretrievable breakdown in civil partners was noticeably constructed as problematic both by clients and by solicitors: 'I think that it does, you know, probably annoy all of us' (Ms James). Consider this story from Heather:

> The only ... aspect that I got frustrated about was the fact that I couldn't apply for it on the grounds of, adultery. [...] Because, I had to apply on the grounds of unreasonable behaviour, and I made that application, but obviously stated the adultery as the unreasonable behaviour, and initially my application got declined. Because, the judge that it obviously went in front of didn't read the form, and it basically got sent back to me just saying that I should have applied on the grounds of adultery. So, I then had to fill in ... I had to photocopy all of the original paperwork and send it all back with a cover letter basically saying, 'I can't, it's a civil partnership'. And, I did get a bit frustrated at that as well because, you know, not only was I not allowed to apply on the grounds of adultery, but they were then saying, 'Well, that's what you should have done.' And, I know that that was a mistake, he obviously didn't look and see that it was a civil partnership, and he probably had loads in front of him every day. But, if you're going to refuse it then you should make sure that you're refusing it correctly, because they put it all back probably a couple of months, by the time that the paperwork came back to me and I had to send it all off again and things. (Heather)

Not all clients were so clear that same-sex relationships were just the same as different-sex relationships, and several thought that there should have been a different approach in the law as a result. The perspectives on what the differences are between lesbian and gay relationships and straight relationships are worthy of further exploration.

One difference that was articulated by these participants was that gay men may be more likely to have multiple sexual partners, even within a committed and formally-recognized relationship. Consider this story, from Isaac:

> ISAAC: I think that it was just difficult for her to understand, because she was married herself and she had—it would have been better if I had gone to a gay solicitor who knew about these things, and knew what gay men did, actually. That would have been better. But, she had no idea of lifestyles that happen and go on.
> INTERVIEWER: Can you think of any examples of that?
> ISAAC: Umm, yeah, she was shocked that, you know, he wanted an open relationship, and that he wanted continual sex with other people and, you know, she found that quite shocking. She told me, 'This is fairly shocking stuff'. But, you know, if that had been a gay solicitor—a gay man especially, or a gay man working in a solicitors' dealing with dissolution—he'd have said, 'I totally understand what's going on here.' And, there would have been a lot more tea and sympathy, rather than a, 'Oh, shock horror, this is happening' type thing.

---

[58] A difference between same- and different-sex divorce which is retained following the insertion of s 1(6) of the Matrimonial Causes Act 1973 by schedule 4 of the Marriage (Same Sex Couples) Act 2013.

Here, Isaac attributes a lack of understanding from his solicitor (a straight woman) to her gender and sexuality, and suggests that a gay male solicitor would have been more likely to have understood gay male non-monogamies.[59] More interestingly, perhaps, the issue of diversity in the legal profession ran through a significant portion of these participants' accounts. It appeared to be significant both that there is still such widespread heterosexuality across the legal profession, and that members of the judiciary will tend to be of an advanced age. Around 97 per cent of those responding to a question in the Law Society's practising certificate-holder survey identified as heterosexual,[60] whilst this figure was closer to 98 per cent amongst recommendations for judicial appointment from October 2013 to March 2014.[61] Indeed, Rackley emphasizes that, while the judiciary of England and Wales is the most diverse that it has ever been, there is certainly more to be done.[62]

The two lesbian solicitors interviewed (Ms James and Ms Field) opined that same-sex partners will be more comfortable when consulting a lesbian or gay practitioner, and this assertion was repeated in the client accounts. Anthony explained having instructed Mr Arnold because he did not want any 'awkwardness' or, 'the barrier of difference in sexuality' in the context of a process that is 'still quite invasive'. Anthony felt that, 'there's just an empathy ... you have the same, let's say, foundational mentality.... If the solicitor had been straight, I would probably have been being prejudiced against the solicitor thinking that the solicitor would be prejudiced to me' (and, likewise, Isaac described the difficulty of relaying personal information to 'a straight woman, actually, err, who didn't understand'). In terms of the latter point concerning judicial demographics, even solicitor Ms Irvine voiced that the legal profession is, 'run by people who have very old-fashioned concepts'. Client Debbie perceived, regarding generational attitudes, that, 'I should imagine that my granddad, yeah, had he still been alive today, would probably not be as accepting of gay people as probably, like, my mum would be.' In fact, she suggested that, in her matter, 'I think that the age of the judge probably went against me', and she attributed her perception of the homophobia of the judge who heard her case with him ultimately having been cited in a note that she wrote prior to a later suicide attempt. This view of homophobia from the judiciary was also related by solicitors in this study:

> And, my experience of the courts making orders about civil partnership finances is that they pretty much throw the case law out. That's been my experience. So, for example, I had two women, one was a well-paid [healthcare professional] and the other was quite a well-paid [financial services professional]. They had two children, umm, and they were sharing the care of the children. There was a big difference in their salary, [my client wanted] half of the equity in the house and wanted a clean break on spousal maintenance. That would not happen ... that would not be allowed to happen if they were straight. Two young children- the judge would say, 'No, we want nominal

---

[59] C Klesse, *The Spectre of Promiscuity: Gay Male and Bisexual Non-Monogamies and Polyamories* (Ashgate 2007).

[60] Law Society, *Diversity Profile of the Profession: A Short Synopsis* [online] (2014) 10 <http://www.lawsociety.org.uk/advice/articles/diversity-in-the-profession> accessed 21 November 2014.

[61] Judicial Appointments Commission, *10th Set of JAC Diversity Statistics Published* [online] (2014) <https://jac.judiciary.gov.uk/news/10th-set-jac-diversity-statistics-published> accessed 21 April 2015.

[62] E Rackley, 'Judicial Diversity, the Woman Judge and Fairy Tale Endings' (2007) 27 Legal Studies 74.

> maintenance', at least. Especially at our local court, nominal maintenance for children. But not for lesbians, apparently. So, I think there's a bit of- I feel that there's some homophobia. (Ms James)

Perhaps related to this perception of the possibility of homophobic responses from formal law, some of the solicitors reported a lack of faith in the legal system from lesbian and gay clients, and a disjuncture between the perceptions and the realities of legal representation in the dissolution process.

> Expectations of the law were a lot lower than maybe a heterosexual client, that the law wasn't going to do anything to help them.... I think, actually, that both of the clients that I dealt with individually were fairly skeptical about the law in general. They weren't big fans of it. (Mr Derrick)
>
> What interests me most about the civil partnership work that I do is that they're generally not litigated. Umm, and my view is that is because until recently there hasn't been a forum for lesbian and gay people to litigate. And it's quite an interesting hangover from that time. [...] There's a study that says that something like 80% of people who ... straight people who break up, the first people that they go and see is a solicitor. It's really high, and I would say that it's much lower for homosexual break-ups. I think that the first person that they go to is not a solicitor. Umm, possibly the last. [...] The law hasn't been seen as particularly friendly, umm, and, on that basis, [they] definitely avoid [law] ... possibly to their detriment ... my view would be that they don't come to law. I think that civil partners generally do now ... they do because they- they know that they have to do something legal. Something legal happened, and they know that something legal has to happen. [...] It's not because they want to argue about everything, they just want a bit of help. But, no, they don't want the bloody help when you give it to them. 'No, we're fine, we've sorted it out'. 'You've got it wrong'. 'It's fine'. (Ms James)

This finding that lesbians and gay men prefer to avoid solicitors, have low expectations of what solicitors can do for them, or prefer to work things out for themselves reflects findings from our previous research into legal consciousness in lesbian and gay family relationships.[63] It is clear that the historical exclusion of lesbian and gay relationships from family law has significantly contributed to this approach, but there appear to be additional factors at play that suggest same-sex couples may have a different approach to finance and relationship breakdown to that which has developed through the 'big-money' heterosexual case law. Consider these reflections from solicitors and clients on this issue:

> In my three experiences both parties have been working, there hasn't really been an expectation that one was going to maintain the other or anything like that, you know. There's definitely been more of an air of, 'We're going our own way, we need to divide our assets and get on with our own lives.' Whereas, when you see a wife who has, perhaps, been working part-time and is very dependent on her husband's income, you get a very different feel from that wife. (Ms Clarke)

---

[63] Harding (n 7).

When they're in a relationship they contribute as much as they can [...], and then when they break-up they say that, 'Our main asset we'll divide equally, but we won't give each other any compensation and we won't pay any maintenance, because we've done everything separately and independently. So, we'll carry on doing that. You've had more money than me, and you always will. I've always had less money than you, and I always will. I've got enough to start again, and that's fine'. (Ms James)

When you've got a same-sex couple, and especially two men- men still earn more money than women these days- and so ... but there's no ... everybody's treated the same. And, I found that really disappointing, actually. And, obviously that's the law, I couldn't change it, and that's how I was going to be judged. I earned more money than he did, so I was the breadwinner, so basically I could have come out a bit- the worst, basically. (Isaac)

Taken together, this discourse would seem to suggest that clients either try to, or would prefer to, 'opt out' of the substantive remedies introduced to address (heteronormative) assumptions about necessary dependency and vulnerability within relationships, in part because of a higher degree of financial independence within their relationships. It may, of course, be the case that the same can be said of heterosexual couples that organize their finances independently (and many different-sex partners do favour the private ordering of their assets). However, the indication within our data is that these opinions may be more common in same-sex matters. Solicitor Ms Field rationalized this by asking, 'Do you think that it's so part of the culture that marriage means sharing, whereas civil partnership ... ? I don't know' (indicating that it may have alternative connotations).

IV. Heteronormativity, Legal Consciousness, and Dissolution

These data suggest that there is a level of divergence between solicitors' and their lesbian and gay clients' perceptions of civil partnership dissolution. As the dissolution framework for civil partnership is identical to that in same-sex divorce, there is no reason to consider that these tensions will not be carried over into same-sex divorce. These pressures appear to cohere around three points of difference between same- and different-sex relationships: first, that same-sex couples are resistant to the negative interpersonal effects of legalized familial-dispute resolution; second, that same-sex couples still do not trust the law to sort out their disputes, in spite of increasing formal legal equality; and third, that there is significant resistance to the redistributive models of financial division that have developed through different-sex divorce cases.

A key reason why same-sex couples prefer to sort out their relationship disputes on their own terms, and settle, rather than leaving it to legal professionals to do so, is likely to be related to the longstanding subcultural importance of former partners within lesbian and gay kinship networks.[64] Previous research suggests that lesbians are even more likely than gay men to report ongoing close friendships with former lovers.[65] Jacqueline Weinstock suggested that drivers for the ongoing relationships come from

---

[64] K Weston, *Families We Choose: Lesbians, Gays, Kinship* (2nd edn, Columbia UP 1991); Weeks et al (n 53).

[65] PM Nardi and D Sherrod, 'Friendship in The Lives of Gay Men and Lesbians' (1994) 11 Journal of Social and Personal Relationships 185.

both positive and negative forces.⁶⁶ Negative forces she identified included suggestions that lesbian relationships were too closely enmeshed, that lesbians struggle with moving on after separation, and the small and close networks that have been necessary in lesbian communities.⁶⁷ In contrast, she also identified several positive drivers for this behaviour in same-sex couples and friendships, including the ways that the dividing lines between friends and family are blurred in same-sex relationship contexts, the need for lesbian friendships in order to develop and maintain non-heterosexual identities, and the shared experience of marginalization, which supports the relationships between lesbians and their ex-partners.⁶⁸ It is not clear, yet, to what extent the rise in the use of online dating websites and the changes that these have sparked in the ways that same-sex couples meet may affect this longstanding tradition of friends as families in lesbian and gay communities. It is also not clear from this small study whether the differences between lesbians and gay men noted in previous research are reflected in approaches to legal representation during relationship dissolution.

A second reason for the lesbian and gay men's resistance to the formalized legal approach to relationship-dispute resolution is that even following the legal recognition of same-sex relationships, lesbians and gay men still do not appear to trust formal law to resolve their disputes. In certain respects this is understandable, because if 'law' does not have the discursive or conceptual tools to understand the different kinship practices that characterize same and different-sex relationships, then engagement with formal law may require lesbians and gay men to fit their relationships into (hetero)normative ways of doing relationships. Harding, in her legal consciousness study of lesbian and gay lives, argued that understandings of law by lesbians and gay men appeared to be characterized as including a form of resistance to law.⁶⁹ This resistance to law included elements of the 'against-the-law' category of legal consciousness outlined by Ewick and Silbey,⁷⁰ but also included more active forms of resistance, which sought to shape and change law, rather than purely avoiding it. Similar tensions are evident in these data, which suggests that formal legal recognition of same-sex relationships has not had entirely assimilatory effects so far. This is evidenced by the reports from both clients and solicitors in this study that same-sex couples are more likely to settle out of court, and that same-sex couples prefer to take their own approach to financial division that does not reflect the 'yardstick of equality' approach developed by the courts in previous heterosexual cases (now a starting point principle in light of *Charman v Charman*⁷¹).

This latter issue requires more careful consideration, particularly as the ways that parties in these same-sex relationship disputes appear to be approaching financial division run contrary to approaches developed in the courts to redress economic power imbalances within relationships. It may be that because none of the clients interviewed for this study had children or other significant caring responsibilities, and similarly the

---

⁶⁶ JS Weinstock, 'Lesbian FLEX-ibility: Friend and/or Family Connections Among Lesbian Ex-Lovers' in JS Weinstock and ED Rothblum (eds), *Lesbian Ex-Lovers: The Really Long-Term Relationship* (Harrington Park Press 2004).
⁶⁷ ibid.   ⁶⁸ ibid.   ⁶⁹ Harding (n 7).
⁷⁰ P Ewick and SS Silbey, *The Common Place of Law: Stories from Everyday Life* (Chicago UP 1998).
⁷¹ *Charman v Charman* [2007] EWCA Civ 503.

solicitors interviewed had little experience of same-sex dissolution proceedings involving children, the differences in the approach to relationship finances were a function of the lack of children, rather than because these were same-sex couples. Though, importantly, the one dispute involving children that was discussed by Ms James suggests that the courts are also not following previous heterosexual case law when addressing same-sex dissolution matters, even where these do involve children and an income disparity. This is, perhaps, the most challenging part of the findings from this project, and one which raises the largest number of questions for future research.

It is recognized that, in reality, 'equal division' is often not the outcome of different sex partners' financial matters, with wives still often getting less. However, the case law stemming from *White* adopts a more generous approach to the economically weaker party than had previously existed, and our data suggest that this approach is being eschewed by lesbians and gay men. Instead, the indications were that they favoured financial settlements reflecting the pre-relationship financial status of each of the parties to the relationship. This raises troublesome questions about how the different economic status of parties to a relationship is reflected by and through formally recognized same-sex relationships, and why and whether individual economic circumstances prior to, during, and after the relationship should be prioritized over redistributive practices that recognize and compensate for financial interdependency. It may simply be the case that same-sex couples are, overall, less financially interdependent than heterosexual couples and continue to rely more on strategies of partial pooling and independent money management than their straight counterparts.[72] Alternatively, it might be the case that the previously 'outside' the law status of same-sex relationships has meant that lesbians and gay men have not had the same opportunity to develop more interdependent financial arrangements. Whereas evidence suggests that different-sex cohabitees engage in financial interdependency in the absence of protection, this was attributed to a lack of awareness of legal vulnerability due to a widespread belief that there is a form of 'common law' marriage.[73] In contrast, the historical lack of legal and financial protection on the breakdown of same-sex relationships has likely mediated against higher levels of financial interdependence in same-sex couples.

The potentially transformational effects of same-sex relationship recognition figured strongly in feminist arguments for same-sex marriage.[74] Yet transformations of money-management practices within relationships that lead to economically weaker parties being less well compensated in financial division on relationship breakdown are unlikely to offer the kinds of gender role transformations that we might have preferred to have seen catalysed by same-sex marriage. Money-management research has consistently found that women perceive that they have less entitlement to shared relationship funds, have less control over household finances, and less access to personal

---

[72] M Burns, CB Burgoyne, and V Clarke, 'Financial Affairs? Money Management in Same-Sex Relationships' (2008) 37 The Journal of Socio-Economics 481.

[73] A Barlow, C Burgoyne, E Clery, and J Smithson, 'Cohabitation and the Law: Myths, Money and the Media' in A Park, J Curtice, K Thomson, M Phillips, M Johnson, and E Clery (eds) *British Social Attitudes—the 24th Report* (Sage 2008) 29.

[74] Hunter, 'Marriage, Law and Gender' (n 6).

spending money than their husbands.[75] Interestingly, Sonnenberg *et al*'s experimental study on attitudes to intra household financial organization found that the pooling of all income with both parties having equal access (despite any differences in income level) was perceived as the most desirable money-management approach.[76] They did, however, also find that 'people's norms regarding the organization of household money may be subtly shaped by who contributes what to household income',[77] with the concept of 'perceived ownership' suggesting that higher earners have a stronger entitlement to relationship funds and personal spending money, and that this was more strongly associated when the higher earner was male. These differences in constructions of ownership and entitlement to shared relationship funds appear to be somewhat amplified in same-sex relationships, with less pooling of resources and greater levels of financial independence in same-sex couples. It is possible that as more same-sex cases are litigated (and there is no doubt that they will be over time, notwithstanding the preference for settlement in these matters), normative constructions of financial interdependence in relationships may be shifted in directions away from equality and towards lower levels of compensation for economically weaker parties.

V. Conclusion

Same-sex relationship dissolution appears to be taking place in ways that pose novel challenges for family law. Some of the differences highlighted here between same and different-sex relationships, such as retaining friendly interpersonal relationships with ex partners, may well provide a positive example for straight couples. Similarly, lesbian and gay couples' apparent preferences for settling their family law disputes, rather than litigating, would appear to be in keeping with wider governmental 'nudges' in the direction of mediation, arbitration, private ordering and avoiding (lengthy, costly) family law disputes. Nevertheless, same-sex couples' different approaches to relationship finance, that tend to emphasize financial independence rather than interdependence, could have the potential to encourage a retreat from redistributive models of resource allocation on relationship breakdown.

It is tempting to see the preference for financial independence in same-sex relationships as a function of greater levels of equality within same-sex relationships, or as a result of relatively similar income or earnings potential between the parties. But the participants in this project suggest that this is not actually the case. Instead, we would argue, the preference for settling dissolution matters, and the relative resistance to both compensation and maintenance found here, reflects pre-civil partnership approaches to relationship breakdown and the previous lack of legal support on the breakdown of longstanding same-sex relationships. As those in same-sex relationships find that they

---

[75] CB Burgoyne, 'Money in Marriage: How Patterns of Allocation Both Reflect and Conceal Power' (1990) 38 The Sociological Review 634; C Nyman, 'Gender Equality in "The Most Equal County In The World"? Money and Marriage in Sweden' (1999) 47 The Sociological Review 766; J Pahl, 'Household Spending, Personal Spending and the Control of Money in Marriage' (1990) 24 Sociology 119.

[76] SJ Sonnenberg, CB Burgoyne, and DA Routh, 'Income Disparity and Norms Relating to Intra-Household Financial Organisation in The UK: A Dimensional Analysis' (2011) 40 The Journal of Socio-Economics 573.

[77] ibid 579.

are no longer positioned outside of or 'against' the law, approaches to money management in legally recognized same-sex relationships may shift towards greater levels of financial interdependence. Given the assumptions around financial interdependence that are inherent in the legal recognition of same-sex partnerships, and the consequent reduction in welfare to support those in same-sex relationships (including those who do not choose to marry or enter into a civil partnership), it seems likely that higher levels of financial interdependence within same-sex couples will result. Fundamentally, however, further research is now needed to explore the extent to which legal recognition of same-sex relationships changes the ways that same-sex couples experience law in their everyday lives.

7
The Rights of Families and Children at the Border

Matthew Lister

I. Introduction

Family ties play a particular and distinctive role in immigration policy. Essentially every country allows 'family-based immigration' of some sorts, and family ties may have significant importance in many other areas of immigration policy as well, grounding 'derivative' rights to asylum, providing access to citizenship and other benefits at accelerated rates, and serving as a shield from the danger of removal or deportation. Furthermore, status as a child may provide certain benefits to irregular migrants or others without proper immigration standing that is not available to adults. Despite the fact that these benefits are extremely widespread, the justification for them remains less than fully clear, and the extent of the benefits required by considerations of justice (as opposed to expediency or other policy considerations) is debated. While essentially all states recognize at least some of these rights, a significant number of them wish to reduce, rescind, or place significant conditions on them. The role of the family in immigration policy, then, stands in need of further clarification. In this chapter I attempt to provide the needed clarification and justification.

The chapter will consider the following topics. First, I will consider family unification and formation,[1] considering what, if anything, justifies the special preference that nearly all states give to family unification in their immigration schemes. I will also consider the extent that considerations of justice place on the discretion states should have in placing limits on family unification, both in terms of which family members are admitted and what conditions may be placed on admission, such as providing material support, language, requirements, and so on. I will also here address worries[2] that providing these preferences for family unification is a violation of liberal neutrality, requiring states that hope to be just either not to give preferences to families or else to extend similar preferences to a very wide range of other relationships. As these worries can be generalized not just to the case of family unification, but to the other preferences given to families in immigration law and policy, the need to meet the challenge is significant. But, I shall show that, when carefully examined, this charge does not pose any serious difficulty for the account I have elsewhere presented, and which I will rely on and expand here.[3]

---

[1] I shall generally use the term 'unification' to cover both the cases of bringing an existing family together and forming a new family.
[2] Worries raised most forcefully and cogently by L Ferracioli, 'Family Migration Schemes and Liberal Neutrality: A Dilemma' (2014) Journal of Moral Philosophy 1.
[3] See M Lister, 'Immigration, Association, and the Family' (2010) 29 *Law and Philosophy* 717.

Next, I will examine the way that family ties play a special role in asylum and refugee protection. The most common way that this happens is that family members of people granted refugee status are often given so-called 'derivative' status, allowing them to receive essentially the same protection and rights as the original applicant, without having to prove that they, as individuals, also have a well-founded fear of persecution on the basis of one of the protected grounds.[4] Since many states are relatively stingy in providing protection to refugees, and hope to keep the numbers admitted as low as possible, it is important to see if this protection is justified, particularly in light of the questions about favouring the family discussed above. Next, I will consider when, if at all, harm to a family member should be considered harm to the person applying for asylum or refugee status.

I will then examine when, if ever, family status should provide protection from removal or deportation, as well as when such ties should make access to certain rights and benefits easier or faster.[5] These protections from removal work in many ways, with some of them being modestly strong and others being very narrow and difficult to qualify for. I will argue that the justifications for giving preference to families in immigration policy discussed above also provide strong justifications for such protections from removal, and that the current protections found in the United States (at least) are significantly under-protective. I will also consider how far the same protections should apply to non-citizen family members of permanent residents and not just citizens. Finally, I will, briefly, discuss issues relating to the rights of children in particular, considering access to membership and special protections for them.

II. Family Unification

Family unification[6] is one of the principal means of legal movement between states. This is both for countries such as the United States and Canada, which provide many other ways of qualifying for immigrant status,[7] and which are traditional 'countries of immigration', but also for countries that have traditionally been net-exporters of

---

[4] See 8 CFR. 207.7 for the US rule. The importance of the 'Principle of Family Unity' is discussed in Chapter VI, ss 181–88 of the UNHCR *Handbook on Procedures and Criteria for Determining Refugee Status* (Geneva 1992).

[5] These topics often interact in important ways, making it reasonable to discuss them in the same section. For example, in the US, non-citizens who gain permanent resident status via marriage may naturalize after three years, rather than the more standard five. Once an immigrant has naturalized, she may no longer be deported, and restrictions on access to public benefits are removed.

[6] In this section I draw on, while expanding and modifying, the account I presented in my papers, M Lister, 'Immigration, Association, and the Family' (n 3); M Lister, 'A Rawlsian Argument for Extending Family-Based Immigration Benefits to Same-Sex Couples' (2007) 37 University of Memphis Law Review 745.

[7] In the US, family unification accounts for approximately 64 per cent of legal migration. See PL Martin, 'The United States: The Continuing Immigration Debate' in WA Cornelius, T Tsuda, PL Martin, and JF Hollifield (eds), *Controlling Immigration: A Global Perspective* (2nd edn, Stanford UP 2004) 52–55. Canada is (rightfully) typically thought to put less emphasis on family ties than does the US in its immigration policy, but even there, family unification accounts for approximately 22 per cent of all legal migration. See R Aldana, W Kidane, B Lyon, and K McKanders, *Global Issues in Immigration Law* (West Academic Publishing 2013) 153.

migrants, such as Spain, and Italy, and also for countries such as Germany and Japan which are, or have been until recently, very reluctant to accept immigrants.[8]

Despite the ubiquity of family unification grounds for immigration, the practice raises several puzzles. The most obvious of these is the question of what justifies this practice, and to what degree states could modify it while not violating any principles of justice. One way of seeing the puzzle here is to note that the heavy emphasis given to family unification in most immigration systems is hard to justify if we think that the purpose of immigration policy should be to maximize, or at least promote, the economic or material well-being of either the current citizens of a state or of people in general.

Consider first the economic well-being of current citizens. While essentially all countries have conditions in place to help ensure that family-unification schemes do not impose significant costs on current citizens,[9] it is widely claimed that family-unification programmes do less to promote economic well-being of current citizens than would immigration programmes that directly take this as their goal.[10] If we do not assume a general right to free migration between countries, and for that reason hold that states may craft their 'discretionary' immigration policies so as to meet any acceptable goal, we must ask whether a state could acceptably eliminate or seriously restrict family unification and other family-based immigration benefits so as to better achieve its goal of promoting national economic well-being.

The argument is perhaps even better made when we consider the economic well-being of not just citizens, but people in general. It is widely accepted that significant economic gain for less well-off individuals could be achieved by allowing more migration.[11] If we think that immigration policy should be focused on helping the globally disadvantaged, then giving priority to family unification will be a very bad way to try to achieve this goal. Because family unification will essentially always involve international travel by at least one party (and often by more than that), and because international travel is expensive (and so often beyond the means of the least well-off globally, and difficult for those somewhat above that level), it is safe to assume that those who benefit from family-unification programmes will typically be more advantaged than

---

[8] Family immigration accounts for approximately 36 per cent of legal immigration to Germany and approximately 29 per cent for Italy. Percentages for Spain and Japan are more difficult to determine, but are thought to be roughly comparable. See, respectively, PL Martin, 'Germany: Managing Migration in the Twenty-First Century', K Calavita, 'Italy: Economic Realities, Political Frictions, and Policy Failures', and WA Cornelius, 'Spain: The Uneasy Transition from Labor Exporter to Labor Importer' in *Cornelius et al* (eds), (n 7) 245–49, 351, 418. See also JP Lynch and RJ Simons, *Immigration the World Over: Statutes, Policies and, and Practices* (Roman & Littlefield 2003) 198.

[9] I will consider the appropriateness of these schemes below.

[10] See, eg, S Macedo, 'The Moral Dilemma of US Immigration Policy' in C Swain (ed), *Debating Immigration* (CUP 2007) 67, 77; G Borjas, *Friends or Strangers: The Impact of Immigrants on the US Economy* (Basic Books 1990) 218–25.

[11] See H Chang, 'Migration as International Trade: The Economic Gains from the Liberalized Movement of Labor' (1998) 3 University of California, Los Angeles Journal of International Law and Foreign Affairs 384. I believe that the strongest of these claims are not well supported, as they depend on assumptions that we have good reason to think are false, ie, that each person would move to the location where she would get the best return for her labour or skills. But, even if we focus on more modest claims, it is clear that many people around the world would be able to achieve significant improvements to their material well-being if they were allowed to move freely between states.

average, or at least not often among the least well-off globally. Therefore, to the extent that we think immigration policies ought to focus on the least well-off globally, we may have some reason to significantly reduce or eliminate family-unification programmes.[12]

I have previously argued that the fact that family unification necessarily involves not just an 'outsider' seeking to enter a state, but also an 'insider'—most typically a citizen, though in some cases a permanent resident—provides grounds for unravelling the puzzling features noted above. The core of that argument is that a state's need to respect certain basic rights held by its members gives it grounds to give priority to family unification even in the face of other pressing goals.[13] The core right here is the right to form and maintain intimate relationships of one's choosing. While the family is not the only intimate relationship one might have, its structure and nature, I shall argue, make it especially appropriate for placing limits on a state's ability to set its own immigration policy in a way that would prevent the desired exercise of this right. Because this is a basic right, it cannot, consistent with considerations of justice, be traded off for gains in material well-being or to satisfy the preferences of a majority.[14]

The right to form intimate associations is a sub-category of the general right to freedom of association. Freedom of association in general is often thought to be an important part of developing a conception of the good and of being able to live a good life of one's choosing.[15] This might seem to raise problems for my account from two directions. First, strong arguments have been raised that freedom of association justifies a state (or, more properly, the majority in a state) in limiting almost all types of immigration, including family immigration.[16] Secondly, we may worry that there is no principled way to limit immigration rights based on freedom of association to families, and

---

[12] See the important work of M Gibney, *The Ethics and Politics of Asylum: Liberal Democracy and the Response to Refugees* (CUP 2004) 14–15. There is, however, significant reason to distinguish so-called 'convention' refugees from others in need of aid (or so I have elsewhere argued—see M Lister, 'Who are Refugees?' (2013) 32 Law and Philosophy 645), and reason to think that programmes other than open immigration might best help large numbers of the least well off globally. For discussion of this last point, see T Pogge, 'Migration and Poverty' in R Goodin and P Pettit (eds), *Contemporary Political Philosophy: An Anthology* (2nd edn, Wiley-Blackwell 2005) 710–20. I will discuss instances when family ties are directly relevant to refugee protection below.

[13] This argument depends on two assumptions which I will not argue for here, but that I think there are strong arguments for. First, I will assume that there is no basic or general right to free movement between states. That is to say, states have some degree of discretion in setting their own immigration policies. This chapter considers many of the limits on that discretion, insofar as they relate to family status. Secondly, I assume a version of 'modest cosmopolitanism', a view which holds that, while liberal (and reasonably prosperous) states have obligations to the global poor, these obligations are less strong and less far reaching than the obligations owed to their own members. We should not underestimate the strength of our obligations to the global poor, but this is compatible with 'domestic' obligations of justice being more extensive and far-reaching than those that apply internationally or across borders. For a particularly clear and cogent version of the position, one I am largely in agreement with, see Jon Mandle, *Global Justice* (Polity 2006).

[14] In my earlier account of this right, I set out this argument in terms of the development of what Rawls calls the 'moral powers'. See Lister, 'Immigration, Association, and the Family' (n 3) at 721–24. For discussion of this idea, see J Rawls, *Justice as Fairness: A Restatement* (Harvard UP 2001) 18–19, and S Freeman, *Rawls* (Routledge 2007) 54–56. I still am largely happy with this account, but do not think it is necessary for the argument, and so will not spend significant time on it here.

[15] For important discussion of this point, see generally N Rosenblum, *Membership and Morals* (Princeton UP 1998).

[16] Arguments along these lines are made by M Walzer and CH Wellman. See M Walzer, *Spheres of Justice* (Basic Books 1983) 31–63; CH Wellman, 'Immigration and Freedom of Association' (2008) 119 Ethics 109–41. Wellman has later come around to a position much closer to my own. See CH Wellman, 'Freedom of

that we will be forced to either extend such rights to many other types of associations, or else to grant them to no associations.[17] I shall argue, however, that each of these worries can be met, showing the distinctive place for family unification (and other family-centred immigration rights) in a just immigration scheme.

Consider first the claim that freedom of association at the level of the state should allow majorities in the state to greatly restrict or eliminate family unification. Here we have claims for freedom of association on both sides of the equation. However, while freedom of association in general is important and protected by all liberal states, not all types of association are given the same level of protection, nor should they be. The general rule is that more intimate and closely-knit associations are, and should be, subject to fewer restrictions than more general and open ones.[18] This point may be illustrated by considering examples from US employment and housing law. Businesses are types of associations, and those who run such associations are allowed a significant amount of discretion in setting the terms of the association. Owners and managers may, for example, set minimum educational and training requirements for positions, may set standards for dress and grooming, and increasingly place restrictions on workers that extend well beyond working hours, refusing to hire smokers, for example. But, in the large majority of cases, employers may not discriminate on the basis of race or sex.[19] The primary exception to this rule applies in the case of quite small businesses. Businesses with fewer than fifteen employees are exempt from these anti-discrimination rules.[20] There are similar rules in relation to fair housing laws in the US. Generally, those seeking to rent housing may not discriminate on the basis of race or family status. But, there is an exception to this rule. If an owner is renting rooms in a home which they occupy, they are exempt from this rule.[21]

In both cases we see a pattern which supports the basic argument of this section of the chapter. We have a trade-off between basic liberties, but the more intimate the association in question, the less it is subject to limitation by non-parties to the association. This rule is not absolute—it too must be balanced against other basic liberties, and if certain forms of association made it impossible for significant numbers of members to live good lives, then we would have strong reason to regulate the association. (This can help explain why we do not give full discretion to parents in deciding how to raise

---

Association and the Right to Exclude' in CH Wellman and P Cole, *Debating the Ethics of Immigration: Is There a Right to Exclude?* (OUP 2011) 93.

[17] This is essentially the argument made by Ferracioli (n 2).

[18] My argument here is not meant to imply that other forms of association, such as political association or labour organization, are not extremely important. They are, and so a just state must protect such associations. But note how the same sort of anti-discrimination limits that I discuss below have been imposed in the case of political and labour organization, showing how, even though these are important forms of association, they may be regulated for broader purposes in a way we do not think intimate associations may. Labour organization may stretch over borders as well, though it is not clear that such activities must involve *immigration*, as opposed to more temporary forms of movement. Taking note of the appropriateness of these restrictions will also help us see how the nature of the association in question is essential for evaluating its place in granting immigration benefits, as I argue below.

[19] Title VII of the Civil Rights Act of 1964 ('Title VII').

[20] The somewhat complex method of determining the number of employees need not bother us here. Some state and local governments in the US have stricter anti-discrimination rules in employment.

[21] Fair Housing Act of 1968, as amended in 1974 and 1988, 42 USC s 3601–19, 3631. Some cities have even stronger fair housing regulations.

their children, even given the highly intimate nature of this relationship.) This pattern continues when we look at the family. Very few regulations on marriage and family life are acceptable. As the family is (typically—I will return to this point and its importance) the most intimate of associations, this is as we should expect. The right to marry and form a family according to one's wishes (assuming no other comparable rights are violated in the process) is widely recognized as a fundamental right, and can therefore be restricted only for the strongest of reasons.[22] This strongly suggests that the right to marry and form a family may legitimately be restricted only to protect other equally important basic liberties, and that it may not be traded off against or limited for the sake of less basic liberties or for gains in economic efficiency. If other forms of association are less fundamental than the family in this sense, then the right to form a family may not be limited because of them.

We are here assuming that states may legitimately[23] seek to limit immigration for many different reasons, including better promoting internal justice, controlling population growth and protecting the environment, and, within certain limits, helping to shape the sort of community found within the state. At least some of these goals may be cast in terms of freedom of association. Assuming that the restriction is not applied in an otherwise discriminatory way (that is, isn't applied unevenly on the basis of racial, religious, or national characteristics), we must ask whether freedom of association at the state level can justify restricting or eliminating family unification.

I argue that freedom of association at the state level cannot justify eliminating or highly restricting family unification. My argument proceeds as such: freedom of association is a fundamental right or basic liberty, and as such can only be traded off against other fundamental rights or liberties. Various types of associations are protected by these rights, but in general, the more intimate a relationship, the less discretion a state has in limiting it. Many types of associations are important for living good lives, but given the (typically) highly intimate nature of the family, and the (typical) importance of living close together for many years for family life, it is plausible to think that family unification deserves very extensive latitude from the state in situations like this, and that any attempt to say who can or cannot form a close intimate relationship, when the fundamental rights of others are not at stake, is a grave infringement on one's liberty. However, no modern society could prevent the formation of intimate bonds between its citizens and non-citizen 'outsiders' without committing other very serious abridgments of liberty.

---

[22] For recognition by the US Supreme Court, see *Turner v Safley* 482 US 78 (1987); *Zablocki v Redhail* 434 US 374 (1978); *Loving v Virginia* 388 US 1 (1967); *Skinner v Oklahoma* 316 US 535 (1942); *Meyer v Nebraska* 262 US 390 (1932), and, most recently, *Obergefell v Hodges* 576 US _ (2015), extending these rights to same-sex couples. The right is also recognized in the UN Universal Declaration of Human Rights and other important human rights documents, as well as by many governments.

[23] Of course, if justice requires open borders, as some have argued, then the ability to use immigration restrictions to reach these goals will be greatly reduced. I do not find any of the arguments for open borders compelling, but, more importantly, this is unlikely to be a problem we will face in the near future anyway, so I will not directly address that issue here. My claim here is that the goals in question are ones that states may legitimately pursue, and that, assuming there is no basic right to free movement between states, states may use immigration restrictions as one way to attempt to meet these goals.

Given this, citizens of any state will sometimes want to form families with non-citizens. Furthermore, it is part of the nature of family life that it can typically only be experienced in a satisfactory way if its members, or at least the core members of spouses and minor children, are able to live in close proximity with each other for indefinitely long periods of time. But, this will only be possible if states allow their citizens to bring in non-citizen partners and family members. This requires making permanent residence[24] available to the entire family. Because of this, states have a duty to allow their citizens to bring in their non-citizen family members. Importantly, this is a limitation on the freedom that a state has in setting its own immigration policies that comes completely from duties owed to current citizens. The right here is the right of a current citizen to bring in an outsider, not the right of the outsider to enter. This right, then, does not depend on any controversial argument for free movement between states and is not subject to the arguments against such a general right to free movement.[25]

III. How Far Does the Association Argument Extend?

At this point a new worry arises. If the right to association can limit the ability of states to set their own immigration policies, as I have argued, then we may wonder if this might not extend so far as to leave the state with very limited powers at all. I have addressed this issue before,[26] but will here focus on an important argument by Luara Ferracioli, contending that other sorts of close and important associations—Ferracioli focuses on friendships and creative collaborations, though there could conceivably be others—must also be seen as grounding immigration rights in a way similar to what I have argued for the family if the state in question is not to violate principles of liberal neutrality. More specifically, Ferracioli argues that just states must extend the sort of immigration rights I have argued for to other sorts of relationships or else offer these benefits to none of them. I will argue that this argument fails, for two reasons. First, Ferracioli fails to properly consider that we are here dealing with the question of developing a just immigration policy, and that, when doing so, we must consider typical cases, not unusual ones. When we consider whether a relationship or association should ground immigration rights, we must consider whether this *type* of relationship or association is one which would *typically or usually* justify immigration rights—the right to enter a state and remain in perpetuity, in contrast with some lesser, more temporary right to enter. But, when we look closely at the sorts of relationships Ferracioli considers, we can see that they would only justify immigration rights in unusual cases, while the converse is true of the family—it would nearly always justify immigration rights for the

---

[24] I have elsewhere argued that permanent residents ought to eventually have access to full citizenship, with very few qualifications. See M Lister, 'Citizenship, in the Immigration Context' (2011) 70 Maryland Law Review 175. For a similar argument, see J Carens, 'Why Naturalization Should be Easy: A Response to Noah Pickus' in N Pickus (ed), *Immigration and Citizenship in the 21st Century* (Rowman & Littlefield 1998) 141–48. I will touch on some of these issues later in this essay, but will leave them aside for now.

[25] I discuss in more detail why the associative rights of majorities in states ought not trump the associative rights of families in Lister, 'Immigration, Association, and the Family' (n 3) at 732–35, but will here stop with this less detailed argument.

[26] ibid 735–38.

reasons I have suggested. Secondly, to implement the sort of policy Ferracioli suggests would itself frequently require intrusive actions by the state that would not be compatible with liberal principles of justice. This is because there would be no principled way to judge whether the relationships in question meet the sort of standards she sets without engaging in illiberal actions. For these reasons, we may reject her challenges to my argument.

The core of Ferracioli's argument is that 'an array of special relationships should be allowed to flourish in a liberal ethos' and that therefore, 'either immigration arrangements ought to be designed to include all sorts of special relationships that give meaning to people's lives, or none at all.'[27] As noted, Ferracioli uses close friendships and creative collaborations as examples of the sort of relationships she has in mind.[28] It is undeniable that friendships are important for people, and necessary in most cases if people are to be able to live good lives. In a smaller number of cases, creative collaborations may also play a deep and important role in the lives of those involved. The question here, though, is whether the value of these relationships should give rise to immigration benefits, where the benefits in question extend to the right to live in and remain in a country in perpetuity (and, eventually, to have access to citizenship), as opposed to lesser rights, such as the right to make temporary visits.

Importantly, the primary question at this point is about the nature of the relationships in question, and not about their relative value. In particular, the question is not about the subjective value of the relationships to the people in question. Individuals may value all sorts of relationships, and as Ferracioli notes, it is not the place of the liberal state to say which sort of relationships the individual should value most. Here, where the question is one of crafting a just immigration policy, the question must be about what is necessary in typical cases for the relationship to be able to achieve its end. This is not a matter of the subjective preferences or desires of the participants, but rather of the common form of the relationship. I shall argue that, when we keep in mind the fact that we are here considering policies, there is good reason to give preference to family unification that does not apply to the other sorts of relationships that Ferracioli considers.

At this moment it is worth pausing to consider a methodological point which has already been alluded to. This essay is, in part, an examination of what sort of immigration policies are compatible with liberal principles of justice. No policy can be crafted so as to always include every case which would fall under the principles that justify the policy, and to exclude all cases which would not be justified by the underlying principles. That is to say, all actual policies will always be both over and under inclusive. To those who work in law and politics, this is almost a banality, but it has an importance that is often over-looked by philosophers. In particular, this fact indicates that purported counter-examples work differently than they do in many areas of philosophy. To show that a policy is the wrong one, it is not enough to show that it sometimes produces

---

[27] Ferracioli (n 2) 3.
[28] It is worth noting that the limits on immigration schemes considered here are limits on democratic action. While not all democratic action is worthy of respect, we should hesitate to place limits on it, doing so only when necessary to protect basic rights. Ferracioli does not address concerns like this in her paper.

'anomalous' results—results which are perhaps not fully in accord with the underlying principle that justify the policy—but rather that they typically produce a large number, or an unacceptable number, of anomalies.[29]

Given the above methodological point, Ferracioli's criticisms of the associative argument for family unification would only have weight if it were typically the case that friendships or creative collaborations could only exist when the people involved were able to live close together in the same country in perpetuity. This claim does not seem plausible to me, and Ferracioli gives no reason to think otherwise. She does note that there will be cases where people are disappointed, perhaps deeply so, if they are not able to live in close proximity to their friends or creative partners. These are considerations that states should take into consideration. But it is not at all obvious that the typical example of friendship or creative collaboration require living together perpetually— that is, that immigration, as opposed to temporary access, is required in these cases. It is not the duty of just, liberal, states to make sure that no ones' desires or goals are disappointed, but because she has not shown, and cannot show, that the sorts of relationships she considers typically require living together in perpetuity in the way that family life requires,[30] Ferracioli cannot show that these relationships justify placing limits on the democratic power of the state in the same way that families do. Again, it is important to see that the essence of this claim is not that the family is (subjectively) more important to the well-being and happiness of most people than are friendships or creative collaborations, but rather that the nature of the relationships in question is such that we typically expect that people can, if they wish, continue friendships and creative collaborations even if they do not live in close proximity in perpetuity, but we do not think this is so of the sorts of goods that come from family life. This justifies treating family unification differently from the cases above, regardless of the subjective importance of the relationships to the individuals. (We can here also easily see why it makes sense to treat same-sex relationships similarly to opposite-sex ones. The good achieved by same-sex relationships will typically require close proximity in a way that is essentially the same as opposite-sex ones, but in a way not typically found in other types of relationships.)[31]

Ferracioli's argument also seems to me to depend on a mistaken notion of what liberal neutrality requires. Ferracioli correctly claims that a liberal state must be, in some appropriate sense, neutral between different conceptions of the good, or what makes a good life. She goes wrong, however, in suggesting that this is tied in a close way to the subjective preferences of different citizens.[32] This is almost exactly backwards. Rather,

---

[29] For defence of this methodological point, see MM Dempsey and M Lister, 'Applied Legal and Political Philosophy', in K Lippert-Rasmussen, K Brownlee, and D Coady (eds), *A Companion to Applied Philosophy* (Wiley Blackwell 2017) 315-18

[30] Ferracioli notes, rightly, that there will be cases where family members who do not in fact desire to live together in perpetuity are able to use their ties to gain immigration benefits. See Ferracioli, 'Family Migration Schemes' (n 2) 11. This, however, is not an embarrassment for the view defended here once we note the methodological point above, as there will always be cases that fall under a policy even though they do not fit the justification for the policy.

[31] For extensive elaboration on this point, see Lister, 'A Rawlsian Argument' (n 6).

[32] Ferracioli, 'Family Migration Schemes' (n 2) 15.

what liberal neutrality requires is policies that can be implemented formally.[33] As Charles Larmore notes,

> [W]hat the state does, the decisions it makes and the policies it pursues, will generally benefit some people more than others, and so some conceptions of the good life will fare better than others.... But this does not impugn the neutrality of the liberal state. Its neutrality is not meant to be one of *outcome* but rather one of *procedure*.[34]

This is also compatible with Rawls's notion of neutrality, because, he notes, not-basic liberties (such as the liberty to move between states) may be limited when this is done for public reasons, as we are here assuming is the case.[35] This predictably contributes to the fact that some ways of life will be better able to flourish in a just society than will others, without this violating liberal neutrality.[36] Ferracioli's proposal would require the state to look into the hearts of its citizens so as to determine their true feelings in a way that is itself illiberal.[37] Furthermore, this proposal would produce a deeply undesirable instability in government action, leading to grave possibility of abuse and the imposition of prejudice by government officials. This, too, is incompatible with liberal neutrality, properly understood. Again, as Larmore notes,

> There are circumstances ... where heeding [the] complexity [of moral life] would be misplaced. In some cases decision making in accordance with a system of rules that yields single directive in almost every case, but that corresponds only *grosso modo* to our considered moral judgments, may outweigh a more faithfully nuanced appreciation of the way things are. Most of all this is true in the political realm. There system can prove more desirable than sensitivity for a very important reason. Whenever the government acts according to publicly known statutes and laws that allow little room for conflicting directives, this gives its actions a *predictability* that can be invaluable for those who must make decisions in other areas of society, or even other branches of government.[38]

---

[33] Of course, the proper notion of neutrality to apply in relation to the family is contested, as the papers in this volume show. See, in particular, E Brake's important argument in 'Paid and Unpaid Care: Marriage, Equality, and Domestic Workers' and *Minimizing Marriage* (OUP 2012).

[34] C Larmore, *Patterns of Moral Complexity* (CUP 1987) 43–44. (Emphasis in the original.)

[35] See J Rawls, *Political Liberalism* (Columbia UP 1996) 292, and, for helpful discussion, Freeman (n 14) 78.

[36] See Rawls (n 35) 193, and, for helpful discussion, see J Mandle, (unreasonably neglected) *What's Left of Liberalism: An Interpretation and Defense of Justice as Fairness* (Lexington Books 2000) 95 (unreasonably neglected). There is some difficulty here in that Ferracioli focuses on the subjective preferences of individuals and not, strictly speaking, comprehensive moral views in Rawls's sense, but if anything, this weakens her claim that not extending immigration benefits to friends or others violates liberal neutrality. Both Rawls and Mandle also note the importance of the family in developing the moral powers—a point I have touched on in other work, but do not depend on here.

[37] From the Kantian tradition, see I Kant, *The Metaphysics of Morals* ([1797] M Gregor ed & tr, Cambridge University Press 1996) 6, 393; see also W Kersting, 'Politics, Freedom, and Order: Kant's Political Philosophy' in P Guyer (ed), *The Cambridge Companion to Kant and Modern Philosophy* (CUP 2003) 345. ('Kant's concept of right concerns only the external sphere of the freedom of action. Only the effects of actions on the freedom of action of others are of interest to it.') While Kant was not a 'political liberal' in Rawls's sense, he did argue for an important strain of liberal neutrality in state action.

[38] Larmore (n 34) 40. (Emphasis in the original.)

Such a programme is easily compatible with family immigration, but not clearly compatible with extending such rights to friends, collaborators, and others. In fact, the system proposed by Ferracioli would make this sort of predictability impossible, simply because it would require looking into the hearts of people involved.[39] Therefore, the scheme would violate one of the most important types of liberal neutrality, rather than protect it. For this reason, too, there is significant ground to reject Ferracioli's challenge to the associational argument for family unification rights.

I have argued that family unification rights, based on freedom of association, provide one major limit on the discretion that states should have in setting their own immigration policy, if they hope to be just.[40] However, this leaves open important questions about the limits of family unification rights.[41] There are two main questions to consider here. First, we must ask about the extent of the right—to which family members does it apply? Second, we must ask what sort of restrictions may be put in place on this right so as to ensure reciprocity and other values among citizens.

I will start with the question of the extent of the right to bring in one's family members. I have several times referred to the fact that 'we' generally believe that it is part of the nature of the family that family members must be free to live together. That is, I have referred to a common understanding of what is important about and to the family. I use this idea to help discuss the limits of family-based immigration rights. I refer to our 'common understanding' here for several reasons. First, because I do not believe that there is a deep or 'real' level of importance that can be assigned to various associations beyond our common understandings of the importance or nature of the various

---

[39] Ferracioli proposes that those making visa decisions might, eg, consider the correspondence between the parties. See Ferracioli, 'Family Migration Schemes' (n 2) 19. This would often be an implausible invasion of privacy, but more importantly, such evidence would often not exist. This differs from family formation, where formal bureaucratic evidence is the norm. Of course, this norm is sometimes violated in practice (though not nearly as often as popular imagination would suggest), but here, at least, formal bureaucratic evidence may typically suffice, while in the cases suggested by Ferracioli, it rarely will. For helpful discussion of the sorts of largely formal, bureaucratic evidence most relevant for adjudicating a family-based immigration application to the United States, see 'Adjudicator's Field Manual' (*United States Citizenship and Immigration Services*, 26 August 2014) <https://www.uscis.gov/iframe/ilink/docView/AFM/HTML/AFM/0-0-0-1/0-0-0-15.html> accessed 3 June 2016. Especially relevant is Chapter 11, 'Evidence' and Chapter 21, 'Family Based Petitions and Applications'. It is notable in particular that the only time in which the existence of sexual relations between spouses is explicitly relevant is in the (rare) case of a 'proxy' marriage. See INA s 101(a)(35). In other instances, sexual relationships between spouses are not required, and enquiring into them is strongly disfavoured. As the Field Manual notes in relation to interviewing spouses, the object of an interview is to determine the (formal and legal) 'bona fides of the marriage, not its "viability"', Adjudicator's Field Manual Chapter 21.3(H). In conversation, S Legomsky, recently retired Chief Council for the USCIS, has confirmed for me that adjudicators are not to ask 'intimate sexual questions'. Of course, this guideline is sometimes violated. Different states take different approaches to this question, with some taking a more intrusive, less liberal track. The important point, however, is that these questions *can* be answered with only formal, bureaucratic documentation.

[40] Other foundations for family immigration rights are possible. See C Yong, "Caring Relationships and Family Migration Schemes", in A Sager, ed., *The Ethics and Politics of Immigration: Core Issues and Emerging Trends* (Rowman & Littlefield 2016) 61–83.

[41] D Jeske, in her chapter, 'Moral and Legal Obligations to Support "Family"', has called for a much broader definition of 'family'—one that might well include some people Ferracioli wishes to cover under immigration benefits. This seems too broad, to my mind, but her arguments are worth considering at this point. Similarly, Brake (n 33), discusses inclusion of paid caregivers. Whether these persons, who fulfil many of the same functions as family members, should be provided immigration benefits is a question I lack space to consider in this chapter.

associations. (So, if we *typically* thought friends must live in close proximity, Ferracioli would have a point, but we do not seem to think this.) Secondly, even if there were 'real' foundations for claims about the nature and importance of various associations, there would be disagreement as to what these foundations were. Therefore, we are likely to get both more agreement and greater legitimacy if we abstract from foundational claims and try to find an overlapping consensus here as to what is most important about various associations. This is, of course, a common methodology in liberal political philosophy, so it should be no surprise that we apply it here, too. Finally, an appeal to common conceptions is especially helpful here in showing how the extent of the right to family-based immigration may vary over time and space.

Now, we may have a hard time agreeing on just what our shared conception of the family is and why it is important. (Recent debates over gay marriage in the US surely helps underline this potential disagreement, though perhaps in a way that is more apparent than real in the end.) I will not attempt to give a full answer to this question here for even one society. Rather, I will look at what I take to be a minimal core and then consider how this might be extended. The minimal core of the family, the unit to which all states must extend immigration rights to their citizens, is, I hold, the spouse or partner and minor children. While different societies conceptualize the family in different ways, this seems to be a common core included in all conceptions, without which the notion of a family hardly makes sense. Therefore, if the family has the importance that we normally associate with it, then all states must allow their citizens to bring in spouses or partners and minor children. To refuse to do so, in the large majority of cases, would be unjust.

Many countries offer family-based immigration benefits much broader than this. In the US, for example, parents of citizens who are over twenty-one are also considered 'immediate relatives' and so are eligible for the broadest immigration benefits.[42] Many other relatives of citizens and permanent residents are also eligible for reduced immigration benefits under US Law.[43] The question we must here ask is whether these broader grants of immigration benefits ought to also be considered a matter of right, or whether they can be left to the political process in individual countries to decide. My

---

[42] See INA s 101(b)(1), (2). The reason this benefit applies only to citizens over twenty-one is to minimize attempts to gain 'back-door' access to immigration benefits by having a child in the US, since all children born in the US, even to unauthorized immigrants, are citizens. If children of any age could petition for their parents, this would create strong perverse incentives for non-citizens to have children in the US. Most states deal with this by having significantly less generous *jus soli* citizenship rules than those found in the US, though this seems to me undesirable. See Lister, 'Citizenship in the Immigration Context' (n 24) 205–09. No immigration policy can be perfectly implemented, but we must seek to minimize injustices in application, even if this can never be fully achieved. My approach to this problem would be to apply a standard somewhat like that found in US law, where 'extreme hardship to a US Citizen or permanent resident' (here the child born in the US) can ground a claim for cancellation of removal, though in a more generous way than is currently applied.

[43] Potential beneficiaries include siblings and adult children, among others. See INA s 203(a). These beneficiaries are subject to numerical and country-of-origin limits in such a way as to create very long backlogs. These backlogs are highly frustrating to those subject to them, and sometimes claimed to be unjust in themselves. Since I hold that the justice of these aspects of immigration policy turn on the details of the country in question, and that the only way to determine these details is via the democratic process and deliberation, I will not here attempt to determine whether, as a matter of justice (as opposed to a matter of sound or efficient policy) the US should strive to reduce or eliminate them.

answer is that each state must look to its common conception of the family to decide which level of benefits are a matter of right. This is, of course, not to offer an easy practical answer, but only to suggest what features ought to be considered. In a liberal, highly mobile society like the US, we might reasonably agree that only the minimal core must be protected as a matter of right, though the US in fact offers much broader benefits. In other more 'traditional' societies, where the extended family is both more common and important, it might be reasonable to include more family members under a strong right of immigration. But, beyond the minimal core that seems to apply to any conception of the family, this matter will be one to be determined by the democratic deliberation of a free people.

The final consideration to be addressed here is what sort of restrictions may be placed on family unification so as to ensure reciprocity among citizens. If, as argued by Rawls and others, reciprocity among citizens is a condition on (domestic) justice, then maintaining reciprocity may be reasonable grounds for limiting immigration. That is, if allowing in immigrants would be expected to make those in the country worse off than they would be without allowing in the immigrants (after relevant considerations of global justice are accounted for, again assuming some form of modest cosmopolitanism), then this might be grounds for a state to limit immigration. For example, this would be the case if immigrants were expected to use more resources than they produced, for example. Rules to prevent such cases are wide-spread in western countries, all of which exclude would-be immigrants who are likely to become public charges.[44] Such rules are, I shall, for now, assume, largely acceptable. The question that remains is how this requirement for reciprocity affects family-based immigration.

The US addresses this issue by requiring that a citizen (or permanent resident) who wishes to bring in family members must be able to support her family at 125 per cent of the poverty level for a family of the given size. This may be done via evidence of employment, proof of assets, or, if the person seeking to bring in her family does not meet this level on her own, by means of a third-party guarantor. Furthermore, the petitioner must promise to maintain this level of support for the would-be immigrant for at least five years. This rule has two practical effects. First, if a citizen is unable to meet this requirement, she cannot successfully petition to bring in her foreign-born non-citizen family members. Secondly, once the foreign family members are in the US, this rule makes it difficult for the foreign-born family member to qualify for means-tested government assistance, since the assets of the sponsor are deemed to be available to the immigrant. When joined with restrictions on access to public benefits to new immigrants (when these are needed to ensure reciprocity—this need not always be the case) such measures can help ensure that allowing family-based immigration does not violate reciprocity among citizens. Measures such as these cannot, of course, ensure that family-based immigration will bring the largest possible benefit to the receiving country that any immigration policy could. This will most likely not be the case. But, to

---

[44] In the US, see INA s 212(a)(4). For the European Union, in addition to member-state laws, see Council Directive 90/365, art 1, 1990 OJ (L 180) 28, Council Directive 90/364, art 1, 1990 OJ (L 180) 26, Council Directive 93/96, art 1 1993 OJ (L 317) 59. Note that several countries, in particular the UK, have or have threatened to impose standards that cannot plausibly be thought to be designed to ensure reciprocity, for they impose burdens that are massively too high for this standard. Such burdens are prima facie unjust.

demand that would be to ask too much. While certain measures may be taken to ensure that no citizens are used as a mere means to the support of another's choices, there is no duty of justice to promote the highest amount of aggregate welfare when this would interfere with the basic liberties of others.

Of course the disabilities discussed above may not continue indefinitely if we wish to comply with justice. This is partly because there is reason to expect that only a temporary deprivation is necessary to ensure reciprocity[45] and also because, after some fairly short period of time, the immigrant family member will be eligible for full membership. After this point is reached, any further deprivation would be unreasonable. At this point we may assume that the immigrant is significantly enough integrated into the society so that a refusal to provide public support, if needed, would be unjust, akin to a refusal to provide benefits to a citizen based on ethnicity.[46] Special rules may also be put in place to help prevent abuses and exploitation within families. Rules of this sort exist now, and though the current rules are not sufficient, there is no good reason why they could not be strengthened.[47] I am, of course, not wedded to the particular details of the US system. And, if a majority in a country wished, they could legitimately choose to have fewer restrictions than this, or even none at all. But, if we are to accept that family-based immigration is something owed as a right to citizens, then we must make sure that this right works in a way that everyone could reasonably accept. Regulations such as I have discussed here can, by ensuring reciprocity, help make sure that this requirement is met. If these features are met, then further requirements such as language proficiency seem redundant and unneeded, since there will be strong natural incentives for immigrants to learn the local language, and second-generation immigrants nearly always learn the local language. If such requirements are not needed to support stability or reciprocity, insisting on them would be illiberal.

I have argued that freedom of association provides grounds for family unification rights. In what follows, I shall discuss several more issues where the family plays a special role in immigration policy and show how the association argument provides important constraints on the discretion that states should have in setting their own immigration policies in these areas, too. I start with questions related to removal or deportation.

IV. Family Ties as a Shield from Removal

All states with any significant immigration law have a wide range of grounds for removal or deportation of non-citizens. My purpose here is not primarily to consider which of these grounds for removal are justified, but rather to consider when family ties should be able to serve as a shield for removal. Given the argument set out above,

---

[45] For discussion on this point, see Chang, 'Migration as International Trade' (n 11).

[46] Again, in many areas of modern life, bright-line rules will be preferable to individual assessments, and more compatible with liberalism, since they both allow greater planning, and hence freedom, and also because they allow for less arbitrary decision making and discrimination. See Larmore (n 34) at 40–42.

[47] See, eg, the relevant provisions in the 'Violence Against Women Act' in the US INA s 204(a)(iii)(II), INA s 240A(b)(2). Immigrants who adjust status under these acts are eligible for public benefits.

I will suggest that family ties should serve as a shield from removal whenever removing the non-citizen would significantly impair the associational rights of a citizen (or, in at least some cases, a permanent resident) and the dangers posed to the community by allowing the non-citizen to remain are not clearly sufficient to outweigh these rights.[48]

One way in which family ties may provide a defence against removal is, I think, largely uncontroversial and may be dealt with quickly. In many countries, immigrants who gain access to permanent residence by means of marriage to a citizen are eligible for citizenship on an expedited time frame.[49] This accelerated access to citizenship is plausibly justified by the faster and deeper integration brought about by family ties. When an immigrant becomes a citizen, she must be treated, at least in the vast majority of cases, the same as any other citizen, and so cannot legitimately be removed from the country, barring very rare circumstances.[50]

But what of cases where the immigrant is not yet a citizen? Here the case is somewhat less clear, though, I argue, there are still grounds for allowing family ties to be used as a shield. This will be most obviously the case when the grounds for removal are largely administrative or formal. For example, in the US, it is officially a ground for removal for an alien to fail to file a change of address form within ten days of moving.[51] Of course, most grounds for removal involve violations of immigration laws, or other laws, that are more serious than this, but many are still essentially administrative or formal in nature. In these instances, the same powerful association rights considered above ought to provide a defence from removal. Of course, there is some question as to which laws and regulations ought to count as merely administrative or formal in this way. I would suggest that all violations that are not criminal in nature should certainly fall in this category, and that at least non-violent crimes should also be included. Even more significant violations of immigration law, such as entering the country without permission, ought to plausibly fall within this scope.[52]

The most difficult case will involve ones where the non-citizen has committed a serious crime.[53] Here the association rights of the citizen family members must be weighed against safety for the larger community. If allowing the non-citizen to remain in the community would pose a serious risk to the safety of the community members, this may outweigh the association rights that the citizen family member has. That

---

[48] Other defences against removal are also plausibly justified. In particular, there may be good reason to not remove a non-citizen when removing her would pose a serious hardship to the non-citizen, even when it would not be detrimental to any current citizens. However, as these cases fall outside of the scope of my investigation of the role of family ties in immigration policy, I will not further consider them.

[49] This is so for the US and France, eg, and probably for other countries, too.

[50] In the US, eg, it is extremely difficult to 'denaturalize' a citizen. This process is usually only possible in the case of serious material fraud in the original immigration application or in the naturalization procedure.

[51] INA s 265.

[52] Currently, in the US, non-citizens who enter without inspection and then have US citizen family members (through marriage or birth) are presented with a deeply unjust 'catch-22'. They may not adjust their status on the basis of their family ties while remaining in the US, but, while they are eligible for immigration benefits if they leave the US, they are then typically barred from re-entry for ten years because of having entered without inspection. This rule has torn apart many otherwise law-abiding families and forced many others into significantly unjust situations.

[53] In the US this would typically be a 'crime involving moral turpitude' or an 'aggravated felony'. Both of these categories are maddeningly vague and include many crimes which are not obviously extremely serious.

the non-citizen has committed a serious crime may be a plausible reason to withdraw the right to remain in the host society from the non-citizen.[54] Still, this consideration must be weighed against the important rights held by citizen family members, and not imposed lightly or without consideration of the other rights in question. The associational rights considered above might reasonably be thought to ground a special right of review, where the non-citizen who has served a sentence for a serious crime may be able to show that his removal is not necessary to provide for the safety of the community, and (or perhaps 'or') would lead to non-trivial hardship to citizen family-members.[55] In this way, family ties may be respected and protected without exposing the wider community to excessive danger.

V. Families and Refugee Protection

Family ties raise a number of important and interesting questions in the area of asylum and refugee protection. Some of these issues have been addressed in the laws or policies of various countries, in conventions such as the Convention on the Rights of the Child, and in the policy of the UN High Commissioner for Refugees (UNHCR). However, the basic justification for these protections has not been clearly worked out or defended. I will attempt to provide a basic justification for so-called 'derivative' refugee or asylum protection, and will discuss when harm or threatened harm to a family member should be considered harm to the person applying for asylum.

To be considered a refugee or granted asylum, an applicant must show that she has a well-founded fear of persecution on the basis of race, religion, nationality, political opinion, or membership in a particular social group. Many people who fit within this definition, however, have family members, and these family members may not themselves fall under the definition.[56] Should states have an obligation to take in these family members if the principle applicant is granted asylum?

I claim that the union of the duties owed to refugees,[57] conjoined with the importance of familial association discussed above, provide good grounds for extending the same rights offered to refugees to at least immediate family members—spouses and minor children—as derivative applicants, even if these family members do not themselves face a danger of persecution. Refugees, recall, are people who cannot safely live in their home country for reasons that they cannot or ought not to be expected to change, such as their political views, race, sexual orientation, or religion. Such a person

---

[54] I do not think that it is always a good reason. Especially in the case of long-term residents, there may be good reason to allow them to remain even after having committed a serious crime. This topic is beyond the scope of this chapter, however.

[55] This may also plausibly apply to non-citizen but permanent-resident family members.

[56] Of course, in many cases, if one family member falls under the definition, the others likely do so, too, for straight-forward reasons. But, there may be significant administrative advantages in treating these claims as derivative claims, parasitic off of that of the primary applicant. In what follows I will focus on cases where other family members do not have, at least obviously, their own asylum claims.

[57] The most basic duty owed to refugees is *non-refoulement*, or the obligation not to return them to a country where they face danger. Beyond this, there is a duty to provide a 'durable solution'—the right to live in and remain in a safe society, at least so long as the refugee cannot safely return to their home country. We may expect this obligation to be on-going and open-ended. For discussion, see Lister, 'Who are Refugees?' (n 12).

must seek another country to live in, if she is going to be safe. Given the importance of family ties discussed above it is not reasonable to expect people who cannot live in their own countries to either abandon their families or live in danger. Such a choice ought not be forced on anyone. If family ties are as important as I have suggested they are, then in refugee cases, we have good reason to allow refugees to bring their family members with them, even if they do not face persecution themselves.

One further case is relevant at this point. Sometimes the harm that an asylum applicant faces is not aimed at them directly, but at a family member. In some cases this is straightforward, and the need for refugee protection is clear. Suppose, for example, that a ruling party tells an opposition member that if she does not stop her political activities, it will kill or imprison her children. While the direct harm would be done to someone other than the opposition member, it is clear here how this is still a harm to her, or a means of harming her, and so the basis for providing her with refugee protection should be straightforward. In some cases, however, the situation may be more complicated. Consider the following case: a native of El Salvador in the US faces deportation (for non-criminal grounds) to that country. She does not herself have a colourable asylum claim. But, she does have a US citizen child. Because the child has no other family member in the US, if the mother is deported to El Salvador, she will have to take the child with her. However, if she is so deported, the child will face forced recruitment or other persecution from gang members in that country. Here the child faces harm, but the harm directed towards the child is not imposed as a means of harming the parent. The child cannot herself apply for asylum (making the mother eligible as a derivative applicant) because she is already a US citizen. The mother does not herself face direct harm from the gang members, or at least not any more than any other citizen of El Salvador. Should the mother be able to use the threatened harm to the child as a ground for applying for asylum? So far US Courts have been extremely reluctant to accept this claim, but if we see family life to be as important as I have claimed it to be above, there may be some justification for granting asylum to the mother in cases such as this. This is, however, a complex case, and I cannot claim to have a fully worked out theory at this point.

VI. The Rights of Children

The rights of children[58] raise a number of distinct issues in immigration law and policy. While I lack sufficient space to provide a full account here, I will mention a few examples that are particularly important. If children are to be able to develop and thrive, they typically need access to secure membership in the society that provides their cultural context, as well as, in most cases, access to the citizenship held by their parents. I have argued that, in relation to children, justice requires that they have access to any citizenship held by their parents (so as to help ensure a stable family life) and also to citizenship in the society where they have grown up and spent a significant amount of time. This second case does not necessarily, I contend, require as strict a form of *jus soli*

---

[58] See CM Macleod's chapter for a very helpful general discussion of children's rights.

citizenship as found in the US, but does require access to citizenship when the child has lived for a significant percentage of her or his life and developing years in the country.[59] A similar argument tells in favour of granting residence rights, and eventually full citizenship, not just to those born within a territory, but also to those who entered after birth but at a young age, if they live in the territory for significant periods of time. Both children born in a particular state and those who enter it while minors (especially very young children) find themselves in the society in a way that differs morally from adults who choose to enter. In this way, the standing of these children is at least very similar to the children of citizens. Most controversially, this claim applies even to those who entered or remained in the country without proper permission—a group often termed 'Dreamers' in the US, but found in many other countries as well.

The previous consideration leads to a final one. It is not unusual for children to arrive in a state without adult accompaniment. Steps must be taken so as to ensure that such children are treated fairly and safely. They must not be housed in jail-like conditions, must be given access to social services, including education, and every step must be taken to evaluate whether they have a colourable asylum claim or other right to enter and remain within the country of arrival. In any case, children should not be forcibly removed from a country when doing so would be expected to place the child at significant risk for her or his safety.[60] I cannot give this important practical issue the time it deserves in this chapter, and so will have to rest with this bare, intuitive, account.

VII. Conclusion

In this chapter I have argued that family ties place significant limits on the discretion that states should have in setting their own immigration policies. In particular, I have argued that the associational rights that underlie these family ties justify significant family-unification programmes, place limits on the removal power of states, and require extending protection similar to that given to refugees to the family members of those granted refugee or asylee status. Furthermore, states, if they are to have just immigration policies, must take steps to ensure the rights and safety of non-citizen children.[61]

---

[59] I make this argument at length, and offer some nuance, in Lister, 'Citizenship, in the Immigration Context' (n 23) 201–04.
[60] A too-weak version of this protection is available in the US as 'Special Immigrant Juvenile' status. See 8 CFR s 204.11.
[61] Thanks to Stephanie Silverman, Alex Sager, Andreas Cassee, Elizabeth Brake, Lucinda Ferguson, Scott Altman, Kerry Abrams, Ayodele Gansallo, Stephen Legomsky, and Colin Macleod for helpful comments on earlier versions of this chapter.

PART III

RIGHTS AND OBLIGATIONS

8
Moral and Legal Obligations to Support 'Family'

Diane Jeske

I. Introduction

Recent decades have seen various social trends and political movements exerting pressures to redefine the notion of family so as to make it more inclusive of non-traditional arrangements. The resultant legal and political debates demonstrate how important it is to many people that they are able to label certain others in their lives 'family', as opposed, say, to labelling them 'friends' or 'lovers'. For example, most of us regard ourselves as having particularly weighty moral obligations to family members, and we regard these obligations as being stronger and of greater moral significance than those that we have to 'mere' friends, for example. And the state grants certain 'familial' relationships a special legal status accompanied with special legal obligations and entitlements. Most importantly, the state defines who can and who cannot enter into the marital relationship, a relationship at the core of many people's understanding of family. Given these facts, previously excluded groups, in particular, gays and lesbians, have been fighting to be able to have their relationships officially recognized as marriages.

Others, however, have begun to ask whether the state should maintain a legal status of marriage, where the state determines who can have that status and then enforces certain legal obligations between and grants certain benefits to the parties involved. Answering this question is extremely complicated because the rhetoric surrounding marriage (and family more generally)—in political debate, in court decisions, in everyday moral and social discourse—is often conflicting and romanticized to the point of having little connection to reality. Current debates about extending marriage rights to previously excluded groups have only served to confuse the issue, because advocates of such extension play upon entrenched assumptions about the nature of marriage and the family in order to gain support for their cause.[1]

I think that we need to reorient the debate about marriage and family if we are ever to make real progress. First, we need to dislodge 'family' as a term of fundamental moral significance: what matters morally in many of the interpersonal relationships that we label 'familial' is the intimacy between the parties involved. But intimacy is not present in all relationships understood to be familial, and it is present in many relationships regarded as 'non-familial'. Once we see intimacy and not family as of fundamental moral significance, we need to re-approach the political and legal issues. We need a

---

[1] The way in which advocates of gay marriage have distanced themselves from polygamists is a good example of this strategy. See C Calhoun, 'Who's Afraid of Polygamous Marriage? Lessons for Same-Sex Marriage Advocacy from the History of Polygamy' (2005) 42 The San Diego Law Review 1023.

more open discussion of the ways in which the state ought and ought not intervene in adult intimate relationships, a discussion unencumbered by the baggage of terms such as 'family' and 'marriage'.

In section II, I will discuss the nature of intimacy and the moral obligations that intimates have to one another. Section III will discuss the role of the state in shaping intimate relationships and in defining who will, officially, count as family. I will then, in section IV, consider the possible ways in which the state might approach protection of or intervention in intimate relationships. Section V will further pursue this issue by examining a particularly contested issue in family law, the issue of spousal support after the dissolution of a marriage (or marriage-like) relationship.

Before continuing I need to address a possible worry that one might have about my use of the term 'family'. In his contribution to this volume, David Archard argues that the term 'family' should be reserved for a 'group of individuals whose adults take primary custodial roles in respect of its dependent children'.[2] I agree with him that social units in which care-taking of dependent children is performed ought to have a special legal status in recognition of their valuable social function and of the unique vulnerability of the children within them. However, it seems clear to me that whatever people mean by 'family', it is broader than Archard's proposed definition allows. People regard their spouses as family, even if they have no children and have no intention of having children, adult children and parents still regard themselves as family even once relations of dependency have been dissolved or re-constituted in a new direction, and grown siblings regard each other as family. In this chapter, I am concerned with intimate relationships between adults, precisely those relationships that Archard wants to exclude from his concept of family. In the end, I am arguing that whatever we take family to be, it is not what is of fundamental moral significance, so my disagreement with Archard may be moot. However, in so far as our ordinary concept leeches into politics and law, it remains an important entry into these issues.

II. Moral Obligations to Intimates

A. The nature of intimacy

In talking about intimate relationships, I am talking about those relationships that we might think of as 'close'. Friendship can be taken as a paradigm of an intimate relationship, where our friends can be contrasted with those who are merely acquaintances, neighbours, sexual partners, or colleagues. I say 'merely' because, of course, we can be friends with, or be intimate with, people who are also our neighbours, sexual partners, or colleagues. Our colloquial usage of 'friendship', however, probably does not stretch to cover all of our intimate relationships, such as those that adult children often have with their parents.

What is involved in being intimate with another person? Let us suppose that Lucy and Ethel have an intimate relationship that exhibits all of the features characteristic of such relationships. If that is so, then Lucy and Ethel (a) have mutual positive attitudes

---

[2] See D Archard's chapter.

toward one another that can be described as liking, loving, etc, (b) have a concern for each other that exceeds that which they have for any person merely in virtue of being a person, and their history with each other exhibits that concern, (c) have desires to spend time with each other and have already causally interacted with each other in some relevant manner, and (d) have or are in the process of acquiring knowledge about each other that goes beyond what a stranger or mere acquaintance would have.

Hopefully, with conditions (a)-(d) I have captured the kind of interpersonal relationship that we have in mind when we think about our relationships with those people to whom we think of ourselves as 'close'. It also, I hope, captures a broad range of intimate relationships, including those that we usually refer to as friendships as well as those we more naturally consider familial. It does not, however, capture all of our relationships to people whom we might label 'friend' or 'family member'. So, for example, Joe might describe Jack, with whom he regularly plays golf, as a friend, and, certainly, given that they enjoy and actually do play golf together, they satisfy condition (c) and perhaps also condition (a). However, suppose that Joe and Jack talk only about recent sports events, the weather, and cars—they fail, then, to meet condition (d). If they are willing to forget about each other when golf is outlawed so that better use can be made of the land composing golf courses, it might seem that they fail to meet condition (b) as well. Joe and Jack are 'buddies', 'friends' in some very minimal sense, but they do not have an intimate relationship. And I think that, on reflection, this seems right to us: we distinguish between people with whom we play golf or drink, or who happen to be in our book clubs, and those with whom we are genuinely intimate, ie our close friends, where these close friends can vary in degree of closeness.

Importantly, we do not have intimate relationships with all of those people whom we consider members of our family. I might see my old Aunt Wilma at family holiday gatherings, and perhaps I have a greater concern for Aunt Wilma than I do for just any random human being—I will be moved when she dies in a way that I will not be moved when I read the obituaries in my local paper. But I would also be quite content if I never see or talk to Aunt Wilma ever again, being content to hear news of her through the family grapevine. I might know more about Aunt Wilma than I do about most people, but if this is the result of family gossip, then I might just as well have read a biography about Aunt Wilma. In such a case, I do not have an intimate relationship with Aunt Wilma, and that would be even truer of blood relatives whom I have never met. It may also be true of family members who share a roof: consider siblings who live with their parents but who lead entirely separate lives. Importantly for my purposes in this chapter, two people can be married and yet not have an intimate relationship. Intimacy, then, is a feature of an interpersonal relationship that is not necessarily connected to any legal or biological status.

B. The moral significance of intimacy

The kinds of relationships that I have picked out as intimate are, I claim, relationships that have significant moral import. We tend to think—and think correctly in my view—that we have moral obligations to those with whom we are intimate *merely because* we are intimate with them. The fact that Lucy and Ethel are intimate friends in and of itself grounds obligations for Lucy and Ethel to care for one another. If Lucy has to choose between taking care of Ethel or taking care of her neighbour Fred with whom she is not intimate, it seems quite clear that, all else being equal, Lucy has a reason to care for Ethel that she does not have to care for Fred, and the source of that reason is the relationship in which Lucy and Ethel stand to one another. It seems that Lucy will have failed, morally speaking, if she forsakes Ethel to care for Fred in a situation where both are equally in need of her help.[3]

So there are some obligations (special obligations of intimacy) which intimates have to one another that occur only in intimate contexts in so far as they are grounded directly on, and only on, the intimate relationship in which the parties stand to one another. But the fact of an intimate relationship also often plays an instrumental role in (a) providing a fertile arena for the generation of other sorts of obligations, and (b) providing the parties to the relationship a privileged position for promoting value.

With respect to (a), we can consider promissory obligations and obligations of gratitude as primary examples. Intimate relationships are contexts in which people naturally make various kinds of commitments to each other, binding themselves via either explicit or tacit promises. Some intimates make grandiose commitments to each other—wedding vows are a good example of such—while others do not. But intimate contexts are contexts of shared projects, shared concern about each other's well-being, and shared emotions and experiences. They naturally, then, are heavily laden with agreements of all sorts: to meet at the movies at six this evening, to provide comments on each other's papers, to keep in touch, to exchange birthday gifts, to never reveal what happened during that drunken night five years ago, and so on. Some of these promises are not explicitly voiced but arise as a result of practice and mutual understanding.

Given intimates' concern for each other's well-being and the time that they spend together, they naturally provide goods of varying magnitude for each other. Because of the mutual love and affection present, we sometimes think that we do not owe our intimates any debt of gratitude for what they do for us—this is just what people who care about each other do, we say. I think, however, once we accept that we have duties of gratitude more generally, we ought to acknowledge them in the context of intimacy. Acknowledging such debts is to acknowledge and appreciate that the other has gone over and above in a certain way, and done so when others, even those to whom one is close, might not have. If my friend brings me groceries and makes me meals every day for a month when I am incapacitated by an injury, I ought to be grateful to my friend and to respond in ways that acknowledge this gratitude. If my friend covers my class when I need to visit my grandmother in the hospital, even though that friend has two classes of his own on the same day, I ought to be grateful and to show it. These kinds of 'favours' occur most often between people who care about one another, and so intimacy is a context rife with debts of gratitude. However, with respect to both obligations of promising and of gratitude, while intimacy may provide special or a great number of instances of such obligations, the obligations of that type can also be present in

---

[3] I argue for this view in D Jeske, *Rationality and Moral Theory: How Intimacy Generates Reasons* (Routledge 2008). See S Keller, *Partiality* (Princeton UP 2013), for a discussion of a range of views on special obligations to intimates, including a critique of the view that I offer here.

non-intimate relationships and are not present in all intimate contexts. These obligations are grounded fundamentally by acts of promising or the receipt of goods, and the context of intimacy is instrumentally relevant only.

To turn to (b), intimacy is also a context which greatly facilitates our ability to promote value. First, it is plausible to think that intimate relationships themselves are valuable: most of us regard our intimate relationships as a very significant part of a good life, independently of any other goods causally produced by such relationships. But, secondly, intimacy is most definitely instrumental in producing other goods, perhaps most importantly, pleasure. Other projects in our lives gain added meaning and significance for us when we can share our achievements and dreams with intimate friends. Intimates know us well and regularly interact with us, and so are both epistemically and causally well-placed to benefit us in various sorts of ways. Intimacy provides a space in which people can care for one another in particularly meaningful and potent ways, not only because they regularly interact and have important knowledge about one another, but also because people often want to be cared for by people with whom they are intimate. It is often easier to accept care from those with whom we have an established relationship with a certain degree of reciprocity. Intimates often trust and feel safe with one another, and this kind of comfort with another person facilitates allowing that other to take care of oneself. So well-being can be fostered in intimate contexts in ways that it cannot be in non-intimate contexts.

In claiming that intimacy is of fundamental moral significance, I am intending to contrast intimacy with family, in so far as, I claim, the latter has no fundamental moral significance. I am not saying that nothing else other than intimacy is of fundamental moral significance. Importantly, in addition to our special obligations grounded directly on intimacy (or on promises or the receipt of benefits under certain conditions), we have duties to promote value. I have already mentioned the instrumental role that intimacy plays in allowing us to promote value. But intimacy is not the only context that is fertile ground for the promotion of value. Consider, for example, the relationship between a parent and an infant. It seems quite clear that infants are not capable of intimacy in so far as they do not have the requisite mental states, and, at least with respect to new-borns, there is no established history of interaction. But parental care for infants flows from parental love and concern and is, at least in part, a response to the extreme vulnerability of the infant. Parental care-giving in this context has great instrumental value, then, in promoting the well-being of the infant and of the person whom the infant will become. Consider another case: academic colleagues may not have a relationship that meets to a significant enough degree the conditions for intimacy. However, they may be dedicated to promoting each other's careers and intellectual development. In so far as such development and achievement may be valuable, this collegial relationship provides a space for the parties to fulfil their duties to promote value and so has moral significance. Finally, two people may come together only to have sex with one another: even with no elements of intimacy present, their interactions provide each with intense pleasure.

Thus, in one important respect, I am entirely in agreement with the position that Elizabeth Brake takes in her chapter.[4] Care-giving is an important function of

[4] See E Brake's chapter.

interpersonal relationships, and, where it occurs, the state has a legitimate interest in at least considering the provision of benefits/obligations. Such is also the case in relationships in which one or both individuals are vulnerable to a certain extent (see Brake's chapter). In so far as care-giving and vulnerability are often features of intimate relationships, the state has an interest in regulating intimate relationships. My concern, however, is considering how the state ought to respond to intimate relationships in virtue of the obligations that intimates have to each other in virtue of their being in such a relationship. Thus, my project is complementary, rather than in opposition to Brake's project.[5]

III. State Interventions in Intimate Relationships

In the United States, Supreme Court decisions have defended the so-called 'right to privacy', and have attempted to establish the bounds of this supposed right. The justices in these cases employed the term 'intimacy' in their attempts to explain the significance of certain kinds of human activity and also in drawing the line around the aspects of human life and endeavour that are protected and private. This understanding of intimacy focused on 'marriage and the family'.

In *Griswold v Connecticut* (1965), the Court declared that the state had no right to enter 'the sacred precincts of marital bedrooms' in order to control decisions concerning the conception of children. Justice Douglas, in delivering the decision of the court, extolled marriage as 'a coming together for better or for worse, hopefully enduring, and intimate to the degree of being sacred. It is an association that promotes a way of life ... a harmony in living ... a bilateral loyalty, *not commercial or social purposes*' (emphasis mine). Justice Goldberg, in a concurring opinion, cites with approval Justice Harlan's dissenting opinion in *Poe v Ullman*:

> the intimacy of husband and wife is necessarily an essential and accepted feature of the institution of marriage, an institution which the State not only must allow, but which always and in every age it has fostered and protected.... [the State acts illegitimately when] 'it undertakes to regulate by means of the criminal law the details of that intimacy'.

In *Eisenstadt v Baird* (1972) the Court extended the right to use contraception to unmarried couples by analogizing the relationship of unmarried sexual partners to that of married sexual partners. *Bowers v Hardwick* (1986), the case which upheld (by a narrow five-to-four margin) as constitutional the Georgia statute criminalizing homosexual sodomy,[6] was a battle over how narrowly the notion of 'marriage and the family' ought to be interpreted and about why marriage and family are protected. Justice

---

[5] However, unlike Brake, I am not a political liberal in the Rawlsian vein. I think that consequentialist appeals are legitimate ways to justify public policy, i.e. claiming that policy P will maximize valuable consequences is a perfectly good reason to offer in support of P. Undoubtedly, disagreements about value and the good life are factors that are relevant in trying to determine what the effects of any given policy would be. Thus, sometimes, as Mill so eloquently pointed out, having the government refrain from promoting a conception of the good life may very well be the best way to promote good lives.

[6] *Bowers v Hardwick* was explicitly overruled in *Lawrence v Texas* (2003).

Blackmun, in his dissenting opinion, grants that earlier privacy cases involved in some way the 'protection of the family'. But, he insists, we must take seriously what was asserted in *Moore v East Cleveland*: we must not close 'our eyes to the basic reasons why certain rights associated with the family have been accorded shelter under the Fourteenth Amendment's Due Process Clause'. Blackmun claims that those 'basic reasons' do not have to do with contributions 'to the general public welfare', but, 'because they form so central a part of an individual's life': "we protect the family because it contributes so powerfully to the happiness of individuals, *not because of a preference for stereotypical households*"' (emphasis mine). In relation to the case at hand's issue of a right to engage in homosexual sodomy, Blackmun says that we have the same sorts of justifications for protecting it, given that 'individuals define themselves in a significant way through their intimate sexual relationships with others'.

Trying to extract a consistent philosophical view from a single Supreme Court decision is difficult enough, whereas attempting to do so across decisions is well-nigh impossible. It does seem, though, that these decisions are saying that family and marriage are important because they involve intimacy, and intimacy is an important component of individual well-being. Thus, if other relationships that may or may not be properly considered familial—such as those between gay or lesbian sexual partners—also involve the important value of intimacy, then the state ought to protect them in the same way that it protects the properly familial.

There is little doubt that the state's attempts to protect a private, intimate realm have and continue to focus on a realm defined by marriage, sex, and reproduction. Marital partners have certain kinds of rights and entitlements that are not available to those in intimate relationships that are not marriages. So, for example, spouses have claims over each other's property, both during the marriage and at its dissolution, are considered each other's next of kin for various purposes, and 'qualify for special tax and immigration status and survivor, disability, Social Security, and veterans' benefits'.[7] Disclosures between spouses are privileged in courts of law, in the same way as are disclosures between clients and their attorneys or physicians/therapists.

Social institutions other than the law also give marital partners a special status. To take just one example, in spheres such as academia, so-called 'spousal hires' are a regular occurrence. In such cases, when the college or university hires one spouse, they then also hire the other even though no search for someone in the latter's field of specialization had been announced or conducted. Another case is that of special couples' rates. This is common with respect to, for example, gym memberships: the gym offers a rate to couples which is often considerably lower than the sum of two individual memberships.

While some of these special entitlements accorded to married persons 'appear to reflect', as Elizabeth Brake points out, 'an assumption of a "traditional" single-breadwinner model, in which one spouse depends on the other for health insurance and income',[8] others such as, most clearly, spousal hires, seem to assume just the

---

[7] E Brake, 'Minimal Marriage: What Political Liberalism Implies for Marriage Law' (2010) 120 Ethics 302–37; 306.
[8] ibid 306–07.

opposite. In all cases, the privileges and entitlements depend only on having the legal status of marriage, not upon any particulars of the individual relationship in question. And most of the privileges and entitlements are unavailable to those who are not in a marital relationship, unless, in certain cases, an unmarried couple is co-habiting in a sufficiently 'marriage-like' relationship or have a legal domestic partnership contract.

Thus, we see the Supreme Court according special protections to the marital and to sexual relationships, and justifying those legal protections by appeal to claims about the moral significance of such relationships. Two issues, then, are important: if the state grants privileges or entitlements to persons in certain sorts of relationships, should it also enforce obligations between those persons, and, if so, which obligations? Also, which relationships are the appropriate candidates for state intervention and under what conditions should such intervention take place?

IV. Justifying State Interventions in Intimate Relationships

Once we accept that persons in intimate relationships have a diverse range of moral obligations to one another, including obligations unique to participants in intimate relationships, we can ask how, if at all, the state ought to intervene with respect to those relationships and their attendant duties. Before beginning, we need to distinguish *moral* obligations and *legal* obligations. Moral obligations between persons are justifying (as opposed to merely motivating) reasons for them to treat each other in certain kinds of ways.[9] To say that S has a legal obligation to do P, on the other hand, merely means that there is a law requiring S to do P. Analysis of the claim that there is a law requiring S to do P will vary, of course, from one philosopher of law to another, but it is not important for me to settle on an analysis of law here. However, I will be taking for granted that there are no *necessary connections* between the having of a legal obligation and the having of a moral obligation. This is not to deny that facts about legal obligations and about the law more generally can affect our moral (and other) reasons for action. To take just one obvious and familiar example: we have no moral obligation to drive on the right-hand side of the road, but, given that in the United States the law dictates that we do so, we come to have a moral obligation to do so. We all have moral obligations to avoid causing harm to others, and, given the law as a coordination mechanism, by conforming to the law and driving on the right-hand side of the road we can thereby avoid causing harm to others. But following the law is only instrumental to acting on my reason to avoid causing harm—I have no obligation to drive on the right-hand side of the road *merely because the law dictates that I do so.*

So our question is: how ought individual *legal obligations* to be structured given the facts about the *moral obligations* that individuals have to their intimates? I will consider the following possibilities: (a) the state should not enforce interpersonal obligations between intimates (beyond the interpersonal obligations that it would otherwise

---

[9] Some philosophers reject the thesis known as 'moral-reasons internalism', ie they reject the claim that a true ascription of a moral obligation to a person implies that that person has any justifying reason to act in accordance with that obligation. I use the term 'obligation' to refer to reasons that have particular kinds of grounds, and so am assuming the truth of moral-reasons internalism.

enforce between any two persons regardless of any intimacy between the two persons[10]), but it should protect individuals' abilities to fulfil their obligations to their intimates as part of a more general protection of the intimate sphere; (b) the state should not enforce obligations between intimates, but it should grant privileges to those in intimate relationships designed to insure that they have the space to fulfil their obligations to one another; (c) the state should enforce either all or some subset of obligations between intimates merely in virtue of the fact that persons have those obligations; or (d) the state should enforce obligations to intimates when and only when doing so is instrumental to achieving good consequences, where those consequences may involve the intimate relationships themselves or some other unrelated (legitimate) goal of the state.

Let's begin by considering (a)—the state protects a space in which individuals are able to fulfil their obligations to their intimates. This might be seen as what is going on in the privacy cases that I discussed in the previous section. In *Griswold*, for example, the Court could be understood as insisting that the state refrain from interfering in decisions that ought properly to be made by the persons involved in the relationship. One reason for such restraint[11] could be a concern to ensure that the state does not, through such intervention, undermine the intimate relationship itself, given that intimacy involves a sharing of experience which can be destroyed if decisions between the parties are mediated or dictated by a third-party. Similarly, state intervention could constrain the action of the parties in such a way that they are unable to fulfil the demands of the relationship itself, ie, they would be unable to meet the obligations that they have to one another merely in virtue of being intimates.

There would certainly be justification for this kind of 'protected spheres' approach. First, intimate relationships are, as the Court reiterates in several places in the privacy decisions, a significant aspect of valuable human lives. While it may be theoretically possible for an individual to live a good life without any intimate ties to other human beings, it remains a fact that the vast majority of us require intimate connections in order to be happy: these intimate connections are not only, in and of themselves, important parts of our happiness, but they are instrumental to our ability to build and sustain the other sources of our happiness, such as a career and hobbies—without the support of those close to us, it is extraordinarily difficult to carry out such projects, and, even when we can continue to carry them out, they provide us with far less satisfaction if we have no others with whom to share our passions, and then it becomes difficult to sustain the passion at all. Given the significant value of intimate relationships, and the ways in which obligations to intimates depend upon the particularities of a given relationship, we have strong reasons to think that the state ought to leave us alone to attend to our intimates in the ways that we determine are best.

So what justification, if any, might the state have for regulating and enforcing obligations between intimates (or some subset of such obligations)? Let's consider option

---

[10] So, eg, to whatever extent the state enforces contracts between individuals, it will also enforce contracts between intimates.

[11] I am not making any claim to the effect that this is the reasoning that underlies or best explains what the court actually says in *Griswold*.

(c) (I will address (b) below)—the state enforces such obligations between intimates merely because of the fact that intimates have those obligations. Even if we were to accept that at least part of the job of the state is to act as enforcer of the fulfilment of individual interpersonal obligations, it seems that we need to have an account of *when* the state is justified as acting as such an enforcer. After all, it is hard to imagine anyone seriously asserting that the state would act legitimately in enforcing any and all interpersonal obligations. For example, imagine that Ricky and Lucy are married sexual partners, where Ricky focuses primarily on his own pleasure and Lucy is generous and attentive to Ricky's sexual needs. Even supposing that Ricky has a moral obligation to be more oriented toward Lucy's sexual pleasure, I cannot imagine supporting the claim that the state ought to enforce such an obligation. Allowing legal enforcement of such obligations is highly likely to be destructive of the intimate relationship involved. Further, fact-finding and enforcement in such cases is almost certainly going to be objectionably intrusive and fraught: trying to sort through the particularities of an intimate relationship to determine who owes whom what is something that should be left to the parties in the relationship.

So the mere fact that two persons have certain obligations to one another as the result of being in an intimate relationship would not be sufficient justification for the state attempting to enforce the fulfilment of such obligations: in many cases, such an attempt would be self-defeating and would have the result of destroying the intimate relationship at issue. Thus, if the state aims to enforce obligations between intimates, it has to be able to determine when its enforcement will be effective and will not destroy the relationship that grounds the relevant obligations. In all such cases, we also need to consider consequences beyond the relationship itself in order to ensure that even if the state effectively enforces obligations between intimates and strengthens intimate bonds that it does not thereby create counterbalancing harms elsewhere.

One reason why enforcement of obligations between intimates who stand in familial relationships to one another might be more effective than enforcement of obligations between non-familial intimates is that we can more easily track the familial correlate to the intimacy, such as co-habitation, paternity/maternity, siblinghood, etc. Of course, as I pointed out earlier in the chapter, there is no necessary connection between such familial status and intimacy. However, if there is a high correlation between certain biological statuses and intimacy, then the state might be justified in putting the burden to disprove intimacy on such parties. The state would then have to show that it does no serious injustice to those who are not in fact intimate but are not able to prove that to the state's satisfaction.

A good case to illustrate here would be the state deciding to force adult children to contribute to the care of their aged parents. Parent/child relationships are easy to track, and a large number of adult children have intimate relationships with their parents. Elder care is becoming a huge financial burden on the state, and so it has good reasons to find sources for funding such care. But this case also illustrates worries about destroying relationships—adding financial burdens to adult children can cause resentment and stress and may alienate them from their parents. Other sorts of injustice are also looming because those least likely to be able to fund their own elderly care are those from the lower to lower-middle socioeconomic classes. These people were also unlikely to have been able to provide their children with the sorts of privileges and benefits that their wealthier counterparts were able to provide to their children. Forcing children to contribute financially to the care of their aged parents is likely then to place extra financial burdens on those who, relative to those upon whom no such burden is placed, received fewer benefits earlier in life. In such a case, then, enforcing obligations between intimates—even assuming that the state can pick out only the intimate parent/child relationships and that such enforcement does not destroy intimacy between adult children and their parents—is likely to increase and consolidate class privilege, making social mobility even less achievable than it currently is.

This suggests approach (b), that the state provide privileges and entitlements to those in intimate relationships aimed at allowing them to fulfil their special obligations of intimacy.[12] In the case of adult children and their parents, this seems like a much better option than (c), for several different reasons. First, when adult children are intimate with their parents, they feel their duty to care for their elderly or ill parents quite intensely. If job and financial pressures make them unable to do this, they, their parents, and the relationship between them will suffer. And adult children often do not feel that they have adequately discharged their duty by taking advantage of state-funded opportunities for placing their parents in nursing care centres—they know that they themselves could provide a kind of care at home for their parents that simply cannot be provided by paid professionals (no matter how caring they might be) in an institutional setting. So, second, better care will be provided if adult children have the resources to offer it (with the aid of, for example, visiting nurses and physical therapists). And, third, if workplaces provided adequate paid leave for elder care, individuals would be better placed to think carefully about their obligations and the value of their relationships without stress and resentment. There is abundant reason to think that this kind of approach will be no more costly in the long run, in financial terms, than is the current system of Medicaid-funded nursing care centres.

To what range of intimate relationships ought such privileges, designed to allow for fulfilment of special obligations of intimacy, be extended?[13] People are very quick to point to potential abuses of extending, for example, paid leave for care-giving to friends: how can we determine that two people are really friends? People will just start taking paid leave to spend time with friends or will take advantage of such paid leave options to travel or undertake some other personal project, it might be said. Here is one place where conventional familial relationships have instrumental significance—we can verify whether, for example, Barbara is my mother when I ask for leave to care for her. Similarly, marital partners have an established legal status that can be verified. But as long as the state does not allow other kinds of intimacy beyond marriage and blood ties any sort of legal status, we must recognize that our current system is arbitrary, and need to at least consider ways in which we could monitor the granting of

---

[12] I would like to thank C Macleod for raising and emphasizing this option.
[13] For further discussion of this issue, see E Brake's chapter.

privileges to a wider range of intimates, at least in cases where other social costs would not be prohibitively high.[14]

And this leads us to the fourth approach that the state may take to enforcement of obligations between intimates: (d) the state enforces obligations between intimates when and only when doing so is an effective means to achieving some valuable end. In order to illustrate this approach, consider again the case of the state requiring adult children to contribute financially to the care of their elderly parents. If the state were taking approach (c), then its concern would be to enforce obligations between intimates, and it would refrain from doing so in cases where such enforcement produces significant enough counterbalancing harms.

If the state were to adopt approach (d), however, its concern would not be with enforcing obligations between intimates. Rather, the state would have certain goals such as providing adequate care to the elderly who are unable to care for themselves, and it would enforce certain select obligations between intimates as a strategy for achieving its goal of adequate elder care. The state might adopt such an approach in order to alleviate resentment about the extra costs, hoping that the love that adult children have for their parents will make it easier for them to bear the additional financial burden. Of course, as I pointed out above, in the case of elder care, this might not be a particularly fair strategy, and it is also unlikely to be an effective one: the state would be attempting to fund elder care by relying on those in the social classes least likely to be able to bear any additional financial burden. It will also thereby create additional social welfare problems: if adult children in the lower socioeconomic classes are forced to contribute to the care of their aged parents, they will have even less than they already have to care for themselves and for their children. Such inabilities will place greater strain on, for example, Medicaid, and other social welfare programmes. This is not to reject the strategy of enforcing obligations between intimates as a way of dealing with other legitimate problems faced by the state. Rather, it is just to point out that if and when the state does so, it needs to ensure that it does not create new problems or exacerbate other existing ones.

Before moving on to consider spousal support as an illustrative case, I want to explain my omission of a further approach to state enforcement of obligations between intimates. (What I say here about enforcement of obligations applies also to provision of entitlements.) It might be said that the state ought to enforce obligations between intimates if and only if they have voluntarily entered a legally defined relationship or voluntarily accepted an established legal status. But this is not really a separate approach at all, because we need to have a justification for having certain legally defined relationships available for intimates to opt in to (eg, marriage or domestic partnership) while we do not provide this option of giving formal legal status to other sorts of intimate relationships (such as 'mere' friendship). And, I am inclined to think that such a justification would take one of the forms of justification (a)-(d) that I have just discussed.

---

[14] Some might say we ought to appeal to co-habitation. However, for many people, too much proximity and loss of personal space is actually detrimental to maintaining intimacy. Many adult children, eg, find that living with their elderly parents places undue stress on their caring relationship.

V. Marriage and its Moral and Legal Aftermath

Marriage is the primary instance of the state offering official legal status to parties to a supposedly intimate relationship, a legal status which is accompanied by state conferral of benefits and state enforcement of obligations. In order to see how the state views its intervention in intimate relationships, it can be helpful to look at what it does in cases in which the parties are attempting to end the marriage. In arriving at a resolution between the parties, the state reveals how it understands its reasons for intervention in this particular intimate relationship. This is particularly true in the case of spousal-support law.

There is a definite 'before' and 'after' when it comes to spousal support law, and the dividing line is the advent of no-fault divorce. Prior to no-fault divorce, marriage was understood as a life-long commitment between the two parties which could be terminated only upon an action that constituted breach of contract by one of the parties. In such a system, divorce proceedings required a guilty party—the one who breached the contract—and the innocent or wronged party. As Christina Fernandez points out,

> The courts viewed a support award as furthering these interests [punishing the guilty and adjusting equities] because of an official belief that one spouse was responsible for the divorce. Therefore, the required payment of support acted as a penalty for the 'guilty' party and as equitable compensation for the 'innocent'.[15]

But there can be no issue about guilt and innocence if parties can divorce with neither being at fault, so this justification for spousal support has been abandoned.

The fault concept of divorce was embedded in a concept of marriage and in a society that involved clear gender-based norms. Husbands and wives had roles and expectations: the husband worked outside of the home, earning an income to support his wife (and children if there were any), while the wife remained in the home, taking care of the domestic realm (including any childcare to be done). Marriage was a life-long commitment, and so the husband had a life-long commitment to support his wife. If he breached the marital contract either by some fault or by leaving the marriage, he retained his obligation to support his wife, as long as the wife herself was innocent of fault.[16] Again, the advent of no-fault divorce and the rising divorce rate have made this justification of spousal support obsolete.

In no-fault regimes, there are several models of spousal support to which the courts have appealed, and I will discuss the following prevalent models: (a) the reimbursive/compensatory model of support, (b) the rehabilitative model of support, and (c) the income-security model of support. We'll start with (a), the reimbursive/compensatory model of support. Under the reimbursement model, one marital partner (historically, this was almost always the wife), devotes her time and energy to the marriage so that the other partner can focus on education and/or career advancement. Supposedly, she

---

[15] In CM Fernandez, 'Beyond Marvin: A Proposal for Quasi-Spousal Support' (1978) 30 Stanford Law Review 359, 365.
[16] See C Rogerson, 'The Causal Connection Test in Spousal Support Law' (1989) 8 Canadian Journal of Family Law 95, 105.

does this so that in the future both parties to the marriage can enjoy a higher standard of living. Thus, if the marriage is ended before such benefits can be enjoyed, the spouse who dedicated herself to the marriage is entitled to spousal support so that she can reap what she has sown, as it were.[17] Compensatory support, on the other hand, is awarded to the marriage-dedicated partner because, supposedly, she has reduced prospects in the job market while her spouse has increased his market value. Thus, the latter owes support to the former in order to compensate her for lost opportunities.[18] As Carol Rogerson says, '[u]nder this model the basic purpose of spousal support is to compensate claimant spouses both for the economic disadvantages which they have suffered as a result of the marriage and the economic advantages which they have conferred on the other spouse during the course of the marriage'.[19]

What does the compensatory/reimbursive theory of spousal support reveal about the state's justification for intervention in this particular intimate relationship? What many see this as revealing is that marriage is being understood as an economic partnership rather than as an intimate relationship. Thus, when the partnership is dissolved, the economic gains and losses need to be distributed equitably between the partners.[20] But, of course, we do not think that the state ought to intervene in order to ensure that economic gains and losses are equitable in other intimate relationships. And it is not at all clear that one of the duties that parties to intimate relationships have to one another is an even sharing of such gains and losses, particularly if we consider such gains and losses in isolation. Consider, for example, a friendship in which one party has considerably more money than the other and is able to provide her friend with nice dinners and trips. The friend may reciprocate in other ways that cannot be economically measured. In any case, there does not seem to be any moral requirement that parties to a friendship do not lose by their friendship. If I decide to stay in my current city because my friend says that she would miss me too much if I moved, it does not seem that, if she decides to end our friendship, that she owes me financial compensation for the larger salary that I would have earned if I had moved. Similarly, suppose that throughout college and graduate school, I devoted less time to my own studies in order to help my less academically gifted friend with hers. When our friendship ends, I may be able to claim truthfully that I would have a better job with better prospects if I had not been friends with her, but it hardly seems right to suppose that she ought to compensate me for the opportunities/money that I lost as a result of being her friend.

---

[17] There are other possible rationales for compensatory support, such as payment for domestic services. See BG Larson, 'Equity and Economics: A Case for Spousal Support' (1978) 8 Golden Gate University Law Review 443, 471, 473; and back pay for childcare, see D Westfall, 'Unprincipled Family Dissolution: The American Law Institute's Recommendations for Spousal Support and Division of Property' (2004) 27 Harvard Journal of Law and Public Policy 917, 937. I will not discuss these here, because they are really special cases to which, I think, my remarks on the more general theory of compensation will also apply.

[18] See JL McCoy, 'Spousal Support Disorder: An Overview of Problems in Current Alimony Law (2005) 33 Florida State University Law Review 501, 508.

[19] Rogerson, 'The Causal Connection Test in Spousal Support Law' (n 16) 110.

[20] ibid. Also, NM Catanzarite, 'A Commendable Goal: Public Policy and the Fate of Spousal Support After 1996' (1998) 31 Loyola of Los Angeles Law Review 1387; MA Freeman, 'Should Spousal Support Be Abolished?' (1973) 48 Los Angeles Bar Bulletin 236.

Someone might object that, typically, marriage involves a sharing of economic resources to an extent that other intimate relationships do not. This is undoubtedly true, but it is also true that it involves a sharing of much else besides. When the court chooses to look only at economic gains and losses, it is clearly not interested in what the parties owe one another in virtue of their intimate relationship. Consider, for example, a case of a wife who decides to stay home in order to care for the couple's children. The husband wanted to be the one to stay home, but he earns more money with better benefits, so he agrees to continue working and allow his wife to be the one to stay at home and take care of the children. When the marriage ends, the compensatory/reimbursive model of spousal support would have the husband owing the wife support because of what she 'sacrificed'. But the husband sacrificed time at home with his family in order to provide for them economically and to allow the wife to stay at home, which is what she wanted to do. Shouldn't the husband be owed some time with his children undisturbed by work obligations?

My point here is that if the state really were concerned with interpersonal moral obligations between intimates, it could not focus on economic losses and gains to the exclusion of less quantifiable gains and losses. For the sake of argument, we might grant that in some cases, intimates at least have obligations to one another not to take advantage of each other's willingness to aid. But then, spousal support would be justified only if one spouse had taken advantage of the other, but showing that such was the case would require showing that the one spouse had not given anything of comparable worth, economic or otherwise, to the other, and had intended to skip out before certain benefits could accrue to both of them. So the compensatory/reimbursive model of spousal support seems to require that we understand obligations between spouses as obligations between business partners, and state justification for the legal status of marriage would require showing why encouraging and making official such economic partnerships furthered some legitimate state interest.[21] Further, the state would have to explain why it provides the kinds of constitutional protections that it does to what is, in essence, an economic partnership; after all, no other economic institution has been extolled by the Supreme Court as 'sacred'.

Now let's consider (b), the rehabilitative theory of spousal support. According to this theory of spousal support, it 'is awarded to help the financially impacted spouse obtain the skills, training, or education needed to become self-sufficient'.[22] Whereas the compensatory/reimbursive theory is backwards-looking (what did the claimant spouse sacrifice in the past?), the rehabilitative theory is forward-looking (what does the claimant spouse need in order to become financially self-supporting?). I think that it is at least somewhat easier to link the rehabilitative theory to moral obligations between

---

[21] I find it hard to see what this reason would be, unless it is related to child-rearing: perhaps the state has a legitimate interest in seeing that children receive maximum parental care, and so, to encourage at least one stay-at-home parent, it might support compensatory/reimbursive spousal support so that people do not find that option too risky in the light of the odds of marital breakdown. (See JM Krauskopf, 'Theories of Property Division/Spousal Support: Searching for Solutions to the Mystery' (1989) 23 Family Law Quarterly 253, 256, 263.)

[22] McCoy, 'Spousal Support Disorder' (n 18) 511; see also Rogerson, 'The Causal Connection Test' (n 16) 115–18.

intimates than it was to so link the compensatory/reimbursive theory. Surely, it might be said, if intimates have duties to care for one another, they have duties to ensure that each of them can at least support themselves at some decent minimal level. If the ending of the intimate relationship results in economic hardship for one of the parties to the relationship, it is not implausible to suppose that the other party has moral obligations to continue to help them until they can support themselves.

I think that here we could understand the state as taking either option (c) or (d) discussed in the previous section. If it was taking option (c), its concern would be enforcing obligations between intimates, and it would intervene, risking the harms raised in discussing the 'protected spheres' option, when the relationship is already irrevocably damaged and poverty looms for one of the intimates. If it was taking option (d), then it would have some other goal—perhaps ensuring that citizens are able to secure the skills needed for gainful employment—and it would enforce obligations between intimates when doing so is an effective strategy for achieving that goal which is extrinsic to concerns about intimate relationships. Option (d) would be problematic in this context, because it is difficult to see rehabilitative spousal support as an effective strategy for ensuring employable, self-supporting citizens.[23] Rather, in lower to lower-middle class families, where such rehabilitative support is likely to be most needed, the financially employable spouse will have little to spare to get their former spouse to the point of self-sufficiency. With respect to option (c), it is difficult to see why the state would support rehabilitative-spousal support but not other sorts of rehabilitative support. Suppose a woman stayed at home to raise her children. Her husband dies when the children are grown, leaving his wife in a precarious financial position. Supposing the adult children are gainfully employed, should we require them to support their mother, at least until she can find adequate employment? Here, it might be said, we have to worry about putting excessive strain on the intimate relationship between mother and adult child. But then why not enforce such an obligation when the adult children are already distant from their mother, perhaps as a result of self-absorption or simply as a result of not enjoying their mother's company? In any case, given that these are unlikely to be successful long-term strategies for addressing the problems of older workers attempting to become self-supporting, it is unclear that we should move away from the protected-spheres approach.

Finally, we can consider (c), the income-security model of spousal support. Spousal-support law focuses on the needs of the claimant spouse and the means of the other spouse, suggesting that a goal of spousal-support orders is to ensure that the claimant spouse is kept off public welfare payments when the other spouse has the means to support her.[24] Like approach (b), the income-security model could be viewed as the state being concerned to enforce obligations between intimates and choosing to do so when broader social policy supports doing so, or as the state having broader social

---

[23] On this point, see L Ferguson, 'Family, Social Inequalities, and the Persuasive Force of Interpersonal Obligation' (2008) 22 International Journal of Law, Policy, and the Family 61.

[24] ibid. See Rogerson, 'The Causal Connection Test' (n 16); also, MV Mackay, 'Spousal Support: Law Reform and the Forms of Justice' (1987) 45 University of Toronto Faculty of Law Review 243; and N Semple, 'In Sickness and In Health? Spousal Support and Unmarried Cohabitants' (2008) 24 Canadian Journal of Family Law 317.

policy goals and using enforcement of obligations between intimates as a strategy for reaching those goals. However, given the emphasis on needs and means, it seems that, in the case of approach (c) the state is not really concerned with obligations to intimates at all, but, rather, simply with finding alternate ways of supporting those who would otherwise end up on the public welfare rolls.

What this foray into justifications for spousal support seems to show is that this particular intervention into intimate relationships is construed by the state as an opportunity to enforce broader social policy, or the state is viewing marriage as an economic partnership, not as an intimate relationship. Is the state approach justified? That depends on the answers to several questions: (a) does the state actually effectively achieve its other social policy goals?; (b) can the state justify characterizing marriage primarily as a valuable and meaningful interpersonal intimate relationship in one context but as an economic partnership in another?; (c) does the view of marriage presented in cases of spousal support justify granting it, but not other intimate relationships, an official legal status?; and (d) what impact on intimate marriages and on other types of intimate relationships does the state's approach to marriage in cases of its dissolution have on those relationships? What is all too apparent is that the state does not have a coherent justification for or understanding of marriage, which is not surprising, given that our current institution is the descendent of an outmoded institution that few would find appealing.

VI. Conclusion

Our foray into spousal-support law shows that, at least when it comes to the dissolution of marriage, the state is approaching it as an economic institution, not as an intimate relationship. We need not draw the conclusion that spousal-support law is not consistent with the Supreme Court's approach to marriage as a 'sacred' intimate relationship. However, I think that putting the two side-by-side makes it clear that we need to justify maintaining our institution of marriage, given that it is viewed in such different ways in different contexts. For this reason, I am sympathetic with the intent behind Archard's limitation of 'family', at least for the purposes of family law, to social units with dependent children:[25] the legitimate state goal of protecting and nurturing vulnerable young people seems to support treating marriage as an economic institution important to providing stable environments for children. But then many of the justifications of spousal-support law would be undermined, given that they make no reference to dependent children.

Justification of marriage requires showing why some intimate relationships are to have special legal status with attendant obligations and entitlements. Some might argue that for many people their most important intimate relationship is the one that they have with their spouse, and, thus, protecting this relationship goes a long way to protecting intimacy. But it is unclear to what extent our society's enshrining marriage in law contributes to the way that people prioritize their relationships. Further, we have to ask whether marriage really does protect intimacy given that somewhere around

---

[25] See D Archard's chapter.

50 per cent of all marriages end in divorce. Is the goal of protecting valuable intimate relationships really best served by maintaining the institution of marriage, or does the state's emphasis on marriage to the exclusion of broader support networks put greater strain on both state and individual purses? By allowing for spousal support does the state make it easier for people to put all of their hopes for intimacy and financial stability in one basket, thereby encouraging a view of non-sexual relationships as secondary and thus, as less demanding? The current social discussion about marriage, both with respect to who gets to enter and with respect to what happens when it all falls apart, needs to take place in the larger context of intimate relationships, how and when the state ought to intervene, and the appropriate interplay between protection of a private intimate sphere and the achievement of broader social policy goals.

9
Are Children's Rights Important?

Colin M. Macleod

I. Introduction: Taking Children Seriously

A satisfactory moral theory that purports to be comprehensive must take children seriously. It must be applicable to children in a way that yields credible judgments about morally salient features of childhood.[1] It should show how these features ground important moral claims of children and it should illuminate the duties or special responsibilities that adults, whether individually or collectively, have to children. A moral theory will be deficient if it is not suitably sensitive to the distinctive interests of children or if it yields wildly implausible judgments about how children should be treated.[2] Given the general normative significance that rights enjoy in both popular discourse and in contemporary moral philosophy, a seemingly natural way to give recognition to at least some of the morally significant facets of childhood is through the attribution of moral rights to children. This chapter discusses whether assigning rights to children is appropriate and important.

In order to be clear about what is at stake in attributing moral rights to children, it is useful to follow Feinberg's distinction between kinds of rights.[3] Some of the candidate rights of children, such as the right to life, may simply be the same rights that are standardly thought to be possessed by adults and attribution of such rights to children gives recognition of some of the important basic moral claims that adults and children have in common. Feinberg terms these 'A-C rights'. Other rights, 'A-rights', are rights uniquely possessed by adults in virtue of moral capacities, interests, or attributes that adults have but children lack, at least to the degree requisite for grounding a right. Basic liberty rights that permit persons to make authoritative decisions about a wide array of important self-regarding matters are often considered to be A-rights.[4] Freedom of

---

[1] Childhood is a complex and multifaceted phenomenon. The morally salient interests of children change and evolve as children mature and acquire cognitive, moral, and psychological attributes. Moreover, there may be some important differences between cultures and political communities about the way in which childhood is interpreted or how facets of childhood are treated. Although my discussion will not address how such complexities affect the articulation of children's rights, it is reasonable to suppose that the specific moral and legal rights of children may vary with the age and stage of moral development. So even if infants and adolescents are considered children, we can allow that their rights will, in some respects, be different.

[2] To the degree that an account of justice is significantly different from a comprehensive moral theory, I assume that a parallel standard of success applies to a theory of justice: it must be suitably attentive to the distinct interests of children and must yield credible judgments about what the justice-based entitlements of children are. It should be able to identify and illuminate ways in which the justice-based entitlements of children should be distinguished from those of adults.

[3] J Feinberg, 'A Child's Right to an Open Future' in W Aiken and H LaFollette (eds), *Whose Child? Parental Rights, Parental Authority and State Power* (Littlefield, Adams & Co 1980).

[4] The view that the standard rights of adults should be extended equally to children has had some defenders, eg, R Farson, *Birthrights* (Collier Macmillan 1974) and JC Holt, *Escape from Childhood: The Needs and*

religion construed as the right to make one's own choices about whether or how to engage in religious worship is a standard A-right.[5] Finally, 'C-rights' are rights that are uniquely possessed by children in virtue of distinctive attributes, interests, or capacities of children. The right to be loved is arguably a C-right.[6] In what follows, I will consider whether it is both appropriate and important to attribute moral rights to children in either of the senses noted by Feinberg. For most of the discussion, the distinction between 'A-C rights' and 'C-rights' will not be especially significant since I am interested in the issue of whether children should, in any sense, be considered bearers of moral rights. So unless otherwise noted, I shall simply refer to children's rights as the set of rights comprising both 'A-C rights' and 'C-rights'. Nonetheless, the distinction is worth keeping in mind because some theorists who doubt the importance of children's rights only raise concerns about the idea that there are 'C-rights'.[7] Such theorists allow that there are some basic human rights enjoyed by both adults and children. However, other theorists (for example, James Griffin) deny that children are bearers of moral rights at all. They deny the existence of both 'C-rights' and 'A-C rights'.[8]

The attribution of moral rights to children is a complex matter for a number of reasons. First, there are lively theoretical disagreements amongst philosophers about the nature, foundation, and importance of the moral rights that are attributed to adults. Controversies about moral rights are not peculiar to the case of children. Second, despite the fact that there is now a rich academic literature on children's rights[9] and that invocations of children's rights are common in political discourse,[10] there are disagreements, even amongst theorists sympathetic to children's rights, both about what moral rights children have and about the precise justificatory basis of children's rights. Third, even where some consensus about the moral rights of children can be achieved, there

---

Rights of Children (Penguin 1975) but has little traction today. For a sustained critique of so-called child liberation see LM Purdy, *In Their Best Interest? The Case Against Equal Rights for Children* (Cornell UP 1992).

[5] Children may have some rights linked to their religious identity or beliefs but the exercise of such rights is usually subject to the authority of adults, especially parents. So children are standardly thought not to have the broad scope of religious liberty that adults have.

[6] M Liao, *The Right to Be Loved* (OUP 2015).

[7] L Ferguson, 'Not Merely Rights for Children but Children's Rights: The Theory Gap and The Assumption of The Importance of Children's Rights' (2013) 27 International Journal of Children's Rights 177.

[8] Sceptics who deny that children have moral rights may nonetheless recognize that children have and should have legal rights. J Griffin, 'Do Children Have Rights?' in D Archard and C Macleod (eds), *The Moral and Political Status of Children: New Essays* (OUP 2002).

[9] *The International Journal of Children's Rights* was established in 1993 and has published hundreds of essays, both abstract and applied, on philosophical, legal, and sociological facets of children's rights. For helpful overviews of core themes in the literature about the justification of children's rights see D Archard, *Children: Rights and Childhood* (2nd edn, Routledge 2004); D Archard, 'Children's Rights' The Stanford Encyclopedia of Philosophy (Summer edn, 2016) <http://plato.stanford.edu/archives/sum2016/entries/rights-children/> accessed 29 August 2016; J Eekelaar, 'The Emergence of Children's Rights' (1986) 6 Oxford Journal of Legal Studies 161; J Tobin, 'Justifying Children's Rights' (2013) 21 International Journal of Children's Rights 395. Other defences of the importance of children's rights include J Eekelaar, 'The Importance of Thinking that Children Have Rights' (1992) 6 International Journal of Law, Policy & the Family 221 and MDA Freeman, 'Why it Remains Important to Take Children's Rights Seriously' (2007) 15 International Journal of Children's Rights 5.

[10] The unanimous adoption by the United Nations General Assembly of the Convention on the Rights of the Child (CRC) in 1989 along with the subsequent ratification of the CRC by 193 nations is a good indication of the broad acceptance of children's rights in contemporary politics. As of 2016, only the United States and South Sudan had failed to ratify the CRC.

are disagreements about the relation between the moral rights of children and the articulation of legal rights that can be feasibly protected and enforced by state institutions. I cannot begin to address all the interesting positions and debates in the now vast literature on children's rights. Instead my focus in this chapter is more narrow and selective. I wish to consider forms of reticence about children's rights that are not grounded in scepticism about moral rights in general. I consider different sources of this reticence with a view to determining whether, or perhaps the degree to which, it is justified. So far as possible, I want to offer an analysis that does not turn on defending a determinate position about the deep philosophical foundations of moral rights. Similarly, I will try to be reasonably agnostic about the precise set of moral rights that is appropriately attributed to children. My interest is primarily in diagnosing reticence about the general idea and practice of attributing rights to children. However, since I am, in fact, very sympathetic to the project of attributing rights to children and since I have elsewhere defended specific claims about some of the rights of children,[11] my analysis will not be completely neutral either about the justificatory basis of children's rights or about some of the rights children actually have. I hope to vindicate their importance by identifying and rebutting different sources of reticence about children's rights.

I will begin by outlining considerations that speak in favour of attributing moral rights to children and to viewing them as important. My strategy is to sketch a case for children's rights that is plausible but which does not depend upon supplying a definitive foundational theory of children's rights. If this strategy succeeds, children's rights can be vindicated as important even if they are incompletely theorized. I will then identify some points of debate within rights theory in general that provide the backdrop for different kinds of reticence about children's rights. Against this framework, I distinguish two basic kinds of reticence about children's rights: (a) *foundational scepticism* and (b) *discourse anxiety*. Foundational sceptics maintain that a proper understanding of moral rights and the moral status of children blocks attribution of rights to children. I distinguish two varieties of foundational scepticism: *capacity scepticism* and *duty distortion scepticism*. Critics who give expression to discourse anxiety can allow that children qualify theoretically as bearers of rights. But they worry that emphasizing rights and seeking to regulate relations between children and adults via the language of rights has various deleterious effects. Within this category of rights reticence, I distinguish three sources of anxiety: *inflation, efficacy,* and *corrosion*. I indicate how each consideration might offer a challenge to the importance of children's rights.

II. The General Case for Children's Rights

To build a case for importance of children's rights we first need a general characterization of moral rights and their place in normative theorizing. Three features of

---

[11] C Macleod, 'Shaping Children's Convictions' (2003) 1 Theory and Research in Education 315; C Macleod, 'A Liberal Theory of Freedom of Expression for Children' (2004) 79 Chicago-Kent Law Review 55; and C Macleod, (2016) 'Constructing Children's Rights' in J Drerup, G Graff, and G Schweiger (eds), *Justice, Education and the Politics of Childhood* (Springer 2016).

moral rights are pertinent. I will label these features: signalling, normative weight, and enforcement. Let me briefly explain and illustrate each of these features.

First, rights have an important *signalling function* in a moral community. Rights pick out particular interests or claims of persons[12] and express the idea that moral agents have reason to be especially attentive to securing a protected interest or respecting a protected claim. To say that a subject, S, has a right to X serves to announce that special normative significance attaches to ensuring that S has reliable access to X and that others should not obstruct S's access to X. Recognizing that S has a right to X may also give rise to a moral responsibility on the behalf of others to ensure that S has reliable access to X. Consider, for example, children's right to be loved. This right expresses the idea that children are entitled to receive care, affection, and emotional support from parents (or other caregivers) who stand in special relationships of intimacy and authority to children. To respect this right, parents must not withhold or deny love to their children. Moreover, non-parents may have responsibilities to ensure that background social conditions (for example, the way the work day is structured, policies of parental leave, etc) are hospitable to children receiving the love to which they are entitled.

Second, rights have significant *normative weight* in the sense that claims or interests protected by genuine rights typically assume priority over the satisfaction or promotion of interests or values that subjects (collectively or individually) have or care about. This does not mean that rights are never defeasible. But a right to X held by S is usually not limited or defeated by another normative consideration unless the right conflicts with another right held by another person that has equal or greater normative significance. Consider, for instance, children's right to an autonomy-facilitating upbringing. This right generates an entitlement by children to be raised in a manner that is conducive to the acquisition by children of the cognitive and moral capacities requisite to meaningful autonomy. Those responsible for rearing children must not impede the development of autonomy and must ensure that children have access to the social and material conditions (for example, good nutrition and education) that are crucial to the development of meaningful autonomy. In this context, recognizing the special weight of rights imposes stringent limits on how parents may pursue highly valued projects or commitments of their own. For example, religious parents who seek to instil their religious commitments in their children are prohibited from pursuing this end through indoctrination or denying their children knowledge of diverse perspectives on religious faith.

Third, since moral rights function as signals to protect especially important and fundamental interests or claims, rights have an *enforcement* dimension. Although not all moral rights may be coercively enforced, the fact that a subject S has a right to X often serves to justify the use of coercive measures to protect or to facilitate S's right to X. The recognition of moral rights thus plays an important role in justifying some legal rights and the institutional mechanisms (for example, coercively enforced laws and policies)

---

[12] I focus on rights attributed to individual persons but nothing in the analysis precludes the possibility that groups have rights.

that may be employed by states to secure them.[13] Children's right to education can justify public funding of primary and secondary education along with laws that require children to attend school.

Given the foregoing, fairly generic, depiction of moral rights, whether it is appropriate to attribute moral rights to children seems to depend only on establishing: (a) that children have significant claims or interests that merit distinct recognition and attention; (b) that protection of some of these claims or interests has a kind of normative priority or urgency over other normative considerations and thereby limits the pursuit of other potentially worthwhile objectives; and (c) that coercive measures designed to ensure protection or facilitation of children's weighty claims or interests are sometimes warranted. It does not take much thought to realize that at least some of the distinct claims or interests of children meet these criteria. Indeed, given the familiar ways in which children are especially vulnerable and hence dependent on others to promote their basic interests or secure their dignity, it seems especially important to attribute rights to them. To take an easy example, it seems clear that children have a weighty interest or claim in continued life that is sufficiently important to warrant attribution of the right to life to them. Coercive enforcement of this right is also obviously warranted.

Note, I am not suggesting that these remarks themselves constitute a full articulation of the normative grounding of children's right to life or other rights. Philosophers can debate whether the right to life is grounded in concern for the welfare of a child or whether it rests on the inherent dignity of children (in a way that is distinguishable from considerations of welfare). My point is only the rather banal one that protecting the lives of children is very important and that a natural way of giving recognition to that fact is to attribute a right to life to children. Assuming that there are other facets of children's lives that have great normative significance that merit distinct recognition and protection then we have the basis for identifying other rights of children and for supposing that such rights are important. Of course, some facets of children's lives that have great normative significance may be facets that they share with adults. So rights that appeal to these facets may be 'A-C rights' since they are grounded in morally salient attributes common to adults and children. But to the degree that children have attributes *qua* children that merit special recognition and protection, we have grounds for articulating some distinctive 'C-rights'. The examples of putative children's rights I have already given—the right to be loved, the right to an autonomy-facilitating upbringing, and the right to education—are arguably 'C-rights'. Each example rests on a claim about a distinctive facet of children's lives and the special normative significance that attaches to protecting or promoting interests or capacities.

These remarks do not, of course, establish what specific moral rights children have nor do they determine the degree to which children's rights are parallel to or distinct from the rights of adults. How such matters are resolved depends on the articulation of a fuller account of the justificatory basis of moral rights along with fuller identification of the facets of childhood that merit special attention. However, I think they are sufficient to

---

[13] This does not mean that all, or even most legal rights, are grounded in moral rights. There is no inconsistency in denying that children have moral rights and yet allowing that they can and indeed should have some legal rights, including legal rights that are specifically tied to distinctive features of childhood.

establish a strong presumption in favour of attributing moral rights to children and to viewing children's rights as important. If this is correct then we can be confident that children have important moral rights even in the absence of consensus on the precise theoretical underpinnings of such rights. To many supporters of children's rights the foregoing is apt to seem obvious or unnecessary. However, since some theorists harbour doubts about attributing moral rights to children, I think it's worth briefly considering the main issues that need to be broached by a more fully developed theory of children's rights.

III. Towards Fully Theorized Children's Rights

Thus far I have presented an argument for taking children's rights seriously that does not rest on a fully articulated theory of rights. Briefly identifying some of the major issues at stake in developing a full theory may provide a helpful backdrop for diagnosing and responding to scepticism about children's rights.

First, there are basic foundational issues concerning the ultimate justificatory basis of moral rights. Here we encounter debates about whether rights themselves are primarily grounded in basic considerations of justice or whether they are best grounded in a sophisticated form of (maximizing) consequentialism.[14] On the former approach, identification of moral rights can be the direct upshot of interpreting the basic moral standing of human beings.[15] This approach holds that some claims or interests of persons have sufficient moral significance to merit recognition and protection as rights without regard to the effect such rights have on promotion of general well-being or the overall goodness realized in a community. By contrast, in sophisticated consequentialist theories, moral rights are treated as devices that play an especially important role in facilitating aggregate well-being or the overall flourishing of a community as a whole.[16] So whereas a non-consequentialist theory of rights might ground a right to free speech in the integral role that free speech has for each individual in the development and exercise of autonomy or Rawls' two moral powers,[17] a consequentialist would link justification of a right to free speech to the beneficial effects (for example, truth discovery, happiness) that are likely to be generated for a community by employing a moral discourse and associated social practices that treat free speech as a basic moral entitlement that individuals can claim.[18] The consequentialist view treats recognition of

---

[14] Consequentialism is the view in moral theory that holds that morally right actions are actions that maximize overall goodness. Utilitarianism is a consequentialist theory in this sense. It holds that right actions are actions that maximize overall happiness. But there are also non-utilitarian forms of consequentialism that offer different and more complex accounts of goodness.

[15] Whether non-human animals can be the bearers of moral rights is an important issue and consideration of the attribution of moral rights to non-human animals may help to resolve some controversies about the foundations of rights (eg, the debate between interest and will theories of rights). However, for the purpose of this discussion, I set aside issues about the moral rights of non-human animals.

[16] LW Sumner, *The Moral Foundation of Rights* (Clarendon Press 1987).

[17] The moral powers that Rawls draws upon in identifying the equal basic liberties that merit special protection are: (a) a sense of justice and (b) a capacity for a conception of the good, J Rawls, *Justice as Fairness: A Restatement* (Harvard UP 2001) 18–19.

[18] For such consequentialists, the limits of moral rights and the conditions under which they may be violated are determined through consideration of the likely effects on overall human flourishing of circumscribing or overriding specific rights.

moral rights as crucial elements of the decision-procedure most conducive to the maximization of overall well-being. The non-consequentialist, by contrast, allows that moral rights are direct expressions of important moral claims that have force irrespective of whether the practice of respecting rights is most conducive to maximizing overall well-being. Indeed, in some instances, the non-consequentialist will insist that a right merits recognition and respect even if it is (predictably and reliably) not maximally conducive to promotion of overall well-being.

A second site of debate in rights theory that is relevant to attributing rights to children concerns interpretation of the protective function of rights. Rights delineate claims of persons that have special moral significance. But there is debate about how the fundamental claims protected by rights are to be understood. On the choice or will theory of rights, moral rights are fundamentally grounded in and serve to protect the autonomous agency of persons. As we shall see below, this construal of the protective function of rights can seem hostile to the recognition of children's rights.[19] The inability of a choice model of rights to accommodate the idea that children can have moral rights is, for many theorists, problematic and provides motivation for adoption of an interest view of rights in which rights serve to protect certain fundamental interests of persons.[20] Yet a different possibility is a hybrid model of rights in which children's rights initially protect basic interests of children but the rights of adults function, primarily, to protect agency.[21] On this view, children gradually acquire choice-protecting rights as they mature.

A third issue that naturally arises in the wake of debates about how to characterize the protective function of rights concerns the substantive content of the claims that merit recognition as rights. If rights protect fundamental interests then what interests of children should be viewed as especially weighty and what is the basis of identifying interests as fundamental? Is children's interest in being loved by parents sufficiently important to ground a right to be loved? If rights protect the choice-making capacities of agents, what kinds of choices are sufficiently important to agency to ground specific moral rights? The background supposition here is that not all forms of choice-making are sufficiently important to ground a moral right. So whereas freedom of speech, freedom of religion, and freedom of association are typically recognized as among the most important rights enjoyed by adults, such rights only extend to children, if at all, in an attenuated sense.

---

[19] Some versions of the choice model can countenance children's rights providing it is allowed that children, though not fully rational and mature moral agents, display forms of juvenile agency that merit protection.

[20] N MacCormick, *Legal Right and Social Democracy: Essays in Legal and Political Philosophy* (OUP 1984). Insofar as persons are thought to have a fundamental interest in developing and exercising autonomy, the interest theory of rights can provide a justificatory basis for many of the liberty rights that are typically emphasized as crucial by defenders of the choice theory of rights (eg, freedom of religion). Similarly, insofar as there are significant social and material conditions that play a crucial role in facilitating meaningful autonomy, the choice theory of rights can provide a justification for some welfare rights commonly associated with the interest theory of rights (eg, a right to basic health care).

[21] S Brennan, 'Children's Choices or Children's Interests: Which Do Their Rights Protect?' in D Archard and C Macleod (eds), *The Moral and Political Status of Children: New Essays* (OUP 2002).

A final general issue concerns the division of moral labour that is necessary in order to secure the moral rights of persons. Who bears responsibility for securing and protecting the rights of different persons? For instance, do parents have special responsibilities in relation to their children to ensure that some or all of their rights are respected? To what degree does meaningful recognition of moral rights depend on providing persons with the social and material conditions hospitable to development and exercise of their rights, as opposed to mere forbearance by other persons? For instance, does the right to life require ensuring that persons have ready access to life-sustaining resources or does it only constrain how others may act towards bearers of the right (for example, refraining from killing them)?

Theorists who endorse the attribution of moral rights to children and who view such rights as important vary in how they address the foregoing issues. Nonetheless, some broad generalizations are possible. First, the scope of children's rights is held to be quite broad. In addition to having many of the basic moral rights of adults (for example, the right to life or the right not to be tortured), children are held to have distinctive rights that have a preparatory facet. Such rights focus on the entitlements children have to resources and opportunities that facilitate children's development as mature, responsible adults who are well-prepared to conduct successful lives as adults. For instance, children's rights to education and to health care are partly aimed at ensuring that children have a fair chance to pursue vocations and are able to meaningfully participate in democratic processes.[22] Children's right to an autonomy-facilitating upbringing similarly is aimed at equipping children with the knowledge, skills, and dispositions requisite to deliberating about conceptions of the good and pursuing chosen life plans.[23] However, some of children's distinctive rights have significant non-preparatory dimensions since they are motivated by a concern with the character of children's lives *qua* children. For instance, the right to play is arguably an important right of children because of the significance of play to the quality of children's lives irrespective of whether play helps to facilitate the healthy development of children or the acquisition of skills that may be valuable in adulthood.[24] Similar remarks apply to children's right to be loved: ensuring that children are loved can be important not only because the absence of love in children's lives impedes healthy psychological development but also because children, *qua* children, have an enormous stake in being loved.

Recognition that children's rights have a broad scope has a significant impact on issues of distributive justice. This is because, for a wide range of rights, meaningful realization of children's rights depends on the provision of resources and opportunities to families and children. Most obviously children's rights to health care and to education

---

[22] E Callan, *Creating Citizens: Political Education and Liberal Democracy* (OUP 1997).

[23] E Callan, 'Autonomy, Child-Rearing, and Good Lives' in D Archard and C Macleod (eds), *The Moral and Political Status of Children: New Essays* (OUP 2002); C Macleod, 'Conceptions of Parental Autonomy' (1997) 25 Politics and Society 117.

[24] For discussion of special goods of childhood that could ground such rights see S Brennan, 'The Goods of Childhood and Children's Rights' in F Baylis and C McLeod (eds), *Family-Making: Contemporary Ethical Challenges* (OUP 2014); A Gheaus, 'The Intrinsic Goods of Childhood and the Just Society' in A Bagattini and C Macleod (eds), *The Nature of Children's Well-being: Theory and Practice* (Springer 2015); C Macleod, 'Primary Goods, Capabilities, and Children' in H Brighouse and I Robeyns (eds), *Measuring Justice: Primary Goods and Capabilities* (CUP 2010).

can only be secured if there is adequate social investment in health care and education. Moreover, if children are assumed to have equal rights to education and health care then respect for these rights will set rather significant limitations on the permissible material inequalities that can obtain between children.[25] Children cannot be held responsible for securing for themselves the social and material conditions requisite to fulfilment of such rights. Similarly, fulfilment of children's rights should not be held hostage to the socio-economic status of their parents. So even if significant inequality between adults in these domains is compatible with respect for the rights of adults, the scope of inequality between children that is compatible with respect for their rights may be much more limited. Since some of children's rights, such as the right to be loved, can only be fulfilled by select adults who stand in a special caring relationship to children, children's rights are also highly relevant to the design of economic policies and social institutions. For instance, labour markets and rules of employment must be structured so as to ensure that parents have adequate opportunities to spend time with children and to engage in valuable shared activities as families. Holiday time, work hours, parental leave policies, and day-care arrangements all have an important link to the realization of children's rights. This does not mean that all families must be structured in the same way or that there is a single set of social policies that respect for children's rights mandates. In many cases, respect for children's rights is realizable in multiple ways: parents can manifest their love for children in a wide array of acceptable ways; loving families can be diverse in structure and there are a variety of educational strategies through which autonomy can be facilitated, and so on.[26]

A final distinguishing feature of children's rights is that the precise claims they protect change as children mature. When children are very young their rights to make important decisions about their own lives or even to access information or entertainment are highly limited. But as they mature, children's right to be consulted about important matters grows as does their authority to make significant decisions (even poor ones) about their own lives. Children start with few liberty rights and gradually acquire rights comparable to or even equivalent to those of adults. The evolving character of children's rights can make practical interpretation of them very complex. It is difficult to gauge what degree of agency children have and what impact the gradual acquisition of mature agency should have on the attribution of rights to children in specific settings.[27]

---

[25] See C Macleod, 'Liberal Equality and the Affective Family' in D Archard and C Macleod (eds), *The Moral and Political Status of Children: New Essays* (OUP 2012); A Swift, *How Not to Be a Hypocrite: School Choice for the Morally Perplexed Parent*, (Routledge 2003); H Brighouse and A Swift, *Family Values: The Ethics of a Parent–Child Relationship* (Princeton UP 2014).

[26] This point can have great practical importance in negotiating controversies involving cultural and religious minorities. Although the rights of children do impose significant limits on the character and scope of parental authority (eg, by prohibiting corporal punishment or religious indoctrination), these limits are compatible with respect for a wide variety of cultural and religious practices. Moreover, we should be extremely cautious about assuming that cultural minorities tend to be more hostile to the rights of children than majority cultures. For instance, sexist cultural norms that diminish the respect for the rights of girls to, say, education are certainly not unique to minority cultures.

[27] One important context in which such interpretive complexities arise involves the competency of children to make decisions about whether to refuse medical treatment. In many jurisdictions, a child who displays sufficient emotional and cognitive maturity can be declared a 'mature minor' and has the right to refuse urgent medical treatment recommended by medical authorities.

Although the foregoing remarks do not provide a fully articulated theory of children's rights that explains and catalogues the full range of children's moral rights, it does illustrate why the articulation of children's rights is both important and complex. One might have reservations about any particular proposal concerning the claims or interests of children that are suggested to be sufficiently important or fundamental to ground a moral right. And disagreements are to be expected over how the evolving capacities of children should affect judgments about what rights should be ascribed to children at different ages and stages of development. Yet it seems extremely difficult to deny that children have distinct (though complex) claims and interests that have great normative significance and merit recognition and protection. Moreover, it seems clear that such fundamental concerns, and the rights they give rise to, ground strong duties, held by various moral agents in different settings, to nurture children and to treat them with respect. All this seems more than sufficient to vindicate the reality and the importance of children's rights. Nonetheless, there are sources of theoretical scepticism about children's rights and it is to different kinds of scepticism we now turn.

IV. Foundational Scepticism about Children's Rights

Foundational scepticism denies the importance of children's moral rights by challenging the theoretical propriety of attributing moral rights to children. The challenge has two main forms. *Capacity scepticism* simply denies that children meet the criteria requisite to being a bearer of moral rights. *Duty distortion scepticism* insists that viewing children as rights bearers fundamentally mis-describes the character of the obligations and relationships that moral agents have to children.[28]

A. Capacity scepticism

Capacity scepticism embraces a general analysis of rights that treats rights as conceptually linked to the possession and exercise of agential capacities (for example, rational autonomy). Rights are viewed as basic moral entitlements that agents can claim and, in many instances, can choose to waive. The status of being a rational, autonomous agent is treated not only as a normatively relevant trait that merits special recognition and respect but also as uniquely grounding moral rights. In terms of the protective function of rights noted above, the fundamental purpose of rights is to protect autonomous agency and the choices that flow from such agency. Since children (or at any rate young children) lack the relevant form of agency, they cannot have rights. Even as children develop agential capacities, it is not until some significant threshold of autonomy is reached that the attribution of rights to children is deemed appropriate. Those who defend this view do not deny that children have important interests that generate

---

[28] A position closely allied to this could also be expressed as a concern about the dangers of overemphasizing children's rights rather than a denial that it is theoretically appropriate to attribute fundamental rights to children. This version can be seen as a form of discourse anxiety since it can allow that children are genuine bearers of (important) moral rights. However, as I interpret it, duty distortion scepticism offers a more fundamental challenge to children's rights by suggesting that the very logic of children's rights, *qua* normative claims, is incompatible with proper recognition of the distinct duties that are owed to children.

duties, even stringent duties, to children held by adults. But for capacity sceptics, the absence of mature agency places children outside the community of rights bearers. Some capacity sceptics, like Griffin, allow that children gradually acquire some rights as they acquire degrees of autonomy, but they insist that infants and other humans lacking normative agency do not have rights.[29]

Capacity scepticism, especially extreme versions that deny that children have any moral rights whatsoever, is deeply counter intuitive. Consider, for instance, the status of the entitlement of children not to be subject to torture. The capacity sceptic is committed to denying that children, *qua* non-agents, have a right not to be tortured and insofar as this implies that children do not have an enforceable basic moral entitlement against being tortured the view is absurd. To avoid this absurdity, the capacity sceptic may allow that children do indeed have an important, enforceable moral entitlement not to be tortured (along with other enforceable moral entitlements) but deny that such entitlements should be termed moral rights. Griffin, for example, favours a 'restricted' use of rights language but he does not wish to deny the grave moral wrongness of killing children.

> It is, or should be quite enough to say that wantonly to take an infant's life is murder, and one of the most grievous kinds of murder. To deny an infant the chance to reach and exercise and enjoy maturity is a far more horrendous wrong than most infringements of human rights.[30]

However, the strategy of restricting rights language in this way seems little more than arbitrary semantic stipulation. It is implausible to hold that adults have a right against torture that entails an enforceable moral claim not to be tortured and yet hold that although children have an enforceable moral claim not to be tortured they lack a right not to be tortured. Ultimately, what matters is not whether the term 'moral right' is used to pick out important enforceable moral entitlements of children but whether children have such entitlements and if they do what those entitlements are. Once the capacity sceptic allows that children, including infants, have enforceable justice-based entitlements of the sort that typically are termed moral rights then the rationale for insisting upon a restricted sense of moral rights becomes hollow. It is worth noting that an interest theory of rights simply does not encounter this problem.

B. Duty distortion scepticism

Duty distortion sceptics hold that attributing fundamental moral rights to children is problematic because it generates a defective conception of the moral relationship between adults and children. In particular, a rights-emphasizing view will not adequately recognize the importance of the imperfect obligations that adults have to children. (Imperfect obligations are obligations for which there are no corresponding rights. Consider, for instance, a duty of beneficence. Although I may have a duty to devote some time and energy to helping people achieve projects they care about, this duty can be discharged in different ways and no particular person can claim a right

---

[29] J Griffin, *On Human Rights* (OUP 2008), 94.   [30] ibid.

to my assistance. I could act on my duty of beneficence by helping you move your furniture but I have some discretion as to whether I help you and you cannot insist that I help you.) This position is most famously defended by the Kantian moral theorist Onora O'Neill.[31] However, similar concerns about the way rights may distort the character of moral relationships have also been discussed in the ethics-of-care literature.[32] O'Neill plausibly contends that a sound ethical theory must give recognition to imperfect duties and that some imperfect duties play an especially important role in caring appropriately for children. She thinks adults have duties to be 'kind and considerate in dealing with children'[33] and the character of these duties differs significantly from the duties adults have to care for other adults. Although imperfect duties to children are not morally optional, they are not duties that adults owe to all children and the care that adults owe children in this respect is not care to which children have a right. Determining how such imperfect duties to care for children should be discharged is highly dependent on circumstances and the nature of the relationship that obtains between particular adults and particular children. Parents, for instance, may have a duty to be emotionally supportive to their own children but not to the children of strangers. Moreover, even in regard to their own children parents have significant discretion in determining how the duty of care is best discharged.

The suggestion that attending to the needs, interests, and special vulnerabilities of children in an ethically appropriate fashion is not wholly a matter of attending to the rights of children is surely correct. But that fact alone cannot ground scepticism about the fundamentality of children's rights because that fact only establishes that attention to the rights of children is not sufficient to meet all of their morally salient interests. To motivate rights scepticism, O'Neill must make a much stronger claim namely, that viewing rights as morally fundamental is inimical to proper recognition of imperfect obligations owed to children. Thus she says: 'If rights are taken as the starting point of ethical debate, imperfect obligations will drop out of the picture because they lack corresponding rights.'[34] As O'Neill sees it, there is a deep divide between ethical theories that assign primacy to rights and theories that assign primacy to obligations that forces us to choose between theories that recognize imperfect duties owed to children and those that do not. This, however, is a false dilemma. To begin with, it is hard to see why, in general, we must choose between rights and obligations as the starting point for ethical theory. Acknowledging that moral rights are fundamental does not preclude acknowledgement that obligations are also fundamental. An overall ethical theory need not have a single fundamental foundation. But even if we think that there must be an ordering of fundamental starting points for ethical theory, and rights are viewed as having theoretical primacy, this does not preclude recognition of the importance of imperfect obligations. For instance, acknowledging that children have a fundamental right to an autonomy-facilitating education does not obfuscate recognition of the idea that adults have duties to be kind and considerate to children or that adults have some

---

[31] O O'Neill, 'Children's Rights and Children's Lives' (1988) 98 Ethics 445.
[32] See the chapters by E Brake and ML Shanley for further treatment of themes in the ethics-of-care literature.
[33] O'Neill, 'Children's Rights' (n 31) 448.   [34] ibid 449.

discretion in determining how kindness and consideration is suitably displayed to specific children in particular settings.

V. Discourse Anxiety

I have suggested that foundational scepticism fails to undermine the theoretical propriety of attributing (fundamental) moral rights to children. But critics of children's rights can adopt a different tactic for questioning the importance of children's rights. They can argue that the discourse surrounding the attribution of moral rights to children has deleterious effects when it comes to dominate our understanding both of what is important in the lives of children and how relations between adults and children should be handled. Here critics are typically prepared to concede that some basic rights (for example, the right to life) are properly attributed to children but they worry that an orientation to the moral claims of children that treats rights as very important and therefore as a principal locus of moral concern obscures or disrupts values that are crucial to regulating relations between children, parents, other adults, and the state appropriately. The critique of rights at stake here is not best understood as holding that recognition of children's rights logically or conceptually entails neglect of other values. (One can hold that children have certain rights and yet recognize that other normative considerations besides rights play an essential role in determining how children should be treated in a wide variety of contexts.) Rather the concern is that assigning special importance to rights in our normative discourse about children tends to crowd out other considerations in a troubling fashion. Three varieties of discourse anxiety can be distinguished (though in practice there may be overlap between them). I label them *inflation, corrosion,* and *efficacy*.

A. Inflation

First, there is the concern that assigning importance to children's rights generates a discourse in which too many of the interests of children, whether trivial or weighty, are wrongly elevated to the status of rights. Appropriately attending to the complex and varied interests of children requires nuanced moral judgment that permits subtle distinctions to be drawn between more and less important ways of responding to children's diverse needs, desires, and interests. Adopting a perspective in which the rights of children are emphasized and prioritized might lead to an excessive proliferation of putative rights. Since rights are generally regarded as especially strong moral entitlements that are only defeasible in very exceptional circumstances, viewing too many of the interests of children as protected by rights stymies deliberation about how competing interests should be assessed, weighed, and balanced. On the one hand, the proliferation of 'rights talk' can, perhaps somewhat paradoxically, devalue the moral currency of basic rights. For instance, if all rights are assumed to have broadly equivalent moral significance then talk of a child's right to play might encourage the view that the right to autonomy facilitation is not especially important. On the other hand, focusing on children's rights might result in an erroneous elevation of modest interests of children to the status of rights. For example, school-age children may have an interest in receiving a weekly allowance from their parents and perhaps good parenting practice, in many settings, includes the provision of an allowance. However, proposing that children have a right to an allowance and that parents who do not provide an allowance have violated their children's rights is not conducive to attending to the interests of children in a sensible fashion. In either case, the general worry is that emphasizing the protection of children's rights as the main locus of moral concern presents obstacles to the proper treatment of children. We will fail to make relevant moral distinctions between children's interests and, as a consequence, reasonable conduct by parents and other adults in caring for children may be (wrongly) scrutinized as threatening their children's rights.

B. Corrosion

The second variety of discourse anxiety focuses on the threat to family values posed by rights talk. The family is frequently identified as an especially important site of special values that are grounded in the close relationships of trust, affection, and mutual concern between parents and children.[35] In their influential discussion of such family values Brighouse and Swift (2014) argue that parenting is an extremely important source of human flourishing and that we must be attentive to the ways social structures and cultural norms can either be hospitable or hostile to the realization of family values.[36] For instance, the good of familial intimacy can only be reliably realized and sustained if parents and children have ample opportunities to spend time with one another and engage in shared activities. Of course, realization of the goods of family also depends crucially on the emotions, attitudes, and dispositions that parents and children have toward one another. Parents who are psychologically cold, highly judgmental or emotionally distant from their children are not well-placed to achieve and sustain rewarding forms of familial intimacy with their children. Similarly, certain kinds of moral discourse could be corrosive to familial intimacy. Rights are often viewed as setting strict boundaries between people and as articulating unconditional demands for treatment that are issued by people who are concerned more for their own well-being than the well-being of others. As Hardwig puts it:

> Thinking in terms of rights does more than reflect an egoistic, atomistic situation; it creates such a situation or reinforces our tendency to move in that direction. Thinking in terms of rights is divisive. It teaches us to think of 'I' and 'I versus you' instead of 'we'. Through accepting this picture and living in it we become more like enemies, antagonists, or traders, at best—less like brothers, sisters, lovers, and friends.[37]

With respect to the damaging impact of rights talk on familial intimacy Ferdinand Schoeman is explicit. He claims that:

> the danger of talk about rights of children is that it may encourage people to think that the proper relationship between themselves and their children is the abstract one that

---

[35] Although I emphasize relationships between parents and children here, the family values in question can be realized in the close relationships children often have with other caregivers (eg, grandparents, aunts, uncles, nannies etc).
[36] Brighouse and Swift (n 25).
[37] J Hardwig, 'Should Women Think in Terms of Rights?' (1984) 94 Ethics 441, 448.

the language of rights is forged to suit. So, rather than encouraging abusive parents to feel more intimate with their children, it may cause parents in intimate relationships with their infants to reassess the appropriateness of their blurring the boundaries of individual identity and to question their consciousness of a profound sense of identification with, and commitment toward, their families.[38]

C. Efficacy

The third variety of discourse anxiety concerns the impact of the discourse of children's rights on actually promoting and protecting salient interests of children. Rights are supposed to play a valuable role in highlighting and protecting the fundamental claims and interests of putative rights bearers. So one might reasonably hold that the importance of children's rights depends on there being evidence that addressing children's core interests via the lens of rights is actually beneficial to them. If the discourse of children's rights does not actually yield significant benefits for children then we have reason to doubt the efficacy and thus the importance of children's rights. Lucinda Ferguson nicely articulates the concern about the efficacy of children's rights. She argues that recourse to a framework of children's rights, especially in contexts where we seek guidance on how to regulate disputes about the appropriate treatment of children, is only justified if it yields better outcomes for children than a non-rights framework (for example, one that focuses directly on children's welfare). She contends 'we have no reason to think that regulating children in terms of children's rights is necessarily better than alternative approaches'.[39]

Ferguson grounds her scepticism about the efficacy of children's-rights discourse in the putative difficulty of adequately articulating a credible 'child-centred' account of the distinctive content of children's rights.[40] On her view, children's rights can only

---

[38] F Schoeman, 'Rights of Children, Rights of Parents, and the Moral Basis of the Family' (1980) 91 Ethics 6, 9. See also Glendon who worries that 'the language of rights has invaded American homes' and that 'rights language not only seems to filter out other discourses; it simultaneously infiltrates them'. M Glendon, *Rights Talk: The Impoverishment of Political Discourse* (The Free Press 1991) 173.

[39] Ferguson, 'Not Merely Rights' (n 7) 202.

[40] Ferguson allows that children have some basic rights in common with adults (eg, the right to life) and she does not doubt that recognition of such basic rights is important. Her reservations concern the utility of deploying a discourse of children's rights (ie, C-rights in Feinberg's terminology). Ferguson is especially interested in whether a children's rights framework is fruitful in yielding good outcomes for children in legal disputes where their welfare is at stake. However, the general critique she raises need not be restricted to legal contexts. Ferguson's overall analysis depends crucially on the claim that 'there is no coherent child-centred way to give content to individual children's rights'. Ferguson, 'Not Merely Rights' (n 7) 199. Ferguson seems to ground this claim on the idea that a genuinely 'child-centred' account of the content of children's rights requires attending to children's own conception of their basic interests or claims. Since children generally lack the capacities to authoritatively articulate their own interests, it seems that the content of children's rights cannot be given by children themselves and thus cannot be supplied in a suitably 'child-centred' way. However, there is a different way in which an account of the content of children's rights can be 'child-centred': it can appeal to plausible claims about the distinct interests that children have in virtue of their distinct capacities, vulnerabilities and potentialities. We can make coherent judgments about the nature and importance of these interests without supposing either that the interests in question are simply those of mature adults or that children, *qua* children, must be able to endorse these interests for them to count as genuine, child-specific interests. For instance, we can recognize the importance that attaches to

have special significance if their content can be articulated in a way that is suitably grounded on the perspective that children take toward their own interests or claims. Yet since children typically lack the capacities necessary to articulate their interests with authority, the content and practical meaning of children's rights will be held hostage to judgments about children's interests made by adults. But this means that adults may ascribe rights to children that are at odds with children's own conception of their own interests. For example, a child may be deemed to have 'a "right" to an outcome she does not want'.[41]

Ferguson's point is not to doubt the propriety of grounding the treatment of children on judgments about children's interests that children do not endorse. She is not opposed to paternalistic treatment of children. Rather her point is that rights themselves do no distinctive work in securing good outcomes for children. So the invocation of children's rights does not, itself, deliver better outcomes to children than a direct appeal to and suitable weighing of their interests. The importance of children's rights is putatively undercut because rights discourse has no demonstrable advantages in yielding better outcomes for children than other approaches (for example, a welfare focused approach).

VI. Assessing Discourse Anxiety

The three varieties of discourse anxiety I have identified provide reasons to resist excessive and exclusive focus on children's rights in the course of normative theorizing about children. But acknowledging that children's rights are important is not the same as claiming that all normatively salient features of children's lives must or should be framed in terms of rights. An attempt to regulate *all* aspects of relationships between adults and children via the language of rights might well present an obstacle to familial intimacy and it would probably lead to a pointless proliferation of pseudo-rights that would impede rather than facilitate the overall well-being of children. But the advocate of children's rights is not committed, either in theory or practice, to the over-extension of rights. Indeed, an important feature of rights is to highlight a certain set of basic interests or claims that are distinguishable from other interests in virtue of the fact that they merit special recognition and protection. There is, therefore, a reason within rights theory itself to resist the proliferation of children's-rights claims. Children's-rights advocates should exercise caution in determining what interests or claims of children have special significance and merit protection by rights. However, as we have already seen, it is extremely difficult to deny that children *qua* children have distinctive interests

---

shielding children from threats to well-being they face in light of their cognitive and moral immaturity. Similarly, we can give recognition to the importance of childhood play both for its own sake and its contribution to healthy development without supposing that children having a genuine and distinct interest in play is contingent on the articulation of such an interest by children. This means there is a way to supply content to the rights of children that does not fall prey to Ferguson's objection. Moreover, any credible non-rights approach to children must also make such 'child-centred' judgments. And if making such judgments were really fraught with theoretical difficulty then any non-rights approach to the treatment of children that appealed to distinct interests of children would be imperilled.

[41] Ferguson, 'Not Merely Rights' (n 7) 193.

and claims that merit special recognition and protection and which are defeasible only under extraordinary circumstances. Rights discourse, as we have seen, helpfully signals the importance of such claims or interests.

The fact that the content of children's rights is fixed by the distinct needs and special vulnerabilities of children is relevant to rebutting the concern about corrosion. The relevant interests protected by children's rights crucially include interests in being nurtured and cared for in loving and affectionate ways. So respect for children's rights entails a concern to ensure that families have access to the social and material conditions that are conducive to the realization of relationship goods. Moreover, recognizing and respecting the fact children have distinct rights is not an impediment to close, emotionally rich relationships between children and parents. Acknowledging that one's children have rights is entirely consistent with loving one's children or nurturing them in a way that is both emotionally spontaneous and responsive to their idiosyncratic personalities. Respect for children's rights does shape relationships by imposing limits on the exercise of parental authority and by mandating concern for some of children's basic interests. However, respecting these rights does not require that daily care of one's children be dominated by constant deliberation about their rights. Rights discourse need not be omnipresent to be important and its presence in families does not inevitably crowd out other valuable forms of discourse. Moreover, care that is not regulated, at least implicitly, by attentiveness to the basic interests and claims protected by children's rights is not likely to be conducive to the realization of real family values.

While it is true that the special importance of attending to the core interests of children could possibly be expressed in a non-rights framework, abandoning rights discourse has both theoretical and practical costs. Consider, for instance, the importance to the lives of children of being loved and being provided with an autonomy-facilitating education. Avoiding discourse that affirms that children have a right to be loved or a right to an autonomy-facilitating education can diminish the significance that attaches, from a societal point of view, to ensuring that children are loved and raised to be autonomous. It suggests that loving children or facilitating their autonomy, though potentially important, are simply considerations to be factored into a general moral calculus alongside a wide variety of other considerations of varying overall weight or importance. Discourse that conflates or tends to conflate highly weighty interests with modest or trivial interests is likely to generate troubling distortions in our assessments of how children should be treated. Reluctance to grapple with the rights of children can also work in the service of dubious conceptions of the rights and prerogatives of parents and other adults in regard to children. Without a discourse of rights that clearly articulates morally essential entitlements of children, adults may abuse their authority over children or fail to adequately attend to some of their basic interests. This is not to say that a discourse of rights necessarily guarantees protection of the fundamental interests of children. But it does provide a standard of moral accountability that can be invoked to guide, motivate, and assess treatment of children that affect especially important facets of their lives. Securing better outcomes for children involves prioritizing some of their interests over others and rights discourse is particularly well suited to give expression to that task.

VII. Conclusion

Although discourse-anxiety concerns have some force against exaggerated depictions of children's right talk gone amok, the concerns do not strike me as sufficient to undermine the basic case for the general importance of children's rights. We have also seen that foundational scepticism about children's rights is unpersuasive and does not jeopardize the importance of children's rights. Of course, there are controversies about exactly which rights should be attributed to children and how the developing maturity of children shapes the interpretation of children's rights. Similarly, the resolution of cases in which children's rights are at stake and in which they seem to collide with other weighty normative considerations will often be difficult. But the theoretical and practical challenges that arise when we deliberate reflectively about how to treat children do not magically disappear if we try to banish rights talk or push it to the margins. We should take children seriously by taking children's rights seriously. But we should also recognize that children's rights do not exhaust what is morally important about children.

10
Parental Control Rights

Scott Altman[1]

I. Introduction

Some parents claim a right to direct their young children's lives—a right to decide where children will live; who children will associate with; what moral guidance and religious activity children will be exposed to; and how children will allocate much of their time. These control rights include two related entitlements: (a) that parents are permitted to set rules for their children and, within limits, to enforce those rules; and (b) that non-parents generally refrain from subverting parental efforts to guide and shape their children. Such rights become important when governments or individuals intervene, and when children seek help from outsiders in resisting parental choices.[2]

By 'rights' I mean special sorts of moral claims.[3] These will only sometimes merit legal protection, depending both on the strength of other conflicting rights and on the political and practical questions that always constrain enforcing moral norms with legal rules. I use the term 'control rights' to distinguish parental entitlements to control their children's lives from other moral claims asserted by parents, such as the right to become a parent, and the right to associate with one's children, including claims for child custody, for visitations, and for limits on relocation by the child and custodial parent. Although control rights and these other claims are related, they have distinct justifications.[4]

---

[1] For helpful comments, I thank Elizabeth Brake, Emily Buss, Mary Anne Case, Lucinda Ferguson, Ron Garet, Greg Keating, Andrei Marmor, Daria Roithmayr, Elyn Saks, Nomi Stolzenberg and participants in the Oxford seminar on philosophical foundations of children's and family law, and the University of Chicago Regulation of Family, Sex, and Gender Workshop.

[2] The sort of immunity I have in mind is against government dictate when the child's parents agree with each other. When parents who are equally entitled to the decision-making authority disagree with each other, government intervention can be understood partly as dispute resolution rather than simple regulation.

[3] The argument advanced here aims to be agnostic on many disputes about the nature of rights. For example, some writers insist that rights within the family should be understood as relational. See, eg, M Minow and M Shanley, 'Relational Rights and Responsibilities: Revisioning the Family in Liberal Political Theory and Law' (1996) 11 Hypatia 4. This means that the good being pursued is constituted by a certain kind of relationship. All of the arguments explored in this chapter can in this sense be understood as claims for a relational right. The fact that the right is relational does not moot the question of whether it is directly justified. Each person can have an individual interest in the specific sort of relationship.

[4] In a prior paper I argued that an interest in intimacy justified parental rights of access—a right to see one's children regularly. I considered whether intimacy could also justify other alleged parental rights, such as a broad right to direct a child's upbringing, but concluded (as have prior writers) that it could not. S Altman, 'The Pursuit of Intimacy and Parental Rights' in A Marmor (ed), *The Routledge Companion to Philosophy of Law* (Routledge 2011).

Obviously, parental control rights do not include the right to succeed in controlling everything that happens to a child. Such control is not possible; fate and children's own preferences conspire so that parents at best have a chance to influence their children's lives without too much interference by government or third parties. None of these rights is alleged to be absolute, and all of them fade as children grow older and claim more control over their own lives.

Parental rights to direct their young children's lives, and possible justifications for such rights, are much disputed. Some theories treat parental rights as subsidiary to parental responsibilities.[5] Other theories offer justifications for parental rights that are indirect; they support parental control rights based on interests other than those of the parent, such as the interests of children or of society. Without discounting such child-centred and society-centred justifications, this chapter explores whether parental control rights can be justified directly based on parental interests.[6] My purpose in exploring a parent-centred justification is not to deny that we have child and society-centred reasons for deferring to parental choices. Nor it is to urge that we should defer to parents more often in practice or protect children less vigorously. Rather, I mean to clarify the nature and basis of parents' moral claims to control their children's upbringing so that we can think more clearly about the topic.

II. Do Parental Control Rights, or their Direct Justification, Matter?

Does it matter whether parents have moral rights to control their children's upbringing or whether those rights can be justified by parental interests? Perhaps not. Even without considering parental interests, we have strong reasons to protect parental decisions from outside interference. First, parents generally know their children well and care about their welfare. So most of the time, parents will make better decisions for their children than will others. This happy coincidence means that there is often little gap between children's welfare and parents' decision making. Second, deference to parental decisions might be necessary compensation for the work parents do—necessary in the sense that some people would not become parents (or would not be responsible parents) absent substantial control, including the ability to make parenting choices that society dislikes. Parental control thus benefits children and society by enticing people

---

[5] The main argument in this chapter could be restated in terms of rights that derive from duties. Certainly, the argument that parents have a right to be fiduciaries can be understood as a right derived from a duty. So too can a parent's interest in educating, counselling, and nurturing a child.

[6] Justifications for parental rights that derive both from children's interests and from the interest of parents are sometimes called dual-interest theories. See M Clayton, *Justice and Legitimacy in Upbringing* (OUP 2006) 54. I accept the basic idea that parents should control their children's upbringing both because it is in the interest of parents that they have these rights and that these rights are in the interests of children and of society. But the most important disputes about parental rights arise when parents have an interest in exercising a right (or exercising it in a specific way) that does not advance their children's interests. In exactly these cases, a theory of parental rights based partly on parental interests will sometimes condone a parental right to harm children. Dual-interest theories sometimes pursue a different strategy; they suggest that parents' interests justify the right to become a parent or the right to associate with children, but not the right to control a child's upbringing. See, for example, S Hannan and R Vernon, 'Parental Rights: A Role Based Approach' (2008) 6 Theory & Research in Education 173, 184.

to become parents or to carry out their parenting duties well. Third, in a pluralist society where views of the good differ, some parents will inevitably want to rear children in ways that others view as non-ideal. Protecting those decisions allows varied ways of life to flourish and limits government efforts to dictate one view of the good.[7]

Not only do we have good reasons to empower parents without positing directly justified parental rights, it is not clear that parental rights add force to those reasons. After all, parental rights must be balanced against other interests. As a result, even with parental rights, states will be able to regulate to prevent serious harms to children, to protect a child's right to an open future or an older child's right to make decisions for himself, or to promote society's need for educated citizens. Indeed, many important disputes in which parental rights are invoked depend not primarily on whether parents have control rights (or on their justification), but instead on the scope and strength of opposing rights.[8]

Nevertheless, practical outcomes sometimes turn on whether parental control rights exist and on whether they derive from parental interests. Parental powers that depend only on child-centred or society-centred justifications are contingent and vulnerable. They guarantee parents no control over their children if child welfare (conventionally understood) can be improved by overriding parental directives.

Consider as an example a law that aims to address three perceived problems among young people: growing timidity, failure to work well in teams, and declining physical fitness. The new law requires that: (a) children participate in a team sport (promoting physical fitness and teamwork); and (b), that they participate in an outward-bound style programme (promoting both physical fitness and confidence in the face of fear).

If parents have no control rights, they would lack any cause to reject this law. The goals might be well supported by science as helpful both to children and society, and therefore appropriate matters of state interest. They are not particularly ideological, and so are not apt to be disallowed by those concerned with government-imposed orthodoxy or the need for diverse views of the good in society. And they are not so intrusive that people subject to such regulation would forego parenting rather than rear children under such limitations.

If parents have control rights that are indirectly justified by child welfare, they might still lack any basis for objecting this law. Indirectly justified rights are just rules of thumb; we authorize parents to decide for children because we believe they will make good decisions. But if this rule of thumb is the main reason for deference, parents have no ground to object if society decides to override parental decisions that are deemed unwise.

---

[7] For a provocative argument against too much state deference toward varied views of the good, see MA Case, 'Feminist Fundamentalism on The Frontier Between Government and Family Responsibility for Children' (2009) 11 Utah Law Review 381.

[8] This point is made by M Clayton. He reviews several accounts of the interest children have in autonomy. On some accounts—especially those that emphasize capacity to revisit commitments—parents may aim to indoctrinate their children so long as the techniques of indoctrination are sufficiently mild as to allow for later reflection. But on other accounts, in which autonomy requires that people have mature capacities before they are intentionally indoctrinated in ideas, many conventionally accepted parental efforts at education would violate children's autonomy rights.

If parents have a directly justified right to direct their children's upbringing, they should be able to resist this law. The law's goals are not urgent enough to override a robust parental right. Children deprived of team sports and outward bound can go on to live happy and fruitful lives. But parents may have strong reasons to oppose the law. Team sports might be thought objectionable by some parents as demeaning to individual effort and skill, and by other parents as supporting tribalism and discrimination against out-groups. Sport in general might be thought to waste time better spent on study or on music. And outward bound might be thought simply unduly risky. Whether parents, rather than governments, are entitled to assess these trade-offs depends on whether parents have control rights and on why they have them.

Similar examples might arise from parental efforts to impart values that the state thinks inappropriate. Consider parents who believe that striving always for excellence leads to happiness and that having soft attitudes toward those who fail (or worse, those who violate rules) is itself a moral failing. The parents instruct their children in these views and express disdain for those who model forgiveness toward failure or wrongdoing. The state where these parents live has concluded that such lessons harm children—that children with unforgiving world views tend to suffer later in life from higher rates of violence, divorce, and illness. So the state mandates that all schools offer instruction in empathy. The parents refuse to allow their children to be so taught. If parents have a parent-centred right to shape their children's values, they are entitled to resist this law (subject to enquiry into conflicting rights of the child and of society). But if parental prerogatives depend on a rebuttable presumption that parents act for their children's welfare, a state might legitimately intervene in this case to provide children with beneficial lessons in empathy.

Yet another example comes from the, perhaps short-lived, controversy over 'free-range parenting'. In reaction to overly-cautious parenting styles, some parents have begun to allow their children to wander unsupervised in settings that would have seemed unremarkable a generation ago, but that now strike many people as too risky. In a few cases, parents have been charged with neglect for allowing children to play unsupervised, even when the children were not harmed and when no evidence of specific danger was present.[9]

Admittedly, these examples (team sports and empathy lessons) are a bit contrived and are hardly the most pressing disputes over parental control rights. In more difficult cases, parental rights will not be so decisive. But they are apt to be important. One such case is the rights of parents to exclude (or limit visitation by) grandparents. Grandparent-visitation disputes are difficult because multiple parties have strong interests, and governments are poorly situated to evaluate conflicting claims with certainty. Children might have strong interests in maintaining or establishing relationship with grandparents (or in being protected from grandparents). And grandparents themselves may have strong interests in these relationships.[10] But insofar as parents have an

---

[9] See C Wergin, 'The Case for Free Range Parenting' *New York Times* (New York, 20 March 2015).

[10] One particular difficulty with grandparent visitation cases is that some arguments for parental rights also counsel protecting grandparent rights. This is true both for intimacy-based claims, and perhaps even for claims based on an interest in nurturing, counselling, and educating, which are discussed later in this chapter.

important interest in controlling their children's upbringing, the balance of interests in these hard cases may more easily fall to strong parental control.

III. The Direct Justification of Parental Rights

The case for deriving parental control rights from parental interests rests on two claims. The first is that parents are people whose interests are no less deserving than their children or than other members of society. Parenting has long been understood to affect important interests of children, parents, and society.[11] Deriving parental rights exclusively from interests of children and society arguably treats parents as means only, rather than as persons whose interests count equally with others.[12]

The second claim is that parents' interest in control is the kind of interest that can warrant a right: an interest that contributes to the fundamental success of a parent's life. The following sections examine candidates for parental interests that might justify control rights.

Before examining these candidates, I should address one parent-centred argument often advanced for control rights: parents are entitled to direct the upbringing of their children because doing so is the inevitable consequence of directing their own lives. Parents profoundly affect their children when they choose where to live, whether to attend church, and how to allocate money between family vacations and charity. A parent's right to shape her own life by making such choices might thus justify parental-control rights.

This argument is not sufficient to establish the sort of broad parental rights often claimed. A parent's right to direct her own life will sometimes protect a parent's power to control a child's upbringing. But it does so only when that power is needed for a parent to pursue non-child-rearing goals. Perhaps a parent is entitled to bring a child to church services because the parent herself is entitled to go and is also entitled not to spend money to hire a babysitter. But this incidental right does not encompass the broad right to direct a child's religious upbringing by, for example, choosing to send the child to a religious school, or preventing the government from insisting that the child study evolution. A broad right to control a child's upbringing requires more than the inevitable effects we have on children when we exercise our rights to live our own lives. A parent-centred justification for control rights thus requires a specific parental interest that control rights advance.

---

[11] For a careful examination of this tripartite balancing in the context of control rights, see E Buss, 'Allocating Developmental Control among Parent, Child and the State' (2004) University of Chicago Legal Forum 27.

[12] W Galston makes this point. On his view, control over children must coordinate three sets of interests: children, parents, and society. While values connected with each 'must find appropriate expression in practical decisions, there is no guarantee that they will fit together into a harmonious whole. Pressed to the hilt, any one of them will entail costs to the others that may well be judged excessive.' WA Galston, *Liberal Pluralism* (CUP 2002) 94. See also C Macleod, 'Conceptions of Parental Autonomy' (1997) 25 Politics & Society 117, 121 (describing the problem of parental autonomy as depending on an egalitarian thesis that interests of parents, children, and society matter equally). This argument has sometimes been rejected as inappropriate, most notably by JG Dwyer. See JG Dwyer's chapter, 'Regulating Child Rearing in a Culturally Diverse Society'. A version of the argument can also be found in Hannan and Vernon, 'Parental Rights' (n 6) 184.

IV. Which Parental Interests Justify Control Rights?

A. Parents' interests in intimacy

Control rights are sometimes said to derive from a parent's interest in intimacy. According to Ferdinand Schoeman, intimacy requires parental control rights because intimate relationships require autonomy and privacy. Regulating intimate relationships 'would inevitably result in a redirection or "socialization" of these relationships'[13] and 'require the parties to think of themselves primarily as serving public ends and as having public duties'.[14]

Schoeman does not explain why regulations inevitably have these effects on relationships. Perhaps he assumes that regulations would be extremely pervasive. Certainly a state would undermine intimacy if it placed cameras in homes to monitor parental behaviour and then intervened to correct every perceived parental misdeed. Intimate relationships cannot thrive without being sheltered from constant observation. Nor are they really relationships if participants lack all control over their actions and merely carry out an outsider's dictates. In this sense, intimacy requires some degree of privacy and autonomy.

That a minimum threshold of privacy and control is necessary for intimate relationships does not establish Schoeman's conclusion of broad parental control rights. Lost intimacy seems far less likely if we contemplate more realistic regulations. For example, there is no evidence that parent–child intimacy is more difficult because governments require car seats for infants. This simple safety regulation does not cause parents to think of themselves primarily as serving public ends. I see no reason to assume intimacy would decline if governments forbid corporal punishment at home or require comparative religion curricula at school. To the contrary, intimacy seems quite resilient.

Narrower claims connecting intimacy to parental control have also been advanced. Harry Brighouse and Adam Swift, for example, though arguing for parental control rights primarily on another ground, urge that parental control rights are occasionally necessary to protect intimacy. Their main example is sharing parental enthusiasms with the child. Sharing enthusiasms is thought important for parent–child intimacy because: an ongoing relationship requires having at least some shared interests, enthusiasms, and values; shared enthusiasms provide the interactions that foster intimacy; and a relationship in which enthusiasms cannot be shared would be constantly self-conscious.[15]

Brighouse and Swift's argument connecting parental rights with intimacy seems to presume extreme governmental intrusion. Intimacy would be difficult if the state forbid parents from ever encouraging their children to prefer one thing over another. But

---

[13] F Schoeman, 'Rights of Children, Rights of Parents, and the Moral Basis of the Family' (1980) 91 Ethics 6, 15.

[14] ibid 16.

[15] H Brighouse and A Swift, 'Parents' Rights and the Value of the Family' (2006) 117 Ethics 80, 104. See also H Brighouse and A Swift, *Family Values: The Ethics of Parent–Child Relationships* (Princeton UP 2014) 151. ('Valuable relationships require parents to be free to engage with their children in ways that produce mutual identification and reflect the parents' judgments about what is valuable in life.')

such a regime is not plausible. No one thinks that an upbringing without viewpoints would benefit children. The question of parental rights arises in the context of asking whether parents are entitled to make decisions that outsiders regard as non-ideal. So a more realistic enquiry about parental rights would ask whether state intrusion limited to correcting perceived errors would undermine intimacy.

Imagine a government that forbids parents from using tobacco products in front of children or allowing young children to see violent video games. This limitation on sharing enthusiasms would not prevent most families from having enough shared values and experiences to maintain intimacy. And it would not require such pervasive self-consciousness as to make intimacy impossible.[16] Only in cases of extravagant regulation (or the rare parent interested in nothing besides tobacco and violent video games) would state intrusion into parental decisions undermine intimacy by preventing mutually enjoyable experiences and shared enthusiasms.

My reply to Shoeman and to Brighouse and Swift—that their imagined extreme interventions are unrealistic and that plausible interventions by outsiders to protect children (or social interests) would not harm intimacy—might be thought mistaken.[17] Plausible interventions in the family might not threaten to destroy all intimacy; any harm to intimacy would be too small to detect. But small, undetectable harms are still harms and might accumulate into large harms.

This response seems to me mistaken for two reasons. First, some harms persist even when they are small: A punch in the face is a large harm; a soft punch is a small harm; a gentle, but unwanted touch is a smaller harm still, but a harm nonetheless. But not all harms follow this pattern. Enclosing a claustrophobic person in a box is a large harm; putting her in a small room is a smaller harm. But putting her in a large room is no harm at all. Once she has sufficient space to feel comfortable, enclosure does not interfere with her interests. Intimacy may be more like personal space than like bodily integrity. Requiring that children wear helmets does not make parent–child intimacy more difficult, even in a small or undetectable way. Rather, it leaves more than enough room for parents to establish intimacy with their children, and therefore harms intimacy not at all.

Second, even if some regulations intrude undetectably on intimacy (thus counting as small harms), and even if such small harms could accumulate into large harms if aggregated, it is not clear what follows. Parental interests in intimacy are the sort of interest that can justify a right. But the right need not be powerful as against trivial harms, or

---

[16] The self-consciousness argument is in tension with Brighouse and Swift's specific account of how parental intimacy differs from other intimacy: unlike intimate adult relationships, fiduciary obligations 'often require [parents] to be less than wholly spontaneous and intimate ... The good parent sometimes masks her disappointment ... She does not inflict on the child ... all her spontaneous reactions or all her emotional responses'. Brighouse and Swift, 'Parents' Rights and the Value of the Family' (n 15) 93–94. The duty to restrain sharing and spontaneity that Brighouse and Swift see at the core of good parenting is surely consistent with at least some duties not to share enthusiasms if the state concludes such restraint is needed for child welfare.

[17] Brighouse and Swift might actually accept my argument. In another context, they note that 'A parent should be able to sustain a successful relationship without any *particular* shared interest or values'. Brighouse and Swift, *Family Values* (n 15) 157.

against harms that could become large if aggregated in circumstances where no such aggregation is likely.

Perhaps, though, the argument from intimacy to control rights has more force for subgroups in the population whose intimacy is peculiarly vulnerable to outside intrusion. For example, separatist groups that seek to shelter their children from modern or secular influences might fear that forced exposure will alienate children from parents and thus undermine intimacy.

Perhaps separatist groups have a good argument for being permitted to shelter their children. But these arguments offer little help in thinking generally about parental-control rights and intimacy. In particular, it is not obvious why those who make their intimate relationships peculiarly vulnerable to outside interference should be able to generate a duty to avoid harms to their intimacy. Perhaps in the case of separatist religious sects, we can see a justification: fundamental-religious commitments require that they live in intimate settings that are highly vulnerable to outside harms. In such cases, we may find ourselves inclined to accommodate their needs. But the accommodation stems from respect for religious needs, and an inclination not to force people to choose between religious obligation and family intimacy. It does not reflect a general deference to those who choose to make themselves unusually vulnerable to lost intimacy and therefore does not offer a general basis for parental control rights.

B. Parents' interest in being fiduciaries

Brighouse and Swift argue for parental control rights based on a second interest often invoked for this purpose: parents' interest in being fiduciaries. Being a fiduciary—acting for the welfare of another—is a fundamental good for many people.[18] Fiduciarity is important for parents (and for their children) according to Brighouse and Swift because it facilitates a relationship 'in which the adult offers love and authority, a complex and emotionally challenging combination of openness and restraint, of spontaneity and self-monitoring, of sharing and withholding'.[19] Fiduciarity is thus valuable because it supports a specific valuable relationship.

Brighouse and Swift connect the interest in being a fiduciary (and the relationship it supports) to parental control rights in part through the role of value inculcation. Parents, they say, are entitled to influence their children's values because influencing values is an integral part of fostering a child's moral development, which is itself key to a parent's fiduciary duty.[20] The argument from a parent's interest in being a fiduciary to a right to provide needed guidance has some appeal. But on reflection, this argument does not work. The interest in acting for children's welfare need not encompass selecting the moral instruction children receive.

---

[18] A similar argument for parental rights is advanced in S Brennan and R Noggle, 'The Moral Status of Children: Children's Rights, Parents' Rights and Family Justice' (1997) 23 Social Theory and Practice 1 (describing parental rights as stewardship rights). For an account of parents as legal fiduciaries, see, E Scott and R Scott, 'Parents as Fiduciaries' (1995) 81 Virginia Law Review 2401. The Scotts understand parental rights as in-kind compensation for performing fiduciary tasks.
[19] Brighouse and Swift (n 15) 93.
[20] Brighouse and Swift, 'Parents' Rights and the Value of the Family' (n 15) 104.

Fiduciary duties are often fulfilled within externally set constraints, including externally selected values. Consider the fiduciary duties of a trustee. If I am appointed to administer a large trust for the benefit of two children, I cannot give half the corpus to a charity merely because I think undue wealth will harm the children whose interests I am charged with advancing. To the contrary, my discretion as a trustee must be guided by conventional understandings of the children's welfare (or by the benefactor's express wishes). On this standard model of fiduciarity, one can successfully work for other people's good without choosing the good one pursues.

Perhaps this response to Brighouse and Swift is unfair, for two reasons. First, their reference to being a fiduciary need not be understood as a literal mirror for legal doctrines. Rather, they are pointing to the human good of acting for the benefit of someone who cannot act for themselves. I accept this point. But the legal example was meant to illustrate more than just actual practice. Being a fiduciary is fulfilling because it allows us to act for another person, setting aside our own aims, and sometimes even our own values. The distinctive good of fiduciarity, not just its practical instantiation, flows from setting aside one's own values to implement someone else's goals.

Second, perhaps analogies to financial fiduciaries are inapt. The fiduciary relationship that parents have an interest in establishing might differ from typical fiduciary relationships in a way that makes externally guided discretion problematic. Brighouse and Swift do not address this question directly. They insist that any relationship demanding spontaneity and openness requires a 'substantial sphere of interaction unmonitored by authorities'.[21] But just as with intimacy, we have reason to wonder whether the good of parental relationships would be undermined by plausible regulation. Indeed the desired relationship that Brighouse and Swift describe includes a mix of spontaneity and self-monitoring and of sharing and withholding. Since some withholding and self-monitoring are at the core of a parent–child relationship, modest intrusion by the state to require that parents withhold some lessons that harm children likely would not undermine the relationship that justifies parental control.[22]

Sarah Hannan and Richard Vernon offer a similar account, but reach a different conclusion: that there are no parent-centred reasons for parental control rights. They begin from the same insight as Brighouse and Swift—that parents have an interest in being fiduciaries toward children, an interest that justifies a right to become a parent and to associate with one's child. But they emphasize that once parents enter a fiduciary relationship, its contours cannot be governed by the parents' interests.[23] Indeed, the vulnerability of children requires that the relationship protects children and not parents.[24] Hannan and Vernon note that although liberal theories generally justify rights based on interests, they never allow individual interests to justify rights to control another

---

[21] ibid.

[22] ibid 119. Brighouse and Swift state clearly that parents have no right to influence their children's values except to the extent that doing so is needed to support an appropriate relationship. They also conclude that on their theory, parents should have much 'less discretion over their children's upbringing than they currently do' 177.

[23] Hannan and Vernon, 'Parental Rights: A Role Based Approach' (n 6) 185. Similarly, Brighouse and Swift argue that adults have the right to become parents based on their own interests, but that their rights *as* parents derive entirely from children's interests. Brighouse and Swift (n 15) 93–94.

[24] Hannan and Vernon, 'Parental Rights: A Role Based Approach' (n 6) 186.

person. For this reason, fiduciary powers exist exclusively to promote the beneficiary's interests.

What do Hannan and Vernon mean when they say that parents have an interest in becoming fiduciaries, but that their interests may not affect the relationship they are entering? They certainly cannot mean that a parent who becomes a fiduciary must thereafter act only for the benefit of children. Fiduciaries are not slaves who must sacrifice their own welfare to benefit those in their care.[25] Parents may allocate resources for their own benefit, even if redirecting those resources might have benefited the children, for example, saving for retirement rather than paying for college tuition. Fiduciary duties require that people who exercise control of others give the interests of those others due consideration, not absolute weight. As even Hannan and Vernon note, 'in a liberal society, premised on equal moral consideration, one's pursuit of one's chosen life project is necessarily constrained, for others have life-projects too'.[26] This certainly means (as Hannan and Vernon intended) that parents cannot make decisions about children without regard to the child's current and future aims. But it also means that parents cannot be required to make decisions about children without regard to the parents' life projects. Liberal theory and actual institutions both recognize that institutional roles must accommodate the reasonable life-projects of all participants, including those who exercise power over others.

Hannan and Vernon must mean something narrower when they claim that parents' fiduciary roles protect only children's interests. Perhaps they mean to distinguish parental actions that incidentally affect children from parental actions authorized by their roles as fiduciaries. When parents act as individuals in ways that affect children (such as when they spend money), parents need not be absolutely selfless. But when parents act exclusively as fiduciaries—using authority granted to them only because children need protection—parents must exercise pure fiduciary loyalty.

This narrower view of fiduciary relationships has some appeal. A person's interest may justify them occupying a role in which power over another is exercised. But once in that role, power can be exercised only based on the reason for creating the role, not on the reason the person wanted to occupy it.[27] This image of a fiduciary seems to match our practices. For example, someone may yearn to be a lawyer because it is lucrative, or interesting, or a way to advance particular social goals. But a lawyer may not exercise power as a fiduciary to advance these goals at the expense of client welfare. In advising a client about whether to settle a case, the lawyer may not offer advice based on which outcome is most financially, intellectually, or politically advantageous to the lawyer.

Despite its appeal, the narrow view of a parent's fiduciary role has a problem. It depends on being able to distinguish cases where parents legitimately pursue their own ends (with due concern for their children's interests) from those where parents exercise power exclusively as fiduciaries and thus must act only for their children's welfare. Presumably this distinction depends on whether the choice involves one of

---

[25] Brighouse and Swift make a parallel point about fiduciaries not being slaves. Brighouse and Swift (n 15) 98, 121–22.
[26] Hannon and Vernon, 'Parental Rights: A Role Based Approach' (n 6) 180.   [27] ibid 184–85.

the parent's life projects (in which case the parent can pursue her own interests).[28] For example, in deciding where to live or whether to spend limited funds on private education, the parents may consider how this affects their own goals. In deciding whether to send the child to a religious school, or to require or forbid the child to participate in sports, the parent must consider only the child's welfare.

I see three difficulties with this distinction. First, it cannot accommodate a parent for whom raising a religious or athletic (or ambitious, or empathic) child is itself part of a parent's life project. In many ways, this example is at the core of disputes over parental-control rights. If the government believes that empathy lessons are important for every child's personal development, but a parent regards creating rigid and unforgiving children as important—not just to the child's welfare, but to their own success as parents—we cannot know what rights the parent has unless we know how to address parents who seek to create children with certain dispositions, talents, or experiences as a core reason for becoming a parent.

Second, the distinction separates permissible and impermissible actions in a way that treats identical effects on child welfare very differently. For example, parents who decide to live in a remote location could do so if they wanted a rugged and isolated life, subject to welfare requirements for their children, including requirements for protecting a child's future autonomy. But a parent who wishes to make the same decision about where to live based centrally on a desire to raise children who are separated from civilization would potentially be subject to restraint if society decided that this outcome was not ideal for children.

Third, an institution in which fiduciary responsibilities must be exercised exclusively for the benefit of children as conventionally understood might be so restrictive toward how parents exercise their fiduciary duties as to preclude parenting from being a meaningful part of a life project. As Hannan and Vernon note:

> If we want to devote a large part of our life to the project of parenting, would that project not include wanting to give to our children the best chance of a good life as we see it? What other idea of a good life should we want to give them, if not our own?[29]

The next section explores an account of parental interest that captures this understanding—that parents have an interest in producing good outcomes for children based on the parents' understanding of the good. But perhaps the value in being a fiduciary can be salvaged as a basis for control rights just by reflecting on the importance of value pluralism and predictive uncertainty. After all, parental control rights would not much matter if we all agreed about what outcomes best served children and what steps best ensured those outcomes. Disagreement between parents and governments

---

[28] One might think the distinction turns on why the parent is given power to decide an issue. If the parent has power because the child lacks sufficient maturity to make decisions, then the power is purely fiduciary. But this approach does not work. If parents want to relocate, we presume that the parents may bring their children. This presumption relies on the idea that the parents are entitled to decide where to live. But we presume that the child will follow because children are not mature enough to live on their own or to decide on their residence. This illustrates that most parental powers to make decisions about children ultimately derive in part from children's incapacity. Therefore incapacity cannot help us to distinguish parenting choices that incidentally affect children from those where pure loyalty is owed.

[29] Hannon and Vernon, 'Parental Rights: A Role Based Approach' (n 6) 181.

often arises over difficult moral questions about which we cannot expect consensus. We have strong political reasons to prevent governments from dictating orthodoxy in such matters.

No doubt appropriate respect for diversity and concern about government abuse strongly counsel deference to parental choice. But these concerns do not tie parental rights to parental interests in being a fiduciary. They are political reasons for protecting parental prerogatives. They justify parental rights indirectly based on the well-known concern for restraining government in the face of value pluralism.

Before providing an alternative account of the interest underlying control rights, I must return to Hannan and Vernon's assertion that we never permit the interests of a person with power over others to shape that relationship.[30] Contrary to Hannan and Vernon's assertion, we do sometimes allow the interests of people who exercise power over others to shape institutions in which they operate.[31] Consider our practice of protecting the custody rights of parents who provide very poorly for their children's welfare: parents who have addictions, or who suffer in terrible poverty, or who lack important skills and dispositions needed by children. In all but the most serious examples of neglect and abuse, we allow children to remain in the care of their parents. No doubt reasons of child welfare and of preventing state abuse can be marshalled in defence of this practice. But overwhelmingly, we allow parents who provide badly for their children to retain custody because we recognize the importance of this association to the parents. If associational rights are protected despite harms to children because such associations are key to parental-life projects, why should we not take the same view of control rights? Our actual practice suggests that a parent's interest in entering a not-purely fiduciary relationship with children can justify having an impurely fiduciary relationship.[32]

Of course, we might be wrong to leave children in the custody of merely adequate parents.[33] But it seems incredible that our duties toward children are so absolute as to require what in any other circumstance would be an obvious injustice. As Matthew Clayton has argued, most children will become parents themselves someday. Reasonable people (not knowing if they were to be parents or children, or both) would

---

[30] This objection might be thought irrelevant to the case of young children, who must be in the control of one or more people, whether a parent, the government, or someone else. But this observation misses the objection's core point. Even granting that children cannot choose for themselves, we need to know whether the person choosing has the right to make choices that harm children to some extent (as measured by some consensus on child welfare) because having this ability advances the chooser's interest.

[31] Outside of family law, this is true for prisons and institutions for the mentally ill, where rules protect workers from danger posed by the residents. Sometimes these rules are oppressive. But even in well-run institutions, rules balance the interest of the residents and the workers who oversee them. Much the same can be said for most schools.

[32] Another example of a significantly parent-centred rule concerns relocation by custodial parents after divorce. Rules about such relocation vary greatly by jurisdiction. But many jurisdictions embrace the view that courts may not use the threat of changing child custody as a means of deterring relocation, even if it seems obvious that continuing the current custody arrangement and deterring relocation is best for the child (and that the threat would work). Concern about justice for custodial parents seems the obvious reason for this rule. See S Altman, 'Should Child Custody Rules be Fair?' (1996) 35 Journal of Family Law 325.

[33] This seems to be the position adopted by JG Dwyer, 'The Child Protection Pretense: States' Continued Consignment of Newborn Babies to Unfit Parents' (2011) 93 Minnesota Law Review 407.

not resolve conflicts between the interest of parents and children by opting for decisions that benefit children only.[34]

C. Parents' interests in nurturing, counselling, and educating

Parents seek to nurture, educate, and counsel their children, helping them to grow into happy, good, or productive adults. Nurturing, educating, and counselling are good activities—good for the person doing them, not just good for the person made happy and productive or for the society in which they live.

How is an opportunity to nurture, educate, or counsel connected to control rights? To be valuable, these activities demand authenticity, which in turn requires discretion. Merely being present when guidance is given and having that guidance come from a parent does not fulfil the core purpose of parenting. Nurturing and guiding another person requires that the lessons taught (and the methods used to teach them) be authentic: that the teacher offer her own lessons, not lessons chosen for her, that the exemplar choose the life she models, rather than have that model imposed on her. Discretion—and the use of that discretion to choose (within constraints) what is good for the child—is constitutive of the good people seek through parenting, rather than being a mere convenience needed by parents in order effectively to act for the child's benefit or to maintain a desirable relationship.[35]

Parenting without substantial discretion over how and what to teach and counsel is no more parenting than reading someone else's text from a teleprompter is being a journalist, painting by numbers is being an artist, or reading aloud from a state-chosen textbook is being a teacher. Perhaps these things, if done well, have some good effects. But they are not good for those who want to participate meaningfully in important tasks. To participate is to offer something of yourself, not just to be a vehicle through which others act.

Parents' interest in nurturing, educating, and counselling with authenticity differs from an interest in being a fiduciary. A fiduciary's task is faithfully fulfilling a mission as an agent for someone else. Perhaps we can describe foster parents in such terms. Although both caretaking and intimacy matter to foster parents, their role does not bring with it an expectation of directing a child's life according to the foster parents' view of the good. As a result, foster parents have far less discretion to make such decisions. Parents, by contrast, do not regard their task as fulfilling someone else's mission. Rather, their life project is to help create a good or happy person within the context of a loving relationship. The point of shaping another person (to the extent this is possible) is lost if we are compelled to shape that person toward a view of goodness or happiness that we ourselves reject.

---

[34] Clayton (n 6) 56.

[35] My argument focuses on the good of nurturing, teaching, and counselling. These goods I assert cannot be meaningful unless authentic, which cannot happen without discretion. I do not mean to make the separate argument that creativity and authenticity are the goods that justify parental control rights. No doubt these are important components of a good life. But they can be found outside parenting. And almost no one manages to have a life in which all of their activities exhibit creative and authentic expression. So the need for creativity and authenticity in general cannot support parental control rights.

Unlike fiduciaries, parents assert a right sometimes to harm children's interests, conventionally understood, exactly because individual parents have unconventional values and predictive theories. This is not to say that parents can cause children serious harm, that they can systematically violate the rights of children, or that parents may go entirely unmonitored. Absolute dominion and immunity from monitoring simply do not follow from parental need for authenticity and discretion. The rights of children and of society constrain parental control rights. But insofar as non-derivative parental rights exist, these other interests will not always take priority.

Authenticity in nurturing, counselling, and educating differs from an image often associated with parental rights: parental prerogatives to replicate themselves.[36] On this caricatured view, parental control rights serve to manufacture 'mini-mes' (or to manufacture the people parents wish they might have become—'mini-couldabeens'). No doubt all parents fall prey to this temptation on occasion; some parents do so to a fault. But focusing on how rights might be invoked by the most vain and self-obsessed parents diverts attention from a more common and important understanding. Parents who want their children to be happy or good, or productive have diverse views on what will lead to those outcomes and on what those outcomes really mean. The desire for self-replication based on vanity, or for self-correction based on regret, are not the interests that warrant parental control rights.[37]

The position I have outlined resembles in some ways William Galston's theory of expressive liberty. Galston explains that people must be free from constraints that make it difficult for them:

> to live their lives in ways that express their deepest beliefs about what gives meaning and value to life. Expressive liberty offers us the opportunity to enjoy a fit between inner and outer, conviction and deed.
> ... Part of what it means to have deep beliefs about how one should live is the desire to live in accordance with them....
> [T]he ability of parents to raise their children in a manner consistent with their deepest commitments is an essential element of expressive liberty. ... [P]arenting is typically undertaken as one of the central meaning-giving tasks of our lives. ... [L]oving and nurturing a child cannot in practice be divorced from shaping that child's values. In so doing, we cannot but draw on the comprehensive understanding that gives our values whatever coherence and grounding they may possess.[38]

Galston's emphasis on authenticity—the need for parental choices to be embraced by the parent in order for parenting to be a meaning-giving activity—seems to me right. One can quibble about using the word 'expressive' to describe the importance of authenticity.[39] But the core concept captures part of the good in parenting.

---

[36] Brighouse and Swift accuse C Macleod and E Page of justifying parental rights based on self-replication, which Brighouse and Swift call selfish and narcissistic. Brighouse and Swift (n 15) 103.

[37] I am not arguing that we ought actually to police parental motives for wanting to control their children. Rather, I am explaining why the desire to shape a child's identity deserves to be treated as a potentially worthy life goal, rather than as a sign of self-obsession.

[38] Galston (n 12) 101–02.

[39] All our important choices in life might be understood as expressive. Our choices reveal (to others and to ourselves) what we most value. But this revelation (the expressive aspect) need not exhaust—indeed need

Galston errs, in my view, by limiting his theory to deep commitments and comprehensive understandings. His position makes some sense in the context of a book about liberal pluralism and education, where conflicting comprehensive views on morality loom large. But from the perspective of parental control rights, the theory provides too narrow a justification. Most parenting decisions rely on simple judgments, which need not be connected to deep commitments. For example, I allow my children to ride horses, but not to play football or ride motorcycles, because I regard the former but not the latter as involving benefits that justify the risks. Nothing in this specific assessment relies on deep commitments or comprehensive understandings. But it is typical of actual parental decisions. On Galston's account, these do not seem to qualify as protected parental choices.

A better account recognizes that authenticity matters to parents in ways analogous to any creative endeavour. It requires very broad discretion in the shaping of outcomes. Small choices matter, even if not connected to deeply held beliefs, because broad control is the essence of authenticity.

My core claim—that the good protected by parental control rights is the ability to counsel, educate, and nurture with authenticity—depends centrally on a factual claim: that most parents regard their roles as meaningful centrally because they can engage in these tasks authentically. I believe this to be descriptively true for most parents in western society. I do not mean to deny the cultural dependency of this claim. Nor do I particularly mean to assert the normative desirability of having children reared by parents who find meaning in their roles largely in this way. Perhaps other ways of rearing children would be better for everyone. I mean only to assert that in our society, parents have a strong interest in control of the sort that can ground a right. The fact that this might not be true in a very different society (or in the best possible society) does not preclude it from underlying control rights in ours.

V. Is the Interest in Nurturing, Counselling, and Educating Sufficient to Justify Parental Control Rights?

Even if nurturing, counselling, and educating are important human goods pursued through parenting, they might not justify robust parental rights. Consider four reasons for doubting the connection: (a) people can satisfy their desire to nurture, counsel, and educate as teachers, ministers, camp counsellors, coaches, or scout leaders. Since parenting is not the only site for pursuing these goods, parents need not be given special privileges; (b) parental rights attach to specific children—biological children, adopted children, or perhaps children cohabiting with the parent. Why should the interest in nurturing, counselling, and educating attach to these specific children?; (c) nurturing, counselling, and educating can be done without exercising control; and (d), authenticity cannot justify strong parental rights because authenticity is not actually threatened by most intrusions on parental authority.

---

not be important to—the goals of parenting. I can value helping others, shaping them to be happy and productive by making thoughtful choices about their lives, without locating the primary value of these acts in what they reveal about me.

The first concern—that parenting is not sufficiently special to warrant a right since the goods of parenting can be pursued by non-parents—is mistaken for reasons of both form and substance. The form of this argument need not be accepted. That there are alternative avenues for pursuing a good does not show that we lack reason to protect one such avenue. Identifying parenting as one site where an important interest is well-pursued should be enough to warrant protecting parental rights, all else equal.

Substantively, parenting differs from being a teacher, camp counsellor, or childcare provider in important ways. The role is occupied as to a specific child for much longer. It thus offers an opportunity for the long-term project of nurturing from start to end, so to speak. Insofar as this is part of the project parents undertake, it is not actually one that can be pursued in many other places.

Second, why does the interest parents have in nurturing, educating, and counselling attach to specific children? Several answers might be given. Insofar as the project of parental nurturing, counselling, and educating derives its meaning centrally from shaping a child over a long period, it must take place within an ongoing structure such as the family. As well, parental rights to control exist within a broader context of parental rights and duties. These include a right of association and a duty of support. These other rights and duties (I have argued elsewhere) derive from interests unrelated to the interest in nurturing, counselling, and educating.[40] But they warrant an ongoing connection between parents and specific children. Insofar as that connection is justified, the parental interest in nurturing, counselling, and educating becomes appropriately focused on the children to whom parents are already connected by a right of association and a duty of support.[41]

The third concern—that educating and nurturing do not necessitate control—requires that we distinguish among several aspects of control rights. As I noted at the start, the control required by parental rights consist largely of two elements: that parents be permitted to set rules for their children; and that non-parents generally refrain from subverting parental efforts to guide and shape their children.

Why should the good of nurturing, counselling, and educating demand either of these elements? The first element, rule-enforcement, does not seem central to counselling or nurturing. Ministers and counsellors pursue these same goods without enforcing rules. Perhaps parents of young children must set rules to keep their children safe. But for children beyond a certain age, parents could pursue the goods of nurturing, counselling, and educating without control rights. Parents can model good behaviour and talk with their children about values—the same tools used by ministers and counsellors who lack power to make and enforce rules.

---

[40] S Altman, 'A Theory of Child Support' (2003) 17 International Journal of Law, Policy & the Family 173; S Altman, 'The Pursuit of Intimacy and Parental Rights' in A Marmor (ed), *The Routledge Companion to Philosophy of Law* (Routledge 2011).

[41] An additional answer to this concern might be found in parental duty. Many parents believe themselves not only entitled to direct their children's upbringing, but also obligated to do so. I have elsewhere argued that parents' associational rights derive in part from parents' duty (as they see it) to care for their own children. Perhaps the duty to nurture and educate children so that they pursue the good as a parent understands that good differentiates parental interests in nurturing and educating from parallel non-parental interests and explains the exclusive nature of parental rights.

This objection overstates the consensus on children and rules. For some parents, the idea of teaching by example and discussion only (rather than by enforcing rules) seems sensible once children become teenagers. But not all parents share this view of appropriate childrearing. If we are to take seriously the idea that parents have an interest in teaching their children about the good as parents see it, which includes giving effect both the parents' view of good outcomes and the parents' view of good means to reach those outcomes, we must accept varied views on when control, rather than discussion, is the best means of nurturing, counselling, and educating.

The second element of control rights—an entitlement that others not subvert a parent's preferences about a child's activities—may seem harder to justify. Non-parents often have an interest in nurturing, counselling, and educating; why should parental rights systematically take priority over the rights of non-parents in directing the upbringing of children? For example, if a school teacher pursues a career wanting to share the values of critical thinking, tolerance, and equality, why should we permit parents to shelter their children from such lessons?

Several distinctions warrant exclusionary rights for parents but not for teachers. Parenting is a project tied to specific children (rather than to whatever children happen to end up in the care of a given teacher or counsellor). And the parental role is occupied as to a specific child for much longer.

Parenting involves a distinctively creative kind of counselling, nurturing, and educating. By creative I do not mean (only) that these tasks require innovative ideas. I mean also that parents want a central role in creating good and happy people. This aspect of creation is rewarding in part because it requires an ongoing effort over many years to help the child become good and happy, as the parent understands these goals. Allowing others to contribute to the project in ways that subvert the parent's efforts undermines this key element of parenting.

The final concern is that I am guilty of the same offence that I accused Shoeman and Brighouse and Swift of committing: announcing an interest that is only threatened by imaginary and oppressive regulation. Authenticity can thrive within constraints just as intimacy can. Totalitarian-parenting regulation would deprive parenting of its core attraction. But that does not mean that any particular intrusion threatens to make parenting pointless.

Certainly, parents can meaningfully nurture, educate, and counsel in the face of unwanted regulatory control. Indeed, the constraints of children's and society's rights require that they must. If I believe that risk-taking is a core value to be encouraged, but the state requires that all children wear helmets for cycling and skateboarding, I am deprived of one means by which I can educate my children in the thrills and virtues of risk. But I can still talk with my children about why I think these laws are immoral, can live a risky life myself to model these virtues, and can engage with my children as teacher, counsellor, and nurturer on all of the less-regulated aspects of our lives. In this regard, nurturing, educating, and counselling with authenticity really are just like intimacy. They require a scope of freedom from regulation, but not an unlimited scope.

Despite these similarities, authenticity in nurturing, counselling, and education differs from intimacy in the scope of control needed to realize the good. Intimacy, and the shared enthusiasm it requires, seems very robust; it can flourish in the face of substantial regulation. Authorship of goals and means—the defining aspect of authenticity—requires significantly more discretion and therefore provides a basis for a more robust parental control right.

I do not mean that all regulation destroys the good of parenting. But significant regulation harms the good of authenticity (even for those whose choices happen to correspond to the regulation's mandate). Whether the harms are trivial will depend on the case—both on how important the choice would have been to the parent as part of nurturing, educating, and counselling, and on whether regulation in the aggregate diminishes discretion to such a point that parents have little room for authentic participating in these goods.

I also do not mean to overstate the harm most people suffer from regulation. Control over many aspects of children's lives seems unimportant. Most parents delegate important aspects of nurturing, educating, and counselling, only sometimes with significant oversight. Nonetheless, most parents value making key choices about moral lessons, practical life skills, and exposing their children selectively.

VI. Conclusion

Parenting involves many basic human goods. Among them are surely a distinctive form of intimacy and working for the good of another person. Although both intimacy and fiduciarity play key roles in parenting, they do not offer the strongest justification for parental control rights. Intimacy does not much depend on control. And fiduciarity turns out to be too self-effacing for the core meaning most parents attach to their roles.

Instead, I have suggested, parental rights depend on the importance of authenticity in key childrearing tasks, such as nurturing, counselling, and educating. This conclusion does not settle most practical disputes over parental rights. But I believe it helps us to think more sensibly about those challenging problems.

11
An Argument for Treating Children as a 'Special Case'

Lucinda Ferguson[1]

Introduction

This chapter's argument stems from the premise that legal language should speak for itself. The 'paramountcy' principle[2] suggests the prioritization of children's interests, and 'children's rights' suggests some aspect of distinctiveness to children's interests. But there is academic consensus in respect of both that children's interests cannot and should not be prioritized over those of others, though they might be 'privileged'[3] in the factual balancing exercise.[4] This chapter examines the justification for the contrary perspective, and for treating children as a prioritized 'special case' in all legal decisions affecting them. Given the current legal language, anyone taking the consensus view needs to justify why the words of prioritization cannot speak for themselves in relation to children.

Four key counter-arguments frame the discussion. First, the 'social construct' objection: as a social construct, childhood cannot sustain the prioritization of children's interests over those of others. Second, the 'vulnerability' objection: children's vulnerability is either not unique or suggests dependency or interdependency, not prioritization. Third, the 'family autonomy' objection: parents' rights and the family unit justify deference of children's interests. Fourth, the 'equality' objection: equal moral consideration makes prioritization unjustifiable.

I. Prioritization and 'Special Case' Defined

To see children as a 'special case' means to prioritize their interests over those of other parties as recognition of children's unique position in society. Elsewhere, I explain that

> [t]his prioritisation can take two forms, namely providing children with additional legal protection over that available to others and, when there is a conflict between

---

[1] Associate Professor of Family Law, University of Oxford; Tutorial Fellow in Law, Oriel College, Oxford. I am grateful to Elizabeth Brake, Stephen Gilmore, and Helen Reece for their comments on the ideas presented in this chapter. Errors, of course, remain my own.
[2] Children Act 1989, s 1(1).
[3] See, eg, J Eekelaar, 'Beyond the Welfare Principle' (2002) 14 Child and Family Law Quarterly 237, 244, 249; S Choudhry and H Fenwick, 'Taking the Rights of Parents and Children Seriously: Confronting the Welfare Principle Under the Human Rights Act' (2005) 25 OJLS 453, 471, 479, 483.
[4] ibid as discussed below in Section II.

children's interests and other parties' interests, prioritising children's interests in the resolution of the dispute.[5]

For non-lawyers, a brief explanation of legal reasoning helps demonstrate this distinctive use of the term 'prioritization'. In reasoning to resolve a particular case, matters of law determine the applicable legal rule(s) or principle(s) that govern, but any rule(s) or principle(s) can only decide the outcome in a particular case through subsequent application to the facts. Thus a legal presumption might be rebutted on the facts. Considerations that relate to the legal phase are of a different, normative nature to those that relate to the factual analysis.

In this chapter, I use the term 'prioritization' to demarcate an approach that favours children's interests at the *outset* of any decision-making exercise, in other words that prefers children's interests as a matter of *law*. This is to be contrasted with all alternative approaches to children's interests, which include both treating their interests just the same as the interests of any others and approaching them the same as a matter of law whilst *privileging* them—placing more weight on them—in the *factual* balancing exercise of competing considerations. In this way, the argument for children as a 'special case' is an argument for recognizing that children's interests have a distinctive *nature*, not just that the *extent* of weight to be attached is greater.

Prioritization is a critical issue because the idea of 'children's rights', properly understood in contrast to 'rights for children', requires us to see children as a 'special case'.[6] Within a welfare-based perspective, the *language* of 'paramountcy' suggests such prioritization, whilst the *language* of 'primacy' does not. As I discuss below, however, the language employed in legislation or judicially is only an indicator of the approach possibly adopted, making the language used simultaneously critical and irrelevant. It is for this reason that my argument cuts across both the larger labels of 'children's rights', 'rights for children', 'welfare', 'duty', as well as the language descriptors selected within categories, such as 'paramountcy' and 'primacy'. My fundamental concern is how children's interests have been conceptualized regardless of the specific framework under discussion, and how this impacts on reasoning about—and outcomes for—particular children affected by legal decision-making.

What if the same outcome might be reached in individual cases regardless whether the child's interests are either prioritized as a matter of law or privileged in the factual balancing of competing interests? Why then might it remain essential to determine whether we can justify treating children as a 'special case'? I suggest that the answer lies in the reality that it is only through 'special case' prioritization that we can ensure that children's interests are not susceptible to being unjustifiably overridden in the outcome reached.

---

[5] L Ferguson, 'The Jurisprudence of Making Decisions Affecting Children: An Argument to Prefer Duty to Children's Rights and Welfare' in A Diduck, N Peleg, and H Reece (eds), *Law in Society: Reflections on Children, Family, Culture and Philosophy – Essays in Honour of Michael Freeman* (Brill 2015) 143.
[6] ibid.

II. Legal and Academic Intuitions

A. Children as a 'special case' in the governing law

Whilst we cannot assume that the way that the language is being used necessarily aligns with the conceptual approach taken by a particular court, one might wonder if courts' choice of legal labels suggests any intuition about whether children should be seen as a 'special case'. The same question might be asked of the governing legislation and international conventions.

Can we justify the assumption within the Section 1 of the Children Act 1989 'welfare' principle that children are a 'special case'? Whilst it is not always clear that the judicial application thereof does likewise,[7] the general understanding of the 'paramountcy' principle is clear. This may be further complicated by context-specific judicial interpretation of the 'paramountcy' principle. How it is understood judicially in the context of medical treatment decision-making, for example, may be quite distinct to the meaning ascribed in relation to relocation disputes or in relation to immigration.

How should we understand the requirement in Section 25(1) of the Matrimonial Causes Act 1973[8] that—when deciding whether to make any financial orders in the context of divorce or separation and, if so, which orders to make—'first consideration' is to be given to the welfare of any minor child of the family? In the Court of Appeal decision in *Suter v Suter and Jones*,[9] Lord Justice Cumming-Bruce reasoned that 'first consideration' did not mean the 'paramount' consideration, but that it was an 'important consideration' to be borne in mind throughout the consideration of all the circumstances, including those specified in Section 25(2)[10]. Cumming-Bruce LJ further commented that the court was also to 'try to attain a financial result which is just as between husband and wife'.[11]

This judicial understanding of Section 25(1) rests on an uncertain view of the status of children's interests. Children's interests need not be the only consideration in order to treat children as a prioritized 'special case', and prioritization does not of itself signal the irrelevance of adults' interests even as regards the content of children's interests. But what is the nature of the balancing envisaged by Cumming-Bruce LJ's encapsulation of the Section 25A 'clean-break' principle? As a procedural concern, one might argue that it cannot be directly weighed against the substantive concerns that inform the Section 25 exercise. Equally, however, the Section 25(1) 'first consideration' cannot override the Section 25A duty, hence it cannot underpin an outcome that is not also 'just and reasonable' to the spouses. This arguably suggests a certain judicial ambivalence about the nature of children's interests as 'first consideration'.

Beyond the domestic position, what of the perspective adopted by the ECtHR on whether children are a 'special case' in relation to conflicts between ECHR rights? Here, I consider conflicts between children's and parents' rights and interests. The ECtHR

---

[7] See, eg, *Re T (A Minor) (Wardship: Medical Treatment)* [1997] 1 All ER 906 (EWCA); *Re M (Child's Upbringing)* [1996] EWCA Civ 1320.
[8] c. 18.   [9] [1987] Fam 111 (EWCA).   [10] ibid 124G (Cumming-Bruce LJ).
[11] ibid 124H (Cumming-Bruce LJ).

adopts a 'fair balancing' formulation in *Johansen v Norway*, which acknowledges that '[i]n carrying out this balancing exercise, the Court will attach particular importance to the best interests of the child, which, depending on their nature and seriousness, may override those of the parent'.[12] By contrast, in *Yousef v The Netherlands*, the Court reasons that 'the child's rights must be the paramount consideration' in such conflicts, such that '[i]f any balancing of interests is necessary, the interests of the child must prevail'.[13] The *Yousef* formulation sees children as a 'special case', yet the *Johansen* formulation has been preferred academically.[14] The expression of preference highlights that language is seen to matter. Yet, the inconsistency in the language adopted by the ECtHR suggests the relative unimportance of language in practice, a view further reinforced by the wide range of language descriptors employed by the ECtHR, such as children's interests being 'of crucial importance'.[15]

To what extent should we see the United Nations' Convention on the Rights of the Child[16] as treating children as a 'special case'? Archard argues that

> [t]here is a straightforward reason to prefer a statement of the welfare principle that is specified in terms of primacy not paramountcy. This is that it is implausible to think that in every case, in which we must determine what is done for or to a child, the child's interests outweigh those of all others.[17]

Contrast General Comment No 14, in which the United Nations' Committee on the Rights of the Child explains its approach to the 'primary consideration' aspect of Art 3(1) as follows:

> The expression 'primary consideration' means that the child's best interests may not be considered on the same level as all other considerations. This strong position is justified by the special situation of the child: dependency, maturity, legal status and, often, voicelessness. Children have less possibility than adults to make a strong case for their own interests and those involved in decisions affecting them must be explicitly aware of their interests. If the interests of children are not highlighted, they tend to be overlooked.[18]

In suggesting that children's interests 'may not be considered on the same level as all other considerations', this seems to treat children as a 'special case'. Yet, the conclusion to that paragraph immediately casts doubt on such a reading: the Committee is concerned to ensure that children's interests are not overlooked, rather than that they are

---

[12] *Johansen v Norway* (1997) 23 EHRR 33 [78].
[13] *Yousef v The Netherlands* (2003) 36 EHRR 20 [73].
[14] See, eg, S Choudhry and H Fenwick, 'Taking the Rights of Parents and Children Seriously: Confronting the Welfare Principle under the Human Rights Act' (2005) 25 OJLS 453.
[15] See, eg, *Elsholz v Germany* (2002) 34 EHRR 58 [48]. Further highlighting the apparent lack of significance to language, the Court in *Süss v Germany* [2006] 1 FLR 522 (ECtHR) both recites the *Johansen* 'particular importance' formulation ([88]) and describes the child's best interests as of 'crucial importance' ([86]). For more language descriptors adopted by the ECtHR, see L Ferguson and E Brake's chapters, notes 197–201, and corresponding main text.
[16] 20 November 1989, 1577 UNTS 3 [CRC].
[17] D Archard, 'Children, adults, best interests and rights' (2013) 13 Medical Law International 55, 60.
[18] United Nations' Committee on the Rights of the Child, *General Comment No 14 (2013) on the right of the child to have his or her best interests taken as a primary consideration* (29 May 2013) art 3, para 1 [37].

prioritized. We might compare the Committee's choice of language and aims to that of leading academics, discussed below. Dixon and Nussbaum reason that the Convention gives 'special priority' to children's welfare or socio-economic rights[19] but, as will be discussed below, it is not clear that that translates to treating children as a 'special case'. This analysis highlights the contrast between the clarity in legal language and the uncertain and varying relationship between the language itself and conceptual understanding it may be thought to invoke.

B. The academic consensus against prioritization

There has been a marked shift in attitude in the English academic literature in relation to the private law treatment of children. Formerly, the consensus for prioritizing children's interests was generally unquestioned, with little concern felt to additionally justify the approach.[20] That says nothing, of course, about how those interests were interpreted and applied in practice. Reece thus comments that 'while everybody agrees that children's welfare should be paramount, nobody knows what children's welfare demands'.[21] This approach has transformed to the current questioning and challenging of the nature and extent of the preference for children's interests. Thus, Gilmore and Bainham argue that '[i]t is certainly open to question whether children's interests should always be given priority'.[22]

This shift should be read in the context of a widespread *belief* that, prior to the current approach—regardless whether one sees the current law as requiring prioritization—children were treated as the property of their parents.[23] This common belief is particularly important in relation to the 'welfare' or 'paramountcy' principle in the Children Act 1989, given that the language of 'paramountcy' preceded the Act.[24] Reece disagrees with the accuracy of this characterization of the earlier approach: she argues that parental rights did not see children as property and suggests that it was 'crystal clear that ... the law treated parental rights as existing for the benefit of the child, not the

---

[19] R Dixon and M Nussbaum, 'Children's Rights and a Capabilities Approach: The Question of Special Priority' (2012) 97 Cornell Law Review 549, 553.

[20] H Reece, 'The Paramountcy Principle: Consensus or Construct?' (1996) 49 Current Legal Problems 267, 270 (noting the lack of justification provided, rather than arguing it was unnecessary).

[21] ibid 271.

[22] S Gilmore and A Bainham, *Children: The Modern Law* (4th rev edn, Jordan Publishing 2013) 326.

[23] See, eg, BB Woodhouse, '"Who Owns the Child?" *Meyer and Pierce* and the Child as Property' (1992) 33 William and Mary Law Review 995; T Gal and BF Duramy, 'Enhancing Capacities for Child Participation: Introduction' in T Gal and BF Duramy (eds), *International Perspectives and Empirical Findings on Child Participation: From Social Exclusion to Child-Inclusive Policies* (OUP 2015) 1. In the English context, Hale, who was involved in the law-reform process behind the 1989 Act (cf M Maclean with Jacek Kurzczewski, *Making Family Law: A Socio Legal Account of Legislative Process in England and Wales, 1985 to 2010* (Hart Publishing 2011) 26 explains that legislation was aimed at 'get[ting] rid of the property lawyers' approach to parenthood as ... in the Children Act 1975', 'at the top [of which] were "parental rights and duties"'. See Baroness Hale, 'Family Responsibility: Where Are We Now?' in C Lind, H Keating, and J Bridgeman (eds), *Taking Responsibility, Law and the Changing Family* (Ashgate 2011) 25, 26.

[24] See Guardianship of Infants Act 1925, s 1; Guardianship of Minors Act 1971, s 1, which describe the welfare of the child as the court's 'first and paramount' consideration.

parent'; the 1989 Act reforms were, she proposes, aimed at further emphasizing this approach.[25]

But, to the extent that this belief in the devaluation of children was widespread, one might wonder if the legal language of prioritization was embraced as a means of *equalization*, rather than genuinely signalling that children were a 'special case'. This might be said to be reflected in Archard's comment that

> Under whatever label it might be captured, some version of the best interests or welfare principle is essential if we are as decision-makers to give some consideration to the child as a distinct human being with her own needs, character, feelings, desires and future. Otherwise, we are in danger, as law was once, of ignoring the child, seeing it as having no distinct or special claim upon us, or as recognising only the powers of the child's guardians.[26]

Archard thus appears to see 'best interests' as a means of avoiding the devaluation of children, rather than as a means of prioritizing their interests. If the intention was to equalize children's treatment from a perceived 'children-as-property' approach, perhaps this explains why, even though the language of 'special case' has remained unchanged, the questioning as to whether it really means 'special case' has taken hold.

By contrast, in the American academic literature, the current general view is that of 'children's subjugation'.[27] Dwyer argues that, historically, children have been seen as inferior in social and moral status.[28] In terms of children's current treatment, Appell contends that, rather than children being prioritized for their vulnerability, they are 'distrust[ed]'.[29] Dwyer suggests that the 'best interests' principle governs rarely and that, when it does, it frequently masks the predominance of adult interests.[30] We might relate children's ongoing place as 'the objects of adult authority'[31] to the constitutional status of the parental rights doctrine in American law.[32] In the context of subjugation, equal treatment is as much of a leap forward as prioritization is in the context of equal treatment.[33]

The broader American perspective also colours the interpretation of the CRC. Appell, for example, contends that the Convention 'fails to challenge, or even problematize, the structural subversion of and the privatization of childhood'.[34] In support, Appell references Rehfeld's comment that 'the CRC prioritizes the welfare of children'.[35]

---

[25] H Reece, 'The Degradation of Parental Responsibility' in R Probert, S Gilmore, J Herring (eds), *Responsible Parents and Parental Responsibility* (Hart Publishing 2009) 85, 87.

[26] Archard, 'Children, Adults, Best Interests and Rights' (n 17) 59.

[27] AR Appell, 'Accommodating Childhood' (2013) 19 Cardozo Journal of Law & Gender 715, 717, 730. Appell sees this as a product of the 'development thesis', which 'holds that children are unwise, weak, unreasonable, and wild' 721.

[28] JG Dwyer, *Moral Status and Human Life: The Case for Children's Superiority* (CUP 2011) 1.

[29] Appell (n 27).   [30] Dwyer (n 28) 191.

[31] LA Rosenbury, 'A Feminist Perspective on Children and Law: From Objectification to Relational Subjectivities' in T Gal and BF Duramy (eds), *International Perspectives and Empirical Findings on Child Participation: From Social Exclusion to Child-Inclusive Policies* (OUP 2015) 17, 20.

[32] See, eg, *Troxel v Granville*, 530 US 57 (2000). This constitutional perspective arguably contributes much to the notion of 'parental control rights', with which Altman's contribution to this volume is concerned.

[33] Exceptionally, and as discussed in Section VI, Dwyer argues for the unequal consideration of children's interests.

[34] Appell (n 27) 717.   [35] ibid note 4.

Given the CRC's status as a Convention on rights, this is problematic if, as I have argued elsewhere, it is theoretically sound to reason in terms of children's welfare but not children's rights.[36] Once we acknowledge that difficulty, as well as that labels are less important than the conceptualization of children's interests within those labels, it is not at all clear that prioritizing welfare necessarily devalues children's status in the way Appell assumes.

Consideration of this American academic response to the CRC suggests a further possible explanation for the lack of fit between the current legal language, and the interpretation of that language together with outcomes for children. Rather than being due to a strategic aim, the language employed in contexts such as the English 'paramountcy' principle may simply reflect a desire to value children whilst not carefully considering what that language requires for practice. Such a conclusion also accords with the relative lack of attention to children in moral and political philosophy.[37] In respect of Rawls, for example, Brennan notes that '[i]n the course of a very thick book, [*A Theory of Justice*], children are only found in a few places and the subject of justice-based obligations to them is not addressed at all'.[38]

C. The academic convergence on equal treatment

Recent English academic proposals for law reform generally do not treat children as a 'special case' in the way that I suggest is envisaged by the English 'welfare' principle and the idea of 'children's rights'. In terms of recognizing children's rights, Freeman contends that they are 'no more or less important than rights generally'.[39] To the non-specialist, this might be baffling. Should the distinctive language not itself indicate the intention of a distinctive approach? Why argue for distinctive language to ground a claim for equal treatment? And yet, the academic consensus is that the language of prioritization should be interpreted otherwise.

Eekelaar argues for a 'least detrimental alternative' approach to the process of decision-making in contexts currently governed by the welfare principle. But his model for balancing the competing interests of children and other parties is a qualified one. An outcome can be adopted that is not the least detrimental alternative for the child if it is much less damaging for the affected parent or parents than the alternative, which would have enhanced the child's interests to a larger extent at great expense to the parent or parents.[40]

In developing his qualifications to this approach, Eekelaar distinguishes between children's interests being 'privileged' and children's interests being 'given priority'.[41] The child's position is privileged to the extent that no solution that actively diminishes

---

[36] Ferguson, 'The Jurisprudence of Making Decisions Affecting Children' (n 5); L Ferguson, 'Not Merely Rights for Children but Children's Rights: The Theory Gap and the Assumption of the Importance of Children's Rights' (2013) 21 International Journal of Children's Rights 177.

[37] S Brennan, 'The Goods of Childhood and Children's Rights' in F Baylis and C McLeod (eds), *Family-Making: Contemporary Ethical Challenges* (OUP 2014) 29, 30.

[38] ibid 31.

[39] M Freeman, 'Why It Remains Important to Take Children's Rights Seriously' (2007) 15 International Journal of Children's Rights 5, 7.

[40] Eekelaar, 'Beyond the Welfare Principle' (n 3) 244.   [41] ibid.

the child's interests can be chosen unless all options would do so.[42] Eekelaar sees his approach as entailing the privileging of children's interests only, and not their prioritization, because of the weighing process.

But I would suggest that even the privileging in the weighing of competing interests is hard to justify if we do not see children as a 'special case'. As outlined, the envisaged weighing is permitted in only two scenarios: first, where the impact on the child's interests for various alternatives are all differing degrees of benefit; second, where all of the alternative outcomes would negatively impact on the child. In a scenario in which one or more outcome is positive for the child's interests, the decision-maker cannot select an outcome that has negative consequences for the child. In this way, I would argue that it is not the particular facts of the case that lead to more weight being placed on the child's interests in the outcome, but rather a principle of privileging, which protects children from situations of active detriment where feasible. In other words, 'privileging' seems to be a matter of law for Eekelaar. As a result of the incorporation of this principle into Eekelaar's model, his distinction between 'privileging' and 'prioritizing' is arguably better seen as one of the extent to which children are a 'special case', rather than one that determines whether they are a 'special case' at all. The difference in extent is that 'privileging' permits some weighing, whereas 'prioritization' does not.

Even if my analysis of the implications of Eekelaar's account is correct, however, it does not accord with his intention. Like Freeman, Eekelaar reasons that children's rights

> should be seen as a species of people's rights .... In themselves, these rights are no different from adults' rights. Due allowance being made for issues of competence and children's special vulnerability, they should be respected just like adults' rights should be; certainly no less, but also no more.[43]

In this way, he also sees the language of prioritization—of 'children's rights'—as a means of achieving equal and *only equal* treatment with adult interests.

Choudhry and Fenwick argue for a 'parallel-analysis' approach[44] that starts by seeing children's and adults' interests 'on a presumptively equal footing'.[45] Making use of Eekelaar's language, they suggest that children's interests would be 'privileged within the processes of reasoning'[46] and that the court would ask whether an 'especially "core" aspect of a child's [Article 8 ECHR] private or family life' is at stake.[47] Yet, when they describe the process of reasoning the 'ultimate balancing act',[48] they do not suggest any 'privileging' along the lines of the two exceptions envisaged by Eekelaar. For this reason, I would suggest that they understand the language of 'privileging' to refer simply to weighing more heavily in the factual balancing exercise, rather than as a matter of law. Their supporting reference to Eekelaar might thus be a misdirection, which highlights the importance of interrogating the language descriptors individual academic arguments employ. That said, their mention of the need to have regard to affected 'core' aspects of children's rights does also hint in the direction of prioritization. Overall, Choudhry and Fenwick may best be described as embracing the notion of equal treatment of children's and others' interests.

---

[42] ibid. [43] ibid 249. [44] Choudhry and Fenwick (n 3) 481.
[45] ibid, 471, 479, 483–84. [46] ibid 485. [47] ibid. [48] ibid 484.

The domestic English-reform argument in favour of securing no more than equal treatment for children's interests is in line with American reform arguments to improve to achieve equal treatment for children's interests. As a result, one might conclude that the normative debates in both jurisdictions have converged on equality. Yet Appell's rejection of an 'equal rights approach'[49] highlights the need to be precise when discussing equality. The account she rejects is one that would remain based on negative rights only,[50] yet her 'accommodation model'[51] for reform does not itself appear to argue for greater respect for children's interests than those of others. Moreover, Fineman sounds a note of caution in relation to any convergence on equality; she argues that 'equality of treatment has provided [.] the passive toleration of inequality and complicity in the conferral of often unwarranted privilege on the few'.[52]

Taking Appell's and Fineman's analyses together demonstrates the need to be precise when discussing equality, especially because, as discussed below, it may be possible to have equal concern or moral consideration for children without equal treatment. As this distinction does not inform the legal literature, this also suggests the need for caution when considering legal academic arguments about equality. In any event, the broader convergence on equal treatment highlights that any case for genuine prioritization of children's interests such as presented in this chapter needs weighty arguments to underpin it.

III. The 'Social Construct' Objection

A. The meaning-making of the social construction of childhood

Given the academic convergence on the idea of treating children's and adults' interests with equal regard, on what basis can we justify the argument that children should instead be treated as a 'special case' and their interests prioritized? I frame the discussion through counter-arguments as it is in the rejection of objections that the argument for prioritization can take shape. The first relates to childhood, and the view that, if childhood is a social construct, it is incapable of comprising a justifiable class of individuals whose interests ought to be prioritized over those of others. In responding to this concern, I develop an account of the concept of childhood centred around children's unique vulnerability, which justifies treating children as a 'special case' in law.

This first concern recognizes that, if the distinction between childhood and adulthood is artificial, it cannot support a theoretically sound argument for prioritizing children. Whilst the existence and embrace of an artificial—socially constructed—distinction highlights a societal choice to value the content of that construct, it does not of itself give a reason to value that content.

---

[49] Appell (n 27) 753.   [50] ibid.
[51] An 'accommodation model' seeks to enhance children's participation at an earlier stage and in a more meaningful way than a model based on formal equality would do: Appell (n 27) 754–78. Yet, equal respect for children's interests could underpin the demand for accommodation. The critical issue is how we interpret equality and understand its requirements for implementation in the legal regulation of children's lives.
[52] MA Fineman, 'Equality and Difference – The Restrained State' (2014) 66 Alabama Law Review 609, 613.

B. The concept of childhood, its social construction, and normative basis

A two-fold response is required. Firstly, it is necessary to distinguish between the definition of childhood, namely its construction, and the underlying concept. Secondly, it is critical to determine the normative basis of the concept of childhood and whether it is justifiable. Whilst it falls outside the scope of this chapter, we would need to add a third step if we wanted to determine the extent to which the current law, the current legal construction of childhood, is justified. This would entail an examination of the nature of the relationship between any established justifiable basis for the concept and the current social construction thereof.

It is vital to distinguish between the conceptual core and the social construction thereof before assessing the claim that it is justifiable to treat children as a 'special case'. At the core, childhood as a concept may justify treating children as a 'special case' even if the definitional representation of childhood for legal purposes is constructed. Age is a critical example of the definitional construction, and there are both general definitions of childhood based on age and specific age-based rules for particular contexts. I argue that the social construction does not and cannot play an independent normative role because it neither relates to, nor seeks to engage directly, with the content of (the concept of) childhood. Whilst the socially constructed aspect of childhood does not perform a normative function, it may—as a proxy for conceptual aspects—reflect one.

Where the social construction straightforwardly reflects the concept's normative core, it is not itself making a normative claim, but simply seeking to reflect the natural limits of the concept, whatever its content. In this way, if the concept's normative basis is justifiable, the social construction is justifiable, but only parasitically, not independently. But the social construction can be arbitrary, either because the intended proxy is not or is no longer accurate, or because the definitional boundary has been drawn for explicitly non-normative reasons that do not seek to connect the construct to the concept.

If the proxy is not or is no longer accurate, such as a legislative rule intended to encapsulate decision-making capacity, the full extent of the construction is not justifiable. That lack of justification, however, does not of itself undermine the normative value of the conceptual core; it might suggest, of course, that reform to the definition is required in order for it to more faithfully serve as a proxy for the underlying concept. By way of contrast, administrative efficiency provides a good example of a non-normative concern[53] that may determine the construct, such as in relation to the voting or driving age. Its use may be justifiable, even if non-normative, because it can be grounded in fundamental concerns about the operation of law as a social construct more generally. Thus any proxy for the requisite capabilities can be rigidly applied regardless of individual differences. It seeks to uphold both the value of consistency and respect for individuals' status.

---

[53] As I have discussed elsewhere in relation to children's refusal of critical medical treatment. See L Ferguson, *The End of an Age: Beyond Age-Based Legal Regulation of Minors' Entitlement to Participate in and Make Health Care Treatment Decisions* (Law Commission of Canada 2005) Part 5: III.

Distinguishing between the social construction and the concept of childhood is not unusual. Where the argument in this chapter differs, however, is in the lack of significance attached to the social construct. Writing in the context of the CRC, Tobin also separates the two aspects of childhood,[54] but appears to suggest that the socially constructed element of childhood is part of its justification. He contends that the 'empirically grounded and socially constructed [conception of childhood] ... provides the foundation for the "special" human rights that are granted to children under international law'.[55] As I argue above, however, the social construction does not seek to and cannot provide this type of foundation.

In her discussion, Appell also separates the concept from the social construct, though less explicitly so; she reasons:

> While acknowledging the 'natural' differences between many children and most adults, I challenge the totalizing categorical distinction between adulthood and childhood, the extent of the limitation on children's agency, and their segregation from public life.[56]

In noting 'natural' differences, Appell identifies factors that might underpin the core of the concept of childhood. She then proceeds to focus on the social construction of childhood, particularly its negative consequences for children, viewing the social construction as responsible for creating rigid, unjustifiable limits on children's treatment in society.

As a strategy for securing better treatment for children, Appell's approach makes sense. The constructed aspect of childhood is isolated and critiqued so that a move from the devalued status of children—generally adopted in the American literature—to a more equal status for children might be justified. Yet, understanding the motivations for this delineation highlights a critical assumption Appell's argument makes about the social construction of childhood, namely that the social construction is *not* tied to the concept of childhood. Otherwise, it would not be possible to assume that the mere fact that the construction draws rigid dividing lines is itself criticizable. As I contend above, however, there are multiple ways in which the social construct might be related to the concept of childhood that could support the justifiability of the construct. As a result, any separation of the social construct from the concept does not necessarily prevent the basis and limits of the construct from depending on the concept: we need to determine whether it is a separation of degree or kind. The former may permit us to question the rigidity of the application of the construction, but only the latter can lead us to reject it. Moreover, it may be that the concept of childhood with which we are concerned should be situationally specific.

---

[54] In similar terms to my account, he reasons that

> a further issue exists as to whether the concept of childhood can actually be justified. The point to stress here is that although the outer boundaries of the concept remain socially constructed and flexible under international law, there remains agreement among states as to the concept of childhood.

See J Tobin, 'Justifying Children's Rights' (2013) 21 International Journal of Children's Rights 395, 400, 401.

[55] ibid 396.   [56] ibid 718.

IV. The 'Vulnerability' Objection

The foregoing makes clear that what becomes critical to an argument for treating children as a 'special case' is the identification of distinctive factors that inhere to the concept of childhood, respect for which requires the prioritization of children's interests. This may be reflected in the CRC's Preamble reference to the 'United Nations ha[ving] proclaimed that childhood is entitled to special care and assistance', which Tobin contends is justified by 'empirical reality'.[57] I argue that children's vulnerability can provide a strong foundation. There are two objections to this positive account of the role for vulnerability: firstly, that children are neither more vulnerable nor uniquely vulnerable compared to other groups; secondly, that, even if children are uniquely vulnerable, the negative consequences to children that result from focusing on their vulnerability outweigh any case to the contrary.

A. 'Everyone is vulnerable'

Writing in the Australian context, Seymour contends that '[c]hildren are not just another disadvantaged group (like a racial minority). Children are vulnerable. Until they are of an age and capacity to make informed judgments for themselves, the state has a role to play in protecting them'.[58] But, are children more or uniquely vulnerable?

In respect of the extent of children's vulnerability, we might readily concede that adults could be just as or more vulnerable in certain respects such as in the case of elderly individuals' loss of physical mobility or capacity, and both children and adults can suffer from disabilities. More generally, we can define and redefine vulnerability, of course, to include the complex ways in which particular groups of adults, and adults in general, are also vulnerable. But, as Reece notes—in the course of her argument against treating children as a special case—'[i]t is self-evident that, as a general rule, children need more protection than adults'.[59] In fact, it is that need for greater protection that she believes has confused academics into assuming children's interests need to be prioritized over adults'. The critical issue is whether children need more protection because they are uniquely vulnerable.

In order for children's vulnerability to justifiably underpin the prioritization of children's interests through legal regulation, however, that vulnerability must be unique.[60] This is a conceptual point, grounded in the nature, and not the extent of vulnerability. But what of the fact that, as Fineman reasons, '[v]ulnerability is inherent in the human condition'?[61] She suggests that seeing vulnerability as a characteristic of only certain

---

[57] ibid 401.
[58] J Seymour, *Children, Parents and the Courts: Legal Intervention in Family Life* (Federation Press 2016) 175–76.
[59] Reece, 'The Paramountcy Principle' (n 20) 277.
[60] The need for 'special vulnerability' also informs the operation of the 'vulnerability' principle as a justification for allocating special priority to children under a capabilities approach: Dixon and Nussbaum (n 19) 573–78.
[61] MA Fineman, 'Equality, Autonomy, and the Vulnerable Subject in Law and Politics' in MA Fineman and A Grear (eds), *Vulnerability: Reflections on a New Ethical Foundation for Law and Politics* (Ashgate 2013) 13, 13.

groups 'is not only misleading and inaccurate, it is also pernicious'.[62] Whilst Herring acknowledges a role for vulnerability, he does not see it as capable of justifying treating children as a 'special case'. He argues that '[t]he law in its treatment of children based on vulnerability exaggerates the vulnerability of children and exaggerates the capacity of adults'.[63] Alderson reasons that 'vulnerability and the need for protection occur at any age or level of competence'.[64] Appell also notes adult vulnerability, as part of her conclusion that the current focus on children's vulnerability underpins age discrimination against children.[65] Beyond suggesting that everyone is vulnerable,[66] Herring draws on the interdependency of caring relationships to conclude that 'it is wrong to regard [children] as especially vulnerable'.[67]

In seeing everyone as vulnerable, however, are we not in danger of not truly seeing anyone's vulnerability? In this way, might we argue that the feminist perspective offers valuable insight into children's position, but cannot of itself provide the necessary solution?[68] Fineman avoids this concern in her 'vulnerability paradigm' by moving beyond recognition of the universality of vulnerability to focus on the inevitable differences between individuals, including how individuals are embodied and embedded within societal institutions and social relationships.[69] Difference permits the possibility for children being elevated to a 'special case' and highlights how focus on vulnerability need not collapse into formal equality.

Alternatively, in focusing on children's vulnerability in particular, might we be inappropriately marking out children as excessively dependent? What if focus on children's vulnerability is not necessarily beneficial for children? Or might it entail overlooking the necessary interdependency within families?[70] In discussing the treatment of children in the CRC, Tobin argues that:

> Indeed the 'children's first' slogan is a highly problematic model which does not reflect a rights based approach. As Cantwell explains, it places children 'on a kind of "more equal than others" pedestal', which reflects a 'charity based approach to children, where sentimentality over children's vulnerability leads to facile 'separate' responses: never mind human rights let's help children' (Cantwell 2004).[71]

I suggest that this risk can be avoided if the case for prioritization grounded in children's special vulnerability is not just negative, but also positive. In particular, I understand

---

[62] ibid 16.
[63] J Herring, 'Vulnerability, Children and the Law' in M Freeman (ed), *Law and Childhood Studies: Current Legal Issues Vol 14* (OUP 2012) 243, 250.
[64] P Alderson, 'Common Criticisms of Children's Rights and 25 Years of the IJCR' (2017) 25 International Journal of Children's Rights 307.
[65] Appell (n 27) 778.   [66] Herring, 'Vulnerability' (n 63) 253, 257.   [67] ibid 262.
[68] This is not a criticism of the feminist perspective to the extent that one of feminism's critical aims is to uncover the way in which legal regulation creates difference and subjective experience as well as reflects it. See Rosenbury (n 31) 30.
[69] Fineman focuses her argument on how the operation of those institutions and relationships have conferred power and privilege. See Fineman, 'Equality and Difference' (n 52) 612–13, 618; Fineman, 'Equality, Autonomy' (n 61) 21–22.
[70] Herring (n 63) 263.
[71] J Tobin, 'Beyond the Supermarket Shelf: Using a Rights Based Approach to Address Children's Health Needs' (2006) 14 International Journal of Children's Rights 275, 277, 278.

'vulnerability' as comprising not only the lack of capacity, means, and opportunity for children to protect their own interests, but also the richness of aspects of the intrinsic goods of childhood.[72] Responding to the former enables us to secure the child's 'right to an open future'[73] and protect children's potentiality. The latter is intended to capture intrinsic goods of childhood such as innocence, imagination,[74] wonder, and trust.[75] In this way, potentiality is intended to move beyond the merely forward-looking notion of the child's 'right to an open future' and to recognise the value of the present, lived childhood.

Conventional reference to vulnerability focuses on its negative aspects, such as lack of capacity. But that arguably requires us to assume an oppositional, 'othering' relationship between children's autonomy or agency and vulnerability.[76] Moreover, such an account turns on accepting impoverished conceptions of both autonomy and vulnerability for mutual exclusion and reinforcement whereas, as Macleod notes, the reality is 'surprisingly complex'.[77] In any event, as highlighted by the previous discussion on the extent of children's vulnerability compared to adults', it is not at all clear that the distinctiveness of children's vulnerability lies in its negative aspects. That is not to say, however, that the dependency on others generated by such vulnerability may not be unique. In the context of a capabilities approach, Dixon and Nussbaum argue that

> By itself, children's physical vulnerability, therefore, will also be insufficient in most cases to justify any *special priority*—as opposed to special scope—for the rights of children, as compared to adults, under a [capabilities approach]. Instead, what is needed is an account that focuses on the more or less unique vulnerability of children to the decisions of others—that is, those adults legally and economically responsible for their care.[78]

Finally, a deficit account of vulnerability might also encourage us to seek to hasten children's development, which would undermine recognition of the value of the intrinsic goods of childhood.[79]

In terms of the positive account of vulnerability, a child's sense of imagination is something that we value for its own sake, but it also makes them vulnerable in their interactions with others since it entails trusting others and being open to adventure.

---

[72] Various lists have been proposed. See, eg, Brennan (n 37), especially 42; A Gheaus, 'The "Intrinsic Good of Childhood" and the Just Society' in A Bagattini and CM Macleod (eds), *The Nature of Children's Well-Being: Theory and Practice* (Springer 2015) 35, especially 39–42; CM Macleod, 'Agency, Authority and the Vulnerability of Children' in A Bagattini and CM Macleod (eds), *The Nature of Children's Well-Being: Theory and Practice* (Springer 2015) 53, 59–62. For a general account of the definition of vulnerability, see C Mackenzie, W Rogers, and S Dodds, 'Introduction: What Is Vulnerability and Why Does It Matter for Moral Theory?' in C Mackenzie, W Rogers, and S Dodds (eds), *Vulnerability: New Essays in Ethics and Feminist Philosophy* (OUP 2014) 1, 4–9.

[73] J Feinberg, 'The Child's Right to an Open Future' in W Aiken and H LaFollette (eds), *Whose Child? Children's Rights* (Rowman and Littlefield 1990) 76.

[74] Macleod, 'Agency, Authority' (n 72).

[75] D Archard, 'Philosophical Perspectives on Childhood' in J Fionda (ed), *Legal Concepts of Childhood* (Hart Publishing 2001) 43, 45. Archard contrasts innocence, wonder, and trust to vulnerability and dependence, positing the general philosophical approach as one of seeing the former as valuable and the latter as not valuable. By contrast, I suggest that such intrinsic goods are part of children's vulnerability, and hence mean that it should not be understood in a purely negative sense.

[76] A Diduck, 'Autonomy and Vulnerability in Family Law: The Missing Link' in J Wallbank and J Herring (eds), *Vulnerabilities, Care and Family Law* (Routledge 2014) 95, especially 97–98.

[77] ibid 57.   [78] Dixon and Nussbaum (n 19) 575 (emphasis in original).

[79] Macleod similarly argues for the significance of juvenile agency as contrasted with mature agency: (n 72) 58–59, 63.

Whilst adults also have a sense of imagination, there is arguably something unique about children's; as an intrinsic good of childhood it is necessarily positive. This distinctive feature of children's vulnerability means that children are not just *more* vulnerable but *uniquely* vulnerable in their relationships within their families and society more generally. If we accept the distinctiveness of children's vulnerability, it can underpin the justification of prioritization without disregarding or devaluing their interdependent relationships, particularly with their parents.

B. Objections even if children are uniquely vulnerable

Those who agree with the foregoing argument that children are distinctively vulnerable might yet raise two objections against a focus on vulnerability. The first concern is that there might be other aspects of childhood that should be seen as just as, or more important than children's vulnerability. Appell, for example, refers to children's participation, growth, and membership (of groups, such as a family).[80] She reasons that

> The construction of childhood as private, dependent, unwise, and vulnerable belies the rich, active, and productive lives of children and deprives them and the state of important and active constituents who are central in shaping society and who perform labor inside and outside home and school.[81]

But this opposition between vulnerability and valued status in society makes two contentious assumptions. Firstly, it unjustifiably assumes that children's distinctive vulnerability can only serve as the basis for subjugation. Hence, vulnerability is downplayed to secure better treatment. Secondly, it further assumes that the normative basis for treating children as a 'special case' must then become the sole guide to the application of the 'special case' approach in resolving individual cases. As I argue below, this is mistaken: the argument for seeing children as a 'special case' may be grounded in children's unique vulnerability, whilst the limits of its application on the particular facts of a dispute may be determined by other considerations.

The second objection lies in the consequences of focusing on children's unique vulnerability. Whilst it is a core aspect of the concept of childhood, and can thereby set justifiable limits on the construct of childhood, there is a risk that this vulnerability could be relied on to over-extend the construct. Herring has expressed similar concerns over the paternalistic interpretation of children's interests and the role of vulnerability as a basis for 'quietening' children's participation in legal decision-making.[82] Unless we can eliminate this risk, this might be said to provide good reason not to ground legal regulation in children's vulnerability. One immediate reply lies in the positive account of the distinctiveness of children's vulnerability developed above: emphasis of the intrinsic goods of childhood, rather than the deficits, does not invite the same oppressive interaction with children since, for example, their developing agency is valued in and of itself for its ability to access intrinsic goods.

A broader concern remains. Does the institutional response to vulnerability create additional, imposed unjustifiable dependency? Appell comments that some child

---

[80] Appell (n 27) 721.   [81] ibid 742.   [82] Herring (n 63) 246–47.

protective and development-oriented interventions are justified by children's vulnerability and inexperience.[83] Rather than seeing vulnerability as belonging to the child, however, she argues that their vulnerability resides in political and legal systems,[84] in other words the social construction of that vulnerability. It is not clear what advantage is gained by describing the liberal institutional response to vulnerability as itself comprising vulnerability, particularly if the intention is to highlight the importance of how we respond to the empirical differences.[85] But Appell's larger point is a good one. As Rosenbury argues, the institutional response to vulnerability may create legal incapacity;[86] it may impose dependency on children in a way that is not inevitable[87] and goes beyond what their vulnerability either demands or excuses.

But, given that the institutional response to vulnerability is not inevitable, why can we not simply ensure that the construct does not unjustifiably over-extend and excessively concretize the conceptual core? Arguably we can and concern to the contrary is driven by preoccupation with vulnerability as implying only institutional dependency[88] and marginalization. Whilst well-intentioned, this concern is misplaced because it overlooks the possibility for the state to respond positively, in an enhancing, empowering, and enabling way, to children's unique vulnerability. For the foregoing reasons, the 'vulnerability' objection is arguably defeated by a proper understanding of the positive aspects of children's unique vulnerability.

V. The 'Family Autonomy' Objection

A. The range of 'family autonomy' counter-arguments

The third counter-argument is grounded in family autonomy and the 'right' to be a parent, and applies even if children are uniquely vulnerable. Archard and Macleod argue that

> It no longer seems possible to posit a simple harmony between the interests of children and those charged with the responsibility of rearing them, such that the existence of authority over children during their development of maturity can be viewed as a fairly straightforward matter. Instead the challenge is to deepen our understanding of children's interests and to explore how the conceptualization of children's interests affects the character of the moral claims they have.[89]

Where children's and parents' rights and interests conflict, the concern is that children's interests cannot be prioritized over those of either the adults or larger family raising them. Rather than vulnerability being seen to demand prioritization, it is seen as justifying deference to familial, especially parental, decision-making.

---

[83] ibid 719.   [84] ibid 718.
[85] This might be said to underpin Fineman's 'vulnerability paradigm'. See (n 52) and corresponding main text.
[86] Rosenbury (n 31) 21.   [87] Appell (n 27) 724.
[88] SF Appleton, 'Restating Childhood' (2014) 79 Brooklyn Law Review 525, 526, 541.
[89] D Archard and CM Macleod, 'Introduction' in D Archard and CM Macleod (eds), *The Moral and Political Status of Children* (OUP 2002) 4.

The 'family autonomy' objection contains a cluster of views. Putting the case in child-oriented terms, we might take the view that parents are best placed to know what is in their children's 'best interests'. For example, in his judgment in the House of Lords' seminal decision in *Gillick v West Norfolk and Wisbech Area Health Authority*,[90] Lord Fraser reasons that '[n]obody doubts, certainly I do not doubt, that in the overwhelming majority of cases the best judges of a child's welfare are his or her parents'.[91] Alternatively, understanding the issue in parent-centred terms, we might see deference to parents as a consequence of liberal neutrality that respects 'the distinctive contribution that parent–child relationships make to the well-being or flourishing of adults'.[92] We might also consider a 'dual-interest' theory, namely one that captures both children's and parents' interests, which settles on a parent–child relationship that does not permit prioritization to children's interests.[93] Finally, considering all parties in relational terms, we might suggest that children's interdependent relationship with their parents means that there may be circumstances in which they may be required to act altruistically in favour of their parents' or the family's interests.[94]

B. Responding to 'family autonomy'

There are strong countervailing arguments to each way of framing the 'family autonomy' objection to treating children as a 'special case'. What of the child-oriented objection to prioritization on the basis that parents and other caregivers are best placed to give content to their child's 'best interests'? In respect of the CRC, for example, the Preamble 'explicit[ly] naturaliz[es.] the family'[95] and Article 18(1) ascribes to parents or guardians the 'primary responsibility for the upbringing and development of the child' and establishes 'the best interest of the child [as] their basic concern'. In such CRC provisions, '[c]hildren are not first of all addressed as part of a public sphere, but as dependents of their parents in need of protection and guidance within the private sphere'.[96]

But is this characterization justifiable? No proxy decision-making can perfectly encapsulate any decision the child would make if mature, not least because there is no such 'mature' child: we can only hypothesize an instantaneously mature child or imagine the child as an adult looking back, neither of which is satisfactory.[97] In that context, the pragmatic resort to parental guidance seems sensible. Yet, whilst parents generally have more exposure to their children's thoughts, beliefs, and behaviours than others, this does not mean that they should be assumed capable of representing them

---

[90] [1986] AC 112.   [91] ibid 173D (Lord Fraser).
[92] H Brighouse and A Swift, 'The Goods of Parenting' in F Baylis and C McLeod (eds) *Family-Making: Contemporary Ethical Challenges* (OUP 2014) 11, 11.
[93] H Brighouse and A Swift, *Family Values: The Ethics of Parent–Child Relationships* (Princeton UP 2014) 51.
[94] C Foster and J Herring, *Altruism, Welfare and the Law* (Springer 2015), especially 4. See also J Herring and C Foster, 'Welfare Means Relationality, Virtue and Altruism' (2012) 32 Legal Studies 480.
[95] Z Clark and H Ziegler, 'The UN Children's Rights Convention and the Capabilities Approach – Family Duties and Children's Rights in Tension' in D Stoecklin and JM Bonvin (eds), *Children's Rights and the Capability Approach: Challenges and Prospects* (Springer 2014) 213, 226.
[96] ibid.
[97] Discussed in relation to the interest theory of rights: *Ferguson*, 'Not Merely Rights for Children' (n 35) 193–94.

impartially. This is especially so where the child's views may conflict with those of one or both of their parents, and it is for this reason that children may be appointed independent representation[98] or a children's guardian[99] in cases affecting them.

The absence of legal mechanisms for separating the representation of children's and parents' interests in other situations invites one of two possible explanations. On the one hand, the situation could be seen as low-risk in terms of potential consequences for the child, hence the concession to the parental role is limited. Alternatively, the situation could be seen to reflect the fact that, as Lotz reasons, '[m]any liberals seem simply to assume that parents will seek to instil their substantive values in their children'.[100] This requires us to consider the parent-oriented account of the 'family autonomy' objection.

Altman presents such a case in his contribution to this collection, grounded in the parental interest in nurturing, counselling, and educating, in which parents must be able to be authentic.[101] His intention is to provide a stronger normative foundation for 'parental control rights' rather than change outcomes in practice. For this reason, it is not clear that it precludes the prioritization of children's interests to the extent they have already been prioritized in law. At a conceptual level, however, it is more difficult to reconcile 'parental control rights' with treating children as a 'special case'. Rather than reconciling the two, however, we may conclude that an account of 'family autonomy' grounded in parental interests alone is unjustifiable in any event.

Altman argues that '[a]uthorship of goals and means—the defining aspect of authenticity—requires significantly more discretion and therefore provides the basis for a more robust parental control right'.[102] But children's unique vulnerability to their parents' decisions and actions highlights the risk of parental domination to which the same liberal values that suggest respect for the parental role in shaping their children's values and opportunities ought to be inimical.[103] This is so even where the values sought to be inculcated are not pernicious.[104] I suggest it is difficult to make the case for 'parental control rights' without some form of child-oriented limits.

Brighouse and Swift seek to present such a case. Their argument for the value of the family highlights its role in protecting and promoting both children's interests as well as parents' interest in being parents, grounded in their uniquely valuable, fiduciary relationship with their children.[105] Their account is particularly noteworthy because the proposed resolution that justifies the parental role to shape their children's values contains inherent limits that ensure that it does not violate the liberal principles of equality of opportunity and meritocratic selection.[106] Brighouse and Swift achieve this move by characterizing the parental interest in their fiduciary role as 'deeply connected to the content of that role. It is because of *what* children need from their parents that adults

---

[98] Children Act 1989, s 10(2)(b) and (8). See, eg, *Mabon v Mabon* [2005] EWCA Civ 634.
[99] Children Act 1989, s 41.
[100] M Lotz, 'Parental Values and Children's Vulnerability' in C Mackenzie, W Rogers, and S Dodds (eds), *Vulnerability: New Essays in Ethics and Feminist Philosophy* (OUP 2014) 242, 249–50.
[101] See Altman's chapter.
[102] ibid 226.
[103] Lotz (n 100) 260–63.   [104] ibid 263.   [105] Brighouse and Swift (n 93).
[106] For an excellent exposition of this 'trilemma', see J Fishkin, *Justice, Equal Opportunity and the Family* (Yale UP 1983).

have such a weighty interest in giving it to them'.[107] Yet, the account remains dualist because children are not seen to have an interest in the relationship being one in which 'parents always act with their "best interests" in mind'.[108] Instead, the type of fiduciary relationship in which the child has an interest is one in which the parent '[has] her own interests and enthusiasms, and the discretion to pursue them to some extent'.[109]

Does this understanding of 'family autonomy' permit the prioritization of children's interests? The normative role for children's interests in Brighouse and Swift's account itself prioritizes children's interests but brings parental interests within a proper understanding of children's interests. Seeing children as a 'special case' does not of itself render parental interests irrelevant since the content of children's interests can be contextualized: the focus remains the child as subject, but the complexity of their lives is included as it impacts on them. [110] Such a contextualized approach may be reconcilable with this account of the 'family autonomy' objection.

Might this mean that seeing children as a 'special case' is also compatible with a relational account of the 'family autonomy' objection? Whilst the 'umbrella'[111] nature of 'relational' here means that we cannot critique specific arguments, the relational aspect on any account requires that social conditions are seen as conceptually necessary to the self, rather than merely contributory factors.[112] As a consequence, it is not clear that a relational perspective can accommodate seeing children as a 'special case': the focus becomes one of maintaining those relations that are constitutive of the self,[113] which may simply reinforce a legal framework that 'keeps [children] in their place'.[114]

Moreover, it is not clear that there are independent reasons to seek to make the approaches compatible. One of the key benefits of a relational approach is argued to be that it takes a long-term perspective whereas the conventional approach, particularly in terms of the 'welfare' principle, can risk a 'snap-shot' view being taken.[115] But it is not at all clear why treating children as a 'special case' whether via the 'paramountcy' principle or otherwise cannot similarly accommodate a long-term view of the child's interests. Indeed, this is a legislative requirement in respect of 'welfare' in the adoption context.[116] A further key aspect, hence also benefit, of a relational approach is the inculcation of particular values in the child. Herring argues:

> It is beneficial for a child to be brought up in a family that is based on relationships which are fair and just. A relationship based on unacceptable demands on a parent is not furthering a child's welfare.[117]

---

[107] Brighouse and Swift (n 93) 92 (emphasis in original); see also 121: 'Parents' rights and duties, then, are entirely fiduciary. Parents have just those rights and duties with respect to their children that it is in their children's interests for them to have.'
[108] ibid 122.   [109] ibid.
[110] I discuss this elsewhere: L Ferguson, ' "Families in all their Subversive Variety": Over-Representation, the Ethnic Child Protection Penalty, and Responding to Diversity whilst Protecting Children' (2014) 63 Studies in Law, Politics, and Society 43.
[111] C Mackenzie and N Stoljar, 'Introduction: Autonomy Reconfigured' in C Mackenzie and N Stoljar (eds), *Relational Autonomy: Feminist Perspectives on Autonomy, Agency, and the Social Self* (OUP 2000) 3, 4.
[112] J Christman, 'Relational Autonomy, Liberal Individualism, and the Social Constitution of Selves' (2004) 117 Philosophical Studies 143, 147 - 148 (writing in the context of relational autonomy in particular).
[113] ibid 156.   [114] Appell (n 27) 717.
[115] J Herring, *Caring and the Law* (Hart Publishing 2013) 205.
[116] Adoption and Children Act 2002, c 38, s 1(2).
[117] Herring, (n 115) 205.

But a contextualized understanding of the child's interests, properly understood, could and would need to accommodate the impact on parents as it will necessarily also affect the child;[118] the landscape is more complex than the opposition of the atomistic, isolated self and the metaphysical,[119] fully relational self. Whilst treating children as a 'special case' does not require a contextualized approach to children's interests, it can accommodate it.

VI. The 'Equality' Objection

The fourth and final objection to treating children as a 'special case' is an argument from equality. The concern is that equality, expressed as equal moral consideration, has no space for prioritizing children's interests as a matter of law. This entails an examination of two issues: first, how equal moral consideration relates to the status and treatment of children compared to adults; second, whether we can justify not only privileging children's interests in the factual outcome but also preferring children's interests at the outset, namely as a matter of law.

A. The idea of equal moral consideration

There is a strong argument from equality that all individuals' interests should be given equal consideration, and there exists only inadequate arguments to justify derogation from such equal consideration. Equal consideration means seeing children's and adults' interests as of equal moral value. As I have discussed elsewhere, treating children as a 'special case' needs to be compatible with equal moral consideration.[120]

At first glance, we might be concerned that prioritizing children's interests means they are being regarded unequally, and unjustifiably so. The very idea of 'children's rights' suggests the possibility of distinctive outcomes that favour children, namely unequal outcomes. Whilst they may be underpinned by equal moral consideration, the distinct terminology that delineates children from adults highlights the potential for differential results. Yet, as Brennan and Noggle recognize, equal consideration does not mean identical outcomes: 'two people can receive equal moral *consideration* without having exactly the same package of moral rights and duties'.[121] For that reason, we need to be cautious in concluding that the approach being explored in this chapter, namely prioritizing children's interests, does not demonstrate equal consideration. Understanding why the conceptual basis for seeing children as a 'special case' does not fall foul of the equal consideration argument enables us to see the natural limits of any account of what it means to treat children as a 'special case'.

In writing about the moral status of children, Brennan and Noggle argue for the 'equal consideration thesis', namely that '[c]hildren are entitled to the same moral

---

[118] Herring discusses the Court of Appeal's decision in *Re S (A Child)* [2002] EWCA Civ 1795 to suggest to the contrary: ibid, 205–06. I discuss this in Section VII, below.
[119] For discussion, see Christman (n 112).
[120] Ferguson, 'The Jurisprudence of Making Decisions Affecting Children' (n 5).
[121] ibid (emphasis in original).

consideration as adults'.[122] Equal moral consideration captures the interrelated aspects of formal and substantive equality that affect the legal regulation of individuals. In terms of formal equality, it suggests that, to the extent that children and adults as groups are alike, the law should treat them alike. Brennan and Noggle explain this in terms of equal moral status:

> [A] certain moral status attaches generally to all persons, including children. To deny this would be to claim either that persons do not derive moral status from their status as persons, or that children are not persons. Because neither of these claims is particularly plausible, it does not seem plausible to deny the Equal Consideration Thesis.[123]

As children and adults are humans, formal equality underpins children and adults as holders of fundamental human rights, who should be accorded equal respect. But this assumes that 'children's rights' are nothing more than a repackaged reference to fundamental human rights. More precisely, it implies that we have changed the label because that is the only way to ensure sufficient attention is paid to children. Are we using the markers of difference to achieve a measure of sameness?

If, as I have argued elsewhere,[124] it is important to recognize when it is a child who is the rights-holder, namely that there is a difference between 'rights for children' and 'children's rights', this entails having regard to substantive equality. Likewise, if 'best interests' are anything more than an articulation of the need to take children's interests into account just like the interests of others. Drawing on the substance of 'children's rights' and 'best interests', this represents a definitional claim that substantive equality is also critical to determining the criteria against which to evaluate whether children can justifiably be treated as a 'special case'. The recognition that equal moral consideration also includes substantive equality enables us to evaluate the criteria for likeness under formal equality. It also provides an independent basis for justifying outcomes and determining when equal treatment is required. Equal moral consideration thus offers a lens through which to evaluate whether equal treatment or unequal treatment is justified. Unequal treatment may be justified only if it does not undermine the equal respect—the equal moral status—that the law needs to express for children and adults.

B. Superior moral status, equal and unequal outcomes

The foregoing makes clear that we should not approach the evaluation of children's status on the basis that equal respect necessarily means equal treatment. As Dwyer explains,

> [b]ecause equal moral consideration can produce unequal treatment and unequal moral consideration can allow for equal legal protection, it is often difficult to

---

[122] S Brennan and R Noggle, 'The Moral Status of Children: Children's Rights, Parents' Rights, and Family Justice' (1997) 23 Social Theory and Practice 1, 2.
[123] ibid 2.   [124] Ferguson, 'Not Merely Rights for Children' (n 36).

determine when decision makers are systematically treating one group as occupying a lower moral status than another, or are instead treating them as moral equals.[125]

Drawing on this insight, Dwyer argues for unequal moral status in order to achieve equal treatment:

> Recognizing children's superior moral status, if the best account of moral status yields that conclusion, might simply push government officials to give children's interests more or less equal weight to that of adults and make adult society somewhat more reluctant to disparage and discriminate against children.[126]

If children and adults necessarily have equal moral status, however, only equal or unequal treatment that does not violate that status is permissible.

Dwyer presents a case for prioritizing children's interests in the sense of giving them unequal—greater—moral consideration compared to the consideration given to the interests of others.[127] He does not use the socially constructed class of children to delineate those whose interests are to be preferred, but instead argues for placing greater moral weight on the characteristics of youthfulness, which are typically possessed by children.[128] In arguing against the 'egalitarian impulse of modern liberalism',[129] however, a key contention is that unequal consideration ought to at least 'shake us loose finally from traditional assumptions of children's inferiority'.[130] In other words, excessive correction at a theoretical level may only lead to moderate, justifiable correction in practice.[131] Dwyer's aim and prediction is rooted in an account of the current regime that views children as inferior.[132] For this reason, his argument may not be directly applicable to the English context where excessive correction via unequal consideration in theory may lead to unjustifiable, unequal factual outcomes. According greater moral status to children is thus not a necessary means of achieving equal treatment in practice.

More fundamentally, I suggest the resort to unequal moral status is neither necessary nor justifiable as a matter of theory. Dwyer reasons that 'children's superior moral status would mean favoring children even when adults have much at stake'.[133] But, as I proceed to explain, children's interests can be preferred both in the outcome and at the outset without needing to see them other than as having equal moral status with adults. This reply needs to engage with the hypothetical scenario envisaged by Dwyer in which 'a child and adult have *equal but mutually incompatible* interests at stake and fairness considerations do not dictate a particular outcome'.[134] The child prefers one activity and the adult another, such as in relation to dinner choices or vacation destinations, or the child prefers one expenditure and the adult another, such as play equipment or sports equipment for the adult.[135] One way to resolve the conflict, Dwyer suggests, is to reason that the child's preferences should be respected because the child is morally superior

---

[125] Dwyer (n 28) 14. [126] ibid 137.
[127] ibid. Dwyer is clear, however, that his argument is one of the plausibility of children's moral superiority, and that he 'make[s] no pretense of advancing a knock-down case' 148.
[128] ibid 145–87. [129] ibid 143. [130] ibid. [131] ibid 148, 137.
[132] Dwyer (n 28) and corresponding main text. [133] ibid 189.
[134] ibid 184–85 (emphasis added). [135] ibid 185.

such that their interests matter more than the adult's.[136] He contends that those who see children as having an equal moral status to adults cannot found an argument for respecting the child's preference in that theoretical stance.[137]

We might test this by examining a dilemma of the type Dwyer contemplates. Imagine that the decision entails choosing whether to go on a beach holiday or take a city break packed with museums. The child expresses a clear preference for the former and the adult for the latter. But it is not clear in what sense the child's and the adult's interests can be said to be 'equal' such that an additional device—children's moral superiority—is needed to determine the outcome on the facts. Having equal respect for individuals' views regardless of their content would suggest equal moral status, hence Dwyer must mean they are equally weighty when applied to the facts.

Yet, in application to the facts, we are tasked to consider not just each individual's expressed preference but the justificatory arguments for not giving effect to that preference. Even if the initial expression of the child's and adult's interests appears equal, therefore, that does not hold true after the interests have been contextualized to the individual expressing them, including justifications for not giving effect to their expression. For example, the aims of the city break might just as well be accomplished through family outings to museums at weekends, whereas the ocean might be too far away to make weekend trips possible. What is evident is that equal moral consideration for the individual expressing the preference does not mean that we cannot prefer one party's view. In her criticism of the 'welfare' principle in English law, Reece argues that there is a 'fallacy ... [of] equat[ing] priority with protection'.[138] Once we recognize this, she argues, we can see that decisions which, in the outcome give more weight to one party's interests than those of others, may have given equal weight to all parties' interests in the process by which that outcome was reached.[139]

The basis for determining which view is to be preferred does not need to derive directly from the idea of equal moral status, but from the range of arguments available to justify *not* giving effect to one party's preference in the context of the other party's known preference. It is because we know the two preferred holiday types and their aims that we can consider in relation to which we can more readily accomplish its aims just on weekends. It is in the justification for infringement of each individual's prima facie equally respected interests that these interests acquire their full content and are rightly no longer seen as of equal weight, all things considered. This resembles the way in which courts resolve conflicts of parties' Article 8 ECHR rights.[140] As a result, whilst Dwyer's aims of improving the treatment of children in the United States are to be supported, any argument in favour of seeing children as having superior moral status should, at the least, be confined to that context.

C. Prioritizing children's interests as a matter of law

Translating equal consideration into outcomes leads to prioritizing children's interests where their interests are elevated within the guiding legal principles and concepts,

---

[136] ibid. [137] ibid. [138] Reece, 'The Paramountcy Principle' (n 20) 277.
[139] ibid 278–79. See also Dwyer (n 28) 12. [140] (n 12) and corresponding main text.

rather than just application to the facts. If children's interests were preferred merely at the final stage, they would not be a 'special case'. Where children's interests are expressed in rights-based terms, for example, the shift from preferring children's interests in the application to preferring them at the legal stage is reflected in the distinction between 'rights for children' and 'children's rights'. The critical difficulty here is whether the argument from equal moral consideration can accommodate not only unequal treatment in the outcome but unequal treatment at the outset.

I suggest that the response to this concern lies in the contextualization of children's interests. The 'paramountcy' expressed by the 'welfare' principle, for example, does not apply to all, but only specific contexts involving children's interests; equal moral consideration is expressed prior to that prioritization in the contextualization. This demonstrates how we do not need unequal consideration for children's interests in order to see them as a 'special case'; we can prioritize children's interests in a way that does not fall foul of this equality concern.

Compatibility with equal consideration is most critical where children's interests are being prioritized in conflicts with other parties' interests. The 'welfare' principle might be best seen as a framework for decision-making that prioritizes children's interests in conflicts with those of others. Yet, it does not fall foul of the equal consideration concern because equal consideration conceptually precedes the 'welfare' principle. Just as with additional legal protection, we approach children's and others' interests on the basis that they are of equal value. Where the context implicates children's interests more than adults', children's interests need to be prioritized. As a result of this recognition of the need to prioritize, the 'welfare' principle is applied to these contexts. This is why the 'welfare' principle does not apply to all situations affecting children; if it did, it would be harder to justify it because that would imply there could have been no earlier point at which all parties' interests were regarded equally. Thus, its limited scope is a strength, rather than weakness as Reece suggests.[141]

Equal consideration of everyone's interests also explicitly allows for consideration of adults' vulnerability. As a factor approached with equal consideration to determine the correct legal approach to regulating children, however, children's vulnerability is distinctive. The inability of young children to make decisions about whether or not to consent to medical treatment or to avoid being taken to a contact session illustrate the distinctive nature and extent of their vulnerability as a class. The extent of children's vulnerability includes the degree of capacity for autonomous decision-making that particular children might have; the distinctive nature of that vulnerability lies in recognizing children's intended and actual increasing capacities as well as their significant and intimate dependence on adults for a large measure of their well-being. When equal consideration of all parties' interests is applied to the concept of childhood, we are entitled to assume the unique character of the vulnerability is possessed by all children. As a consequence, we are justified in adopting a legal approach that prioritizes children's interests. Which legal approach best recognizes this priority becomes the key issue.

---

[141] Reece, 'The Paramountcy Principle' (n 20) 281, 285.

VII. Implications for the Current Law

A. Fit with the current law

As this account of children as a 'special case' relates to the concept of childhood, it has natural limits that may not accord with the law on the regulation of children in practice. For example, legislative limits that differ may be justifiable for other reasons such as administrative efficiency in respect of a universal rule like the driving age, where there are comparatively low stakes consequences for affected children. More generally, in order that treating children as a 'special case' is workable in a legal context, this account arguably needs to accept that we are entitled to assume that we can consider vulnerability for 'children' as a class, rather than relying on the premise that every child—every member of that class—is vulnerable in a way and to an extent that they require additional protection. Thus, I do not propose a full defence of the current law. At times, the argument presented in this chapter justifies going further, and at times it is more restrictive.

Compatibility with equal moral consideration is most straightforward where children are being afforded additional recognition of rights and interests in law. For example, we recognize that all individuals are vulnerable and are equally concerned about the vulnerability of all, but there are certain contexts in which children's vulnerability is greater than that of adults. Article 24 of the CRC provides a helpful illustration. It is concerned to recognize the child's interest in healthcare. Adults and children alike have an interest in access to the 'highest attainable standard of health and to the facilities for the treatment of illness and rehabilitation of health'.[142] Yet, children are particularly vulnerable to the imposition on them of 'traditional practices prejudicial to ... health',[143] so their interests are specifically noted in this regard. Recognition of this additional right to protection is not because we have less consideration for adults, but because children are less able to protect themselves against such infringement. In this sense, additional protection, which treats children as a 'special case', is a way of implementing equal consideration.

From an English perspective, the debate over which language descriptors treat or indicate an intention to treat children as a 'special case' is of most concern as regards the compatibility of domestic English 'welfare' principle and the ECtHR's approach to expressing children's relative position within an ECHR framework and balancing exercise. Because the 'welfare' principle does not apply to every situation in which a child is affected by a legal decision, it is clear a decision has been made that particular contexts raise more significant issues for affected children than others, hence their position needs to be prioritized. For example, we do not prioritize children's position when deciding whether to hear an application for a declaration of parentage.[144] Adults' interests are conceived as sufficiently critical here that the child's 'best interests' can only comprise an exception regarding when to hear the application, rather than the

---

[142] CRC, Art 24(1).   [143] ibid Art 24(3).
[144] Family Law Act 1986, c. 55, s 55A ('best interests' exception to application for declaration of parentage: '[T]he court may refuse to hear the application if it considers that the determination of the application

presumptive starting-point to the analysis. This serves as a useful illustration of the compatibility between equal consideration and treating children as a 'special case'.

To test the 'special case' argument against the current law, it is valuable to consider a typical scenario in which interests conflict: relocation of children when their parents are separated. In respect of the first, in the recent Court of Appeal decision in *Re M (Children)*,[145] King LJ reasoned that

> There is only one principle in relocation cases and that is that the welfare of the child is paramount; there are no presumptions and any guidance is exactly that, guidance, and, as such, designed to be of assistance (or not) depending on the circumstances of the case. It is unnecessary and inappropriate to trawl through the myriad of authorities in relation to relocation cases; after all in how many different ways is it necessary or helpful for it to be said that the welfare of the child is the paramount consideration?[146]

This seems suggestive of seeing children as a 'special case'. Yet cases are more difficult than dicta. Consider, for example, *Re S (A Child)*,[147] which concerned an appeal by a mother against an order restraining her from relocating internally with her nine-and-a-half-year-old daughter, who had Down's Syndrome, moderate learning difficulties, and other serious medical issues. The mother wanted to move there to be with her new partner, and had been suffering depression since initially being prevented from relocating. The Court had to ask whether the judge at first instance, His Honour Judge Ellis, was entitled to treat this as a 'truly exceptional' case[148] in which it would be justified not to permit the mother to relocate. The Court held that he was, and focused on the daughter's difficulty in understanding and coping with a reduction in contact with her father.

In his analysis of *Re S*, Herring argues that this analysis overlooks the very significant sacrifices the mother has made and would continue to make in caring for the child, and the consequent loss of support of her partner as a result of the dismissal. By contrast, the father, Herring reasons, has been free to remarry and move on with his life. Though it is noteworthy that, in the evidence before the County Court, both families were described as being 'desperate about the situation',[149] and the father was also said to have been unable to work because of the proceedings.[150]

Herring criticizes this decision for focusing entirely on the child's welfare at the moment, and failing to take a sufficiently long-term perspective.[151] But a view to the future is evident in Butler-Sloss P's reasoning that the case 'turns on the assessment of future risk to the emotional wellbeing of a delightful but seriously disadvantaged child'.[152] Moreover, the fact that the court also weighs in the balance the negative consequences for the father highlights that the court is not viewing the child's interests in isolated atomism. Finally, one could argue that *Re S* was wrongly decided on a

---

would not be in the best interests of the child.'). A further example where the child's interests are not paramount is the decision whether a child should give oral evidence in court: *Re W (Children)* [2010] UKSC 12, [24] (Lady Hale).

[145] [2016] EWCA Civ 1059.   [146] ibid [34] (King LJ).   [147] See Herring (n 118).
[148] *Re S* (n 145) [23] (Butler-Sloss P).   [149] ibid [30] (Butler-Sloss P).
[150] ibid [32] (Butler-Sloss P).   [151] Herring (n 115) 206.
[152] *Re S* (n 145) [37] (Butler-Sloss P).

conventional understanding of the 'welfare' principle, or it could also simply be a hard case in which, Butler-Sloss P reasons, '[t]here is no obviously correct decision' such that the judge 'was faced with an impossible task'.[153] Understood in this light, it is not clear that *Re S* evidences any difficulty with the 'paramountcy' of children's 'welfare', hence the possibility of treating children as a 'special case'.

More generally, it should be conceded that there could be a situation in which a relocation dispute is decided in a way that does not secure the ideal outcome for the child because of significant negative consequences for the affected adults, usually their parents. But this would not necessarily undermine seeing children as a 'special case', and prioritizing their interests as a matter of law. Firstly, it would be the extent of the adult's vulnerability that would lead to such an outcome, thus it would not be an assertion that adults' vulnerability has the same nature as children's. Secondly, whilst children's special vulnerability forms the justification for prioritizing children's interests, that is not the same as assuming it is a directly applicable criterion for weighing against other interests in determining individual disputes. Seeing children as uniquely vulnerable, therefore, is not at odds with recognizing adults' vulnerability.

B. Implications for future cases

If we accept this argument that children are a 'special case', what does it mean for how cases will be decided? Could this underpin the 'missing ... coherent vision'[154] that Appleton suggests is a critical difficulty for the recently launched work by the American Law Institute on the legal regulation of children.[155] What would be different? Do we need to be able to point to better outcomes? Or is it enough to render more justifiable apparent, existing inconsistencies? In other words, might we be able to explain that a number of alleged or assumed inconsistencies are not inconsistencies at all?

One key implication is that seeing children as a 'special case' obviates the need to resolve the difficult debate over how Article 3 of the CRC relates to domestic English law, most recently highlighted by the Supreme Court's decision in *SG*,[156] a case concerned with whether the 'benefit cap' was discriminatory against women because of the impact on single-parents, hence predominantly single-mother households. If children are a 'special case', there is a necessary domestic prioritization required. Thus, we do not need to determine either how Article 3 of the CRC fits with domestic law[157] or whether Article 3 itself views children's interests as a 'special case' either as written or

---

[153] ibid.   [154] Appleton (n 88) 529.
[155] The American Law Institute, 'Restatement on Children and the Law: Current Project' (ALI, 15 May 2015) <http://www.ali.org/index.cfm?fuseaction=projects.proj_ip&projectid=36>; The American Law Institute, 'The American Law Institute Launches Restatement on Children and the Law' (CISION PR Newswire, 15 May 2015) <http://www.prnewswire.com/news-releases/the-american-law-institute-launches-restatement-on-children-and-the-law-300044672.html>.
[156] *R (on the application of SG) and Others v Secretary of State for Work and Pensions* [2015] UKSC 16.
[157] ibid, whether compatibility with a child's Art 3 'best interests' simply replaces the usual proportionality stage of the analysis under Art 14 ECHR (Lord Reed and Lady Hale (dissenting)), whether Art 3 might be directly enforceable despite not being incorporated (Lord Kerr (dissenting)), or whether compatibility with Art 3 might be a political, rather than legal issue (Lord Carnwath).

as interpreted and applied by domestic courts and by the United Nations' Committee on the Rights of the Child.

If we accept that children are a 'special case', it may be that we need to categorize contexts in which children's interests at stake. Might Eekelaar's distinction between decisions 'affecting' children and decisions 'about' children be of assistance for this purpose?[158] Alternatively, might we need to distinguish cases involving fundamental human rights from other types of case? But, even if this were a useful starting-point, how would this intersect with any distinction we might wish to draw between disputes between parents and children, and other types of dispute involving children?

Conclusion

One potentially significant objection remains unexplored, namely that grounded in the idea of justice between generations.[159] Might this become a more pressing concern over time? If so, do we need to address it now when determining how to approach children's interests in particular?

The context for the preceding debate may be critical. It may be that recent academic convergence on equal treatment and debate over the need for prioritization within the 'welfare' principle is possible only because of the benefits secured by the politics—the rhetoric and language—of 'children's rights' since the CRC came into force. In this way, arguing for a move away from the language of prioritization *meaning* prioritization may suggest that the rhetoric of 'children's rights' and the 'welfare' principle have achieved much of their aims. But have they? If they have not, might there be reason to be cautious about suggesting any approach other than treating children as a 'special case'? Might there be very practical reasons for this perspective, irrespective of how one evaluates my own conceptual arguments?

Regardless of the conclusion one reaches on whether children are a 'special case', we need to have language that clearly fits with its meaning so as to ensure consistent interpretation and application. Otherwise, we risk fragmented, inconsistent developments in the legal regulation of children. This chapter has sought to show what theoretical basis we might have for the current language of prioritization. Whether the case made here is sufficient to sustain that language is another matter.

---

[158] J Eekelaar, 'The Role of the Best Interests Principle in Decisions Affecting Children and Decisions about Children' (2015) 23 International Journal of Children's Rights 3.

[159] Eekelaar, 'Beyond the Welfare Principle' (n 3).

PART IV
REGULATION AND INTERVENTION

12
Private Ordering in Family Law

Brian H. Bix[1]

I. Introduction

There has been a significant increase of private ordering in family law[2] across a range of topics[3] (though this remains an area of law where status rules remain highly significant).[4] This chapter will give an overview of some of those developments, and the changes in themes, values, and justifications that have accompanied the move from scarce and reluctantly permitted private ordering to more pervasive and occasionally encouraged private ordering. It will consider the philosophical arguments, past and present, relating to support for or opposition to private ordering, both arguments that support private ordering generally and those distinctive to the particular context of family agreements.

Section II briefly discusses some distinctions among different kinds of 'private ordering'. Section III gives an overview of past justifications for refusing or restricting private ordering in family law. Section IV gives examples of substantive agreements and their current legal treatment, while section V looks at procedural agreements. Section VI returns to arguments for and against private ordering in family matters, before concluding.

II. Private Ordering

The general idea of private ordering is that the parties set the terms of their relationship rather than the terms being set by the government (or some other external source).[5]

---

[1] Frederick W. Thomas Professor of Law and Philosophy. I am grateful for the comments and suggestions of Barbara Atwood, June Carbone, Lucinda Ferguson, Jill Elaine Hasday, and Mary Lyndon Shanley.

[2] On the proper understanding of 'family' and 'family law', see D Archard's chapter. Maine was analysing historical changes in family life when he famously wrote: 'We may say that the movement of the progressive societies has hitherto been a movement from Status to Contract.' HS Maine, *Ancient Law* (John Murray 1861) ch 5.

[3] The primary focus of this article will be private ordering in the state and federal law of the United States, though examples will also be drawn from other jurisdictions. (The author's impression is that many other jurisdictions are following the same trend of greater private ordering that one finds in the United States, if not as quickly or as broadly.) The private ordering in countries outside the US is discussed in many sources, including K Boele-Woelki, J Miles, and JM Scherpe (eds), *The Future of Family Property in Europe* (Intersentia 2011); JM Scherpe (ed), *Marital Agreements and Private Autonomy in Comparative Perspective* (Hart Publishing 2012); The Law Commission, *Matrimonial Property, Needs, and Agreements* (The Stationary Office 2014).

[4] See, eg, JE Hasday, *Family Law Reimagined* (Harvard 2014) 120–32.

[5] There are some forms of private ordering that are not of interest for the present inquiry (which is not to deny that they may be significant for other inquiries). Eg, it is 'private ordering' when an individual chooses whether to marry at all, and whom to marry. Also, individuals and families could be said to be choosing the

The focus of this chapter will be on *express agreements* that displace or supplement the (legal) terms that would otherwise apply to the contracting parties.

There is another sense of private ordering in family law that will not be discussed at length in the present chapter. This sort of private ordering involves parties avoiding state norms in favour of certain social (community) norms:[6] for example, some commentators have argued that many women from poorer and minority communities in the United States may be avoiding marriage to follow community norms that give mothers greater control over child custody (in comparison with judicially imposed norms and upper-class social norms that tend towards greater sharing of custody after a marriage or relationship ends).[7]

What is then meant here by 'private ordering'? As noted, the primary focus is not on the fact of private ordering (the mere fact of party agreement), but on the question of *state recognition* or *state enforcement* of private choices. To clarify by an example: spouses could expressly (or implicitly) agree to conduct their marriage in a certain way, or to make certain payments to one another during the marriage or after its dissolution, and then voluntarily abide by the terms of that agreement. This would be private ordering, but because it is private ordering that succeeds through ongoing voluntary cooperation, it is not relevant to the present *legal* analysis.[8] What this chapter is concerned with is whether or when these sorts of agreements will be *enforced by law* if one of the parties refuses to abide by its terms. One can thus think about agreements at different levels: (1) agreements between parties where the state is *not asked* to enforce the agreement;[9] (2) agreements where state enforcement is involved, but the terms being enforced involve only the parties to the agreement; and (3) agreements where state enforcement or state recognition involves (also) rights against the state or against third parties. On the distinction between the second and third levels, one could imagine, for example, at the second level, cohabitants agreeing to a marital-like status, but asking the courts only to enforce rights *inter se*, like provisions involving the division of property at the point that the parties stop cohabitating or requiring one cohabitant to make periodic compensatory payments to the other after the break-up; by contrast, the third level might involve allowing parties to agree to a marital or parental status that the state (and employers, schools and hospitals, etc) might then have a legal duty to recognize.[10]

---

legal terms that govern them when they move from one state/province or country to another, as any such move changes significantly the laws that apply (but it is rare for such moves to be motivated primarily by the applicable laws).

[6] On social norms and their relationship to public/legal norms, see, eg, S Macaulay, 'Non-Contractual Relations in Business: A Preliminary Study' (1963) 28 American Sociology Review 55; RC Ellickson, *Order Without Law: How Neighbors Settle Disputes* (Harvard 1991).

[7] J Carbone and N Cahn, 'The Triple System of Family Law' [2013] Michigan State Law Review 1185.

[8] Though, there of course would be many interesting questions that could be asked, eg, regarding why parties enter such agreements, and when and why they abide by them, etc.

[9] For an overview of the informal contracts of intimate life (and how they interact with enforceable contracts and other legal rights), see MM Ertman, *Love's Promises: How Formal and Informal Contracts Shape All Kinds of Families* (Beacon Press 2015); MM Ertman, 'Marital Contracting in a Post-Windsor World' (2015) 42 Florida State University Law Review 479.

[10] Compare FH Buckley and LE Ribstein, 'Calling a Truce in the Marriage Wars' [2001] University of Illinois Law Review 561 (encouraging *inter se* enforcement of same-sex quasi-marital agreements) with D Zalesne, 'The Contractual Family: The Role of the Market in Shaping Family Formations and Rights' (2015) 36 Cardozo Law Review 1027 (encouraging full enforcement of co-parenting agreements).

Additionally, where the focus is on which agreements to enforce, one can distinguish agreements regarding substantive outcomes (eg, who has parental rights or what the financial consequences would be of divorce), and agreements regarding procedure (eg, having certain types of disputes settled by arbitration, and perhaps by *religious* arbitration, or limiting the grounds for filing for divorce or the frequency with which modifications of custody or support orders can be sought). Substantive and procedural agreements will be treated separately below.[11]

III. Justifications for Enforcing or Refusing Enforcement of Agreements

A. Autonomy

The basic idea of autonomy is that an individual should be the author of his or her own life. The modern idea of autonomy goes back to Immanuel Kant, though Kant's view of autonomy was distinctly different from the modern view.[12] Autonomy is often connected to the idea of 'consent'; consent, in turn, is often analysed as something present to different degrees, depending on various factors, including knowledge of the nature and likely consequences of an action, and the availability of reasonable alternatives.[13] Arguments for enforcing agreements (in any area of law) are often tied to consent, by the idea that with contracts, distinctively (compare criminal law or the law of accidents), the standard being applied is one chosen by the parties, rather than being imposed on the parties by society—this is the idea, or ideal, of 'freedom of contract'.[14]

Knowing in advance that an agreement will be enforceable allows individuals to make choices: eg, if someone is only willing to marry (or only willing to marry *this person*) on certain financial terms (or with certain financial protections for children from a prior marriage), or a member of a same-sex couple is only willing to go forward with helping to raise a child if assurances are given that his or her parental rights will not be challenged later, then making such premarital or co-parenting agreements enforceable will allow the couples in question to go forward to marry and have children (respectively).[15]

And if all the contracting parties, with full information and not under duress, are willing to go forward, what reasons are there not to enforce the agreements? This 'rhetorical question' is sometimes presented as a conclusive argument; it is clearly *not* conclusive, but it reflects an argument that should not be lightly dismissed. As discussed

---

[11] It must be recognized that it is sometimes very difficult to distinguish or disentangle substance from procedure.

[12] JB Schneewind, *The Invention of Autonomy: A History of Modern Moral Philosophy* (Cambridge 1998) offers an excellent overview of the development of the idea of autonomy from before Kant, through Kant's ideas, to the modern view. For Kant, one acts autonomously only when one acts according to the moral law; acting according to desire or inclination (even benevolent inclinations) is not autonomous under his view.

[13] See, eg, BH Bix, 'Consent' in FG Miller and A Wertheimer (eds), *The Ethics of Consent* (Oxford 2010) 215, 252–56.

[14] See, eg, C Fried, *Contract as Promise* (2nd edn, Oxford 2015) 7–20; RE Barnett, 'A Consent Theory of Contract' (1986) 86 Columbia Law Review 269; RE Barnett, *Contracts* (Oxford 2010), 128–47.

[15] See, eg, *WW v HW* [2015] EWHC 1844 (Fam), paras 9, 47 (emphasizing autonomy as a reason to give weight to the parties' premarital agreement).

below, the potential countervailing reasons include protection of third parties (in particular, children), protection of vulnerable parties, and general societal interests.

One response to an autonomy argument is to complicate the analysis: speak of 'present selves' and 'future selves', and how enforcing agreements increases the autonomy of present selves at the expenses of future selves (who must act according to the choices of the now-past self, be forced to do so by the courts, or (more commonly) have to pay damages if they do not).[16] One could argue that there is also an autonomy interest in *not* being bound by the earlier choice, in being able to change one's mind.[17]

A second response to a consent/autonomy argument is that consent to family agreements is often faulty or incomplete, due to a variety of cognitive biases, bounded rationality, and the like.[18] The context of love, optimism, and trust in which such family agreements are often entered stops parties from being sufficiently reflective and self-protecting; and individuals are generally unable to think with sufficient care about the costs and benefits of waiving rights that will not have effects until the distant future. There are also frequently imbalances of bargaining power and sophistication, and the pressure of circumstances that can make parties' assent to these agreements less than fully voluntary.

B. Social benefit (utility)

While the terms of an agreement may have been chosen by the parties (or chosen by one party and acquiesced to by the other), an agreement is an enforceable contract only when the state offers its own resources to enforce the terms. Thus, there is a line of analysis that emphasizes the question of whether society is sufficiently benefited to justify enforcing a particular promise or agreement (or a particular *category of* promises or agreements).[19]

One can start from the view that enforcing agreements is presumptively for the common good, in that (it is claimed) parties would not enter agreements if they did not think they were better-off agreeing than not agreeing, and the promise of enforcement is what allows parties to make reliable commitments regarding their future behaviour. Also, as discussed earlier, there may be some marriages, births, and adoptions that would not occur if parties could not make enforceable agreements (premarital agreements, co-parenting agreements, open adoption agreements, etc), and that such marriages, births, and adoptions are generally things to be encouraged.

However, the common good may not always argue for enforcement. There are vulnerable third parties who should be protected: agreements between adults should

---

[16] In states that authorize gestational surrogacy agreements, one common requirement is that the surrogate be a woman who has given birth before. Eg, Illinois Compiled Statutes, 750 ILCS s 47/20(2). The justification for this is that women who have not given birth before will not know how much their future selves may think differently about the baby they are carrying.

[17] D Kimel, 'Personal Autonomy and Change of Mind in Promise and in Contract' in G Klass, G Letsas, and P Saprai (eds), *Philosophical Foundations of Contract Law* (Oxford 2014) 96.

[18] These are of course limitations to apply to decision making and agreements generally, not just in family law. See generally RH Thaler, *Misbehaving: The Making of Behavioral Economics* (W Norton & Company 2015).

[19] MR Cohen, 'The Basis of Contract' (1933) 46 Harvard Law Review 553.

not be enforced if they would lead, directly or indirectly, to harm for minor children. Also, as indicated in the prior section, there may be parties who sign agreements that are not in their best interests, but sign under pressure, who are misled, or who simply have no reasonable alternatives. And while most marriages, births, and adoptions work to the common good, not all do, and there could be arguments (eg) that a marriage on extremely one-sided financial terms is worse than no marriage at all (especially if there are indications that the person pressing for the extremely one-sided terms might have been willing to go forward with the marriage even on more reasonable terms).

C. Privileged sphere

John Eekelaar argued that family should be treated as a 'privileged sphere', 'free from institutional constraint and censure'.[20] If there is intrinsic value to marital or family life, what implications does that have for the choice the state has to make regarding whether to enforce or to refuse enforcement to agreements that purport to modify marital or parental terms?

At first glance, the value of government non-interference in the family does not seem an apt argument, as these are not circumstances where the government is telling individuals how to behave; to the contrary, it is the contracting parties who are coming to the state asking it to enforce the agreements the parties themselves have previously entered. However, the state's willingness to enforce these sorts of agreements obviously affects family life, and enforcement encourages more parties to enter agreements.

This analysis may work simply as a reminder that there is no real option of non-interference.[21] When agreements are not enforced, the parties are left to the default terms already set by the state. And refusals to 'intervene' leave parties to the imbalances of (physical, emotional, psychological, commercial, or legal) power already existing in the relationship. This in turn is not to imply that there is never good reason to refuse to enforce agreements, only that this decision should probably not be done on the basis that the alternative would be a situation of government 'non-intervention'.

D. Dignity and exploitation

All human beings have intrinsic dignity and worth, and some activities undermine or demean that dignity. Some argue that activities that are contrary to human dignity should be prohibited, or at least not encouraged through state recognition or contract enforcement, even if everyone involved in the activity or agreement in question

---

[20] J Eekelaar, *Family Law and Personal Life* (Oxford 2006), 82. A similar notion in US law is often discussed under the rubric of 'family privacy', with the usual case cited being *McGuire v McGuire* 59 NW2d 336 (Neb 1953).
[21] See FE Olsen, 'The Myth of State Intervention in the Family' (1985) 18 University of Michigan Journal of Law Reform 835.

consents (with full knowledge and despite having reasonable alternatives[22]). For many of these agreements, the argument is related to issues of commodification—that it is undignified or shameful (or just contrary to the long-term common good) to have certain items or practices made a matter of market sale.[23] The argument often comes up in debates about enforcing agreements relating to egg donation, sperm donation, and surrogacy.[24] With some extension, one might argue that concerns about dignity might also be relevant to the decision whether to enforce extremely one-sided premarital and marital agreements.

The related concept of exploitation is one that many people think they understand, and it reflects a judgment regularly made (that a relationship or transaction is 'exploitative'), but it is notoriously difficult to articulate the meaning and criteria of the concept. Exploitation is generally equated with taking undue advantage of the vulnerable. Some commentators would have the moral judgment (whether something should be criticized as 'exploitation' or not) turn on baseline issues: does the offer given to the vulnerable party lower that party's baseline (starting point)?; the offer, 'Do this or I will hurt you' is different from the offer, 'I will pay you $100 if you do this'.[25] By contrast, the everyday use of the label, 'exploitation', as form of criticism, often seems to entail only some combination of an imbalance of sophistication and bargaining power on one hand, and (what appear to be) one-sided terms on other.

One difficulty with the concept and its application is that market conditions may lead to vulnerable parties entering agreements that appear to be one-sided but which are in fact as good as could be expected in that market at that time. For the same reason, the alternative to one-sided transactions may be no transactions at all—that is, market conditions are such that no one would be willing to enter agreements (eg, loans, sales of goods, employment, apartment rental) with the vulnerable on fairer or more favourable terms.

Arguments about exploitation in family agreements are often connected to arguments about dignity and commodification. A recent example in the United States has an interesting twist, in an argument that an individual might be exploited by being paid *too much*: the American Society for Reproductive Medicine established guidelines that tried to *limit* the amount of money egg donors are paid, in part based on the argument that very large payments would lead to coercive exploitation of poor women, who might lie and make bad decisions (affecting their health) because of the lure of large amounts of money.[26]

---

[22] MC Nussbaum has argued that whether we should respect the choice to do certain activities should depend in part on whether the person in question had reasonable alternatives. MC Nussbaum, *Sex and Social Justice* (Oxford 1999) 276–98.
[23] See, eg, MJ Radin, *Contested Commodities* (Harvard 1996).
[24] In other contexts, the examples range from prostitution to the sale of body organs to dwarf tossing.
[25] See, eg, A Wertheimer, *Exploitation* (Princeton 1996).
[26] T Lewin, 'Egg Donors Challenge Pay Rates, Saying They Shortchange Women' *New York Times* (New York, 16 October 2015). A similar argument is sometimes raised about surrogates from third-world countries: that the large amount of money offered (relative to the women's needs and relative to other opportunities) could coerce the women into becoming surrogates despite the health risks. See, eg, F Joelving, 'Surrogate Mothers in India Unaware of Risks' Reuters (2 March 2015).

E. Past attitudes—against private ordering

Private ordering in family law matters was, until recently, generally discouraged. The moral and policy justifications that were offered often involved claims that important individual and social goods were assured by the terms of marriage, parenthood, etc, set by the state, so that any modification by the parties would harm those significant goods. There was also a concern (still present today) about protecting vulnerable third parties, in particular, children (though women—as wives and mothers—were also sometimes considered as a class to be vulnerable parties, unable to fully protect themselves). Family law agreements were thus frequently refused enforcement under the rubric, 'void as against public policy'. As noted, many of these considerations are still present in the evaluation of when family agreements should be enforced, but blanket bans on enforcement are giving way to either case-by-case analyses or guidelines for determining when agreements are consistent with the public concerns.

IV. Substantive Private Ordering

A. Terms of marriage

Many of the best-known forms of private ordering in contemporary family law involve agreements partners enter just before marriage, or during marriage, that alter the financial terms that would apply to the parties under state law at the time of the parties' divorce (eg, division of property or alimony), or at the time that one spouse dies (eg, spousal elective share[27]). For a long time, agreements that purported to waive or alter rights upon divorce were treated, almost universally, as void because they were contrary to public policy. (Agreements altering or waiving rights at the death of a spouse were enforced in some jurisdictions under some circumstances.[28]) The current law in the United States makes these sorts of agreements in principle enforceable,[29] at least in connection with the topics of alimony, property division, and elective share, with states varying significantly in the extent to which these agreements must meet requirements of procedural or substantive fairness beyond those that are applied to conventional commercial agreements.[30] And many states vary the standards applied to premarital and marital agreements (agreements purporting to alter rights at divorce or the death of the other spouse, but entered after the parties are already married), with greater procedural and substantive fairness requirements imposed on marital agreements. Additionally, states generally will not enforce provisions of premarital or marital agreements relating

---

[27] Under the laws of many US states, a spouse can choose between whatever rights he or she has under a deceased spouse's will, or a set fraction (often one third) of the deceased spouse's estate.

[28] In Anglo-American law, the recognition of such agreements goes back to the English Statute of Uses of 1535, which allowed a woman to waive her dower rights (her right to receive a one-third interest in her husband's estate upon his death).

[29] In England, *Radmacher v Granatino* [2010] UKSC 42 [75] created a somewhat different standard: 'The court should give effect to a nuptial agreement that is freely entered into by each party with a full appreciation of its implications unless in the circumstances prevailing it would not be fair to hold the parties to their agreement.' For the standard (as of 2012) in other countries, see, eg, Scherpe (ed), (n 3).

[30] States also vary regarding whether fairness is judged only at the time of formation or also at the time of enforcement.

to children—child custody, child support, rights of relocation by the custodial parent, etc. Finally, courts are generally reluctant to enforce agreements that entail paying for care or for other work in the home,[31] or agreements that create penalties for marital misbehaviour.[32]

The cautious and somewhat suspicious legal treatment of premarital and marital agreements is in sharp contrast to the legal treatment of separation agreements, another form of private ordering. Separation agreements are agreements entered when divorce is imminent or at least jointly contemplated. Such agreements set the financial (property division, alimony, child support) and child custody terms of the marital dissolution. While these agreements are, by statute or case-law, subject to judicial review for reasonableness and fairness, in general practice courts generally enforce the terms agreed upon by the parties without significant review or revision.[33] The sharp difference in treatment of these different sorts of agreements indicates that what may be at stake is less a desire to exclude parties from (enforceably) setting the terms of their marriages and divorces and more a matter of procedure—in the sense of the timing of the negotiations. When parties are about to divorce or have at least already begun the process, we think that they are in a position to think clearly about the consequences of their agreements. By contrast, those about to marry or at an early stage of marriage are less likely to be able to imagine that they will get divorced, let alone to think clearly about what they would want or need should that occur.[34] Additionally, separation agreements have the beneficial consequences of saving judicial resources—setting the terms of dissolution by agreement rather than by the court after a trial—reducing the acrimony of divorce, and perhaps creating terms the parties are more likely to follow, because they helped to determine them.

There is a limited sort of private ordering that occurs when the state creates a small 'menu of options' for structuring marital rights, the parties are free to choose among those alternatives, and either the parties are forced to make an express choice, or one option is the 'default' that is applied if no express agreement to the contrary is made. For example, in France, partners can enter an agreement either just before marriage or during marriage regarding the treatment of properties acquired before or during the marriage (the 'matrimonial regime').[35] In the United States, three states have the option of 'covenant marriage'. Under this legal alternative (which varies slightly across

---

[31] See, eg, *Borelli v Brusseau* 12 Cal App 4th 47, 16 Cal Rptr 16 (1993); *Miller v Miller*, 42 NW 641 (Iowa 1889).

[32] See, eg, *Diosdado v Diosdado* 118 Cal Rptr 2d 494, 97 Cal App 4th 470 (Cal App 2002); In re *Marriage of Cooper* 769 NW2d 582 (Iowa 299).

[33] The doctrinal law may indicate that the judge is to be deferential only to the financial terms of property division and alimony, and is to review critically the terms relating to the children of the marriage (custody and child support); however, it is widely understood that child-related terms are also generally approved with minimal review, unless one of the parties changes his or her mind and challenges the agreement that party had signed prior to its presentation to the court for approval. RH Mnookin and L Kornhauser, 'Bargaining in the Shadow of the Law: The Case of Divorce' (1979) 88 Yale Law Journal 950.

[34] A reluctance to enforce premarital and marital agreements may also be a way to discourage the sorts of discussions and negotiations needed to create such agreements, negotiations that may themselves undermine the marriage.

[35] W Pintens, 'Marital Agreements and Private Autonomy in France and Belgium', in Scherpe (ed), (n 3) 68.

the three adopting states),[36] couples about to marry or who have already married can opt for a more binding form of marriage, where divorce is generally only available on fault grounds or after a significantly longer waiting period. Covenant marriage also requires premarital and pre-divorce counselling.[37]

With both covenant marriage and the French matrimonial regime, the state has offered alternatives that were both fully delineated and authorized for all; whatever choice a couple made would be accepted and (absent extraordinary circumstances) not subject to questioning later. This is in contrast to the treatment of premarital and marital agreements in many American states, where there are no 'safe harbors', no forms of agreement that are guaranteed enforceable; all are potentially subject to challenge on grounds of substantive or procedural fairness, with the success of the challenge turning on the specific facts of the negotiation of the agreement, the factual context in which the agreement was signed, and (sometimes) the particular subsequent developments.

B. Parental rights

Agreements relating to parental rights vary widely: they include agreements about open adoption, surrogacy, co-parenting agreements, and gamete-donor agreements.

'Open Adoptions' (also known as post-adoption 'contact agreements') involve an agreement between a birth parent (or birth parents) of a child being adopted and the person(s) adopting that child. The default legal standard in the United States is for adoptive parents, upon adoption, to obtain all of the legal rights and duties of parenthood while the birth parents lose all of their rights and obligations. And as the process of adoption in most American states traditionally involved the birth parent(s) and the adopting parent(s) having no information about one another, the usual result was one of there being no contact between birth parent(s) and adopted child. This strict confidentiality is no longer universally the case. Open adoption involves an agreement between the parties to an adoption to maintain some level of contact between birth parent(s) and adopted child. The motivations for these agreements vary: sometimes it reflects a shared belief among the parties that it is in children's best interests to be in contact with their genetic parents; sometimes it reflects a compromise, whereby a parent will only give up a child for adoption if continued contact is allowed; sometimes it is a compromise imposed by the state on a parent when the threatened alternative would be full termination of that person's parental rights.[38] For a long time, open adoption agreements were unenforceable in all states (they remain unenforceable in a number of states), as being 'contrary to public policy', the public policy that proclaims that confidentiality and 'clean breaks' are the best approach to adoption. Even as a growing number of states are willing to recognize (enforce) these post-adoption contact agreements,

---

[36] See Arizona Rev Stat ss 25-901 to 25-906; Arkansas Code Ann ss 9-22-801 to 9-11-811; Louisiana Rev Stat Ann ss 9:272 to 9:276.

[37] In the states that have covenant marriage—to the surprise of both supporters and opponents—only a very small percentage of couples have chosen it.

[38] C Sanger, 'Acquiring Children Contractually: Relational Contracts at Work at Home' in J Braucher, J Kidwell, and WC Whitford (eds), *Revisiting the Contracts Scholarship of Stewart Macaulay: On the Empirical and the Lyrical* (Hart 2013) 289, 298–312.

they tend to keep such agreements under regulatory supervision: generally requiring judicial approval (based on an assessment of the best interests of the child involved), and subject to judicial modification (under the same standard).[39]

Surrogacy agreements involve a woman agreeing to carry a child for its intended parent(s) while waiving her own parental claims. A small number of states allow this waiver to be enforced, at least if certain procedural and substantive safeguards have been met.[40] A larger number of states do not allow a waiver of parental rights prior to the birth of the child, the surrogacy agreement may be enforceable only in part, and the intended parent(s) and the surrogate need to go through a formal adoption process after the birth of the child. A few states make surrogacy arrangements entirely forbidden and potentially subject to criminal sanctions. There is clearly an unease with this seeming sale of gestational services and parental rights, as well as doubts about the full consent of the women who agree to be surrogates.[41] Mary Lyndon Shanley's chapter has argued forcefully that claims of contract (volition, intention) in surrogacy arrangements must give way, at least in part, to claims based on caregiving: in particular, that a gestational surrogate who carried a child to term has a parental claim that should not be negated by a contract she signed purporting to waive her parental rights.[42]

Co-parenting agreements are agreements by which parties agree that each will respect (not challenge) the parental rights of the other. Such agreements were most common among same-sex couples in jurisdictions where same-sex couples could not marry or enter any other marriage-like status; for such couples often only one of the partners would be a genetic or adoptive parent for a child the couple is raising, while the other partner might have no legal grounds (other than a co-parenting agreement) to claim parental rights. Opposite-sex unmarried couples also sometimes entered co-parenting agreements (often as a requirement established by IVF clinics for going forward with assisted reproduction treatments). Most courts have not been receptive to enforcing co-parenting agreements.[43] As with surrogacy, the basic idea is that parental status is not something to be given (or taken away) lightly, and not a matter to be delegated to party choice:[44] there are strict legal rules for who is and who is not a legal parent, and parental status and its prerogatives are constitutionally protected.[45] Those

---

[39] See, eg, Washington Statutes Ann s 26.33.295; US Department of Health & Human Services, Administration for Children & Families, 'Postadoption Contract Agreements between Birth and Adoptive Families' (*Child Welfare Information Gateway*, November 2014), available at https://www.childwelfare.gov/topics/systemwide/laws-policies/statutes/cooperative/, accessed 24 October 2017.

[40] See, eg, The Illinois Gestational Surrogacy Act, Illinois Compiled Statutes, 750 ILCS ss 47/1–47/75.

[41] These concerns and doubts are summarized in re *Baby M* 537 A2d 1227 (NJ 1988). For a more supportive view of surrogacy, and the enforceability of (gestational) surrogacy agreements, see *Johnson v Calvert* 5 Cal 4th 84, 851 P2d 776 (1993).

[42] See ML Shanley's chapter.

[43] See, eg, *TF v BL* 813 NE2d 1244 at 1251 (Mass 2004): '"Parenthood by contract" is not the law in Massachusetts, and, to the extent that plaintiff and the defendant entered into an agreement, express or implied, to coparent a child, that agreement is unenforceable' (footnotes omitted).

[44] cf *ST* 467 SW3d 720 (Tex App 2015) (parties cannot enter binding stipulation on paternity of child); *TF v BL* 813 NE2d 1244 (Mass 2004) (parties cannot enter binding agreement to create parental status or parental/child support obligation).

[45] See *Troxel v Granville* 530 US 67 (2000) (third-party visitation statute interfered with parental rights to determine with whom a child spent time); *Santosky v Kramer*, 455 US 745 (1982) (heightened standard of proof required to terminate parental rights); *Stanley v Illinois*, 405 US 645 (1972) (states cannot create conclusive presumption that unmarried fathers are incompetent parents).

courts that have recently given some weight to such agreements have often done so indirectly: eg, seeing the agreement as evidence that the legal parent had waived his or her legal rights to exclude the other party from contact with the child in question.[46]

With gamete donation, most American states have laws supporting or encouraging sperm donation by holding the sperm donors to have neither legal rights nor legal obligations in any child resulting from the donation.[47] This is the result that is assumed to be preferred by most donors and most people using sperm donors. However, what if the relevant parties *want* the sperm donor to have an ongoing role in the life of the resulting child?[48] Many states (by legislation or case-law) have held that this can be done by express agreement (though many have required the agreement to be in writing, and have refused enforcement categorically for agreements not in writing[49]). In this sort of case, it is likely less a case of the state preferring one arrangement to another, as believing that there are good public-policy reasons for both outcomes (excluding sperm donors from parental rights or affirming the parental rights of such donors), and requesting some clear indication, to guide courts and limit litigation, as to which outcome the parties intended.[50]

C. Division of embryos

Couples who use the in-vitro fertilization (IVF) process to have children often create more embryos than they use (with the idea that these embryos will be available if the earlier efforts to have a child with created embryos do not succeed). Who controls the disposition of unused embryos if the couple breaks-up? IVF clinics now, as a matter of course, require couples going through IVF to agree ahead of time, in writing, regarding disposition of the embryos in case of a break-up (or the death of one of the partners). While some courts have simply enforced the agreements as written,[51] a few state courts have refused to enforce the terms of such agreements if one of the parties subsequently changed his or her mind.[52] As mentioned above, there is a sense in which enforcing current preferences rather than prior agreed preferences is still a protection of autonomy and party choice. However, our legal system (and our social norms of promising) generally gives priority to past commitments over current preferences, as a way of allowing parties to plan and to rely on others. Where we do *not* make commitments enforceable,

---

[46] Eg, *Mason v Dwinnell* 660 SE2d 58 (NC App 2008).
[47] Sperm donor statutes are also generally applied to egg donor agreements. This approach to gamete donation is an exception to the usual preference of having both genetic parents having a (legal) tie to their genetic child (including the legal duty of support), an exception created to encourage a structure and process that would help infertile couples have children. Where parties outside the gamete-donation process attempt by agreement to excuse a genetic parent from parental duties, the courts usually refuse to enforce that agreement.
[48] As J Carbone pointed out to me, what some intended parents want is for the sperm donor to have a role in the child's life, but a role significantly short of full parental rights. I am aware of no cases where the state has legally enforced such an arrangement among the parties.
[49] See in re *KMH* 169 P3d 1025 (Kan 2007).
[50] At least one court has held that a sperm donor could become the child's legal parent based on post-birth behaviour. *Jason P v Danielle S* 226 Cal App 4th 167 (Ct App 2014), review denied, 30 July 2014.
[51] Eg, *Kass v Kass* 696 NE2d 174 (NY 1998).
[52] See, eg, In re *Marriage of Witten* 672 NW2d 768 (Iowa 2003); *JB v MB*, 783 A2d 707 (NJ 2001).

it is usually because of some combination of distrust of the consent given or concern about the importance of the choice. Thus, in many states, one cannot make a decision to give up a child for adoption until some number of days after the child's birth,[53] and that commitment may be freely revocable for an additional period of time.[54]

V. Procedural Private Ordering

Sometimes agreements do not concern (directly) the substantive rights of the parties, but rather the procedure, forum, applicable law, or timing of enforcement. Such agreements about process can be an agreement entered at the time a dispute is being resolved, or it can be a term in a prior contract determining the process to be used for a later conflict about the interpretation or application of that contract.[55]

Parties can agree, either long in advance or at the time of a dispute, to resolve their disputes through binding arbitration rather than through the courts. There are growing numbers of cases in the US,[56] England,[57] and elsewhere, relating to the arbitration of family disputes. Also, many US states allow parties in their separation agreements to create binding agreements that alter (eg) how frequently custody decisions can be challenged,[58] whether alimony awards can be altered,[59] and even the threshold standard that needs to be met for altering child custody.[60]

It is also becoming increasingly common for premarital agreements (and marital agreements) to include choice of law provisions.[61] These provisions may direct a court to the law of a state (or country) whose rules are more receptive to enforcement or more developed in connection with these sorts of agreements. A recent New York case, *Ofer v Sirota*, involved not a choice of law provision, but a choice of forum provision: a New York court enforced a provision in a premarital agreement requiring the couple to bring any divorce action in an Israeli court.[62]

---

[53] Eg, Massachusetts Code Chap 210, s 2 (no valid consent by birth mother until the fourth day after birth).

[54] Comparable concerns about consent can also be found in more conventional (commercial) commitments, eg, when commercial contracts entered for door-to-door sales—with the suspicion of unfair pressure tactics in the sale—can be freely revoked for a certain period of time.

[55] A term can set the process for resolving disputes arising from the agreement itself, as a premarital agreement might require arbitration or the application of a particular state's law to resolve questions about the proper application of the premarital agreement's terms. Alternatively, the process might refer to an entirely separate dispute, as a premarital agreement might require that any divorce petition be filed in a particular forum, as in the *Ofer v Sirota* case, discussed in the text.

[56] In 2016, the Uniform Law Commission promulgated the Uniform Family Arbitration Act. http://www.uniformlaws.org/Act.aspx?title=Family%20Law%20Arbitration%20Act, accessed 24 October 2017. A number of states already have legislation directed specifically to family law arbitration. See, eg, North Carolina Family Law Arbitration Act, *North Carolina Statutes* ss 50–41 to 50–62.

[57] See, eg, *S v S* [2014] EWHC 7 (Fam); L Ferguson, 'Arbitral Awards: A Magnetic Factor of Determinative Importance–Yet Not to Be Rubber-Stamped?' (2014) 37 Journal Social Welfare & Family Law 99.

[58] Eg, Minnesota Statutes s 518.18(a).

[59] See, eg, Connecticut General Statutes s 46b-86 (authorizing no-modification provision relating to alimony and child support obligations).

[60] See, eg, Minnesota Statutes s 518.18(e).

[61] *Hussemann v Hussemann* 847 NW2d 219 (Iowa 2014) (choice of law provision for marital agreement enforced).

[62] *Ofer v Sirota* 116 AD3d 509, 984 NYS 2d 312 (2014).

Sometimes the premarital agreements have terms of importance to the religious community of the couple—eg, *mahr* provisions of an Islamic marriage contract, or certain provisions of a Jewish *ketubah*. *Ketubahs* may include provisions agreeing to bring marital disputes to a Jewish arbitration panel.[63] (Under United States law, the attempted enforcement of religious terms or the orders of religious tribunals may raise constitutional freedom-of-religion issues that are unrelated to the policy and philosophical concerns of this chapter.)

VI. Themes and Concerns

The argument for private ordering is a general one: that parties (if competent adults) are in the best position to know what is in their interests and to protect those interests. What family structures work best for some, or even for most, may not work best for all. Additionally, the (libertarian) argument is that if parties want to enter an (enforceable) arrangement on terms others may consider unfair, one-sided, or even oppressive, the parties should still have the option to go forward on their chosen terms.

As noted earlier, the traditional response to private ordering in family law had been to argue that family law is special (in certain ways), and because it is special, private ordering should not be allowed or should be restricted and regulated in significant ways. While there are still concerns distinctive to family law (on one hand, the state interest in protecting children; on the other hand, a concern that some parties about to marry may be too much in love to be appropriately self-protective), today many of the concerns raised are ones that are raised *generally* about private ordering, rather than concerns distinctive to family law. The worries about agreements between spouses, or between birth parents and adoptive parents, are comparable to the concerns raised about agreements between businesses and consumers, employers and employees, and so on. The concerns are that agreements can be oppressive and exploitative, and that one party to the agreement has neither good knowledge of the terms nor any real choice about whether or not to agree to those terms. The debate about family law agreements thus parallels current debates about regulation or enforcement of pre-dispute (mandatory) arbitration provisions[64] and boilerplate provisions generally.[65] Government has duties to protect the vulnerable, and an interest in encouraging fair terms. At a minimum, courts are reluctant to see themselves as complicit in injustice.[66]

---

[63] Under the Jewish tradition, a religious divorce can only be given by the husband to his wife. Without the religious divorce document (a 'get'), the wife cannot remarry under Jewish law, even if the couple has obtained a divorce in the secular courts. Some of the *ketubah* provisions agreeing to dispute resolution by a religious arbitration panel are there so that the panel can order the husband to give his wife the needed *get*.

[64] J Resnik, 'Diffusing Disputes: The Public in the Private of Arbitration, the Private in Courts, and the Erasure of Rights' (2015) 124 Yale Law Journal 2808.

[65] Eg, MJ Radin, *Boilerplate: The Fine Print, Vanishing Rights, and the Rule of Law* (Princeton 2012); NS Kim, *Wrap Contracts: Foundations and Ramifications* (Oxford 2013).

[66] One can structure the same argument another way, related to the earlier discussion of instrumental justification: that court enforcement is the government's way to offer significant public resources for enforcing private agreements, and this is (or should be) done only where the types of agreements contribute, directly or indirectly, to the public good. Where the agreements are of a type that they tend to detract from the public good, the state properly refuses to use its resources for enforcement.

Still, the concerns will vary across different types of family agreements. As already noted, the primary concern with premarital agreements arguably is cognitive bias ('bounded rationality'), in that parties about to be married (especially those about to marry for the first time) may not be able to think rationally about that marriage ending in divorce, and the consequences of such a divorce.[67] The primary concern of marital agreements or post-adoption contact agreements ('open adoption') is arguably coercion.[68] Of course, what counts as (unacceptable) coercion may differ across cultures as well as across individual circumstances. While some people might think that it cannot be coercive for an individual to choose who to marry *and* to have that decision turn in part on the acceptance of certain terms and conditions, for others, the refusal to marry except on one party's (one-sided) terms could appear highly coercive—eg, (a) to a pregnant partner who cares deeply that the child be born within wedlock;[69] (b) to an immigrant whose ability to stay in a country turns on whether he or she is able to marry her citizen-partner;[70] or (c) a partner who would be deeply embarrassed by having to cancel a wedding after the invitations had already been sent or perhaps after some of the guests had already arrived from out of town.[71] There may also be many cases where a party is so desperate to maintain a marriage or to complete an adoption that a threat to leave the marriage or not go forward with an adoption unless certain terms are agreed to would be comparably coercive.

Many family agreements are meant to control events and effects many years into the future. The concern of cognitive bias/bounded rationality is that we tend to be very poor at evaluating the likelihood of certain events—eg, individuals just starting a job not guessing the *likelihood* that they may be terminated (with or without cause) at a later point, and individuals about to marry (who have not been divorced before) miscalculating the chances that the coming marriage may end in divorce (and the likelihood that during the marriage they may give up their career to take care of children). Part of the concern with (eg) premarital agreements is that parties will not be sufficiently

---

[67] In *MacLeod v MacLeod* [2008] UKPC 64, the Privy Council [36], [37] took the opposite view—that there is *less* to worry about in marital agreements than in premarital agreements. However, there is little analysis or argument grounding the court's conclusion in *MacLeod*. More interesting is Emma Hitching's empirical finding that 'a solid proportion of post-nuptial agreements are really pre-nuptial agreements that have run out of time'. E Hitchings, 'From Pre-Nups to Post-Nups: Dealing with Marital Property Agreements' [2009] Family Law 1056, 1060. She also notes, however, that this is based on a small sample size, and that a number of the marital agreements were of a different form: what some commentators call 'reconciliation agreements', 'where the ongoing status of a marriage is dependent on one party signing a post-nuptial agreement'. ibid. Reconciliation agreements clearly raise the potential for coercion mentioned above.

[68] American Law Institute, *Principles of the Law of Family Dissolution: Analysis and Recommendations* (LexisNexis 2002) 37–39; Sanger, 'Acquiring Children Contractually: Relational Contracts at Work at Home' (n 38) 298–312. A marital agreement is like (in the commercial context) an effort to modify an existing commercial relationship; there is the question of whether the request to modify has been made for a good reason ('in good faith') and whether the modification was only agreed to under duress. See, eg, Uniform Commercial Code s 2-209; *Roth Steel Products v Sharon Steel Corp* 705 F2d 134 (6th Cir 1983).

[69] See, eg, *ex parte Williams* 617 So2d 1033 (Ala 1992) (where a woman was pregnant at the time of signing, importance of legitimacy to her may ground conclusion of coercion sufficient to make the premarital agreement unenforceable).

[70] See, eg, *Holler v Holler* 612 SE2d 469 (SC App 2005) (premarital agreement unenforceable in part because of pressure on woman who would have had to leave the US if she did not marry).

[71] See, eg, *Zimmie v Zimmie* 464 NE2d 142 (Ohio 1984) (premarital agreement not enforced; wife first learned of agreement on the day of the wedding).

protective of their long-term interests, and part of the concern reflects the view that courts *should* respond to the equities of what has happened.[72]

Family law agreements thus commonly raise the issue about whether it is better to have bright-line rules or flexible standards, and the tension between predictability (*ex ante*) and doing justice between the parties (*ex post*). In theory, it would be valuable for courts to have a more nuanced understanding (eg) of the imbalances of bargaining power that occur both at the time of entering agreements and at the time of enforcement,[73] but one might also be concerned about the ability of courts to make such judgments, and the way such enquiries would likely undermine the value of the agreements by reducing the predictability of enforcement.[74]

In some ways, parties to family law agreements are in better positions than the parties to conventional commercial (standard form) agreements regarding doubtful terms. Many family agreements are drafted especially for the particular occasion,[75] rather than being an 'off the rack' boilerplate agreement used in dozens, hundreds, or perhaps thousands of similar agreements. Also, in many family agreements the terms are created or altered based on the input of both parties, again in contrast to the 'take-it-or-leave-it' nature of most consumer and employment agreements. And unlike sale, employment, lease, or franchise agreements, where the primary focus is elsewhere (on the money terms), and parties understandably do not focus on the provisions waiving rights in case of termination or dispute, in the family agreements discussed the waiver of rights is usually salient.

In general, different concerns are in play when parties wish to modify default terms in a relationship status in contrast to when they are trying to enter or mimic a status they are otherwise excluded from. A state or country that has a strongly held public policy about (say) excluding same-sex couples from marriage or parenthood,[76] or refusing recognition to 'group marriages', may resist enforcing private agreements whose purpose and effect is to circumvent that public policy by mimicking the withheld status.

The objectives of procedural agreements are often sharply different than those for substantive provisions.[77] There is a sense, eg, with a premarital agreement or a post-adoption contact (open-adoption) agreement, that there is a clear outcome to which the parties are consenting, while the objective with a chosen procedure or forum may

---

[72] Eg, J Herring, *Relational Autonomy and Family Law* (Springer 2014) 35–41.

[73] See S Thompson, *Prenuptial Agreements and the Presumption of Free Choice: Issues of Power in Theory and Practice* (Hart Publishing 2015).

[74] By contrast, the *Law Commission* (n 3) recommended legislation that would create 'qualifying nuptial agreements'—agreements that, if they met certain procedural requirements would be applied, though only after the financial needs of both partners and any children had been met. (As of this writing, no legislation supporting this proposal has been passed.)

[75] This is especially true for marital or premarital agreements, likely less frequently true for the surrogacy, gamete donation, and IVF (embryo division and co-parenting) agreements, which may be standard forms provided by clinics for their customers.

[76] Eg, the Ohio State Constitution (art XV, s 11) stated: 'Only a union between one man and one woman may be a marriage valid in or recognized by this state and its political subdivisions. This state and its political subdivisions shall not create or recognize a legal status for relationships of unmarried individuals that intends to approximate the design, qualities, significance or effect of marriage.' Of course, that state constitutional provision was overridden by the United States Supreme Court decision holding that same-sex couples have a federal constitutional right to marry. *Obergefell v Hodges*, 135 S Ct 2584 (2015).

[77] Ferguson, 'Arbitral Awards' (n 57).

be more focused on a more confidential process or having a decision-maker with a particular kind of competence (different from the kind of competence one finds in the local judiciary).[78] It may thus be harder to discern if and when the terms are one-sided or otherwise unfair.

VII. Conclusion

As William Eskridge argued, American family law is moving from a view that there is a single right or best way to structure family life towards a view that accepts that there is a plurality of different family forms, and which form is best may vary from family to family.[79] This change entails a move from exclusively mandatory rules to a greater use of default rules combined with standards for when and how those default rules can be modified.[80]

As the issues of how much private ordering should be regulated or deferred to remains controversial in general commercial life, it is not surprising that controversies about private ordering persist in family law. The move towards greater private ordering in family law has been uneven (across jurisdictions and across topics within jurisdictions). The belief that parties should be able to enter enforceable agreements to modify family structures remains in tension with the desire to protect vulnerable contracting parties and vulnerable third parties (in particular, children). The result is often a compromise, involving regulated choices or pre-set options.

---

[78] One party may know that he or she is more likely to prevail, down the road, under a certain chosen forum, procedure, or applicable law, while this information may not be obvious to the other party when that other party is presented with the provision in question.

[79] WN Eskridge, 'Family Law Pluralism: The Guided-Choice Regime of Menus, Default Rules, and Override Rules' (2012) 100 Georgetown Law Journal 1881.

[80] ibid.

13
Regulating Child Rearing in a Culturally Diverse Society

James G. Dwyer[1]

I. Introduction

What role should culture play in legal regulation of child rearing—in particular, in the state's setting of specific limits to parents' power over children? Confusion as to the nature of the state's role in children's lives and as to the source of parental liberty and authority muddles most attempts by political theorists and legal scholars to answer this question. Section II below clarifies what the state is doing, as a conceptual matter, when it defines the boundaries of parental decision-making power and permissible behaviour. Section III then presents an appropriate framework for analysing demands for state toleration and accommodation of child-rearing practices and values in minority-culture groups that are at odds with majoritarian child-rearing norms.

Preliminarily, we can distinguish different types of real-world situations raising the 'culture question', in order to help us focus on the ones which raise interesting ethical questions. In one type of situation, state actors might simply misunderstand what members of particular cultural groups are saying or doing, because differences in language, social arrangements, and mannerisms create false impressions. For example, a child-protection worker might view a parent as indifferent to a child's needs because of the way the parent acts when interviewed, but that way of acting might be normal within the minority culture for a parent who is actually very concerned. This type of situation is easily addressed; state actors should receive training in how to assess situations accurately and avoid such 'translation' problems.

A second type of situation involves child-rearing practices that have developed within a minority-culture group and that the majority deems harmful, but that are a matter of historical happenstance rather than conviction. This might be true, for example, of severe corporal punishment by African-American parents; some suggest (I take no position on whether they are correct) that there is a 'culture' of beating children among African-American families traceable to treatment of slaves and to black parents' reaction to the dangers a racist society presents for black children. This type of situation is somewhat more complicated to deal with as a practical matter; it raises questions about, inter alia, what motive (for example, instilling lessons vs venting rage) or disposition (for example, willingness to change) child protection workers should impute to such parents and whether such a form of discipline is more justifiable on child-welfare

---

[1] Professor of Law, College of William & Mary, Virginia, USA.

grounds for black Americans (for example, if the need for vigilance and conformity is in fact more pressing). But it is not so challenging philosophically, because the practice is not a matter of conviction; the minority group is not asserting a right to substitute its non-majoritarian values, nor is it challenging majoritarian assumptions about the equal personhood or legal status of children. Everyone agrees on the goal of minimizing the physical and psychological suffering of children while also instilling in them the self-discipline they need to stay safe and succeed in a challenging environment. Disagreement arises principally as to the best means of achieving that shared goal, which is more an empirical question than an ethical one. Few would defend a practice that inflicts on children what mainstream society views as harm solely on the grounds that it is a longstanding practice.

A third type of situation is what most philosophers have in mind when raising the culture question. It involves a clash of ideology, values, and convictions between mainstream society and minority cultures. It includes corporal punishment that is more severe than the state deems acceptable and that is inflicted not simply because 'this is how we've always done it', but because 'God commands that we do this'. It includes refusal of medical care for a child because of a belief that this would imperil the soul, which parents holding this belief would say is of greater moral importance than physical well-being and even continued corporal life. And it includes what most political theorists focus on when analysing the culture question—namely, forms of schooling antithetical to the educational aims that modern, secular, liberal states have established for children, such as development toward autonomy, full awareness of mainstream scientific knowledge, and gender equality. This chapter focuses on this third type of situation, which is the most challenging theoretically, because many people believe the state should be more tolerant of parental conduct and choices the majority deems detrimental to children if they arise from conviction and conscience rather than indifference or unreflective continuation of longstanding practice.

II. The State's Role in Children's Lives

A great variety of laws affect children's lives. We might usefully divide them into these two categories.

One type of law affects children simply as citizens, along with older citizens. These laws resolve conflicts of interests and rights that arise simply by virtue of sharing social space and scarce community resources. They include laws allocating state-budgetary spending, laws allocating other scarce resources (for example, public fora for speech), and laws prohibiting behaviour that harms others. Adults are subject to and affected by such laws and so are children. Some such laws—for example, those relating to free speech or criminal conduct—do treat children differently than adults, in most instances because children's needs or capacities are believed to differ from those of adults. But these laws govern aspects of life as to which, for both children and adults, a balancing of interests and rights among all potentially affected persons is appropriate. In enacting and enforcing these laws, the state acts as an agent for society collectively, balancing the interests and rights of individual members in order to effect a fair distribution of rights and well-being. Legal theorists refer to this as the 'police power' role of the state, even though it extends far more broadly than the scope of criminal law.[2]

Another type of law affecting children's lives governs aspects of life as to which adults in liberal societies are generally deemed entitled to decide for themselves without limitations based on supposed rights of others and without balancing their interests against those of others.[3] These include formation of relationships, consent to or refusal of available medical care, and choice among available education options. Subject only to the equal right of others, we adults are entitled to decide whether we will enter a relationship with another autonomous adult or decline to do so.[4] Resources for medical care are scarce and their allocation subject to the police power, but if I do as a practical matter have the option to receive certain treatment, and if I would harm no one else by refusing it,[5] it is entirely up to me whether I will receive it, regardless of others' preferences regarding it. Similarly, we adults get to choose which career path we will pursue, which among available universities we will attend, and what other educational experiences we will have, without legal restrictions reflecting collective aims like employment-market needs or other private parties' preferences—not even our family members' preferences. We might choose gratuitously to let collective aims or other individuals' preferences influence our decisions as to our relationships, medical care, and education, and the state might create incentives to choose one path rather than another, but legally we are entitled to make these decisions based exclusively on what we deem in our own best interests, period (subject, again, to the equal rights of others).

In what capacity, then, does the state act when it presumes to pass laws governing those same aspects of life for children—that is, as to what legal relationships children

---

[2] See Merriam Webster Dictionary, 'police power' (*Merriam Webster*, 2017) <http://www.merriam-webster.com/dictionary/police%20power> accessed 20 October 2017 (defining police power as 'the inherent power of a government to exercise reasonable control over persons and property within its jurisdiction in the interest of the general security, health, safety, morals, and welfare').

[3] Matters might be quite different in more collectivist societies lacking a strong norm of individual rights of self-determination, so this paper's analysis, extending to child-rearing norms that prevail in adult-only contexts is limited in its application to what I will refer to as 'liberal-western societies', where the law embodies strong rights of self-determination for autonomous adults. The analysis is, therefore, a 'coherentist' one, arguing essentially that 'if you believe X, then you should, as a matter of rational consistency, also believe Y'.

[4] Dissolution of relationships is also generally a matter of absolute 'self-determining individual right in these societies. With respect to what historically has been the most binding of relationships, marriage, this is more clearly so today, when 'no-fault divorce' is pervasive. But now as well as before the no-fault age, any obstacles to dissolving a marriage have been justified as voluntarily chosen by the parties to the relationship at its inception, so subsumed within the norms of contract, which treat as an expression of personal autonomy the power to impose certain restrictions on oneself in order to be able to secure reciprocal commitments from others.

[5] Situations posing the problem of effects on others appear to prove the strength of this norm, because the law in western-liberal societies generally does not mandate medical treatments for adults even when failing to secure them does adversely affect others. Even the most justifiable such impositions, such as universal immunization to eradicate a serious disease like smallpox, would trigger vehement protest and protracted court challenges. See, for example, *Jacobson v Massachusetts*, 197 US 11 (1905). A law mandating pre-natal care would likewise give rise to adamant opposition in such societies, even though a pregnant woman's failing to obtain it endangers a baby's well-being and development, and the opposition would rest on assertions of women's absolute self-determining right to sovereignty over her body. People who fail to get preventive care for themselves, or fail to get treatment for conditions likely to worsen without professional care, can also impose costs on others in more attenuated ways, by disrupting workplaces, increasing insurance costs, making themselves worse drivers, etc, yet the law in such societies entitles them to make this choice.

will enter, whether children will receive certain medical treatments, and what sort of schooling children will receive, if any? It is important to answer this question about the nature of the state's role before attempting to reach any conclusion about how the state should respond to non-majoritarian cultural beliefs about child rearing. In answering it, we must eradicate two fundamental errors that plague philosophical and legal writings about child rearing in minority cultural groups: one mistake is to assume that when parents or cultural community leaders are able to control children's lives as they wish that the situation is one in which the state is not acting at all, and so then the question just posed simply does not arise. The other is to assume that, if the state acts at all with respect to these aspects of children's lives, then the state acts in a police-power role. The remainder of this section explains why these assumptions are false.

A. The illusion of non-intervention

Scholars and the general public commonly speak of legal restrictions on parental treatment of or choices regarding children as 'state intervention into the family', as if there exists a practical alternative of the state's 'leaving families alone'. But there is no such alternative. The state is heavily and inevitably intervening into children's lives regardless of how much legal freedom and authority parents have. The state first creates legal parent–child relationships (who else could create a *legal* relationship?), and for that legal relationship to have practical significance the state must also confer on the persons whom it has made legal parents some particular privileges and powers. Granting them more privileges and powers cannot sensibly be characterized as state non-intervention; it instead amounts simply to intervening more in children's lives by one means (delegation of power) than by another (direct exercise of power).

As with any long-standing universal practice, we tend to assume that what we as a society do or believe is 'natural' in the sense of being extra-legal and pre-political. But that is a false assumption. The reality is that people occupy legally protected custodial and caretaking roles as to children because the state places them in that role. This is as true of biological parents as it is of foster parents and adoptive parents. If there were not state statutes stating that the persons believed to be the biological parents of a child shall (in nearly all cases) become that child's first legal parents, birth parents would have no legal recourse should someone else (for example, the medical staff who delivered a baby) take possession of the child. Chaos regarding custody and control of children would reign, and no sane person would want this. Many people believe natural law commands that biological parents are entitled to raise a child, but trying to call the natural police or to file suit in a natural court is not going to do one much practical good. (And, it is worth noting, other people might just as plausibly assert that natural law commands that the best available and willing caretakers should be a child's custodian, even if those persons are not the child's biological parents.) One might convince real-world legal actors to rule in one's behalf by invoking natural law, or by saying 'this is how it has always been', but it is still the state that is in charge and making the effective decisions. Natural-law belief and historical practice are simply two among many possible reasons why a legislator might rule thus.

Further, people occupying a parental role clearly need the state to confer on them special legal privileges and powers in order for them to raise a child as they wish, as against any contrary wishes of the state or of other private parties. Lawfully to assume a caregiving role at all as to a particular child, one needs a special set of legal privileges that other people do not possess as to that child, including permissions to assume physical control of the child, take the child into one's home, and manipulate the child's body in various ways (dressing, feeding, bathing, etc)—conduct toward another, non-consenting person that our criminal laws generally prohibit.[6] In addition, to enjoy the authority to dictate such things as a child's schooling experience and medical care, persons in a legal-parent role as to a particular child need the state to confer on them extraordinary powers that other people do not possess as to that child. I might wish that all children in my town attend the school my church operates, but were I to pronounce that this shall occur, as a matter of my right, anyone hearing me would assume I am joking or insane, and my pronouncement would have no practical effect, because the state has not given me any such legal right. If I made a similar pronouncement as to only the children as to whom the state has made me a legal parent, it would have practical effect, precisely because the state has also given me the legal power to make such decisions for those particular children.

Thus, any struggle over the content of laws relating to children's education, medical care, or other aspects of child rearing is not between more and less intervention, but rather over the form that state intervention will take—that is, whether the state will confer more or less power on the persons whom it has made legal parents, and conversely how much power the state will repose in its own employees (for example, education agency officials, courts). With non-autonomous persons of any age, the state either exercises decision-making power itself or confers it legally on some private parties, and in either case the state is acting, intervening in the lives of those persons.

Speaking of legal commands regarding parents' treatment or decision making regarding children as state intervention in the family is thus not inaccurate, but it is highly misleading, because as a matter of conversational implicature it falsely suggests there is some alternative possible situation of state non-intervention whereby certain persons (and only those persons) have greater practical freedom and effective decision-making authority as to a particular child. And it has a pejorative sense to it that is unwarranted given the actual absence of such an alternative. Similarly, characterizing as state intervention the initial introduction, decades ago, of legal prohibitions on wife-beating was not inaccurate, but if that characterization carried the implicature that the old coverture legal regime of marriage, within which husbands held the legal privilege physically to chastise their wives, was a situation of state non-intervention, then it

---

[6] This is true even as to *de facto* child-rearers whose parent-like role has never received overt legal recognition; to the extent their physical control of a child is lawful, rather than falling into the legal category of kidnapping, it is because the law empowers 'official' parents explicitly or implicitly to delegate legal permissions to others. Third parties, such as doctors and schools, need not—and, indeed, should not—pay any heed to the preferences of such unofficial caregivers, in the absence of a law directing them to do so, and those caregivers would have no basis for legal complaint in that case should a third party refuse to respond to their wishes.

would be highly misleading. It is preferable, therefore, to dispense altogether with the term 'intervention' in discussing the law governing child rearing.

Like the intervention/non-intervention distinction, three other distinctions on which much deliberation about legal regulation of child rearing rests are also highly problematic in light of this reality about the state's inevitable role in child rearing—namely, the state action/inaction distinction, the public/private distinction, and the negative rights/positive rights distinction. The difference between the state's commanding that all children attend a state-operated school versus the state's conferring on legal parents the power to decide where children will attend school (or whether children will attend school at all) is not a difference of state action vs inaction or of public vs private. Both scenarios crucially involve state action in determining the fate of children, and either type of law involves the public (through the legal institutions that carry out its will) in the lives of every child. Similarly, the coverture legal regime that once governed marriage, conferring on husbands the effective legal power to dictate certain aspects of their wives' lives, constituted state action that involved the public profoundly in the intimate life of spouses.[7]

Relatedly, it is a mistake to characterize parental demands for the latter regime—that is for legal entitlement to parental decision-making power—as invoking negative rights (ie, rights to the state's forbearance). Demands for greater parental authority are actually positive rights claims, demands that the state affirmatively do something—namely, give persons in a state-created legal-parent role more of something that they desire—namely, more effective power, backed by state legal enforcement apparatuses. Objections to legal restrictions on one's behaviour toward any child—for example, a prohibition of corporal punishment or sexual contact—might fairly be viewed as assertions of negative right, but that right is not properly characterized as an entitlement to be 'left alone' any more than assertion of a right to beat one's wife is a demand to be left alone; one is not alone when acting upon another person. Recognizing these points is important because negative rights to be 'left alone' in the 'private' sphere carry greater moral purchase in public discourse (and in much philosophical writing) than do (a) positive rights, or (b) negative rights to treat some other, vulnerable person however one wishes within a living situation that exists only because the state gave one special legal privileges (ie, to take the vulnerable person to one's home and keep them there).[8]

---

[7] F Olsen, 'The Myth of State Intervention in the Family' (1985) 18 University of Michigan Journal of Law Reform 835. When family law scholars today speak of 'private ordering', they generally mean the state's enforcing contracts between autonomous persons in an intimate relationship, as opposed to the state's dictating particular outcomes (with respect to, eg, property distribution upon dissolution of a relationship) regardless of any agreement between the parties. See, eg, BH Bix's chapter. Although not entirely accurate, given the role state enforcement of the contract plays, characterizing this as 'private ordering' might be tolerable in connection with some aspects of family law, a non-misleading shorthand for 'agreement between autonomous private parties (ie, not state actors) as to matters within the scope of their self-determination, backed by the state's commitment to force compliance'. It is misleading, however, in connection with contractual terms relating to custody and control of children (which are, as a matter of positive law, generally less legally enforceable), because characterizing those terms as a matter of private ordering obscures the reality that those terms presuppose a state-conferred status and set of powers over persons who are presumed non-autonomous and who are not parties to the agreement.

[8] Whether they should carry greater moral purchase is the subject of some debate among philosophers, but I cannot present or enter that debate in this chapter. The opposing view comes principally from those

What underlies pervasive confusion, among philosophers as well as legal scholars and the general public, about the essential nature of state regulation of child rearing, is a set of 'intellectual illusions'. The more it seems things could not or should not be otherwise, the less we recognize the state's role in making things as they are. But the normalcy or seeming naturalness or inevitability of a law does not make it any less a law, a product of state action. In addition, we recognize state action more readily when it is unusual and individualized—in particular, a court decision dictating a departure from the norm. Thus, statutes applying to a great number of cases, operating automatically without individualized adjudication, are often invisible to us. Yet they are just as effective practically, and equally constitute state action, as individualized-court decisions. Both illusions operate in people's thinking about creation of parent–child relationships. With adoption of a child by persons who are not the child's biological parents, there must be a court order, which usually occurs only after another court order terminating the parental status of biological parents following protracted litigation intensely scrutinizing the individual case, and so the state action is obvious, the public nature of the event is evident, and no one would make the mistake of characterizing the would-be adopters as asserting a negative right when asking to be made legal parents. In contrast, a child's first legal parent–child relationship generally arises by virtue of state statutes that operate without any court involvement (though court decision making is quite common with respect to paternity), so the state action is unrecognized by most people, but it exists nonetheless and it is no less state intervention in a child's life than is a court order of parentage. And biological parents' expectation of receiving legal parent status actually rests on presupposition of possessing a positive right; the state's declining to bestow that status on a particular biological parent would in no way constitute an infringement of negative right.

B. Role confusion

Though typically unstated, the assumption that the state acts in a police-power capacity when legislating about children's relationships, schooling, and medical care is evident from the way scholarly analysis of such legislating typically proceeds, with a balancing of children's interests against interests and supposed rights of other people—most often parents, but sometimes society as a whole.[9] The assumption is unstated because it is not a

---

aiming to bolster claims of entitlement to state provision of basic physical necessities for persons unable to provide for themselves, and certainly not from theorists aiming to strengthen the case for the state's giving some persons legal powers to control the lives of other persons.

[9] See, eg, R Reich, 'Testing the Boundaries of Parental Authority over Education' in S Macedo and Y Tamir (eds), *NOMOS XLIII: Moral and Political Education* (New York UP 2002) 295 (arguing circularly that because parents and society, as well as children, have interests at stake in children's education, state allocation of decision-making authority over schooling must rest on a balancing of the interests of the three parties, lest there be a 'despotism' of one party's interests); W Galston, *Liberal Pluralism* (CUP 2002) 94 (urging a balancing of children's interests, parents' interests, and societal interests in establishing the content of parental authority over children's lives, simply because all those interests exist and might not be coincident); A Gutmann, *Democratic Education* (Princeton UP 1989) 27 (asserting that even if the state were omniscient regarding children's educational interests, it should design a society's educational system so that it also serves 'our good as parents and as citizens' even if this means sacrificing children's good to some extent).

considered judgment; scholars and others debating these topics simply do not consider whether the state might be operating in a different capacity, such that a different sort of analysis is in order. But there is an alternative to police-power jurisdiction—namely, the state's long-recognized *parens patriae* authority to act in behalf of non-autonomous persons, enforcing their rights and protecting their welfare. Scholars and legal actors do sometimes mention the state's *parens patriae* authority and responsibility, yet then go on to recommend or simply proceed with a balancing of children's interests along with interests and supposed rights of parents and minority-cultural communities or the state as a whole. Can the state carry on in both a *parens patriae* and police-power role at the same time? If so, should it? If not, which of the two roles should the state assume?

In answering these questions, we should begin by asking what justification there is for the state deciding these matters at all—that is, with whom children will have family relationships, whether and where children will attend school, what medical care children will receive. As noted above, these are types of decisions as to which in the 'normal case'—that is, the case of autonomous persons—the state is generally deemed to have no say; they are matters of self-determination for autonomous adults, decisions persons are entitled to make for themselves without limitations based on the preferences or interests of others (subject to equal rights for all). For the state in a liberal society to make these decisions for particular individuals, or for the state to empower some private parties to make these decisions for other private parties, is extraordinary and in need of justification.

The obvious justification for the state's presuming to make these decisions for children is that children need for these decisions to be made, they are unable (at least before a particular developmental stage, which differs by type of decision) to make the decisions themselves, and the state is the only feasible substitute decision maker. There must be laws—that is, state enactments embodying state decisions—dictating who will be a newborn's custodians and caretakers and what powers they will have. Again, the only alternative is chaos. Importantly, the same is true with respect to incompetent adults; they need for certain decisions to be made about their lives, they cannot make those decisions themselves, and state decision making—including delegation of particular choices to private caretakers—is the only feasible substitute for their self-determining choices.

In short, the state decides who a child's legal family members will be, whether children must attend certain types of schools, and whether children must receive medical care of certain kinds in certain situations, *because* children *need* the state to make these decisions. And crucially, the state's power cannot exceed the justification without becoming unjustified, and its exertion of power over children's lives cannot be contrary to the justification. Children's need in no way justifies the state's using their lives for the direct purpose of satisfying preferences or interests of other persons. It does not warrant or excuse treating children's lives instrumentally in this way. This is a fundamental point that defenders of 'parental rights' routinely fail to recognize.[10] Similarly, the

---

[10] See, eg, S Altman's chapter. Some theorists offer up a sort of 'contractualist' defence of the state's conferring on legal parents some modicum of child-rearing authority solely for the sake of gratifying parents, on the assumption this is necessary in order to incentivize people to become parents. See, eg, ES Scott and RE Scott, 'Parents as Fiduciaries' (1995) 81 Virginia Law Review 2401. The factual conjecture of practical

incapacity of adults who have never been autonomous or who have lost their autonomy does not create a legitimate opportunity for the state to use them for ends other than their own well-being. It justifies solely the state's acting in their behalf to attempt to make for them the decisions they would have made for themselves as to such things as who will be their custodian and what powers their custodian will possess.[11]

In other words, children's inability to make self-determining choices justifies the state's making choices about aspects of children's lives that are ordinarily, for autonomous persons, matters of individual right not subject to state police-power jurisdiction, solely in a *parens patriae* capacity, as an agent for the child, subject to the normal expectations for a fiduciary. Among the expectations for a fiduciary is conformity to a strict obligation of undivided loyalty; the fiduciary may not use its authority to serve its own interests or the interests of third parties. To sacrifice the well-being of the principal or ward to any degree for the direct purpose of satisfying third parties[12] would be a breach of fiduciary obligation and an affront to the rights and dignity of the principal or ward. This is well-recognized in contexts where autonomous adults employ fiduciaries—for example, when lawyers or persons with a power of attorney must act in their behalf. The law proscribes self-dealing and conflicts of interest. That it might be difficult in many circumstances to say definitively what is in the best interests of the principal or ward does not alter the ethical obligation to make that the sole object of decision making.

Consistent with this understanding, the state must act solely in a *parens patriae* role when legislating parentage, compulsory schooling, and mandatory medical care for children. The police-power role is incompatible with the *parens patriae* role, so the state cannot occupy both at the same time. This is not merely unethical but in fact a conceptual impossibility; if the state acts as agent for all, then *ipso facto* it is not acting as a fiduciary for an individual. And the justification for the state's acting at all with respect to these basic aspects of children's lives cannot support acting in a police-power role, balancing children's well-being against preferences and interests of parents or cultural-community leaders. It justifies solely acting as an agent for a child.

---

necessity lacks evidentiary support, but more importantly this is not an argument for parents' having a moral right to greater rather than less legal authority; it is an argument for the state's carrying out a moral duty to children in a particular way, and so really an elaboration of children's moral rights (even if the state finds it expedient to misleadingly characterize parents' legal authority as a matter of parents' legal 'right' rather than, more accurately, privilege).

[11] This is conceptually tricky, because imagining 'what an incompetent person would have decided if able' would seem to entail imagining them being competent, contrary to the very reality we are addressing. But we can coherently conceptualize this surrogate decision making as what a competent person would have set forth in an advance directive if they had had perfect information about their future situation of incompetence. This is essentially how the law approaches 'substituted-judgment' decisions for adults who have lost their competence, and with respect to such persons it has the virtue of allowing for consideration of the particular values they held as well as generic interests. In the case of persons who have never been competent, including both infants and older persons who have always been mentally disabled, we can imagine the person having had a prior life in which they made such an advance directive. This conceptualization has the advantage of facilitating a form of 'behind a veil of ignorance' way of thinking about state decision making for children that I develop below.

[12] 'For the direct purpose' is in contrast to 'because this incidentally serves the interests of the principal or ward'.

C. What about parents' rights?

Many readers will find it odd that I discuss the state's role in child rearing without mentioning parents' rights. Parents, most people think, are not simply other persons who take an interest in how children's lives go. They have 'fundamental interests' at stake and therefore 'rights' to control 'their' children's lives. Even if the state legitimately acts on a concern for children's well-being, most people in western societies would say, it must respect rights of other affected persons—specifically, parents.

The concept of parents' rights is another instance of long-standing, unexamined dogma utterly lacking rational justification. Its retention for many people rests in part on the mistake of supposing that for parents to have any child-rearing authority they must have rights against the state (and perhaps against other private parties as well). However, as is evident from many other social roles that entail special authority—for instance, guardianship for incompetent adults, lawyers representing clients in negotiations or court, and persons occupying government roles such as legislator, regulator, or judge—it is possible to possess and exercise authority without possessing any right to have such authority, such that one could complain in one's own behalf about denial of some modicum of such authority. Authority can be enjoyed as a matter of legal and moral privilege, a privilege held because one's having that authority serves collective aims or fulfils rights of other persons. Likewise, parents can and should possess authority with respect to children's lives as a matter of privilege—just as the state does—in order to promote children's welfare and fulfil whatever rights children might have to care and governance. Reasoning from children's needs to parental entitlement is therefore illogical; to the extent any rights protect children's welfare, they should be rights of the children.

The practical difference it makes to reject the concept of parents' rights is to force parents or minority-cultural groups who object to the state's constraining parental or community choices about children's lives to express their objection in terms of children's welfare, and on the basis of assertions about children's welfare that the state can accept. Conversely, the real work that recognition of parental entitlement does, relative to conceptualizing the parental role as a fiduciary one occupied as a matter of privilege (the way we view a guardian for an incompetent adult, an attorney acting for a client, and public officials), is to shift focus away from the child and to the parent and to gratification of parents' wishes for their own sake. Or else it is to further collective ends like cultural diversity and fostering 'experiments in living'. For the state to ascribe legal *rights* to parents, rights to deference to parental wishes for parents' own sake, is therefore in derogation of the state's *parens patriae* role. The state is, as explained above, not justified in doing this. Children's incapacity does not generate justification for treating them as objects of others' rights, for making them instruments for gratification of other individuals, regardless of what role those other individuals might occupy in the children's lives.

Giving up the idea of parental right is quite difficult for most people, just as giving up the idea of husbands' entitlement to control wives' lives was once very difficult. The idea is deeply ingrained, so much so that it is difficult to stand apart from it and assess it objectively and rationally. The normal inclination is to reject all comparisons with ostensibly like situations and to insist the parent–child relationship is different. Thus even philosophers, trained to examine fundamental assumptions with a critical eye, tend to devolve into *sui generis* pseudo-reasoning about family life, making no effort to appeal to general principles or to think about analogous situations. Rather than endeavouring to reconcile the parental role with other caretaking or agency roles that people occupy, participants in scholarly and public debates about child rearing unreflectively treat it in an entirely different way, conflating this intrinsically 'other-determining' human activity (a child being a distinct person, 'other' relative to the parent) with situations involving only self-determining actions and choices by autonomous persons that conflict with societal norms. They approach a parental objection to government regulation of religious schools the same way they would approach an individual's objection to government regulation of his or her own religious training—that is, as pitting the individual's right to free exercise of religion against the state's police-power concern for the impact of that exercise on the rest of society.[13] But that is the wrong approach. Control of a child's life is not a matter of the parent's self-determination, and so it simply falls outside the protections that constitutions create for persons' free exercise of religion, just as does one adult's religiously motivated desire to control the life of another adult, whether there is an intimate relationship between them or not. If pro-lifers asserted that their right to free exercise of religion includes a right to prevent pregnant women from having abortions, the legal system would respond that the pro-lifers misunderstand the nature of rights in our legal culture, and so they cannot even make out a prima facie case that would require a state response. It is not that they have such a right and it is simply outweighed by an autonomous woman's own right, but rather that they have no such right at all; their rights simply do not extend to control over basic aspects of another person's life (and so their desire would have no moral or legal weight even as to a non-autonomous woman who is pregnant).

Another source of resistance is the view that parental interests in how their children's lives go are fundamental ones.[14] Western legal systems generally accord rights to individuals to protect their fundamental interests, at least to some extent. The parental interest is different from the interest one adult might have in the direction of another adult's life, even a spouse's or that of an incompetent adult ward. The developmental aspect of childhood appears to distinguish the parent–child relationship from other relationships, even other intimate or family-like ones.

One could fault this reasoning from fundamental interest to entitlement by pointing out that the law does not protect every fundamental interest with a right, so more would need to be said than simply that parents have a fundamental interest in receiving plenary legal authority over children. A person might have a fundamental interest in receiving an organ transplant, but neither law nor common moral beliefs ascribes to anyone a right to an organ transplant.

But there is the further problem that ascribing a fundamental interest to parents is empirically false. It wrongly conflates caring greatly about something and having a fundamental interest at stake. One can readily think of innumerable examples of persons

---

[13] See, eg, Galston (n 9) 252–55.   [14] See, eg, S Altman's chapter.

caring intensely about something yet not having a fundamental interest at stake. To name a few: pro-lifers care intensely what choices pregnant women make with respect to abortion, presidential candidates care greatly about being elected, and persons in love tend to feel their lives will disintegrate if their adoration is not reciprocated. Yet none of these people actually has a fundamental interest at stake in these situations. 'Fundamental' means basic, and in connection with human interest means, properly understood, a prerequisite to carrying on at all and pursuing higher-order aims. Fundamental interests are basic necessities, including such things as physical security, food and shelter, medical care, and cognitive development. Controlling another person's choices, becoming president, and marrying a particular other person are not basic necessities of this sort and so not fundamental interests. One can fail to have these things yet pursue innumerable aims in life. The same is true of parental control over children's upbringing and, indeed, of occupying a parental role at all. A significant percentage of adults never become parents yet have flourishing lives. And if what is at issue is merely state denial to parents of some modicum of authority regarding children's upbringing, so that parents otherwise remain able to enjoy a full family life with their children, it is implausible to suggest the parents have even a substantial interest at stake, let alone a fundamental one. What they have at stake is a desire, period, however strongly felt that desire might be.

To summarize this section: the state is inevitably and profoundly involved in children's lives, first creating their legal family relationships and then deciding how much authority over them their legal parents will possess. There is no non-intervention position the state can realistically take regarding child rearing. In making these decisions, the state must act exclusively in a *parens patriae* capacity, as an agent for the child, governed by the state's best judgment as to what will best promote each child's well-being, without any compromise for the direct purpose of gratifying parents, or other third parties, or serving collective societal aims. Parenting is not an aspect of self-determination nor a matter of fundamental interest for persons who do it, and the very notion of parents' rights is therefore conceptually and morally illicit, an affront to the equal moral personhood of children. This is all rather abstract, but it is important to establish a clear and appropriate conceptual framework before delving into the messy facts of real families' lives, which is the task of the next section.

III. What the State Should Make of Cultural Difference

We should imagine ourselves, then, as state actors—legislators, state agency officials, judges, etc—who have cleansed our minds of illicit notions of parents' rights, state's rights, citizens' rights, and police power in connection with child rearing. We are tasked with acting as agents for each individual child with respect to those aspects of the child's life, from the moment of birth (and perhaps before) until achievement of autonomy, that fall within the realm of self-determining rights for autonomous adults, such as relationship formation and dissolution, education, and medical care. We must aim to establish legal rules to govern those aspects of children's lives, with children's welfare our sole concern. Those rules will either dictate particular choices or delegate authority to make such choices to private decision makers—in particular, parents.

A. Basic considerations in allocating authority

Let us suppose (contrary to present-day reality) that we have made appropriate decisions about who each child's legal parents and custodians will be.[15] Certainly we will delegate a substantial amount of authority over child rearing to those adults. We have ample empirical evidence that children's lives go best when families operate as cohesive units insulated in a practical sense to a substantial degree from the outside world, with presumptively loving caregivers managing most aspects of children's daily lives. All of us parents do this imperfectly, but child-centred state decision making about family life will recognize both that state actors are also imperfect and that child-centred regulation is always a matter of balancing benefits to children against costs to children. Disrupting family life in and of itself usually entails a cost for children.[16] So we would choose, for children's sake, to confer on parents substantial freedom and discretion in how they structure family life.

On the other hand, no sane person would seriously maintain that the state should confer absolute childrearing freedom and power on parents. Everyone acknowledges that the law must impose some limits. Even 'parentalists', for whom parental entitlement is a bedrock starting point, concede that the state may prohibit 'unreasonable' or 'seriously harmful' parental choices and behaviours. They have given us no guidance on how to give meaning to these terms, perhaps because they realize that presuming to draw the line themselves would render them vulnerable to the same charge of presumptuousness that they level against liberals who favour more robust state decision making about such things as education and discipline. How could anyone presume to judge what scope of parental authority is best for children without presupposing that they themselves know what is best for children in a great variety of circumstances? They also fail to see the self-contradiction inherent in the assertion that 'only parents know what is best for a child'; one cannot judge that a parent knows best without presuming to know oneself what is best for that parent's child. We form a belief that substantial parental authority is generally good for children by looking at outcomes for children in a large number of individual cases and judging, based on our own standards of child welfare, that they are good.

In any event, parentalists' views on how to divide authority among state actors, parents, and other private parties are impertinent, because they arise from an illicit perspective that ascribes entitlement where none properly exists. We state actors must reject as morally inappropriate any perspective on decision making about fundamental aspects of children's welfare that presupposes an entitlement in anyone other than the

---

[15] For discussion of the tragic consequences of the states' ham-fisted approach to initial legal parentage, see JG Dwyer, 'A Constitutional Birthright: the State, Parentage, and the Rights of Newborn Persons' (2009) 56 UCLA Law Review 755; JG Dwyer, 'The Child Protection Pretense: States' Continued Consignment of Newborn Babies to Unfit Parents' (2008) 93 (2) University of Minnesota Law Review 407.

[16] Of course, parents themselves disrupt family life far more often than the state does, by dissolving the relationship between them, and the disruption is especially threatening to children's well-being when parents wage a legal battle over custody and/or decisions about particular aspects of children's upbringing. The marginal cost of state exertion of decision-making authority might be less in such circumstances than when parents' relationship is stable and harmonious (even if it is not a cohabiting relationship). See JG Dwyer, 'Parents' Self-Determination and Children's Custody: A New Analytical Framework for State Structuring of Children's Family Life' (2012) 54 Arizona Law Review 79.

children, and indeed any perspective presupposing that the interests of anyone other than the children are of direct relevance.

B. The indirect relevance of parents' interests

Interests of parents, or of other private parties besides the children, might nevertheless be of *indirect* relevance, insofar as children's interests are intertwined with those of other persons. All else being equal, it is better for children that their parents and others in their lives are happy and that they enjoy the role they play in a child's life. A moral hazard lies in making known to parents that the state will give them more power if it seems denying that power would make them unhappy, to the detriment of their children, but the state cannot simply ignore the ways in which children's interests are inextricably intertwined with those of their parents, other family members, teachers, and others.

This is relevant to the topic of culture, of course, because culture gives pronounced meaning to certain activities and choices, and child rearing comprises an activity and set of choices that are typically central to a group's culture. When culture entails religious beliefs and ties activities and choices today to prospects for life after earthly death, or even just to one's relationship today with a deity, values and commitments tend to take on particular intensity. Preventing adults from acting on such beliefs in connection with child rearing therefore has the potential to be unusually upsetting, which can indirectly adversely impact the children at issue.

It is wrong to suppose, however, that cultural meaning or religious belief alone injects intense significance into parental decision making. Listening to defenders of parental religious freedom, one gets the impression that they believe religious belief is unique in this regard—that is, that if certain parents' religion commands them to do something with their children, then the stakes for those parents (and perhaps their children) are categorically greater than the stakes for other parents in connection with that aspect of children's lives. The implicit supposition is that religion is a stronger or more important motivator than any other, including love. What basis is there for that supposition? One might justifiably presuppose that child welfare counsels in favour of greater deference to parental religious commitment than to parental indifference or laziness, but what basis is there for elevating religion over love?

I think, for example, of friends who have agonized over the decision whether to circumcise their son, where religion played no role in their decision making. Or my own concern with the sex stereotyping I saw at the local public elementary school when my daughters attended it, and with vaccinations my girls' doctor recommended for them in middle school. Would our interest in these things necessarily be greater if infused with religious command of some sort? And what if we had no concerns on secular grounds, but only religious beliefs telling us we should do one thing rather than another; how would that religion-alone situation compare to a love-alone situation in terms of how unhappy contrary state action would make us? These are empirical questions, and I am unaware of anyone having done the empirical research that would enable us reliably to answer it. Certainly one can find examples of parents holding religious beliefs about child rearing yet not caring all that much when the state tells them they may not act on those beliefs—that is, manifesting a sort of indifference or laziness regarding their religious adherence. And also examples of parents voluntarily foregoing acting on their religious beliefs because they have sufficient humility about their access to religious truth that they believe it more respectful to their children to let the children decide for themselves later in life—that is, allowing love to override their religious beliefs.

As state actors operating as agents for children, then, we should be sensitive to the possibility that denying parents some modicum of power over their children's lives could make them unhappy to an extent that redounds to the detriment of their children, but we should not assume that religion or other beliefs and practices falling under the heading of 'culture' create a unique situation in this regard. Parents can be upset for all sorts of reasons when not able to do what they want to do.

C. Direct relevance of culture to child welfare

Potential for parental upset is not the sole culture-related concern for us, however. The culture of a society or community in which a child's parents live inevitably shapes a child's life in significant ways. Conflicts between minority-cultural groups and the state typically arise because state actors, whose outlook ordinarily reflects majoritarian norms and values, view certain culture-driven practices or choices as detrimental to children's health, intellectual growth, or other aspects of well-being. But even a secular-liberal state that refrains from making judgments about the truth of religious faiths or other transcendental belief sets should recognize that being brought up in a non-mainstream culture can entail experiences that are beneficial for children. Culture tends to bond members of families and communities, and this solidarity can generate a sense of belonging, security, and being valued. Culture can infuse life and personal identity with special meaning that is gratifying, connecting the individual psychologically to a greater good, an historical mission, and ancestors. Along with family disruption, therefore, we state actors would take into account in deciding how much to empower parents that withholding from them some element of power over their children's lives could mean taking away from the children a cultural experience with potential to benefit them.

But we should not exaggerate the impact of legal rules on children's cultural experiences. So long as we repose custody of children in particular persons, those persons are going to have an extraordinary influence on the children's lives. Even if we were to mandate that all children attend public school, that would still leave more than 80 per cent of the time that children are not sleeping for them to spend time immersed in family and community cultural life, under parental control. Parents would thus still have ample time to teach their beliefs to children and to engage children in cultural practices. Certainly among the 90 per cent of children in the United States who attend public schools, there are many with very rich minority-culture experiences. Notably, when Amish parents in the United States successfully petitioned the courts for an exemption from compulsory schooling laws, they did not contend that those laws precluded them from sharing their way of life with their children, which would have been implausible, but rather that school attendance would expose the children also to other ways of life and as a result increase the danger that their offspring would, upon reaching adulthood, choose a different way of life. There is nothing in that concern that should give us child-centred state actors the slightest pause in rejecting the parents' request for exemption. The only legitimate basis we might have for exempting the Amish parents would be the possibility that the parents would be so upset by our not doing so that this would indirectly generate more of a cost for the children than the benefit they would realize by receiving a high school education, but that possibility seems too improbable to act on.

Likewise with prohibiting specific aspects of cultural practice; this does not prevent parents and communities from immersing children in the culture in every other way. For example, prohibiting all forms of ritual female genital alteration does not preclude Muslim parents and communities from giving their daughters a recognizably Muslim upbringing, as demonstrated by the innumerable Muslim families in which this has not been done to daughters. Is it precisely the kind of Muslim upbringing the parents might want? No, but from our perspective, recognizing the value of having *some* cultural experience in childhood is not equivalent to ascribing to children an interest in having precisely the sort of cultural experience their legal parents might prefer. The interest at stake for children in such situations seems just that of having somewhat happier parents, an interest more likely to be outweighed by the child-welfare benefits of the state's declining to confer on parents that additional modicum of legal power.

Prohibiting some sorts of cultural practices might interfere with children's experience of culture to a greater degree, so to do that we might need to find a greater child-welfare gain from doing so in order for the cost-benefit analysis to cut in favour of prohibition. But as agents for the state, we should be prepared to judge some cultures as fundamentally harmful to children. For example, we might find that intensive sexist indoctrination so thwarts the life prospects of girls that efforts to prevent it are warranted on child-welfare grounds even if they would seriously interfere with girls' immersion in their parents' culture. The hesitation to pass judgment on cultural practices that we ordinarily think appropriate for a liberal state should not apply, at least not to the same degree, when state actors operate in a *parens patriae* role, protecting non-autonomous persons, rather than in a police-power role in which they should respect individuals' self-determining choices even when they seem irrational and self-destructive. Contrary thinking rests on illicit adult-centred suppositions about parental entitlement to dictate the aims for a child's life. As explained above, parents have no such right, and they need to give the state *child-centred* reasons that the state can accept (and so ruling out reasons grounded in religious faith) to empower them to do something the state deems seriously harmful to the children. If all the parents can come up with is 'I'll be upset and my daughters won't fully experience my culture', the state should in such cases say, 'I'm sorry, but our best judgment as agents for your child, based on a balancing of the child's different interests, is to prohibit you from doing this.'

It bears mention here that religious and other cultural groups, as well as individual parents, have generally proven to be adaptable to the legal environment. When faced with a choice between losing their relationship with children altogether and conforming to the state's maltreatment laws, they nearly always choose the latter, and they find ways to ease their conscience and calm their tempers. For example, the US Supreme Court rejected a claim by Jehovah's Witness parents to a religious exemption from child medical neglect law, so they could refuse blood transfusions doctors deem necessary for their children. The congregation adjusted in a couple of ways. One was to work with the medical profession to develop alternatives to normal transfusions for cases in which such alternatives can be effective. The other was to take the theological position that they have not failed in their religious duty so long as it is a court rather than they themselves that authorizes a transfusion.[17] That is how state laws are now set up; the state does not charge the parents with neglect for refusing to consent to transfusion, but doctors can obtain a court order to go ahead with it. And Jehovah's Witnesses appear to be content with how things have played out; they continue procreating and raising children, and legal battles involving them have all but disappeared. A concern that defenders of parental 'rights' sometimes express, that too many people will decide they don't want to be parents at all if the state should start bestowing less power on legal parents, is unsubstantiated, silly even. As economists might put the point, demand for the basic good of simply being in a parent–child relationship, having the opportunity to live with and love a child, is quite inelastic, not much affected by the price one must pay for it in terms of complying with legal duties inconsistent with one's predispositions or ideological commitments.

D. Humility about values

Even if one acknowledges that the state must be the ultimate decision maker as to who a child's legal parents will be and what privileges and powers legal parents possess, and even if one concedes that the notion of parental entitlement is illicit, one might still want justification for the state's imposing majoritarian norms on families in minority cultures. As agents for a young child who, let us suppose, has no self-chosen values or conception of the good, we might think it a complete toss-up as to what values should dictate the course of the child's life, and that in that circumstance deference to parents is as valid a choice as any other, and it has the added benefit of making the parents happier, which indirectly benefits the children. In thinking about whether this is a valid line of reasoning, we should keep in mind that the same presumptively would apply also to incompetent adults subject to a guardianship—that is, that assuming they have no conception of the good, letting their guardians' values control is as legitimate a decision on our part as any other, and has the benefit of making the guardians happier.

Also helpful in thinking about this matter is a 'veil-of-ignorance' approach alluded to above. Imagine that you will die tonight and will be reborn tomorrow, that you can have no idea what values your biological or legal parents will have in your new life, and that you must decide now what legal rules will govern allocation of authority over important aspects of your life such as education, medical care, and discipline. Would you reason from a supposition that there is no way to decide among conceptions of the good to a conclusion that the state may, and perhaps should, empower your parents—whoever they might turn out to be—to act on whatever values they happen to hold? Any actual person undergoing this thought experiment today would have to take into account the possibility that the values of his or her parents in the next life could be

---

[17] See, eg, Re *President and Directors of Georgetown College*, 331 F2d 1000, 1007 (DC Cir), cert denied, 377 US 978 (1964); Re *EG*, 515 NE2d 286, 288–289 (Ill App Ct 1987).

quite antithetical to the values he or she holds now. Thus, for example, a fundamentalist Christian should consider 'what if I were reborn to biological parents who are atheist libertines or Orthodox Jews or adherents to a belief system in which men are subordinate to women', and vice versa.

My intuition is that in this position I would reach two conclusions: (a) governance of my future life should be divided, with neither state agencies (with their values) nor whoever my parents are (with their values) holding monopoly power 'on the ground' over important aspects of my life; and (b), I would aim to ensure I receive an upbringing conducive to my becoming autonomous and having substantive freedom to choose for myself, when I (again) become an adult, what values I will adopt for my life. I would reach these conclusions because, (a) I am sceptical of both the state's and parents' ability to discern 'truth' about values, so dividing authority might minimize the downside risk of 'error'; and (b), as Kant explained, in making decisions as an autonomous person (as anyone presumably is who is reading this) I necessarily value my being autonomous, and that valuing presumably would carry over to what I want for myself in a hypothetical next life.

The latter point also suggests an answer to autonomous members of minority cultures who assert a right to engage in child-rearing practices that thwart development toward autonomy—that is, that presumably they ascribe inherent value to their own autonomy and freedom to choose a conception of the good (beyond the inherent value they see in holding the conception of the good they have), and so they should acknowledge that autonomy and freedom to choose are inherently valuable for their children as well. And accepting autonomy as a desideratum for all children can be the basis for substantial restriction on parents and on minority communities' cultural practices, given that physical and psychological health and a more-or-less liberal form of education arguably are all necessary to proper development toward autonomy.[18]

This line of reasoning is not entirely satisfactory, however, because it presupposes an autonomy-valuing perspective. What can we say to parents or minority-group leaders who are not autonomous in a full liberal sense and who do not see value in the idea of choosing a conception of the good different from the one they actually hold? Some might say they have not chosen their values or belief system, that they simply received these things as their fate. But if they view their beliefs as true and their culture as correct, then reasoning behind the veil of ignorance should lead to the conclusion I reached above, because they would want to ensure that if they were reborn to parents with an erroneous belief system that they could ultimately find their way to the truth.

Others, though, might be cultural and moral relativists who ascribe no truth status to their conception of the good or superiority to their culture. We each have our own fate, and that is that, they might say. One has the beliefs one has, and there is no reason to question or judge or compare. On the basis of this outlook, such persons might endorse a legal regime giving parents complete freedom to act on the values of their culture, or they might endorse a state that imposes the same particular conception of

---

[18] For fuller defences of autonomy as a morally requisite aim for the schooling of all children, and discussion of the prerequisites to becoming autonomous, see M Levinson, *The Demands of Liberal Education* (OUP 2002); H Brighouse, *School Choice and Social Justice* (OUP 2003).

the good on all. The choice between those two extreme regimes would seem to be a matter of indifference to thorough-going relativists, unless the particular conception of the good they now possess happens to be one containing values that dictate a choice of one or the other. Valuing cultural preservation for its own sake, ideological continuity over generations for its own sake, or parental pre-eminence for its own sake would support a *laissez-faire* legal regime. Valuing collectivist spirit might lead one to support the statist extreme.

Thus, as fiduciaries for individual children, we state actors must decide whether we should act on the majoritarian values of our society, which happen to be secular and liberal and individualistic, or some other set of values or no values. The last of these options would appear impossible; having no desiderata is paralysing. Even merely aiming to maximize happiness presupposes a value. That leaves a choice between acting on majoritarian values or some other set. But what other set and for what reason? If we are initially deciding who a newborn child's first legal parents will be, we cannot adopt the values of the legal parents, as we do not yet know who they are. We could adopt the values of biological parents, but what reason do we have to do that? We have already rejected the notion of parental entitlement. We would have to do so on the basis of some values, but that leads to an infinite regress. We could choose based on our best guess of what values the child will adopt when an adult, but the very act of our choosing will likely largely determine what that is, so there is a circularity problem. And in any event, the motivation for acting on a person's expected future values must be a respect for the individual that itself is a non-universal value.

Thus, absent convincing philosophical demonstration of the truth or superiority of some conception of the good, it would seem an arbitrary choice on what set of values we act when we occupy the role of surrogate for a child. This is a problem inherent in surrogate decision making for a person who has never had a conception of the good. Political theory addressing cultural and ideological diversity generally presupposes that the people with whom it is concerned are all individuals who already have a conception of the good and need the state to mediate conflicts among them. It has largely ignored the thorny issue of decision making for non-autonomous persons. Ultimately, we who are liberals will endorse the state's acting on liberal values, as this chapter has done, because those values seem best to us, but that is merely a description or explanation rather than justification. I have provided here simply a 'coherentist' account of what we should believe about the law governing parent–child relationships if we are committed to liberal values.

IV. Conclusion

In any society, it must be the state that ultimately decides what legal rules govern children's lives—both rules for determining who a child's parents will be and rules conferring or withholding child-rearing privileges and powers on parents. A liberal state committed to respecting the separate and equal personhood of all will view its role in deciding core aspects of children's lives as a *parens patriae* role, that of a fiduciary for each child, and it will reject the notion of parental entitlement. With respect to culture, the state should grant parents substantial freedom in conveying their beliefs and involving children in cultural practices, not because parents' desire to do this is of direct relevance, but because cultural experiences can be beneficial for children and parental happiness redounds to children's benefit. But a liberal state should withhold from parents the freedom and power to act on minority-cultural norms that would inflict what it (the state) regards as harmful, including anything that undermines children's development toward autonomy. Our acting on the basis of liberal values might not be justifiable at a foundational level, but it is also not clearly unjustified; the choice of ultimate values might be arbitrary. This chapter has aimed simply to clarify how we should view legal treatment of minority-cultural practices if we do presuppose a state committed to liberal values.

14
Surrogacy
Reconceptualizing Family Relationships in an Age of Reproductive Technologies

Mary Lyndon Shanley

I. Introduction

Surrogacy, the practice whereby a woman agrees prior to conception to bear a child and permanently relinquish it at birth to the person(s) who commissioned the pregnancy, has been a highly controversial practice. In arguments about the ethics of surrogacy, the focus is nearly always on the respective rights of the commissioning parents and surrogate, some seeing surrogacy as a mutually beneficial agreement, others regarding it as potentially exploitative and dehumanizing for the surrogate. The dominant questions asked concern whose rights should prevail, and whether genetics, gestation, or contract should ground legal parental status when a child is born through the use of assisted reproductive technology and surrogacy.

In this chapter I argue that we should shift the lens through which scholars and policy-makers view surrogacy from one that focuses on the rights of individual adults to the intrinsic and on-going relationships entailed in any surrogacy agreement. This approach draws on recent work in the ethics of care and theories of relational rights. It emphasizes the ways in which all persons are embedded in and shaped by relationships of mutual dependency and by both providing and receiving care. Several theoretical and practical commitments follow from this relational analysis. One is that the interests and needs of the person who will come into being if the pregnancy is successful must be part of the ethical and policy considerations. The relationships to be considered are not only those between surrogate and commissioning parents, but those among commissioning parent, surrogate, and child. Genetics, gestation, and contract are all relevant to these relationships and must receive due consideration and recognition; none of them 'trumps' to the exclusion of others. Finally, I argue that relational analysis makes clear that surrogacy entails not the creation of a traditional nuclear family by non-coital means, but rather joins other non-traditional families in creating new forms of family and kin relationships.

My exposition follows a rough chronological progression. I describe how different positions emerged over time both through philosophical conversation and in response to developments in reproductive medicine and technologies. While the development of various positions does not follow an unswerving straight line, this chronological approach highlights how positions have changed or developed in response to lived experience, scientific advances, and philosophical dialogue. Technological change and theoretical perspectives that paid attention to the significance of relationships each contributed to new understandings of how to ground legal parental status. And given the continuing advances in reproductive technologies and philosophical attention to care and relationship, there is every reason to think that the philosophical and legal understanding of parenthood is far from settled.

I focus primarily on the United States in tracing the evolving discussions of the role of genetics, contract, and gestation in establishing legal parental status because it is the country with which I am most familiar and because the wide variation in the regulation of surrogacy among the fifty states has generated rich discussion. Section II discusses the traditional cultural and legal assumption that genetic parents are a child's 'real' parents. Section III traces the development of the notion that in cases involving reproductive technologies, contract or intent is the proper grounding of legal parenthood. Section IV considers arguments that gestation creates indefeasible parental status for a woman who bore and gave birth. Section V considers the ways in which theories of care and relational rights encompass commissioning parents, surrogates, and the person created by their joint efforts, and argues that this framework is more satisfactory than those that focus on competing individual rights. Section VI suggests how the perspective of relational rights and care could shape regulations or practices that would give better cultural and legal recognition to the complex familial and kin relationships arising from surrogacy than do most current practices.

Before plunging into the main discussion, I want to make two observations that are beyond the scope of this paper but have great importance for those concerned with helping people establish parent–child relations. The first is that the point of using assisted reproductive technologies is the creation of a parent–child relationship, not simply conception, gestation, and birth. Those receiving medical treatment for infertility too often move from relatively non-invasive measures to ever more expensive and risky procedures without fully considering bringing an existing child into their lives through adoption. Because adoption, like conception achieved using assisted reproductive technologies (ARTs) leads to loving family relations, reproductive technologies and medicine should always be joined with consideration of adoption. The second is that those concerned about the formation of parent-child relations should also be concerned to put in place social policies that will support and sustain family relationships. The proper role for a liberal state is not 'hands off' the family, but the creation of an economic and social environment in which family relationships can thrive.[1]

II. Genetics and Natural Inevitability

The traditional or 'taken-for-granted' view of family formation and the establishing of a parent-child relationship was that 'by nature' men and women had sex, that this led

---

[1] M Eichner, *The Supportive State* (OUP 2010); L Ferguson, 'Family, Social Inequalities, and the Persuasive Force of Interpersonal Obligation' (2008) 22 International Journal of Law, Policy, and the Family 61; E Brake's chapter, 'Paid and Unpaid Care: Marriage, Equality, and Domestic Workers' argues that the importance of relationships suggests the need to grant legal recognition and state support to non-marital caregiving relationships.

to conception and childbirth, and that those who engaged in this procreative act were the parents of the resulting child. In American culture, 'family' meant biological parents and their children, and '[t]he relationship which is "real" or "true" or "blood" or "by birth" can never be severed, whatever its legal position', observed anthropologist David Schneider. The blood relationship 'is culturally defined as being an objective fact of nature, of fundamental significance and capable of having profound effects, and its nature cannot be terminated or changed'.[2] Social and legal constructions of parenthood were regarded as growing out of or resting upon the natural occurrences of coitus, pregnancy, and childbirth, simply ratifying or codifying existing natural relationships.

The general cultural understanding that the biological mother and father were the people who should exercise parental rights and assume parental responsibilities was thrown into question by social changes and, most dramatically, by the changes in conceptualizing human reproduction and family formation resulting from reproductive technologies. The birth of the first child conceived through *in vitro fertilization* (IVF) in 1978, the use of third-party gametes (eggs and sperm), and the practice of surrogacy all challenged traditional theories of parenthood based on the 'natural' relationship between parent and child arising from the genetic tie.

Until medical technology made it possible to remove and fertilize ova outside a woman's body, the identity of the genetic mother was always known when a woman gave birth, but not that of the genetic father. Marriage, therefore, became important to legal recognition of a man's parental status. Any child born to a married woman was considered the offspring of her husband; only if he had been 'beyond the seas' for a year and could not possibly have fathered a child did this 'marital presumption' give way. By contrast, a child born to a woman whose husband was abroad, or to a woman who was not married, was legally her child, but '*filius nullius*', the child of no man.[3]

Before the age of reproductive technologies, the main impetus for identifying genetic paternity was the desire by the state to create an obligation on unwed fathers to contribute financial support for the maintenance of non-marital children. In colonial New England there was community pressure to make sure that the father of an out-of-wedlock child either paid child support or married the mother.[4] That practice collapsed by the nineteenth century and unwed mothers became much more socially and legally isolated; but in the aftermath of the Civil War some effort was made to protect women from the loss of a male breadwinner. Although from the New Deal to the late twentieth century US welfare policy provided support to dependent children and their unmarried mothers as an entitlement, the Welfare Reform Act of 1996 required mothers receiving aid to identify the father(s) of their children, and to engage in paid work

---

[2] DM Schneider, *American Kinship: A Cultural Account* (University of Chicago Press 1968) 24. D Roberts, 'The Genetic Tie' (1995) 62 University of Chicago Law Review 209 discusses the difference in understandings of the significance of the genetic tie among African-Americans and other ethnic groups.

[3] M Grossberg, *Governing the Hearth: Law and the Family in Nineteenth-Century America* (University of North Carolina Press 1985). On England, see RH Helmholz 'Support Orders, Church Courts, and the Rule of Filius Nullius: A Reassessment of the Common Law' (1977) 63 Virginia Law Review 431.

[4] Midwives played a central role in this, formally asking the mother, 'at the height of travail', to name the father and then reporting that to authorities. See L Ulrich, *A Midwife's Tale* (Knopf Doubleday 1990). I am grateful to Professor L Murdoch for information regarding the history of state-imposed support obligations of unwed fathers in the United States.

('workfare'). This concern to link genetic fatherhood to financial obligation (but not to parental rights) continues to the present.[5]

Some unwed fathers invoked the genetic tie to claim rather than avoid parental rights and responsibilities, arguing that their genetic tie to a child supported legal recognition of parental status. While decisions across jurisdictions were not uniform, in a series of cases the Supreme Court articulated a standard that in instances when an unmarried biological father has established a relationship with his child, the father's right to continue the relationship may be constitutionally protected.[6] But this 'biology-plus-relationship' standard did not always lead to an order of filiation, and courts sometimes gave less weight to unwed fathers' claims when a mother opposed them and had remarried.[7]

Prior to the spread of alternative insemination and IVF, therefore, there was no undisputed consensus about the role genetics should play in establishing legal parental status for men, and while the law recognized any woman who gave birth as the legal mother, this was because she was *both* the genetic and the gestational mother (no one thought to make the distinction until embryo transfer was possible). It is fair to say, however, that the general assumption was that for women and men alike, moral and legal parenthood arose from the genetic tie.

As early as the 1940s and 1950s the use of alternative insemination to deal with male infertility initiated efforts to sever the link between genetic fatherhood and support obligations. Something like the marital presumption prevailed—a child born to a married woman was presumed to be the offspring of her husband. But this was sometimes done without the husband's (or offspring's) knowledge of the sperm donation. In 1973 the Uniform Parentage Act (a guideline for states) sought to lay to rest both secrecy and any claims from sperm donors by stating that if a husband gave written consent and insemination was done by a licensed physician, then the husband would be the legal father, and the sperm donor would have no parental rights or obligations. Contract or consent was henceforth to replace genetics as the basis for paternity in such situations.

And then, in 1978, the first human conceived outside the womb, Louise Brown, was born. Initially, IVF was promoted as a way for infertile married couples to have a genetically related child. Sperm and eggs from the couple were fertilized *in vitro*, and the resulting embryo(s) introduced into the woman's uterus. The only difference in conception through IVF and coitus for married heterosexual couples was where egg and sperm met.

Once fertilization occurred outside a woman's body, however, a host of possibilities expanding the array of families and family-like relationships emerged. The fact that both male and female gametes (sperm and eggs) could be separated from the body that

---

[5] D Archard and D Benatar (eds), *Procreation and Parenthood: The Ethics of Bearing and Rearing Children* (Oxford University Press 2010) contains several essays that discuss obligations of unwed parents.

[6] *Stanley v Illinois* 405 US 645 (1972); *Quilloin v Wolcott* 434 US 246 (1978); *Caban v Mohammed* 441 US 380 (1979); *Lehr v Robertson* 463 US 248 (1983). See ML Shanley, 'Fathers' Rights, Mothers' Wrongs?: Reflections on Unwed Fathers' Rights and Sex Equality' (1995) 75 Hypatia 74.

[7] *Michael H v Gerald D* 491 US 110 (1989) denied an unwed father's suit for a filiation decree and visitation despite the fact that he had lived with his daughter and her mother at various times and was known to the child as her father.

produced them meant that third-party gametes could be used to create an embryo.[8] Same-sex couples could create embryos genetically related to one partner. Single persons could use gametes from anonymous or known donors. And any female body of a suitable age could receive the embryo and carry the foetus to term. Initially, surrogate mothers were inseminated by the intended father, and so had both a genetic and gestational relationship to the child born at the end of their pregnancy (surrogacy using alternative insemination and the surrogate's eggs is now called 'traditional' or 'complete' surrogacy). But rising success rates in IVF, testimony from surrogates that they felt less conflicted about relinquishing a baby to whom they had no genetic connection, and the disposition of courts to grant custody more readily to commissioning persons when the surrogate did not have a genetic tie to the baby, all helped shift the practice of surrogacy to 'gestational' surrogacy.[9]

The use of donor eggs, sperm and embryos in a variety of contexts undercut the genetic grounding of parental status when formation of families took place through the use of reproductive technologies

III. Contract and Individual Autonomy

The development of gamete donation and surrogacy spurred efforts to declare contractual agreement rather than biological ties to be the proper ground for establishing legal parental status when assisted reproductive technologies were used. As long as the contracts were entered freely, without coercion or undue inducement, and with fully informed consent, proponents argued, they should be binding and enforced by the state. The notion that a pre-conception contract could be the basis of a legal parent–child relationship marked a new understanding of family formation.[10]

The Uniform Parentage Act of 1973 (a proposal for state statutes since family law in the US is governed by each state) was an early attempt to make contract rather than genetics the basis of legal parenthood. The Uniform Parentage Act applied only to married couples, and stated that if a husband gave written consent and insemination was done by a licensed physician, medical records were to be sealed and the husband would be the legal father and the donor would have no parental rights. In amendments adopted in 2002 the act treated egg donation as equivalent to sperm donation, stipulating that an egg or sperm donor is not a parent when a child is conceived through assisted reproduction or reproduction not involving sexual intercourse.[11] Naomi Cahn suggests that 'the UPA became a comprehensive framework for establishing the parents of any child, marital, nonmarital, or produced through reproductive technology,

---

[8] R Ameling, *Sex Cells: The Medical Market for Eggs and Sperm* (University of California Press 2001).
[9] M Strasser, 'Traditional Surrogacy Contracts, Partial Enforcement, and the Challenge for Family Law' (2015) 18 Journal of Health Care Law and Policy 85.
[10] The revolution in family formation sparked by assisted procreation was not the first time in American culture and law that people other than biological parents assumed parental responsibilities—apprenticeship was common during the colonial and early Republican periods and foster care and adoption both placed a child with non-biological caregivers. Each of these differed in significant ways, however, from pre-conception contracts.
[11] NR Cahn, *Test Tube Families* (New York UP 2009) 83–87.

setting the stage for "normalizing" children not born through traditional, marital intercourse'.[12] However, the UPA did not eliminate disputes that pitted biological groundings of parental status against contractual ones. In the US, these disputes led to no definitive resolution of the issue of how to ground parental rights in cases of the use of third-party gametes, embryos, or gestation, with state statutes, courts in different states, and at trial and appellate levels in a given state, reaching different conclusions.[13]

These differences and the significance of contracts were glaringly apparent in the multiple decisions in the landmark case of *Davis v Davis* (1992), all of which grappled with questions of whether gametes should be considered possessions, and if so, who should control their disposition when the gamete donors disagreed. The case involved the cryopreserved pre-embryos of Mary Sue and Junior Lewis Davis. The couple married in April 1980 and began trying to conceive a child. Six attempts in 1985 to conceive through IVF failed. In 1988 they again tried IVF treatments; nine embryos were created of which two were transferred unsuccessfully, and seven were cryogenically preserved. The couple divorced the following year, but could not agree on what to do with the seven cryopreserved pre-embryos. Mary Sue wanted to use the pre-embryos for future attempts at pregnancy, while Junior wanted them to remain cryopreserved because he did not want to be the genetic father of a child that he would not raise. The trial court and the Court of Appeals disagreed on what principles to use in resolving this case. On appeal, the Tennessee Supreme Court in 1992 held that both gamete providers had an interest in whether the embryos would be transferred, and that in the event of a dispute, a court should enforce any prior agreement between the gamete providers.[14] In the absence of such an agreement, the Court said, courts should weigh the interests of the parties, ordinarily ruling in favour of the party who wishes to avoid procreation, and so the Court supported Junior's right not to become a father. But in strong language the Court said that the case demonstrated that it was imperative that people using reproductive technologies make binding written agreements prior to beginning any attempt at procreation.

A more multi-faceted dispute involving genetic ties, gestation, and contracts had galvanized national attention only a few years previously in the *Baby M* case (1988). *Baby M* remains the best-known legal contest involving 'surrogate motherhood' in the United States, and the litigants appealed to a wide range of criteria for awarding legal parental status. The final decision used a genetic understanding of legal parental status, holding that the surrogate, Mary Beth Whitehead, was the legal mother of the baby who was her genetic offspring and to whom she gave birth, and William Stern, the child's genetic father, was the legal father.[15]

---

[12] ibid 85.
[13] In 2017, surrogacy was legal in thirty-four states and the District of Columbia but in some only a post-birth parentage order is available or additional post-birth legal procedures may be required; in eleven states surrogacy is practised but there are serious legal hurdles; five states prohibit commercial surrogacy contracts or will not issue a birth certificate to both intended parents. Creative Family Connections, 'Gestational Surrogacy Law Across the United States' (Creative Family Connections, 2017) <https://www.creativefamilyconnections.com/us-surrogacy-law-map/> accessed 24 October 2017.
[14] *Davis v Davis*, 842 SW 2d (1992).
[15] Re *Baby M*, 525 A2d 1128 (Superior Court, Chancery Division, 1987); reversed on appeal, *Baby M*, 536 A2d 1227 (NJ 1988). Trial testimony is discussed in C Sanger, 'Developing Markets in Baby-Making: In the Matter of Baby M' (2007) 30 Harvard Journal of Law & Gender 67.

In 1985 Mary Beth Whitehead, a married mother of two, agreed to be inseminated with the sperm of William Stern and to give up any child born as a result to him and his wife for a fee of $10,000. 'Baby M' was born in March 1986; three days later Ms Whitehead turned the baby over to the Sterns, but shortly thereafter persuaded the Sterns to let her take the baby temporarily, promising to return with her later. She then told the Sterns that she had changed her mind and could not relinquish the baby, fleeing with her husband from New Jersey to Florida. Over the next three months she moved from one motel to another with the baby, periodically speaking with Mr Stern by phone to tell him that the baby was all right. At the end of July, Florida police found and took possession of the baby, and New Jersey authorities delivered Baby M to the Sterns; in response, Ms Whitehead began a custody proceeding in New Jersey. On 31 March 1987, the trial court ruled that the contract by which Ms Whitehead had agreed to bear the child for the Sterns was valid; he declared that Mr Stern was the legal parent and he issued an order of adoption making Elizabeth Stern the baby's legal mother. On appeal, the New Jersey Supreme Court reversed that decision, holding that surrogacy contracts are invalid and unenforceable. The Court ruled that Ms Whitehead was 'the natural mother' of the child, and therefore was the child's legal mother. The Court granted custody to Mr Stern but ordered that Ms Whitehead be allowed visitation with the child, leaving it to the trial court to work out what kind of visitation would be in the child's best interest.

The turbulent litigation and heated public debate pushed legal reform efforts in the direction of insisting that people engaging in collaborative procreation should make explicit written agreements and be held to them—and that this should apply to intentional parents, to third-party gamete and embryo providers, and to surrogate mothers. That is, despite the courts' granting legal parental status to the genetic parents in both *Davis v Davis* and *Baby M*, the long-term effect of these cases was *not* to solidify and sustain the notion that legal parental status should be based on genetics, but rather to challenge and undermine that position. Proponents of using contracts to establish a legal parent–child relationship pointed out that had there been a binding contract in these cases, the cases could have been resolved quickly, avoiding lengthy litigation and also, in *Baby M*, uncertainty for the child as well as the parents.

As these cases were moving through the courts, some legal scholars like John Robertson argued that 'preconception rearing intentions should count as much as or more than biologic connection' in establishing legal parenthood in cases of collaborative procreation. Robertson saw 'compelling reasons for recognizing the pre-conception intentions of the parties as the presumptive arbiter of rearing rights and duties, as long as the welfare of the offspring will not be severely damaged by honoring these intentions'.[16] Marjorie Shultz agreed, asserting that when procreative agreements are 'deliberate, explicit and bargained for ... as they are in technologically assisted reproductive

---

[16] Robertson took the position that the right to control what happens to one's genetic material is part of what it means to be a self-possessing individual: 'Although the bundle of property rights attached to one's ownership of an embryo may be more circumscribed than for other things, it is an ownership or property interest nonetheless.... [T]he persons who provide the egg and sperm have the strongest claim to ownership of the embryo.' JA Robertson, *Children of Choice: Freedom and the New Reproductive Technologies* (Princeton UP 1994) 104–05.

arrangements, they should be honored'.[17] Carmel Shalev argued that autonomy should be understood as 'the deliberate exercise of choice with respect to the individual's reproductive capacity'.[18] These and other scholars saw enforceable contracts as a way to enhance individual freedom and responsibility for all involved.

The rubric of reproductive freedom, contractual agreement, and individual choice in thinking about family formation using reproductive technologies resonated with other aspects of late-twentieth century culture in the United States. The abortion debates used the terms 'choice' and 'reproductive freedom' to emphasize the right of each individual woman to control her reproductive life. Proponents of a contractual grounding of parental status in cases of gamete donation and surrogacy invoked these understandings of 'choice' and 'reproductive freedom' in making their case that both those seeking to become parents and those selling genetic material or gestational service should be able to decide what to do with their bodies free of government prohibition or regulation.

Also influencing the reception of contracts for collaborative procreation was the fact that when egg extraction and IVF became possible after 1978, eggs and embryos were viewed as analogous to sperm, as separable from the body, and as capable of being exchanged and commodified. When gametes are separable from the provider they can appear to have certain characteristics of commodities, objects 'produced' by the body that become part of a common store, as the term 'sperm bank' suggests, a generalized 'resource' that can be traded in the market. Marilyn Strathern emphasized the enormous power of market thinking: 'we think so freely of the providing and purchasing of goods and services that transactions in gametes is already a thought-of act of commerce'.[19] Gestational surrogacy, like eggs and sperm, could be sold on the market, including the global market.[20]

The combination of pro-choice insistence on individuals' authority to choose to do as they wished with their reproductive capacities and the equation of market choice with consumer freedom created a receptive environment for agreements that contractual agreement was the proper grounding of legal parental status in cases of procreation using ARTs.

IV. Gestation and Women's Bodies

In response to *Baby M* and other contested surrogacy cases, 'traditional' or 'complete' surrogacy declined significantly, replaced by the more difficult and costly procedure of 'gestational' surrogacy, in which the surrogate has no genetic relationship to the

---

[17] MM Shultz, 'Reproductive Technology and Intention-based Parenthood: An Opportunity for Gender Neutrality' (1990) 1990 Wisconsin Law Review 300.
[18] C Shalev, *Birth Power: The Case for Surrogacy* (Yale UP 1989) 103.
[19] M Strathern, *Reproducing the Future* (CUP 1992) 37.
[20] As contracting for gestational services increased in the twenty-first century, concerns about the economic disparity between intentional parents and surrogates, and the potential for exploitation of poor women gained public attention. I do not consider intercountry surrogacy here, but economic disparity and the difficulty of future contact among surrogate, intentional parents, and offspring make it nearly impossible to structure this as an ethical practice. See P Laufer-Ukeles, 'Mothering for Money: Regulating Commercial Intimacy' (2013) 88 Indiana Law Review 1223; A Phillips, 'Exploitation, Commodification, and Equality' in M Deveaux and V Panitch (eds), *Exploitation: From Practice to Theory* (Rowman & Littlefield 2017).

embryo created through IVF, thus removing the genetic component of a surrogate's claim to parental status, leaving only gestation. But neither the push to create enforceable contracts nor the effort to eliminate the surrogate's genetic relationship to the foetus quelled the bitter controversies over surrogacy and, in particular, the surrogate's claim to recognition as a parent.

Carole Pateman and Margaret Jane Radin, for example, both argued that gestational labour is far more closely tied to a woman's identity than other kinds of labour, and that the enforcement of a pregnancy contract against the will of the surrogate entails an alienation of the self that renders the agreement void.[21] The 'work' of pregnancy is not external to the body: during the nine months of pregnancy, the foetus is intimately connected with the woman's body: nutrients and oxygen cross the placenta to provide nourishment, and waste material is eliminated through the flow of blood. Indeed, the placenta is formed from tissue provided by both the mother (the decidua) and the embryo (the chorion); the habit of saying that the foetus resides 'within' the woman's body obscures their interconnectedness.

Barbara Katz Rothman argued that maternal caregiving during pregnancy gave the gestational mother a particularly strong claim to recognition as a legal parent at the birth of a child. In Recreating Motherhood (1989) Rothman contended that 'Infants belong to their mothers at birth because of the unique nurturant relationship that has existed between them up to that moment. That is, birth mothers have full parental rights, including rights of custody, of the babies they bore'.[22] Rothman emphasized that her rejection of the assignment of legal parenthood based on the genetic tie rested on her understanding of pregnancy as 'a social as well as a physical relationship', and that 'any mother is engaged in a social interaction with her foetus as the pregnancy progresses'. Rothman gave the gestational mother an absolute claim for six weeks after giving birth (during which time any adoption decision would rest solely in her hands). After six weeks, 'custody would go to the nurturing parent in case of dispute'.[23]

James G Dwyer, although very unlike Rothman on other issues, also privileged the birth mother. Men could become legal parents automatically, without petitioning,

> only if they are married to the birth mother and the mother consents to their parenthood. This approach treats the mother-child relationship as presumptively the core relationship for a newborn child, on the assumption that being the birth mother of a child creates a psychological bond with the child even before birth.[24]

Anca Gheaus, arguing that biological parents have a right to parent their child, noted that 'pregnancy [is] a uniquely privileged context for developing a bond that is both physical and imaginative with the future child'. This bond gives birth mothers parental rights, and the significance of the bond to the baby 'may ground a parental right to

---

[21] C Pateman, *The Sexual Contract* (University of California Press 1988) 216; MJ Radin, 'Market Inalienability' (1987) 100 Harvard Law Review. A Rich had expressed her subjective experience of this connection: 'In early pregnancy, the stirring of the foetus felt like ghostly tremors of my own body, later like the movements of a being imprisoned within me; but both sensations were my sensations, contributing to my own sense of physical and psychic space.' A Rich, *Of Woman Born: Motherhood as Experience and as Institution* (Norton 1970) 47.

[22] B Katz Rothman, *Recreating Motherhood: Ideology and Technology in a Patriarchal Society* (Norton 1989) 254.

[23] ibid 255.   [24] JG Dwyer, *The Relationship Rights of Children* (CUP 2006) 265.

keep and raise that baby based on the child's interest'.[25] While it can be severed, for these scholars the relationship between woman and foetus is intrinsic to gestation.

Many people who thought that gender had to be taken into account in assessing the biological, social, and cultural significance of surrogacy did not agree with Rothman that surrogates should have exclusive parental rights for six weeks after birth, but did contend that pre-conception or pre-implantation pregnancy contracts should not be enforced when a surrogate changed her mind. Some argued that to enforce such contracts 'seems to belie notions that [parent-child] relationships should not be bought or sold in the marketplace'.[26]

The difference in economic and other resources between commissioning parents and surrogate reflects and creates imbalances of class and gender in both contract negotiation and relations during the pregnancy. Despite the inextricable interdependency of foetus and surrogate, surrogacy is a practice in which one woman's body is valued as a means to meet the needs of (by implication more significant) others. Surrogacy inescapably reflects and re-inscribes class and gender inequality and when a poorer woman of colour carries a foetus for a white woman, the practice re-inscribes racial hierarchy as well.[27]

I have, for twenty years, considered and felt the pull of the argument that surrogacy contracts should be enforced when the woman bearing the child changes her mind about relinquishment.[28] The great value of enforceable contracts is that they avoid uncertainty, delay, and litigation, and timely permanent placement is beneficial to a child. And giving surrogates the opportunity to rescind their agreement to relinquish parental rights would cause great suffering to the commissioning parents (although they might be awarded custody after a court hearing). But it is not possible to eliminate the pain of custody adjudication, and potential adoptive parents (including foster parents who have bonds to a child that they hope to adopt) also live with uncertainty and, occasionally, the pain of having their expectations and dreams denied.

We must weigh against the pain of unfulfilled parental hopes not only the anguish of the gestational mother faced with losing a child with whom she was in the closest possible physical intimacy during pregnancy, but the cultural reverberations of appropriating the reproductive labour of women. The latter is especially significant in the United States, where such appropriation was sanctioned by the laws of slavery. Although the

---

[25] A Gheaus, 'The Right to Parent One's Biological Baby' (2012) 20 The Journal of Political Philosophy 432, 449, 452 n 46.

[26] Laufer-Ukeles, 'Mothering for Money' (n 20) 1257.

[27] A Phillips noted that surrogacy is 'an intrinsically inegalitarian trade' due not only to the unequal bargaining position of the surrogate and the commissioning parents, but also to the fact that 'commercial surrogacy is a luxury good that depends on treating some people's childlessness as a matter of more consequence than that of others.' Phillips, 'Exploitation' (n 20). M Goodwin discusses both race exploitation and poverty as 'tolerated components of assisted reproductive technology' in 'Reproducing Hierarchy in Commercial Intimacy' (2013) 88 Indiana Law Journal 1289.

[28] See ML Shanley, '"Surrogate Mothering" and Women's Freedom: A Critique of Contracts for Human Reproduction' (1993) 18 Signs: Journal of Women in Culture & Society 618; ML Shanley, *Making Babies, Making Families: What Matters Most in an Age of Reproductive Technologies, Surrogacy, Adoption, and Same-Sex and Unwed Parents* (Beacon Press 2001); ML Shanley and S Jesudason, 'Surrogacy: Reinscribing or Pluralizing Understandings of Family?' in D Cutas and S Chan (eds), *Families: Beyond the Nuclear Ideal* (Bloomsbury Academic Press 2014).

woman who bargains and enters a contract for gestational service is clearly not a slave, the assertion of another person's legal ownership of the baby to whom she gives birth, 'turn[s] women's labour into something that is used and controlled by others'. This, in addition to the reinforcement of gender stereotypes that have been used to justify the unequal treatment of women, perpetuates a 'traditional gender-hierarchical division of labour'.[29]

The number of disputed outcomes in surrogacy cases is very small. The possibility that parental status could be adjudicated following birth would make doctors, counsellors, lawyers and any others facilitating a surrogacy take great pains to screen both surrogates and commissioning parents.

In the end, I find that to deny parental status to a woman who has borne and birthed a child commodifies human reproduction, fails to give adequate recognition to the unique character of gestational labour, reflects and reinforces women's subordinate status in the contemporary United States, and values the reproductive aspirations of some over those of others. The social harm, at least in our contemporary context, outweighs the good. Jennifer Nedelsky observed that 'we are likely to experience our responsibilities differently as we recognize that our "private rights" always have social consequences'.[30] Contracts for human reproduction are undeniably important tools in the creation of family relationships; but assigning parental status *exclusively* by contract obscures the multifaceted, complex, and profound relationships generated by genetics, gestation, and contract alike.

V. Care and Relationship

In the final decades of the twentieth century, thinking about parental rights was influenced by the work of philosophers and political theorists who were engaged in rethinking classical liberal notions of the self, autonomy, and individual rights. The ethics of care, developed by feminists beginning in the 1980s, brought women's traditional activities into philosophical discussions that had largely ignored them, along with the profound interdependence and relationships that characterize all human existence.[31] During the same period, other theorists who shared the concern that traditional-liberal theory did not give adequate recognition to the role relationships played in the development of autonomy were developing what they called a theory of relational rights.[32] By the turn of the century, theories of the ethics of care and of relational rights

---

[29] D Satz, 'Markets in Women's Reproductive Labor' (1992) 21 Philosophy & Public Affairs 123.

[30] J Nedelsky, 'Reconceiving Rights as Relationship' (1993) 1 Review of Constitutional Studies/*Revue d'études constitutionnelles* 17.

[31] C Gilligan, *In a Different Voice* (Harvard UP 1982); J Tronto, *Moral Boundaries: A Political Argument for an Ethics of Care* (Routledge 1993); EF Kittay, *Love's Labor* (Routledge 1998); M Harrington, *Care and Equality* (Knopf 1999); V Held, *The Ethics of Care: Personal, Political and Global* (OUP 2005).

[32] ML Minow, 'Rights for the Next Generation: A Feminist Approach to Children's Rights' (1986) 9 Harvard Women's Law Journal 1; J Nedelsky, 'Reconceiving Autonomy: Sources, Thoughts and Possibilities' (1989) Yale Journal of Law & Feminism 7; ML Minow and ML Shanley, 'Relational Rights and Responsibilities: Revisioning the Family in Political Theory and Law' (1996) 11 Hypatia 4; MM Kavanagh, 'Rewriting the Legal Family: Beyond Exclusivity to a Care-based Standard' (2004) 16 Yale Journal of Law & Feminism 83; R Zafran, 'Children's Rights as Relational Rights: The Case of Relocation' (2010) 18 American University Journal of Gender, Social Policy & the Law 163; Laufer-Ukeles, 'Mothering for Money' (n 20).

had proven themselves powerful tools for conceptualizing family relationships created through use of assisted reproductive technologies.

Carol Gilligan's *In a Different Voice* (1982) is often taken as the first significant articulation of ideas that inspired the development of the ethics of care.[33] Gilligan challenged Lawrence Kohlberg's claim that ethical reasoning progressed up a six-stage ladder of moral reasoning, culminating in the articulation of universal principles. Gilligan charged that Kohlberg's methodology was male-biased, privileging men's accounts of their (abstract) moral reasoning. Examining interviews with women contemplating whether to have an abortion, Gilligan identified 'a different voice' that articulated forms of moral perception and reasoning other than those based on rules, universal principles, and rights.

Applying Gilligan's epistemological insights to political and legal theory, Seyla Benhabib showed how the notions of the 'social contract' and the 'state of nature', central to classical–liberal theories from Thomas Hobbes to John Rawls, mask human interdependency and exaggerate the separation between public and private spheres.[34] Sara Ruddick, focusing on women's lived experience as a source of knowledge, insisted that forms of thinking are linked to distinctive practices, and that the activities of mothering generated moral insights as significant as those derived from abstract ratiocination.[35]

Theorists developing what became known as theories of relational rights also challenged classical–liberal individualism. Jennifer Nedelsky pointed out that 'Most conventional liberal rights theories ... do not make relationship central to their understanding of the human subject.... The selves to be protected by rights are seen as essentially separate and not creatures whose interests, needs and capacities routinely intertwine.'[36] The notion that autonomy requires protection and separation from others is 'deeply misguided'; rather, 'what makes autonomy possible is not separation, but relationship.'[37] The shift from focusing on individual autonomy and rights to relational autonomy and rights is not to abandon liberal theory but rather to add an important dimension to it.[38] Laufer-Ukeles similarly argued that the way 'to optimize autonomy [is] by recognizing circumstances, conditions, and surrounding relationships.'[39] If society 'structure[es] relationships so that they foster autonomy', then 'dependence is no longer the antithesis of autonomy, but a precondition in the relationships—between parent and child, student and teacher, state and citizen—which provide the security, education, nurturing, and support that make the development of autonomy possible'. Nor is this a singular or static event, but 'a capacity that requires ongoing relationships that help it flourish; it can wither or thrive throughout one's adult life.'[40]

---

[33] Gilligan (n 31).

[34] S Benhabib, 'The Generalized and Concrete Other: The Kohlberg-Gilligan Controversy and Moral Theory' (1986) 5 Praxis International 38. Like Benhabib, Held pointed out that 'Western liberal democratic thought has been built on the concept of the "individual" seen as a theoretically isolatable entity. This entity can assert interests, have rights, and enter into contractual relationships with other entities. But this individual is not seen as related to other individuals in inextricable or intrinsic ways.' Held (n 31) 124.

[35] S Ruddick, *Maternal Thinking: Towards a Politics of Peace* (Beacon 1989).

[36] Nedelsky, 'Reconceiving Rights as Relationship' (n 30) 12.   [37] ibid 8.

[38] 'The liberal tradition has been not so much wrong as seriously and dangerously one-sided in its emphasis.' ibid 13.

[39] Laufer-Ukeles, 'Mothering for Money' (n 20) 1228.

[40] Nedelsky, 'Reconceiving Rights as Relationship' (n 30) 8.

Theories both of care and relational rights provided a rich and innovative approach to thinking about who should be recognized as the legal parent of a child born through gamete transfer and surrogacy. Each of the components of a surrogate pregnancy—genes, contractual agreement, gestation—creates relationships that need to be recognized in both social practice and legal discourse.

Take genetics: sperm and eggs are currently commonly treated as commodities, and donors are anonymous. Some donor-conceived children and adults, like adoptees who sought to end the practice of sealed adoption records, pressed for reforms to do away with anonymous sperm and egg donation. Significantly, they did not voice a desire for medical information alone, but also for social information and identity; their focus was on every person's interest in a full narrative of his or her origin.[41] Many donor-conceived persons also wanted information about 'donor siblings': persons conceived with genetic material from the same donor. Some said they wanted to avoid inadvertent incest, while others said they had a sense of affinity with possible genetic relatives, and identity concerns linked in the imagination to nationality and religion.[42] There are not yet studies of what persons born of surrogacy arrangements think and feel about the circumstances of their conception and birth, but the experiences of adoptees and donor-conceived persons seem relevant to children born of surrogacy arrangements.

Sally Haslanger argued that insistence on non-anonymous gamete transfer 'entrench[es] and naturalize[s] the value of biological ties' and in so doing fails to disrupt and displace 'old ideologies of the family'.[43] She refuted David Velleman's contention that anonymous sperm and egg donation for purposes of procreation is morally wrong. Velleman believes that it is not enough to fill out extensive questionnaires, or even to have open records; rather, face-to-face meetings are required because knowledge of biological progenitors is necessary for successful identity formation. Haslanger remarks that 'it is hard to even entertain the idea that contact with birth families is necessary for a good life' when innumerable adoptees lead excellent lives without contact with birthparents.[44] The problem for some adoptees is not lack of contact, or even of information, Haslanger insists, but the cultural stigma of not being able to fit the bionormative model of the nuclear family. Rather than taking steps to fit donor-conceived families into the dominant cultural schema, we should instead make every effort 'to combat the dominance of the schema'.[45]

---

[41] Adult adoptees made the public aware of the importance of open records. Recently, donor-conceived offspring filed a lawsuit in British Columbia seeking to establish that donor-conceived offspring have equal rights with adoptees to know their genetic forebears. The lower court decision granted a donor-conceived person the right to know the identity of her sperm donor, but the Appeals Court overturned this, declaring that there was no right 'to know one's past'. British Columbia Court of Appeal (BCCA) in *Pratten v British Columbia*, 2012 BCCA 480. Despite the final outcome, however, the case made an impact on people's attitudes. In 2011, Washington became the first US state to ban anonymous sperm and egg donation. When offspring conceived from sperm and egg donation banks or agencies in Washington reach age eighteen they can access their donors' medical histories and their full names, unless a donor has specifically refused to have his or her name released. WA Legis 283 (Westlaw 2011).

[42] N Cahn, 'The New Kinship' (2012) 100 The Georgetown Law Journal 367; W Kramer and N Cahn, *Finding Our Families* (Penguin 2013).

[43] S Haslanger, 'Family, Ancestry and Self: What is the Moral Significance of Biological Ties?' (2009) 2 Adoption & Culture 91, 92.

[44] ibid 102.   [45] ibid 113.

The requirement of open records upon request of the donor-conceived person, however, is not necessarily bio-normative; it disrupts other cultural tropes about families. For example, open records challenge the idea that there are two and only two adults with whom the child may have a relational interest and who may have an interest in maintaining some kind of relationship (letters, phone calls, visitation, or even periodic information) with the child. Indeed, unsealed birth records in adoption and non-anonymous gamete donation seem to me to undercut the notion that progenitors are the 'real' parents, and such policy also respects the testimony of some adoptees and donor-conceived persons about their experiences while leaving requests for information or contact up to future persons.

Acknowledgement of genetic forbearers as well as gestational mothers does not, it seems to me, contribute to genetic essentialism but to a sense of responsibility for procreative potential and activity, and to a more capacious understanding of 'family' and 'kinship' that could have salutary effects on social inclusion and acceptance of a plurality of family forms. Not only offspring but commissioning parents benefit from full stories of origin. Melanie Thernstrom, who became a parent of two children born with donor eggs and surrogacy, points out that the family narrative can be important to the commissioning parents as well as their children: 'When I tried to think about why I don't want to have donor-and-surrogacy amnesia, it isn't that it seems unfair to them (although it is), but that it erases our own experience of how our children came to be.'[46] In surrogacy, '[P]arental rights are disaggregated and deconstructed in a manner that rejects the exclusive binary rights of traditional parenthood and embraces a more kin-like, extended, and functional family structure.'[47]

Contracts, too, create intrinsic and on-going relationships, and are not simply vehicles by which competent adults agree to mutually beneficial arrangements: '[t]he commissioning couple does not just enter into a *contract* with the surrogate: they embark on a *relationship* with her.'[48] The process of drawing up a surrogacy contract could be tremendously helpful in clarifying the priorities and expectations of both the surrogate and the commissioning parents. Doing this would help them to articulate and share their hopes, desires and expectations, along with the conditions of their continuing involvement.[49] Studies show that in domestic surrogacy, surrogates and commissioning parents are affected by their relationship with one another. That relationship begins in discussions of their agreement, continues through pregnancy, and persists after birth. Empirical studies reveal that surrogates experience their commissioned pregnancy 'as an intimate relationship in which attachments and emotional relationships are formed, if not with the foetus, then with the commissioning parents'.[50] Heléna Ragoné speculated that the language of 'gift' ('the gift of life') that often appears

---

[46] M Thernstrom, 'My Futuristic Insta-Family' *New York Times Magazine* (New York, 2 January 2011) 43.
[47] Laufer-Ukeles, 'Mothering for Money' (n 20) 1252. See also Kavanagh, 'Rewriting the Legal Family' (n 32), P Laufer-Ukeles and A Blecher-Prigat, 'Between Function and Form: Towards a Differentiated Model of Functional Parenthood' (2013) 20 George Mason Law Review 419.
[48] JA Parks, 'Care Ethics and the Global Practice of Commercial Surrogacy' (2010) 24 *Bioethics* 331, 338.
[49] See BH Bix's chapter, 'Private Ordering in Family Law'. Also D Zalesne, 'The Contractual Family: The Role of the Market in Shaping Family Formations and Rights' (2015) 36 Cardozo Law Review 1027.
[50] Laufer-Ukeles, 'Mothering for Money' (n 20) 1226–27.

in accounts by both surrogates and commissioning parents suggested that their relationship extended beyond the commercial transaction. She noted that despite the fact that 'surrogates are discouraged from thinking of their relationship to the couple' as a permanent one, 'surrogates recognize that they are creating a state of enduring solidarity between themselves and their couples'. And the commissioning parents, in acknowledging that the surrogate is giving them the 'gift' of a child, seem to 'accept a permanent state of indebtedness to their surrogate'.[51]

Contract begins a process that creates both a physical and an emotional relationship between the surrogate and foetus. While for observers pregnancy may appear to be 'a time of waiting and watching, when nothing happens', the pregnant woman experiences herself as a 'participant in a creative process. Though she does not plan and direct it, neither does it merely wash over her; rather, she *is* this process, this change.'[52] The fundamental fact that mother and foetus are at one and the same time distinct and interrelated entities, means that to speak of the 'freedom' of the mother as residing in her intention as an 'autonomous' agent misunderstands both the relationship between woman and child and that of the woman to her ongoing self. Despite this close relationship, most surrogates navigate the transfer of their maternal status to the commissioning parents during the course of pregnancy and birthing. After birth, some surrogates describe their relationship to that child as like that of an aunt or family friend and hope for (and expect) a continuing relationship with both the parents and the child.[53]

The contract also creates a relationship between the commissioning parent and the foetus. Their aspiration to parent initiates the process of conception and gestation. Their financial support of the surrogate during pregnancy is care not only for her but also of the foetus. During the nine months of pregnancy they plan for the child's entrance into their family, and imagine their future family life together. It is, indeed, the relationship that the contract establishes between commissioning parents and the foetus that makes it unacceptable for commissioning parents to refuse legal parental status upon the birth of a child whose life their actions initiated. (They may, like other parents, relinquish their parental rights if they feel they cannot raise the child but at birth they are legal parents unless the surrogate asserts a parental claim.)

VI. Practices that Help Reframe Parenthood and Family Relationships

Framing surrogacy either as one of a series of medical procedures or as a mutually beneficial employment agreement fails to encompass fully what the practice entails. As

---

[51] H Ragoné, 'The Gift of Life: Surrogate Motherhood, Gamete Donation, and Constructions of Altruism' in R Cook, SD Sclater, and F Kaganas (eds), *Surrogate Motherhood: International Perspectives* (Hart Publishing 2003) 215–16. E Teman's study of surrogacy in Israel, where national policy actively supports surrogacy, found that strong bonds between surrogate and commissioning mother developed over the nine months of pregnancy. Israel has a long and detailed protocol to 'transfer motherhood', a recognition of the significance of the transfer of parental status to all those involved. See E Teman, *Birthing a Mother: The Surrogate Body and the Pregnant Self* (University of California Press 2010).

[52] IM Young, *'Throwing Like a Girl' and Other Essays in Feminist Philosophy and Social Theory* (Indiana UP 1990) 167.

[53] Shanley and Jesudason, 'Surrogacy' (n 28).

Naomi Cahn observed of medical personnel facilitating surrogacy, they are 'focused on gamete safety or truth in advertising, [and] cater only to the parents as patients, not to the families they are creating'.[54] The same is true of lawyers drafting pregnancy contracts; they are focused on insuring informed consent, full disclosure, and lack of coercion for their clients, not the families these clients are creating. But surrogacy is a process that creates new family relationships and family forms. A person born through a surrogate arrangement is linked in significant ways to gamete donor(s) (who may be the commissioning parents), surrogate, and commissioning parents, and these persons, too, are linked by their collaboration in creating another human life, a parent–child relationship, and hence a new form of family.

People who have been concerned that members of the medical and legal professions do not give adequate attention to the complex relationships entailed in family creation using ARTs, have suggested a variety of measures such as stricter guidelines for fertility clinics,[55] the licensing of commissioning parents,[56] or regulatory legislation[57] to shift attention from individual patients and clients to the complex relationships of which they willy-nilly become part. I am not going to choose here among these mechanisms; what I want to do is explain why I think we must shift the discourse surrounding surrogacy from one of protecting individual rights to one of recognizing and promoting the multiple and complex relationships involved in creating parent–child relationships through surrogacy, and in doing so promote our understanding and acceptance of multiple family forms.

Various practices could help give the complex relationships involved in surrogacy practical expression. Commentators have suggested measures like extensive pre-conception counselling and counselling during pregnancy to identify, in the first instance, 'familial, economic, and social pressures that may compromise autonomy' and freely-chosen obligations.[58] But it would also focus on the complexity of the new relationships that the commissioning parents and surrogate are entering, and would examine their expectations concerning post-birth contact with one another and between surrogate and child. Christine Overall advocated screening and counselling '*before* the contract is signed and before conception … or implantation' in order that commissioning parents and surrogate understand their responsibilities to one another *and* to the 'needs, interests, and wellbeing' of the person who might come into being as a result of their actions.[59] As one commenter observed, 'The staff (at a fertility clinic) should be rooting for the child. They should be aware that what they are doing is more than giving medical treatment. It is about creating a life for someone who will grow up to be an individual with rights and possibilities.'[60] Measures such as non-anonymity of

---

[54] Cahn, 'The New Kinship' (n 42) 49.

[55] G Pennings, 'Reproductive Tourism as Moral Pluralism in Motion' (2002) 28 Journal of Medical Ethics 337; S Golombok et al (eds), *Regulating Reproductive Donation* (CUP 2016).

[56] A Asch, 'Licensing Parents: Regulating assisted reproduction' in D Cutas and S Chan (eds), *Families— Beyond the Nuclear Ideal* (Bloomsbury Academic 2012); C Overall, 'Reproductive "Surrogacy" and Parental Licensing' (2015) 29 Bioethics 353.

[57] Laufer-Ukeles, 'Mothering for Money' (n 20); Teman (n 51).   [58] ibid 1263.

[59] Overall, 'Reproductive "Surrogacy"' (n 56), 359, 354.

[60] AC Lalos, C Gottlieb, and O Lalos, 'Legislated Right for Donor-insemination Children to Know their Genetic Origin: A Study of Parental Thinking' (2007) 22 Human Reproduction 1759, quoted in Asch, 'Licensing Parents' (n 56) 138. IG Cohen and others have countered the notion that it is proper to set policy

gamete donors and surrogates, in-person meetings between surrogate and commissioning parent(s), and post-birth contact between surrogate and commissioning parent and between surrogate and child are valuable practices. Each one helps shift the focus from the moment of decision to establishing and maintaining connections that support identity formation and the continuing development and exercise of autonomy.

One of the most important needs of the person who will come into being is a story of origin. Jennifer Parks noted that the child born of surrogacy deserves 'the same opportunity to be enveloped in a family history and narrative as their naturally conceived counterparts', a narrative that begins well before birth.[61] It is not simply medical information that is at stake, but a full sense of social location.[62] Having a story of origin, with information about the persons who made one's existence possible, is something that practices and policies regarding ARTs and surrogacy should make possible.

Counselling, therefore, would focus on how to tell children where they came from, and why this is important to the child and the future adult the child will become. The right of donor-conceived persons and those carried by a surrogate to as full a narrative of their origins as possible creates an obligation of disclosure for gamete donors, surrogates, and commissioning parents. Although a requirement of non-anonymity runs the risk of suggesting that successful identity formation depends on knowing one's progenitors, the right to access the information could belong only to the donor-conceived person and only after reaching a certain age (probably somewhere in the teenage years). The message would not be that the progenitor is the 'real' parent or that knowledge of his or her identity determines the offspring's own. Rather, it reflects respect for the donor-conceived person's right not to be shut out from information that he or she determines is important, that is, to be as far as possible given agency. It also emphasizes that gamete transfer is not simply sale of a commodity, but is integral to the creation of a human life. Gamete donors would learn why some donor-conceived persons seek information about their genetic progenitors, and why they should agree to terms that are in the interest of the future person. If they cannot agree to be named in a donor register, they cannot donate. The issue of anonymity does not arise as often in surrogacy, since surrogate and commissioning parents enter into a contractual agreement, although any person born of surrogacy should be able to know whether the woman was the genetic as well as the gestational mother.

---

based on the supposed interests of future persons. IG Cohen, 'Regulating Reproduction: The Problem with Best Interests' (2011) 96 Minnesota Law Review 423. Yet this does not do away with the question of what persons living now should do out of respect for future persons who cannot speak for or represent themselves. We have enough information about the experiences and expressed desires of adoptees and donor-conceived persons to know that some, at least, want open records and a possibility of contact with birthparents and genetic forbearers. It is also important to bear in mind that the person who comes into existence should not be thought of simply as a child, but rather as someone who may have a long lifetime that extends through adulthood and into old age, with desires and needs we cannot know in the present.

[61] Parks, 'Care Ethics and the Global Practice' (n 48) 337.

[62] E Blyth and L Firth, 'Donor-Conceived People's Access to Genetic and Biographical History: An Analysis of Provisions in Different Jurisdictions Permitting Disclosure of Donor Identity' (2009) 23 International Journal of Law, Policy, & Family 174; V Ravitsky, 'Knowing Where You Come From: The Rights of Donor-Conceived Individuals and the Meaning of Genetic Relatedness' (2010) 11 Minnesota Journal of Law, Science & Technology 655.

Counselling of both surrogate and commissioning parents should include detailed conversations about their expectations concerning both non-anonymity and possible post-birth contact between surrogate and child. Here, drawing up a contract can be tremendously valuable as part of a process of establishing a relationship between surrogate and commissioning parents both during pregnancy and after birth.[63]

Pre and post-birth contact between commissioning parents and surrogate requires conceptualizing what is involved in this method of creating a parent–child relationship. Building a family through surrogacy should be seen not simply as a one-time transfer of a child from one 'rights bearer' to another, but as a process—hopefully ongoing—that entails 'reciprocity, gratitude, responsibility, and compulsory solidarity'.[64] In surrogacy, post-birth contact 'gives credence to the relationships that surrogates tend to build with commissioning families during the surrogate process'.[65] For both surrogate and the person she bore, the possibility of post-birth contact 'can promote autonomous decision-making'—for the surrogate entering the pregnancy agreement and for the person born as a result of that agreement.[66] Post-birth contact may help construct both narrative and lived relationships. This dimension of surrogacy is akin to the relationships established in open adoption. Judith Modell's observation that 'the adopted child in an open arrangement is alienated neither from his blood parent nor from "his legal parent"' articulates the vision of possible relationships among the adults and children linked through ARTs and surrogacy.[67]

Both surrogacy and open adoption are part of the movement in family law toward 'more extended, flexible notions of parenthood, custody and visitation', and I think this movement could suggest new definitions of what constitutes 'family' and 'kin'.[68] Even before reproductive technologies, the emergence of same-sex families and non-nuclear households, many of which included children, led sociologists and anthropologists to identify 'families of choice' that they contrasted to biologically related families, and to assert that 'kinship' is a socially constructed as well as a genetically defined relationship.[69]

---

[63] See BH Bix's chapter.
[64] J Modell, 'Open Adoption and the Rhetoric of the Gift' in LL Layne (ed), *Transformative Motherhood: On Giving and Getting in a Consumer Culture* (New York UP 1999) 57.
[65] Laufer-Ukeles, 'Mothering for Money' (n 20) 1251.   [66] ibid 1228.
[67] Modell, 'Open Adoption and the Rhetoric' (n 64) 40.
[68] Laufer-Ukeles, 'Mothering for Money' (n 20) 1252. See also D Archard's chapter 'Family and Family Law: Concepts and Norms'.
[69] J Stacey chronicled the late-twentieth century emergence of what she called 'the postmodern family' in Silicon Valley, California, one not tied to traditional heterosexual forms. See J Stacey, *Brave New Families* (Basic Books 1990) 270–71. She continued this exploration in, J Stacey, *Unhitched: Love, Marriage and Family Values from West Hollywood to Western China* (NYU Press 2011). PH Collins wrote about the custom of "othermothers" in African American communities, where women would assist biological mothers in raising their children. (PH Collins, *Black Feminist Thought* (Routledge 1991). K Weston, in *Families We Choose: Lesbians, Gays, Kinship* (Columbia UP 1991) also reassessed US-family structures. Weston described households and 'extended families' defined not by legal recognition (ie heterosexual marriage) but by common residence and mutual caregiving. Her goal was to dislodge the privileged status of the nuclear, biological family, and to insist upon the equal status and worth of a number of family forms. For an exploration of biotechnology's impact on notions of kinship, see M Strathern, *After Nature* (CUP 1992); M Strathern, *Reproducing the Future* (CUP 1992); M Strathern, *Kinship, Law and the Unexpected* (CUP 2005).

Other instances of families that do not fit the two-and-only-two caregiver paradigm are plentiful. Foster parenting does not transfer the status of legal parent to the foster parents but is a reminder both of society's obligation to provide care for children and of adults' capacity to act cooperatively on behalf of children.[70] Blended families, step-families, and multi-generational households also demonstrate that more than two adults can be in significant relationships with a child.[71] Some scholars call for some kind of legal status for significant 'other' adults in a child's life: 'Legally recognizing a plurality of parental relationships may go a long way toward valuing and validating a variety of relationships valued by both adults and children and may move us away from viewing children as entities over whom adults should be driven to seek exclusive possession'.[72] 'Permanent guardianship' that gives custodial authority to guardians without totally severing the parental ties of original parents who cannot raise their child has protected contact and visitation rights for some parents.[73] Efforts to cabin families created by ARTs into a model of the two-parent nuclear family fail to recognize the complex relationships that these families—like so many others—engender.

VII. Conclusion

Reflecting on her experience of becoming a parent through two surrogacy arrangements, a commissioning mother wrote,

> If you consider third-party reproduction to be simply a production detail in the creation of a conventional nuclear family—a service performed and forgotten—then acknowledging the importance of outsiders could make it all seem like a house of cards. But if you conceive of the experience as creating a kind of extended family, in which you have chosen to be related to these people through your children, it feels very rich.[74]

That richness is associated with the web of relationships that make assisted procreation possible, create new persons, and generate new relationships.

---

[70] On foster care in the United States see DF Wozniak, 'Gifts and Burdens: The Social and Familial Contexts of Foster Care' in LL Layne (ed), *Transformative Motherhood: On Giving and Getting in a Consumer Culture* (New York UP 1999); J Duerr Berrick, 'When Children Cannot Remain Home: Foster Family Care and Kinship Care' (1998) 8 The Future of Children: Protecting Children from Abuse and Neglect 72.

[71] Kavanagh, 'Rewriting the Legal Family' (n 32). On polyamorous families, see E Brake, 'Recognizing Care: The Case for Friendship and Polyamory' (2014) 1 Syracuse Law and Civic Engagement Journal <http://slace.syr.edu/issue-1-2013-14-on-equality/> accessed 27 May 2016.

[72] U Narayan, 'Rethinking Parental Claims in the Light of Surrogacy and Custody' in Uma Narayan and JJ Bartkowiak (eds), *Having and Raising Children: Unconventional Families, Hard Choices, and the Social Good* (Penn State UP 1999) 86. Michele Goodwin has proposed "baby cooperatives" to provide care to children in single-parent households. (M Goodwin, 'Baby Cooperatives: Rethinking the Nature of Family' (2013) 2013 Illinois Law Review 1337.

[73] Women in Prison Project, Correctional Association of New York, 'When "Free" Means Losing Your Mother: The Collision of Child Welfare and the Incarceration of Women in New York State', (Correctional Association of New York, 2006) <http://www.correctionalassociation.org/resource/when-free-means-losing-your-mother-the-collision-of-child-welfare-and-the-incarceration-of-women-in-new-york-state> accessed 11 November 2017.

[74] Thernstrom, 'My Futuristic Insta-Family' (n 46) 44–45.

It is not surprising that focus on the web of relationships involved was not initially part of the way medical and legal practice regarded surrogacy. Surrogacy emerged from advances in medical technology and was regarded as a 'last step' in infertility treatment, and therefore as a private matter, and one in which the primary responsibility of the physician was protecting the health of the patient. Lawyers negotiating the transfer or assignment of parental rights also focused on the rights of the negotiating parties as traditional–liberal theory and law suggested. But this individualistic approach does not adequately characterize or reflect the complex relationships entailed, including those of the person who will come into being as a result of a successful surrogacy agreement.

Rather than thinking about surrogacy as a practice that substitutes for procreation through sexual coitus, creating 'a child of our own' for heterosexual couples, it is wiser to recognize that—like adoption, step-parenting, parenting in blended families, co-parenting in same-sex families, and foster parenting—surrogacy stretches our understanding of what constitutes a 'family'. Debates and discussions about surrogacy, therefore, are important not only for refining medical practice, legal regulations, and cultural understandings of contract pregnancy and the families created by surrogacy contracts, but also for prompting us to consider the grounding of parent–child relationships in general. Examining the intricacies of surrogacy enables us to consider anew the role of relationships, relational autonomy, and caregiving in forming and sustaining all parent–child relationships.

Bibliography

Note, 'Looking for a Family Resemblance: The Limits of the Functional Approach to the Legal Definition of Family' (1991) 104(7) Harvard Law Review 1640

Aldana R, Kidane W, Lyon B, and McKanders K, *Global Issues in Immigration Law* (West Academic Publishing 2013)

Alderson P, 'Common Criticisms of Children's Rights and 25 Years of the IJCR' (2017) 25 International Journal of Children's Rights 307

Almond B, *The Fragmenting Family* (OUP 2008)

Aloni E, 'Deprivative Recognition' (2014) 61 University of California, Los Angeles Law Review 1276

Altman S, 'Should Child Custody Rules be Fair?' (1996) 35 Journal of Family Law 325

Altman S, 'A Theory of Child Support' (2003) 17 International Journal of Law, Policy & the Family 173

Altman S, 'The Pursuit of Intimacy and Parental Rights' in A Marmor (ed), *The Routledge Companion to Philosophy of Law* (Routledge 2011)

Ameling R, *Sex Cells: The Medical Market for Eggs and Sperm* (University of California Press 2001)

American Law Institute, *Principles of the Law of Family Dissolution: Analysis and Recommendations* (LexisNexis 2002)

Anapol D, *Polyamory in the Twenty-First Century: Love and Intimacy with Multiple Partners* (Rowman & Littlefield 2010)

Anderson ES, 'John Stuart Mill and Experiments in Living' (1991) 102 Ethics 26

Antokolskaia MV, 'Development of Family Law in Western and Eastern Europe: Common Origins, Common Driving Forces, Common Tendencies' (2003) 28 Journal of Family History 52

Appell AR, 'Accommodating Childhood' (2013) 19 Cardozo Journal of Law & Gender 715

Appell AR, 'Parental Rights Doctrine: Creating and Maintaining Maternal Value' in MA Fineman and K Worthington (eds), *What is Right for Children?* (Ashgate 2009)

Appleton SF, 'Restating Childhood' (2014) 79 Brooklyn Law Review 525

Archard D, 'Philosophical Perspectives on Childhood' in J Fionda (ed), *Legal Concepts of Childhood* (Hart 2001)

Archard D, *Children: Rights and Childhood* (2nd edn, Routledge 2004)

Archard D, *The Family: A Liberal Defence* (Palgrave Macmillan 2010)

Archard D, 'Children, Adults, Best Interests and Rights' (2013) 13 Medical Law International 55

Archard D, 'Children's Rights', *The Stanford Encyclopedia of Philosophy* (Summer edn, 2016) <http://plato.stanford.edu/archives/sum2016/entries/rights-children/> accessed 21 August 2017

Archard D and Benatar D (eds), *Procreation and Parenthood: The Ethics of Bearing and Rearing Children* (OUP 2010)

Archard D and Macleod C, 'Introduction' in D Archard and C Macleod (eds), *The Moral and Political Status of Children: New Essays* (OUP 2002)

Archard D and Macleod C (eds), *The Moral and Political Status of Children: New Essays* (OUP 2002)

Arnold J, *The Marriage Law of England* (Staples Press 1951)

Asch A, 'Licensing Parents: Regulating Assisted Reproduction' in D Cutas and S Chan (eds), *Families—Beyond the Nuclear Ideal* (Bloomsbury Academic 2012)

Auchmuty R, 'Same-Sex Marriage Revived: Feminist Critique and Legal Strategy' (2004) 14 Feminism & Psychology 101

Ayres I, 'Ya-HUH: There Are and Should Be Penalty Defaults' (2006) 33 Florida State University Law Review 589

Ayres I and Gertner R, 'Filling Gaps in Incomplete Contracts: An Economic Theory of Default Rules' (1989) 99 Yale Law Journal 87
Baldwin R, 'From Regulation to Behaviour Change: Giving Nudge the Third Degree' (2014) 77 Modern Law Review 83
Barker N, *Not the Marrying Kind* (Palgrave Macmillan 2013)
Barlow A, Burgoyne C, Clery E, and Smithson J, 'Cohabitation and the Law: Myths, Money and the Media' in A Park, J Curtice, K Thomson, M Phillips, M Johnson, and E Clery (eds), *British Social Attitudes – the 24th Report* (Sage 2008)
Barlow A, Duncan S, James G, and Park A, *Cohabitation, Marriage and the Law: Social Change and Legal Reform in the 21st Century* (Hart 2005)
Barlow A and Smithson J, 'Legal Assumptions, Cohabitants' Talk and the Rocky Road to Reform' (2010) 22 Child and Family Law Quarterly 328
Barnett RE, 'A Consent Theory of Contract' (1986) 86 Columbia Law Review 269
Barnett RE, *Contracts* (OUP 2010)
Barrett M and M McIntosh, *The Anti-Social Family* (2nd edn, Verso 1991)
Bartlett KT, 'Re-Expressing Parenthood' (1988) 98 Yale Law Journal 293
Bartlett KT, 'Feminism and Family Law: Family Law and American Culture' (1999) 33 Family Law Quarterly 475
Batra M, 'Organizing in the South Asian Domestic Worker Community: Pushing the Boundaries of the Law and Organizing Project' in S Jayaraman and I Ness (eds), *The New Urban Immigrant Workforce: Innovative Models for Labor Organizing* (ME Sharpe Inc 2005)
Bayne T and Kolers A, 'Parenthood and Procreation', *The Stanford Encyclopedia of Philosophy* (Summer edn, 2006) <http://plato.stanford.edu/archives/sum2006/entries/parenthood/> accessed 21 August 2017
Beaman LG, 'Introduction' in G Calder and LG Beaman (eds), *Polygamy's Rights and Wrongs: Perspectives on Harm, Family, and Law* (University of British Columbia Press 2014)
Beck-Gernsheim E, *Reinventing the Family: In Search of New Lifestyles* (Patrick Camiller tr, Polity Press 2002)
Bedi S, *Beyond Race, Sex, and Sexual Orientation: Legal Equality Without Identity* (CUP 2013)
Bendall C, 'Some Are More "Equal" than Others: Heteronormativity in The Post-*White* Era of Financial Remedies' (2014) 36(3) Journal of Social Welfare & Family Law 260
Benhabib S, 'The Generalized and Concrete Other: The Kohlberg-Gilligan Controversy and Moral Theory' (1986) 5 Praxis International 38
Bennett C, 'Liberalism, Autonomy, and Conjugal Love' (2003) 9 Res Publica 285
Bennett TW, 'Comparative Law and African Customary Law' in M Reimann and R Zimmermann (eds), *Oxford Handbook of Comparative Law* (OUP 2006)
Bennion J, *Polygamy in Primetime: Media, Gender, and Politics in Mormon Fundamentalism* (Brandeis UP 2012)
Bernardes J, 'Do We Really Know What "the Family" Is?' in P Close and R Collins (eds), *Family and Economy in Modern Society* (Macmillan 1985)
Bernstein A (ed), *Marriage Proposals: Questioning a Legal Status* (NYU Press 2006)
Berrick JD, 'When Children Cannot Remain Home: Foster Family Care and Kinship Care' (1998) 8 The Future of Children: Protecting Children from Abuse and Neglect 72
Bhandary A, 'Liberal Dependency Care' (2016) 41 Journal of Philosophical Research 43
Bhrolcháin MN and Beaujouan E, 'Education and Cohabitation in Britain: A Return to Traditional Patterns?' (2013) 39 Population and Development Review 441
Bird A and Tobin E, 'Natural Kinds', *The Stanford Encyclopedia of Philosophy* (Spring edn, 2016) <http://plato.stanford.edu/entries/natural-kinds/> accessed 21 August 2017
Bix BH, 'Consent' in FG Miller and A Wertheimer (eds), *The Ethics of Consent* (Oxford 2010)
Bix BH, 'Private Ordering and Family Law' (2010) 23 Journal of the American Academy of Matrimonial Lawyers 249
Bix BH, *The Oxford Introductions to US Law: Family Law* (OUP 2013)
Blackstone W, *Commentaries on the Laws of England* (HW Ballantine edn, Blackstone Institute 1914)

Blyth E and Firth L, 'Donor-Conceived People's Access to Genetic and Biographical History: An Analysis of Provisions in Different Jurisdictions Permitting Disclosure of Donor Identity' (2009) 23 International Journal of Law, Policy & the Family 174

Boele-Woelki K and Fuchs A (eds), *Legal Recognition of Same-Sex Relationships in Europe* (Intersentia 2012)

Boele-Woelki K, Ferrand F, Beilfuss CG, Jäntera-Järeborg M, Lowe N, Martiny D, and Pintens W, *Principles of European Family Law Regarding Property Relations between Spouses* (Intersentia 2013)

Boele-Woelki K, Miles J, and Scherpe JM (eds), *The Future of Family Property in Europe* (Intersentia 2011)

Boele-Woelki K, Mol C, and van Gelder E (eds), *European Family Law in Action. Vol. V – Informal Relationships* (Intersentia 2015)

Boris E and Klein J, *Caring for America: Home Health Workers in the Shadow of the Welfare State* (OUP 2012)

Borjas G, *Friends or Strangers: The Impact of Immigrants on the U.S. Economy* (Basic Books 1990)

Bottomley A, 'From Mrs. Burns to Mrs. Oxley: Do Co-habiting Women (Still) Need Marriage Law?' (2006) 14 Feminist Legal Studies 181

Bottomley A and Wong S, 'Shared Household: A New Paradigm for Thinking about the Reform of Domestic Property Relations' in A Diduck and K O'Donovan (eds), *Feminist Perspectives on Family Law* (Routledge 2006)

Boyd SB, 'Autonomy for Mothers? Relational Theory and Parenting Apart' (2010) 18 Feminist Legal Studies 137

Brake E, 'A Voluntarist Account of Parental Role Obligations' in D Archard and D Benatar (eds), *Procreation and Parenthood* (OUP 2010)

Brake E, 'Minimal Marriage: What Political Liberalism Implies for Marriage Law' (2010) 120 Ethics 302

Brake E, 'Marriage and Domestic Partnership', *The Stanford Encyclopedia of Philosophy* (Fall edn, 2012) <http://plato.stanford.edu/archives/fall2012/entries/marriage/> accessed 21 August 2017

Brake E, *Minimizing Marriage: Marriage, Morality, and the Law* (OUP 2012)

Brake E, 'Recognizing Care: The Case for Friendship and Polyamory' (2014) 1 Syracuse Law and Civic Engagement Journal <http://slace.syr.edu/issue-1-2013-14-on-equality/> accessed 21 August 2017

Brake E (ed), *After Marriage: Rethinking Marital Relationships* (OUP 2016)

Brake E, 'Equality and Non-Hierarchy in Marriage: What Do Feminists Really Want?' in E Brake (ed), *After Marriage: Rethinking Marital Relationships* (OUP 2016)

Brake E and Millum J, 'Parenthood and Procreation', *The Stanford Encyclopedia of Philosophy* (October 2013) <http://plato.stanford.edu/entries/parenthood/> accessed 21 August 2017

Brannen J, 'The Study of Sensitive Subjects' (1988) 36(3) Sociological Review 552

Braun V and Clarke V, 'Using Thematic Analysis in Psychology' (2006) 3(2) Qualitative Research in Psychology 77

Brennan S, 'Children's Choices or Children's Interests: Which Do Their Rights Protect?' in D Archard and C Macleod (eds), *The Moral and Political Status of Children: New Essays* (OUP 2002)

Brennan S, 'The Goods of Childhood and Children's Rights' in F Baylis and C McLeod (eds), *Family-Making: Contemporary Ethical Challenges* (OUP 2014)

Brennan S and Cameron B, 'Is Marriage Bad for Children? Rethinking the Connection between Having Children, Romantic Love, and Marriage' in E Brake (ed), *After Marriage: Rethinking Marital Relationships* (OUP 2016)

Brennan S and Noggle R, 'The Moral Status of Children: Children's Rights, Parents' Rights and Family Justice' (1997) 23 Social Theory and Practice 1

Bridgeman J, 'Parental Responsibility, Responsible Parenting and Legal Regulation' in J Bridgeman, H Keating, and C Lind (eds), *Responsibility, Law and the Family* (Ashgate 2008) 242

Brighouse H, *School Choice and Social Justice* (OUP 2003)

Brighouse H and Swift A, 'Parents' Rights and the Value of the Family' (2006) 117 Ethics 80
Brighouse H and Swift A, *Family Values: The Ethics of a Parent-Child Relationship* (Princeton UP 2014)
Bromley PM, *Family Law* (Butterworth 1957)
Brook H, 'How to Do Things with Sex' in C Stychin and D Herman (eds), *Sexuality in the Legal Arena* (Bloomsbury 2001)
Brooks T, 'The Problem with Polygamy' (2009) 37(2) Philosophical Topics 109
Bruno L, 'Contact and Evaluations of Violence: An Intersectional Analysis of Swedish Court Orders' (2015) 29 International Journal of Law, Policy & the Family 167
Buckley FH and Ribstein LE, 'Calling a Truce in the Marriage Wars' [2001] University of Illinois Law Review 561
Burgoyne CB, 'Money in Marriage: How Patterns of Allocation Both Reflect and Conceal Power' (1990) 38 The Sociological Review 634
Burns M, Burgoyne CB, and Clarke V, 'Financial Affairs? Money Management in Same-Sex Relationships' (2008) 37(2) The Journal of Socio-Economics 481
Burton F, *Family Law* (Cavendish Publishing Ltd 2003)
Buss E, 'Allocating Developmental Control among Parent, Child and the State' (2004) 2004 University of Chicago Legal Forum 27
Butler J, *Gender Trouble: Feminism and the Subversion of Identity* (2nd edn, Routledge 1999)
Cahn NR, *Test-tube Families: Why the Fertility Market Needs Legal Regulation* (NYU Press 2009)
Cahn NR, 'The New Kinship' (2012) 100 The Georgetown Law Journal 367
Calavita K, 'Italy: Economic Realities, Political Frictions, and Policy Failures' in WA Cornelius, T Tsuda, PL Martin, and JF Hollifield (eds), *Controlling Immigration: A Global Perspective* (2nd edn, Stanford UP 2004)
Calder G, 'The Personal *Is* Economic: Unearthing the Rhetoric of Choice in the Canadian Maternity and Parental Leave Benefit Debates' in R Hunter and S Cowan (eds), *Choice and Consent: Feminist Engagements with Law and Subjectivity* (Routledge 2007) 125
Calhoun C, 'Who's Afraid of Polygamous Marriage? Lessons for Same-Sex Marriage Advocacy from the History of Polygamy' (2005) 42 San Diego Law Review 1023
Callan E, *Creating Citizens: Political Education and Liberal Democracy* (OUP 1997)
Callan E, 'Autonomy, Child-Rearing, and Good Lives', in D Archard and C Macleod (eds), *The Moral and Political Status of Children: New Essays* (OUP 2002)
Carbone J and Cahn N, 'The Triple System of Family Law' [2013] Michigan State Law Review 1185
Card C, 'Against Marriage and Motherhood' (1996) 11(3) Hypatia 1
Carens J, 'Why Naturalization Should be Easy: A Response to Noah Pickus' in N Pickus (ed), *Immigration and Citizenship in the 21st Century* (Rowman & Littlefield 1998)
Carrington C, *No Place Like Home: Relationships and Family Life Among Lesbians and Gay Men* (University of Chicago Press 1999)
Case MA, 'Marriage Licenses' (2004–2005) 89 Minnesota Law Review 1758
Case MA, 'Feminist Fundamentalism on the Frontier Between Government and Family Responsibility For Children' (2009) 11 Utah Law Review 381
Catanzarite NM, 'A Commendable Goal: Public Policy and the Fate of Spousal Support After 1996' (1998) 31 Loyola of Los Angeles Law Review 1387
Chambers C, 'The Marriage-Free State' (2013) 113(2) Proceedings of the Aristotelian Society 123
Chambers C, 'The Limitations of Contract: Regulating Personal Relationships in A Marriage-Free State' in E Brake (ed), *After Marriage: Rethinking Marital Relationships* (OUP 2016)
C Chambers, *Against Marriage: An Egalitarian Defense of the Marriage-Free State* (OUP 2017)
Chambers L, 'Women's Labour, Relationship Breakdown and Ownership of the Family Farm' (2010) 25 Canadian Journal of Law and Society 75
Chan W, 'Cohabitation, Civil Partnership, Marriage and the Equal Sharing Principle' (2013) 33 Legal Studies 46

Chang H, 'Migration as International Trade: The Economic Gains from the Liberalized Movement of Labor' (1998) 3 UCLA Journal of International Law & Foreign Affairs 384

Chloros A (ed), *International Encyclopedia of Comparative Law* IV (Mohr Siebeck 1971, 2007)

Choudhry S and Fenwick H, 'Taking the Rights of Parents and Children Seriously: Confronting the Welfare Principle under the Human Rights Act' (2005) 25(3) Oxford Journal of Legal Studies 453

Christman J, 'Relational Autonomy, Liberal Individualism, and the Social Constitution of Selves' (2004) 117 Philosophical Studies 143

Clayton M, *Justice and Legitimacy in Upbringing* (OUP 2006)

Clisham MR and Wilson RF, 'American Law Institute's *Principles of the Law of Family Dissolution*, Eight Years after Adoption: Guiding Principles or Obligatory Footnote?' (2008) 42(3) Family Law Quarterly 573

Cohen IG, 'Regulating Reproduction: The Problem with Best Interests' (2011) 96 Minnesota Law Review 423

Cohen MR, 'The Basis of Contract' (1933) 46 Harvard Law Review 553

Collins PH, *Black Feminist Thought* (Routledge 1991)

Comaroff J and Roberts S, *Rules and Processes: The Cultural Logic of Dispute in An African Context* (University of Chicago Press 1981)

Cornelius WA, 'Spain: The Uneasy Transition from Labor Exporter to Labor Importer' in WA Cornelius, T Tsuda, PL Martin, and JF Hollifield (eds), *Controlling Immigration: A Global Perspective* (2nd edn, Stanford UP 2004)

Cornelius WA, Tsuda T, Martin PL, and Hollifield JF (eds), *Controlling Immigration: A Global Perspective* (2nd edn, Stanford UP 2004)

Correctional Association of New York, 'When "Free" Means Losing Your Mother: The Collision of Child Welfare and the Incarceration of Women in New York State' (*Correctional Association*, 2006) <http://www.correctionalassociation.org/wp-content/uploads/2012/05/When_Free_Rpt_Feb_2006.pdf> accessed 21 August 2017

Cossman B, 'Family Feuds: Neo-Liberal and Neo-Conservative Visions of the Reprivatization Project' in B Cossman and J Fudge (eds), *Privatization, Law, and the Challenge to Feminism* (University of Toronto Press 2002) 169

Dagan H, 'The Limited Autonomy of Private Law' (2008) 56 American Journal of Comparative Law 809

Davis AD, 'Regulating Polygamy: Intimacy, Default Rules, and Bargaining for Equality' (2010) 110 Columbia Law Review 1955

Day Sclater S, *The Psychology of Divorce: A Research Report to the ESRC* (University of East London 1998)

de Sousa R, *Love: A Very Short Introduction* (OUP 2015)

Dempsey MM and Lister M, 'Applied Legal and Political Philosophy' in K Lippert-Rasmussen, K Brownlee, and D Coady (eds), *Blackwell Companion to Applied Philosophy* (Wiley-Blackwell forthcoming)

Den Otter RC, *In Defense of Plural Marriage* (CUP 2015)

Den Otter RC, 'Three May Not be a Crowd: The Case for a Constitutional Right to Plural Marriage' (2015) 64 Emory Law Journal 1977

Denscombe M, *The Good Research Guide for Small-Scale Social Research Projects* (3rd edn, Open UP 2007)

Department for Children, Schools and Families, *Support for All* (Green Paper, Cm 7787, 2010)

Dewar J, 'The Normal Chaos of Family Law' (1998) 61 Modern Law Review 467

Dewar J, 'Can the Centre Hold? Reflections on Two Decades of Family Law Reform in Australia' (2010) 22 Child and Family Law Quarterly 377

Diduck A, 'Shifting Familiarity' (2005) 58 Current Legal Problems 235

Diduck A, 'Ancillary Relief: Complicating the Search for Principle' (2011) 38 Journal of Law and Society 272

Diduck A, 'What is Family Law For?' (2011) 64 Current Legal Problems 287
Diduck A and Orton H, 'Equality and Support for Spouses' (1994) 57 Modern Law Review 681
Dixon R and Nussbaum M, 'Children's Rights and a Capabilities Approach: The Question of Special Priority' (2012) 97 Cornell Law Review 549
Dodds D, 'Dependence, Care, and Vulnerability' in C Mackenzie, W Rogers, and S Dodds (eds), *Vulnerability: New Essays in Ethics and Feminist Philosophy* (OUP 2014)
Douglas G, *An Introduction to Family Law* (OUP 2001)
Dworkin R, 'The Model of Rules' (1967) 35 University of Chicago Law Review 14
Dworkin R, *Law's Empire* (Belknap Press, Harvard UP 1986)
Dwyer JG, *The Relationship Rights of Children* (CUP 2006)
Dwyer JG, 'The Child Protection Pretense: States' Continued Consignment of Newborn Babies to Unfit Parents,' (2008) 93 University of Minnesota Law Review 407
Dwyer JG, 'A Constitutional Birthright: the State, Parentage, and the Rights of Newborn Persons' (2009) 56 University of California, Los Angeles Law Review 755
Dwyer JG, *Moral Status and Human Life: The Case for Children's Superiority* (CUP 2011)
Dwyer JG, 'Parents' Self-Determination and Children's Custody: A New Analytical Framework for State Structuring of Children's Family Life' (2012) 54 Arizona Law Review 79
Dwyer JG, 'The Moral Basis of Children's Relational Rights' in J Eekelaar and R George (eds), *Routledge Handbook of Family Law and Policy* (Routledge 2014) 279
Easton D and Hardy JW, *The Ethical Slut: A Practical Guide to Polyamory, Open Relationships, and Other Adventures* (2nd edn, Celestial Arts 2009)
Eekelaar J, 'The Place of Divorce in Family Law's New Role' (1975) 38 Modern Law Review 241
Eekelaar J, 'The Emergence of Children's Rights' (1986) 6 Oxford Journal of Legal Studies 161
Eekelaar J, 'The Importance of Thinking That Children Have Rights' (1992) 6 International Journal of Law, Policy & the Family 221
Eekelaar J, 'Families and Children: From Welfarism to Rights' in C McCrudden and G Chambers (eds), *Individual Rights and the Law in Britain* (OUP 1994)
Eekelaar J, 'Family Law: Keeping Us "On Message"' (1999) 11 Child & Family Law Quarterly 387
Eekelaar J, 'Beyond the Welfare Principle' (2002) 14 Child and Family Law Quarterly 237
Eekelaar J, 'Judges and Citizens: Two Conceptions of Law' (2002) 22 Oxford Journal of Legal Studies 497
Eekelaar J, *Family Law and Personal Life* (OUP 2006)
Eekelaar J, 'Why People Marry: The Many Faces of an Institution' (2007) 41 Family Law Quarterly 413
Eekelaar J, 'Then and Now: Family Law's Direction of Travel' (2013) 35 Journal of Social Welfare and Family Law 415
Eekelaar J, 'Family Justice on Trial: re A' (2014) 44 Family Law 543
Eekelaar J and George R, 'Children's Rights: The Wider Context' in J Eekelaar and R George (eds), *Routledge Handbook of Family Law and Policy* (Routledge 2014)
Eekelaar J and Maclean M, 'Marriage and the Moral Bases of Personal Relationships' (2004) 31 Journal of Law and Society 510
Eekelaar J and Maclean M, *Family Justice: The Work of Family Judges in Uncertain Times* (Hart Publishing 2013)
Eichner M, 'Marriage and the Elephant: The Liberal Democratic State's Regulation of Intimate Relationships between Adults' (2007) 30 Harvard Journal of Law & Gender 25
Eichner M, 'Principles of the Law of Relationships among Adults' (2007) 41 Family Law Quarterly 433
Eichner M, *The Supportive State: Families, Government, and America's Political Ideals* (OUP 2010)
Ellickson RC, *Order Without Law: How Neighbors Settle Disputes* (Harvard 1991)
Ellman I, 'The Theory of Alimony' (1989) 77 California Law Review 1
Ellman I, '"Contract Thinking" was *Marvin*'s Fatal Flaw' (2001) 76 Notre Dame Law Review 1365
Ellman I, 'Why Making Family Law is Hard' (2003) 35 Arizona State Law Journal 699
Emens EF, 'Monogamy's Law: Compulsory Monogamy and Polyamorous Existence' (2004) 29 New York University Review of Law & Social Change 277

Ertman MM, *Love's Promises: How Formal and Informal Contracts Shape All Kinds of Families* (Beacon Press 2015)

Ertman MM, 'Marital Contracting in a Post-Windsor World' (2015) 42 Florida State University Law Review 479

Eskridge WN, *Equality Practice: Civil Unions and the Future of Gay Rights* (Routledge 2002)

Eskridge WN, 'Family Law Pluralism: The Guided-Choice Regime of Menus, Default Rules, and Override Rules' (2012) 100 Georgetown Law Journal 1881

Ettelbrick P, 'Since When is Marriage a Path to Liberation?' in S Sherman (ed), *Lesbian and Gay Marriage* (Temple UP 1992)

Etzioni E, *The Spirit of Community: Rights, Responsibilities and the Communitarian Agenda* (Crown 1993)

Evershed FR, 'Foreword' in R Graveson and F Crane (eds), *A Century of Family Law: 1857 – 1957* (Sweet & Maxwell 1957)

Ewick P and Silbey S, *The Common Place of Law: Stories from Everyday Life* (Chicago UP 1998)

Family Justice Council, *Sorting out Finances on Divorce* (Family Justice Council 2016)

Farson R, *Birthrights* (Collier Macmillan 1974)

Fehlberg B and Smyth B, with L Trinder, 'Parenting Issues after Separation: Developments in Common Law Countries' in J Eekelaar and R George (eds), *Routledge Handbook of Family Law and Policy* (Routledge 2014)

Feinberg J, 'A Child's Right to an Open Future' in W Aiken and H LaFollette (eds), *Whose Child? Parental Rights, Parental Authority and State Power* (Littlefield, Adams & Co 1980)

Feinberg J, *Harm to Self* (OUP 1986)

Feinberg J, *Harmless Wrongdoing* (OUP 1990)

Ferguson L, *The End of an Age: Beyond Age-Based Legal Regulation of Minors' Entitlement to Participate in and Make Health Care Treatment Decisions* (Law Commission of Canada 2005)

Ferguson L, 'Family, Social Inequalities, and the Persuasive Force of Interpersonal Obligation' (2008) 22 International Journal of Law, Policy & the Family 61

Ferguson L, 'Not Merely Rights for Children but Children's Rights: The Theory Gap and the Assumption of the Importance of Children's Rights' (2013) 21 International Journal of Children's Rights 177

Ferguson L, 'Arbitral Awards: A Magnetic Factor of Determinative Importance—Yet Not To Be Rubber-Stamped?' (2014) 37 Journal of Social Welfare & Family Law 99

Ferguson L, 'The Jurisprudence of Making Decisions Affecting Children: An Argument to Prefer Duty to Children's Rights and Welfare' in A Diduck, N Peleg, and H Reece (eds), *Law in Society: Reflections on Children, Family, Culture and Philosophy—Essays in Honour of Michael Freeman* (Brill 2015)

Ferguson L, 'The Curious Case of Civil Partnership: The Extension of Marriage to Same-Sex Couples and The Status-altering Consequences of a Wait-and-See Approach' (2016) 28 Child and Family Law Quarterly 347

Ferguson L, 'Hard Divorces Make Bad Law' (2017) 51 Journal of Social Welfare and Family Law (forthcoming)

Fernandez C, 'Beyond Marvin: A Proposal for Quasi-Spousal Support' (1978) 30 Stanford Law Review 359

Ferracioli L, 'Family Migration Schemes and Liberal Neutrality: A Dilemma' (2014) 13 Journal of Moral Philosophy 1

Fineman MA, *The Neutered Mother, The Sexual Family, and Other Twentieth Century Tragedies* (Routledge 1995)

Fineman MA, *The Autonomy Myth: A Theory of Dependency* (New Press 2004)

Fineman MA, 'Equality, Autonomy, and the Vulnerable Subject in Law and Politics' in MA Fineman and A Grear (eds), *Vulnerability: Reflections on a New Ethical Foundation for Law and Politics* (Ashgate 2013)

Fineman MA, 'Equality and Difference—The Restrained State' (2014) 66 Alabama Law Review 609

Finnis J, *Natural Law and Natural Rights* (2nd edn, OUP 2011)
Fish J, 'Making History Through Policy: A Field Report on the International Domestic Workers Movement' (2015) 88 International Labor and Working-Class History 156
FitzGibbon S, 'Marriage and the Good of Obligation' (2002) 47 American Journal of Jurisprudence 41
Folbre N and Nelson J, 'For Love or Money—Or Both?' (2000) 14 The Journal of Economic Perspectives 123
Foucault M, *Power: Essential Works of Foucault 1954-1984, volume 3* (JD Faubion ed, R Hurley et al tr, Penguin 2002)
Fox R, *Kinship and Marriage: An Anthropological Perspective* (CUP 1983)
Frantz CJ and Dagan H, 'Properties of Marriage' (2004) 104 Columbia Law Review 75
Freeman MA, 'Should Spousal Support Be Abolished?' (1973) 48 Los Angeles Bar Bulletin 236
Freeman M, 'The Right to Responsible Parents' in J Bridgeman, H Keating, and C Lind (eds), *Responsibility, Law and the Family* (Ashgate 2008)
Freeman MDA, 'Why It Remains Important to Take Children's Rights Seriously' (2007) 15 International Journal of Children's Rights 5
Freeman S, *Rawls* (Routledge 2007)
Fried C, *Contract as Promise* (2nd edn, Oxford 2015)
Fry R, 'New Census Data Show More Americans are Tying the Knot, but Mostly It's the College Educated' (*Pew Research Center*, 6 February 2014) <http://www.pewresearch.org/fact-tank/2014/02/06/new-census-data-show-more-americans-are-tying-the-knot-but-mostly-its-the-college-educated/> accessed 20 August 2017
Gal T and Duramy BF, 'Enhancing Capacities for Child Participation: Introduction' in T Gal and BF Duramy (eds), *International Perspectives and Empirical Findings on Child Participation: From Social Exclusion to Child-Inclusive Policies* (OUP 2015)
Galston W, *Liberal Pluralism* (CUP 2002)
Gardner J, *Law as a Leap of Faith* (OUP 2012)
Gavison R, 'Feminism and the Public-Private Distinction' (1992) 45 Stanford Law Review 1
Gerstman E, *Same-Sex Marriage and the Constitution* (CUP 2004)
Gheaus A, 'The Right to Parent One's Biological Baby' (2012) 20 The Journal of Political Philosophy 432
Gheaus A, 'The Intrinsic Goods of Childhood and the Just Society' in A Bagattini and C Macleod (eds), *The Nature of Children's Well-Being: Theory and Practice* (Springer 2015)
Gibney M, *The Ethics and Politics of Asylum: Liberal Democracy and the Response to Refugees* (CUP 2004)
Gilbert N, *Researching Social Life* (3rd edn, Sage 2008)
Gilligan C, *In a Different Voice* (Harvard UP 1982)
Gilmore S and Bainham A, *Children: The Modern Law* (Jordan publishing 2013)
Gilmore S and Glennon L, *Hayes and Williams' Family Law* (4th edn, OUP 2014)
Girgis S, Anderson RT, and George RP, *What is Marriage? Man and Woman: A Defense* (Encounter Books 2012)
Gittins D, *The Family in Question* (Macmillan 1985)
Glendon M, *Rights Talk: The Impoverishment of Political Discourse* (The Free Press 1991)
Glennon L, 'Obligations between Adult Partners: Moving from Form to Function?' (2008) 22 International Journal of Law, Policy & the Family 22
Goldfeder M, *Legalizing Plural Marriage: The Next Frontier in Family Law* (Brandeis UP 2016)
Goldfeder M and Sheff E, 'Children of Polyamorous Families: A First Empirical Look' (2013) 5 Journal of Law and Social Deviance 150
Golombok S et al (eds), *Regulating Reproductive Donation* (CUP 2016)
Goodwin M, 'Baby Cooperatives: Rethinking the Nature of Family' (2013) 2013 Illinois Law Review 1337
Goodwin M, 'Reproducing Hierarchy in Commercial Intimacy' (2013) 88 Indiana Law Journal 1289

Goody J, *The Development of The Family and Marriage in Europe* (CUP 1983)
Gordon L, *Heroes of Their Own Lives* (Viking 1988)
Gordon L and Batlan F, 'The Legal History of the Aid to Dependent Children Program' (*Social Welfare History* 2011) <http://www.socialwelfarehistory.com/programs/aid-to-dependent-children-the-legal-history/> accessed 21 August 2017
Govier T, *A Practical Study of Argument* (3rd edn, Wadsworth 1992)
Gray KJ and Gray SF, *Elements of Land Law* (5th edn, OUP 2009)
Griffin J, 'Do Children Have Rights?' in D Archard and C Macleod (eds), *The Moral and Political Status of Children: New Essays* (OUP 2002)
Griffin J, *On Human Rights* (OUP 2008)
Grossberg M, *Governing the Hearth: Law and the Family in Nineteenth-Century America* (University of North Carolina Press 1985)
Gutmann A, *Democratic Education* (Princeton UP 1989)
Hale B, 'Family Responsibility: Where Are We Now?' in C Lind, H Keating, and J Bridgeman (eds), *Taking Responsibility, Law and the Changing Family* (Ashgate 2011)
Hall C, *Clarke Hall and Morrison's Law Relating to Children and Young Persons* (Butterworths 1967)
Hannan S and Vernon R, 'Parental Rights: A Role Based Approach' (2008) 6 Theory and Research in Education 173
Harding LF, *Family, State and Society Policy* (Macmillan 1996)
Harding R, *Regulating Sexuality: Legal Consciousness in Lesbian and Gay Lives* (Routledge 2011)
Harding R and Peel E, 'Surveying Sexualities: Internet Research with Non-Heterosexuals' (2007) 17 Feminism & Psychology 277
Hardwig J, 'Should Women Think in Terms of Rights?' (1984) 94 Ethics 441
Harrington M, *Care and Equality* (Knopf 1999)
Hart HLA, 'Social Solidarity and the Enforcement of Morality' in HLA Hart, *Essays in Jurisprudence and Philosophy* (OUP 1983)
Hart HLA, *The Concept of Law* (Clarendon Press 1961, 2nd edn, Clarendon Press 1994, 1997)
Hasday JE, *Family Law Reimagined* (Harvard 2014)
Haskey J, 'Marriage Rites—Trends in Marriages by Manner of Solemnisation and Denomination in England and Wales, 1841–2012' in J Miles, P Mody and R Probert (eds), *Marriage Rites and Rights* (Hart Publishing 2015)
Haslanger S, 'Family, Ancestry and Self: What is the Moral Significance of Biological Ties?' (2009) 2 Adoption & Culture 91
Hasson E, 'Setting a Standard or Reflecting Reality? The "Role" of Divorce Law, and the Case of the Family Law Act 1996' (2003) 17 International Journal of Law, Policy & the Family 338
Hayward A, 'Family Property and the Process of Familiarisation of Property Law' (2012) 24 Child and Family Law Quarterly 284
Hayward A, 'The "Context" of Home: Cohabitation and Ownership Disputes in England and Wales' in M Diamond and TL Turnipseed (eds), *Community, Home, and Identity* (Ashgate 2012)
Hayward A, 'Finding a Home for "Family Property"' in N Gravells (ed), *Landmark Cases in Land Law* (Hart 2013)
Held V, *The Ethics of Care: Personal, Political and Global* (OUP 2005)
Helmholz RH, 'Support Orders, Church Courts, and the Rule of Filius Nullius: A Reassessment of the Common Law' (1977) 63 Virginia Law Review 431
Herman D, *Rights of Passage: Struggles for Lesbian and Gay Legal Equality* (University of Toronto Press 1994)
Herring J, 'Farewell Welfare?' (2005) 27 Journal of Social Welfare and Family Law 159
Herring J, 'Why Financial Orders on Divorce Should Be Unfair' (2005) 19 International Journal of Law, Policy & the Family 218
Herring J, *Older People in Law and Society* (OUP 2009)
Herring J, 'Sexless Family Law' (2010) 11 Lex Familiae 3

Herring J, 'Vulnerability, Children and the Law' in Michael Freeman (ed), *Law and Childhood Studies: Current Legal Issues Vol 14* (OUP 2012)
Herring J, *Caring and the Law* (Hart Publishing 2013)
Herring J, *Relational Autonomy and Family Law* (Springer 2014)
Herring J, *Family Law* (8th edn, Pearson 2017)
Herring J and Foster C, 'Welfare Means Relationality, Virtue and Altruism' (2012) 32 Legal Studies 480
Hitchings E, 'From Pre-Nups to Post-Nups: Dealing with Marital Property Agreements' [2009] Family Law 1056
Hochschild A, 'Love and Gold' (2009) 8:1 The Scholar and Feminist Online <http://sfonline.barnard.edu/work/hochschild_01.htm> accessed 21 August 2017
Hochschild A, *The Outsourced Self: What Happens When We Pay Others to Live Our Lives for Us* (Picador 2013)
Holt JC, *Escape from Childhood: The Needs and Rights of Children* (Penguin 1975)
Hopkins N, 'The Relevance of Context in Property Law: A Case for Judicial Restraint?' (2011) 31 Legal Studies 175
Howes C, Leana C, and Smith K, 'Paid Care Work' in N Folbre (ed), *For Love and Money: Care Provision in the United States* (Russell Sage Foundation 2012)
Hull KE, 'The Cultural Power of Law and The Cultural Enactment of Legality: The Case of Same-Sex Marriage' (2003) 28 Law & Social Inquiry 629
Hunter ND, 'Marriage, Law and Gender: A Feminist Inquiry' (1991) 1 Law & Sexuality 9
Hurka T, *The Best Things in Life* (OUP 2011)
Institut de la statistique du Québec, *Le Bilan Démographique du Québec* (Gouvernement du Québec 2014)
Jackson J, *The Law Relating to the Formation and Annulment of Marriage and Allied Matters in English Domestic and Private International Law* (Sweet & Maxwell 1951)
Jeske D, *Rationality and Moral Theory: How Intimacy Generates Reasons* (Routledge 2008)
Joelving F, 'Surrogate Mothers in India Unaware of Risks' (*Reuters*, 2 March 2015) <http://www.reuters.com/article/us-surrogate-mothers-india/surrogate-mothers-in-india-unaware-of-risks-idUSKBN0LY1J720150302> accessed <1 November 2017>
Johnson R, *Taxing Choices: The Intersection of Class, Gender, Parenthood, and the Law* (University of British Columbia Press 2002)
Judicial Appointments Commission, *10th Set of JAC Diversity Statistics Published* [online] (2014) <https://jac.judiciary.gov.uk/news/10th-set-jac-diversity-statistics-published> accessed 21 August 2017
Kant I, *The Metaphysics of Morals* ([1797] Mary Gregor ed & tr, CUP 1996)
Kaspiew R, Gray M, Qu I, and Weston R, 'Legislative Aspirations and Social Realities: Empirical Reflections on Australia's 2006 Family Law Reforms' (2011) 33 Journal of Social Welfare and Family Law 397
Kavanagh MM, 'Rewriting the Legal Family' (2004) 16 Yale Journal of Law & Feminism 83
Keller S, *Partiality* (Princeton UP 2013)
Kersting W, 'Politics, Freedom, and Order: Kant's Political Philosophy' in P Guyer (ed), *The Cambridge Companion to Kant and Modern Philosophy* (CUP 2003)
Khalidi MA, 'Kinds (Natural Kinds vs Human Kinds)' in B Kaldis (ed), *Encyclopedia of Philosophy and the Social Sciences* (Sage 2013)
Kilbride PL, *Plural Marriage for Our Times: A Reinvented Option?* (Bergin & Garvey 1994)
Kim NS, *Wrap Contracts: Foundations and Ramifications* (OUP 2013)
Kimel D, 'Personal Autonomy and Change of Mind in Promise and in Contract' in G Klass, G Letsas, and P Saprai (eds), *Philosophical Foundations of Contract Law* (OUP 2014)
Kittay EF, *Love's Labor* (Routledge 1998)
Kitzinger C and Wilkinson S, 'The Re-branding of Marriage: Why We Got Married instead of Registering a Civil Partnership' (2004) 14 Feminism & Psychology 127

Klein DJ, 'Plural Marriage and Community Property Law' (2010) 41 Golden Gate University Law Review 33

Klesse C, 'Polyamory and Its "Others": Contesting the Terms of Non-Monogamy' (2006) 9 *Sexualities* 565

Klesse C, *The Spectre of Promiscuity: Gay Male and Bisexual Non-Monogamies and Polyamories* (Ashgate 2007)

Koppelman A, *The Gay Rights Question in Contemporary American Law* (University of Chicago Press 2002)

Kramer W and Cahn N, *Finding Our Families* (Penguin 2013)

Krauskopf JM, 'Theories of Property Division/Spousal Support: Searching for Solutions to the Mystery' (1989) 23 Family Law Quarterly 253

Kurdek LA, 'The Allocation of Household Labor by Partners in Gay and Lesbian Couples' (2007) 28 Journal of Family Issues 132

LaFollette H, 'Licensing Parents' (1980) 9 Philosophy & Public Affairs 182

Lalos A, Gottlieb C, and Lalos O, 'Legislated Right for Donor-Insemination Children to Know Their Genetic Origin: A Study of Parental Thinking' (2007) 22 Human Reproduction 1759

Larmore C, *Patterns of Moral Complexity* (CUP 1987)

Larson BG, 'Equity and Economics: A Case for Spousal Support' (1978) 8 Golden Gate University Law Review 443

Laufer-Ukeles P, 'Mothering for Money: Regulating Commercial Intimacy' (2013) 88 Indiana Law Review 1223

Laufer-Ukeles P and Blecher-Prigat A, 'Between Function and Form: Towards a Differentiated Model of Functional Parenthood' (2013) 20 George Mason Law Review 419

Law Commission, *Cohabitation: The Financial Consequences of Relationship Breakdown* (The Stationary Office 2007)

Law Commission, *Matrimonial Property, Needs, and Agreements* (The Stationary Office 2014)

Law Commission of Canada, *Beyond Conjugality: Recognising and Supporting Close Personal Adult Relationships* (Law Commission of Canada 2001)

Law Society, *Diversity Profile of the Profession: A Short Synopsis* [online] (*Law Society*, 2014) <http://www.lawsociety.org.uk/advice/articles/diversity-in-the-profession> accessed 21 August 2017

Leckey R, *Contextual Subjects: Family, State, and Relational Theory* (University of Toronto Press 2008)

Lee RM, *Doing Research on Sensitive Topics* (Sage 1993)

Levine C, 'AIDS and Changing Concepts of Family' (1990) 68 The Millbank Quarterly (Part 1) 33

Levinson M, *The Demands of Liberal Education* (OUP 2002)

Levinson S, 'The Meaning of Marriage: Thinking About Polygamy' (2005) 42 San Diego Law Review 1049

Lewin T, 'Egg Donors Challenge Pay Rates, Saying They Shortchange Women' (*New York Times*, 16 October 2015) <https://www.nytimes.com/2015/10/17/us/egg-donors-challenge-pay-rates-saying-they-shortchange-women.html?mcubz=0> accessed 1 November 2017

Liao M, *The Right to Be Loved* (OUP 2015)

Lifshitz S, 'Married against Their Will? Toward a Pluralist Regulation of Spousal Relationships' (2009) 66 Washington and Lee Law Review 1565

Lister M, 'A Rawlsian Argument for Extending Family-Based Immigration Benefits to Same-Sex Couples' (2007) 37 University of Memphis Law Review 745

Lister M, 'Immigration, Association, and the Family' (2010) 29 Law & Philosophy 717

Lister M, 'Citizenship, in the Immigration Context' (2011) 70 Maryland Law Review 175

Lister M, 'Who are Refugees?' (2013) 32 Law & Philosophy 645

Lloyd M, *Judith Butler: From Norms to Politics* (Polity Press 2007)

Lynch JP and Simons RJ, *Immigration the World Over: Statutes, Policies, and Practices* (Rowman & Littlefield 2003)

Macauley S, 'Non-contractual Relations in Business' (1963) 28 American Sociology Review 55, reprinted in S Halliday and P Schmidt (eds), *Conducting Law and Society Research: Reflections on Methods and Practices* (CUP 2009)

MacCormick N, *Legal Right and Social Democracy: Essays in Legal and Political Philosophy* (OUP 1984)

Macedo S, 'The Moral Dilemma of US Immigration Policy' in C Swain (ed), *Debating Immigration* (CUP 2007)

Macedo S, *Just Married: Same-Sex Couples, Monogamy, and the Future of Marriage* (Princeton UP 2015)

Mackay MV, 'Spousal Support: Law Reform and the Forms of Justice' (1987) 45 University of Toronto Faculty of Law Review 243

Maclean M, Hunter H, Wasoff F, Ferguson L, Bastard B, and Ryrstedt E, 'Family Justice in Hard Times: Can We Learn from Other Jurisdictions?' (2011) 33(4) Journal of Social Welfare and Family Law 319

Maclean M and Eekelaar J (eds), *Managing Family Justice in Diverse Societies* (Hart Publishing 2013)

Maclean M with Kurzczewski J, *Making Family Law: A Socio Legal Account of Legislative Process in England and Wales, 1985 to 2010* (Hart 2011)

Macleod C, 'Conceptions of Parental Autonomy' (1997) 25 Politics & Society 117

Macleod C, 'Shaping Children's Convictions' (2003) 1 Theory & Research in Education 315

Macleod C, 'A Liberal Theory of Freedom of Expression for Children' (2004) 79 Chicago-Kent Law Review 55

Macleod C, 'Primary Goods, Capabilities, and Children' in H Brighouse and I Robeyns (eds), *Measuring Justice: Primary Goods and Capabilities* (CUP 2010)

Macleod C, 'Liberal Equality and the Affective Family' in D Archard and C Macleod (eds), *The Moral and Political Status of Children: New Essays* (OUP 2012)

Macleod C, 'Constructing Children's Rights' in J Drerup, G Graff and G Schweiger (eds), *Justice, Education and the Politics of Childhood* (Springer 2016)

Mahoney J, 'Liberalism and the Polygamy Question' (2008) 23 Social Philosophy Today 161

Maine HS, *Ancient Law* (John Murray 1861)

Malik M, 'Family Law in Diverse Societies' in J Eekelaar and R George (eds), *Routledge Handbook of Family Law and Policy* (Routledge 2014)

Mandle J, *What's Left of Liberalism: An Interpretation and Defense of Justice as Fairness* (Lexington Books 2000)

Mandle J, *Global Justice* (Polity 2006)

March AF, 'Is There a Right to Polygamy? Marriage, Equality and Subsidizing Families in Liberal Public Justification' (2011) 8 Journal of Moral Philosophy 244

Markovits D, 'Sharing *Ex Ante* and Sharing *Ex Post*: The Non-Contractual Basis of Fiduciary Relations' in AS Gold and PB Miller (eds), *Philosophical Foundations of Fiduciary Law* (OUP 2014)

Martin PL, 'Germany: Managing Migration in the Twenty-First Century' and 'The United States: The Continuing Immigration Debate' in WA Cornelius, T Tsuda, PL Martin, and JF Hollifield (eds), *Controlling Immigration: A Global Perspective* (2nd edn, Stanford UP 2004)

Martin W, *Primates of Park Avenue: A Memoir* (Simon and Schuster 2015)

Martin-Casals M and Ribot J, 'Damages in Family Matters in Spain: Exploring Uncharted New Land or Backsliding?' in B Atkin (ed), *International Survey of Family Law 2010* (Jordans, Family Law 2010)

Mason MA, 'The Roller Coaster of Child Custody Law over the Last Half Century' (2012) 24 Journal of the American Academy of Matrimonial Lawyers 451

Masson J, Bailey-Harris R, and Probert R, *Cretney Principles of Family Law* (8th edn, Sweet & Maxwell 2008)

May T, *Social Research: Issues, Methods and Process* (3rd edn, Open UP 2001)

McAdams RH, *The Expressive Powers of Law* (Harvard UP 2015)
McClain L, 'Love, Marriage, and the Baby Carriage: Revisiting the Channeling Function of Family Law' (2007) 28 Cardozo Law Review 2133
McClain L, 'The Other Marriage Equality Problem' (2013) 93 Boston University Law Review 921
McCoy JL, 'Spousal Support Disorder: An Overview of Problems in Current Alimony Law' (2005) 33 Florida State University Law Review 501
Mead M, 'Constraints and Comparisons from Primitive Society' in BJ Stern (ed), *The Family, Past and Present* (D Appleton-Century Co 1938)
Mee J, '*Burns v Burns*: The Villain of the Piece?' in S Gilmore, J Herring, and R Probert (eds), *Landmark Cases in Family Law* (Hart 2011)
Metz T, 'The Liberal Case for Disestablishing Marriage' (2007) 6 Contemporary Political Theory 196
Metz T, *Untying the Knot: Marriage, the State, and the Case for their Divorce* (Princeton UP 2010)
Metz T, 'Review: The Family, A Liberal Defence' (*Notre Dame Philosophical Reviews*, 16 July 2011) <http://ndpr.nd.edu/news/24762-the-family-a-liberal-defence/> accessed 21 August 2017
Mikkola M, 'Feminist Perspectives on Sex and Gender' (2016) *The Stanford Encyclopedia of Philosophy* <https://plato.stanford.edu/entries/feminism-gender/#SexDis> accessed 24 August 2017
Milan A, *Marital Status: Overview, 2011* (Statistics Canada, Minister of Industry 2013)
Miles J, 'Property Law v Family Law: Resolving the Problems of Family Property' (2003) 23 Legal Studies 624
Miles J, 'Marriage and Divorce in the Supreme Court and the Law Commission: For Love or Money?' (2011) 74 Modern Law Review 430
Miles J, 'Marital Agreements: "The More Radical Solution"' in R Probert and C Barton (eds), *Fifty Years in Family Law: Essays for Stephen Cretney* (Intersentia 2012)
Miles J, Mody P and Probert R (eds), *Marriage Rites and Rights* (Hart Publishing 2015)
Miles J and Scherpe J, 'The Legal Consequences of Dissolution: Property and Financial Support between Spouses' in J Eekelaar and R George (eds), *Routledge Handbook of Family Law and Policy* (Routledge 2014)
Mill JS, *Utilitarianism* (G Sher ed, Hackett Publishing 1979)
Mill JS, *Utilitarianism, On Liberty, and Considerations on Representative Government* ([1859] Everyman 1993)
Mill JS, 'The Subjection of Women' in S Collini (ed), *On Liberty and Other Writings* ([1869], CUP 1989)
Mills C, '"Ideal Theory" as Ideology' (2009) 20 Hypatia 165
Minow M, 'Rights for the Next Generation: A Feminist Approach to Children's Rights' (1986) 9 Harvard Women's Law Journal 1
Minow M and Shanley ML, 'Relational Rights and Responsibilities: Revisioning the Family in Political Theory and Law' (1996) 11 Hypatia 4
Mnookin RH and Kornhauser L, 'Bargaining in the Shadow of the Law: The Case of Divorce' (1979) 88 Yale Law Journal 950
Modell J, 'Open Adoption and the Rhetoric of the Gift' in LL Layne (ed), *Transformative Motherhood: On Giving and Getting in a Consumer Culture* (New York UP 1999)
Morgan P, *Family Policy, Family Changes: Sweden, Italy and Britain Compared* (Civitas 2006)
Mount F, *The Subversive Family: An Alternative History of Love and Marriage* (The Free Press 1992)
Müller-Freienfels W, 'The Emergence of Droit de Famille and Familienrecht in Continental Europe and the Introduction of Family Law in England' (2003) 28 Journal of Family History 31
Munoz-Dardé V, 'Is the Family then to be Abolished?' (1999) XCIV Proceedings of the Aristotelian Society 37
Murray M, 'The Networked Family: Reframing the Legal Understanding of Caregiving and Caregivers' (2008) 94 Virginia Law Review 385

Narayan U, 'Rethinking Parental Claims in the Light of Surrogacy and Custody' in U Narayan and J J Bartkowiak (eds), *Having and Raising Children: Unconventional Families, Hard Choices, and the Social Good* (Penn State UP 1999)

Nardi PM and Sherrod D, 'Friendship in the Lives of Gay Men and Lesbians' (1994) 11 Journal of Social and Personal Relationships 185

National Conference of Commissioners on Uniform State Law, 'Family Law Arbitration Act' (*Uniform Laws*, November 2015 Draft) <http://uniformlaws.org/> accessed 21 August 2017

Nearing R, *Loving More: The Polyfidelity Primer* (PEP Publishing 1992)

Nedelsky J, 'Reconceiving Autonomy' (1989) 1 Yale Journal of Law & Feminism 7

Nedelsky J, 'Reconceiving Rights as Relationship' (1993) 1 Review of Constitutional Studies/Revue d'études constitutionnelles 1

Nedelsky J, *Law's Relations: A Relational Theory of Self, Autonomy and Law* (OUP 2011)

Newport F and Wilke J, 'Most in U.S. Want Marriage, but Its Importance Has Dropped' *Gallup Polling* (2 August 2013) <http://www.gallup.com/poll/163802/marriage-importance-dropped.aspx> accessed 1 November 2017

Nicholson L, 'The Myth of the Traditional Family' in HL Nelson (ed), *Feminism and Families* (Routledge 1997)

Nolan D, 'Temporary Marriage' in E Brake (ed), *After Marriage: Rethinking Marital Relationships* (OUP 2016)

Nussbaum MC, *Sex and Social Justice* (Oxford 1999)

Nussbaum MC, 'A Right to Marry?' (2010) 98 California LR 668

Nyman C, 'Gender Equality in "The Most Equal County in The World"? Money and Marriage in Sweden' (1999) 47 The Sociological Review 76

Office for National Statistics, *Families and Households, 2014* (2015)

Office of National Statistics, *Statistical Bulletin: Divorces in England and Wales, 2012* (ONS, 2014) <http://www.ons.gov.uk/ons/dcp171778_351693.pdf> accessed 21 August 2017

Office of National Statistics, *Statistical Bulletin: Civil Partnerships in the UK, 2013* (ONS, 2015) <http://www.ons.gov.uk/ons/dcp171778_395000.pdf> accessed 21 August 2017

Okin SM, *Justice, Gender, and the Family* (Basic Books 1989)

Okin SM, 'Introduction' in SM Okin (ed), *Is Multiculturalism Bad for Women?* (Princeton UP 1999)

Olsen FE, 'The Family and the Market: A Study of Ideology and Legal Reform' (1983) 96 Harvard Law Review 1497

Olsen FE, 'The Myth of State Intervention in The Family' (1984-5) 18 Michigan University Journal of Law Reform 835

O'Neill O, 'Between Consenting Adults' (1985) 14 Philosophy & Public Affairs 252

Overall C, 'Reproductive "Surrogacy" and Parental Licensing' (2015) 29 Bioethics 353

Pahl J, 'Household Spending, Personal Spending and the Control of Money in Marriage' (1990) 24(1) Sociology 119

Parizer-Krief K, 'Gender Equality in Legislation on Medically Assisted Procreation in France' (2015) 29 International Journal of Law, Policy & the Family 205

Parks JA, 'Rethinking Radical Politics in the Context of Assisted Reproductive Technology' (2009) 23 Bioethics 20

Parks JA, 'Care Ethics and the Global Practice of Commercial Surrogacy' (2010) 24 Bioethics 333

Parreñas R, *Servants of Globalization: Women, Migration, and Domestic Work* (Stanford UP 2001)

Pateman C, *The Sexual Contract* (University of California Press 1988)

Patterson CJ, Sutfin EL, and Fulcher M, 'Division of Labour among Lesbian and Heterosexual Parenting Couples: Correlates of Specialized Versus Shared Patterns' (2004) 11 Journal of Adult Development 179

Peel E and Harding R, 'Divorcing Romance, Rights, and Radicalism: Beyond Pro and Anti in The Lesbian and Gay Marriage Debate' (2004) 14 Feminism & Psychology 584

Pennings G, 'Reproductive Tourism as Moral Pluralism in Motion' (2002) 28 Journal of Medical Ethics 337

Phillips A, 'Exploitation, Commodification, and Equality' in M Deveaux and V Panitch (eds), *Exploitation: From Practice to Theory* (Rowman & Littlefield 2017)

Pintens W, 'Marital Agreements and Private Autonomy in France and Belgium' in JM Scherpe (ed), *Marital Agreements and Private Autonomy in Comparative Perspective* (Hart Publishing 2012)

Piska N, 'Constructive Trusts and Constructing Intention' in M Dixon (ed), *Modern Studies in Property Law* (Hart 2009) 222

Plato, *The Republic* (Desmond Lee tr, Penguin 1955)

Pogge T, 'Migration and Poverty' in R Goodin and P Pettit (eds), *Contemporary Political Philosophy: An Anthology* (2nd edn, Wiley-Blackwell 2005)

Polikoff ND, 'We Will Get What We Ask for: Why Legalizing Gay Marriage Will Not "Dismantle the Legal Structure of Gender in Every Marriage"' (1993) 79 Virginia Law Review 1535

Polikoff ND, 'Why Lesbians and Gay Men Should Read Martha Fineman' (2000) 8 Journal of Gender, Social Policy & Law 167

Pollock L, *Forgotten Children: Parent-child Relations from 1500 to 1900* (CUP 1983)

Poo A, 'Domestic Workers Bill of Rights: A Feminist Approach for a New Economy' (2009) 8 The Scholar & Feminist Online <http://sfonline.barnard.edu/work/poo_01.htm> accessed 21 August 2017

Posner E, 'There Are No Penalty Default Rules in Contract Law' (2006) 33 Florida State University Law Review 563

Probert R, 'Family Law and Property Law: Competing Spheres in the Regulation of the Family Home' in A Hudson (ed), *New Perspectives on Property Law, Human Rights and the Home* (Cavendish Publishing Limited 2004)

Probert R, (ed), *Family Life and the Law: Under One Roof* (Ashgate 2006)

Probert R, *The Changing Legal Regulation of Cohabitation: From Fornicators to Family, 1600-2010* (CUP 2012)

Probert R, Gilmore S, and Herring J, 'A More Principled Approach to Parental Responsibility in England and Wales?' in J Mair and E Örücü (eds), *Juxtaposing Legal Systems and the Principles of European Family Law on Parental Responsibilities* (Intersentia 2010)

Probert R, Miles J, and Mody P, 'Introduction' in J Miles, P Mody and R Probert (eds), *Marriage Rites and Rights* (Hart 2015)

Purdy LM, *In Their Best Interest? The Case Against Equal Rights for Children* (Cornell UP 1992)

Rackley E, 'Judicial Diversity, the Woman Judge and Fairy Tale Endings' (2007) 27 Legal Studies 74

Radin MJ, 'Market Inalienability' (1987) 100 Harvard Law Review 1849

Radin MJ, *Contested Commodities* (Harvard 1996)

Radin MJ, *Boilerplate: The Fine Print, Vanishing Rights, and the Rule of Law* (Princeton 2012)

Ragoné H, 'The Gift of Life: Surrogate Motherhood, Gamete Donation, and Constructions of Altruism' in R Cook, SD Sclater and F Kaganas (eds), *Surrogate Motherhood: International Perspectives* (Hart Publishing 2003)

Rajczi A, 'A Populist Argument for Same-Sex Marriage' (2008) 91 The Monist 475

Ravitsky V, 'Knowing Where You Come From: The Rights of Donor-Conceived Individuals and the Meaning of Genetic Relatedness' (2010) 11 Minnesota Journal of Law, Science & Technology 655

Rawls J, *A Theory of Justice* (Harvard UP 1971; rev edn, OUP 1999)

Rawls J, *Political Liberalism* (Columbia UP 1993, 1996)

Rawls J, *Justice as Fairness: A Restatement* (Harvard UP 2001)

Raz J, *The Morality of Freedom* (OUP 1986)

Raz J, *Between Authority and Interpretation: On the Theory of Law and Practical Reason* (OUP 2009)

Reece H, 'The Paramountcy Principle: Consensus or Construct?' (1996) 49 Current Legal Problems 267

Reece H, *Divorcing Responsibly* (Hart Publishing 2003)

Reece H, 'The Degradation of Parental Responsibility' in R Probert, S Gilmore, and J Herring (eds), *Responsible Parents and Parental Responsibility* (Hart 2009)

Reece H, 'Leaping without Looking' in R Leckey (ed), *After Legal Equality: Family, Sex, Kinship* (Routledge 2015) 122

Regan MC Jr, *Alone Together: Law and the Meaning of Marriage* (OUP 1999)

Reich R, 'Testing the Boundaries of Parental Authority over Education' in Stephen Macedo and Yael Tamir (eds), *NOMOS XLIII: Moral and Political Education* (New York UP 2002)

Resnik J, 'Diffusing Disputes: The Public in the Private of Arbitration, the Private in Courts, and the Erasure of Rights' (2015) 124 Yale Law Journal 2808

Rich A, *Of Woman Born: Motherhood as Experience and Institution* (Norton 1986)

Roberts D, 'The Genetic Tie' (1995) 62 University of Chicago Law Review 209

Roberts M, *Mediation in Family Disputes: Principles and Practice* (4th edn, Ashgate 2014)

Robertson J, *Children of Choice: Freedom and the New Reproductive Technologies* (Princeton UP 1994)

Rodger J, 'Family Policy or Moral Regulation?' (1995) 15 Critical Social Policy 5

Rogerson C, 'The Causal Connection Test in Spousal Support Law' (1989) 8 Canadian Journal of Family Law 95

Rogerson C, 'The Canadian Law of Spousal Support' (2004) 38 Family Law Quarterly 69

Rogerson C, 'Child Support, Spousal Support and The Turn to Guidelines' in J Eekelaar and R George (eds), *Routledge Handbook of Family Law and Policy* (Routledge 2014)

Rogerson C and Thompson R, 'Spousal Support Advisory Guidelines' (*Department of Justice Canada*, July 2008) <http://www.justice.gc.ca/eng/rp-pr/fl-lf/spousal-epoux/spag/index.html> accessed 6 November, 2017

Rosenblum N, *Membership and Morals* (Princeton UP 1998)

Rosenbury LA, 'A Feminist Perspective on Children and Law: From Objectification to Relational Subjectivities' in T Gal and BF Duramy (eds), *International Perspectives and Empirical Findings on Child Participation: From Social Exclusion to Child-Inclusive Policies* (OUP 2015)

Rotherham C, 'Proprietary Relief for Enrichment by Wrongs: Some Realism about Property Talk' (1996) 19 University of New South Wales Law Journal 378

Rothman BK, *Recreating Motherhood: Ideology and Technology in a Patriarchal Society* (Norton 1989)

Ruddick S, *Maternal Thinking: Towards a Politics of Peace* (Beacon 1989)

Sanders A, 'Nuptial Agreements, Comparative Law and the Notion of Contract' in A Popovici, L Smith and R Tremblay (eds), *Les intraduisibles en droit civil* (Thémis 2014) 217

Sanger C, 'Developing Markets in Baby-Making: In the Matter of Baby M' (2007) 30 Harvard Journal of Law & Gender 67

Sanger C, 'Acquiring Children Contractually: Relational Contracts at Work at Home' in J Braucher, J Kidwell, and WC Whitford (eds), *Revisiting the Contracts Scholarship of Stewart Macaulay: On the Empirical and the Lyrical* (Hart 2013)

Satz D, 'Markets in Women's Reproductive Labor' (1992) 21 Philosophy & Public Affairs 123

Satz D, 'Relationships and Responsibilities' (1997) 26 Philosophy & Public Affairs 189

Scheffler S, 'Morality through Thick and Thin: A Critical Note of Ethics and the Limits of Philosophy' (1987) 96 The Philosophical Review 411

Scherpe JM (ed), *Marital Agreements and Private Autonomy in Comparative Perspective* (Hart Publishing 2012)

Scherpe JM, 'Towards a Matrimonial Property Regime for England and Wales' in R Probert and C Barton (eds), *Fifty Years in Family Law: Essays for Stephen Cretney* (Intersentia 2012)

Schneewind JB, *The Invention of Autonomy: A History of Modern Moral Philosophy* (Cambridge 1998)

Schneider CE, 'The Channelling Function in Family Law' (1992) 20 Hofstra Law Review 495

Schneider D, *American Kinship: A Cultural Account* (University of Chicago Press 1968)

Schoeman F, 'Rights of Children, Rights of Parents, and the Moral Basis of the Family' (1980) 91 Ethics 6

Schoenbaum N, 'The Law of Intimate Work' (2015) 90 Washington Law Review 1167

Schrama W, 'Marriage and Alternative Relationships in The Netherlands' in J Eekelaar and R George (eds), *Routledge Handbook of Family Law and Policy* (Routledge 2014)

Scott ES, 'Pluralism, Parental Preference, and Child Custody' (1992) 80 California Law Review 615

Scott ES, 'Marriage, Cohabitation and Collective Responsibility for Dependency' [2004] University of Chicago Legal Forum 225

Scott ES and Scott RE, 'Parents as Fiduciaries' (1995) 81 Virginia Law Review 2401

Scruton R, *Sexual Desire* (The Free Press 1986)

Semple N, 'In Sickness and In Health? Spousal Support and Unmarried Cohabitants' (2008) 24 Canadian Journal of Family Law 317

Sen A, 'What Do We Want from a Theory of Justice?' (2006) 103 Journal of Philosophy 215

Seymour J, *Children, Parents and the Courts: Legal Intervention in Family Life* (Federation Press 2016)

Sezgin Y, *Human Rights Under State Enforced Religious Family Laws in Israel, Egypt and India* (CUP 2013)

Shaher S, *Childhood in the Middle Ages* (Routledge 1990)

Shalev C, *Birth Power: The Case for Surrogacy* (Yale UP 1989)

Shanley ML, 'Fathers' Rights, Mothers' Wrongs?: Reflections on Unwed Fathers' Rights and Sex Equality' (1995) 75 Hypatia: Journal of Feminist Philosophy 74

Shanley ML, '"Surrogate Mothering" and Women's Freedom: A Critique of Contracts for Human Reproduction' (1995) 18 Signs 618

Shanley ML, *Making Babies, Making Families: What Matters Most in an Age of Reproductive Technologies, Surrogacy, Adoption, and Same-Sex and Unwed Parents* (Beacon Press 2004)

Shanley ML and Jesudason S, 'Surrogacy: Reinscribing or Pluralizing Understandings of Family?' in D Cutas and S Chan (eds), *Families—Beyond the Nuclear Ideal* (Bloomsbury Academic 2012)

Sheff E, 'Polyamorous Families, Same-Sex Marriage, and the Slippery Slope' (2011) 40 Journal of Contemporary Ethnography 497

Sheff E, *The Polyamorists Next Door: Inside Multiple-Partner Relationships and Families* (Rowman & Littlefield Publishers 2013)

Sheff E and Hammers C, 'The Privilege of Perversities: Race, Class, and Education Among Polyamorists and Kinksters' (2011) 2 Sexuality & Psychology 198

Shiffrin SV, *Speech Matters: On Lying, Morality, and the Law* (Princeton UP 2014)

Shultz MM, 'Reproductive Technology and Intention-based Parenthood: An Opportunity for Gender Neutrality' [1990] Wisconsin Law Review 297

Simpson A, *A Treatise on the Law and Practice relating to Infants* (Stevens and Haynes 1875)

Skorupski J, *Why Read Mill Today?* (Routledge 2007)

Smart C, 'Regulating Families or Legitimating Patriarchy? Family Law in Britain' (1982) 10 International Journal of the Sociology of Law 129

Smart C, *The Ties That Bind: Law, Marriage and the Reproduction of Patriarchal Relations* (Routledge & Kegan Paul plc 1984)

Smart C, 'Divorce in England 1950-2000: A Moral Tale?' in SN Katz, J Eekelaar and M Maclean (eds), *Cross Currents: Family Law and Policy in the US and England* (OUP 2000)

Smart C, *Personal Life: New Directions in Sociological Thinking* (Polity Press 2007)

Smart C, 'Law and Family Life: Insights from 25 Years of Empirical Research' (2014) 26 Child & Family Law Quarterly 14

Smith L, 'Parenthood is a Fiduciary Relationship' (working paper, 24 July 2017) online: <https://papers.ssrn.com/sol3/papers.cfm?abstract_id=3007812> accessed 20 Aug 2017

Sonnenberg SJ, Burgoyne CB, and Routh DA, 'Income Disparity and Norms Relating to Intra-Household Financial Organisation in The UK: A Dimensional Analysis' (2011) 40 The Journal of Socio-Economics 573

Stacey J, *Brave New Families: Stories of Domestic Upheaval in Late Twentieth Century America* (Basic Books 1990; with a new Preface, University of California Press 1998)

Stacey J, *Unhitched: Love, Marriage and Family Values from West Hollywood to Western China* (New York UP 2011)

Stalford H, 'Concepts of Family under EU Law—Lessons from the ECHR' (2002) 16 International Journal of Law, Policy & the Family 410

Statistics Canada, *Portrait of Families and Living Arrangements in Canada: Families, Households and Marital Status, 2011 Census of Population* (Minister of Industry, 2012)

Stemplowska Z, 'What's Ideal about Ideal Theory?' (2008) 34 Social Theory and Practice 319

Stemplowska Z and Swift A, 'Ideal and Nonideal Theory' in D Estlund (ed), *The Oxford Handbook of Political Philosophy* (OUP 2012)

Stevenson C, 'Persuasive Definitions' (July 1938) 47 Mind 331

Stevenson M, 'Mediation and Settlement-Broking' (2015) 45 Family Law 575

Strassberg MI, 'The Challenge of Post-Modern Polygamy: Considering Polyamory' (2003) 31 Capital University Law Review 440

Strassberg MI, 'Scrutinizing Polygamy: Utah's *Brown v. Buhman* and British Columbia's *Reference Re: Section 293*' (2015) 64 Emory Law Journal 1815

Strasser M, 'Traditional Surrogacy Contracts, Partial Enforcement, and the Challenge for Family Law' (2015) 18 Journal of Health Care Law & Policy 85

Strathern M, *After Nature: English Kinship in the Late Twentieth Century* (CUP 1992)

Strathern M, *Reproducing the Future: Essays on Anthropology, Kinship, and the New Reproductive Technologies* (Routledge 1992)

Strathern M, *Kinship, Law and the Unexpected: Relatives Are Always a Surprise* (CUP 2005)

Stychin CF, '"Las Vegas is Not Where We Are": Queer Readings of The Civil Partnership Act' (2006) 25 Political Geography 899

Sumner LW, *The Moral Foundation of Rights* (Clarendon Press 1987)

Sunstein C, 'On the Expressive Function of Law' (1995–96) 144 University of Pennsylvania Law Review 2021

Sunstein C and Thaler RH, 'Libertarian Paternalism Is Not an Oxymoron' (2003) 70 University of Chicago Law Review 1159

Sutherland EE, 'Unmarried Cohabitation' in J Eekelaar and R George (eds), *Routledge Handbook of Family Law and Policy* (Routledge 2014)

Swift A, *How Not to Be a Hypocrite: School Choice for the Morally Perplexed Parent* (Routledge 2003)

Swift K, 'Child Abuse Reporting Systems in Canada' in N Gilbert (ed), *Combatting Child Abuse: An International Perspective on Reporting Systems* (OUP 1997)

Tamanaha B, *Realistic Socio-Legal Theory* (Clarendon Press 1997)

Tamanaha B, 'Understanding Legal Pluralism: Past to Present, Local to Global,' (2008) 30 Sydney Law Review 375

Taormino T, *Opening Up: A Guide to Creating and Sustaining Open Relationships* (Cleis Press, Inc 2008)

Taylor R, 'Responsibility for the Soul of the Child: The Role of the State and Parents in Determining Religious Upbringing and Education' (2015) 29 International Journal of Law, Policy & the Family 15

Teman E, *Birthing a Mother: The Surrogate Body and the Pregnant Self* (University of California Press 2010)

Thaler RH, *Misbehaving: The Making of Behavioral Economics* (W W Norton & Company 2015)

Thaler RH and Sunstein CR, *Nudge: Improving Decisions About Health, Wealth and Happiness* (Yale University Press 2008)

Thernstrom M, 'My Futuristic Insta-Family' *New York Times Magazine* (January 2, 2011)

Thompson C, *Making Parents: The Ontological Choreography of Reproductive Technologies* (Massachusetts Institute of Technology Press 2005)

Thompson S, *Prenuptial Agreements and the Presumption of Free Choice: Issues of Power in Theory and Practice* (Hart Publishing 2015)

Tobin J, 'Beyond the Supermarket Shelf: Using a Rights Based Approach to Address Children's Health Needs' (2006) 14 International Journal of Children's Rights 275

Tobin J, 'Justifying Children's Rights' (2013) 21 International Journal of Children's Rights 395

Tobin J, 'Fixed Concepts but Changing Conceptions: Understanding the Relationship Between Children and Parents under the CRC' in MD Ruck, M Peterson-Badali and M Freeman (eds), *Handbook of Children's Rights: Global and Multidisciplinary Perspectives* (Routledge 2017)

Tribe LH, *American Constitutional Law* (2nd edn, Foundation Press 1988)

Trinder L, 'Finding Fault?' (Interim research findings, *University of Exeter*, March 2017) <findingfault.org.uk/wp-content/uploads/2017/03/Finding-Fault-interim-research-findings.pdf> accessed 21 August 2017

Tronto J, *Moral Boundaries: A Political Argument for an Ethics of Care* (Routledge 1993)

Turley J, 'The Loadstone Rock: The Role of Harm in the Criminalization of Plural Unions' (2015) 64 Emory Law Journal 1905

Ulrich L, *A Midwife's Tale* (Knopf Doubleday 1990)

United Nations High Commissioner for Refugees, *Handbook on Procedures and Criteria for Determining Refugee Status* (Geneva 1992)

United States Citizenship and Immigration Service, 'United States Citizenship and Immigration Services Adjudicator's Field Manual' (*USCIS*, 26 August 2014) <https://www.uscis.gov/iframe/ilink/docView/AFM/HTML/AFM/0-0-0-1/0-0-0-15.html> accessed 21 August 2017

US Department of Health & Human Services, Administration for Children & Families, 'Postadoption Contract Agreements between Birth and Adoptive Families' (*Child* Welfare, 2014) <https://www.childwelfare.gov/topics/systemwide/laws-policies/statutes/cooperative/> accessed 21 August 2017

Waaldijk K, 'Small Change: How the Road to Same-Sex Marriage Got Paved in the Netherlands' in R Wintemute and M Andenaes (eds), *Legal Recognition of Same-Sex Partnerships: A Study of National, European and International Law* (Hart 2001)

Waddams S, *Dimensions of Private Law: Categories and Concepts in Anglo-American Legal Reasoning* (CUP 2003)

Waddams S, 'Private Right and Public Interest' in M Bryan (ed), *Private Law in Theory and Practice* (Routledge 2007)

Wall S, 'Perfectionism in Moral and Political Philosophy', *The Stanford Encyclopedia of Philosophy* (Winter edn, 2012) <http://plato.stanford.edu/entries/perfectionism-moral/> accessed 21 August 2017

Wall S, 'Introduction' in S Wall (ed), *The Cambridge Companion to Liberalism* (CUP 2015)

Wallbank J, 'Parental Responsibility and the Responsible Parent: Managing the "Problem" of Contact' in R Probert, S Gilmore, and J Herring (eds), *Responsible Parents and Parental Responsibility* (Hart Publishing 2009)

Walzer M, *Spheres of Justice* (Basic Books 1983)

Warner M, *The Trouble with Normal: Sex, Politics, and the Ethics of Queer Life* (Harvard UP 1999)

Wedgwood R, 'The Fundamental Argument for Same-Sex Marriage' (1999) 7 Journal of Political Philosophy 225

Weeks J, Heaphy B, and Donovan C, *Same Sex Intimacies: Families of Choice and Other Life Experiments* (Routledge 2001)

Weinrib EJ, 'Private Law and Public Right' (2011) 61 University of Toronto Law Journal 191

Weinrib EJ, *The Idea of Private Law* (OUP 2012)

Weinstock JS, 'Lesbian FLEX-ibility: Friend and/or Family Connections among Lesbian Ex-Lovers' in JS Weinstock and ED Rothblum (eds), *Lesbian Ex-lovers: The Really Long-term Relationship* (Harrington Park Press 2004)

Wellington AA, 'Why Liberals Should Support Same Sex Marriage' (1995) 26 Journal of Social Philosophy 5

Wellman C, 'Immigration and Freedom of Association' (2008) 119 Ethics 109

Wellman C, 'Freedom of Association and the Right to Exclude' in C Wellman and P Cole (eds), *Debating the Ethics of Immigration: Is There a Right to Exclude?* (OUP 2011)

Wergin C, 'The Case for Free Range Parenting' *New York Times* (20 March 2015)

Wertheimer A, *Exploitation* (Princeton 1996)

Westfall D, 'Unprincipled Family Dissolution: The American Law Institute's Recommendations for Spousal Support and Division of Property' (2004) 27 Harvard Journal of Law & Public Policy 917

Weston K, *Families We Choose: Lesbians, Gays, Kinship* (2nd edn, Columbia UP 1997)

Westwood S, 'Complicating Kinship and Inheritance: Older Lesbians' and Gay Men's Will-Writing in England' (2015) 23 Feminist Legal Studies 181

Williams B, *Ethics and the Limits of Philosophy* (Harvard 1985)

Williams B, 'Truth in Ethics' (1996) 8 Ratio 227

Williams R, *Keywords* (Fontana Communications Series, Collins 1976)

Wintemute R and Andenaes M (eds), *Legal Recognition of Same-Sex Partnerships: A study of National, European and International Law* (Hart 2001)

Wittgenstein L, *Philosophical Investigations* (GEM Anscombe and R Rhees eds, GEM Anscombe tr, Blackwell 1953)

Woodhouse BB, '"Who Owns the Child"? *Meyer* and *Pierce* and the Child as Property' (1992) 33 William and Mary Law Review 995

Wozniak DF, 'Gifts and Burdens: The Social and Familial Contexts of Foster Care' in LL Layne (ed), *Transformative Motherhood: On Giving and Getting in a Consumer Culture* (New York UP 1999)

Young IM, *'Throwing Like a Girl' and Other Essays in Feminist Philosophy and Social Theory* (Indiana UP 1990)

Zafran R, 'Children's Rights as Relational Rights: The Case of Relocation' (2010) 18 American University Journal of Gender, Social Policy & the Law 163

Zakaras A, *Individuality and Mass Democracy: Mill, Emerson, and the Burdens of Citizenship* (OUP 2009)

Zalesne D, 'The Contractual Family: The Role of the Market in Shaping Family Formations and Rights' (2015) 36 Cardozo Law Review 1027

Zeitzen MK, *Polygamy: A Cross-Cultural Analysis* (Berg 2008)

Index

abortion 283–4, 304
abuse 6, 47, 83, 86–7, 93, 100–2, 162, 166, 207, 220, 311
adoptees 305–6, 309
adoption 9, 13, 26–7, 32, 46, 56, 67, 197, 245, 260, 265, 268, 270, 279, 294, 297, 299, 302, 306, 310, 312
adoptive parents, *see* parents, adoptive
adult intimate relationships 7, 11, 17, 21, 27, 36, 48, 75–6, 82, 93, 121, 123, 128, 133, 174, 215
adultery 109, 134, 144–5
   grounds of 145
affection 17, 84, 89, 176, 194, 204
agreements
   binding 121, 266, 268
   contractual 297, 300, 305, 309
   in family law 263, 269, 271
   marital 37, 262–5, 268, 270
   premarital 259–60, 268–71
   prenuptial 42, 51, 121, 127–8, 132, 271
   separation 121, 264, 268
Alberta's Family Law Act 6
Alderson, P 28, 239
alimony 25, 263–4, 268; *see also* spousal support
Almond, B 60
Altman, S 7, 9, 16, 30–1, 34, 170, 209–27, 244, 280, 283
American constitutional law 95–8, 114
American family law 103, 272
American law 95, 103, 114, 232
Amish 287–8
Anapol, D 97, 106, 110, 113
Appell, AR 31, 232–3, 235, 237, 239, 241–2, 245
Appleton, SF 253
arbitration 151, 259, 268–9
Archard, D 12–15, 23, 42, 59–72, 174, 189, 192, 197–9, 230, 232, 240, 242, 257, 296, 310
Asch, A 308
association, freedom of 156–8, 163, 166, 197
asylum 153–4, 156, 168–9
Auchmuty, R 134–5
Australia 50, 53
authenticity 91, 221–3, 225–6
autonomy 36, 86, 112, 118, 126, 132, 199–201, 207, 214, 219, 240, 259–60, 267, 274, 281, 284, 290–2, 300, 303–4
   development of 194, 303–4
   exercise of 104, 196, 309
   see also relational autonomy
Ayres, I 130

Baldwin, R 50
Barker, N 10
Barlow, A 6, 130, 150
Barnett, RE 259
Baroness Hale 25, 37, 117–21, 126–7, 129, 231, 252–3
Batra, M 90
Beck-Gernsheim, E 61

Bedi, S 95, 97
Bendall, C 4–6, 8, 78, 134–52
Benhabib, S 304
Bernardes, J 61
best interests principle 1, 53, 232; *see also* child's interests, welfare principle
Bhandary, A 87
biological parents, *see* parents, biological
biological ties 13, 297, 305
birth mother 268, 301
   birth parents, *see* parents, birth
Bix, BH 9–10, 36, 42, 51, 257, 259, 278, 306, 310
black feminist thought 310
Boele-Woelki, K 5, 55–6, 257
Boris, E 84, 89, 92
Bottomley, A 72, 124
Bowers v Hardwick 178
Boyd, S 54, 115
Brake, E 3, 7, 10, 15, 22–4, 75–94, 96, 98, 102, 110, 113, 127, 162–3, 177–9, 183, 202, 294
Brennan, S 82, 197–8, 216, 233, 240, 246–7
Brighouse, H 69, 198–9, 204, 214–18, 222, 225, 243–5, 290
Britain 20, 48, 60, 131
British Columbia 305
Brooks, T 81, 106, 144
Burden case 3, 79
Butler, J 136
Butler-Sloss, P 252–3

Cahn, N 258, 297, 305, 308
Calhoun, C 81, 98, 173
Callan, E 198
Canada 10, 26, 33, 50, 87, 116–17, 120–1, 123–4, 127, 129–31, 154
capabilities approach 231, 238, 240, 243
capacity scepticism 193, 200–1
Carbone, J 258, 267
Card, C 75, 77, 82, 98, 132, 311
care ethics 52, 76, 202, 293, 303–4, 306, 309
care chains 91, 94
care work 75–6, 84–94, 129
   paid 87, 89, 92
caregivers 15, 22–3, 36, 75–6, 82, 84–90, 92, 194, 204, 243, 277
caregiving 23, 36, 77, 83–4, 86, 90–1, 93, 122, 221, 266, 283, 312
Carens, J 159
caring relationships 23, 75–6, 78–9, 81–92, 94, 184, 239
Case, MA 77, 209
causal connection test 185–6
Chambers, C 10, 48, 75, 78, 126
Chang, H 155, 166
child, adopted, *see* adoption
child custody 6, 30, 32, 71, 102, 209, 220, 258–9, 264, 268, 278, 285, 299, 301, 310–11
child welfare, *see* children's welfare

childcare 84, 91, 121, 131, 185–6
childhood
  intrinsic goods of 198, 233, 240–1
  social construction of 235, 237
children
  in polyamorous families 80–1
  protecting 82, 245, 269, 311
  rights for 27, 29, 31, 228, 247, 250
  rights of 29, 154, 169, 192–3, 195, 198–9, 202–7, 214, 222, 240
Children Act 6, 17, 21, 30, 48, 227, 229, 231, 244–5
children's interests 34, 36, 52–4, 195, 197, 200, 203–4, 210, 228, 230, 233–4, 242, 245–6, 251–2, 302; *see also* best interests principle, welfare principle
  prioritization of 29–30, 227, 231, 238, 244–9, 253
children's rights 191–208
  content of 205, 207
  discourse of 205
  importance of 192–3, 200, 203, 205–6, 208
children's vulnerability 227, 238–42, 244, 250–1
  distinctiveness of 240–1
children's welfare 31, 34, 50, 103, 195, 205–6, 210–12, 215–20, 231, 233, 243, 245, 252, 282, 284–5, 287, 311
child's interests, *see* children's interests
choice
  individual 50, 95–6, 103, 118, 128, 300
  marital 96–7, 103, 108
Choudhry, S 35, 227, 230, 234
Church law 46
Church Courts 295
citizenship 104, 153, 159–60, 164, 167, 169–70
civil partnership 4–5, 10, 19, 25, 27, 126, 134–6, 139, 143–6, 148, 152
Civil Partnership Act 27, 143–4
civil partnership dissolution 134, 139–40, 144–5, 148
Civil Rights Act 157
civil unions 6, 75, 77–8, 81, 95, 135
Clayton, M 210–11, 221
co-parenting 271, 312
co-parenting agreements 258–60, 265–6
coercion 83, 99, 102, 270, 297, 308
cohabitants 16, 18, 25, 27, 115–33, 258
cohabitation 6, 9, 17–18, 24, 87, 115–33, 140, 150
Collins, PH 310
Comaroff, J 54
commissioning parents, *see* parents, commissioning
commitments 42, 67, 83, 116, 123, 126–7, 130, 176, 194, 205, 223, 267, 286
  life-long 185
common law 9, 19, 37, 116, 120, 123–4, 130, 132, 144, 295
community property 101–2
compensation 116, 122, 128, 132, 148, 151, 186
consent 6, 8, 19, 51, 88, 99, 102, 118, 126, 128–9, 132, 250, 259–60, 266, 268, 275, 289, 296
consequentialism 103, 196–7
contact agreements 6, 21, 33, 252, 265, 267, 305–6, 309

corporal punishment 48, 273–4, 278
CRC (Convention on the Rights of the Child) 32, 168, 192, 230, 232–3, 237, 239, 243, 251, 253–4
criminal law 178, 259, 275, 277
cultural groups 276, 288
cultural practices 287–8, 290, 292
custody, *see* child custody
Cutas, D 302, 308

Dagan, H 122, 124
Davis v Davis 298–9
Day Sclater, S 141
death 263, 267
Den Otter, RC 15, 19–20, 24, 80, 95–114
Denscombe 138
dependence, economic 23, 86, 121, 123, 240, 304
Dewar, J 8, 50
Diduck, A 12, 14–15, 22, 55, 72, 120, 129, 228, 240
dignity 37, 86, 195, 261–2, 281
dispute resolution 54, 130, 209, 269
dissolution of relationships 12, 50, 78, 132, 139–40, 142–4, 148, 174, 179, 189, 258, 264, 278, 284
diversity
  of views 2–3, 220
  of family forms 12, 61, 71
  in the legal profession 146
divorce 2, 6, 8, 12, 23, 26, 41–2, 46–7, 50–2, 55, 82, 121–2, 124, 127, 139, 141, 144, 185, 259, 263–5, 269–70
  no-fault 25, 107, 185, 275
Dixon, R 119, 231, 238, 240
domestic partnerships 75, 77, 81, 95–6, 184
domestic workers 8, 75–9, 81, 83, 85–7, 89–93, 113, 162, 294
donors, gamete, *see* gamete donors
Douglas, G 62–3
duties
  children's 45
  custodial 69, 72
  fiduciary 216–19
  imperfect 202
  legal 45, 53, 65, 127, 258, 267, 289
  moral 176–7, 186, 188, 191, 200–1, 246
  parental 21, 27, 30, 45, 211, 216, 224, 245, 265, 267, 299
Dworkin, R 9, 43, 115
Dwyer, JG 9, 22, 30–2, 34, 36, 53, 213, 220, 232, 247–9, 273–92, 301

ECHR (European Convention on Human Rights) 13, 35, 41, 48–9, 71, 229, 234, 249, 251, 253, 329
ECtHR (European Court of Human Rights) 3, 13, 35, 41, 48–9, 71, 79, 229–30, 234, 251, 253
education 9, 48, 78, 81, 131, 170, 193–5, 198–9, 202, 207, 211, 219, 225, 274–9, 284–5, 289–90, 304
Eekelaar, J 15–16, 24, 32, 34, 37, 41–58, 125, 127, 192, 227, 233–4, 254, 261
egg donation 262, 305
Eichner, M 12, 122, 294
elder care 182–4
Ellman, I 25, 42, 127
Embryology Act 8, 56, 70

embryos 41, 267, 296–301
Emens, EF 80, 95, 101, 107, 114
enforcing agreements 259–60, 262
England, law in 1, 5–6, 9, 19, 21, 25–6, 30, 37, 41–2, 45, 48, 50, 54–5, 116, 120, 123–5, 127–8, 139–40, 143–4, 146, 231, 248–9, 263, 268, 295
entitlements, functional 77, 81
equal moral consideration 7, 218, 227, 246–7, 249–51
equal treatment 10, 15, 31, 76, 79–81, 84, 86, 92, 96, 98, 101, 103, 108, 232–5, 247–8, 254
equality 5, 7, 10, 75, 77, 79, 81–3, 85, 87–9, 91, 93, 96, 98, 101–3, 151, 235, 238–9, 244, 246, 300
equality and difference 235, 239
equality objection 227, 246
Ertman, MM 258
Eskridge, WN 128, 272
ethics 3–4, 52, 202, 293, 296
Europe 55, 257
Ewick, P 136, 137, 149
experiments in living 103–5
exploitation 37, 54, 87, 90, 102, 106, 166, 261–2, 300, 302

Fair Housing Act 157
fairness 4–5, 7, 12, 123, 144, 156, 162, 196, 263–4
familial forms 14, 68–71, 123
family 23, 59–66, 72, 122
 as privileged sphere 261
 defining 61–72
 extended 80, 110, 165, 310–11
 family resemblances approach to 13, 66
 formal approach to 66–7
 functional approach to 21–4, 66–7
 nuclear 102, 305, 310–11
 regulating the 48, 122, 124
 traditional 60, 62, 67, 69
family autonomy 242–4
family-based immigration 9–10, 13, 18, 153, 164–6; *see also* family unification
family disputes 54–5, 115, 268
Family Justice Council 26
family law 5, 12, 16, 41–58
 private ordering in 257–92
 protections of 76, 78, 88, 92–3
 scope of 1, 23, 69, 72
Family Law Act 124, 251
family privacy 87, 261
family relationships 46, 50, 280, 294, 303, 307
family unification 153–8, 160–1, 163, 165–6; *see also* family-based immigration
family values 204, 207, 214
fathers 14, 19, 45, 47–8, 53–4, 252, 295–6, 298
 genetic 295, 298
 legal 296–8
 unmarried 295–6
Feinberg, J 28, 48, 191–2, 240
feminism 47–8, 51, 67, 82, 102, 122, 134–6, 239
feminist theory 51–2, 76, 82, 86, 100, 102, 110, 122, 128, 134–5, 150, 239, 303, 307; *see also* care ethics
Ferguson, L 5–8, 19, 22, 26, 29–31, 35–6, 122, 188, 192, 205–6, 227–56, 268, 271, 294
Fernandez, C 185
Ferracioli, L 153, 157, 159–64

fertility treatment 19, 32, 70
fiduciaries 31, 210, 216–22, 245, 281–2, 291
fiduciarity 31, 216–17, 226
fiduciary duties, *see* duties, fiduciary
fiduciary relationship 16, 217–18, 220, 244–5
fiduciary responsibilities 219
fiduciary roles 31, 34, 218, 244
filius nullius, rule of 295
financial independence 148, 151
financial orders 8, 25–7, 50, 121, 229
Fineman, M 22, 31, 42, 51, 122, 235, 238–9, 242
Finnis, J 57–8
FitzGibbon, S 126
Fitzpatrick 42, 44
flourishing, human 109, 196, 204
foetus 297, 301–2, 306–7
Folbre, N 76, 87, 89, 91
formal equality 235, 239, 247
foster care 71, 87, 221, 276, 297, 302, 311–12
Fox, R 42
France, law in 49, 55–6, 167, 264
freedom, reproductive 300
freedom of religion 28, 103, 197; *see also* religion
Freeman, M 21–2, 32, 156, 162, 186, 228, 233–4, 239
friendship 25, 68, 78, 82, 84–5, 91, 108, 111, 113, 140, 143, 148–9, 159–61, 174–5, 184, 186, 311

Galston, W 213, 222, 279, 283
gamete donation 267, 271, 297–9, 300, 307
gamete donors 33, 298, 308–9
Gardner, J 43
Gavison, R 48, 51
gays and lesbians 80, 97–8, 113, 126, 128, 134–43, 145–51, 173, 179, 310
gender 7, 12, 19, 76, 81, 99, 106, 129, 134–5, 137, 146, 150, 302–3
gender equality 56, 93, 102–3, 121, 132, 151, 274, 300; *see also* feminism
gender inequality 76, 96, 100, 102, 122, 302
genetics 293–8, 296–7, 299, 301, 303, 305, 309
George, R 32, 34, 50, 56–7
Germany, immigration in 155
Gerstman, E 98
gestation 19, 91, 293–4, 298, 301–5, 307
gestational services 266, 300, 303; *see also* surrogacy
Gheaus, A 198, 240, 302
Gibney, M 156
Gilligan, C 303–4
Girgis, S 109
girls, rights of 199, 288
Gittins, D 61
Glendon, M 52, 205
global justice 89, 155–6, 165, 300
Goldfeder, M 80–1, 102
goods of childhood, *see* childhood
Goodwin, M 302, 311
Goody, J 46
Griffin, J 192, 201
Griswold v Connecticut 178, 181
Gutmann, A 279

Hannan, S 31, 210, 213, 217–20
happiness 50, 104, 110, 161, 179, 181, 196, 212, 221

Harding, LF 61
Harding, R 4, 6, 8, 78, 134–52
Hardwig, J 204
Hart, HLA 43, 63, 65, 117, 119, 121, 125–6, 130, 132, 135, 265
Haslanger, S 305
Haynes 41
Hayward, A 117, 119–20, 125
health care 77, 179, 198–9; *see also* medical care
Herring, J 8, 19, 21–2, 25–6, 28–9, 52–3, 121–2, 125, 232, 239–41, 243, 245–6, 252, 271
heteronormativity 4, 134–7, 140, 143, 148
heterosexual 59, 71, 137, 140, 146
Hitchings, E 270
Hochschild, A 89, 91
honesty, radical 111–12
Hopkins, N 125
household 45, 59–60, 68, 71–2, 117–19, 123, 131, 150–1, 179, 253, 310–11
Human Fertilisation and Embryology Act 8, 56
human rights 29, 47–9, 57, 120, 128, 158, 192, 201, 237, 239, 247, 254
Human Rights Act 35, 120, 227, 230
Hunter, ND 26, 134–5, 150
Hurka, T 103
husbands 16, 46–50, 121, 128, 136, 151, 178, 185, 187–8, 229, 269, 277–8, 282, 295–7, 299
Hyman v Hyman 121

ICGU (intimate caregiving union) 82, 87
ideal theory 7
illegitimacy, of children 47
immigrants 8, 76, 86, 154–5, 165–7, 270
immigration 17, 93, 153–9, 161, 163, 165, 229
immigration law 89, 153–6, 159–60, 163–7, 169–70; *see also* family-based immigration and family unification
immigration rights 65, 156, 159, 164
income 12, 45, 133, 151, 179, 185
inequality 82, 86, 199, 235
infidelity 51, 100, 113
inheritance 50, 86, 128
insemination 296–7
interdependence 12, 42, 71, 124, 151, 227, 239, 250, 303–4
  economic 121, 123, 150–2
interests
  basic 195, 205–7
  state's 97, 103, 115, 122–3
  see also best interests principle; children's interests; parents' interests; public interest
interpersonal relationships 10, 136, 173, 175, 178
intimacy 173–90
  familial 204, 206
  intervention in 178–84
  moral significance of 106, 175–8
  nature of 174–5
  protecting 189
  special obligations of 26, 176, 183
Israel 268, 307
Italy 13, 155
IVF 266–7, 271, 295–8, 300–1

Japan, immigration in 155
jealousy 96, 104, 106, 110

Jeske, D 8, 10, 16, 18, 22–4, 26–7, 31, 37, 51, 67, 78, 106, 163, 173–90
Johansen v Norway 35, 230
justice
  considerations of 153, 156
  theory of 7, 63, 76, 191, 233
  see also global justice
justifiability 3, 5, 14, 18–19, 27, 237
justification, legitimate 79–80

Kant, I 162, 259, 290
Kavanagh, MM 303, 306, 311
kinship 42, 60, 67, 71, 131, 148, 293–4, 306, 310
  next of 78, 179
Klein, J 84, 89, 92

labor 90–2, 122, 155, 241
  women's 126, 303
LaFollette, H 191, 240
Larmore, C 162, 166
Laufer-Ukeles, P 300, 302–4, 306, 308, 310
law
  and philosophy 2–11, 153, 156, 257
  as social construct 3–4, 32
  expressive function of 5–6, 20, 24, 29, 30, 33, 86, 91, 98
law reform, judicial 115, 119, 125, 132
Leckey, R 8–9, 15–16, 18, 24, 27, 56, 78, 115–33
legal consciousness studies 129, 135–7, 147–9
legal equality 143, 148
legal norms 13, 42–4, 46, 48–9, 51, 55, 57
legal obligations 10, 23, 26, 31, 51, 53, 67, 106, 163, 173, 175, 177, 179–81, 183, 185, 187, 189, 267
legal parenthood, *see* parenthood, legal
legal parents, *see* parents, legal
legal recognition of relationships 23, 49, 69, 72, 95–9, 101–5, 144, 152, 294–5, 310
legal recognition of same-sex partnerships 4, 134–5, 144, 149, 152
legal status 17, 32, 51, 66, 77, 79–81, 91, 96, 99–100, 122, 183–5, 230, 271, 274, 311
  formal 15, 17, 77, 184
legitimacy, of children 46–7, 270
Levine, C 67
Liao, M 192
liberal neutrality 10, 36, 60, 70, 79, 96, 98, 101, 153, 159, 161–3, 243
liberal societies 96, 103, 218, 275, 280
liberal state 82, 97–8, 103, 157, 160–2, 274, 288, 291–2, 294
liberal theory 217–18, 303–4, 312
liberal values 10, 244, 291–2
liberalism 79, 81, 96, 98, 103, 113, 162, 166, 244, 285, 291
  political 76, 79–80, 82, 96, 98, 162, 179
liberties, basic 157–8, 166
liberty 7, 10, 36, 47, 76, 91, 100, 103, 158, 162
  expressive 222
Lister, M 9–10, 13, 18, 79, 98, 153–4, 153–70
Lord Collins 119–20
Lord Hope 119–20
Lord Neuberger 118, 125
Lord Nicholls 33
Lord Simon 19

Lord Walker 119–20, 127
Lotz, M 244
love 69, 71, 80, 85, 87, 89, 96–7, 103–4, 108–10, 116–17, 125, 127, 184, 194, 198–9, 260, 269, 284, 286, 289

Macaulay, S 138
Macedo, S 78, 81, 99, 155, 279
Macleod, CM 28–30, 34–5, 169–70, 183, 191–208, 240, 242, 270
Mandle, J 156, 162
marital status 70, 121, 127, 131
marriage
  abolition of 10, 75, 78, 82, 98
  and cohabitation 18, 87, 126, 128
  covenant 264–5
  different-sex 18, 137, 144
  extension of to same-sex couples 5, 10, 27, 136
  institution of 37, 42, 134, 178, 189–90
  legal status of 77, 97–8, 173, 180, 187
  meaning of 37, 52, 95–6
  monogamous 96, 102, 106, 113–14
  polyamorous 104, 106, 114
  see also polygamy; same-sex marriage; agreements, marital
marriage breakdown 1, 27, 121, 127
marriage law 10, 75–9, 98, 124, 179
marriage licenses 77, 97, 101, 105, 107, 114
Marvin 185
McClain, L 94, 125
McGuire v McGuire 261
McLachlin, J 118–20
Mead, M 68
medical care 274–5, 277, 279–80, 284, 289; *see also* health care
Metz, T 23, 67–8, 82, 87, 98, 110
migration 89, 155
Mill, JS 7, 25, 47, 96, 100, 104–5, 113, 178
minimal marriage 10, 77–8, 80, 83, 86–8, 90, 93, 98, 113, 179
minority cultures 199, 273–4, 289–90
Minow, M 52, 209, 303
Modell, J 310
monogamy 71, 78, 80, 95–6, 99–108, 110, 112–14
  compulsory 80, 95
moral norms 43, 51, 53
moral obligations 18, 26, 51, 173–5, 180, 182, 187–8
moral philosophy 98, 153
moral pluralism 103, 308
moral rights, bearers of 192, 196, 200; *see also* rights, rights bearers
moral status 193, 232, 246–8
  of children 216, 246–7
mothers 14, 19, 42, 45, 54, 89, 91, 100, 169, 183, 188, 252, 258, 263, 295–6, 301, 307, 311
  gestational 11, 19, 296, 301–2, 306, 309
  legal 296, 298–9
  single 253, 295
Munby, P 6
Munoz-Dardé, V 68
Murray, J 90, 93, 257

nannies 84, 88, 91, 204
Narayan, U 311
natural kinds 62

natural law 45, 109, 276
Nedelsky, J 22, 52, 303–4
Netherlands 35, 55–6, 135, 230
neutrality, *see* liberal neutrality
Noggle, R 216, 246–7
non-human animals 196
non-intervention, illusion of 261, 276–9
non-parents 194, 209, 224–5
normative questions 66–7, 69, 75
Norway 35, 230
Nussbaum, MC 98–9, 231, 238, 240, 262

Obergefell 10, 55, 97, 158, 271
objectification 232
obligations
  enforcement of 181–4, 188–9
  financial 18, 25–6, 296
  imperfect 201–2
Okin, SM 12, 76, 82, 100
Olsen, FE 48, 124, 129, 261, 278
O'Neill, O 111, 202
opposite-sex couples 96–8, 142
Overall, C 308

paramountcy principle 229, 231, 233, 238, 245, 249–50
parens patriae role 281, 288, 291
parental authority 191, 199, 207, 223, 278–9, 285
parental autonomy 198, 213
parental control rights 7, 9, 16, 30–1, 34, 209–26, 232, 244, 284, 287
parental entitlements 30, 209, 282, 285, 288–9, 291
parental interests 31, 34, 36, 46, 210–14, 216, 219–20, 224, 244–5, 283
  in intimacy 31, 215
  in nurturing 212, 223–5
parents licensing 308
parental responsibility 17, 21, 30, 32, 56, 69, 74, 210, 232, 242, 295–7
parental rights 9, 30–2, 34, 36, 47, 78, 205, 209–26, 231–2, 245, 259, 265–7, 280, 295–8, 301–3, 307, 312
parental rights doctrine 9, 31, 232
parental status 47, 70, 258, 266, 279, 295–8, 300–1, 303, 307
  legal 11, 21, 293–4, 298–300, 307
parenthood 14, 16, 21, 31, 33, 129, 231, 263, 265, 271, 294–6, 301, 307, 310
  legal 93, 294, 296–7, 301
parenting, free range 212
parents
  adoptive 87, 265–6, 269, 276
  biological 56, 64, 276, 279, 290–1, 295, 297, 301
  birth 265, 269, 276
  commissioning 33, 293–4, 302–3, 306–10
  custodial 30, 209, 220, 264
  genetic 265, 267, 294, 299
  intended 266–7, 298
  intentional 13, 299–300
  interests of 32–3, 210, 213, 281, 286
  legal 8, 13, 34, 93, 266–7, 276–80, 284–5, 288–91, 297, 299, 301, 305, 307, 311
  surrogate 33, 293, 303, 306–7, 309–10
  unwed 296, 302

parents' interests, *see* parental interests
parents' rights, *see* parental rights
Parks, J 306, 309
Pateman, C 128, 301
patriarchy 138, 301
Peel, E 137, 139
perfectionism 70, 96, 103–4
Phillips, A 300, 302
philosophy 2–11, 15, 22, 60, 62, 96, 115–16, 123, 160, 233, 257, 278–9, 283, 303; *see also* law, and philosophy
Pickus, N 159
Piglowska 2, 50
Plato 62, 68
plural marriage 19–20, 24–5, 95–114; *see also* polyamory; polygamy; polygyny
political theorists 3, 273, 303
polyamorous families 80–1, 102, 106, 111, 311
polyamory 19, 24, 76, 78, 80–1, 95–114, 311
polygamy 76, 81, 95, 98–100, 106, 108, 173
polygyny 95, 99, 101, 114
Polikoff, ND 134
Poo, A 92
Poor Relief Act 45
post-White era 136
post-Windsor era 258
power 15, 43, 47–9, 51–3, 56–8, 86, 88, 132, 137, 213, 218–20, 261, 271, 273, 275–8, 280–1, 285–7, 289, 291–2, 300
pregnancy 293, 295, 297–8, 301–2, 306–8, 310
pregnancy contracts 301, 306, 308
premarital agreements, *see* agreements, premarital
primary goods 83, 198
private ordering 5, 9–11, 17, 32, 36–7, 143, 148, 151, 257–72, 278
private spheres 190, 243, 278, 304
 protected 12, 37, 51, 261
privatization 122, 232
Probert, R 1, 17, 21, 37, 55–6, 65, 118, 125–6, 128, 232
procreation 33, 56, 296–8, 300, 305, 311–12
property 1–2, 16, 21, 26, 45–6, 48–50, 55, 62, 65, 115, 117–18, 120, 126, 128–9, 131, 179, 186, 231, 258, 263–4
 matrimonial 1, 9, 26, 257
  disputes 115, 120
  division 1, 25–6, 78, 82, 122, 258, 263–4, 278
property law 59, 118–20, 125
public interest 6, 27, 32, 37, 115–34
public/private boundaries 129

Québec 115, 129, 131–2
queer theory 106, 143

race 7, 79, 86, 92, 157, 168, 302
Rackley, E 146
Radin, MJ 262, 269, 301
Ragoné, H 307
Rajczi, A 79
Rawls, J 7, 12, 63, 76, 79, 83, 156, 162, 165, 196, 233, 304
Raz, J 37, 44, 48, 126
Reece, H 22, 50, 131, 227–8, 231–2, 238, 249–50

refugees 154, 156, 168–70
Reich, R 279
relational autonomy 22, 245, 271, 293, 304, 312
relational rights 11, 52, 209, 293–4, 303–5
 and parenting 54
relationships
 different-sex 134, 145, 148–9, 151
 familial 14, 72, 173, 182–3
 interdependent 116, 122, 241, 243
 parent-child 24, 30, 294
 plural 96, 100–1, 106–7
 sexual 51, 78, 80–1, 163, 180
 recognition of 25, 27; *see also* caring relationships, interpersonal relationships
religion 28, 48, 82, 103, 168, 192, 197, 213, 277, 283, 286–7, 305
 free exercise of 48, 95, 283
removal from parental care, grounds for 166–7
reproduction 47, 56, 103, 108, 138, 179, 293–312
reproductive technologies 293–312
responsibility, sense of 300, 306, 310
responsibilities 15, 48–9, 59, 65, 71, 127, 194, 198, 280, 303, 308
 privatizing 122
 special 191, 198
 see also parental responsibility
right to marry 97, 99, 108
rights
 A-rights 28–9, 191
 AC-rights 19, 33, 117, 121–2, 127, 243
 associational 167–8, 170, 220, 224
 basic 156, 160, 203, 205
 C-rights 28–9, 192, 195
 equal 199, 275, 280, 305
 fundamental 103, 132, 158, 200
 interest theory of 197, 201, 243
 liberty 28, 197, 199
 see also children's rights and parental rights, moral rights
rights bearers 193, 200–1, 310
rights discourse 193, 201, 205–7
Roberts, S 54
Robertson, J 299
Rogerson, C 26, 50, 115, 127, 185–8
Rosenbury, LA 232, 239, 242
Rothman, B 301–2
Ruddick, S 304

same-sex couples 4–5, 7–8, 10, 25, 27, 41–2, 76, 78, 99, 135–6, 143, 147–52, 154, 158, 258–9, 266, 271, 297
same-sex divorce 134, 144, 148
same-sex marriage 5, 19, 41, 55, 78–9, 95, 97–8, 106, 126–7, 134–6, 150, 164, 173
 legal recognition of 97–9
same-sex relationships 13, 18, 41, 55, 70, 99, 107, 134–67, 302
 assimilation of 134–5, 137
 breakdown of 5, 134, 137, 150
 recognition of 134–5, 150; *see also* legal recognition of same-sex relationships
Sanger, C 265, 270, 298
Satz, D 303
scepticism, duty distortion 193, 200–1

Scheffler, S 4, 127
Scherpe, JM 1, 26, 50, 121, 257, 263–4
Schneider, D 295
Schoeman, F 205, 214
Schoenbaum, N 75, 88–90, 92–3
school choice 199, 290
schools 20, 195, 212, 214, 220, 241, 258, 277–80; *see also* education
Scruton, R 78
self-determination 275, 278, 280, 284
sexual orientation 95, 97, 106, 168
sexual partners 72, 80, 112, 174, 179
sexuality 106, 146
Seymour, J 238
Shalev, C 300
Shanley, ML 11, 24, 33, 52, 89, 91, 94, 202, 209, 257, 266, 293–312
Sheff, E 80–1, 95, 105–6, 111–12
Shultz, M 300
Silbey, S 136–7, 149
Simpson, A 41
Sir James Munby P 9
Sir Roualeyn Cumming-Bruce LJ 229
social construction 4, 236–7, 242; *see also* childhood, social construction of; law as social construct
social inequalities 8, 26, 122, 188, 294
social institutions 47, 68, 83, 124, 179, 199
social justice 76, 84, 262, 290
social kinds 62–3
social norms 15, 37, 42–52, 55–7, 104, 258, 267
Social Security Act 46
social stigma 20, 104, 114, 128
Spain 51, 55, 155
sperm donation 262, 267, 295–300, 305
sperm donors 267, 296–7, 305
spousal support 8, 18, 23, 25–6, 31, 50, 82, 101, 127, 174, 184–90
    income-security theory of 185, 188–9
    reimbursive/compensatory theory of 185–7
    rehabilitative theory of 185, 187–8
    see also alimony
spouses, claimant 186–8
Stacey, J 61, 310
state intervention 31–2, 34, 37, 45, 48, 129, 180–1, 261, 276–9
status relationships 18–21, 27
Stoljar, SJ 44
Strassberg, MI 99
Strathern, M 300, 310
substantive equality 247
Sunstein, CR 5, 50, 129
support orders 46, 259, 295
Supreme Court
    of Canada 117, 129
    US 55, 97, 158, 178–80, 187, 271, 288, 296
surrogacy, gestational 8, 11, 91, 262, 266, 297–300, 305, 307, 311; *see also* gestational services
surrogates 11, 33, 260, 262, 266, 291, 293–4, 297–8, 300–3, 306–10
Sweden 50, 60, 94, 151
Swift, A 7, 33, 69, 199, 204, 215–18, 222, 225, 243–5

Tamanaha, BZ 43–4
Teman, E 307–8

Thaler, RH 50, 129, 260
Thernstrom, M 306, 311
Tobin, J 32, 192, 237–9
transgender persons 49
Tronto, J 303
Troxel v Granville 32, 232, 266
trust 108, 111, 117–18, 120, 131, 148–9, 177, 204, 240, 260

Uniform Parentage Act 296–7
United Kingdom 3, 35, 41, 48–9, 79
United Nations 230, 254
United States 9, 32, 87, 89, 96–7, 99, 154, 163, 178, 180, 249, 257–8, 262–5, 269, 287, 295, 298, 300, 302, 311
unjust enrichment 117–18, 120, 131, 133
unmarried cohabitation 41, 56, 117, 123; *see also* cohabitation
US v Windsor 97
Utilitarianism 25, 47, 196
utility 66, 124, 129, 205, 260

Vernon, R 210, 213, 217–19
violence 9, 47, 51, 212
vulnerability 8, 12, 22–3, 82, 85, 87, 92, 111, 128, 148, 227, 232, 234, 238–42, 244, 250–3, 260, 262–3
vulnerability objection 227, 238–42

Waddams, S 124–5
Wales 1, 5–6, 9, 21, 26, 37, 50, 55, 116, 123, 125, 139, 146, 231
Wall, S 37, 70, 96, 98
Wallbank, J 21, 240
wealth 46, 50, 116–17, 144
Wedgwood, R 79, 98
Weinrib, EJ 124
Weinstock, JS 148–9
welfare 22, 36, 53, 57, 70, 129, 152, 216, 218, 228–9, 231–2, 243, 245, 252–3, 275, 280, 299; *see also* children's welfare
welfare principle 35, 227, 229–30, 232–3, 245, 249–51, 253–4; *see also* best interests principle, children's interests
Welfare Reform Act 295
well-being
    individual 47, 53, 58, 179
    material 155–6
Wellman, CH 156
Wertheimer, A 259, 262
Weston, K 148, 310
Whitehead, Mary Beth 298–9
Whitford, WC 265
Williams, B 4
Williams, R 60
Wittgenstein 13
wives 6, 46–9, 90, 100, 121, 136, 147, 150, 178, 185, 187–8, 229, 263, 269–70, 277–8, 299
women 70, 97–8, 100–3, 109–10, 112, 136, 188, 260, 263, 266, 270–1, 293–6, 302–3, 307, 309
work, intimate 75, 88–90, 92–3

Yousef 35, 230

Zalesne, D 258, 306